TANGU TRADITIONS

1. New garden, new baby

TANGU
TRADITIONS

*A study of the Way of Life
Mythology, and Developing Experience
of a New Guinea People*

———

KENELM BURRIDGE

FELLOW OF ST. CROSS COLLEGE
OXFORD

OXFORD
AT THE CLARENDON PRESS
1969

Oxford University Press, Ely House, London W. 1

GLASGOW NEW YORK TORONTO MELBOURNE WELLINGTON
CAPE TOWN SALISBURY IBADAN NAIROBI LUSAKA ADDIS ABABA
BOMBAY CALCUTTA MADRAS KARACHI LAHORE DACCA
KUALA LUMPUR SINGAPORE HONG KONG TOKYO

PRINTED IN GREAT BRITAIN

TO MY MOTHER

ACKNOWLEDGEMENTS

M ANY friends and colleagues have indirectly helped to form the climate of ideas in which this book was written; and while it would be inappropriate to name each one, I hope it will be accepted that in collectively thanking all who may have contributed I acknowledge each several debt. In particular, however, I would like to thank Dr. John Layard, who read some early pieces, helped me sort out some initial problems, and provided most of the inspiration; Mrs. Eva Krapf-Askari, who was kind enough to read and comment upon an early draft; Professor F. G. Bailey, a friend always in deed; and Mrs. Camilla Raab, who compiled the index and helped me deal with the proofs. Each has made this book better than it might have been.

Since the ideas of an original scholar tend to become transmuted into something different in the mind of a reader or listener, it is not easy to record one's more general intellectual and personal debts. Nevertheless, I welcome the opportunity to be specific about some. I have always felt myself guided by the many published works of Professor E. E. Evans-Pritchard, and I must emphasize what I owe both to him and to Mr. T. K. Penniman, Curator Emeritus of the Pitt Rivers Museum, in stimulus and warmth of friendship. Professor R. M. Berndt's *Excess and Restraint*,[1] which appeared whilst this book was in draft and deals, in part, with much the same themes, was a definite fillip. I found *The Origins of European Thought*,[2] by Professor R. B. Onians, a mine of ideas. And though he himself might have preferred a quite different kind of book, my debt to the genius of Professor Claude Lévi-Strauss will be obvious.[3] But of course the responsibility for what is set down here is all mine.

[1] R. M. Berndt 1962 *Excess and Restraint*, University of Chicago Press.
[2] R. B. Onians 1951 *The Origins of European Thought*, Cambridge University Press.
[3] Claude Lévi-Strauss, in particular 1958 'The Structural Study of Myth', in Thomas A. Sebeok (ed.) *Myth: A Symposium*, The American Folklore Society, Bloomington, Ind.; 1958 *Le Geste d'Asdiwal*, École Pratique des Hautes Études, Paris; 1960 'Four Winnebago Myths: A Structural Sketch', in *Culture in History*, Columbia University Press, New York.

The field research on which the book is based was carried out in 1952 as a Scholar with the Australian National University under the supervision of the late Professor S. F. Nadel. In revering the memory of the latter, I thank the former for its generosity. Mr. Arthur Ewing of the Australian Administrative Service, and Father Cornelius Van Baar, S.V.D., were always hospitable and companionable whilst I was in the field, and I would like them to know how much I valued their help and friendship. I thank, too, my friends in Tangu and in other parts of New Guinea, whose kindness and patience seldom seemed to wear thin. If Tsieke, Bak'n, Mienai or Randi or any of their brothers and sisters ever come to read this book I wish them enjoyment of it, and I hope they will forgive me if I have, unwittingly, taken any liberties I ought not to have done. For Kwaling, Reamai, and Mangai, great tellers of stories, I reserve my especial thanks.

K. O. L. B.

St. Cross College
Oxford

LIST OF CONTENTS

LIST OF ILLUSTRATIONS

INTRODUCTION

NEW GUINEA is a hard and difficult country without much in the way of natural resources to attract European settlement. Yet it has strategic value and, to Australians, has always been a challenge to enlightened colonialism. While all sorts and conditions of men have explored the island and made their homes there, missionaries and administrative officers have done most of the pioneering, have been the primary vehicles of European civilization. Other kinds of European are relatively thin on the ground, being generally confined either to the coastal fringes, or to the central highland massif, where roads, post offices, telegraph, schools, hospitals, markets, and law courts are evident and efficient. Between these European settled areas, however, is a never-land of foetid bog or marsh, or of impossible hills or mountains clothed in forest and slashed with deep ravines. Here there are only jungle trails which may disappear overnight in a rainstorm, a temporary airstrip perhaps, and outlying mission stations and administrative posts. Most Europeans hurry through these regions as quickly as they can. Only administrative officers working through a lonely tour of duty, or missionaries dedicating their lives to the peoples in their charge, stay for any length of time. In just such a place live the people now known as Tangu, whose experience is our concern.

Tangu have known Europeans and their ideas and artifacts for over fifty years. A traditional culture rich in ceremonial and art forms has been dying, a generation that knows little about a life that lacked the supervision of missionaries and administrative officers is coming of age. But—and here lies the rub— Tangu have nothing to sell. Lacking the specie with which to enter the wider economy, only their souls and their muscle seem to have value in the European ambience. Isolated from the mainstream of European influences, Tangu remain a bush people whose largely traditional subsistence activities have tended to throttle the enthusiasms of new experiences. Nevertheless, the enthusiasms are there. Through administrative officers, missionaries, traders, and the massing evidence of returned contract labourers Tangu have become aware that they might enjoy a new and different kind of life. Their minds and imaginations pricked by what they have seen and heard, Tangu covet, and have started to feel their way towards, a new social order which, they suppose, will enable them to retain their own integrity whilst commanding prestige and respect in the wider community. This 'putting on of the new man', the process whereby a 'neolithic' people are gaining wider and deeper perspectives of action and understanding against the demands of subsistence and the pulls of tradition, is our primary theme.

A number of essays on a variety of aspects of Tangu life have been published in professional journals,[1] and a more lengthy but none the less preliminary account was presented in *Mambu: A Melanesian Millennium*,[2] a book mainly concerned with Tangu and other cargo or millenarian activities.[3] The present work is

[1] Georg Höltker 1941 'Die Mambu-Bewegung in Neu-guinea. Ein Beitrag zum Prophetentum in Melanesien', *Annali Lateranensi*, tom v; 1945 'Ethnografia aus Neu-guinea', *Annali Lateranensi*, vol. ix; 1950 (with Robert Rootil) 'Ein papuanisches Zwillingspaar beim Stamm der Tanggum in Neu-guinea', *Anthropos*, vol 45; 1951 'Die Steinvögel in Melanesien', *Sonderdruck aus Südseestudien*, Basel.

A. Capell 1952 'Languages of Bogia District, New Guinea', *Oceania*, vol. xxii, pp. 130–47, 178–207; [1950] 'Survey of Linguistic Research', *South Pacific Commission*, Project S. 6, Report no. 1, vol. 1.

Burridge: B–1954(a) 'Cargo Cult Activity in Tangu', *Oceania*, vol. xxiv, no. 4. B–1954(b) 'Racial Tension in Manam', *South Pacific*, vol. 7, no. 13. B–1956(a) 'A Note on Tangu Dreams', *Man* 130 Sept. B–1956(b) 'Social Implications of some Tangu Myths', *Southwestern Journal of Anthropology*, vol. 12, no. 4. B–1957(a) 'Friendship in Tangu', *Oceania*, vol. xxvii, no. 3. B–1957(b) 'A Tangu Game', *Man* 100 June. B–1957(c), 'The *Gagai* in Tangu', *Oceania*, vol. xxviii, no. 1. B–1957(d) 'Disputing in Tangu', *American Anthropologist*, vol. 59, no. 5. B–1957(e) 'Descent in Tangu', *Oceania*, vol. xxviii, no. 2. B–1958 'Marriage in Tangu', *Oceania*, vol. xxix, no. 1. B–1959(a) 'Adoption in Tangu', *Oceania*, vol. xxix, no. 3. B–1959(b) 'The Story of Mazienengai', *Anthropological Quarterly*, vol. 32, no. 4. B–1959(c) 'Siblings in Tangu', *Oceania*, vol. xxx, no. 2. B–1959(d) 'The Slit-gong in Tangu', *Ethnos* 3–4. B–1965 '[The Religious practices of] Tangu, Northern Madang District', in *Gods, Ghosts and Men in Melanesia* (ed. P. Lawrence and M. J. Meggitt), pp. 224–49, Oxford University Press, Melbourne. B–1966 'Tangu Political Relations', *Anthropological Forum*, vol. nos. 3–4.

[2] Burridge: B–1960 *Mambu: A Melanesian Millennium*, London.

[3] Cargo cult activities may be described as activities of a millenarian or even messianic nature, generally associated with political and cultural changes and adjustments in the face of a colonial administration and complex economic and technological procedures, and particularly associated with Christian teaching on the one hand, and a desire to possess European manufactured goods or cargo on the other.

For general accounts see: Peter Worsley 1957 *The Trumpet Shall Sound*, London; Vittorio Lanternari 1965 *The Religions of the Oppressed*, New York; Peter Lawrence 1964 *Road Belong Cargo*, Manchester University Press.

supplementary to this, stands beside *Mambu*,[1] re-explores some
of the main themes argued there, and offers for inspection a
collection of Tangu myths, stories, legends, folk-tales, and fairy
stories which are conveniently brought together under the
generic term 'narratives'. Yet there is no intention here of for-
warding or proposing a particular 'theory of myth'. Though
any examination of myths or folk-tales, or narratives as they are
called here, must allude to their relations with time, space,
history, drama, dreams, ritual, and religion; must have a bearing on general theories of myth, their functions, purposes, and
relations to scientific thought; and cannot but be made to
appear as grist to the mills of any one of a variety of anthropological, sociological, or psychological orthodoxies or eccentri-
cities; these considerations are by the way, aside from the main
concern.[2] This is an exploration of the ways in which the
narratives, reservoirs of Tangu thought about themselves and

---

[1] Where relevant and appropriate, summaries of previously published materials
are given in the text. But where the matter does not seem to warrant such a re-
hearsal the reader is referred directly to the source in question.

[2] Few major authors have not written on these topics, but I have in mind
particularly, and acknowledge my debt to, Janet Ruth Bacon 1925 *The Voyage of
the Argonauts*, London; Frank Baker 1931 *Myth, Nature, and Individual*, London;
H. G. Baynes 1940 *Mythology of the Soul*, London; David Bidney 1958 'Myth, Sym-
bolism, and Truth', in Thomas A. Sebeok (ed.) *Myth: A Symposium*, Bloomington,
Ind.; Jerome S. Bruner 1959 'Myth and Identity', *Daedalus*, vol. 88, no. 2;
Joseph Campbell 1960 *The Masks of God*, London; Ernest Cassirer 1944 *An Essay
on Man*, Yale; F. M. Cornford 1912 *From Religion to Philosophy*, London; Mircea
Eliade 1958 *Patterns in Comparative Religion*; 1960 *Myths, Dreams and Mysteries*,
London; Raymond Firth 1960 'The Plasticity of Myths: cases from Tikopia',
Ethnologica, ii (N.S.); Sigmund Freud 1928 *The Future of an Illusion*, London; Erich
Fromm 1952 *The Forgotten Language*, London; A. Van Gennep 1910 *La Formation
des légendes*, Paris; Robert Graves 1958 *Greek Myths*, London; C. G. Jung 1943 *The
Psychology of the Unconscious*, London; C. G. Jung and C. Kerenyi 1951 *Introduction
to a Science of Mythology*, London; E. R. Leach (ed.) 1967 *The Structural Study of Myth
and Totemism*, London; Claude Lévi-Strauss 1964 *Le Cru et le cuit*, Paris; 1966 *The
Savage Mind*, London; 1966 *Du Miel aux cendres*: *Mythologiques*, Paris; Ursula
McConnel 1957 *Myths of the Munkan*, Melbourne; Bronislaw Malinowski 1926
Myth in Primitive Psychology, London; R. R. Marett 1920 *Psychology and Folk-lore*,
London; H. J. Massingham 1927 *The Golden Age*, London; F. Max Muller 1871
Essay on the Philosophy of Mythology, London; 1895 *Chips from a German Workshop*, vol. iv,
London; E. Neumann 1954 *The Origins and History of Consciousness*, London; Dora
and Erwin Panofsky 1956 *Pandora's Box*, London; Helmuth Plessner 1958 'On the
Relation of Time to Death', in Joseph Campbell (ed.) *Man and Time*, London;
F. C. Prescott 1927 *Poetry and Myth*, New York; Raglan 1945 *Death and Rebirth*,
London; Theodor Reik 1958 *Myth and Guilt*, London; Lewis Spence 1921 *An
Introduction to Mythology*, London; W. E. H. Stanner 1961 'The Design of a Riteless

their condition, throw light on Tangu traditions and their transformations, yield up the possibilities of awareness which their culture provides. By interrelating these possibilities with the events and patterns of Tangu life, as well as with those historical developments for which there is evidence, we hope to be able to discover what may be meant by the developing experience implied in putting on the new man. A relatively simple procedure, even though at times it requires juggling with several balls in the air at once, it implies an exploration of social change through the homologues of varieties of kinds of experience.

The process of retrieving and then interrelating the different expressions of, or abstractions from, Tangu culture may be conveniently summed up as 'entering a conversation between Tangu narratives and other aspects of their culture'. And since a conversation implies a dialectic, such is the pattern of presentation and argument. The first three chapters deal with the more positive grounds of experience and awareness: Tangu history, subsistence activities, and social relations. Then come three chapters of narratives, together with analyses or interpretations: these last are based partly on what has gone before, partly on the interior evidence provided by a particular narrative, partly on the suggestions contained in the *corpus* of narratives regarded as a whole. A final chapter attempts to draw the threads together. To achieve such a synthesis, as well as to provide a necessary sense of continuity, the argument is pursued at varying levels in different contexts by the use of certain shorthand terms and phrases which indicate successive breakdowns of the primary dialectic. These terms need a brief introduction.

Although there may be several alternative ways of containing the primary dialectic, the words 'moral' and 'divine' seem to suit the case best. Always used as contraposed and relative or relational terms, what is moral in one situation may be divine in another; and the same relativity of relationship goes for the other pairs of oppositions mentioned below. While moral refers generally to the normative interrelations of men and women

Myth', *Oceania*, vol. xxxi, no. 4; Wilhelm Wundt 1916 *Elements of Folk Psychology*, London.
These are but a few works, representative of the wide variety of interests which the subject of myth evokes or may serve. We agree with Baker (1931: 124) that 'mythical facts are not to be explained, they explain all others'.

bound in community, and in particular to the quality of such relations demanded of adult Tangu—reciprocity of obligation—the word divine refers to a field of non-reciprocal relations which is critically defined, but not exhausted by the relations between Tangu themselves and phenomena or manifestations or images or notions or beings or representations that are not human. Reciprocity is to non-reciprocity as moral is to divine, and he who acts non-reciprocally is divine in relation to those who, behaving reciprocally, are moral. Similarly, 'siblingship' and 'filiation' refer to contrasting characteristics adhering to categories of moral relationship. Thus, while siblingship connotes mutually enforceable reciprocities of obligation, filiation connotes normative but not necessarily mutually enforceable non-reciprocal relationships. And since among Tangu reciprocity of obligation is characteristic between those of roughly the same age and generation, brothers, sisters, brothers-and-sisters, friends, brothers-and-sisters-in-law, sweethearts, betrothed couples, and spouses are in this sense all relationships of siblingship. On the other hand, while in a general sense filiation may refer to mother–son and father–daughter, it particularly refers to father–son or grandfather–father–son (male filiation), or to mother–daughter or grandmother–mother–daughter (female filiation). And this indeed is how Tangu themselves appreciate the situation. Further, however, because filiation connotes the normatively non-reciprocal, relationships of filiation are only enforceable within the terms of a fourth opposition between 'self-restraint' and 'self-willedness'.

The four pairs of oppositions (moral/divine, reciprocity/non-reciprocity, siblingship/filiation, self-restraint/self-willedness) provide a general framework. Within this framework the word 'value' sums up the implications of a predicative term, and 'tension' refers to the situation in which opposed values are simultaneously or almost simultaneously engaged. Thus tension connotes the dialectic in action, the possible resolution or synthesis of one or more of the four pairs of theses/antitheses. To attempt to analyse social relationships in terms of rights and duties would not do justice to the field material. For Tangu situations are characteristically fluid and dynamic. Tangu have only loose expectations of others and attempt to exercise claims in the face of counter-claims within a context of choice, priorities, and ambitions related to the precedents of the past and the demands of the present and future. Hence the phrase 'communication of parts', the active engagement of a relationship whether between Tangu themselves, Tangu and their narratives, or Tangu and the characters or events in a narrative. While many features of Tangu life cannot be said to have either rights or duties, they are movers or activators, and they communicate their parts in much the same ways as Tangu pressure each other.

Situations or relationships which just happen to exist, for which there is no generally accepted and abiding *a priori* principle of explanation, are referred to as 'existential'. Contingent and varied or *ad hoc* attempts to explain why a situation should exist is good evidence of an existential situation. And the state of mind and degree of understanding which the existential situation seems to imply is summed up in 'apprehension'—to know that something exists, to appreciate it in the flat as it were, to accept it without the aid of a generally acknowledged principle which accounts for or explains it. Again, contingent or *ad hoc* attempts to explain or rationalize are indications of apprehension. By contrast, the word 'comprehension' refers to the mind which knows why a situation exists, which is able to appreciate a situation in the round, relating it to other situations and explaining it in terms of premises commanding the consent of all or most of those involved. To move from an apprehension to a comprehension, 'awareness' is required. Awareness, one may say, perceives a situation, leaps forward to rationalize and explain it in terms that command consent, pursues comprehension, is poised to comprehend. Since among Tangu today comprehension implies at least a working knowledge of both European and Tangu assumptions and categories of understanding, large numbers of situations are existential, apprehended merely, and Tangu may be described as groping towards an awareness which may enable them to comprehend.

Summing up Tangu myths and stories as narratives—or as tales or stories where the prefatory 'narrative' may be taken for granted—follows Tangu tradition and has analytical value. For whether traditional or of more recent genesis,[1] all the narra-

---

[1] Narratives N. 1–N. 29 inclusive are traditional narratives, and N. 30 and N. 31 are of more recent origin.

tives are for our purposes evidences of the same kind. They are modes of cognition, communicate awareness. And though particular individuals may interpret a narrative differently—which means that the kinds of awareness being communicated may differ—this is the very nature, stuff, and life of a narrative. For the differing kinds and levels of awareness predicate the possibilities of change in the social order. On the other hand, allowing that the two kinds of interpretation are bound to interact, here an attempt is made to derive the meanings of narratives, and so the kinds of awareness communicated, from the conversation between the narratives and other aspects of Tangu culture. This procedure yields a cultural awareness—the possibilities of awareness available to individuals within the culture—an awareness that is on the level of the collective and objective. It also indicates those principles of the social order which, though they may receive varieties of expression at different times, appear to guide the process of change and development. As within a given cultural awareness individuals attempt to comprehend and realize the different awarenesses communicated by their narratives, so change is generated, new narratives come into being, old narratives take on new meanings, and the cultural awareness is enlarged.

For a variety of reasons that need not detain us, no tape recorder was available in the field.[1] Narratives were written down, repeated back, 'corrected', and rewritten. The stress, it became clear, was on the situations being evoked rather than on an immutable ordering of words and sentences. Often when a narrator was at a loss for words he broke into mime. So that whilst no one will deny the importance of the words, especially of those key words which go to the heart of the situation being evoked, the fact that mime or gesture was accounted as good as words seemed to render unsatisfactory any sustained formal analysis based upon language. Then again, because the Tangu language itself no longer suffices to contain the total experience of Tangu[2]—Pidgin and Latin terms are frequently used—an undue concentration on the Tangu language as such would seem to be methodologically wrong. More positively, the

[1] Fieldwork took place in 1952. The present tense refers to Tangu as of that time.
[2] In summary, *infra*, pp. 32–4. In detail, B–1960: 196–200.

absence of a tape recorder drew attention to the importance of situational content.[1] Thus while the translations of the narratives are free, attempting to recapture a situational texture rather than a quite misplaced literal accuracy, certain key phrases and terms keep imagination within bounds.

Because most of the narratives have to do with men and men's activities it may be thought that they are tales only for men. On the contrary. For while some Tangu hazard a guess that women may have secret narratives of their own, these never came to light, if indeed they existed, and the narratives set down in this book are as well known to women as to men. They are community narratives, pertaining to all, not just men's tales.

The events of Tangu history cannot be documented as a historian might like them to be. Such earlier documentation as there may have been was destroyed during the Japanese invasion of New Guinea. Still, there are memories. And these, checked against life histories, genealogies, material remains, and the content of narratives yield up an intelligible and consistent developmental process. While such events as we think we know occurred provide the guidelines, the series of oppositions mentioned above contain not only the logic of Tangu social relations, a 'preliminary' dialectic, but also illumine the sociological relevance of the historical events, the 'historical' dialectic.

Tangu are egalitarians, aggressively so. Their moral order is characterized by a fierce insistence on equivalent reciprocities and by a minimum of delegated responsibilities. But while much time and energy are spent in coping with, and countering, expressions of self-willedness and the non-reciprocal in others, there are many who covet that reserve of self-willed and non-reciprocal power which will enable them to assert themselves against their fellows. Highly competitive, Tangu egalitarianism is maintained by competition: and resolutions of this generalized condition fill out most of the content of the preliminary dialectic. Since, however, expectations of reciprocal and non-reciprocal behaviour are, and so far as it is relevant always seem to have been, tied to particular kinds of situation and categories of relationship, Tangu social history—the historical dialectic—

[1] In extracting a virtue from necessity let it not be thought that the absence of a tape recorder was anything less than tragic!

becomes intelligible within the same set of oppositional and predicative terms. More recently Tangu have become involved with Europeans, are becoming Christians, assist in the administrative process, have engaged in cargo activities, and hanker after European goods, capacities, and ways. And because in the Tangu view the colonial apparatus cannot but appear, and be categorized—initially at least—as simply non-reciprocal, the same pairs of oppositions contain the logic of Tangu–European relations. Predicated by a contraposition between, on the one hand, a moral order based upon hierarchy, delegated responsibilities, money, and a profuse differentiation of types of obligation and relationship, and, on the other hand, a moral order based on equivalent reciprocities and a relatively simple differentiation of the parts, the developing experience of Tangu is necessarily a story of increasing differentiation—a continuing process in which traditional and new categories of understanding and self-definition are adopted or rejected, or combined, distinguished, and permuted as one way of life gives way to another.

Some account of this extremely complex process is the main burden of what follows. But it can only be a partial and incomplete account. Even if there were not deficiencies and imperfections in the evidence and its import it is difficult to see how it might be 'complete'. So, since with this as with most stories there comes a time when, in spite of its defects, it seems useful and economical to tell it, I do so.

PART ONE

SOCIAL STRUCTURE

I

HISTORY, LAND, AND WORK

ONE of several culturally similar communities settled in the hills of the Bogia region of the Madang District of northern New Guinea, Tangu live in a knot of steep and forested ridges which rise sharply from gentle downland some fifteen miles inland from Bogia Bay.[1] Westward into the hinterland the peoples of Igom, Igamuk, Reng, Sung, Aber, and Barit are Tangu speakers who generally enjoy friendly relations with Tangu, but who neither regard themselves nor are regarded by others as Tangu. South-west, on tongues of raised land in marsh and forest, are the Tangwatt settlements, where a variant of the Tangu language is spoken. To the north are the Diawat peoples, speaking a language structurally similar to Tangu but with a different vocabulary; and between the Tangwatt and Igom groups is Andarum country, where the language, though akin to Tangu, is not intelligible to Tangu speakers. Elsewhere in the region, east and north-east towards the coast, through Dakwenam, Pariakenam, Kangwan, and Bolivol to Lilau over rolling grasslands picked out with woods and copses, or south to the forested ridges of the Jump people and beyond to Moresapa, the languages are quite different from Tangu. Everywhere, however, pidgin English is used, and in most settlements there are one or two who can, in the pidgin phrase, *tonim tok*, speak the language of a neighbouring people.[2]

All these people live similar kinds of lives with much the same equipment. Everywhere men wear wide waistbelts of woven cane with breechclouts of barkcloth or trade cloth; women wear full skirts of shredded pandanus over an underskirt or petticoat of soft banana fibre; small children of both sexes

[1] In approximately 4° 25′ South, 144° 55′ East. Maps 1 and 2 follow.
[2] For the languages of this area see A. Capell, 'Languages of Bogia District, New Guinea', *Oceania*, vol. xxii (1951–2), pp. 130–47, 178–207, 317 (corrigenda). Survey of Linguistic Research, *South Pacific Commission*, Project S. 6, Report no. 1, vol. 1.

generally go naked. Like their neighbours, Tangu are horticul-turalists who, clearing and planting and tending a fresh site each year, supplement this main subsistence activity of growing root crops by hunting and foraging in the bush or forest, as well as by going away to the European settled area to work for cash. Most adults have had some kind of 'European experience', either as labourers working on the coast, or through significant contacts with administrative officers, missionaries, or itinerant traders and labour recruiters. Though steel and iron heads and cutting edges have replaced, or are replacing, the traditional stone implements, the primary tools and weapons remain the digging-stick, axe, adze, spear, and knife. Bows and arrows are for boys and youths. In the past homesteads were generally small, built on floors of hardened earth. Today they are larger and, following a coastal fashion, are more often raised on stilts. Settlements, usually sited astride a ridge or spur within a fringe of banana, areca-nut, and coconut palms, may comprise four or five homesteads clustered round a central feasting and danc-ing space known as the *pekas*, but may be much larger, con-sisting of several such clusters straggling along the spine of a ridge, or disposed about the flanks of a hilltop. Communications are by word of mouth, on foot, or by slit-gong.[1]

Tangu number today some 2,000 souls, distributed through approximately[2] thirty settlements of varying sizes which, located fairly close to each other, are roughly grouped, but not formally organized, into four named neighbourhoods: Wanit-zir, Biampitzir, Mangigumitzir, and Riekitzir.[3] Each of these neighbourhoods contains one or more major settlements of some twenty or more homesteads, and several of much smaller size, decreasing to one or two homesteads only. A comparatively densely settled population,[4] Tangu are an association of small communities bound to each other by tightly knit kin, trading, and exchange relationships. They are, and consider themselves

---

[1] An instrument made from the hollowed section of a tree trunk, and used for making sound signals (*infra*, pp. 275–8).

[2] Smaller settlements tend to be abandoned, reinhabited, and then abandoned again.

[3] The suffixes -*itzir* or -*tzir* may be translated 'neighbourhood' or 'the people of' or 'those who live in the vicinity of'. Thus Tanguitzir, Jumpitzir, Igomitzir, Igamukitzir, Diawatitzir, Andarumitzir, Tangwattitzir, etc.

[4] Taking an area including Tangu and their neighbours, Tangu account for 27 per cent of the total population in 9 per cent of the area.

to be, a polity distinct from their neighbours, a feature which is more precisely defined by a common and virtually exclusive participation in a political activity known as *br'ngun'guni*[1]—the formal occasion for airing grievances, making claims and disputing in public assembly, a 'talking out' before peers, neighbours, and kin.

Four or five generations ago, however, the peoples settled in the Tangu ridges probably numbered about 4,000 persons, concentrated into eight settlement assemblages, each of which, though their social systems differed slightly, had numbers of features in common with others, including, so far as may be ascertained, language. At that time the name Tangu referred to a small spur in Wanitzir close to the now deserted site of Tangumar or Sangumar.[2] Today, though still retaining this particular reference, the name Tangu has come to connote the unity of the four neighbourhoods. The years between, during which the ridges were depopulated and the survivors found the basis of a common experience, were years of conflict and trouble, years of migrations and mobility of settlement to which the present generation are heirs. Today smaller settlements tend from time to time to be wholly or partly abandoned, and later partly or wholly re-established. There is no family which does not at some time temporarily free itself from the involvements of community life by going to a small settlement in the bush for a period of several weeks, sometimes for a year or more. Situated as they are athwart a traditional and much-used trade route from coast to hinterland—in the marches between peoples living a largely traditional life and others, towards the coast, who have been much influenced by European penetration— passing fashions and new ideas and modes of behaviour, and the oppositions and discords these would cause in any community, are part of the present Tangu way of life, as well as of their past experience.

Political unity, however, by no means connotes a uniformity. Traditional activities differ in their details from neighbourhood to neighbourhood in Tangu, and even from settlement to settlement. Some Tangu are Christians, others are baptized pagans, many have taken to Christian or vaguely

---

[1] For detail see B–1957(*d*): 763–80, and *infra*. pp. 124–33.
[2] The sounds represented by 's' and 't' are generally interchangeable.

'European' ways without being baptized. Though many traditional ideas and activities are virtually defunct, and others are
losing ground in the face of new, generally European conceits,
much remains, and a body of behaviour in which all Tangu
participate to a greater or lesser extent has survived, or has been
produced by, their years of trouble and change. General attachment to a few important and interrelated notions and activities
delineate a common way of life, a single moral order which
exists in its own right alongside and together with Christianity
on the one hand and a hotchpotch of 'European' traits on the
other. All over Tangu first loyalties are to the self, and to the
household within terms of whose relations with other households
the capacities, desires, and ambitions of an individual may
develop and mature. Common ground in the meaning and
significance of marriage and the formation of the household
lend point to the frequent intermarriages between members
of different settlements, co-operation between households, and
the numerous and regularly maintained trading and exchange
relationships. Over a wide range of other matters, however,
consensus is often limited. Internal and quasi-political solidari-
ties tend to be temporary and on a small scale. Outside the
household relationships are generally guarded and cautious.

The casual visitor to Tangu in 1951–2, the period of field-
work, would have found the people polite, but cagey, obstinate,
and recalcitrant. They were in the aftermath of disappointed
cargo or millenarian expectations. Not close enough to the
European settled areas for their traditions and social order to
have been completely disrupted—and so, perhaps, feel themselves compelled to adopt new ways—they are yet not so
distant as to be able to select from, or ignore, the effects of the
European presence. Borne on events over whose consequences
they have had little control, from a variety of relatively 'closed'
systems of group allegiances, exchange alliances, and collective
responsibilities in which custom, the precedents of the ancestors,
and conformity ruled, Tangu have been moving towards a
relatively 'open' and inclusive social order in which choices
abound and consequences are not always predictable. From
1880, say, until the establishment of European order in the late
twenties, as the original settlement assemblages disintegrated,
life became more solitary and precarious, characterized by

growing anomy. With the collapse of traditional values the
struggle for power and prestige became bleaker and more
definitive. Then, roughly since the coming of Europeans to
Tangu, but having its roots in the preceding years, there follows

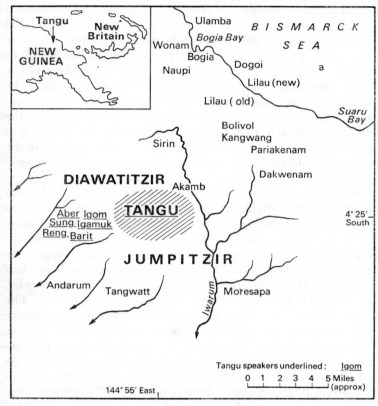

Map 1. Tangu and environs

a period of rebuilding, a phase of reintegration combined with
widening comprehensions in which Tangu are still involved.
The patterning of this process of breakdown followed by reintegration is our main theme.

The Tradition of Movement

So far as we are concerned, Tangu history starts with the dis-
integration of the original eight settlement assemblages in the

Tangu ridges. And two terms, connoting social groupings in space, together with the memories of older folk, guide the account. In the past the word *mwenk* (pl. *mwenker*) referred to a named cluster of between, say, four and ten homesteads grouped about a *pekas*, a dancing and feasting space. But today the word *mwenk* may refer to any named habitation: to a single isolated homestead, or to a collection of proximate homesteads. The other word, *gagai* (pl. *gagawa*), translatable as 'division' or 'section', though still a part of the general vocabulary of the Tangu language, is an archaism scarcely used today. The young confess ignorance, the mature say they have 'given up' *gagawa*,[1] the elderly preface statements about *gagawa* with the word *arin*, long ago, in the past. So that while the meaning of *mwenk* has changed, the meaning of *gagai*—which referred to the group of people associated with a *mwenk* or cluster of *mwenker*— is historical only.

According to elderly Tangu, each of the original settlement assemblages was divided into an upper portion known as Mnduor, and a lower known as Ginunk—names which identify what Tangu distinguish as 'big' *gagawa* (*GAGAI*). Others Tangu distinguish as 'small' (*gagai*).[2] Where *gagai* usually referred to the people of a *mwenk*, *GAGAI* referred to the upper or lower half of a settlement whether these comprised one or several *mwenker*. Both *GAGAI* and *gagai* were exogamous categories. The members of a *gagai* seem to have constituted a co-operative group, carrying out feasting exchanges with similar groups. Members of a *GAGAI* joined together to carry out feasting exchanges with those in the other *GAGAI* of an assemblage. As between different assemblages co-*GAGAI* membership indicated the presumption of mutual aid and support. Where there were no *gagawa*, as in parts of Wanitzir, *GAGAI* groupings provided the predicative terms. The names of both *GAGAWA* and *gagawa* seem to have been identificatory only, and though some were named after, or had the same name as trees, rocks, plants, and animals, the names of others could be translated as 'bald', 'tall', 'big-footed', and 'one-eyed' or 'squint-eyed'. There is no

---

[1] '*Nai mandarate gagawa*, We have given up *gagawa*.' See B–1957(*c*): 56–72.

[2] From here on the division of a settlement into upper and lower halves, what Tangu distinguish as 'big' divisions, will be written as *GAGAI*, and the 'small' divisions will be written as *gagai*.

evidence of any taboos or ritualized attitudes of avoidance or respect by the members of such groups towards the species or minerals which identified their *gagawa* or *GAGAWA*, though of course a member of *gagai* Mnamnier (*mnamnier* = bald-headed) and *GAGAI* Ginunk (*ginunk* = tall with big feet) would be bound to be associated with baldness and tallness, even though he was small with a full head of hair.

If we take as a start-line, say, a couple of decades or so before the turn of the century, the neighbourhood of Riekitzir consisted of about a dozen severally named and proximately grouped clusters of homesteads, *mwenker*, known collectively as Randam.[1] Each *mwenk* was associated with a *gagai*, and the whole assemblage was divided into two portions: an upper known as *GAGAI* Mnduor, and a lower known as *GAGAI* Ginunk. A rather larger assemblage than Randam, but similarly organized into *mwenker*, *gagawa*, and *GAGAWA*, the homesteads of Biampitzir were disposed on the summit and flanks of the highest feature in the region.[2] Randam is generally considered to have been founded by colonizers who came south across the valley from Biampitzir. North-west across the valley from Randam and separated from Biampitzir by a shallow saddle, on the same main ridge which marches round from Randam through Wanitzir and Biampitzir, Mangigumitzir presented a third similarly organized pattern of *mwenker*. Set in thick tropical forest, which begins to thin out on the northern slopes of Biampitzir, within sight of each other, and well within sound of handdrum and slit-gong, these three neighbourhoods were very alike. Culturally and in physical appearance affinities point to the hinterland, putative ancestries lead to Igamuk, Igom, Sung, Reng, and Aber as well as to Barit, Andarum, Jump, and Diawat. By contrast, markedly different in physical appearance, being slight and copper skinned where their western neighbours are heavy and dark skinned, the Wanitzir people have, and had, affinities with the peoples to seaward and eastward, ancestries leading to Sirin, Dakwenam, Akamb, Bolivol, and Lilau.

The Wanitzir settlements were bedded in the outer curve of the main Tangu ridge, commanding a view over grassy downs rolling to the coastal hills. The settlement of Tangumar

---

[1] See Map 2, p. 10.   [2] 1,500 feet above sea level.

consisted of three *mwenker*: the topmost, Daviai, associated with
GAGAI Mnduor; and Rambun and Tangumar—from which
last the whole assemblage took its name—built lower down the

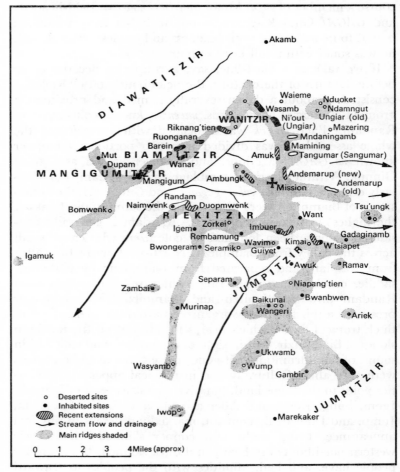

Map 2. Contemporary Tangu Settlement

slope and associated with *GAGAI* Ginunk. There were no
gagawa; the effective landholding and co-operative groups would
seem to have been composed of those who lived in a *mwenk*.[1]

[1] The larger feasting categories were called '*rumbar*, senior', and '*tumbar*, junior'.
How these fitted into the *GAGAI* categories I could not discover.

Mamining, little more than a furlong from Tangumar, also consisted of three *mwenker*: Vangenai on the lower ground associated with *GAGAI* Ginunk; and Resane and Ngurinap on slightly higher ground associated with *GAGAI* Mnduor. Of Mndaningamb, a third assemblage situated on the escarpment face a hundred feet or so below Mamining, only the bare site and memory of what must have been a large settlement remain.[1] People say it was 'like Tangumar', consisting of three *mwenker*. At the other end of Wanitzir, Wasamb and the present Ungiar (formerly Ni'out) were similar to each other, but different from the three assemblages just considered. Ni'out, or Ungiar, consisted of two *mwenker*: an upper known as Ngurinap and associated with *GAGAI* Mnduor; and a lower known as Ni'out, associated with *gagai* Tzengatzing and *GAGAI* Ginunk. Wasamb, across a deep saddle from Ungiar and on a high crown of the ridge, consisted of three *mwenker*: Mbam and Wasamb on the higher ground, associated with *GAGAI* Mnduor and *gagawa* Rienung and Moiruk respectively; and Resane, a few yards down the hill and associated with *GAGAI* Ginunk and *gagai* Resane.[2] Elderly Tangu consider that the dual division of each of the assemblages into *GAGAWA* originated in Tangumar and was adopted by the others. And it is a legitimate inference, since *GAGAWA* were exogamous categories, that *GAGAI* membership guided intermarriages between the assemblages.

Randam (or Riekitzir), Biampitzir, and Mangigumitzir were matrilineally biased. Each *mwenk*, or *gagai*, seems to have been composed of a core of matri-kinsfolk: matri-brothers and their families, or matri-sisters and their families, or matri-brothers-and-sisters and their families—a corporate group based on co- or proximate residence. Though claims to land derived through the matriline seem to have been received with the most sympathy, residence after marriage could be either uxorilocal or virilocal. Children normally lived with the parents. Boys, however, were expected to spend parts of their lives with a mother's brother,[3] and such an arrangement could result—and often

[1] One old man lives there by himself.

[2] Ngurinap, therefore, is a possible *gagai* in Ni'out: and also the name of a *mwenk* associated with *GAGAI* Mnduor both in Ni'out and in Mamining. And Resane, the name of a *mwenk* associated with *GAGAI* Mnduor in Mamining, is the name of a *mwenk* and a *gagai* associated with *GAGAI* Ginunk in Wasamb.

[3] I have used the full mother's brother throughout rather than an abbreviated

seems to have resulted—in youths' gaining prima facie claims over two sets of lands through habitual user[1] and association. For, despite a formal preference for the matriline, it seems that as far back as, say, the turn of the century, familiarity with, and actual user of, particular lands constituted the strongest evidence for continuing to exercise such claims.[2] In Ni'out (present Ungiar) and Wasamb, *mwenker* were composed of a core of patri-kinsmen and their families. Land was formally in the male patriline, and residence was normally both patrilocal and virilocal. Yet not only could a son opt out to join a mother's brother, but the latter seems to have been able to demand that a sister's son should join him. So that whether a youth was living in Ni'out or Wasamb under a system emphasizing the patriline, or in Riekitzir, Biampitzir, or Mangigumitzir where the matriline was emphasized, he had to balance the advantages of going with a mother's brother against those of continued association with the father. Yet these alternatives do not seem to have been necessarily mutually exclusive. On the contrary, the situation provided an opportunity for attempting to exercise claims on both hands.

In a rather different way this same tension between Ego and his father and mother's brother (Ego-father/mother's brother) also seems to have existed in Tangumar, Mamining, and, one supposes, Mndaningamb.[3] In each of these places, it will be remembered, there were three *mwenker* and two *GAGAWA*. And while it is more likely than otherwise that the effective exogamous groups were contained in the *mwenker*, membership of the exogamous *GAGAI* categories was a matter of residence—which itself seems to have been grounded in choice. Young children were associated with the *GAGAI* of residence but, as they came to puberty, formal membership of one or other *GAGAI* was bestowed upon them in alternation as between siblings of the same sex. Thus, if eldest child had been allocated to Ginunk,

MB, and likewise sister's son, mother's brother's daughter and father's sister's son instead of ZS, MBD, FZS. So too with the other relationships mentioned. On the whole, in an extended text which may be of interest to those who are not professional anthropologists, this probably adds to clarity.

[1] 'Usufruct' or 'use of' have different connotations from 'user'. 'User' = continued use or enjoyment of a right; right to use; presumptive right arising from. (*Concise Oxford Dictionary.*)

[2] Considered *infra*, pp. 77–83.

[3] Mndaningamb was 'like Tangumar' (*supra*, p. 11.)

the second sibling of the same sex would have been allocated to Mnduor. Yet the elderly are adamant when they say that upon entering the club-house in preparation for their puberty rites, youths, and in some instances maidens,[1] could choose for themselves whether to be Ginunk or Mnduor. No doubt pressures could be brought to bear either way, and perhaps in fact the choice was less real than it appears to have been. Still, one must allow that the choice existed. And because *GAGAWA* were exogamous categories, and since all over Tangu the preferred, and in terms of categories virtually the only, form of marriage was (and is)[2] one between those standing to each other as mother's brother's daughter and father's sister's son, the choice in these communities also resolves itself into an association with the father, evoking values in filiation, or an association with the mother's brother, evoking values in siblingship.[3]

Everywhere in Tangu, therefore, whatever the formal bias of the lineal transmission of claims to user of land, youths generally, and maidens in some parts, might attempt to exercise claims over two sets of lands, each of which was formally associated with a different residential group. Providing that settlement remained stable, that the ratio between lands available and land-holding group sufficed for ample subsistence, and that the numbers of persons attempting to exercise claims on both hands remained at a controllable minimum, then there seems no reason why a system founded on the corporate residential group should not work as well as one based upon corporate descent groups. The composition of groups would change with shifts in residence; the allegiance of particular individuals and their families might often be ambiguous. But the categories of corporateness would persist, and households would have been free to find their most appropriate ambience of corporateness. Indeed, as we shall see, just these features of mobility between corporate residential groups, and of temporary ambiguities of group memberships, are characteristic of Tangu social relations.

In fact, however, the conditions noted did not persist. Whether there was a sudden increase in population, or whether Tangu

---

[1] *Sic.* But it does not seem likely.

[2] *Infra*, pp. 60-73.

[3] For preliminary definitions of filiation and siblingship see *supra*, pp. x-xi. As we shall see, the mother's brother–sister's son relationship may itself be broken down into an opposition between filiation and siblingship.

were so pressured from the north that the size of the Tangu communities increased in relation to the lands then available to them, is debatable. Much more certainly, there was an increase in the range and numbers of interactions available to those who lived within the Tangu ridges. Also, not only were inter-marriages between the several Tangu communities beginning to provide those ambiguities which could allow too many the opportunity to attempt to exercise claims deriving both from the father and the mother's brother, but, given that there was then, as there is today, generalized competition for resources, such intermarriages between communities with different biases towards the lineal transmission of claims to land could only have served to aggravate an increasingly unsettled situation.[1]

Tangu themselves are not in any doubt when they trace the origins of their troubles to the widening choice of mates, to growing ambiguities, to the tensions inhering in the Ego-father/mother's brother relationship (filiation/siblingship). And that Tangu are still involved in the same predicament suggests not simply a projection into the past, but that the tension is inherent in the structure of Tangu social relationships. Today, as fathers, men try to keep their sons under their exclusive control. Further, many are attempting to insist on a formal patriliny in the transmission of claims over land. On the other hand, as mother's brothers these same men attempt to extend their influence over sister's sons: it enhances their fame and prestige. But in an egalitarian society such as Tangu the only way to influence another is to give him something—lands, specie, resources. And the simplest solution is to allow sister's sons a user of one's lands. Then, seeing their opportunity, the youths and young married men who are sons and sister's sons strive to maintain and exercise claims deriving from both sources. Later, these very sons and sister's sons, competing against each other for prestige and resources, themselves become the fathers and mother's brothers of the succeeding generation —and the tension perpetuates itself.

From the available evidence it is not unreasonable to suppose

[1] For example, to take an extreme instance, in point of form the son of a 'patri-lineal' father and a 'matrilineal' mother would have been well placed as against the son of a 'matrilineal' father and a 'patrilineal' mother. Given the nature of the Tangu terrain, 'boxed in', and given the nature of *br'ngun'guni* (*infra*, pp. 124-33), it was an invitation to continue disputing.

that for at least a couple of generations before the coming of Europeans the several communities within the Tangu ridges were drawing closer and closer, creating the basis of a common experience. Rather more certainly, the decade before the turn of the century seems to have seen an acceleration of mutual interdependences and a sharing of such features as club-house rituals, dances, and narratives, which, hitherto, had been regarded as belonging exclusively to one or other particular community. At that time rather more than at present, perhaps, some of the Wanitzir communities enjoyed a virtual monopoly in the region of the manufacture of clay cooking-pots, utensils much in demand.[1] They also exercised a control on the entry into Tangu from seaward of goods such as salt, iron, beads, cloth, and hunting-dogs—all of which found a keen demand among the peoples of the other three neighbourhoods. And as the soils and climate of the seaward slopes of the Tangu ridges do not support the same quality or quantity of areca-nut, tobacco, sago, and pandanus[2] as do the damper westward-facing slopes of Mangigumitzir, Biampitzir, and Riekitzir, there was a regular traffic in these commodities. Further, although today there are some who are beginning to engage in casual and *ad hoc* commercial transactions without the safeguard of an accompanying relationship expressible in the kinship idiom, no Tangu will engage in regular economic relations outside the categories of the kinship idiom. Indeed, the categories of kinship are for Tangu a set of moral categories which express economic relations as much as relationships derived from marriage. So that the existence of these economic relations between the four neighbourhoods may be taken to imply either frequent intermarriages, or a significant extension of the kin idiom, or both of these features. They reveal the four neighbourhoods as formally constituting, or as beginning to constitute, a single moral entity.

Apart from the probable regulation of these economic matters through the *GAGAWA* categories as well as through particular links of kinship, since feasting and dancing today provide, and may be supposed to have provided, the explicit and formal

---

[1] The manufacture of these pots has recently spread to Biampitzir.
[2] Areca-nuts and tobacco are stimulants; sago is a valuable food resource; pandanus fibre is used in the manufacture of skirts, string bags, and string.

opportunity for *br'ngun'guni*, the discussion of claims and grievances in public assembly, and as the members of the four neighbourhoods seem to have spoken the same language, it is not unreasonable to take the evidence of the elderly at face value and assume that disputes arising from the economic relationships were already being settled without a necessary resort to open war. Further, owing in part at least to the kin links between the several communities, which tended to involve members of different settlements in a common cause, it had at about this time become habitual for members of the four neighbourhoods to combine in defence against outsiders.[1] Such a defensive alliance, which could not have involved the total fighting strength of all Tangu, but which does seem to have recruited kinsfolk and neighbours from different communities, did not necessarily mean, however, that there was no internal raiding, feuding, and occasional resorts to violence. For if all could participate in *br'ngun'guni*, this institution is, and always seems to have been, as well adapted to making and exacerbating disputes as to settling them. The transmission of claims to land was biased in different directions. And certain acts, such as murder or a death diagnosed as due to sorcery, obligated the *mwenk* and near kin to vengeance. Also, if many single individuals were beginning to appreciate slightly different ways of life, there existed no authoritative institution through which new formal rules to rationalize a changing situation might be initiated. Since *br'ngun'guni* is and was a democratic institution in which all could participate, the initiatives of the far-sighted and more comprehending few could always be thwarted by the more selfish and near-sighted many—an example of self-willedness imposing itself on self-restraint.

There were, too, troubles over marriage, troubles which led to internecine fighting, for which Tangu today blame the tensions contained in the Ego-father/mother's brother triangle. Competition for wives was closely bound up with the competition for land and material resources, and because of the greater freedom of action within an expanding range of possible mates, many of the formally eligible, who, within a narrower single

---

[1] Tangu say that the Diawat people had been pressing from the north and were trying to expand round the north-east through Akamb, thus partially cutting off Wanitzir, and so the other neighbourhoods, from the coast and its valuable trade.

community, had been betrothed by their parents in infancy,
either refused to comply with the arrangements that had been
made for them, or, on account of other such refusals, were themselves denied the spouses they had contemplated marrying.
Since both 'valuables' (such as chaplets of dogs' teeth, or bird-
of-paradise feathers) and more immediately fluid and conver-
tible forms of wealth (such as pigs, foodstuffs, pots, and a
variety of artifacts) had changed hands at the betrothals, disputes arose over repayments and compensation. In themselves
the material losses were not serious: they could have been made
good. But not to insist upon repayment or compensation would
have been considered unmanly and disgraceful, whilst to accede
or accept would have been greeted with contempt and derision.
Either way prestige and moral standing were at stake. Moreover, since marital affairs are one of the foci of sorcery and
witchcraft, disputes over marriage—entailing as they do today,
and seem to have done in the past, a mass of personal resentments and possible losses of prestige—could only give rise to
mutual suspicions of sorcery and, finally, attempts to resolve
the situation by an appeal to arms.

Then, aggravating what seems to have been already a tense
situation, there came into Tangu along the trade route from the
coast through Wanitzir numbers of artificial dogs' teeth which
had been introduced by the Germans—then setting up plantations in the Bogia region—as currency. Now there is not today,
nor does there ever seem to have been, a consensus among
Tangu concerning the relative values of natural and artificial
dogs' teeth. And the substitution in many instances of artificial
teeth for natural teeth in a bride-wealth payment—and chaplets of dogs' teeth bound to a string base were the central valuable in such payments—threw doubt on, or could be made
to throw doubt on, the adequacy or legitimacy of particular
payments. Disputing seems to have increased, and one of the
consequences, certainly, was a limited fragmentation of the
original communities.[1] From Tangumar some families moved
south to found old Andemarup, formerly a temporary settlement

---

[1] That the two sets of events occurred at roughly the same time is supported by
the estimated ages of old coconuts on the deserted sites. Old folk in Tangu connect
them as cause and effect, and on the whole the connection made here seems
reasonable.

at the centre of a group of gardening sites. Others moved up to the crest of the ridge from Tangumar to found Amuk, and still more moved north to Akamb—itself a border settlement between Tangu and the Diawat peoples. In a few years, it seems, the whole settlement assemblage of Tangumar was left derelict. Ambungk in Biampitzir; Zorkei, Igem, and Bwongeram in Riekitzir; perhaps the Ndamngut and Nduoket settlements in the north of Wanitzir; and some of the tiny, now deserted, settlements within the central Tangu basin also probably date from about this time.

At this juncture in their affairs, at about the turn of the century, as they were beginning to scatter over former hunting lands within the Tangu boundaries, Tangu were visited with an epidemic sickness.

Apart from the deaths it caused directly, this epidemic, which is today associated with coughing and diarrhoea, was interpreted by Tangu as resulting from an inordinate increase in sorcery. Even if the situation had been other than it was, such an interpretation is to have been expected. Diarrhoea is almost certain evidence of sorcery, and, the sickness occurring when it did, in an atmosphere already corroded with malice and re-sentments over spouses and lands, current animosities seemed wholly justified, suspicions of sorcery became certainties, and the customary resort to vengeance led to more virulent disputes and further scattering in consequence. *GAGAWA* and *gagawa* fragmented. Households dispersed and resettled themselves over a relatively wide area in differently composed units.[1] Over a period of some years families from Randam pushed south and south-east through the forest and over the ridges into what, at that time, was Jumpitzir. In time Randam was entirely deserted. In addition to Bwongeram, Igem, and Zorkei, the new settlements of Zambai, Murinap, Iwop, Wasyamb, Marekaker, Wump, Ukwamb, Wangeri, Baikunai, Bwanbwen, Niapang'-tien, Separam, Seramik, Awuk, Rembamung, Wavim, Imbuer, Guiyet, Kimaimwenk, W'tsiapet, Want, Ramav, and Gadagi-namb were founded. The Jump people were either displaced or absorbed in intermarriages. Some few from Randam followed the Murinap ridge and made their way to Tangwatt. From Biampitzir families moved north-east along the ridge, founding

[1] See Map 2.

Ruonganan, then joined with emigrants from Wasamb to found the group of *mwenker* known as Riknang'tien. Some crossed the valley southwards, finding a home in Ambungk. Others pressed on into the new Riekitzir where they settled with refugees from Randam and Wantizir and allied themselves with remnants of the retreating Jump people. Mndaningamb was entirely deserted, so was Ni'out. Some families moved out to Waieme, Nduoket, Ndamngut, and old Ungiar; others joined forces with emigrants from old Andemarup to found Tsu'ungk. And many from Wanitzir went even further afield, taking refuge with kinsfolk or friends in Akamb, Dakwenam, Bolivol, Kangwan, and Lilau. Movement out of Mangigumitzir, however, was limited. A few came across into Riekitzir, others went to Mut, Dupam, and Bomwenk.

Quarrelling and wife stealing—for Tangu are polygynous, two wives are economically more advantageous than one, the sickness is said to have affected women more than men—together with vengeance killings seem to have become endemic, continuing until well into the twenties. Women, who in the days of agreed bride-wealth payments seem to have had no little influence on affairs, if only indirectly, became much as chattels: they had to rely on the strong arms of their husbands and were not always effectively within reach of brothers whose duty it was to protect them. Nevertheless, combinations against outsiders, especially against Andarumitzir, Diawatitzir, and Jumpitzir seem to have remained viable. Movements from *mwenk* to *mwenk* were as much or more a means of avoiding an otherwise inevitable dispute as the result of a quarrel that had already occurred. So far as it was possible to do so, the elderly say, compensation was eventually paid for stolen wives, thus virtually and in effect legitimizing the new unions. Widows were quickly remarried. Trading, exchanging, dancing, and feasting continued. Club-houses were built and used. Provided that English standards of 'stability' and 'good order' are not imposed on the situation, the circumstances of life in those days are not so difficult to envisage as one might at first think. Tangu live with sorcery today. Suspicions, resentments, and animosities are close to the surface. Well aware that they might lose control of their passions, Tangu take pains to avoid overt explosions. Though fragmentation of the original communities was severe, the distances between the many new *mwenker* were small, most settlements were within twenty minutes' walk of several neighbours. Life continued more or less as it had done, albeit much less securely and predictably, with more frequent emergencies requiring *ad hoc* arrangements. In principle the normative moralities seem to have continued unchanged. If a man wanted to survive, keep wives and children in reasonable health, and receive honour and respect from others, killing would not take him far. It invited the counter-attack, made life more dangerous. On the other hand, with foresight and cunning, by judicious withdrawals, by distancing himself, by working hard in field and in forest, he might realize desire and ambition. By living in small groups apart from each other internal resentments could be contained, and passions could be, and were, channelled against the outsider, either in defence, or aggressively to take over new lands.

The effect of these movements and migrations upon *GAGAWA* and *gagawa*, however, was decisive. As new *mwenker* were founded so new *gagawa* in association with the contiguous lands were invented. Old *gagawa* and *GAGAWA* memberships were residually retained, and by moving from *mwenk* to *mwenk*—thereby becoming associated with *gagai* after *gagai*—some families collected many *gagai* names: thus devaluing the significance the *gagai* once had. At that time, too, it seems that the basic fighting group was recruited from the members of a *mwenk* which was also, essentially, the *gagai*. At first, it appears, men who at one time had been members of the same *mwenk* and *gagai*, but who had become associated with different *mwenker* and *gagawa*, might still feel mutually obliged to rally as a fighting group. After all, they would have been boys together and probably close of kin. On the other hand, such a category of mutual aid could not have lasted for long, nor could it have had the value of a compelling imperative. Even in the case of a family which had not left a particular *mwenk* precisely because co-operation had become difficult, with *mwenker* so small and scattered, and with primary loyalties necessarily tied to the *mwenk* of residence and its adjacent lands, if helping those in another *mwenk* was not impracticable it could not at any time have been convenient. But against the outsider the situation was otherwise. He was a threat to all, and, since he could not speak the Tangu language,

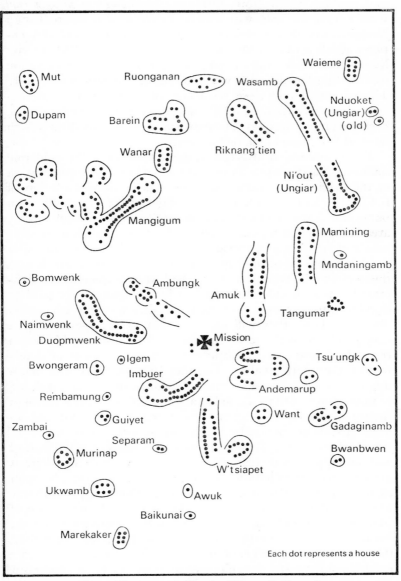

Each dot represents a house

Fig. 1. Diagrammatic Sketch of Tangu Settlements

and could not, therefore, satisfactorily engage in *br'ngun'guni* with Tangu, the issue with him had to be settled before Tangu themselves could quarrel with each other in terms of conventions which provided for more peaceful solutions. 'Where you lived—that was your *gagai*', Tangu remark. 'Where you worked (gardened)—that was your *gagai*. The others were lost.' Ties of actual and close residence, of common interests, co-operation, and habitual inter-association, values in siblingship, became emphasized at the expense of those loyalties which derived from parentage or filiation.

The introduction of artificial dogs' teeth, and the epidemic sickness, clearly played an important part in the fragmentation of the original communities, as well as in the destruction of *GAGAWA* and *gagawa*. But their effects were dependent on particular features of social relations. Tangu beliefs in sorcery are closely related to, and in terms of action depend upon, sickness and residence.[1] Central to the competition for lands and resources, the Ego-father/mother's brother relationship is also the nucleus of witchcraft beliefs.[2] And when suspicions of witchcraft become specifically linked to land disputes they tend to develop into sorcery cases.[3] Newly-weds are vitally concerned about the lands they will use, and seek to exercise as large a range of claims as they can; and the marital troubles which often result lead into sorcery disputes.[4] Perhaps a means of determining the relative values of artificial and natural dogs' teeth might have been found, perhaps the consequences of not doing so might have been mitigated. Tangu might have come through the epidemic—as Mangigumitzir virtually did—reduced in numbers but not otherwise much changed. But containment of the tensions in the Ego-father/mother's brother relationship, and an appropriate transmission of claims over land, must always have depended on a close regulation of choice. So soon as, in Biampitzir, Riekitzir, and Wanitzir at any rate, a relatively narrow and normative range of claims to land and choice of spouses became so broadened as to allow for effective manœuvre, events could be made to serve particular interests rather than the common good, and exploiting both the choice itself and the resulting ambiguity in relationships seems to have become a

---

[1] *Infra*, pp. 137–40.   [2] *Infra*, pp. 143–4.
[3] *Infra*, pp. 144–6.   [4] *Infra*, pp. 141–3.

useful ploy for the ambitious if not for the less able. The exercise of self-willedness might reap a present advantage, while restraint and conformity with the rules of the past could lead to poverty and loss of prestige. In Mangigumitzir, on the other hand, intermarriages with the Wanitzir people were relatively few, patrilineal influences were minor, the lands of the two neighbourhoods did not march together, and ambiguities seem to have remained under control.

Given the predicative situation as between three of the neighbourhoods, however, and given Tangu modes of thought, deaths due to the epidemic could hardly have been interpreted otherwise than as the all too probable outcome of the malice and suspicion which informed existing relationships. If there were some who comprehended what was happening, and who wished to restore or establish anew such normative rules as might have contained the broadening bases of action, there existed no institutional machinery by means of which they might have obtained the necessary consensus for enforcement. So, feeling their way through changing circumstances, Tangu remained prisoners of their own traditions and selfish ambitions until the time came when Europeans brought a new order, peace, and more change.

European Penetration

With the coming of Europeans to supervise their affairs, Tangu became the appendage of a large and complex system of economic, social, and political relations. But they possessed neither the means nor the ability to enter this wider community on a level of equality. Compared with the goods which Europeans brought to New Guinea, Tangu valuables, artifacts, and produce—all that they had in the past striven to make or nurture, possess, trade or exchange in order to express their notions of manhood and humanity—seemed as so much junk. Their own material resources had no value whatever for the newcomers, who appeared to express and realize their humanity on a quite different level. Unable to sell what they had, even at a loss, Tangu could become Christians or labourers or both. They could not remain themselves. Faced with European capacities and equipment, their own culture, no longer the most worthwhile to which Tangu themselves could aspire, seemed to

its bearers of little account. 'We were like pigs', the elderly
remark. 'We were like the wild pig which scuttles into the
forest when a man approaches.' Tangu had to make new men
of themselves.

German administrative officials penetrated to Tangu shortly
before the First World War, but they made little impact.[1] Much
more significant were the stories about white men which probably came up from the coast along the old salt route through
Bolivol, Kangwan, and Lilau. Partly on account of these
stories, but also because of the anxious conditions at home, some
Tangu made their way to the coast and plantation labour.
Rather later, youths were indentured by itinerant labour
recruiters. In many instances these adventurers were to return
to Tangu to find their families regrouped: fathers had been
killed, mothers remarried, brothers and sisters separated. After
the war, missionaries of the Society of the Divine Word came
to Tangu to reconnoitre the area. It was not until the early
twenties, however, at about the same time as the mission was
attempting to establish a catechist in Wanitzir, that the Australian administration began to bring Tangu under control.
Within the context of the stories they had heard about Europeans, Tangu gave both mission and administration a mixed
reception.[2] Yet it was not long before a majority—particularly
women, who saw in the mission security, stable marriage, and
an assured status—had begun to accept the inevitable more
positively. Though attempts by both the mission and administration to persuade Tangu to concentrate into larger settlements—where they could be more easily supervised and taught
—availed little, the decade before the Second World War was a
period of relative calm and steady development. By the time of
the Japanese invasion of New Guinea a sizable mission station
and church had been almost completed, and many Tangu had
become Christians. European administrative officers toured
Tangu about once a year. Locally appointed officials—Luluai,
Tultul, and Doctor boy[3]—were expected to maintain order and
liaise with sub-District headquarters in Bogia. The peace was
kept, village hygiene was supervised, migrant labour to the

---

[1] B–1960: 126.   [2] See B–1960: 125–7.
[3] The Luluai was nominally the agent of the administration: the Tultul was
constable to the Luluai; and the Doctor boy maintained the medicine hut.

coast was controlled. Indeed, going away to work on the coast had become an accepted part of Tangu life, the cash earned being used to buy tools for more efficient hunting and cultivating, or to purchase decorative paraphernalia.

Two features of the 'tween-war years require a special note. In 1937 a man named Mambu—who came from the coast, and who later became the leader of a cargo movement in the Suaru Bay area—visited Tangu.[1] A man of some ability, Mambu left Tangu with a self-conscious awareness of their unsatisfactory relations with Europeans. There were one or two incidents. Still, after Mambu had been gaoled for his activities along the coast, feeling and tension in Tangu itself seemed to subside; on the surface life continued much as it had done. Nevertheless, the strains and animosities engendered by the Europeanized environment persisted. The creation of a new man, a man fully able to cope with the new environment, became more urgent. Then, too, there was the decay and final abolition of the Tangu club-houses.

The creation of the new man could not but be intimately related to the passing away of the old or traditional man— a mode of being closely associated with club-house life and its attendant ritual activities.[2] And the mission, realizing the importance of these club-houses as vehicles of tradition, and seeing in them a rival to Christian teaching, made it clear to Christian converts that if they wanted to be new men they would have to free themselves from the old. Younger Tangu and most of the women made their choice, and gradually club-houses began to fall into disuse. By the end of the war, after more positive action by both the administration and the mission, not a club-house remained. While elderly conservatives grumbled and shook their heads in dismay, they did little else. Younger folk, women and Christians, on the other hand, were quite happy to have done with them. The club-houses had served their purpose, the traditional activities associated with them seemed quite out of place in the new order to which Tangu were becoming accustomed. The new man beckoned, and the old man, figured in the baleful looks of the elderly still living, seemed wholly unattractive.

[1] For Mambu's activities see Höltker 1941: 181–219. B–1960: 182–8.
[2] *Infra*, pp. 170–5.

During the war, most of which Tangu spent under a loose Japanese military administration without effective access to courts, there was some reversion to feuding. With the end of the war, and after a period under military government, both the Australian administration and the mission returned to the supervision of Tangu affairs.[1] Renewed efforts were made to persuade Tangu to concentrate into larger, more easily administrable settlements in which schooling would also be more effective; and a few families moved closer to the mission station. But it was not until Yali,[2] at that time enjoying administrative support, but later a well known leader of cargo movements, advised them to do so, that Tangu began to move into larger settlements. Old Andemarup was almost wholly abandoned, new Andemarup was built close to the mission. New Ungiar (old Ni'out) and Wasamb took in the inhabitants of old Ungiar and Waieme. Most of those who had been living in the Riekitzir forests to the east and south came into the new Duopmwenk, hard by old Randam. Imbuer, W'tsiapet, Amuk, Ambungk, and Riknang'tien were extended and enlarged to take in families which had been living in the small and scattered *mwenker* in adjacent areas.

These arrangements, satisfactory as they were both to the administration and the mission, also entailed more frequent interactions and an acceleration in the dissemination of news, gossip, and rumours. In essence, the pre-sickness period was being repeated. After what had by this time become a tradition of withdrawal, of avoiding trouble by living in small groups and moving elsewhere as vexations increased, the closer concentration and extended range of interactions certainly contributed towards a heightening of tension. Rumours, moreover, became more and more millenarian in nature, charged with expectancy. Then, in 1951, Tangu sought to realize their new man. They engaged in explicit and overt cargo activities.[3]

---

[1] Tangu refer to the 'tween-war years as the '*gud taim*', a pidgin phrase meaning 'good times' or 'good old days'.

[2] About Yali see Peter Lawrence 1954 'Cargo Cult and Religious Beliefs among the Garia', *International Archives of Ethnography*, vol. xlvii, no. 1, pp. 1–20, and 1964 *Road belong Cargo*, Manchester University Press, *passim* and especially pp. 141–79. See also B–1960: 196–207.

[3] B–1960: 1–3.

TABLE 1

Population Distribution 1951

	Houses	Population		Houses	Population
Wanitzir	135	664	*Riekitzir*	141	667
Wasamb	25	101	Naimwenk	1	4
Waieme	8	18	Duopmwenk	36	186
Ungiar (new)	27	162	Igem	1	5
Ungiar (old)	3	13	Bwongeram	2	7
Mamining	21	106	Murinap	7	15
Mndaningamb	1	1	Zambai	1	3
Amuk	22	108			
Andemarup (new)	23	138	Catechist: 1.		
Andemarup (old)	2	7	Luluai: 1. Tultul: 1. Doctor boy: 1.		
Tsu'ungk	3	9			
Luluais: 4. Tultuls: 4.			Separam	3	12
Doctor boys: 4.			Rembamung	2	7
			Imbuer	30	167
			Want	4	15
Biampitzir	67	347	Guiyet	3	9
			Awuk	1	3
Wanar	9	47	W'tsiapet	31	176
Barein	14	80	Gadaginamb	9	20
Ruonganan	8	45	Ramav	1	3
Riknang'tien	14	73	Bwanbwen	1	6
Ambungk	22	102	Baikunai and		
Catechists: 3 for Biampitzir and			Baitikai	2	7
Wanitzir together			Ukwamb	6	22
Luluai: 1. Tultul: 1.			Catechist: 1.		
Doctor boy: 1.			Luluai: 1. Tultul: 1. Doctor boy: 1.		
Mangigumitzir	85	336			
Mut	7	13			
Dupam	3	6	Catechist: 1.		
Bomwenk	1	2	Luluai: 1. Tultul: 1. Doctor boy: 1.		
Main cluster	74	315			

Notes:

1. Approximately 1,700 of the above are nominal Christians. Of these about 500 are reasonably regular in their religious duties, and most of these are female.

2. Approximately 15–20 per cent of the male population is liable to be away on extended periods of contract labour.

3. Catechists are literate in pidgin English. Otherwise a moderate competence is confined to those youths and maidens who have attended school regularly, and who are about to leave school.

Tangu and Cargo

The European presence in Tangu solved some problems, created new ones, but made little difference to the central dilemmas of Tangu social relations. Under the aegis of mission and administration, conditions for stable and well-regulated marriage were ensured. The peace had to be kept, some of the consequences of the beliefs attaching to sorcery could be mitigated, habits of hygiene and cleanliness were developed, migrant labour to the coast was controlled so that villages should not be denuded of the young and able-bodied. School houses were built, mission teachers or catechists taught the young and maintained contacts between the mission station and outlying settlements, attendance at Sunday mass became habitual for many pagans as well as Christians, administrative procedures were accepted. But the primary tensions cohering in sorcery and the opposed values of filiation and siblingship remained. There was no institution through which Tangu could themselves make explicit adjustments to the changes taking place. Because essentially non-reciprocal and unpredictable, relations with Europeans were a strain. And if Tangu could apprehend, see, and experience facets of the new and Euro-peanized environment, there is little evidence that they could comprehend them.

Having access to wage labour, Tangu were in a position to buy a variety of goods instead of having to make them for themselves. No more the sweat of working in and with stone. Iron and steel hoops, bars, springs, and wires could be beaten cold into spear or adze blades and hunting knives. Cheap enamel ware replaced carved wooden bowls and cups of coconut shell. Castaway cigarette and tobacco tins were handier as lime containers than incised gourds. For daily wear, if not for ceremonial purposes, the old clothes of Europeans or the cheap multi-coloured textiles at the trade store seemed more economical, and perhaps more progressive, than the traditional bark-cloth. Ribbon, coloured braiding, and service webbing found favour at the expense of the more laboriously woven cane anklets, wristlets, armbands, and waist-belts. It was not difficult to pick up or buy a large variety of articles originating in the factories of Europe, Australia, China, and Japan. On the other hand, though some traditional artifacts—in decreasing numbers—continued to be made, that vital relation between a man and what he creates with his own hands from his own mind lay dormant. When the club-houses disappeared a tradition of fluting, of painting, of carving, of canework, and of sculpture was lost to the rising generation. And because such activities were for Tangu indicative of that creativity in man which distinguished him from the beasts, with them went much of the self-respect and distinction in manhood. Mission activities could not, overnight, be a satisfactory substitute. The young had money which they could give to, or withhold from, their elders: either way, and with the best will in the world, parents in the mellowness of their maturity and experience were placed in a position of dependence on their children. In addition, brought up as Christians, learning to read and write in pidgin English and becoming familiar with, and dealing in, the terms of the new environment, the young began to be isolated from their parents and their own tradition.

Life in this new environment depended significantly upon a particular attitude towards the giving and obeying of orders, upon delegation of responsibilities, upon a conception of what was legal, upon recourse to courts of law. Such conventions were foreign to Tangu—yet they had to act within terms of them in their relations with Europeans. While the administration attempted to deal with sorcery by insisting on habits of hygiene, the mission, more subtly, was using these beliefs to teach Tangu a Christian way of life.[1] Such differences of approach were also expressed at the organizational level. So that, competing for the trust and confidence of Tangu, administrative officers and missionaries often found themselves in rivalry—enabling Tangu to play off one against the other.[2] More importantly, perhaps, taking the sum of their experiences with Europeans into account, it became clear to Tangu that if they were men, then Europeans were something more. Or, if Europeans were but men, then they were something less.[3] Though there were certain occasions when Europeans could be cajoled or persuaded, they had powers which they appeared to wield quite freely, which Tangu did not possess, to which Tangu had no access, over which Tangu had no control. Europeans

[1] See B–1960: 69.   [2] See B–1960: 140–6.   [3] See B–1960: 160.

were a problem, not simply because Tangu had to get on with
them in a very practical sense, but because their presence alone
forced Tangu to look into themselves and question their own
nature as men and women. At this point, one might say, Tangu
began to covet a future in which they and Europeans would
confront each other on equal terms, with similar kinds of powers,
able to deploy and dispose of equivalent amounts of wealth.

Quite early in their European experience Tangu explained
their relations with white men in the form of a narrative.[1]
'Once upon a time', runs the gist, 'there were two brothers. One
was the ancestor of white men, the other of black men. They
lived together as brothers should, in amity and co-operation.
One day, however, the brother who was the ancestor of black
men did what he should not have done. In consequence the
descendants of that brother have forfeited intelligence, understanding, and all the things that white men have. Yet, since
white men were in fact the brothers of black men, they should
behave as such, sharing their inheritance with their black
brothers.' On the level of apprehension the narrative carried
the notion of change, of an equable settlement.[2] In 'explaining'
an initial situation the narrative gave some guidance as to the
development of that situation. In practical terms, white men
could and should be persuaded to share their goods and attributes—because they would.[3]

The narrative about the two brothers was the seed from which
there grew what has elsewhere been called a myth-dream—
myth-dream rather than aspirations, because the latter implies
an intellectualization which the former does not.[4] No static
summation, once the myth-dream began to take shape subsequent events and experiences not only added to the content but
tended themselves to be interpreted in the light of its previous
postulates.[5] On the level of apprehension Tangu began to act out
the terms of the myth-dream. If the first ancestor had done what
he should not have done, they themselves were in a position
to mitigate the consequences. White men must be persuaded
into brotherhood. Yet while few Europeans were disposed to
such intimacy, attempts by Tangu to take the initiative were

---

[1] Narrative N. 30, *infra*, pp. 400–3 (but see also B–1956(*b*): 415–31 and
B–1960: 154–76).   [2] See B–1960: 172–6.
[3] See B–1960: 172–6.   [4] See B–1960: 148.   [5] See B–1960: 177–9.

condemned as insolent, rebellious, or presumptuous. Then
Mambu appeared. He told Tangu that white men were not
brothers who might be persuaded into sharing their inheritance. On the contrary, he said, they were thieves and robbers
who were stealing what by rights belonged to the black man.
White men were intercepting the cargo—manufactured goods
—and changing the labels on the cases. So, Mambu went on,
white men should not be obeyed. They should be thrown out of
New Guinea.

As events turned out, Mambu failed to energize a coherent
movement in Tangu itself. But he left behind him memories
of his supposed exploits which themselves became a myth or
legend, part of the total myth-dream. In the narrative about
Mambu,[1] however, the vehement opposition to Europeans of
Mambu the man emerged as toned down and in rough conformity with the first of the cargo narratives. Co-operation, the
linking of black and white in a reciprocal relationship, was again
the theme—with this difference: whereas the first narrative had
referred to 'black' and 'white' peoples as wholes, personalized
as brothers, with the Mambu narrative a process of differentiation becomes noticeable, and a new conception, that of the
'moral European'—the European who, unlike the general run of
Europeans, will act like a brother and share his inheritance—is
given shape. Further, touching the springs of individual responsibility welded to competence and integrity which had been
developing in Tangu, from the Mambu narrative there emerges
the model of a new man, an individual, a black man with
primary Christian virtues and characteristics.[2] And this aspect
of the encounter with Europeans, the making of a new man
able to deal with Europeans on their own terms, began to
overshadow the others.

Well it might. For until Tangu had made new men of themselves they were in no position to persuade Europeans into
adopting more nearly reciprocal relations. Nor could they gain
that access to manufactured goods which might enable them to
do so. It was, too, within the context of the new man that Yali—
a cargo leader from the Rai coast who had become known all
over the Madang District—had most significance for Tangu.

[1] Narrative N. 31, *infra*, pp. 403-4 (but see also B–1954(*a*): 245–6 and
B–1960: 188–96).   [2] See B–1960: 254–9.

For Yali had been known to enjoy friendly relations with administrative officers. He was not just another black man. His manhood, bravery, and competence during the war had been recognized by Europeans with an award for gallantry. As the central figure in several cargo movements, and because he was believed to be behind the labour troubles at that time quite frequent in the Madang District, Yali was accorded the signal honour by those Europeans who were opposed to him of being treated not as an impoverished and impotent kanaka, but as an opponent demanding a full deployment of their resources. So far as Tangu were concerned, Yali, a black man, had become a full man in the terms of European notions of manhood. And in the rites Tangu performed when they engaged in their cargo activities, the theme of creating a new man, a competent and responsible individual of integrity who could encounter Europeans on their own terms, receives as much or more emphasis than the theme of sharing an inheritance of material goods.[1]

The suggestion of guilt involved in the first of the cargo narratives not only forced Tangu to look into themselves as human beings who were not as competent in the new environment as the white men of their experience seemed to be, but it also explained why the social organization which the closer ancestors had left to them was incapable of providing cargo— what Europeans had, and by which all Europeans could be classified together.[2] In the notion of the new man, however, all this was contained and overleaped. From a resigned acceptance, coupled with the hope that white men would take the initiative, the more positive notion of making the new man developed. For in the new man, exemplified first by Mambu and then by Yali—both of whom had explicit ideas about new institutions and new modes of living[3]—lay just that competence which

[1] See B–1960: 254–9.

[2] Within terms of the distinction 'shame/guilt', traditional Tangu culture could be described as a 'shame' rather than a 'guilt' culture. But apart from the fact that 'shame' does not necessarily exclude 'guilt', after a generation of Christian influence and the adoption into the Tangu language of '*pekato*, sin', it would be surprising if 'guilt' were not present. After questioning Tangu on the nature of the brother's act in this narrative, and after observing their behaviour and reactions in relation to it, there is little doubt that they themselves feel that the act is characterized by, or characterizes, 'guilt' rather than 'shame'. (Compare Ruth Benedict 1947: 222–7 *The Chysanthemum and the Sword*, London.)

[3] See B–1960: 246–59.

might conceive the new, proper, and necessary institutions. The
new man was a solution as much for the individual as for the
community as a whole. And though, as men, both Mambu and
Yali could be seen by Tangu to have failed in their own particular endeavours, as concrete representations of the new man
they succeeded in making explicit what for Tangu had hitherto
been largely hidden in feelings. By taking the initiative, by
expressing this initiative both in word and deed, Mambu and
Yali articulated and externalized for Tangu what they had
felt to be so rather than known to be so, apprehended rather
than comprehended.

Ideally, comprehension would have required of Tangu a
knowledge of the new environment in the terms of a language
which could describe and analyse all its aspects and relations.
Pidgin English on Tangu tongues is largely a vocabulary
syntactically ordered as in the Tangu language. Economical in
simple directives and closely related to traditional life, even at
its most verbose straining at the meaning in English, it is not
a language with the contextual referents necessary to a full
understanding of the new world that is forming. It is a language
adapted to relations between superior and inferior. The attempt
to use the Tangu language to explain the parts of the new
environment, on the other hand, puts a European into a situation of complete *rapport* with Tangu themselves. Conceptions of
space, time, number, causation, and relationship cannot but be
reduced to Tangu terms. Then, as Tangu remark, one is either
a liar, speaking of marvels beyond the imaginative grasp, or
implying the existence of a 'secret' which white men possess and
are withholding from the black man.[1] Yet whilst for the vast
majority of Tangu their native tongue is the only one in which
they are fully articulate, their total experience includes many
varieties of 'European situation' to which they have to respond.
Not wholly comprehended through pidgin, these 'European
situations' may be completely misinterpreted through the vernacular. Thus, though virtually the only terms in which Tangu
can think articulately, intellectualize, or fully express themselves are those of the Tangu language, related to a traditional
environment and social order, much of their present experience
is bound up with an environment and social order which

[1] See B–1960: 199.

require very different terms of expression if the experiences are to be adequately described, related, and so comprehended. Mambu and Yali brought comprehension that much nearer.

Contexts of Being

If cargo activities signal the attempt to bring different sectors of experience and being into a single coherent whole, a process of cognoscence or gathering comprehensions, outside the cargo situation separate fields of being tend to fall apart, eliciting processes of oblivescence, the abandoning of particular beliefs and practices. Both processes together contribute to the making of history, and the differing kinds and degrees of understanding characteristic of Tangu are pertinent in all aspects of their lives. Though, through their common participation in *br'ngun'guni*, Tangu form a polity, they are not so much a social group with clearly designated bases of action as an aggregate of individuals with a common experience. The mission is bringing literacy to Tangu, an awareness of membership of a greater community, some perception of Christian thought and doctrine. Through the mission the past is being forgotten, partial comprehensions of the present and future are deepening. But while Christian values are implanted in the mind, a largely traditional subsistence economy fosters and recreates traditional ways and thought. Experience of the administration has given Tangu some further understanding of hygiene and cleanliness, and it is accustoming them to that delegation of authority so necessary to being in the greater political community. But in present circumstances Tangu find it difficult to abandon the idea that in practice a man speaks only for himself and perhaps his wife and younger children. Whereas missionaries and administrative officers tend to require of Tangu conformity to their own ideals, and so make demands on their loyalty, affection, and moral confidence, the commercial experience derived from encounters with traders, planters, and recruiters has taught Tangu that an exchange of goods and services for cash need not be accompanied by a continuing sense of moral obligation.[1]

---

[1] For a discussion of the relations between Tangu and various categories of European see B–1960: 30–42.

PLATE II

a. A part of Riekitzir

b. A part of Mangigumitzir

Within the interactions and syntheses taking place between Tangu tradition and the three different systems represented by missionary work, moneyed commerce, and the administration, the notion of the 'moral European' is of crucial importance. An imaginative or ideal rather than a pragmatic category, potentially inhering in every European though unlikely to be realized in any particular one, the moral European represents the kind of European Tangu themselves would like to encounter because he would engage in reciprocal relations with them. An idealized synthesis of the more agreeable sectors of the European experience, the moral European both defines and is defined by the new man. For this new man, figured as black with European capacities, appears as the kind of man Tangu would like themselves to be when engaging with the moral European: an encounter between equals.[1] Still, such a synthesis is for the future to realize. Today, outside the cargo situation, different fields of being and experience remain separate and distinct. When an administrative officer comes on his rounds Tangu behave as though personal hygiene, cleared paths, a spruce village, and the giving and acceptance of orders with military smartness were the most naturally important features of their lives. But when the officer proceeds to a census and begins to ask questions, the occasion palls. At church, or when a missionary pays a visit, a friendly and almost jocular demeanour is thought to be proper. Pidgin English is spoken, vociferous greetings exchanged. Youths and maidens test each other in mental arithmetic. But passing inquiries as to attendance at mass, school, confessional, or communion rails are met with uneasy grins and promises. And though one cannot be sure that possible alternatives are not in the mind, traditional transactions tend to be effected in traditional ways, formal and dignified ways, quite different from going into a mission or trade store to make a purchase.

Such contextual definitions of being should not, however, blind one to the gathering undercurrents of convergence. Parts at least of the behaviour proper to one context tend to be carried over into others—even if only temporarily or by way of jest. In this sense every present situation is pregnant with new forms and precedents. When because of some alteration in circumstances or a slight nonconformity someone is hurt or aggrieved,

[1] For more about the 'moral European' see B–1960: 264–70.

the matter is argued and discussed in terms of traditional usages, mission teaching, the possible or probable reactions of the missionary himself, administrative policies and procedures, the probable consequences of going to court or seeking administrative advice, the conventions of other New Guinea peoples, the motives of the individuals concerned, the advantages to be gained by emphasizing one aspect rather than another. Lacking collective groups such as the clan, lineage, or association, the Tangu householder is forced to make shift for himself. He confronts the varied situations of present-day Tangu life with his own and his household's interests in view. Engaging in temporary alliances, since no one is bound to help him he has to go carefully and initiate slowly.

That the Tangu social order has not completely disintegrated seems to be due to three main factors. First, there is the administrative presence which, by enforcing the peace, has prevented any further self-destruction. Then there is the missionary endeavour. This, in attempting to educate Tangu, has given them the opportunity to develop their prospects in the greater community. Finally, and perhaps most importantly, there is that stream of tradition which, as we shall see it emerging from the narratives, still gives shape to the meaning of man. Yet there is neither consistency nor complementarity in the variety of features subsumed in these three terms. On the contrary, they are in conflict with one another. Hence the search for the new man and the moral European, syntheses of antithetical features.

Subsistence Activities in Perspective

Had Tangu history been more adequately documented, the summary of its main features might differ in particulars from what has been said above. But the primary themes, one may suggest, would run parallel. Though much has doubtless grown large with the telling, and may in parts be fictional, or suffer from projections from the present—what history does not?— still, that which is said to have occurred is part of the experience of the living or of their parents or grandparents—who were known and seen. It does not represent lore of the ancestors, what has been handed down from time immemorial. Tangu themselves make this distinction. And as far as individuals resort to this 'history' to explain the present, justify themselves, or give depth to their reasons for disputing, so far is it contained in the present. Changes in settlement and social organization, tensions in relationships, events, and the growing influence of Europeans—all represent a historical experience against which Tangu appreciate their present condition. On the other hand, contrasting with those features which have served to widen Tangu horizons, subsistence activities have altered little —and the narratives bear this out. Tangu have more efficient tools than they used to have—of European manufacture, or of natively hafted steel or iron blades instead of stone. Men and youths go away to the coastal areas to work for cash, which they can use to buy tools, trinkets, gewgaws, and medicines. Some of their produce may occasionally be sold to the administration or the mission or other natives for money. And more recently the administration has tried to encourage the cultivation of rice as a cash crop.[1] Nevertheless, life in Tangu still depends on shifting horticulture, on arboriculture, hunting, foraging for wild nuts, fruits, leaves, and relishes, bartering manufactures, making formal food and harvest exchanges, providing feasts.

There is no doubt, however, that the organization of these activities has changed. Whereas in the past co-operation would have been based on the *gagai* or *mwenk*, everywhere in Tangu today the basic and most permanent co-operative group is the household, composed of a husband, his wife or wives, their natural and adopted children, and perhaps an ageing parent of either spouse. It is reasonable to assume that in the past Tangu led a busy and variegated village life. Security from enemies lay in the settlement. Adult men and youths could meet and gossip in the club-houses. Members of reasonably stable co-operative groups could take it in turns to work in the garden, hunt, or idle. There were decorative paraphernalia, tools, weapons, personal and other gear and equipment to be made. But today during daylight hours settlements are deserted, and households are scattered over the surrounding countryside, gardening, hunting, or visiting friends or kinsfolk. Many prefer to spend days or nights at a time in their garden shelters or hunting lodges, and only at dusk, or at week-ends, or when an administrative officer is expected, or on festive occasions, is any large

[1] See B–1960: 225–7 for a comment on rice growing.

proportion of a settlement present. For particular purposes such
as clearing land, fencing gardens, providing feasts, taking in the
harvest, or building new houses, households combine together.
But they do so not necessarily because certain spouses in the
households concerned form a kin group based on a common
descent, but rather from a convenience and preference which
resolve themselves into economic and political advantage.
Though the kin idiom is used to describe these alliances and
their interrelations, and residential propinquity appears as a
correlate, further scrutiny shows these combinations to be
temporary only. Householders live where they do, or shift
residence, in relation to the claims to land which they can
exercise, as well as in relation to the ambience of their interactions with particular neighbours. The kin idiom, as also that of
friendship,[1] indicates continuing moral relationship and categorizes economic and political relations rather than biological
connection.

Combining and co-operating to their mutual advantage, a
group of households tends to be held together by able and
industrious men whom Tangu call 'big men', *wunika ruma*, and
whom we may designate 'managers'. Shrewder and wiser than
most, possessing qualities of leadership, managers succeed in
maintaining an alliance principally through a notable productive capacity and prominent and effective oratorical prowess in
br'ngun'guni. In the past, it may be supposed, such features as
age, range of closer kin, warrior values, influence in the club-
house, and ritual and other specialist knowledge would have
filled out and broadened the managerial role. Today, however,
managers cannot rely on the unhesitating aid of kin or neighbours, nor can they exert influence through a club-house or
count on their fighting skill and generalship. Instead, they are
invited continually to maintain, prove, and demonstrate anew
their ability to provide large quantities of foodstuffs for feasting
exchanges. Yet because Tangu are fiercely egalitarian, and
insist upon equivalent reciprocities in exchanges of foodstuffs,
in order to show precisely how equal they are managers require

[1] Friends are formally not kin, but the moral content is much the same (*infra*,
pp. 118–22).

[2] On managers and the managerial role see *infra*, pp. 124–33, and also
B–1957(*d*): 763–6; B–1960: 108–11.

rivals of similar ability, and co-operative alliances stand in opposition to each other.

A generally competitive economy as between households and co-operative groups—however these latter are, or may have been, formed—it is exactly the tensions implied in the phrase 'competitive egalitarianism' which, going to the roots of being Tangu, engenders the conflict in European as well as traditional situations. Not yet much concerned with raising standards of living for their own sake, unable to conserve the wealth they produce, Tangu exploit the resources of their environment not simply to subsist but to show they are worthy of living in it. Each successive generation has to re-create the total wealth of the community, each household competes with others to contribute the most. Those who work hard gain prestige and credit by disposing of their produce through a more rapid turnover and wider ranges of equivalent exchanges. For Tangu the point, or value, in producing foodstuffs for exchange, making artifacts, or having access to, or possession of, European manufactured goods, lies in the way they reflect skill, competence, shrewdness, cunning, wisdom, foresight, industry, and moral integrity. A mound of yams, or a fistful of feathers, or plaques of dogs' teeth, or a chest of European goods that did not directly reflect these qualities in their possessor would be pointless, of no value. And since, first and foremost, prestige and influence depend upon competence in the subsistence activities, abilities not supported by competence in this field do not normally count for much.

Work and its Values

Tangu and the immediate environs are relatively high. To the north the cloud-capped top of Manam volcano is visible, and on a clear day the lofting Bismarcks may be seen far to the west. Looking eastward over grasslands across to the Adelbert mountains, one may see the winding strip of forest that marks the course of the Iwarum. Rain squalls which form over the coastal range rush southwards over river and forest. Yet little rain falls in Tangu, for most such squalls are deflected either side of the Tangu knot, leaving the central areas dry. While the north and eastward aspects of Wanitzir and Biampitzir are dry and grassy, within the hollow formed by the main Tangu ridge and thence south and west, the country is forested, steep, and rugged, the ridges gradually dropping in height until, beyond Andarum, the traveller debouches into the Ramu swamps. Here the climate is moist. Still, storms and squalls originating over the Ramu and roaring eastwards over the tree tops may be channelled between two Tangu ridges at the expense of the valleys on the further sides. Subject to such vagaries, which provide Tangu rain-makers and rain-checkers with their opportunities, most of the year is generally wet, with an expectable if not wholly reliable dry spell in the period from July to October. Topsoils are fertile, though there are barren patches. Steep slopes and, in most parts, an underlay of clay, make for a rapid run-off after rain, and consequent sudden and dramatic flooding of the valley floors. Earthquakes and tremors are frequent.

All the permanent settlements in Tangu are built on high ground. The older ones within the main Tangu knot are sited on soft and workable sandstone, which drains well after rain and is free from dust in dry weather. But through into Riekitzir, where the ridges are limestone formations usually well covered with soil, the settlements are badly drained, extremely sticky in wet weather and dusty in dry. Garden plots, each with a garden shelter sufficiently robust for a family to eat and sleep in comfort, are distributed over the surrounding country. Though some households have more, all have at least two plots, a main cultivation reasonably close to the permanent settlement, and a smaller one next to the hunting lodge, which is usually in the depths of the forest or out in the bush. Where a family is polygynous it is usual for each wife to have a separate plot for herself and her children, and normally, though not always, co-wives have contiguous plots. In their gardens, which must be remade each year, either by clearing away tracts of forest or, as in the easterly parts of Wanitzir, by clearing away *kunai* grass, Tangu cultivate in rotation numerous varieties of four main staples:[1] yams, *mami*,[2] taros, and bananas—which are supported by sugar-cane, pitpit-cane, gourds, squashes, beans, and shrubs with edible leaves. Maize, tapioca, sweet potatoes, melons, pumpkins, tomatoes, and other vegetables have been introduced

[1] See Table 2, *infra*, for a summary of subsistence activities.
[2] A species of yam.

comparatively recently by missionaries and returned labourers. Out in the forest or across the downs, using the hunting lodge as a base, Tangu hunt pigs, cassowaries, lizards, wallabies, phalangers, and the smaller marsupials. There too they forage for wild edible leaves, nuts, chestnuts, and fruits. Breadfruit trees are planted in suitable places, a wild variety of breadfruit is nurtured but not planted, and sago, a fifth staple, is planted in damp cups in the hillsides where it will prosper. Coconut and areca-nut palms are planted around settlements, though areca-nut groves are often found in the bush or forest—they were planted when that part of the bush or forest was under cultivation. In their settlements Tangu keep pigs and cockerels. Hunting dogs follow their masters.

A husband begins seriously to think about making a new garden towards the end of July and the beginning of August, at the start of the dry season, when the leaves on the yam vines have begun to curl and turn brown. The yam harvest and making a new garden proceed concurrently. Yet the site will have been chosen some months earlier. For though the main work does not start until the yams are ready, if ripening taros are to cut short the dearth from December through January and into February, a damp and spongy plot will have had to be cleared by May or early June for the planting of taro shoots. The most convenient site for a new garden is one adjacent to the old: distances for transplanting are at a minimum, the old garden shelter may be used for another year, and a section of the old fence will enclose the new garden. On the other hand, no man wants land that has been in fallow for less than three years, the wise prefer a seven-year rest, and primary forest— which is free of undergrowth—is much easier to clear than secondary scrub with weeds and seedlings in profusion. A humus of dead and rotting leaves is desirable, so is a steep and well-drained slope. Then, since the wife will have to carry the produce from garden to settlement, the distance between them has to be considered.[1] Finally, both husband and wife remember well the sites of past gardens and the kinds of harvests they yielded. Personal convenience must be set against sufficient

---

[1] Though women often carry heavy loads of produce from garden to settlement, what at first sight appears to be gruelling and arduous is also matter for pride. Women like it to be known how far they can carry heavy loads.

subsistence, contributions to feasts, exchange obligations, and the ambition to be more equal than others.

As yams start to ripen, so the work of clearing the main area of the new site commences. It proceeds slowly at first, for attention often reverts to digging up the ripened yams, cleaning them, sorting, stacking, and later carrying the bulk to the settlement for storage, exchanges, and feasts. Then, as the yam season advances, more and more time is given over to the

TABLE 2

Summary of Subsistence Activities

1. *Gardens*

    Median size of:

    main household plot, monogamous family   1·6 acres
    main household plots, polygynous family   1·8 „
    plot at hunting lodge   0·6 „

    Average acreage worked by:

    renowned managers   2·8 acres
    mature men, not managers   2·1 „
    men with managerial ambitions   2·2 „

    Median number of plots worked by one household 2
    Largest number of plots worked by polygynous household 4

2. *Main staples*

	planted	harvested
Taro (*Colocasia* spp.)	May–June	Feb.–Apr.
Taro (*Xanthosoma* spp.)	July–Sept.	June–Aug.
Bananas (*Musa* spp.)	July–Oct.	July–Oct.
Mami (*Dioscorea alata* spp.?)	Oct.–Dec.	May–July
Yams (*Dioscorea esculenta* spp.)	Nov.–Jan.	July–Oct.
Sago (*Metroxylon rumphii* spp.?)	Nov.–Feb.	Nov.–Feb.
Coconut (*Cocos nucifera*)	perennial	

3. *Annual household garden crops*

Bananas	Beans	Cabbage	Ginger	Gourds
Maize	*Mami*	Melons	Peas	Pepper
Pitpit-cane	Pumpkins	Squashes	Sugar-cane	Sweet potatoes
Tapioca	Taro	Tobacco	Tomatoes	Yams

4. *Cash crops*

    Yams, taros, sago, and vegetables are sold to the mission in small quantities: either (*a*) for immediate use by mission personnel,
            or   (*b*) for distribution free, or at a nominal price, to the sick and needy.

Hill or dry rice is cultivated in plots varying from 0·1 to 0·5 acres:

> co-operative task group (say 30 households) recruited by local administrative officials within the area of their responsibility and residence;
>
> seed provided by administration;
>
> sale virtually guaranteed if brought to administrative headquarters.

5. *Crops planted, nurtured if found wild, access to the fruits of which is particularized*

Areca-nut palms	Planted around settlements, hunting lodges, and garden shelters. Presence in forest or bush indicates a previous settlement or garden site.
Bananas	Planted around settlements and hunting lodges, as well as in gardens. Wild varieties nurtured for fibres.
Breadfruit	Domestic variety planted out from cuttings and nurtured. Wild variety watched, but allowed to grow and propagate itself.
Coconut	Planted and nurtured around settlements and hunting lodges.
Deamar tree	Found wild, nurtured for the inner bark from which barkcloth is made.
Juatak'mba	Wild chestnut, found in swampy places, nurtured.
Pandanus	Found wild, species also planted and nurtured in and about settlements, hunting lodges, garden shelters. Fibres used to make string and skirting.
Paw-paw	Recent plantings around settlements and hunting lodges.
Poison roots	Found wild (*Derris trifoliata*?). Sometimes planted in gardens.
Edible leaves	From shrubs planted in gardens and around settlements and hunting lodges; nurtured when site is in fallow.

6. *Wild stuffs, access generally unparticularized, though disputes may follow takings by certain people in lands not directly associated with them*

Bamboo	Rattan cane
Croton	Edible leaves of trees
Tangked palm	Hardwood (*limbom*) palms (*Kentiopsis archontophoenix*)
Pepper	
Wild taros	South Seas almond (*galip*) (*Canarium* spp.)
Wild yams	Vines

7. *Domesticated or partially domesticated livestock*

Pig   Cockerel   Hunting dog   Cat

8. *Animals and birds hunted for their flesh*

Bandicoot	Cassowary	Pig
Bush rat	Marmot	Possum
Cuscus	Monitor lizard	Wallaby

9. *Additional animals taken for their flesh*

Cicadas, grasshoppers	roasted, a delicacy for children.
Frogs	delicacy for adults.
Land crabs	for children (but rarely).
Small snakes	roasted, for children.
Small lizards	roasted or smoked, for children.
Tree grubs	delicacy for adults.

10. *Birds shot primarily for feathers; flesh may be eaten*

Bird of paradise (*Paradisea apoda, Uranoris rubra*)
Guria pigeon
Hornbill
(Domesticated cockerel also kept only for feathers)

11. *Hunting and fishing*

Land animals	tracked and brought to bay by dogs, dispatched with spear;
	trapping (deadfall, maze fence, pit).
Birds	shot with bow and arrow from 'hides' in trees.
Fish	netted with hand nets by women (obsolescent);
	speared by men with light multi-pronged spear in shallows;
	speared by men by the light of bamboo torch at night;
	stunned in pools by using poison roots.

12. *Supplementary activities for cash*

Migrant labour to coast or further afield.
Contingent tasks (house building, repairs, porterage) for administrative
   officers and mission personnel.

new garden. Gradually, day by day, wives and daughters
helped by younger sons clear away the underbrush and weeds.
With clearing well forward, older and unmarried sons start lopping the trees while their fathers clean off the cut branches and
stack them against the time when they will be needed as supports for yam and *mami* vines. After the lopping comes felling,
work for men and older boys. The larger trunks are left where
they fall, most of them effectively dividing the site into plots
which will be marked out to the names of members of the
household. Smaller trunks may be used for the same purpose,

or be rolled across or down the slope to make a base for the garden fence. Trunks are cleaned, the larger branches being stripped and laid aside as fencing material. Saplings and younger trees are left standing to provide shade, to be the central supports of pyramids of yam stakes, and to provide a nucleus of growth for the return to forest when the site is eventually abandoned. There is little apparent urgency. With plenty of yams available, and each household within a co-operating group taking its turn to help the others with cleaning, lopping, and felling, the atmosphere is gay and cheerful. Breadfruits are ripening, calling for impromptu parties or flirtations either on the site or in the bush,[1] feasts and dances are in preparation, food is plentiful.

The site cleared, the next task is to burn off the dried litter of sticks, weeds, and leaves. It should be done as soon as possible. Fresh shoots begin to spring up almost immediately, and so fast is their growth that sometimes, if there happens to be a wet spell, it is easier to start clearing all over again elsewhere than to attempt to pull up the mass of freshly germinated weeds and seedlings. Burning the litter is normally done in two stages. First, at about noon on a hot sunny day when the dew and damp have dried off and the rubbish is like tinder, a torch is put to it. Hopes are for a short, swift, and fierce conflagration. Then, a day or so later, depending on the yam harvest, the site is cleaned by firing small piles of sticks and ashes and raking them over the ground—a long and painful task usually done by the women. As cleaning is completed so a husband marks out plots to the names of the members of his household, and starts to plant *mami*. Shortly after the site has been cleared *mami*-planting is almost at an end, shoots of the giant taro have been thrust into the ground here and there, suckers from early bananas have been transplanted, and fresh young sprouts from the *mami* first planted have come into view. In the old garden, meanwhile, though the weeds have been allowed to grow un-checked—they can no longer make any difference to the size and quality of the ripened crops—there is still much to be done. Bananas are fruiting, and transplanting the suckers continues through November to March. During the same period pitpit-canes yield their edible flower buds and are cut back and

[1] See N. 11, *infra*, pp. 259-60.

transplanted as their harvest is gathered. Seed yams, some of which remain in the old garden until late in November, are planted in the new garden right through until February. The old garden fence, brittle and dry, is systematically broken down by wife and daughters for use as firewood throughout the following year.

December and January are months of dearth. Tubers are in short supply, and Tangu have to decide whether to put a yam into the cooking-pot, plant it, or compromise by eating the inside and planting the outside where the 'eyes' are protruding. In Riekitzir, Biampitzir, and Mangigumitzir, as the last breadfruits are eaten, householders turn to leaching sago. In Wanitzir, on the other hand, where the drier climate and drainage are inhospitable to sago, the dearth is eked out with breadfruits, the remains of the yam harvest, and edible leaves. But the dearth is also the proper season for making clay cooking-pots and bartering them against sago flour from the other three neighbourhoods. For here, in swampy cups and basins in the hillsides, enough sago palms have been imported, planted, and nurtured to see householders through the period of shortage of tubers. By February, however, new taros are coming up and being eaten, most of the yams have been planted, *mami* and the earlier yam vines are spreading and in leaf. The garden fence, begun when all the *mami* was planted, is almost completed, and the shelter, a rough wind-break in October, has been transformed into a house, small, but large enough for the family to live in and hold the *mami* harvest in June and July. Women are busy weeding. Husbands sleep in their gardens in order, on the one hand, to stop wild pigs from ravaging the young crops, and, on the other, to ambush and kill them for meat, either as they try to break through the garden fence, or as they come through specially constructed gaps which have been laid with traps or snares.[1] In March there are chestnuts to be gathered from the forest. These are picked, parcelled in leaves bound with staves

---

[1] Pigs rut in this period, and sows, farrowing in the bush, find the gardens a relatively easy source of food. It is a man's duty to seek out piglets in the forest and bring them into the village to domesticate them. At the same time, though taros are coming up, there is little variety in the human diet and men are after meat. And the garden fence is rarely completed. Thus building fences, sleeping in the garden, man's desire for meat and piglets, and the sows' and piglets' need for easier nourishment all coincide at one point in time and space: the garden.

and vines, and left to ferment in stagnant pools for a fortnight or so before eating. From April until June—when the main taro crop has been eaten, and *mami* are beginning to be dug up —a husband has relatively little to do in the garden. He spends most of his time hunting, whilst wife and daughters continue with the seemingly interminable work of weeding and cleaning the garden. Then, as *mami* ripens, to be followed by the giant taros, bananas, and yams, he is kept fairly busy. Apart from the work itself, as each crop comes to maturity in its turn there are exchange obligations, feasts, and dances to organize and attend. And the political problems involved in these activities keep him occupied until the time comes when, with these same matters in mind, he begins to think about the size and site of his new garden.

Though the cycle is the same in each of the four neighbourhoods, and everywhere the planting and so harvesting of each crop is spread out over several weeks, Mangigumitzir is usually in advance of the other three neighbourhoods, whilst Biampitzir and Riekitzir, keeping roughly abreast, follow on. Wanitzir comes last, a feature which earns them a local reputation for laziness.[1] Of the five staples (yams, *mami*, taros, bananas, and sago), all Tangu ascribe most importance to yams, and each neighbourhood takes pride in the special varieties it produces. When carefully stored and well ventilated, yams will keep for an appreciable time.[2] Indeed, were it not for the feasting exchanges after the harvest, there would probably be sufficient quantities of yams in Tangu to see all four neighbourhoods safely through to the new taros in February.[3] *Mami* will keep for a short while, and sago flour will store for some months if packed into well-stoppered barrels. But all other crops perish fast.

[1] However, the seasons do, in fact, appear to start somewhat later in Wanitzir than elsewhere. The reputation for laziness of Wanitzir people is probably much more closely connected with the fact that they manufacture cooking-pots, use cash more frequently than others, and often tend to rely on the mission to help them out of temporary difficulties. On these counts, of course, Wanitzir people are envied.

One may add here that Riekitzir, unlike the other three neighbourhoods, engages in large feasting exchanges only in alternate years.

[2] Stored in the past in yam bins. Now stored in conical pyramids on the floors of hunting lodge, garden shelter, or hut in the settlement.

[3] The idea of a surplus can, of course, only arbitrarily be imposed. The first essential is to meet exchange and feasting obligations. Thus, though a man may provide a large feast, it is always possible that he and his family have been going short in order to provide it.

Though sago is sometimes provided for feasting purposes, properly it ought not to be, and *mami* is regarded as second-rate, inferior to the finer-grained yams. Taros, bananas, sugar-cane, pitpit-cane, sweet potatoes, tapioca, and maize may all find a place in exchanges and feasts—but they are generally regarded as supplementary makeweights that one should not presume seriously to offer as main items. Yams take first place.

Of all the crops grown in Tangu, yams are the most difficult to bring to the cooking-pot. And prestige and standing in the community primarily depend on matching productions of yams. Coconuts and areca-nuts always figure prominently in feasts, but once they are seen through the first few weeks and planted out there is little to be done. In themselves they indicate friendship, solidarity, and hospitality rather than work and industry.[1] Sago suckers must be planted out from the parent palm. Yet every child knows how to tell when the flour is being secreted in the fibres, and though leaching requires a few days' hard work it does not present many problems. Taros require a damp and puddingy soil, but as soon as they have germinated, their broad spade leaves shade the ground and effectively prevent the growth of many weeds.[2] *Mami* are rather more difficult. Yet they are hardy, more reliable than yams if not such pleasant eating.

Successful cultivation of any crop reflects diligence and industry. And, in a poor year, he who provides a good feast is openly admired for the self-restraint that has enabled him to deny himself and his family a wholesome daily meal so that he can meet his exchange obligations; secretly envied for the dogged self-willedness that has enabled him to be more equal than others. But a good yam harvest reveals in detail all that a man should be. It points to a wise choice of site, for if the ground is too damp the yams will rot; to skilful and careful planting, for the soil should be loosened and aired to a depth of at least a foot, and the seed yam should be placed so that there is an air cushion beneath it; to many hours of careful weeding, for the vine is exposed to sun and rain and weeds grow quickly,

---

[1] But see *infra*, pp. 251, 395–6.
[2] A new weed, supposedly introduced by the Japanese, and locally known as *jap'n*, may sometimes harm taros, but is particularly associated with the destruction of tobacco plants.

strangling the developing tubers; to deft and judicious digging out, for yams may proliferate in any direction underground, and a damaged yam is no use in exchanges; and to careful storage, for badly stored yams will rot very quickly. All this requires good team-work and foresight; harmonious relations as between husband, wife, and children; skilful direction. Lastly, because yams are vulnerable to blight, and will rot in the ground if there is too much rain or if there happens to be a layer of clay too close under the topsoil, a good yam harvest is evidence of that quality of not having engaged the damaging attentions of other people, non-human beings or animals, which, Tangu feel, ought to go along with moral integrity.

Apart from fermented chestnuts, which are a delicacy not available to all, and which require a certain amount of skill and supervision to prepare; and breadfruits which, again, need some supervision; foods gathered from the forest or bush do not of themselves find a place in exchanges. Used to provide tasty relishes which set off a dish of cooked food—especially at feasts —on the whole the wild harvest is for individuals to gather when and how they please. Social relevances in relation to values in prestige and influence in the community are concentrated on the nurtured foods, primarily on those grown in the garden; on those wildstuffs which require supervision and processing; and on animal life.

Women fish in the streams with hand-nets; men use fish-spears, particularly at night, aided by torches of dry bamboo stuffed with faggots. White grubs,[1] fat and about an inch long, are to be found inside the rotting bark of wild sago palms and, more rarely, in other trees. Men gather them. Two varieties of frog,[1] a red and a yellow, are caught in handfuls as they come out to spawn, and cicadas and other animals of the same family are caught by children, briefly roasted, and then eaten by them. Adults scorn such food. Small snakes, occasionally encountered, are immediately killed and handed over to young children for roasting and eating. Men and youths concern themselves mainly with the trapping, snaring, or pursuit with dogs, of pigs, casso-waries, wallabies, monitor lizards, possums, cuscus, and bush-rats. Piglets are captured in the forest, then brought to the

---

[1] Unidentified.

village which they are trained to regard as their home. And since domestic sows mate with wild boars and farrow in the bush or forest, it is one part of a man's duty to find out where the litter is and capture the piglets for rearing in the village. There they are named and allocated slit-gong call-signs to which they are trained to respond. No feast is complete without meat, pork is especially desirable. As yams produced for a feast are the measure of a competent gardener and householder, so are wild pigs taken in chase the measure of a hunter, and domestic pigs the measure of a careful and far-sighted husbandman or wife.

As a general rule no animals are purposefully bred in Tangu. Cockerels are kept for their feathers, and may ultimately go into the pot: but no one keeps hens. Eggs are not wanted, and hawks, of which there are plenty, have proved to some innovators the virtual impossibility, in the circumstances, of successfully rearing chicks.[1] As soon as they start to grow into boars, village pigs are castrated. Traditionally the operation was carried out with a bamboo sliver; today a razor blade or a knife is more usual. When a bitch carries a litter the pups are reared, often being suckled at the breast. But the occasion is more by chance than judgement. For while Tangu keep bitches—they hunt reasonably well—a dog is not regarded as a useful hunting companion unless it has been emasculated. The majority of Tangu hunting-dogs and cockerels are imported either from Tangwatt in exchange for cloth, iron, or beads, or from the coast against cash, tobacco, areca-nuts, string bags, or cooking-pots.

Despite the entry into Tangu of varieties of manufactured goods, mainly through the mission and returned labourers, the large mass of the population still relies on the resources of the immediate environment for a number of products. Tangu grow and cure their own tobacco, and barter or trade the dried or cured leaf among themselves as well as with members of neighbouring communities. Traditionally the leaf was rolled into a cigar for smoking, and smoking itself was for men rather than

---

[1] Whether of bamboo strips or wire netting, cages do not seem to be proof against Tangu hawks. Eggs may be full of protein, but have no social relevance.

women. Today both sexes smoke, and the cured leaf is more often stuffed into a cheap briar pipe bought from a trade store.[1] Though cloth may be bought quite cheaply from the mission or other trade stores on the coast, Tangu women still prefer to make their petticoats or underskirts from soft banana fibres, and their overskirts from combed and shredded pandanus fibres. From the pandanus, too, by twisting the fibres between palm and thigh, women make string, which is itself used to make fishing-nets; to make string bags and pouches in which to carry crops, gear, and personal trinkets; to knit and crochet plaques and masks and hats to which dogs' teeth or shiny buttons are fixed; to mark out the plots of a new garden site;[2] to illustrate narratives by means of string figures and cats' cradles. Though many men and youths have taken to wearing trade cloth *lava-lavas* or *lap-laps*—shin-length kilts—for routine or daily tasks, most of them still go out into the forest to make themselves a breech-clout of barkcloth, which they can wear proudly at dances and feasts. Trade store bracelets, bangles, belts, garters, ribands, and armbands exert a certain fascination, but many still find a satisfaction in weaving strips of cane—dyed red or black, or left the natural yellow—into waistbelts, anklets, wristlets, and arm-bands for brides and sweethearts. Men make their own wide waistbands, through which the working breechclout passes. Youths and maidens, buying or collecting new materials such as beads, braiding, and ribbon, spend much of their leisure time making ornaments and personal accessories to their own patterns and designs.[3] Tangu still make slit-gongs: they are necessary for making public announcements, for signalling and communicating over difficult country. But the associated rites and ceremonies are no longer practised. Instruments are plain, without the traditional carving, incising, pigmentation, and decoration.[4] The manufacture of handdrums, still marginally

[1] Tangu say that tobacco first grew from a woman's vulva.

[2] The string was reeled on a spindle and, with string in hand, the marker hurled the spindle through the air across the garden. The unreeled string marked the borders of a plot, the landing points of the spindle marked the corners. After the plots had been marked out thus, and after planting, the string was recovered and used to illustrate narratives, which, traditionally, were told and retold in the slack period before the new taros.

[3] Most of these items are personal, being made either for oneself or for a sweet-heart, fiancée, or spouse.

[4] For a discussion of the slit-gong see B–1959(*d*): 136–50.

pursued, is tending to die out in the face of imports from other areas against cash, areca-nuts, pots, string bags, and tobacco.

At one time slivers of bamboo were used for elementary surgery, for shaving, and for circumcising youths on completion of their probationary period in the club-house. Many older folk still prefer to shave with these bamboo slivers, but there is no longer any circumcision, and most Tangu use the razor blades available from trade stores for a variety of purposes, including shaving head, face, or body hairs. The trump or Jew's harp, traditionally made from a section of hard bamboo and used in courting or in illicit love affairs, or by men and youths simply to charm the solitary hour, is no longer made. Nor are models of European manufacture imported. A few skilled potters in Wanitzir and the hither portions of Biampitzir, men as well as women,[1] supply all Tangu with open-fired clay cooking-pots against tobacco, areca-nuts, string bags, sago flour, or cash. Other peoples within a radius of about twenty miles come to Tangu to trade for cooking-pots as well as to bring or gather news and gossip.

Though in general Tangu dislike travelling through the neighbouring areas—for fear of sorcerers—they go to Tangwatt for medicines and hunting-dogs, and to the coast—to or through villages where, having a 'friend' or 'sister', they know they will be safe from sorcerers—for salt, lime, iron, dogs, and a variety of goods which they can obtain for cash or against their local produce. Within Tangu itself trade and barter take place between households in the four neighbourhoods chiefly in terms of the interchange of cash, European manufactured goods, cooking-pots, string bags, sago, tobacco, and areca-nuts. Though cash and European manufactured goods come into Tangu through returned labourers, the mission store in Wanitzir is the most permanent and regular source of the cash and goods in circulation. The wages and stipends of mission employees, when not spent in the store directly, are distributed to various kinsfolk in payment or repayment for past gifts and favours. Most of it, eventually, finds its way back to the mission store in pay-

---

[1] Refusing opportunities to use, and to learn how to use, a wheel, Tangu potters hold fast to the traditional method of 'coil' manufacture. Once made and smoothed off, the pots, about 12 inches in diameter at the largest, are placed in the house and allowed to stand, drying, for a fortnight or more. Later on they are dried in the full sun. After this they are fired in a bonfire of dried coconut fronds.

ment for trade goods. Some cash is hoarded, the rest pays for imports. Trade goods, at second or third hand, are always a useful 'decider' or makeweight in a particular transaction, besides being always acceptable to hinterland peoples in exchange for dogs or medicines.

Perhaps the most significant trade and barter transactions within Tangu are those which concern the distribution from Wanitzir and parts of Biampitzir of clay cooking-pots against sago, string bags, tobacco, areca-nuts, and cash. While it is true that the soils and climate of Wanitzir appear to inhibit the growth of as much sago, pandanus, tobacco, and areca-nuts as are available in the more westerly neighbourhoods, clay is equally available to all. Members of the other neighbourhoods might have made their own pots, the Wanitzir people might have been able to manage without the benefit of produce from the other three neighbourhoods. But, though cooking in pots is certainly easier than pressure steaming in green bamboo barrels, the latter method results in a more palatable meal. Yet, as Tangu point out, though in a material sense each of the four neighbourhoods might have been able to exist independently of the others, if there were no such economic links between them there would be no explicit opportunities for visiting kinsfolk and friends. That the economic relationship should appear, and be thought of, as contingent on the moral engagement is a general feature of Tangu life. If, historically, the traffic in pots seems to have been crucial in bringing the four neighbourhoods together as a unity, it would be more consistent with the themes of Tangu life to say that the traffic in pots provided Tangu with the opportunity to give concrete expression to a moral relationship that had already started to exist. Upon the prior and more general moral engagement, that is, other kinds of relationship tend to depend.[1]

[1] Two further examples:

(a) In a dispute (B–1957(d): 774–9) an embargo on the trade in pots by one community on another incommoded the latter not so much because they could no longer get pots—they could use bamboo barrels for cooking—as because the breach of the moral relationship made it difficult to interact satisfactorily in other fields. Similarly, the community enforcing the embargo was also prevented from engaging satisfactorily in these other fields. Reconciliation, and the lifting of the embargo, were inevitable.

(b) There are several salt pools in Tangu, one of them centrally situated. In the past this central pool probably played an important part in bringing Tangu

Though, apart from pots and string bags, the demand for the products of particular traditional skills is fading, each adult in Tangu is nominally master of some specialist activity, whether it be painting, carving, plaiting, dyeing, mixing a medicine for snake-bite, elementary surgery, telling stories, or making a love potion. On the other hand, all—even mission employees, who are paid in cash for their services to compensate them at least partly for the time lost from gardens and hunting—participate in the main subsistence activities. Relative competences in these, in gardening, hunting, and foraging, provide the basic measures of prestige and virtue: the prestige system demands the common engagement if men are to measure themselves against each other. Withdrawal from them into some full-time specialist activity would, in present circumstances, be tantamount to withdrawing from community life.[1] When backed by productive capacity, a high turnover in the passage of treasure articles and in initiating and meeting food-exchange obligations, the frequent provision of feasts, and competence in *br'ngun'guni*, part-time specialist skills further inform a man's stature. But without the evidence of skill and hard work in garden and bush, part-time specialist skills tend to measure themselves and not the man.

The qualities among Tangu are agglutinative rather than differentiated, add to a man's standing when they cohere in a single whole-status, but do not separately and severally in themselves measure a status that is independent of productive capacity. Money in Tangu, though frequently used, is not yet a thorough-going common medium of exchange. It buys the kinds of things which, traditionally, would have been made in part-time specialist or recreative activities; and it has made

together. Today, neither this nor the other pools are used at all. Whether or not these pools could provide Tangu with the salt they want is impossible to say. Tangu themselves assert that they prefer to get their salt either through Wanitzir, or by walking down to the coast where they can evaporate sea water in pots, or collect driftwood permeated with salt—'In this way we can visit our friends and our sisters.'

[1] Native mission teachers, for example, though themselves natives of Tangu, are on the whole outside the prestige system because, teaching being a full-time occupation, they cannot give sufficient time to hunting and gardening. Teachers who want an over-all prestige must either neglect their school work in order to tend their gardens or go hunting, or try to gain prestige from their association with the Christian and European ambience.

certain traditional tasks seem unnecessary. But money among Tangu does not—as it does in a cash and market economy—as yet differentiate and measure occupations and qualities. It is no basic measure of man. Traditionally, a man's belongings, including his treasures, were buried with him. Today, nobody knows where a dead man has buried his money. Tangu judge a man on his performance, particularly by the way in which, in his generation, he communicates his parts and makes his productive capacity morally relevant. As the wealth of the community is re-created by the sweat and labour of each succeeding generation, so is the moral system, expressed through these same labours, regenerated and sustained with each generation. But—and this touches the heart of the Tangu dilemma—if the new man is to be made, the traditional man must go: competence in other kinds of skills will have to match the status gained by productive capacities. If Tangu are to gain access to, and realize the meaning of, cargo, they will have to abandon their present moral system and traditional measures of man in order to separate and further differentiate the significant parts of man. Manufactured goods are bought with money, money makes possible full-time specialization. Until money is used as money in Tangu, playing a basic role in differentiating and measuring the qualities of man, cargo will remain out of reach, and equality with Europeans, or equality of opportunity to participate with Europeans in the wider economy and community, will remain a part of the myth-dream. Money, the common measure of differentiated statuses, is the key to cargo.

The pursuit of game or, as Tangu put it, 'getting meat', is generally regarded as being more difficult and dangerous[1] than successful gardening. And if a man's reputation lies as much in his garden, because hunting is a male affair the garden and gardening have, thereby, a weighted association with women and the obligations men incur on their behalf. Rarely does a

---

[1] The dangers are not simply the more ordinary ones of being on one's own at the risk of being caught in a sudden flood, or of breaking an ankle or leg without a companion to help, or of being injured by a wild boar or cassowary. Sorcerers inhabit bush and forest, enemies might lay an ambush, a variety of non-human beings may have at him.

man work in his garden without wife or daughter present. More commonly, while women garden, men sit and smoke in the garden shelter or are away hunting. Yet hunting is not simply an economic task, a search for protein. When a husband retires to his hunting-lodge he goes there to find privacy, to free himself from the ties of family and community, to think things over, to nurse a grudge, to dream, to make holiday and have time to

TABLE 3

Summary of Tangu Trading Relations

1. *European manufactured goods.* Mission maintains a trade store for sale against cash or kind; migrant labourers return to Tangu with; administrative officers may distribute in part payment for services; bought for cash in trade stores on coast; second-hand articles obtained in private transactions against cash, services, other European manufactured goods, game, local manufactures, either internally or from neighbours.

2. *Cash.* Mission pays regular employees in, makes *ad hoc* payments for contingent tasks in, buys produce for; administrative officers make payments for porterage and other services in; rice may be sold for; pots may be sold to outsiders for; may form a part of any transaction.

3. *Clay cooking-pots.* Made in Wanitzir and Biampitzir only; trade with outsiders mainly against cash; people come from coast to buy; people come from hinterland to buy; traded within Tangu against foodstuffs, sago, string bags, tobacco, areca-nuts, cash, dogs, beads.

4. *String bags.* Made particularly by Riekitzir and Mangigumitzir to obtain pots from Biampitzir and Wanitzir; also sold to coastal peoples for cash.

5. *Sago.* Produced by Riekitzir, Mangigumitzir, and hinterland peoples for subsistence and exchange or sale to mission (which redistributes during dearth period), Wanitzir, Biampitzir, and coastal peoples against cash, iron, hunting-dogs, beads, pots.

6. *Hunting-dogs.* From coastal peoples against cash and sago; from hinterland peoples against cash, iron, beads, pots, spears, and other local or European manufactures.

7. *Tobacco.* Grown and cured everywhere locally; mostly in Riekitzir; for personal use, trade, and exchange.

8. *Areca-nut.* Grown everywhere, but in rather larger quantities in Riekitzir, used personally or for trade and exchange.

9. *Sundry manufactures, of local or European origin.* The worn or second-hand article traded among Tangu themselves, or with hinterland peoples against hunting-dogs, pigs, and sago, as well as medicines.

himself. There is somewhere to sleep, a fire, food in the garden hard by. And when his family, or a friend, or a close kinsman accompanies him, the lodge is still a haven from the envies and rivalries associated with community life. There in the quiet depths of the forest a father tells his son stories, teaches him how to trap and stalk game, spins out the hours happily carving the haft of an adze, enjoys a pipe at his ease. In like vein wives and daughters may cook, weed, look after young children, cure tobacco, gather pandanus and banana fronds to make string bags or skirts. In their hunting-lodges Tangu are at their friendliest, most inclined to hospitality, most gracious and relaxed. It is a place where, in particular, a man may be truly himself. The ambience of the hunting-lodge emphasizes the values of filiation, distances those of siblingship and community life.

The main garden nearer to the permanent settlement is where a man can be most at his ease as a member of community. In the village itself a man is exposed to criticism, must seek approbation if he is not to be adversely criticized. From this the main garden is a refuge. Still, the accent is on siblingship and community rather than on filiation and family. The household larder, the source of foodstuffs, the garden is also the vehicle through which a man develops his moral experience and sense of responsibility. Where hunting-lodges are more or less permanently sited, the associated gardens moving round the lodge as year succeeds to year, main garden sites have a considerably greater variation of movement. So it is that Tangu remember their main gardens as sections or cycles of their life span, relating events in time to garden plots in particular places, and, by counting and locating plots either before or after an event, so converting relations in space to relations in time. Nursery to the child, the main garden is also a play-ground for the young. The context of growth and maturation as well as a mnemonic for social relationships—for the bulk of each harvested crop is destined to be exchanged against those of others—in gardening Tangu work for a livelihood and also act out their notions of the good life. Not so much attached to the land as to the meaning of the activity of gardening in itself, while hunting throws into prominence those qualities which are specifically masculine, the reputation of a man and his wife and his household lies in the garden, in the way it is kept, in what it is made to produce. The hunting-lodge evokes that part of man which he reserves to himself and perhaps to his intimates. The main garden evokes the responsible man, the householder who uses the wealth he creates to participate in, and manage, community affairs. For Tangu gardening is 'work, *'uap*', a criterion of the creative, cultural, human, and moral. Hunting brings out the predatory self-assertion of maleness.

If some in Tangu work harder than others, no man or woman or child who can wield the necessary implements is ignorant of the techniques that go to make a good gardener. Gardening is the common activity in which each individual may express and realize himself or herself through interaction with others. Maidens whose wedding-day is drawing near, and who have worked in the gardens of their natal households ever since they could walk, look forward to having gardens of their own. And the transition from maiden to wife, from daughter to mistress of her own household, from working under parents and brothers to working with a husband, appears and is represented as an even progress. But for a youth who is becoming independent and looking for self-assurance the parallel transition is uneven. On the whole he prefers hunting to gardening. He likes clearing a new site because he can show off his strength and skill with an axe. He enjoys the firing and planting because a blaze is always exciting, there are opportunities for larking, and by wielding a digging-stick with vehemence he may impress with his vigour and endurance. But he shies from the more gruelling and less spectacular forms of garden work. He likes to laze, take his ease, throw advice to mothers and sisters. Treasuring the self-reliance that hunting has fostered in him, yet still reluctant to quit the security which garden and family have offered, by playing the boss in his parents' garden he has the best of both worlds. Soon he will have a garden of his own, a wife and family to manage, protect, and feed.

Women in Tangu tend to regard their gardens with a practical air that spells security and nourishment for themselves and their children. Garden, women, and children belong together. While they participate in the prestige of an achievement explicitly accorded the husband, like the earth in which a man plants the crops that are to nourish his physical and moral being women are the fertile soil which a man makes fruitful and morally relevant, and through whom he takes his tradition into the future. As a man looks out over his garden the broad and shining taro leaves and rows of climbing yam vines warm his heart. There will be plenty to eat, enough and more for feasts and exchanges. Clean and well-weeded plots tell of a contented wife and dutiful daughters; sons will have their portions in plenty. He feels big, is affable, life glows. But as he glances across at the garden of a neighbour his eyebrows draw together in a frown, muscles tense, unbidden envies tumble in the mind, the venom courses in his veins. In a moment he is on his feet, poised to cuff an irritating son, spurring his women with rough-tongued admonition. . . . By and by, as he looks at his own again, he calms, sits by the fire at his shelter, lights a pipe, thinks and makes plans: even if this matter of cargo is difficult, his yams will earn him respect.

2

THE AMBIENCE OF THE INDIVIDUAL

TANGU history and subsistence activities provide grounds of experience that are widened and deepened by the ways in which Tangu themselves interact and communicate their parts. Aware of history, Tangu recognize that the interactions of the past differed from those that obtain today, and, as their cargo activities bear witness, they look to a future that is different again. But, as was the case in traditional times, moral virtue is still coupled to performance in the subsistence activities. And because these last are often described in narratives and bulked large in the lives of their forefathers, they link Tangu through history to a past beyond it, representing an incapsulation of the past in the present, in rudimentary cash economy, contract labour, an enforced peace, Christian teaching and organization, and subordination to administrative procedures. Subsistence tasks accomplished still sculpt the contours of self-revelation, and provide public evidence of knowledge, skill, thought, cunning, industry, organizational competence, and resilience of character: qualities which are chiselled into prominence or eroded in encounters with others. Given that an individual is to be found in particular resolutions of the normative claims and obligations attaching to categories of relationship, Tangu are accurately described as an aggregate of individuals with a common experience. Not only is there room for manœuvre as between categories and persons, but the content or expectations of the categories themselves are and have been changing. To these matters we now turn.

The Model[1]

The reciprocal communication of parts among Tangu may be either formal or informal, is expressed in services, co-operation,

---

[1] In essence the model is not unique—compare, for example, Claude Lévi-Strauss 1949 *Les Structures élémentaires de la parenté*, Paris, where it receives masterly

exchanges, barter, and sometimes in trade, and is characterized by the fact that obligation does not cease with a completed *do ut des* but continues. Thus A's repayment to B obliges B to give to A, who, in turn, is obliged to repay B, and so on. . . . And defining this continuing engagement by antithesis there are arrangements for specifically agreeing not to communicate the parts. Equivalence in communication is a moral imperative; the actual or potential capacity to participate in reciprocities indicates the range and nature of moral relationships; and the explicit agreement not to communicate the parts, usually entered into after a series of formal exchanges and known as *mngwotngwotiki*—'enough, sufficient, equivalent'—points to a plateau of achievement, an approximate but mutually acknow-ledged moral equivalence. Further, as both active and formally negatived reciprocities are contained within the categories of the kinship idiom, or within institutionalized friendship, these categories describe the limits of the moral order.[1] One not so categorized is called *rangama*, stranger, one with whom there are no regularized reciprocities, no necessarily foreseeable potential of them, and from whom, in consequence, loss or evasions or damage or trouble are likely.[2] Europeans, who cannot partici-pate in Tangu reciprocities, but with whom Tangu have other kinds of relations, are known by special terms outside the idioms of kinship or friendship.[3]

Among Tangu the categories of the kin idiom have an exten-sive range of emphasis, order particular kinds of moral and normative relations, but do not necessarily imply biological

exposition; and the same author 1963 *Structural Anthropology*, London (pp. 120–66), where variants are similarly dealt with. See also Gregory Bateson 1936 *Naven*, Cambridge University Press (pp. 35–53), which deals with a case closely corres-ponding to the Tangu situation. What is of interest here is the way in which the model works, its flexibility, and its persistence through a variety of vicissitudes. Finally, when the model is related to the narratives, we gain some idea of the way in which it is being transformed.

[1] Though friendships may lapse in fact, they do not lapse in principle, and friends cannot become *mngwotngwotiki*.

[2] The Tangu word for sorcerer (*infra*, pp. 133–55) is *ranguma*, and his and the stranger's expected behaviour are often identical. As the two words sound much alike, Tangu often make play with them, implying the one by using the other. While a *rangama* is potentially a *ranguma*, the latter is not necessarily a stranger.

[3] Such as *kiap* (administration, administrative officer); *kampanimasta* (trader, planter); *misin* (mission, mission employee); *pater* (missionary); *waitsikin* (Euro-pean); *masta* (employer). For details see B–1960: 35.

connection. As the members of a household normally consist of a husband, his wife or wives, and their children, within that context the kin idiom implies close biological connection or, as in the case of an adoption, a relationship which should be treated as though there were such a close biological connection. Within the household relations are informal, characterized by mutual help and co-operation, eating together, and a mutual sharing and interest in the property and prosperity of the household— qualified only by the fact that each member exercises claims over property regarded as peculiarly his or her own. Quarrels within the household, which usually turn on expressions of non-reciprocal behaviour, should be amicably settled internally, and are not normally referable to *br'ngun'guni*, to resolution in public assembly. Outside the household, however, and beyond the range of the half-blood or first cousinship, relations between the members of different households are characterized either by formal co-operation, or by formal exchange, barter, and trading relationships, or as *mngwotngwotiki*. And in this field issues are answerable in *br'ngun'guni*. Relationships are still categorized in the kin idiom but the expectations evoked are of a political kind. Outside the household but within the range of first cousinship, depending on the degree of formality actually being observed in the communication of parts, the same kin idiom may evoke either a formal, that is political, relationship, or the informal relationship associated with close biological connection. By referring a dispute to *br'ngun'guni* a formal and so political relationship is made explicit. Yet a particular amicable settlement outside *br'ngun'guni* need not indicate anything more than a contingent if mutual desire not to make the issue one of public concern. The potential of a political relationship is inherent in any category conjoining males, and the most virulent disputes take place within the area between known informal and known formal reciprocities, in the field where expectations are uncertain or ambiguous.

Attempts to extract certainty and explicitness from situations where relations are uncertain or ambiguous clearly play an important part in the dynamic of social relationships. Indeed, ambiguity in relationships, whether in the simple terms of group membership, or as it may be more personally and subtly expressed in word, gesture, or glance, lies at the heart of the con-

flicts which maintain equivalence within a generally competitive ambience. Yet in whatever field of activity the kin idiom is
used it predicates moral obligation of a continuing kind. Since
there is no explicit and delegated enforcement, he who goes
too far beyond the bounds of conformity is faced with three
basic choices: expressly to reacknowledge and so re-enter the
system of reciprocities by confession followed by a compensation exchange;[1] to remove himself from Tangu and so from the
moral order which, by his act, he has already rejected; or, today,
to remain in Tangu and do the best he can from an equivocal
position, neither accepted as part of the community, nor wholly
rejected by it. In the past the choice would have been between
conformity and, virtually, death at the hands of outsiders who
were enemies, or death at the hands of members of the community who had now become enemies. Today, with the administration keeping the peace, and with opportunities to go away
on contract labour, there is more latitude, and the third alternative—usually involving a man becoming like a sorcerer[1]—
has become possible. Still, the essentials of the choice remain.
Equivalent reciprocities carry their own sanctions, are either
mutually enforceable through *br'ngun'guni* or entail disbarment
from community life.

   Because among Tangu mutually enforceable reciprocities are
contained in and derived from sibling relationships, the culture
is one based upon siblingship rather than descent, on the interrelations of brothers, sisters, brothers-and-sisters, friends, siblings-in-law, sweethearts, betrothed couples, and spouses rather
than upon the corporate group defined by categories of parentage or quasi-parentage. The term 'siblingship' connotes reciprocal relations, is defined by the element of reciprocity in
relationships, and thus, in the most general context, refers to
any relationship within which there exist mutual expectations
of reciprocal obligation. Hence, although the quality of reciprocal obligation between friends differs from that between,
say, brothers-in-law, so that the reciprocities of friendship and
kinship may be distinguished, because friendship is reciprocal
we can regard the relationship between friends as a particular
variant of the general meaning contained within siblingship.
As between grandparents and parents and children, on the

---

[1] *Infra*, pp. 133–55.

other hand, reciprocity of obligation cannot exist, but normative non-reciprocal relations do. So that relationships of filiation
are defined by non-reciprocity. And again, because friendships
are inherited non-reciprocally, the inheritance of a friendship
may be regarded as a variant within the general meaning of
filiation. Since, too, relationships of filiation and siblingship
are contained within the idioms of kinship and friendship, and
are subject to normative expectations, they are moral relationships. But while relationships of filiation carry values crucial
to being as Tangu, and provide for continuity between one
generation and the next, because they are not normally mutually
enforceable, and may so often be abused, they depend on resolutions between self-restraint and self-willedness: which features
illumine the inner kernel of meaning in 'moral'. By contrast,
relationships of siblingship, always expressed in the reciprocal
communication of parts, are mutually enforceable in *br'ngun-
'guni* and depend upon action and reaction.

For Tangu the behaviour actually being experienced within
a relationship gives a category its nuance and often predicates
the category itself. Category and behaviour tend to define each
other. Where, for example, two or more households are co-
operating, either formally or informally, the husbands are
behaving as brothers should, and in the past supposedly did,
behave; and the wives are behaving as sisters should, and in the
past supposedly did, behave. Hence, irrespective of biological
connection, the husbands concerned are categorized as *ndwanger*,
brothers; and the wives as *nuomanger*, sisters. That is, married
siblings of the same sex should co-operate; and since those who
in fact do co-operate are behaving as though they were married
siblings of the same sex they are categorized accordingly. Conversely, married siblings of different sex should be in exchange
relationships. So it is that husbands and wives of households in
exchange relationships are regarded as being related to each
other as brothers and sisters, *ndwanger–nuomanger*,[1] a situation
referred to in the phrase 'We brothers are feasting our sisters',
or 'We sisters are feasting our brothers'.

In practice the flexibility and pragmatism as between category and behaviour that today characterize relationships of

---

[1] The plural forms. Brother(s) = *ndwang(er)*; sister(s) = *nuomang(er)*.

siblingship may also occur within relationships of filiation. But whereas relationships of siblingship are concerned with exchange obligations. and turn upon that ambiguity which allows for competing for resources, prestige, power, and influence, the central values in filiation tend to be attached to the biological facts of fatherhood and motherhood—fatherhood especially. Opposed co-ordinates of being, filiation is to siblingship as the natural is to the cultural, the ideological to the practical, the dogmatic to the pragmatic. And the Ego-father/mother's brother triangle has already briefly indicated how the more immediate, pragmatic, and mutually enforceable values in siblingship may outweigh the dogmatic but mutually unenforceable values in filiation.

As members of the same household or group of co-operating households, the youths and maidens who are sons and daughters of co-operating couples are categorized as brothers and sisters. They co-operate. Brother provides for, shelters, and protects sister, who cares for him and cooks for him. But after their several marriages the households of brother and sister come into potential exchange relationships. Within the full blood these exchange relationships are initially, and usually remain, informal: in-laws or *mwerkindanger* (a man's sister's husband, or a woman's brother's wife)[1] expect hospitality as matter of course, give each other gifts, even trade informally. And though the same might be said ideally to apply whatever the former relationship of *mwerkindanger*, the further the distance in blood relationship, or the more irksome the previous or current emotional or economic relationship between the pair, the more is an informal relationship apt to become a formal one answerable in *br'ngun'guni*. If *mwerkindanger* elect to become co-operators, although they do not cease to be *mwerkindanger* in one sense, they become as *'ndwanger*, brothers', and as *'nuomanger*, sisters', in another sense. Overtly and formally they are as brothers, or sisters, but on the personal and informal level they remain *'mwerkindanger*, in-laws'. And if, later, they decide to break the co-operative relationship and come into a formal exchange relationship, then they become *mwerkindanger* in a political sense. The *mwerkindang* relationship implies exchange,

---

[1] *Mwerkindanger* is the plural, *mwerkindang* the singular. As we shall see (*infra*, pp. 109–13), *mwerkindang* also means 'son-in-law'.

and, depending on the formality with which exchanges are made, differences are settled as between themselves or in *br'ngun'guni*. Despite close biological connection all informal reciprocities carry the potential of becoming formal: small quarrels over informal exchanges tend to grow more and more intractable and generally result in the households concerned coming into formal relationships. Yet the latter are not necessarily bitter, malicious, or inimical—though they may be. Exchange relationships are necessary to achieve *mngwotngwotiki*, to arrange a marriage between the offspring of the households concerned, and indeed, to find a new mutual respect.

Preferred or ideal marriages among Tangu are of two kinds: within the terms of the kin idiom, or within friendship. In the first case the marriage is between youth and maiden of the same generation who are not, normally, first cousins or closer, and who stand to each other as father's sister's son and mother's brother's daughter. Where possible this cross-cousin marriage is accompanied or followed by an exchange marriage: groom's sister marries bride's brother; the categories in both instances being derived chiefly from the co-operative or exchange relationships obtaining—though they may, of course, also coincide with classificatory genealogical relationships. The model (see Figure 2 below) consists essentially of two lines of male filiation and two lines of female filiation linked as husband and wife and as brother and sister. The parents of bride and groom, it will be noted, are *mwerkindanger*, in exchange relations across the brother and sister link: so that both bride and groom marry into a household with which the natal household is, or has been, in an actual or nominal exchange relationship. Marriages are contracted between the children of households in exchange relationships, and upon or before deciding to marry their offspring the households concerned become *mngwotngwotiki*: the two decisions are interdependent. Conversely, children of co-operating households should not intermarry. Their fathers are brothers and their mothers are sisters: they themselves are, or are categorized as, brothers and sisters; sexual relations between them are incestuous. If, in relation to the model, brother and sister were to marry each other they would not be able to form pairs of households in exchange relationships. On the other hand, while a youth (maiden) may not marry father's brother's daughters (sons) or mother's sister's daughters (sons), between father's sister's daughter and mother's brother's son a marriage is permissible: the natal households are in a nominal exchange relationship, and, observing the model, patrilateral and matri-

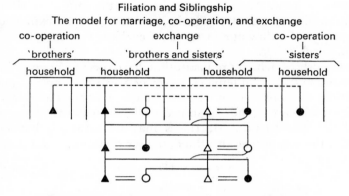

Filiation and Siblingship
The model for marriage, co-operation, and exchange

Two lines of male filiation, and two lines of female filiation.
Siblings who are husbands or wives (heads or mistresses) of
households and of the same sex co-operate; those who co-operate
are as though siblings of the same sex.
Siblings who are husbands or wives (heads or mistresses) of
households and of different sex exchange; those who make
exchanges are as though siblings of different sex.

Fig. 2.

lateral cross-cousins may coincide. At the same time, it is considered more proper that between a youth and the father's sister's daughter, or between a youth and a mother's brother's daughter, where in both cases there is quite specifically no intention to marry, there should exist a sweetheart relationship known as the *gniengi* or *gangarin* relationship:[1] a relationship which implies mutual petting and joking, fondling breasts and penis, but no coital satisfactions.

Whoever a man marries, his bride is regarded after the marriage as though she had been a mother's brother's daughter: a wife is a mother's brother's daughter but a mother's brother's daughter is not necessarily a wife. Or, to put it in another way, since a man ought to marry a matrilateral cross-cousin, and marriage connotes a previous nominal or actual exchange

[1] *Infra*, pp. 96–7.

relationship between the natal households of groom and bride, then the woman a man marries is regarded as conforming to the category. Thus, though matrilateral cross-cousin marriage is not prescriptive *ante hoc*, it is difficult to have avoided *post hoc*. Again, behaviour and category define each other: the model maintains itself. And it does so because the lateral or sibling relationships and their categories, and the concrete expressions of reciprocal behaviour in terms of exchange or co-operation, define each other.

Friendships, which are institutionalized, occur between pairs of males and pairs of females, never between man and woman. Further, the sons of men who are friends, and the daughters of women who are friends, inherit the friendships of their parents and are also friends. Marriages may be arranged between, firstly, the son of one and the daughter of another of a pair of

Marriage and Friendship

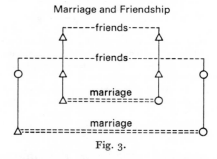

Fig. 3.

friends, and secondly, between a son and daughter of each of the two friends' full blood sibling of different sex (see Figure 3 above). Once the marriage is concluded the household so formed becomes, as all households do, an independent unit, nominally in exchange relationships with the households of the bride's married brothers and the groom's married sisters. Since, however, friendships are usually formed between men, or women, who live in different settlements, and upon marriage one spouse must become an immigrant, the couple take departure for both co-operating and exchanging from the position of the native spouse.

Friendship, and marriage under friendship, links individuals in two separate communities, and is ancillary to the system which operates within a local community. As regards the latter

—and the model described is one to which Tangu attempt to conform—a local community would consist of two exogamous intermarrying moieties: a feature which, historically, was contained in the fact that each local community comprised two exogamous *GAGAWA*. Fathers of households in exchange relationships, it will be noticed, transmit the exchange relationship to their sons; and to daughters are transmitted the exchange relationships of their mothers. Such a pattern could allow of each *GAGAI* being composed of several smaller exogamous groups, and, if access to land were restricted, it could be combined with transmitting land either patrilineally, or matrilineally, or to males in the patriline and females in the matriline —providing that one alternative was adhered to in a particular local community, and that, to surmount the difficulty of equal numbers of households having to have equal numbers of intermarriageable sons and daughters, there was some method of equalizing the numbers of households in each moiety. And in fact two devices do and did exist: a son could leave the natal household and become associated with another; ambiguity in relationships is correlated with precisely this point. Further, if circumstances arose to break the pattern of residence—as they did—then the models of marriage and concomitant reciprocities could still be maintained without reference to any kind of lineal descent group. Noting that there are no named lineal descent groups in Tangu today, and that on the evidence available they do not seem to have existed in the recent past, one may add that, given the model and the characteristics of siblingship, descent groups would have been unnecessary or superfluous, and that within the terms of 'competitive egalitarianism' it would be necessary to explain why descent groups should exist.

It is important to distinguish filiation, a series of mutually unenforceable claims and engagements attached to the facts of fatherhood and motherhood, from descent, the existence of corporate groups defined by criteria of real or putative genealogical connection. Maintaining equivalence in formal feasting exchanges demands that groups of households in exchange relationships should be roughly equivalent in numbers,[1] a

---

[1] If a group of five households were to exchange against a group of three, and offered more than the latter, it would be considered disgraceful. It would be equally scandalous if five households could only offer as much as three others.

feature which results in a local community being composed of two main groups—unnamed and existential and temporary moieties, whose households may shift membership or withdraw altogether—in complementary opposition to each other. Further, because equivalence also demands that capacities should be equally distributed, to show their qualities ambitious householders must have rivals worthy of themselves, rivals who will allow them to communicate their parts to advantage. Thus, though two full brothers would be expected, initially, to co-operate with one another, should they begin to emerge as the two most capable men in the community such pulls of biological connection as there may be are, and must be, waived in favour of political realities, without necessarily wholly expunging the potential of obligation implied in the biological connection. They cease to co-operate, pause awhile in an ambiguous relationship, then enter the *mwerkindang* relationship in formal oppositional exchange as political rivals. At the same time, as they remain brothers in the narrower sense, in situations of witchcraft or sorcery, for example, they might temporarily dissolve their political rivalry and behave as brothers.

Provided that behaviour (as reflected in the deployment and disposal of skills, services, commodities, and foodstuffs) and category remain mutually interdependent, and provided that neither term becomes rooted in a formal absolute such as biological connection, the model as described above remains inviolate, and capable of containing a variety of personal and organizational relationships. Though the manipulation of people in relation to categories results in temporary ambiguities, individuals have the opportunity to exercise their talents and earn recognition for them. Membership of a formal descent group would impose impossible limitations. With the system as it is, within the context of mutual interactions, on the one hand individuals may seek their own preferences and levels in relation to productive capacity and co-operative and residential group; on the other the industrious and competent are forced into positions of maximum relevance, whilst the lazy and incompetent are marked and so spurred, if not forced, into greater efforts. Competitive egalitarianism demands temporary ambiguities, or flux, of group memberships. Given that in the further past war, feud, and conformity would have imposed a narrower scope, an individual would still have been able to find his own appropriate ambience. Indeed, whatever his own delusions regarding his ability, the nature of the system would have steered him into the position he should occupy in relation to others. Further, given the circumstances of Tangu history—the mixing of traditions, the movement of ambiguity from ancillary device to a value in itself, fragmentation, expansion over territory, Christian teaching, and the alternative of being able to withdraw from the community in comparative safety—it would be surprising if there had not been a movement from group to individual responsibility. Ambiguities of group membership impose their own patterns of self-reliance.

TABLE 4

Vocabulary of Kinship Idiom and Friendship

Abwvai, avai—father, father's brother, head of household co-operating with father.

  Yapwerk—father, father-boss, boss, head of household.

Amai—mother, mother's sister, mistress of household co-operating with mother.

  Ameung, yameung—mother, mistress of household, ancestress.

Amat—daughter, man's brother's daughter, woman's sister's daughter, daughter of household with whom husband or wife has co-operative relationship, unmarried female member of household junior to mistress.

Ambwerk—eldest sibling of same sex, elder sibling of same sex, senior sibling of same sex, eldest or elder or senior co-operator of same sex, father-deputy, mother-deputy.

Amuthek—wife, fiancée, mother's brother's daughter, daughter of household with which one's own household exchanges and whom one proposes to marry.

Aran—man's sister's son, son of household the mistress of which is as sister to Ego (male), son of household with which Ego (male) exchanges; also used of sister's daughter with same extensions.

Awuk—mother's brother, father of fiancée, father's *mwerkindang*, head of household with which own natal household exchanges, circumcisor.

Azein, zai—wife's mother.

Aziuv—husband, fiancé, father's sister's son, son of household with which one's own household exchanges and whom one proposes to marry.

GAGAI—one of two divisions into which a settlement cluster used to be divided.

gagai—corporate residential co-operative group.

Gangarin, gniengi—sweetheart (male and female mutually), mother's brother's daughter and father's sister's son NOT intending to marry, father's sister's daughter and mother's brother's son, boy and girl of households exchanging who are sweethearts.

Geumeung, geumeunga—son's wife.

Iwok, juok—wife's father (particular).

Java—grandchild, son's son, daughter's son.

Kwav, wvert—friend (male or female).

Mnjiep—mother's brother (Wanitzir only), as under *Awuk*, above.

Moringer—(mainly Wanitzir; see under *Ndwang* below).

Mum—son, son of sibling of same sex, son of co-operator, unmarried male member of household junior to head.

Mumai, mumang—father's sister, man's sister's daughter, mistress of household with which father may be exchanging.

Murimbar—man's brother's wives, wives of households in co-operative relationship.

Mwanbar—(see under *Ndwang* below).

Mwerk—man's sister's daughter, woman's brother's son, sometimes used with same meaning as *aran* (above).

Mwerkamum—man's sister's daughter's son, woman's brother's son's son.

Mwerkindang—daughter's husband, son-in-law, man's sister's husband, woman's brother's wife, wife's brother, husband's sister, those of same sex with whom one has exchange relationships.

Mwerz ungunwan—same mother, same mother's mother.

Mwerz indin—different mother, different mother's mother.

Nanai—grandfather, grandmother, grandchild.

Ndwang (also *ndwanger, moringer, wvertzir* (Wanitzir), *mwanbar*, all plural forms)—brother, brothers, those with whom a man has co-operative relations, those with whom an unmarried sister co-operates, those to whom an unmarried sister owes services, those who should protect a sister; those heads of households with whom a married woman, a sister, has exchange relationships; those who exchange with and protect a married sister; see also under *nuomanger-ndwanger* below.

Ndyung, tuman—younger or youngest sibling of same sex.

   Ndyunger—younger siblings of same sex.

Nuakai, nuak'nyum—grandmother, mother's mother, ancestress in the matriline, old woman.

Nuandin—(see under *Ringertiam* below).

Nuomang, nuomanger—sister, sisters, those with whom a woman has co-operative relationships; those with whom an unmarried brother co-operates, those who owe services to brothers, those to whom brothers owe protection, those mistresses of households with which a married man exchanges.

Nuomanger-ndwanger—sisters-brothers, unmarried daughters and sons of co-operating households, married women and men in exchange relations.

Nyambanyek—habitually co-operating and co-mensal group larger than the household.

Riena 'gunwan—'one blood', exogamous category.

Ringertiam, nuandin—co-operating group, exogamous category.

Tuman—(see under *Ndyung* above).

Wvertzir—in plural (Wanitzir), brothers; in singular, *wvert*, friend.

Yameung—(see *Amai* above).
Yapwerk—(see *Abwvai* above).

Note:

1. The word 'exchange' above may be preceded by actual, or nominal, or potential, or informal, or formal.

2. Tangu often use the possessive -*ka* to indicate a specific person. Thus *avaikameung*, father's mother, instead of the generalized *nanai*.

Filiation and Siblingship: Categories of Action

In the further past, one may reasonably suppose, membership of *GAGAI* and *gagai*, closely associated with filiation, gave residential propinquity a determinative rather than contingent value. But today, as well as in the recent past, it is the other way about. Householders who want to co-operate become close neighbours, and close neighbours who enter an exchange or oppositional relationship shift residence and distance themselves. Traditional values in filiation are at a discount. On the other hand, as the narratives will bear out, and more positive evidence confirms, in traditional times the opposed values of filiation and siblingship were more equally balanced.

The phrase '*mwerz ungunwan*, one womb', seems in the past to have evoked the collective action of those of the same sex and generation well known to belong to the same uterine line. And the phrase '*mwerz indin*, another womb', or more emphatically— usually to indicate a degree beyond the first cousin—'*zin mwerz indin*, yet another womb', differentiated. Whilst there are some in Tangu today who would like 'one womb' to include all those of the same sex who can trace descent from a common ancestress exclusively through women, the most common usage is to unite, *ad hoc*, those of the same sex with a mother or maternal grandmother in common. And while 'one womb' never seems to have connoted a persistent and corporate group of matrilineal kin, in the past men who were 'one womb' seem to have formed a fighting group which sought vengeance for a death diagnosed as having been caused by sorcery. Today, however, despite the fact that being 'one womb' with a victim of sorcery is generally prima facie evidence of innocence, historically based expectations of support are not infrequently disappointed. The *Pax Australiana* prevents regular recruitment for offensive or retaliatory action, present tendencies are towards attachment to the father rather than the mother, and Tangu feel on the whole that if an individual is not the best judge of his own interests he is to blame. As an explicit moral imperative, that is, 'one womb' lacks reinforcement in terms of pragmatic interests and reciprocities. Moreover, the attempt to recruit support by the reminder '*Mwerz ungunwan!*'—which reveals a feeling, historically derived, that there ought to be common interests and fellowship in being 'one womb'—can usually be countered by '*Mwerz indin!*' 'another womb', or '*Abwvai indin!*' 'another father'. Or again, if, as sometimes happens today, 'one womb' is made to refer to those of different sex, then 'one womb' may be used to obstruct a marriage, and 'another womb' may be used as evidence to allow it. The category has become ambiguous, a weapon of ploy in which a supposed past and a future-in-the-present are point and counterpoint.

In contrast to the filiatory values of the womb idiom, the terms *ringertiam* (or *dingertiam*)[1] and *nuandin* and *nyambanyek*, bearing directly upon marriage, co-operation, and exchange, remain significant categories connoting existential and temporary groupings. Coterminous alternatives, *nuandin* and *nyambanyek* mean roughly 'we who work and live together'. Both terms refer in the first instance to the household, then to the smaller co-operative group of households. They carry a feeling of first cousinship, imply informality of interaction, free sharing, no intermarriages between the children of the constituent households. Sons and daughters of such households are regarded as brothers and sisters, are not 'afraid' (*bareipi*) of taking and eating food from each other's households; sexual relations between them are regarded as incestuous. The overriding connotations of the three terms are, firstly, working and sharing and eating together; and secondly, the prohibition on intermarriages and sexual relations between the offspring of the households concerned. And both sets of features refer to the pragmatic interests and reciprocities contained within siblingship.

Ringertiam has additional nuances contained in the word itself. Particularly and adjectivally it describes boy and girl brought up within the same household or more persistently co-operating group of households—brother and sister. And the term is also

---

[1] The sounds represented by 'r' and 'd' are interchangeable.

used of a co-operating mother's brother of the full blood, who had a special responsibility for the care of sister's children, and on whose bounty sister's children had an especial claim. But the more general indications of the word are more revealing. For the word *ringer* (*ringer-tiam*) usually refers to the source of a stream and includes the fact that a stream may be fed from several sources; and *ringertingertiki*, an active form, refers to the convergence of a number of streams into one, anastomosis, or a stream branching out into distributaries. These features bear directly upon marriage, exchanges, and the reproductive process.

When a couple marry and set up on their own as an independent household, they bring to their first new garden site seed crops from the plots which have been marked out to their names in the natal household plots, the groom his share of his father's original seed and increase, the bride her share from both mother and father.[1] In traditional times, before planting their several 'fortunes' in their new garden, husband and wife would lie together, mix their sexual secretions with prepared leaves and earth, and sometimes coconut milk, and scatter portions of the mixture in and over the new site.[2] Today virtually obsolete, this ritual was repeated every year when the new garden site had been cleared for planting. Now, as in the past, as children are born to the couple, or are adopted, and as the household works up its productive capacity by hard work and by keeping ripened tubers for seed rather than for eating, the garden grows larger and separate plots are marked out in the names of the children. In due course, as the children grow into adulthood, marry, and form households of their own, they take with them the seed and increase of their plots until, finally, when the last child has married, the parents usually have insufficient to maintain themselves and must go to live with one or other of their children—an event which roughly coincides with the father's failing physical powers. The evocations of

[1] Since in the past it was customary to destroy a person's foodstuffs upon his or her death, it was important for the succeeding generation that a parent should not die before the marriage of the child, or at least not before a plot had been marked out to the name of the child. The untimely death of a parent could, thus, be a disaster; and there was a more than sentimental grievance against the sorcerer or murderer who killed a parent before the children could claim their inheritance of crops.

[2] Reiterated in narratives, see *infra*, N. 26, pp. 347–50.

ringertiam are, then, the union in marriage of crops and spouses from different sources, the formation of the household as a co-operative unit, the begetting of children, the increase in crops accompanied by an increase in offspring, and the eventual dispersal of the children and redistribution of the seed crops as the children marry. Not only are the fertility of crops and that of humans interassociated, but formally and in terms of the model, the arrangements for exchange, disposal, replacement, and increase roughly coincide.

While *ringertiam* connotes a balance between the values of filiation and siblingship, with the category '*riena 'gunwan*, one blood', we see again the decay in filiatory values. Like the womb idiom, *riena 'gunwan* may be made to mean different things by different people. Within the general agreement that those who are one blood should neither marry nor have sexual relations, some in Riekitzir say that the category describes those begotten by the one father, others give it an extended reference which approaches the meaning of agnates, and yet others elsewhere assert that it is equivalent to *ringertiam* or *mwerz ungunwan*. Confronted with these inconsistencies, Tangu are evasive. '*Arin* . . .' they say, 'In the past . . .' And they continue to exploit its ambiguities. But, given the common agreement on a prohibition of marriage and sexual relations, consistently with the requirements of formal exchange relationships the field is restricted to males and their mother's sisters' daughters and father's brothers' daughters. And by giving 'one blood' limited biological value one would be justified in holding that the category referred to parallel cousins of different sex. Bearing in mind the association of males with the line of male filiation, and the association of females with the line of female filiation, we might go further and say that for males the category referred to father's brothers' daughters, and for females to mother's sisters' sons. Alternatively, remembering the different biases in the several neighbourhoods relating to the transmission of land claims, it could be maintained that each meaning applied in different neighbourhoods . . .[1]

[1] A generalized prohibition on marriage between parallel cousins is consistent with the systems obtaining in each of the communities, but particularly in Tangumar, Mamining, and Mndaningamb. A male bias and reference is consistent with the systems obtaining in Wasamb and Ungiar; a female bias and reference is consistent with the systems obtaining in Mangigumitzir, Randam, and Biampitzir.

Because, however, such precisions of meaning as *riena 'gunwan* may have had must be traced to the point when the name 'Tangu' referred only to a spur by Tangumar, to try to give *riena 'gunwan* a single and definite meaning would be to miss the point. Both blood and womb idioms, expressing traditional values in filiation, are in oblivescence. And this, in turn, is connected with the increasing reliance on ambiguity. A necessary concomitant of the merging of different variations of a single structural system, ambiguity provided and still provides the more ambitious with opportunities for enlarging claims and exercising influence within the total growing community. Again, while the tension between filiation and siblingship is revealed in the Ego-father/mother's brother triangle, exploitation of the tension itself shows a lack of self-restraint and a decline in the values attached to filiation on the one hand, and an increasing reliance on self-willedness and ambiguity on the other. Further, dependent as they are on stable residence, the values evoked by the blood and womb idioms could not but be weakened by the dispersals over territory that followed the introduction of artificial dogs' teeth and the epidemic sickness. In contrast, but entirely consistently, the values attaching to the categories *nuandin, nyambanyek,* and *ringertiam,* dependent on the pragmatic if existential interactions of siblingship, seem to have come down to the present almost unaltered. 'Almost', because, whereas in the past the groups connoted by the categories would have had some permanence, today they are only temporary. And again, this impermanence seems due to the movements over territory, the advantages of ambiguity, and the decline in the values attaching to filiation. Tangu, one might say, accepted the expedient at the expense of principle.

Filiation and Siblingship: Land

By selecting grandparents who are young, and accepting hearsay evidence, it is possible to spell out a line of filiation of some six to seven generations. But collaterals will have been forgotten; the ascendant genealogies of most Tangu informants go only to the grandparents, whose collaterals are only rarely remembered. Though some men assert a knowledge of the fourth ascendant generation in the line of male filiation, it is more usual to remember only the father's father and mother's mother, and if only one grandparent is remembered it is most often the mother's mother. All have some knowledge of her. Those women who succeed in surviving into old age generally live longer than their brothers. As grandmothers in daughters' households, sometimes in the households of sons, old women are competent cooks, string makers, and knitters until the day comes when they drop, knife in one hand and half-peeled yam in the other. Grandmothers look after grandchildren, tell them stories, teach them games, rock them to sleep, free a mother for other tasks. No household begrudges such workers their keep. Old men, on the other hand, live apart and alone, hapless and unwanted, a burden on the households which feed and support them. Few old men survive beyond the fifth or sixth year of retirement from active life. So that while a child is likely to know a grandmother quite intimately, particularly the maternal grandmother, an image of 'grandmother' becoming fixed in his or her mind, even if a grandfather should be long-lived he is an isolate, inter- acting only briefly and spasmodically with grandchildren.

The bias towards maternal kin which these circumstances indicate is of some significance to a woman, and co-residence is generally re-established between a woman and one of her daughters. A man, however, takes departure from his father. And if he is to maintain himself and his household, and gain prestige, he must manœuvre within the categories of siblingship in order to extend his claims on material resources. These acti- vities demand the greater part of his energies, and, since they often conflict with the interests of a father, father and son tend to move apart from each other. Not until after a father has died does he reassume, as a ghost, that generally beneficent relation- ship he had with his sons when they were boys.[1]

If today a husband is asked why he hunts over or gardens in one tract of land rather than another, he replies that he does so because the land is his, because he knows the land, because he has always hunted or gardened there, or because the land be- longs to his wife who has always been associated with it in the same ways. The children of a household become associated with, and get to know, the lands the natal household is using. Other things being equal, this association and knowledge places them in a position of strength as against those who have not used the

[1] *Infra*, pp. 164–6.

land as much, or who do not know it as well. If sons are garden-ing lands previously associated with the father, they point out that they are using the lands because they are sons of the father. He showed them over the place when they were small, he showed them the better gardening sites, the best fishing pools, where game was most likely to be taken. A more accurate assessment, however, would be that they were using the lands associated with the natal household, and that the land happened to be associated with the father. *Mutatis mutandis*, they might have said that they were using the land because they were 'one womb', sons of the mother. Yet such associations with lands are never exclusive. For just as sons have often visited the parents' siblings, have become acquainted with their lands, and have had trees planted there to their names, so do the children of the parents' siblings have a variety of claims on the lands being used by their cousins.

Maintaining the full sum of such claims is desirable for pur-poses of prestige, no less important for simple subsistence. For no claim is invulnerable. And because laxness in exercising claims is sure to invite the inroads of another, attempting to maintain, extend, or challenge particular claims results in frequent disputes which tend to be between *mwerkindanger*, who, either in formal or informal exchange relationships, thus com-pete in overlapping fields of resources. Fruits, nuts, and edible leaves may be gathered; hunting dogs may be taken when crossing a cousin's land; a fishing spear or net is useful when stopping by a stream for a rest. Should one object to such a 'trespass', the 'trespasser' might reply that as he had been shown over the land in childhood it is, in a sensible way, land asso-ciated with himself. At which point the alternatives are amicable persuasion, forcible ejection, or bringing the issue to *br'ngun-'guni*. The last resort is employing a sorcerer or taking mystical measures oneself. Again, and especially where *mwerkindanger* are biologically closely related, the indignation of one who con-siders that it is his fruit which has been taken may be countered by those on the spot who point out that he should have come earlier. For only by industry, by himself gathering and disposing of the fruit, may a man maintain his claim to continue doing so. He who gathers or occupies is presumed to have a claim to do so. And if such a claim goes unchallenged, the presumption is that if anyone had, or thought he had, a stronger or prior claim, he has allowed it to lapse. Conversely, a claim that appears to have lapsed may be revived by the attempt to exercise it.

It happens that Tangu have plenty of land available. But this does not stop them from trespassing. Some parts are more conveniently situated than others, game from another man's land always seems sweeter than one's own. Challenge, counter-claim, disputation, and the consequent definition of the self by interacting with others would probably occur even if land were more restricted and hence more stringently allocated. Men who leave Tangu for periods of contract labour take mystical measures to ensure that their claims are maintained while they are away. They also ask brothers to use their spears if necessary. Yet, in spite of such forethought, a man may return from the coast to find that another, tentatively at first, and then more and more confidently, has gone a fair way to establishing a user. If such a trespasser suffers no harm from the mystical safeguards, his continuing good health is evidence of the strength of his own claims. Conversely, a trespasser who sickens remembers his trespass, confesses it, and makes restitution. On the other hand, should a successful trespasser attempt to consolidate his user by himself using mystical means for his protection, and these result in the sickness of, say, the returned labourer, the evidence of right in terms of claims made good is almost conclusive. No man will continue to attempt to use lands on which the mystical techniques of another are more effective than his own.

That a 'right' to land only exists as such so long as the claims to exercise it can be maintained in the face of counter-claims is partially a historical inheritance. But it is also contained within the logic of Tangu social relations. As Tangu migrated over lands comparatively new to them, building new settlements, the only initial right they had to settle on, hunt over, or garden in particular tracts was the right they could maintain by might. Even though some of the new settlements were built on former hunting lands, establishing a user generally gave the first trespasser a prior claim to the second. Removal necessitated force or mystical measures. In fact, it seems, migrating households could always move on over the next ridge and oust the Jump people. But if a trespasser chose to face the con-

sequences, and was sufficiently robust in mind and body to
remain in possession, then, by exercising his claim he came
near to establishing what might be regarded as a primary right.
Yet such a right would not for long go unchallenged by those
who felt they derived claims from the former circumstances.
And the stability of the new situation seems to have been a
function of the alternatives available and the energy and deter-
mination either party could bring to bear on the matter.

Such flexibility and ambiguity concerning the user of lands
persists into the present. Claims to cultivate, hunt, or gather
may be announced, either formally at *br'ngun'guni*, or informally
whilst gossiping, even though the derivation of the claims may
be vague, whimsical, or based on a parental anecdote. Quite
frequently in disputes a man or woman will assert claims to
lands which he or she may never have seen. Usually a pretext, a
goad, an invitation to be challenged on this or some other
matter, those in the assembly accept it as such—but note that
the claim has been made. One who has been shown lands has a
prima facie claim to use them. He who is, or has been, hunting
or gardening there without opposition is more strongly placed.
Those who have been making regular use of the land and maintaining their claims against trespassers may feel confident of
continuing to do so—providing that they do not get lazy. But,
given the realist and pragmatic approach, open argument in
marginal cases requires the support of a form. Other things
being equal, everywhere men should argue from men, women
from women: the incoming spouse derives claims from actual
user or from the natal spouse. In Wanitzir and the hither
portions of Biampitzir a man's association with father's land
provides advantage; but in Mangigumitzir and the neighbouring parts of Riekitzir and Biampitzir a derivation from the
mother or mother's brother finds more general favour. Nevertheless, a household has to make its way, find the food and
meat to live, and meet the needs of exchange and prestige. And
the first one to be elbowed aside is usually a *mwerkindang*. Which
is another way of noting that the Ego-father/mother's brother
tension persists.

Each of the individuals comprising a household has claims
which, though they may be put to work for the household as a
whole, do not necessarily coincide with those associated with

the household as a unity: in practice the claims of the household as such comprise only the claims of husband and wife together. As children grow older and become familiar with the natal household and parents' siblings' lands, they gradually build up for themselves a series of claims of varying strengths. One son, for example, being fond of a certain mother's brother, may through frequent visiting create for himself stronger claims on his uncle than another brother who might dislike the uncle, and who, in consequence, finds something else to do when a visit is projected. In such and similar ways the children of a household become engaged in a variety of personal relationships with kinsfolk and others, both adult and of their own generation. Likes, dislikes, rivalries, interests—all develop during childhood through to adolescence. And later on in life it is this complex of early personal encounters that forms the background to those claims which an individual may attempt to exercise. As the sum of the claims held by the individuals comprising the household begins to be divided among the households of the married children, the parents age, their visits to others become less frequent, the claims they themselves can exercise become fewer. And as they lapse they are taken over by the succeeding generation. Sister's sons attempt to assert their claims, sons try to curb the inroads of cousins whilst at the same time trying to make good claims deriving from the mother's brother. Persistent endeavours to make good some claims and widen others result in minor quarrels, then in open disputes. And these, while rarely yielding any permanent reallocation of 'rights', necessitate seeking out allies and co-operators. Partial retreats and shifts of alliance are involved, and those who cannot make good their claims in one direction may find that by concentrating their efforts elsewhere they may be able to realize a part of what they claim.

Partly owing to historical circumstances, particularly the migrations after the epidemic sickness, and also because inter-community marriages are common, everyone in Tangu has kinsfolk in other parts of Tangu.[1] Starting on the basis of these kin ties each individual is so placed within a unique constellation of personal relationships created by his own interactions with others that some claims, not necessarily exclusive, are more

---

[1] See Appendix II for an example.

easily exercised than others. And it is towards these that he
gravitates. While the facts of filiation provide the initial placement from which youth and maiden view their world, upon
marriage, when the pursuit of power begins to be serious, and
when adjustments to the powers of others begin to be critical,
couples take a hard look at themselves and their circumstances,
and settle where, as Tangu say, 'they think the prospects are
best'. And these prospects depend on how relationships of
siblingship are managed.

Recruitment to the Household

A bride and groom are members of households which, previously either in nominal or actual exchange relations, have
now become *mngwotngwotiki*, morally equivalent. And after
living and working turn and turn about in and with each
other's households, the couple leave their natal households to
form an independent household of their own.[1] The husband
removes all the crops in his name from the parental site to his
own newly cleared site, but the wife leaves behind with her
parents a small stock of taros. Tangu say of this last that it is
purely sentimental, that parents, more attached to daughters
than to sons, like to retain something closely associated with the
daughter. But the usage also indicates that, in addition to her
brothers who are always responsible for her, a married daughter
has a line of retreat back to the natal household. When a son
marries, on the other hand, he goes off on his own, a man, self-
reliant and ultimately responsible for and to himself and his
household.

An ambitious young husband sets to work at once to develop
the store of seed crops at his disposal. And he can manage,
fairly early in married life, informal exchanges with married
wife's brothers and his own married sisters. But his future is
bound up with children. Natural affections apart, children are
spurs to more strenuous activity, and, as they grow older and it
becomes more necessary, they become additional working hands
who help to boost the production of the household as a whole.

[1] Formerly and formally, the departure of husband and wife to form a household
of their own should not occur until it is seen that the wife is pregnant. Pregnancy
and making the first new garden should run in parallel. Few today observe this
practice, but until the newly married couple do set up on their own they are still
said to be *mnuomnuom*, not quite independent.

Further, the conventional pretext for initiating feasting exchanges is in order to celebrate the births and anniversaries of children, particularly of daughters[1] who, in terms of the model, are destined to marry the sons of those households with which the natal household is in exchange relationships.[2] Although childless couples are not debarred from giving feasts, not having any children considerably narrows the scope of an ambitious husband. He must either adopt some children, or see if he can do better with another or second wife.

The traditional view of birth among Tangu is that the woman holds in her womb that which may be thought of as the 'seed' or 'germ' of being, today a rather vague notion associated with blood, the menstrual flow, and the onset of sexual maturity: a woman has inside her that which may grow into a child. This 'germ' of being is not thought of as male or female: it is simply a 'something' that is capable of becoming a 'he' or a 'she'. During pregnancy the foetus is in the process of becoming a 'he' or a 'she', and not until after birth can it be known whether the 'germ' of being has developed into a 'he' or a 'she'. But if the 'germ' is to develop into anything at all, Tangu say, it has to be 'fed'[3] with the 'milk'[4] of the husband. And for the babe to emerge from the mother's womb healthy and strong, Tangu hold that it has to be constantly and continuously 'fed' by the husband. Though the theory of birth is the same for a child of either sex, a boy is said to grow up on his 'father's milk', and a girl is said to grow up on her 'mother's milk': a distinction which may be referred to the line of male filiation on the one hand and the line of female filiation on the other. A moment of conception is not recognized; the androgynous, neutral, bisexual or ambisexual 'germ' of being develops and differentiates within

[1] But to feast a daughter before she can walk is considered presumptuous and an invitation to sorcery.

[2] The potential marriage of offspring presently engaged in exchanging against each other, together with the knowledge that the crops now crossing from one household to the other must unite in the marriage, are correlatives of the tension that exists between households in exchange relationships. But when such households become *mngwotngwotiki*, equivalent, the crossing crops are considered equivalent, and the offspring may marry.

[3] The vernacular word is *'brami'*, to eat or partake of. Thus *warinda brami*, to eat tubers, yams, or taros; or *rapai brami*, to 'eat', or as we would say, smoke, tobacco.

[4] The word for semen is *wvigoea*. But this word is hardly ever used. Semen is most often referred to as *geumb*, milk, where *geumb* may be milk from a coconut, milk from the breast, milk from a tin, or any milky or whitish fluid.

the womb. After birth, *post hoc*, a girl—who looks to her mother to teach her how to be a woman—grows up on her mother's milk, and a boy—who looks to his father to teach him how to be a man—grows up on his father's milk.[1]

Once a wife is clearly pregnant, but not until it becomes more tiresome than otherwise, sexual intercourse ceases and the expectant mother arranges either to go to her own mother for the birth of the child, or for her mother to come to her. Sisters come to witness the birth and to help in the labour and parturition; at least one sister will remain with the new mother to suckle the child and help with the household chores until mother and babe can fend for themselves. Though the woman who bears a child is held to be ultimately responsible for nursing her babe, and for caring for him or her in the early years, the idea or notion of motherhood tends to be contained in the suckling and caring rather than in the carrying, labour, and issue. Possibly connected with deaths in childbirth, more certainly related to the unequal distribution of fecund women,[2] and clearly related to the arrangements for adoption,[3] if the biological mother must be referred to the womb, the idea of motherhood is contained in the suckling, nourishing, and caring, and is extended to all those who in fact do these things— usually the biological mother and her sisters.

Tangu take it for granted, or like to assume, that a wife's husband is the father of her child. Unlike motherhood, where the emphasis lies on what happens after a birth, on what a woman does for a child, both father (or genitor) and fatherhood—particularly in the case of a male child—are critically contained in the feeding of the child in the womb with the 'milk' of the penis. Marriage, regular sexual relations, and feeding the babe in the womb imply each other and, traditionally, barred the casual adulterer from claiming fatherhood. Today, should a husband happen to be away on the coast on contract labour, for example, and is obviously not the genitor, he is still regarded as the father, pater, providing that the woman remains his wife. If the child is a boy he is told who the genitor

---

[1] See *infra*, pp. 384, 396.

[2] Most women in Tangu suffer series of still-births and early mortality of the babies that survive birth. But some few women appear to be extremely strong, robust, and fecund: they have many children, most of whom seem to survive, and many of whom are adopted by the childless.   [3] See *infra*, pp. 93-4.

is, or is thought to be, when he leaves his mother's skirts and comes under the care of the father.[1] Then, if the genitor is agreeable and the boy so wishes, he may leave the household of the pater for the household of the genitor. Most Tangu feel that the link between father-genitor and son is such that a boy ought to want to know who his genitor is, and further, that tutor and genitor should be the same man if possible.[2] Still, choice of household is generally left to the boy himself, and so long as the adults concerned put up no objections he may switch from household to household. It is not long before he sees where his best interests lie. For a girl the problem of genitor hardly arises: her being is linked to mother and sisters, not to her genitor.

If a mother has insufficient milk in her breasts, while she will not forgo the child fondling her nipples a sister will actually feed the babe. Even if a mother is amply endowed sisters will suckle the child, or allow it breast play, as the mother in her turn will give of her own to their children. Fathers, on the other hand, keep their distance for about three or four weeks after the birth of a child. They prefer not to sleep in the same hut as a new-born babe and they normally make alternative arrangements. And when a father eventually handles a new baby he does so awkwardly, gingerly holding it with arms outstretched lest it piddle or defecate on him.[3] Some while later, as the child grows, mother's brothers pay visits, bring small gifts for members of the family and coconuts to plant in the name of the child. They too insist upon handling the child much as the father does. By the time a child is four years old he or she knows the mother's sisters intimately, and there has been little hesitation in seeking their breasts, whether to play, titillate, or feed. Yet there is usually a clear distinction, expressed as a preference for the one rather than the others, between the mother and her sisters—as, for example, when to its own intense annoyance a child is passed from breast to breast in an intimate gathering of sisters. If, as sometimes occurs, a child begins to

---

[1] *Infra*, pp. 87–8.

[2] Upon the death of father, son communicates with the ghost or dream-image of father. Ghost and tutorial period are closely connected, both are closely connected with the 'feeding' in the womb, and, indeed, with the transmission of self-restraint or conscience (*infra*, pp. 396–8).

[3] Progressive young scoffers regard this practice as 'mere superstition', *samting bolong bus kanaka tasol*! As all fathers will know, they have something to learn.

show a marked liking for a mother's sister rather than the mother, the situation is resolved either by allowing the child its preference, eventually perhaps transferring it from the one household to the other, or by making it difficult for the sister in question to have access to the child.

On the whole, however, the natal household very soon appears to become a definable and exclusive environment. And within this environment a girl's life history until she marries and becomes the mistress of a household of her own is relatively tranquil. Little boys, on the other hand, have tantrums, fight, and squabble. When he is about six, following a phase of furious outbursts of temper, a boy leaves his mother and begins to spend more and more time with his father.[1] He begins to use a jungle knife, scorning the small and jerky movements of a woman and imitating the full swinging slash and smooth overhand stroke associated with men. He batters trees with a tomahawk, plays at spearing a pig at bay, follows his father around—doing him small favours such as fetching, filling, and lighting his pipe for him. And father, who has already planted trees and palms in the name of his son, begins to make the boy familiar with household lands and water, teaches him magical spells, minor rituals, and the special skills of which he may be a master: treatment for snake-bite, constipation, or boils; painting or carving or modelling clay cooking-pots; or tracking, drumming, dancing, plaiting, building, trapping, fishing. . . . So father and son come into a close and affectionate relationship, father wielding tutorial authority, son willing.

Father is both *abwvai* or *avai*, an affectionate term and translatable as 'dad' or 'papa', and '*yakwerp*, father-boss', head of the household.[2] Through the father's tutorial role in relation to the young son, the latter is being shown the lands father is using, and he is obtaining prima facie claims which he will attempt to exercise in the future. And by virtue of the son's affectionate attachment to the father the former regards the lands in question in a somewhat sentimental way. On the other hand, mother's brothers are also becoming known to the boy. Trees

[1] It is at about this time that a boy may be told of his genitor, if pater and genitor are different.

[2] Though *abwvai* or *avai*, and *yapwerk*, might be distinguished as 'genitor' and 'pater', the distinction could only hold in particular circumstances. *Yapwerk* is formal, the recognition that father is also boss. *Abwvai* and *avai* are affectionate.

have been planted in his name, he goes hunting with them, is shown their lands. Though the educative role is not as marked as father's, claims deriving from actual user are being created. If the relationship is not as close or affectionate as the father-son, by tradition it is all the more explicitly authoritative. Moreover, as between father and mother's brothers—already in oppositional exchange relationships—there enters more surely an element of jealousy, even malice, as each competes for the affections of the growing boy. As the son approaches puberty—begins actively to co-operate with other households, hunt, trap, fish, clear new garden sites, and help with the fencing and harvesting, becomes more and more able to do a man's job without help and advice—father becomes less and less the fount of tutorial affection, more and more the boss whose authority chafes.

While a growing boy comes into contact more frequently and more significantly with a wider range of kinsfolk and others, particularly with male siblings on either side of the marriage link, and is made aware of conflicts in relationships fairly early, until she begins to menstruate a girl is almost exclusively associated with the mother, the mother's sisters, and her brothers within the household. From her mother and sisters she learns the skills and crafts of women. She knows when still very young what wild leaves to gather as relishes, how to cook, carry, draw water, clear underbrush, weed, roll string, make skirts and string bags. On the whole she knows more stories, more games, more lore than her brothers. Almost as soon as she can walk a girl is looking after younger siblings. It is not uncommon to see a small and spindly maid carrying a brother as well as a bag of tubers on her back. And, far from objecting, a sister is at worst amicably resigned to a brother being given the best and the most to eat. From her earliest days she is accustomed to continuous hard work and apparent subservience to men. Later on, as she comes of age, a girl may see something of youthful sweethearts, play with her age-mates, enjoy going to dances. Soon afterwards she is married, with children and a household of her own. Then, when her children are married, she becomes a working grandmother. Formally favoured and protected, though a woman is denied, or freed from, the anxieties of political decision she is always of value to the household that keeps her.

In the past, towards puberty, both girls and boys were admitted into the club-house: the boys to be circumcised and
initiated, the girls, not yet nubile, as companions simply. Today,
with the disappearance of the club-houses and the discontinua-
tion of circumcision, the girl makes a smooth passage through
puberty to becoming mistress of a household. Sometimes there
is trouble from persistent young men, but on the whole nubile
maidens stick together, playing girlish games in the evening
when they are not working, or going in pairs to meet their
sweethearts, their *gangariner*. Though a newly-wed wife may
lack experience, she has a complete command of womanly
skills, and, with the help of mother and married sisters, very
soon learns how to overcome any deficiencies. For a boy, however, the progress into adulthood and political responsibility is
much more difficult. At about the age when in the past he would
have gone into the club-house under the supervision of mother's
brothers, circumcisors and disciplinary authorities,[1] a boy begins
to resent his father and to express his independence of him.
He refuses, point-blank and in public, to fill his father's pipe.
And father, pipe held out at arm's length, grumbling and
scolding, has to fill his pipe for himself. While son grouses about
household tasks, is continually impertinent, and seizes the
occasion to assert himself, authority sits uneasily on the shoulders
of a householder who knows he cannot put it to the test. In the
past the seclusion of a son in the club-house would have
made for minimal interaction between father and son. And it is
possible that father, distanced, would have continued to be
thought of, at least until son's marriage—as he is today until
puberty—as a source of affectionate protection, the seat of
learning and wisdom, a model of firm but gentle manhood,
hardworking and brave. But today, finding it difficult to
reconcile affection towards, and authority over, a son who is
fast becoming a man, a father often appears either raucously
over-authoritative or unbecomingly meek. Mother's brothers
exacerbate the situation where in the past they would have
buffered it. For, refusing responsibility for the activities of

---

[1] Mother's brothers were entitled to strike or thrash a sister's son. The conventional greeting between a mother's brother and sister's son, sometimes still seen,
took the form of mother's brother raising his adze in a threatening manner whilst
sister's son bowed and turned away.

sister's sons, they attempt to detach son from father in their own favour. And though a youth may take advantage of the approaches of a mother's brother to score off his father, realizing that the former only wishes to exert control over him and that an exchange of authorities is no solution, he endeavours to maintain an equivocal position. Becoming his own master, resenting authority in others, a young man must still try to nurture those claims he thinks he can make good in the future.

Mother and son remain in a close and affectionate relationship through this period and, indeed, throughout their lives. They compete for nothing. The rages to which a boy is prone do not appear to be directed at either of the parents, who are generally permissive. Rather are they expressions of frustration which signal the boy's own realization that he belongs to the world of men, is an individual in himself, and is no longer merely an extension of his mother. For, once freed of mother and taken under the father's wing, the son's rages cease. Father it is who sets a son on the road to independence, father who teaches him the rudiments of manhood: 'a boy grows up on his father's milk'. And as youths come into manhood they copy their fathers more seriously, cocky and a little unsure of themselves maybe, but upbraiding mother and sisters for lazing in the garden, for a meal not as well cooked as it might be. Mothers accept such treatment with good humour and pride; sisters jump to a brother's instructions. The boy is becoming a man, a master whose wishes, if they may be circumvented in a variety of ways, may not be directly challenged by a woman.

From a father's standpoint a maturing son may be a source of pride, but is nearly always an infliction also. A recalcitrant youth is little help to his own household and may involve it unnecessarily with others. Demanding independence yet not responsible, feeding at their parents' expense, adolescent youths gang up together, laze about the village, gossip, mock the mature, tease the girls, and indulge in escapades which their elders seldom find amusing, and over which they may be forced to dispute. Yet a youth must test his strength, explore his limitations, find and assert himself. In the end, therefore, a father accepts the boy's claim to deal with his own life as he wishes. And his wisest course under current conditions is to suggest, obliquely and through third parties, that the boy should go away on contract labour. So that behind the expressions of sorrow when such a youth sets off there is usually a feeling of relief. On his return to Tangu a proportion of his savings will go into the household pool, and if he is still not ready to marry and accept responsibility he will go away to the coast again.

When a man grows old and is unable to provide for himself, he has recourse to the household of a son. But unlike grandmothers, grandfathers tend to be tiresome passengers. Their claims for sanctuary and subsistence derive from sentiment and past services. They are not based upon current contributions. They grumble, bemoan the old days, and constantly ask for titbits of food, tobacco, lime, and areca-nut. They are experienced, know much, may be wise; they are also soured, often malicious. As soon as an old man dies, however, as soon as his physical presence ceases to be a concrete problem, he becomes a ghost or dream-image to his sons. And in this guise he confides equivocal advice. In one sense the father–son reverts to the pre-puberty phase; in another, since the father is dead, a quite new but none the less non-reciprocal relationship commences.

Starting by being dependent on mother and sisters, a boy frees himself from female attachments to associate himself with father. Then, rejecting his father, at puberty son seeks experience in self-reliance, becomes independent, marries, defines himself to others in terms of the reciprocal exchanges which marriage demands, and eventually returns to a partial dependence on father as ghost or dream-image. Though it is always a non-reciprocal relationship, father is normally willing to expend his energies on son at least until puberty. But after puberty a son is reluctant to waste his resources on father: the younger man's interests lie in the concomitants of siblingship and advancing his prestige and standing. The re-engagement of the father–son through the ghost or dream-image is, as we shall see, of political relevance. But women, politically dependent on their men, are not acknowledged to experience ghosts. Unlike men, women work without having to decide why they should.

Though, normally, recruitment to the household is by the natural bearing of children, the latter are not necessarily tied to

the natal household, and households may expand their membership by adoption. Initially, however, natal household membership is definitive: a child 'belongs' to the parents who are
presumed to have begotten and borne it, and if a parent should
die the eldest surviving male of the household assumes responsible guardianship. Where an orphan[1] is very young, mother's
sisters who have actually suckled the child have first claims and
responsibilities. Where the child is a boy over four years old,
father's brothers may have preference, for the boy is about to
enter a man's world in any case. If father's brothers are lacking,
father's sisters may have claims on brothers' sons, but on the
whole the onus shifts back to mother's sisters. Should a husband
die, the widow keeps her children and sets about finding a
replacement for the husband. She might marry a bachelor, or
a widower, or become some man's second wife. Or, most likely,
she would join a husband's brother as first or second wife. If she
has a son who is mature but unmarried, he would take the place
of his father, maintaining the household as an economic unit
and making himself responsible for the exchanges devolving
from the mother's marriage. If the son himself should marry,
however, he and his wife become the core of a new household,
and if the widow and her small children remain with the
married son they become subordinate members of the new
household, the son's young brothers and sisters being regarded
for most purposes as though they were his own children. An
ageing widow who still has young children, and who cannot
or will not marry or join a husband's brother, may herself
join the household of sister or daughter, whilst the husband's
brother, or a mature son, might insist on taking charge of the
youngsters.

While there tends to be some competition for the widow and
her children, a widower who does not have a daughter to work
for him is forced to distribute his children either among the
households of his married sisters, or among those of his wife's
sisters. He repays the board, care, and attention given to the
children by produce from his garden. His difficulty is to get a

---

[1] The word 'orphan' is here used in its English sense—without father or mother.
The Tangu word which translates as 'orphans' is *mnduner*, a plural noun which,
encountered only in narratives, refers to completely kinless pairs of children,
usually brother and sister. In life no one can be an orphan in such a sense.

woman to work in his garden. On the one hand providing produce for the benefit of other households necessarily puts an end to his political ambitions; on the other hand any able woman whom he gets to work for him probably has a husband —who will dispute the time given to another's garden. Finally, those householders who have temporarily adopted his children will not think well of him unless he can supply them with plenty of foodstuffs. The alternative of dispensing with his children altogether is not really open to him. For, apart from the fact that while he lives he is nominally responsible for them until they reach adult years, he would like to pass on his seed crops to his sons, he is fond of them, wants them for his own in his own household. His only realistic solution is to find a new wife.

A relatively large number of Tangu children are members of 'adoptive' households.[1] In part this is due to deaths. It is also because the likes and dislikes of children are given full scope. Even where a child has both parents alive but prefers for one reason or another to live, for example, with a mother's sister or a father's brother, such a preference will be accommodated. Similarly, should a child wish to return to the natal household after having lived with adoptive parents, in the end, despite possible objections from one side or the other, the child will have its way. No household wants children who do not show their appreciation in affection and services, and, since there is no family name and no lineage to perpetuate, a perverse child is allowed to find its most suitable and satisfactory ambience.[2] Because father's brothers are alternative fathers, and mother's sisters are alternative mothers, for boys and girls respectively these are the most appropriate adoptive households. Yet if, overtly, a child is allowed to choose his or her own household, unless a parent or parents have died there is no obligation on households other than the natal to accede. The only household which may not veto a choice is the natal. Into this household the child was born, and the onus of educating and nurturing is

[1] Approximately 19 per cent.
[2] A feature which, it will be remembered (*supra*, pp. 69–71), echoes those implications of adhering to the equivalent reciprocities contained within sibling-ship that, combined with a concomitant weakening of the values in filiation, movement, and the advantages of ambiguity, entail an individual finding his own level.

squarely on those who are presumed to have brought the child into the world.

Though community life leaves little escape from the inter-actions and obligations of siblingship, parents may give to, withhold from, or be careless about, their children; in later life children may ignore the claims of parents on their bounty; 'one womb' and 'one blood' exert only equivocal pressures. As com-pared with the mutually enforceable obligations of siblingship, filiation entails alternations of dominance/dependence, and turns on how far self-restraint can overcome self-willedness. Siblings with the same mother and father may possess an identical filiation. Yet sons appear to have different dream-images of their father, and both sons and daughters behave differently in relation to mothers. Thus, so far as relationships of filiation must resolve themselves largely in terms of what either party is prepared to give without the expectation of an equivalent return, to that extent is uniqueness or individuality attached to filiation. In the past, as the narratives will show, club-house life, the disciplinary authority of the mother's brother, and a more stable pattern of residence did much to offset and con-trol the possibilities of evasion inherent in filiation. Today, within the context of traditional activities, interactions and the communication of parts are generally predicated by the recipro-cities of siblingship. At the same time, Christian teaching and the larger environment are beginning to encourage new modes of expressing values in filiation, new modes of controlling the interactions within it, a new consensus regarding the norma-tive values filiation should carry.

Marriage and Divorce

A traditional but still firmly asserted division of labour between the sexes among Tangu requires that an efficient working group should consist of males and females in partnership. Men cut down trees, lop, make fences, build houses, dig, plant, hunt, trap, and fish with spears. Women weed, carry, cook, draw water, clear underbrush, fish with nets, and look after children. Men help with the cooking of foodstuffs, particularly meat, on public feasting occasions; they make their own gear, equip-ment, dress, and decorations; they work in wood, paint, carve, incise, and weave cane waistbands, armbands, anklets, and wristlets. Women make skirts, string, string bags, dogs' tooth plaques, and their decorative accessories; they also work in cane. Most potters are men, but some are women. Men regard it as degrading to have to do work specifically associated with women. Their traditional role, which they see no reason to relinquish, is to think, plan, invent, create, initiate, manage, and, freed from encumbrances, be ready with a spear. Since warfare has ceased, a woman can, it is true, do some of the man's work and vice versa. But the distinction between the two sets of tasks does not necessarily lie in how arduous or dangerous they are or might be. If skill and endurance are common to both, men's tasks are generally associated with sudden bursts of energy, forethought, inventiveness, improvisation, and tactical adroitness. Women's work is generally hard, dull, monotonous, and routinized. Men are supposed to think and plan before and as they work. Women simply work.

Tangu say, 'A man must have a wife else how would he eat? And a woman must have a husband else how could she live?' Sometimes middle-aged widows are looked after and protected by their mature, unmarried sons, and at other times brothers and sisters help each other, or a daughter will do a wife's work for a widower father. But such partnerships are regarded as temporary makeshifts. The ideal basis is the marital union. Without a wife a man becomes a member of someone else's household. He has sisters and *mwerkindanger* maybe, but he cannot make politically relevant exchanges with them. He may speak in *br'ngun'guni*, but only as a virtually disinterested party. Productive ability he may have, but he has no opportunity to demonstrate managerial capacities. To participate fully in the complex of reciprocities that characterize Tangu community relationships, youth and girl must marry. Only through marriage can a man translate industry, competence, and astuteness into prestige, influence, and power. And though there are, in spite of the disadvantages, a few confirmed bachelors in Tangu,[1] there are no spinsters much beyond the age of puberty. A mature woman who had not been married at some time would be an anomaly.

Before marriage both bride and groom will have had some

---

[1] Three in all.

limited sexual experience within the *gangarin* or *gniengi*, or sweetheart relationship. Existing formally between a youth and father's sister's daughter or, when the latter coincides with mother's brother's daughter, between youth and mother's brother's daughter whom he is not going to marry, the designatory terms of the relationship derive from, or are the source of, the verbs '*managangari, managniengi*, to laugh, tease, joke, or jest'. Those who are *gangariner* or *gnieng'gniengi* (plural forms) sport with each other, their quips having bawdy or sexual overtones, and engage in love play. As children *gangariner* play with each other, enjoying mutual confidences. As youth and maiden they take advantage of balmy evenings and dances to sit next to each other, jest, whisper sweet nothings, fondle and stroke each other. Breast play and penis and nipple titillation are the most marked features: there may even be penis penetration. But the latter, and *a fortiori* coital satisfaction, are not formally permitted. If before their several marriages *gangariner* should have sexual congress it is thought that their stomachs will swell, that boils will break out over the body, and that they will have diarrhoea. Eventually they may die. Both sickness and possible death may be avoided, however, by confessing either to a friend or to an old man—both of whom are, in the context of the reciprocities of siblingship, neutrals—and then undergoing a purificatory ritual in the presence of the third party. Through the last the rest of the community—should they know of, or suspect, the transgression—comes indirectly to learn that confession and at-one-ment have been made. They are reaccepted into the community. After marriage *gangariner* may still see a lot of each other. . . . But much depends on the attitudes of the wives or husbands of the *gangariner* involved. The relationship might, after all, become simply adulterous.

Though *gangariner* stand to each other in otherwise marriageable categories, marriage between them is not permitted. On the other hand, if parents betroth a son and daughter to each other, and the marriage does not take place, then the couple may become *gangariner*. Moreover, as in all Tangu relationships, if the relationship is not actively maintained and concretely expressed it lapses. Conversely, those who are not initially in the required categories as derived from the parents' siblings may still become *gangariner*. Thus if a boy and girl are told by their parents that they are *gangariner*, and they do not take to each other, the relationship lapses. And when a boy and girl who are not initially *gangariner* discover a mutual attraction and start behaving like *gangariner*, then providing their households are not co-operating they become *gangariner* or *gnieng'gniengi*.

The Tangu word for husband is *aziuv*, and that for wife *amuthek*. The same terms are used to describe those who are betrothed, whether they are infants, children, adolescents, or more mature. They are also used in relation to a youth and his mother's brother's daughter where a betrothal is intended but not concluded. Where both partners are being married for the first time initiative is in the hands of the groom and his parents. In subsequent unions it is the groom, again, who traditionally 'captured' or 'took' a wife, and today 'takes' or 'buys' a wife. But despite the overtones in the English words, in all cases a properly completed marriage rests upon the mutual consent of both bride and groom and their families—particularly the brothers of the bride—and the marriage itself predicates a partnership between individuals as equals. If the husband has formal authority and control, neither is more beholden to the other and, unless they are Christians, each is formally free to dissolve the marriage at any time. In the past, before the sickness, it may have been the case that 'partnership between individuals as equals' remained true during the marriage as well as in terms of later possible consequences. After the sickness, however, during the period of migrations, the reverse seems to have been the case: if women were highly valued and fought for, they were still at the mercy of a strong right arm. And today, while a man who is not a Christian may go through several divorces and still find it possible to live in Tangu, after her second divorce a woman has almost exhausted the possibilities of satisfactory community relationships.

Currently the interval between betrothal—or 'marking'—of the spouses to an initial union, and the wedding itself, is normally some two or three years—though it may be a few months, or very much longer if the betrothal takes place in infancy. Popularly, the time chosen for a betrothal today is just before the man goes away to the coast on contract labour. The parents of the groom visit the parents of the bride, present a pig and some trade goods, including perhaps chaplets of dogs' teeth, *liandahr*, and, upon agreement, the young man goes off to work to earn money so that he can buy tools and gear. Now, as in former times, in contrast to *gangariner*, the relationship between betrothed couples is one of strict avoidance. They keep their distance, do not speak to each other, take care that covert glances shall not meet. When the youth goes on contract labour avoidance is simple. But when he does not it is something of a strain. Indeed, the period immediately preceding the wedding, whether the groom has been away or not, is spent in slowly breaking down the attitudes of avoidance and substituting for them a relationship more consistent with living and working together.

The natal households of bride and groom, it will be remembered, have been in an actual or potential exchange relationship. Now they become *mngwotngwotiki*, or as though *mngwotngwotiki*: the projected marriage envisages a confluence of actual or potential rival foodstuffs, a passage from actual or potential mutual obligation and reciprocity to conjunction. Bride and groom go to work in each other's households, exchanged against each other to start with, but later working as a pair, now in one household, then in the other. They maintain avoidance, neither of them eating the food produced and cooked by the other household until the moment comes when, after some weeks of working both severally and together in each other's households, mutual oppositions are gradually broken down and the couple begin to eat and work together as easily and informally as brother and sister brought up in the same household. Then the projected marriage is ripe for confirmation. The first meal cooked by the maiden and accepted by the young man is the signal that the wedding may take place.

So soon, then, as the tensions inherent in the formal reciprocities of the past have been broken down, the couple, if they are Christians, repair to the mission and announce their intention of marrying. The groom buys a ring, the banns are read in the usual way and, there being no substantial objections, the couple are married by Christian rites. Many who are not Christians buy a ring in the same way and seal the marriage by handing the ring to the bride in the presence of her parents and brothers. In either case the brothers of the bride present her with food bowls, cloth, pots, string bags, and a variety of domestic utensils; and the bride's family feast that of the groom. This last not only nominally clears the debt created by the presentation of betrothal pig and valuables but, coming from the brothers of the bride rather than from her household—the households of bride and groom are *mngwotngwotiki*—it is, so far as the new household is concerned, the first in a series of exchanges with wife's brothers that will continue until divorce or until they become *mngwotngwotiki*. In the past, though not often today, the brothers of the bride demonstrated a hostility before which the groom was expected to show some anxiety—an illustration of the facts that the groom is not only beholden to the brothers for exchanges, and is initially in debt to them, but will have to face their wrath if he maltreats his wife. Formerly, too, after the presentation of the household goods, the bride was closeted with a mother's brother of the groom[1] and deflorated, *coitus interruptus*. The sexual secretions of the couple were collected, mixed with certain herbs and portions of the bride's underskirt, then introduced into the milk of a bisected coconut. This mixture the groom drank. The purpose of the rite, Tangu say, was to ensure the birth of children and the fertility of garden crops.[2]

The most convenient time to marry is sometime before the later spring or early summer, when new garden sites are being cut from the bush. By so arranging it the newly-weds may help their natal households with the harvest, and gain assistance in shifting their seed crops and clearing and planting their new site. As soon as they set up on their own, however, they can no longer rely on their natal households for help; they pass out of an ambience of personal problems and delights into one characterized by obligation and responsibility. There is work to be done in garden and bush, claims must be made good, allies sought; other households will be demanding their equivalent exchanges, children will have to be nurtured and trained. Their relations with other households will depend on the way they cope with co-operating with some, making exchanges, bartering, and trading with others. And their own personal relationship with each other will be affected by the same factors. Wife will have to help husband so manœuvre as to gain security as well as influence in community affairs; and husband will have to satisfy both wife and wife's brothers.

---

[1] Not, apparently, the *ringertiam* mother's brother.
[2] Compare the rite at the making of a new garden, *supra*, p. 75.

Second or subsequent unions tend to crystallize out of *ad hoc* situations, do not normally involve an exchange of spouses, brother and sister, and are not invested with the ritual of a first marriage. A second wife provides a man with another set of exchange relationships through which he may make his productive capacity and industry yield him political influence. Sometimes, especially if the wives are sisters, polygynous households work as a single unit. But if the wives are not sisters and each has children, they are lodged separately with their own gardens. The husband works in, and organizes, both sets. If a man has two wives he should be capable of doing more work than the average, and if he is stronger or more competent than most, he will seek out an additional wife in order to have another set of exchanges through which he can make his working capacity politically significant.

When the proposed second wife is not a sister of the first, the husband normally has to contend with several sorts of opposition. The first wife will object because there is bound to be a division of attentions. But if the husband can convince her that a co-wife will be an economic advantage, he will usually get his way. Then the brothers of the intended co-wife like to assure themselves that the husband is really capable of dealing with two wives and two sets of exchanges. Being ambitious themselves, and bound by equivalence, they would not want to have to make small exchanges. Similarly, if the brothers of the first wife think they can foresee a falling-off of current obligations, they will oppose a second marriage. Finally, there are generalized objections to taking a second wife: it may be denying a bachelor the opportunity to marry; the intention to take a second wife shows that a man thinks himself more competent than others. Still, since second wives serve more than one interest, a keen husband usually succeeds in obtaining one—especially if the woman is a widow, a woman whom no one else seems to want, or a sister of the first wife. For though some polygynous unions are between a man and two 'unrelated' women, the more common arrangement is for two sisters to share a husband. Full sisters, in a close and affectionate relationship, are often inseparable. Following on a first marriage a bride's sister may come more and more often to stay with her married sibling, the visits becoming longer and longer until, eventually, the second sister becomes

PLATE III

a. A meal on the new garden site

b. In a new garden shelter

part of a multiple household. But to take her to wife, ex-
cepting the case where the second wife is the widow of the
husband's brother, the husband must make a payment to the
brothers. There is no ritual, the payment contracts the marriage.

Payment for a woman makes her the 'property' of the husband. She is his, bought, *pungkwojuoki*. He incurs no obligations
on her behalf. But if the husband is a reasonable man he will
accept a conventional repayment from the brothers. The repayment frees the wife from the husband and at the same time ties
her to him in terms of exchange obligations to the brothers. The
latter will not accept an exchange relationship unless the husband accepts a repayment. A true marriage implies the formal
freedom of either spouse to break off the relationship, but it also
includes the exchange relationships which tend to prevent them
from doing so. In the more recent past wives used to be 'taken'
(*puginie*) by force, and kept by force. The claim to have her
rested on a man's ability to take her and keep her. On the other
hand, the union could be regularized as a marriage by exchange
payments and the acceptance of exchange obligations. Today,
although Tangu no longer capture women, they have the
opportunity to marry women who come from villages some
way from Tangu. Since, in such circumstances, maintaining the
exchange relationship would tend to be impracticable, a single
payment for the wife is sometimes made. But again, though
there may be no insistence on regularly maintaining an exchange relationship, a repayment creates a better atmosphere.
The brothers have nothing on their consciences, and the woman
is free to return to them or marry elsewhere should the union
turn out to be odious to her. In former times a marriage payment, whether initially or on a subsequent marriage, always
included a pig and chaplets of dogs' teeth. Today various
amounts of goods, cash, and possibly a pig, are bargained and
argued out in relation to particular circumstances.

Men evaluate wives in economic terms: 'She is a hard worker,
A strong woman like that will always be a good wife, She can
carry more yams than most—and the baby too! She makes the
best string bags, She can walk for miles with the heaviest loads,
She is a good cook, She wastes nothing . . .' The measure of
worth is working capacity. Maidenly charms are a delightful
addition, but by themselves simply an invitation to sorcerers,

adulterers, damaging gossip—Trouble. A good wife does well all those necessary tasks which provide the basis, and leave a man free, for significant—that is political—interaction with others. A husband is the boss of the household. He directs the activities of its members, protects them, provides the environment in which children may grow up, learn, and become fitted to take their parts as adults in the community. He needs a wife through whom to make exchanges, and he requires children in whose names he may give feasts. His claims are put to work for the household, and while he lives his industry and mode of managing his household redound to his credit. Maintaining a marriage pulls the couple into the centre of conformity with community values, and may give the husband a certain control over them. Broken unions tend to force both men and women out to the fringes of community life. For a man the political and economic implications of a marriage overshadow the personal or emotional relationship with the wife or wives. For a woman a husband and household spell children, protection, security, and sexual satisfactions. From being a subordinate member of a household, after marriage a woman becomes mistress of her own. Her personal qualities, her working capacity, and her fecundity may make her well known and respected. But her effectiveness in the community can only be felt through her husband, and through having a husband.

When couples part company it is not necessarily on account of an adultery, but because, for one reason or another, they cannot get on with each other. And in this the initiative would seem to come most often from the woman—who requires a satisfactory personal relationship within the marriage. In principle, no kind of stigma attaches to divorce as such. Tangu feel that a woman should have the opportunity of living with a husband she likes, and the husband's repayment to the brothers is virtually an acknowledgement of her claim to do so. While a dissatisfied wife is a nuisance, inviting adulterous unions and consequent quarrels and trouble, a contented wife makes for more stable interactions all round. Reciprocities are more conveniently maintained than changed. A man's political interest in a wife has to be reconciled with a woman's desire for a husband who, in satisfying her sexually and emotionally, also protects her and provides her with economic security. The major problem for those who wish to part company is to find alternative spouses. Because she is the channel through whom they themselves make exchanges, a woman's brothers will attempt to prevent a divorce unless an alternative husband is immediately available; and because her best security is within a household, a woman will not normally leave her husband unless a remarriage is likely. A retreat back to the parents is always possible, but since an unattached woman who has been married is considered a standing invitation to sexual adventurers and sorcerers, unless a new husband is definitely in view divorce occurs in an atmosphere of general unease and disapproval. An unsatisfactory marriage, that is, tends to be solved in terms of an alternative marriage; and divorce is closely related to the prospects of remarriage.

A man finds little difficulty in marrying or remarrying—though he may have to wait or find a wife from an outside village. But a woman who leaves her first husband, or who is deserted by him, finds it hard to do more than become another man's second wife. And a second divorce or desertion renders a third marriage unlikely: whatever the reason, maritally the woman is a proven bad risk. Though some brothers would be willing to look for a husband for her in some outside community, most would be only too ready to wash their hands of her entirely: sooner or later she will involve them in trouble. Further, since brothers and sisters who are or have been married ought not to live within the same household,[1] a divorced woman without a husband is only of limited personal help to a brother, besides being politically valueless. Finally, as no man in the community appears to want her as a wife, but she is a marriageable woman likely to cause trouble, she may be forced to leave Tangu and take her chance elsewhere by herself—'where people do not know her so well', as Tangu say.

Though certain women in Tangu are pointed out by men as generous with their favours, good for a casual adultery should the opportunity offer itself, their marriages tend to persist. While it is true that the husbands of such women tend to dream about sorcerers more often than others—a feature which has the

---

[1] Married brother and sister in the same household, co-operating, are in a formally incestuous relationship, even if there is no co-habitation in the sexual sense.

effect of mobilizing public opinion against a suspected adulterer, thus making it difficult to gain access to another man's wife[1]— because for men marriage means so much more than regular sexual satisfactions, they are apt to place their unions beyond and above suspicions of adultery. And the same is true of women: on both hands the present advantages of actually being married have to be weighed against not being married, being married to someone else, or not being able to find an alternative spouse.[2] Discoveries of adultery *in flagrante* are dealt with on the spot, in hot blood, by an injury or a killing. In any case the act will involve arranging a compensation exchange if, as is usual, the married couple or couples do not intend to part. The stigma, or shame, lies on the man especially. A woman cannot but be herself, prone to sexual activity, Tangu say. But a man should behave responsibly. And, because a discovered adulterer has not behaved responsibly, he comes to be thought of as a sorcerer or like a sorcerer; he becomes a focus of suspicions.[3] But an adultery carried out with some finesse is treated rather differently. All Tangu 'know' or 'feel' that such adulteries are common. They say they are 'always' going on. Yet while the realities behind such statements are inaccessible, and though boasting and talking of such conquests in contexts of ribald escapade is freely indulged, the idea of seriously setting out to steal someone's wife is regarded as very nasty indeed. On the one hand no end to the marital union is envisaged, on the other only a sorcerer or someone like a sorcerer would set out to steal another man's wife. And against the sorcerer the whole community is united.

Perhaps because what starts as bright and careless might develop into something dark and broody, adultery is for Tangu

[1] *Infra*, pp. 139, 145.

[2] If after marriage, for men a political rather than a personal act, husbands tend to channel their suspicions over women and wives into sorcery, itself a complex of political relevance (*infra*, pp. 151–5), wives, whose jealousies turn on personal and economic matters, favour a more directly personal approach. When N's wife, herself not blameless, found out that her husband had been having an affair with another woman, she bit him in the arm and chest and laid about him with a hunk of firewood. N thereupon decided to go away to the coast on a spell of contract labour. The wife, in herself perhaps further enraged, but overtly becoming much more tractable, weepy, and stricken, reminded her husband that he had a wife and children, a household to support, exchange obligations to meet. The husband stayed. Her security was his political opportunity.

[3] *Infra*, pp. 140–5.

a wrong, a sin, requiring confession.[1] Since the fabric of community reciprocities hangs on the principle of the marital union, the integrity of particular marriages has to be defended. Yet what is at stake is not so much the maintenance of the family—children, as we have seen, are expected to find their own most satisfactory household ambience—as the stability of households mutually engaged in co-operative and exchange relations. Stealthy and malicious adulteries, carried out by men who are by definition sorcerers, not only disrupt a single household but vitiate the relations between numbers of households. Those who divorce and who do not remarry, or who cannot maintain a subsequent marriage, eventually find themselves, like adulterers, excluded from a full participation in community life, or even exiled. Broken marriages and adultery are evaluated against maintaining a system of households in more or less stable reciprocal relations.

As with sister to brother, a wife's obligations to her husband are summed up in the phrase 'She must cook for him', the implications being obedience, nourishment, and services. And as is the case between brother and sister, a husband's obligations to his wife are summed up as 'He should protect her'. He must so initiate and manage affairs that she and her children are maintained in security. Some couples are, as we might say, truly in love with each other, enjoying mutual affections and understanding. Other couples tolerate each other—foreseeable alternatives seem worse than the current arrangement. But there are no obviously miserable marriages among Tangu. Either an initially unsuited couple will have parted company in favour of alternative unions, or they will have so interacted and communicated their parts as to reach a reasonable accommodation with each other.

Tangu men compare their wives to the beautiful and highly prized bird of paradise. 'Ah!' they exclaim with a sigh, hands evoking the dip and flow of paradise plumes at a dance. 'So lovely! But what a voice the bird has—Kaak! Kaak! Kaak!'

Siblings of Different Sex

Marriage, forming a household, having children, and engaging in reciprocities with other households provide the individual in

---

[1] For Christians, and also many pagans, a wrong as well as a sin, *pekato*. For confession see *infra*, pp. 150–5.

Tangu with his or her widest scope and opportunity. Unmarried, the range and significance of interactions is limited; divorce not followed by remarriage entails diminishing interactions and may even result in total exclusion. And the framework within which these interactions take place is provided by siblingship.

The relationship between those categorized as brother and sister is formally one of mutual affections and respect expressed in reciprocal services. And these services define the relationship. Thus, although the relationship is modelled on that which is supposed to exist within the household between brother and sister of the full blood, should such siblings become members different households through adoption, and the households concerned come into exchange relationships, then it is arguable whether the siblings may marry. Most Tangu say 'No'. Others point out that since the natal households are in exchange relationships, youth and maiden are not categorized as brother and sister, and so can marry. On the other hand, the children of co-operating households are categorized as brothers and sisters and, while they remain so categorized, may not marry. The incest taboo, that is, is tied to the kinds of reciprocities obtaining as well as, or rather than, to the biological connection.

Before marriage sister cooks for brother, works for him, accepts his demands and has his confidence, is always encouraging, never nags. After marriage she cooks for him through their exchange relationship, may look after him and his children in an emergency. But it would be incestuous for her to become a member of his household. In return brother protects sister and provides her with food through exchanges. For Tangu the relationship is summed up in the formula 'A sister cooks for her brother', the corollary being that brother makes it possible for her to do so. And, as we have seen, sexual relations apart, precisely this act of cooking for a man characterizes the relationship between wife and husband. Cooking, indeed, is the common and mediating link between the two relationships. Though the intimacy between brother and sister within a co-operating group may develop into something approaching sexual play, occasioning expressions of horror, both in dreams and in narratives brother and sister marry or have sexual relations. Moreover, just as it is well-nigh inconceivable that a sister-as-wife (where the component 'sister' is drawn from the pre-marital phase) could nag or make trouble for a brother-as-husband (where the component 'brother' is also drawn from the pre-marital phase), so does it seem to most men that a sister, or a sister-like woman, would make an ideal wife.

That a sister who becomes a wife will no longer be a sister is most of the problem. The troubles, pushes, and pulls within the marital union are the price of espousal, sexual relations, bearing children, community life and, for men, the assumption of responsibility. Whether sisters are idealized as mates because they seem the best helpmeets, or because their brothers may not marry them, the best qualities of a sister are desirable in a wife, 'sister' and 'wife' figure in each other. For a woman on the other hand, though an image of 'brother' should figure in 'husband', since in fact husbands are normally more attentive and affectionate than brothers, it might well be wished that 'good husband' were figured in 'brother'. Among Tangu, one may epitomize, social life is possible, and individuals reach maturity, by satisfactorily resolving the sibling-to-marital relationship. Within the household, sexual relations excepted, brother and sister behaviour echoes the patterns set by father and mother who are husband and wife. Sons model themselves on fathers, involving themselves in men's work and prejudices as their fathers teach them to do. Similarly, daughters follow their mothers. Like mother to father, sisters assume a role of subservience to their brothers, attending to their needs and demands. Unlike mother to father, before marriage sister does not nag brother. When the brother has become a man and is able to do so effectively, he is expected to protect his sister. For after marriage a woman needs the kind of protection a husband cannot give: protection from the husband himself. Yet brothers are not always placed to protect their sisters; such protection may be against their interests and, as responsible men, it may be appropriate not to protect their sisters.[1] On the other hand, in spite of harsh words, quarrels, or threats, the services of sisters for their brothers are only rarely withdrawn. That is, from childhood on, the brother–sister relationship is based not upon necessary mutual reciprocities actually maintained, but upon the surrender of sisters to their brothers. The onus is more critically on sister to provide for brother.

[1] For example, after a second divorce.

Between men who have to play their responsible parts, and women who, as Tangu point out, may be themselves, precisely reciprocal services can rarely exist. But, Tangu hold, it is up to a man to choose between self-restraint and self-willedness, to decide what action is appropriate. The responsibility is his.

The relationship between brother and sister is most sharply defined where the siblings concerned have the same mother and father within the same household, and where both siblings are as yet unmarried. The incest taboo is at its strongest, opportunities to give in to temptations are most numerous and easily taken, the surrender of sister to brother is most complete, the brother's demands are most wilful and random, the co-operative relationship in producing, processing, consuming, and proffering food the most intimate. But as one moves outside the household and beyond the full blood, the relationship becomes more and more formal until the co-operative relationship alone defines the categories. Upon their several marriages, however, both brother and sister make a significant substitution. The sister consents, conditionally, to accept as chief protector a husband for whom she has to work and cook, and to whom she owes on an initially formal basis the same kinds of services as she has hitherto given her brothers as a matter of course. She also gains claims to sexual satisfaction and bearing children. For his part the husband gains the same kinds of services as he would get from a sister, as well as that which no brother of the woman he is marrying has: sexual access. But he does not obtain at once that surrender which a woman unconditionally gives her brother. He has to earn it. And it is evident from the behaviour of some married couples that virtually this has been done: husband has become as though 'favourite brother with whom sexual relations are possible', and wife has become as though 'favourite sister with whom sexual relations are possible'. The progress of a marriage, that is, may be seen as an attempt to realize the significance of a brother-and-sister union: stasis, neither obliged nor unobliged in exchanges; the inner core of meaning in becoming *mngwotngwotiki*.

When a sister marries and her brother remains single, the latter visits the former and continues to make demands on her time, strength, and resources. At first the *mwerkindang* (sister's husband) resents, though he suffers with good grace, these attempts to maintain the initial brother–sister relationship. Meanwhile, he is doing what the brother may not do: giving sexual satisfaction and the promise of children. He completes legitimately a relationship which, so far as the brother is concerned, can only be completed on an imaginative plane. And where the brother remains unmarried the relations between the three persons involved are clearly invidious. But symmetry is achieved through a brother-and-sister exchange marriage: each *mwerkindang* in the foursome completes the brother-and-sister relationship. Husbands and wives provide and cook food for a feast, handing the food to sisters and brothers to eat; sisters continue to cook food for their brothers, though they do so through a basic opposition of households in an exchange relationship. Then, as each *mwerkindang* becomes, or is identifiable as, a husband-brother or sister-wife, so he or she realizes a culturally determined role which touches differing levels of awareness according to the individuals concerned.

Mwerkindanger through full siblings walk together, fingers intertwined. They use each other's belongings, eat together from the same bowl, help each other in garden and bush, or with children, without making demands or taking it amiss if for some reason one or other cannot comply. They interact on a basis of mutual identification. Beyond the tie between full siblings, however, the relationship becomes more and more formal until, indeed, it becomes a quarrelling relationship. For *mwerkindanger* are in exchange relationships. And because exchanges should be equivalent, but being made in foodstuffs cannot be so, there is always the potential of trouble and disputation between *mwerkindanger*. Yet if two disputants are reminded that they are *mwerkindanger*, however distant the sibling link which joins them each will deny that a quarrel exists. 'How can I be angry with my *mwerkindang*?' each will protest. So that, though individuals may quarrel within terms of their personalities and competing claims, when the category of relationship is explicitly invoked, the ideal associated with it, drawn from the full blood relationship, operates. Overtly, the quarrel dies. But as the evocations of the category fade, so the dispute between individuals with competing claims emerges again. Those who are looking for trouble find little difficulty in making it. *Mwerkindanger* in accord make their exchanges in peace, without trouble; and *mwerkindanger* who wish to dispute an equivalence can always find a pretext for doing so.

If *mwerkindanger* quarrel because they make exchanges, they can make their temporary peace with each other—and so continue to dispute within limits—because they are *mwerkindanger*. Moreover, since marriages are arranged between the offspring of households in exchange relationships, when their exchanges come to be habitually regarded as in accordance with equivalence, when they are *mngwotngwotiki*, equivalent, neither exchanging nor co-operating with each other, then formal mutual identifications as husband-brother and sister-wife may be seen as achieved. Interactions between *mwerkindanger* have developed to the point when, through communicating their parts, each is identifiable in terms of the other: they neither exchange nor co-operate; actively maintained reciprocities are at an end.[1] Just such a situation of stasis, of neither co-operating nor exchanging, would occur if brothers indeed married sisters.

When a man from Tangu goes away to the coast on contract labour and meets there, and likes, a man from a stranger village, the two men may become friends, *kwaver*, or they may become *mwerkindanger*. The wife of each becomes, or is thought of as, the other's sister, and the wives also become *mwerkindanger*. When the two labourers return to their villages, they and their families visit each other, bring gifts, trade informally, and stand as sponsor for each other whilst in the stranger village. And though husbands and wives, severally, entertain each other, the expedition is thought of as 'a visit to my sister' or 'my brother is coming to see me'. Gifts and informal exchanges are not as between wife and wife, or husband and husband, but as between two pairs of brothers and sisters. Tangu like to have such brothers and sisters residing in neighbouring villages, or in settlements along a trade route. Visitors become as kin, and therefore less vulnerable to, and less likely to be thought of as, sorcerers. For sorcerers, considered to be wantonly malicious and dangerous, are particularly associated with strangers and

---

[1] An approximation only. For the reciprocal obligation of NOT co-operating or exchanging, of NOT acting so as to put the other under an obligation, remains while the state of being *mngwotngwotiki* lasts.

stranger villages; and travelling and trading demand that sure expectation of hospitality and sponsorship which friends and *mwerkindanger* will provide. Sisters cook for their brothers and, because they are sisters, will not tamper with the food. Indeed, mothers and wives apart, if a man accepts food from a woman she must be either a sister or one who, through the acceptance of food, becomes as though a sister, if not a mistress.

Such sibling or *mwerkindanger* relationships extend through the different settlements within Tangu and outside to hinterland and coast. They constitute networks of interaction, exchange, and communication; they enhance prestige by enabling a man to dispose of his superior production; the number of sisters or *mwerkindanger* a man has indicates his standing. If some are genealogically based, others are created *ab initio*. They are also inheritable: son and daughter of the two households concerned may become brother and sister. Or, since the two households exchange specie, and the spouses of the same sex are *mwerkindanger*, a marriage may be arranged between a son and daughter of the two households. Brother and sister slide easily into husband and wife. *Mwerkindanger* arrange intermarriages between members of different communities, and, the question of sorcery aside, they also provide the links through which intercommunity disputes may be settled. Having free access to both communities, *mwerkindanger* act as spokesmen and go-betweens, seeking formulae on the basis of which their several communities might come to an accord.[1]

In general usage the word *aran* means 'good', 'proper', 'fitting', 'right'. But as a category within the kin idiom, *aran* refers to a man's sister's son and often to a woman's brother's daughter. *Arandar* (plural form) are a man's sister's sons or a woman's brother's daughters. The term *mwerk* (pl. *mwerker*), today frequently interchangeable with, and used as a synonym for, *aran*, more properly refers to a man's sister's daughter or a woman's brother's son. *Arandar* of brother-and-sister (see Figure 4 below) marry each other, so do *mwerker*. But whereas the son of *mwerker*, specifically designated *mwerkamum*,[2] conjoins the brother-and-sister lines of male and female filiation, as though

---

[1] See, for example, B–1957(*d*): 775–6.

[2] *mwerk-ka* (possessive) *-mum* (son).

the product of a brother-and-sister union, the son of *arandar* conjoins the other lines of brother-and-sister male and female filiation. So that with each alternate generation, though spouses may not be related as brother and sister,[1] as representatives of lines of filiation which are derived from brother and sister, brother marries sister. Moreover, since the term *mwerkindang*, whose substitutive content we have already noted in its reference to spouse of sibling-of-different-sex, also refers to a man's daughter's husband, the defloration of a bride on her wedding day[2] by a mother's brother of the groom is not only an enactment of father–daughter incest,[3] but, so far as it represents a union between a line of male filiation and a coincident line of female patrifiliation, thus far is it a representative brother-and-sister union. Moreover, since thereafter the husband is son-in-law, *mwerkindang*, the son of the bride's father's *mwerkindang*, and it is he who continues the sexual experience initiated by the father-in-law, the elements of substitution and projection of the self contained in the meaning of *mwerk-* become the more explicit. The suffix *-indang* contains the oppositional connotation.

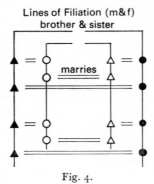

Lines of Filiation (m&f)
brother & sister

marries

Fig. 4.

In the narratives, as we shall see, brother-and-sister unions are common. Without a knowledge of the behaviour patterns of brother-and-sister, and husband-and-wife, and in ignorance of the relevances of the kin categories, the meanings of brother-and-sister unions can be interpreted only on the most general *a priori* lines. Relationships traceable across the brother-and-sister link are characterized by tension. They ring the changes between substitution and identification, and opposition and exchange, as between those of the same generation; they entail alternations of dominance/subservience as between those of

---

[1] Which is to say, genealogically, that a woman's patrifiliation should not coincide with a man's male filiation, and that a man's matrifiliation should not coincide with a woman's female filiation.   [2] *Supra*, p. 99.

[3] Father–daughter sexual relations are only marginally incestuous. Tangu regard them as silly and unnatural rather than incestuous, and, providing that a daughter maintains her widower father's exchange relations, are prepared to laugh them off.

successive generations. Because women incline to the company of mothers, sisters, and daughters, the lines of female filiation, related to each other as female *mwerkindanger*, interact relatively infrequently. Male *mwerkindanger*, on the other hand, interact and dispute much of the time, and sons and sister's sons also become embroiled. The model of two lines of male filiation and two lines of female filiation conjoined on the one hand as brother and sister and on the other as husband and wife, with a merging of brother-and-sister and husband-and-wife in each alternate generation, frames the dynamic of Tangu social relations. The communication of parts and incest stand to each other as thesis and antithesis. Where a communication of parts is abjured, it is bound to connote that self-concern or self-willedness which refracts a part of the meaning contained within 'incest'. Becoming *mngwotngwotiki* is the organizational hinge of these structural requirements. For while the activities involved in becoming *mngwotngwotiki* entail the communication of parts and the competition for prestige, attaining *mngwotngwotiki* connotes that stasis which is equivalent to husbands and wives being as though brothers and sisters.

Siblings of the Same Sex

Whether male or female the elder or eldest sibling of the same sex in a particular context is referred to in the vernacular as *ambwerk*, and the younger or youngest sibling of the same sex is known as *tuman* or *ndyung*. And though one who is *tuman* in one context might be *ambwerk* in another, specificity of meaning can be obtained by turning to the household model. *Ambwerk* is the link between successive generations. He or she carries responsibility without concomitant powers, is both senior child and junior parent without being fully accepted by either generation as quite one of themselves. Lacking the force and authority that come from actually being a parent, he or she is expected to protect or nurse the younger siblings. If a father should die, *ambwerk* (male) takes his place, becoming as father; and similarly, eldest daughter may have to take over the duties of a mother. But in neither case will father's brothers or mother's sisters consider *ambwerk* as on a par with themselves; and in both cases junior siblings tend to regard *ambwerk* as an usurper. Destined for responsibility, but not necessarily able to carry it;

accorded, but not necessarily commanding, respect; *ambwerk* categorizes a position of dilemma whose best solution is conformity with custom and established usage.

As is the case with all Tangu categories, but perhaps rather more so in this instance, *ambwerk* and *tuman* are categories of more general understanding, as well as categories of specific relationship. In the narratives Ambwerk and Tuman are presented as contrasting personality types. Where Ambwerk is proper and conformist, assuming cautious responsibility, Tuman is rebellious, the daring initiator in whose plans Ambwerk becomes involved. Where Tuman uses his wits, Ambwerk has recourse to time-honoured procedures. Where Tuman is forthright, bright, and full of fun and mischief, Ambwerk has responsible doubts. When Tuman decides, Ambwerk prevaricates. When Tuman acts, often disastrously, Ambwerk follows behind, grumbling and anxious to save his brother from the consequences of his folly. Whilst Ambwerk is always concerned for the welfare of Tuman, uneasy lest he stray and come to harm, Tuman is concerned only for himself. Without Tuman there could be no Ambwerk, and without Ambwerk there could be no Tuman: each exists in virtue of the other. And if every man and woman is sometimes Ambwerk and at other times Tuman, *ambwerk* and *tuman* are in close correspondence with Ambwerk and Tuman.

Contrasting personalities of the same class who cannot mature and develop in terms of each other's capacities by an intercommunication of the parts unless they shift categories and become *mwerkindanger*, siblings of the same sex are co-operators, but none the less rivals. Sisters become co-wives, but may also differentiate themselves through separate husbands. Brothers co-operate, but if both are able and ambitious they will become *mwerkindanger*. As children full brothers compete for the attention of mother, for the breast, for affection; girls are placid and obedient, not aggressive like their brothers. If father takes one son hunting, another will want to go too. If father is teaching a younger boy how to use an axe, the elder stands by and jeers: he knows already. If father asks elder son to fill and light his pipe, a younger son clamours to be allowed to do so instead. Some fathers, aware of this rivalry between their sons, often try to get elder to teach younger. But without much success. The issue is father's time, trouble, and attention, not how to handle an axe. And when elder brother begins to assert his independence, father naturally turns to the younger—who leaps at the opportunity. So, as elder brother gangs up with his peers, younger brother comes into his own within the household, becoming *ambwerk* and accepting the challenge of *tuman*, the third son.

The comradeship that exists between the young and unmarried men of a village tends to overlay the rivalries of brothers. Strong and fit, doing little work and virtually without responsibilities, they lead a life that consists of escapade, dances, larking with maidens, and thoughts of contract labour, cash, and adventure. After marriage, when brothers become involved in exchanges, providing feasts, trading, affording food and shelter to wives and children, exercising claims to land, and face the problem of who is going to care for which ageing parent, the rifts begin to show again. Sorcery may still draw them together, especially if they are *mwerz ungunwan*, but, lacking recurrent crises such as feud and warfare, and with added opportunities for independent action, households with a common pool of resources are apt to find grounds for dispute. Then, as we have noted, able brothers are likely to shift into the *mwerkindanger* relationship, engage in exchanges, and define themselves to each other until they become *mngwotngwotiki*. Common fatherhood does not necessarily unite the sons. A father is the pivot of rivalry in all those male skills—such as hunting lore and ability, clearing a new site, hewing down trees, fencing, planting, knowledge of spells—which are not only related to competitive activities but themselves foster the competitive spirit. In turn, each son frees himself from the father to become independent and self-reliant. And as father ages, so the sons compete to inherit a share of his claims. When father dies each of the sons has a private and separate dream-image of him, and, since such dream-images or ghosts appear to be selective in their visitations, and the relationships between sons and their dream-images or ghosts vary considerably, each brother is effectively seized of a different father. Which means that each man has a component in filiation and inheritance uniquely his own, an individual identity which he gains through his male filiation.

Through the father, then, sons are specifically not equivalent persons. They are unique individuals. Common motherhood, on the other hand, as the category *mwerz ungunwan* implies, evokes that well-known phrase 'the equivalence of siblings', and invites expressions of that which brothers have and hold in common. But if in the past 'one womb' demanded co-operation in work and war, a responsibility emphasized by the mother's brother who circumcised his sister's sons, today it is the individuality gained through the father which seems more pertinent.

Unlike males, who have significant relationships with both father and mother, and whose individuality can be related to varying relationships with the father, girls and women, completely submissive to fathers, are united and separated only in relation to their mothers. Girls and maidens and women, females together, show a marked solidarity that contrasts with the differences, envies, and rivalries found among males. If Tangu women are not immune to spite and malice, husbands and brothers are quick to smother overt expressions, and females do not normally have the opportunity to make their differences yield a relevant reward. Either female animosities grate in broody privacy, or they are made relevant by husbands and brothers. Still, given their capacities for work and services, the subservience of Tangu women to their menfolk must surely play its part in the serene confidence and quiet power that are their outstanding characteristics. No man can afford to maltreat or lose a good wife: she has too high an economic and political value. When, as sometimes may occur, a woman enters a man's world and, for example, speaks in *br'ngun'guni*, the assembly falls silent and she has her say without the interruptions that accompany speeches by men. Yet if what she has to say is to resolve itself into events it must be quite explicitly endorsed by husband or brother. For though she has a right to speak, she is offering a comment on matters which are being managed by men, which are integral to the competitive interactions of men. And should she show herself unaware of the differences between the overt issues as expressed in the oratory, and the underlying motives which move the orators to express themselves thus, she is soothed and gently but firmly led away to her cooking-pot. For Tangu a woman, having quite other spheres of aptitude and competence, and regarded traditionally as possessing a quite distinct nature and being, cannot also be, and behave like, a man.

Tangu women work, bear and nurture children, render services. And they are valued for doing these things well. Not considered to have the necessary restraint, foresight, and initiative, they are not held responsible for the management of community affairs. If a woman wants to initiate she has to do so through a husband or brother: they will bear responsibility for the consequences; other men, not women, will react to the initiative. So long as a woman attends to her duties—and husband and brothers should see that she does so—varying qualities of temperament, ability, and character are indulged. The final sanction, which solves the problem quite neatly, is that after her second divorce she will probably have to shift for herself among strangers. At once more secure than a man ever could be, after a woman marries her personal satisfactions carry elements of risk that may well be decisive: her security exacts its own price. But while Tangu women may be themselves, are what they do, and are expected to act in accordance with what they are, men pay for the privileges of initiative and responsibility by having to conform to the idea of a man. Men manage community affairs in the knowledge that a man is defined by particular qualities and abilities, and that those who fall short do not rate as responsible men, though they may be males. A timid boy must put a brave face on it and act the swashbuckling warrior; a frail or crippled young man must spear a wild boar if he is not to be shamed or laughed out of countenance. No other qualities or competences will offset an inability to meet exchange obligations, take game, and provide feasts. If a man may experience several divorces and still be able to find a wife and maintain himself, it is because he has the privileges of manhood, may use his initiative and enforce his will. It is also because, considered responsible, it is thought that he will not have left his wife without good reason. If, on the other hand, he is not considered to have behaved as a responsible man should, then he comes to be thought of as a sorcerer and suffers exclusion.

Setting themselves the task of continuously proving their manhood in interactions among themselves as well as in relation to Europeans, men compete with each other in making exchanges, co-operating, feasting, dancing, oratory, hunting, gardening, and in their knowledge of particular skills, narratives, and current affairs to show each other how much they are worth. They are considered positively to create their culture, and they are responsible for maintaining it. That is why they sometimes take risks, why they must answer for the consequences. In Tangu males have to be men—or nothing.

Friendship

A one-to-one relationship occurring in pairs between two individuals, between men or between women, but not between a man and a woman, friendship is formally free of the obligations characteristic of the kin categories. Friendships are made, may be allowed to lapse. And though friendships may be inherited, interactions proceed in principle from the initiative of those who choose to become friends. If friends feel the same kinds of obligation towards each other as they experience within the categories of the kin idiom, then either they are not true friends, or their friendship is pointless. Friendship is explicitly not a relationship between kin, nor an active political relationship, though it may have political consequences. But just as brothers may become *mwerkindanger*, so those who are kin, categorized within the terms of the kin idiom, may also become friends. And while such a course tends to defeat the advantages of friendship, the ambiguities involved are typical, useful to the able, confusing to others.

Normally entered into *ad hoc*, friendships are generally confined to those of the same generation. But the sons of two men who are friends, or the daughters of two female friends, are likewise friends. And, as we have seen, friendship contains the potential of kinship by providing for marriage. Inheritance apart, choice of friends is limited only by mutual consent and advantage. Men institute the relationship by formally exchanging, winding on, and knotting their own breechclouts on their friends; women and girls do the same with their skirts. In the past the ceremony took place in or by the club-house, and was witnessed. Today, though the exchange of breechclouts, or skirts, is still usual, since the period of contract labour is the nursery of most friendships among men, the public ceremonial is forgone. While girls and women have the same formal freedom of choice in their friendships as youths or men, their opportunities are not as extensive, they do not travel as much as men, nor do they have the same interests in maintaining friendships as men do.

Most Tangu form the bulk of their friendships with members of other settlements both within and outside Tangu itself: friendships within the local community tend to be self-defeating. Friendship entails mutual aid, hospitality, informal gift-giving, trading and exchanging; brooks neither rivalry nor quarrelling. The stress is on giving, not taking; on a loose expectation which cannot be put in issue in public proceedings if there is a default, or if a default is imagined. Friendship is personal, between individuals, contraposed to the implications of the categories of the kin idiom. No man should want, or expect, a friend to embroil himself in matters which are the proper concern of those who interact within the terms of the kinship idiom. Friends should gain from a friendship, not lose or be forced into improper risks because of it. Because they are not involved in the same complex of active political relations, friends tell each other about their illicit sexual adventures. Not simply a matter of gossip or sympathy, telling a friend of such wrongdoings is confessional and is expected to preclude the sickness or death which might otherwise follow.[1] When Tangu go down to the coast to buy salt, or gather news, or visit a trade store, or when they travel inland to buy hunting dogs, sago, or dogs' teeth, they visit friends and choose routes which will take them through villages in which they have sisters or *mwerkindanger* or friends. Like the sisters or *mwerkindanger*, friends will provide hospitality, may trade, are an insurance against sorcerers, will gossip and give information useful to the purpose of the journey.

Through his friends a man's name becomes known outside the narrow community circle. His achievements become the more widely admired, his standing the more securely confirmed. The more friends a man has in the surrounding country, the more solid his prestige and influence at home, the easier it is to buy the right kind of pig at short notice, the more conveniently a holiday is arranged when there is trouble brewing in the village at home. Few in Tangu are not parts of innumerable networks of friendships spreading from Tangu to the coast, along the foot-hills of the Adelberts to Josephstaal and around in a wide arc towards the confluence of Iwarum and Ramu, and thence

[1] *Infra*, p. 140.

to Hansa Bay. Friends introduce Tangu to feasts and dances where they have no kin, or where in any case being the guest of a friend carries the privilege of immunity without denying the visitor an audience if he has anything to say. Like *mwerkindanger* too, friends mediate and arbitrate in intercommunity disputes, making it possible to settle outstanding issues without a necessary resort to sorcery.

Though friendship can in no way replace the political and economic interactions of the kin categories—friends as such may not become *mngwotngwotiki*—it extends the range of moral relationships outside the existential local community, plays an important part in regulating relations between two or more such communities, links individuals in a wider and greater community. Whilst friends are neutrals, outside the involvements and reciprocities of community life, marriage under friendship entails exchanges just as any other marriage does, and creates kin. Where the marriage is between youth and maiden whose natal settlements are some distance from each other, few problems are involved. But when, as sometimes happens today, the friends live in the same settlement, the informal *mwerkindanger* relationship is apt to become strained, making a formal relationship answerable in *br'ngun'guni* almost inevitable—thus defeating the ends of friendship.[1] On the other hand, marriage under friendship can also be used to circumvent the formal prohibitions relating to marriage within the terms of the kinship idiom. Thus if, for example, those formally categorized as brother and sister are not first cousins or closer, instituting friendship between the parents will allow of a marriage. Should the parents in fact have been co-operating, they cease co-operating, pause in an ambiguous relationship, and after a suitable interval become friends and arrange the marriage.

As in marriage within the kin idiom, friendship entails avoidance between those who, otherwise coming into fairly intimate contact with each other, might marry or have sexual relations. Thus there are avoidance relationships between Ego (male) and the friend's sister, the friend's father's sister, and the friend's sister's daughter: and between Ego (female) and the friend's brother, the friend's mother's brother, and the friend's

[1] See B–1957(*a*): 187–9.

brother's son. The pattern (Figure 5) formally prevents friends from becoming *mwerkindanger* or child and parent-in-law, whilst at the same time preparing for a marriage through the preceding avoidance relationships. And since a marriage between those of different generations is not usual, in effect those who inherit a friendship have the choice of continuing as friends, of allowing the friendship to lapse, or of becoming *mwerkindanger* as well as friends. Where the last alternative is in fact adopted the avoidance relationships are slowly broken down as in marriage within the kin idiom.

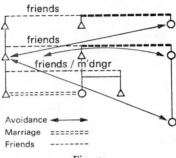

Fig. 5.

Though friendship is distinct from kinship, it is a moral relationship which remodels the principles of filiation and siblingship. Friendships descend through the generations as though in a line of male filiation, or as though in a line of female filiation. And since marriage and the formation of the household are the fulcrum of active reciprocities and so of social and community life, it is to be expected that the themes of siblingship, already apparent in the avoidance relationships, should be reiterated in friendship. And indeed they are. Thus, whether male or female, the more general term for 'friend' is *kwav* (pl. *kwaver*); and the word for the self or 'I' or 'myself' in emphatic reference is also *kwav*. This suggests some kind of mutual identification between the self and a friend, and lays the basis, when a marriage under friendship is envisaged, for that mutual identification and substitutional relationship which we have seen exists between *mwerkindanger*. Moreover, friends not only exchange, but gird each other with breechclout or skirt—items of dress which for men and women respectively are their most private possessions, concealing their most intimate and significant parts. When, therefore, the male projection of one friend marries the female projection of the other, what is being represented in the marriage of the son and daughter of two friends is a marriage between brother and sister. At a further

---

[1] An alternative word for 'friend', in Wanitzir only, is *wvert* (pl. *wvertzir*). But whilst *wvert* means 'friend', *wvertzir* may also mean 'brothers'.

remove the same representation is being effected in the case of a marriage between the son and daughter of the friends' full blood siblings of different sex. The full content of meaning in the relationship between brother-and-sister and husband-and-wife goes to the heart of being as Tangu.

Community life, a process of differentiating and communicating the parts, is made possible by the incest taboo, critically contained among Tangu in the prohibitions relating to brother and sister. Males and the male are opposed to females and the female, lines of male filiation are opposed to lines of female filiation. On the one hand, through the generations these lines are related to each other as brother and sister, on the other, as husband and wife. In each generation the *mwerkindang* consummates a sexual relationship which Ego may not, Ego and *mwerkindang* are substitutes for each other. With each alternate generation brother and sister lines converge as husband and wife, only to separate again with the succeeding generation— one may recall the imagery of a stream with its sources and distributaries. Values in filiation are opposed to those of siblingship. Where filiation, critically seen in the father–son, mother–daughter, and in the inheritance of friendship, is non-reciprocal, affective and affectionate, matter of volition and exerting self-restraint against self-willedness, siblingship connotes degrees of mutually enforceable reciprocal obligation and rivalry. While filiation provides males with a unique inheritance, individuality, this individuality is developed in terms of those mutually enforceable reciprocities contained within siblingship. Parents hand on to their children the values of their culture, and these the children may preserve or change as their ambitions and interests are limited by the values in siblingship.

With each generation the wealth of the community is re-created, with each generation the basis of community life, the incest taboo, is reiterated. The onus is on father to bring up son, on mother to bring up daughter. Mother nourishes her children, father protects them. Though siblings of the same sex are generally in rivalry, sisters are often in accord, and, whether male or female, a special relationship is typical between elder and younger sibling. Son always maintains a relationship of affection with mother. Until son reaches puberty father is a source of pride; father and son are close and intimate. While the mother's brother carries authority and attempts to win the affections of a sister's son, father tries to use the devotion of son to exercise authority over him. But before either can expand into the field proper to the other the youth enters into his parts as a man, becomes self-reliant. Real independence goes with the marriage that follows soon after. Exercising his parts, a man matures by working out his equivalences with *mwerkindanger* through wife and sisters. Until he dies and becomes a dream-image or ghost to his son, father recedes into the background; mother's brother steps forward, the equivocal father-in-law. Before marriage a daughter is bound to her mothers and sisters, rendering services to father and brothers. Not until after her marriage do the brothers have effective obligations towards her. Then, through her husband, she enforces reciprocities with her brothers until, having intercommunicated their parts and become *mngwotngwotiki*, in stasis, neither obliged nor unobliged, the four lines of filiation are interrelated as brother and sister who are also husband and wife. At this point the incest taboo operates, exchange marriages are arranged, the cycle restarts.

The formal design of the Tangu social order not only ensures a differentiation of the parts, allowing an individual his scope, but it also incapsulates a representational return to wholeness or an undifferentiated unity. While the normative interactions of the differentiated parts are characterized by obligedness, mutually enforceable or derived from self-restraint, a particular cycle ends in individuals becoming *mngwotngwotiki*, equivalent. And this, humanly speaking, constitutes redemption—aware and unobliged with a clear conscience. Internally, in short, there is a formal total coherence: the parts are differentiated into a variety of desires, interests, and kinds of awareness which may be reagglutinated into wholeness or unity; the life cycle and maturation of an individual harmonizes with the design of the community as a whole. But men are not puppets. With each generation the cycle must be reworked, self-restraint and conformity must be fostered, self-willedness and nonconformity countered. There are, too, problems of evil, pride, and self-assertion. For while the moral community is characterized or internally defined by obligedness, it is externally or diacritically defined by the self-willed and unobliged.

3

THE MORAL AND DIVINE

PIVOTING on the full relationship between brother-and-sister and husband-and-wife, the categories of friendship and kinship describe the field of moral relationships: outside them reciprocities do not form a part of general expectations. But whilst relationships within these categories are knit together and given meaning through marriages and the formation of households, the obligations contained within them are maintained, enforced, and brought to issue in the central institution known as *br'ngun'guni*. Filiation and the household provide initial placement and an early environment; siblingship and friendship widen the horizon to include risk and the more positive communication of parts; maturity comes through *br'ngun'guni* and a purposeful exercise of ambiguity.

The Moralities Observed

Br'ngun'guni, a debating and talking or disputing in public assembly, is an institutional form which Tangu share with their neighbours. But since it is a 'debating and talking', virtually only those who can speak the Tangu language may participate in *br'ngun'guni* in Tangu. On some occasions, it is true, a speaker may break into snatches of pidgin English. But such lapses are deprecated and earn stony stares of deliberate incomprehension. Tangu speakers from Igamuk and beyond sometimes attend *br'ngun'guni* in Tangu itself, and in their turn some from Tangu who have business in those parts will go to Igamuk and the neighbouring settlements to attend *br'ngun'guni* there. Mostly, however, being ethnocentric and suspicious of strangers, Tangu tend to *br'ngun'guni* amongst themselves,[1] reacting forcefully to champerty.

---

[1] *Br'ngun'guni* is an active verbal form, effectively corresponding to a present participle, which may be used either as a verb or a noun.

Formal *br'ngun'guni* occurs at feasting exchanges, which are also dances. In the intervals between different phases of the dance, which usually continues from nightfall to sunrise, as food is placed before the exhausted dancers, men from either group of households engaged in the feasting exchange make speeches. Handdrum in hand, an orator stands in the centre of the ring of assembled villagers. As he talks he accompanies himself with staccato beats on the drum, the pace and emphasis of his drumming accurately matching the passion, tempo, and significance of what he is saying. Points are impressed on the audience by resoundingly swashing the buttocks, and by high leaps. Usually the oratory is concerned with food production, with prowess in garden and bush. Astute self-praise is mixed with comments on the produce or abilities of the *mwerkindanger*. More critically, *br'ngun'guni* is the explicit opportunity for bringing up any matters which may be of concern to the community. Managers, administrative officials, mission personnel—all may have their say, reminding the assembly that it is time to harvest yams, to cut new garden sites, to repair the medicine hut or administrative officer's rest house, to renovate the school house, weed the rice field, dig new latrines, clear the approach paths, or clean up the settlement. . . . And others may bring up their grievances, whether these relate to hunting, fishing, gardening, administrative, mission, or kin matters, exchange obligations, allegations of trespass, or suspicions of sorcery. Visitors from other communities come to a feast not only because they enjoy a party, but because in formal *br'ngun-'guni* they will get a hearing, whether they want to put forward a claim, state a grievance, or simply goad another into an oratorical combat.

Br'ngun'guni may also occur *ad hoc*, outside the context of a feast. Following on a slighting remark, or a brazen trespass, or some oppression that cannot wait on ceremony, a man will commence *br'ngun'guni*. He runs up and down the dancing-space, leaping, swashing, boasting, threatening, complaining, exhausting his passion if he is angry, making public whatever is on his mind. Villagers gather round to listen, argue, or sympathize. But whether formal or *ad hoc* the procedure, ends, and means of *br'ngun'guni* are much the same. Managers are concerned to show their qualities and make names for themselves;

some, perhaps more cunning than is immediately apparent, may not involve themselves as positively; others interject remarks, mediate between the primary contestants, soften the lines of thrust and parry, calm the rage and indignation of a solo performer. What is being sought is a temporary equilibrium, the restoration of overt amity, an accommodation to a current distribution of power. For while *br'ngun'guni* is a political rather than legal device, selecting managers and influencing the composition of household alliances, there is never any specific and explicit reallocation of claims. Providing implicit authority for a number of activities, *br'ngun'guni* may initiate, continue, contain, or resolve most kinds of dispute. Nevertheless, it is for each man to gauge the feelings and interests of others, draw his own conclusions, and act accordingly. Amity in the community depends not upon some vague and emotional goodwill, but on the maintenance of equivalence. And *br'ngun-'guni* is the crucial and public test of equivalence as well as the means of maintaining it.

Equivalence, however, has to contain the desires of individuals to enlarge both personality and claims: competitive egalitarianism. When an orator begins to assume a dominance, feelings turn against him, sympathies dry, interjections from those assembled become barbed and contrary, brothers stare at the ground in silence. A wise man will give ground and allow his antagonist a point. And though formally as exacting in relation to exchanges of words, insults, quips, threats, or facial contortions, in the end equivalence is related to the concrete, to food and what is done with it. So that critical assertions of equivalence occur in food exchanges, whether they are between individuals, households, groups of households, or local communities. But foodstuffs, particularly tubers, are difficult to measure, weigh, or evaluate against each other; and unless and until those who are making exchanges are prepared to decide that enough is equivalent—become *mngwotngwotiki*—the equivalence of particular exchanges can always be made subject to doubts. In turn, such doubts tend to harden and come to be seen as indications of either contempt or an assertion of dominance. Futher, both or either of the parties concerned may be suspected by each other, or onlookers, of attempting to imply the suspicion of resorting to sorcery. No man of good will nurses his doubts and his grudges in private: he brings them to issue in *br'ngun'guni*, where each man's behaviour—and, for the discerning, perhaps even his motives—are open to public scrutiny. In *br'ngun'guni* a man challenges himself and others in an effort to prove his prowess, his manhood: maintaining equivalence is competitive. But his own desire to enlarge the self is accompanied by a hypercritical attitude towards others. And although a variety of facets of temperament and character are also in question during *br'ngun'guni*, the primary referents are productive capacity and equivalence in exchange. Given the evidence of piles of foodstuffs and meat, it is in *br'ngun'guni* that a man is most tempted in the moment, in *br'ngun'guni* that he has to balance self-restraint against self-willedness within the accepted conventions of talking, shouting, leaping, drumming, boasting, and swashing. Here doubts are externalized, brought openly to issue.

The breach of equivalence invites trouble, dissatisfactions, expressions of anger or opposition, and further breaches of amity. Tangu have no noun to denote anger. Men are angry with one another or something, not merely abstractly angry.[1] And an angry man should come out with it cleanly and publicly: for anger kept in the heart is reckoned to lead into sorcery— which may mean sickness or death for a person who has caused the anger. Anger made public by a rapid onomatopoeic drumming signal on a slit-gong, on the other hand, will lead into an explicit complaint and counter, and thence into *br'ngun'guni*. Yet an angry man is always a dangerous man. So that when anger is signalled on the slit-gong—a first essay in self-restraint —it is both a warning to keep clear and an invitation to a kinsman or friend to inquire what the matter might be. Then, whether the anger has been assumed, in order to unsettle, or whether it derives from a substantial antecedent cause, it can be, and almost always is, explicitly related to food and its production. A theft is denying another man food, or the means to procure food; a trespass implies the intent to take game, fish, or fruits from within the claims of another. Both render the wronged person less able to maintain equivalence. Just as the breach of reciprocities finds concrete expression in relation to food, so restitution of the equilibrium requires further and

[1] The word is *mangumbini*, or *managambini*, transitive.

public activities in relation to food: *br'ngun'guni* and feasting exchanges. Lacking the public expression of anger, however, Tangu assume that it will work itself out in some sorcerer-like way.

Besides being a necessary preliminary to the intermarriage of the offspring of households which are in exchange relationships, becoming *mngwotngwotiki* is the expression of households in open equivalence. After and through a long series of exchanges in which faultfinding and criticism have played a dominant part, each household has, overtly at least, no weakness to find in the other. Even if the pressures to have children married must tend to smother those critical faculties with which Tangu are so well endowed, becoming *mngwotngwotiki* still represents a considerable achievement. All suspicions of foul play or resorting to sorcery must have been laid; accusations of cheating, of malpractice in accepting foodstuffs from other households in the course of exchanges, must have been resolved. Fears that oneself, or the other, may have been justified in asserting a dominance, or in showing contempt, should have been quieted; the stinging retort in *br'ngun'guni* should rankle no longer. So far as their respective equivalences go each household should be mirrored in the other, and each should be equally unaffected by the goading and gossip of others. Yet who can say as between two men or two women or two households that there do not remain some gnawing doubts? Again, for Tangu the test lies in behaviour over food. Because it is so easy explicitly or implicitly to criticize food[1]—whether in kind or quality or quantity or cooking—when no fault is found, when an equivalence seems fitting, then *mngwotngwotiki* is achieved.

The explicit importance of food in becoming *mngwotngwotiki* should not obscure the numbers of other features that are also being brought together and held in the balance. Food is, rather, the conventional touchstone which is taken to reveal other and more complex relations. Exchanges do not take place in private. Collusion is well-nigh impossible. Expressions of doubt from onlookers cannot be ignored. So that, whereas on the one hand becoming *mngwotngwotiki* cannot but indicate a deep and truly moral equivalence, on the other hand—with a people such as Tangu—two households cannot remain *mngwotngwotiki* for long

[1] Wrinkling the nose, for example, is a sufficient criticism

unless one or other shifts residence. Arrangements for marriage apart, households which are *mngwotngwotiki* usually practise avoidance. Sooner or later, however, a chance encounter may re-energize dormant envies thought to have been resolved, and households tend to re-engage in active relations. The redemptive process entailed in becoming *mngwotngwotiki* is continuously engaged and re-engaged.

The failure to meet one's obligations may occasion shame.[1] And accompanying the notion of shame is 'sorrow' or 'sympathy', which, like anger, is an active and transitive verb. One is sorry, or feels sympathy, for someone.[2] To steal or trespass or commit adultery maliciously is to be like a sorcerer, a *ranguma*, one who in his actions does not appear to acknowledge the reciprocities of the moral order. To do the same things without malice—'under a fellow's eyes', as Tangu say—may result in the expectable reactions of one who has suffered a loss. Yet the matter is overt, the acts are viewed as attempts to establish claims, the circumstances may be argued out in *br'ngun'guni*. But to do very much the same kinds of things inexpertly, without finesse, and then to be found out; to be maladroit or behave unbecomingly; to be childishly wilful or obstinate in the face of developing public opinion; to boast and then, when challenged, to be found wanting in the deed—such gaffes and blunders occasion shame. And those who would have shared in the benefit which might have flowed from the act, had it been more deftly executed, feel sorry for the culprit and sympathize with him. The fellow has made an ass of himself and, instead of being driven into a corner of bitterness, he is given the opportunity to re-engage community values. Just as an outward show of anger expresses the moralities because it opens the way to reciprocal interaction in *br'ngun'guni*, so shame, indicating a surrender to the moral order, and sympathy, the reciprocal acknowledgement of the other's surrender, are the attributes of a moral being.

When in *br'ngun'guni* an orator goes just so much too far for the requirements of equivalence, he is halted by the cry 'Shame!' Co-operators feel sorry for one of their number who has been publicly rebuked, found out. And if the orator shows shame,

[1] *Agumi*, a quality or attribute.
[2] *Mandyungungarai*, which translates into the pidgin *sari* or *sori*.

the sympathy of the co-operators deepens and spreads so as to inform the actions and reactions of all in the community. He who feels shame, or who has been shamed, may cover his face with powdered lime or chalk and sit in the porch of his hut in silence for all to see. Those who pass on their daily round feel sorry for him—sitting alone, so grim, so sad. Some may give him good-day, others may tease. Gradually, however, attempts to engage him in conversation become more and more successful; it becomes evident to the shamed man that he is being invited to rejoin the community. So he washes his face, retires to his hunting-lodge for a few days, and afterwards takes up normal community life without remark. Alternatively, more usual to-day, instead of staying in the village with whitened face one who feels shame will go off to his hunting-lodge for a fortnight or more. There he will stay by himself, or perhaps with his household for company, slowly regaining contact with the community through those who feel sympathy for him, who come to visit him and talk. But once sympathy has succeeded in bringing a shamed man back into the reciprocities of the moral order, sympathy dries. To feel sorry for a man who is wholly capable of looking after himself on equal terms with others is to patronize, to erect a façade for contempt, to breach equivalence.

Shame, then, characterizes the moral being who breaches equivalence, knows that he has done so, and overtly appears to wish he had not. While the breach of equivalence places a wrongdoer outside the complex of reciprocities which in his act he has already denied or ignored, his shame is a recognition of the validity of these reciprocities, and the sympathy accorded to him both acknowledges his claim to re-enter community and draws him back into the complex of reciprocities that makes up the moral community. But the whole process must be open and explicit, public. An act which is or might be a breach of equivalence, but which in fact goes unnoticed, is not, strictly, a breach of equivalence at all. No one appears to have been hurt. On the other hand, it is possible that a man will find a fault in himself although no one else does so at the time. And if he is a good man, carefully maintaining his equivalences, he will confess such a breach either to a friend, or to an old man—each of whom is formally outside the focal range of reciprocities clustering about marriage and siblingship, and therefore uninvolved. Nevertheless, a confessor is not bound to secrecy, and the content of confessions quickly becomes general knowledge. So that through a private confession, which is covertly disseminated through the community, an individual who feels guilty, who feels that by some act or omission he has temporarily placed himself outside the complex of reciprocities which connote the community, covertly surrenders to the moral and is covertly reaccepted into the moral community.

Within the terms of maintaining amity by competing for equivalence, participating in *br'ngun'guni*, becoming *mngwot-ngwotiki*, showing anger and shame and sympathy, and making use of confessional procedures, Tangu managers emerge as an ideal of manhood. Extrovert and outward looking, ably communicating their parts, in them the limits of moral behaviour are most finely drawn and expressed. The reverse of incestuous on any behavioural projection, if managers make more opportunities for themselves than do others the responsibilities they incur are concomitantly greater. In their larger productions there is more room for error, more scope for faultfinding. When experts are disputing or arguing, a subtlety cuts deep even when unwittingly dealt. Temptations to equalize or get one's own back by resorting to the covert and stealthy are the more compelling, requiring qualities of skill and courage to eschew. Moreover, as managers are known to be more open to temptation than others, they are the more readily suspected of yielding. Yet these same men set the pace of community life, provide an example for the rising generation. They work hard, talk well, use their skills with economy and foresight. A manager is expected to be generous, but a good manager chooses his time, avoids uselessly squandering his resources, always has a reserve of food, areca-nut, and tobacco against the unexpected arrival of a distinguished visitor from another village. A manager keeps himself informed of affairs and developments. With a sharper sense of situation than others, he gets to know the members of his community well enough to be able to predict their likely courses of action. But he must avoid giving the impression that he knows he is more able or thoughtful than others, or that he thinks himself inherently more worthy than they. The air and demeanour of a man dealing with food and food exchanges is as important as the amount laid out: humility and pride of performance should so mingle as to produce that grave confidence which barely hides a certain anxiety. If a manager has merit and virtue, these are their own reward and do not entitle him to treat others with contumely. Managers may guide or steer, influence others, and suggest courses of action: but they have no authority as such, and may not give orders outside the household. He who works hard in field and bush or forest, who is shrewd, skilful, and competent, and who at the same time is able to maintain his equivalences amicably and openly, is considered a good man, more able in himself—because more stringently tested—to become better yet. And a manager is such a man.

Since they live in a changing world, Tangu allow for particular deviations of form by judging issues in their substance against amity, equivalence, and due process in *br'ngun'guni*. For though the forms of expression might change, as between those who communicate their parts in *br'ngun'guni* overt amity and equivalence continue to be maintained. All are involved. No one may stand on a privileged position. The manipulation of ambiguities ensures that each individual finds his own level in relation to others. But again, while Tangu outwardly respect and admire a man for being open and frank, so acquiescing in the criticism of others, few do not covet an astuteness that will enable them to escape such a scrutiny. If others are expected and exhorted to be straightforward and candid, opening themselves to censure if they are not, oneself ought to have something in hand. Indeed, this is the context wherein one man differs from another, here the self combined with the knowledge and experience implanted by father begins to be relevant. Yet the imperative to equivalence keeps this differential to a minimum: disputes can be seen as attempts to drive an opponent into a committal of those powers and resources which he may be holding in reserve. To become truly *mngwotngwotiki* just these reserves ought to have been committed. Only then is each *mwerkindang* fully in possession of the parts of the other.

Since managers are more able than others, and are, therefore, the more readily suspected of holding resources in reserve for ends not wholly apparent to others, when a manager springs to his feet to engage in *br'ngun'guni* it is all to the good. He is incited to commit his reserves, forced to submit himself to his critics, compelled to acknowledge his dependence on others. He redeems himself by fulfilling his generality as intensely as possible. What Tangu deplore and fear is that a man may try to realize ambition and desire covertly, outside *br'ngun'guni*, by asserting his singularity: a circumstance which brings him within the range of meaning of *ranguma*, sorcerer.

Sorcery and Witchcraft

The word *ranguma* is conveniently translated as 'sorcerer', though in many situations 'witch' or 'criminal' or 'assassin' or 'scapegoat' or 'outlaw' or 'villain' or 'knave' might be more accurate. While allowing that there are different kinds of *ranguma*, Tangu have but the one word. A nasty fellow, a bad man who has no shame, the description '*ranguma*' has meaning when contrasted with the good man, crucially the manager who, while himself the most exposed to temptation, yet maintains overt amity and public equivalences through *br'ngun'guni*. Used of men, but not of women, almost always of a particular man in a specific context, though he may not be otherwise identified, the word *ranguma* is used less often of a man all the time, and only rarely today of a co-ordinated group of men—though the idea of *ranguova*[1] working together in gangs is certainly not absent. While a man may be thought of as a *ranguma*, only in certain situations does the thought become explicit. In different circumstances he may be regarded as any other man—a good father, a hard worker, a careful husband. 'When the *ranguma* came into the world', Tangu say, 'he was the last man to come out of the hole in the earth. He brought with him poison and [the means and ability to cause] sickness and death. He was arrogant and proud, and proclaimed that all things were his.' Not only is there no guarantee, Tangu continue, that all men will openly engage their reciprocities in *br'ngun'guni*, but inevitably there will be some who will not. These men are *ranguova*, or like *ranguova*.

The fact that men and women become sick and die long before they reach old age reveals to Tangu the presence of a power or powers which they cannot control, and which may dominate their lives in ways that represent a defeat of the implicit aims and purposes of the moral community. That this power, or powers, may kill is of consequence. That it, or they, working

[1] Plural.

in or manipulated by men, may cause sickness or death is of more immediate concern. For, whether as vehicles or as originators, men and what they do are the interest of members of the moral community. Irrespective of final consequences, causing sickness is wrong, a denial of equivalence; so also, except in self-defence, is killing. And these are precisely what a *ranguma*, a particular kind of man, does or is thought of as doing. If a man has a grudge he should out with it openly in *br'ngun'guni* and quarrel it through in public. This is what a *ranguma* does not do. He is *imbatekas*.

Imbatekas has a wide range of possible translations: 'uncontrollable, odd, unobliged, eccentric, unusual, useless, unfortunate, awesome, remarkable, queer, singular, anomalous, evil, wicked, bad . . .'. It is a word which may be used of almost any act, situation, being, place, or thing which does not belong to the normal, preferred, expectable, commonplace order of society or nature. A two-headed dog or pig would be *imbatekas*, a kinless person is *imbatekas*, so too are unusually severe storms, thunder and lightning. Enormous snakes are *imbatekas*, certain patches of forest are *imbatekas*, and earthquakes, wild boars that kill men, and those who provide too much food at a feast also figure as *imbatekas*. On the whole, *imbatekas* spells trouble, and trouble is itself associated with the new, the strange, the odd, the unusual, the unobliged, that which is not under control. Unlike the average and reasonable man with whom one has reciprocities, a *ranguma* is most often thought of as an outsider or stranger from whom there is no assurance of reciprocal and continuing obligation.[1] He is an odd fellow, one who does not belong to a community acknowledging reciprocal obligations. Because all ordinary folk would, rightly in the Tangu view, regard a *ranguma* and the things he does or is supposed to do with extreme distaste, he must be exceptional who would be a *ranguma*. Because he does not conform to the community ethic he is a bad man doing evil things in an evil way. Supposedly possessed of powers denied to the majority, his nonconformity breeds trouble and often brings about a situation of moral conflict. He is arrogant, self-willed, and self-concerned, claiming to possess all things. Figuring a refraction of the incestuous, he is *imbatekas*, denies obligation to others.

[1] *Supra*, p. 61, n. 2.

Tangu do not normally separate act from actor, and by insisting that a *ranguma* is a man who does certain kinds of things they are able to exert a measure of control over what some might be tempted to regard as manifestations of a principle of evil. And if some such principle might be deduced from the activities associated with *ranguova*, it must be remembered that while a *ranguma* may be described as bad or wicked or evil, these terms have meaning only in relation to the Tangu idea of the good man, the man who maintains equivalent reciprocities in amity through *br'ngun'guni*. Just as Tangu do not conceive of anger in the abstract, but remain convinced that a man who is angry must be angry with someone, so it is that—other than containment in *imbatekas* which, as we shall see,[1] spans the unobliged and uncontrolled, and includes what a European might designate as good as well as what he might think of as bad—they do not refer to a principle of evil, but to the man who is a *ranguma*. If Tangu see a man whom they believe to be a *ranguma* presently bent on some nastiness,[2] they will attack him if they can, using spears or clubs. If a *ranguma* is considered to have been at work, and the label *ranguma* can be attached to a particular man, then he may be beaten up, persuaded to make restitution or pay compensation, or dispatched entirely. Because a *ranguma* is a man, and not the instance of a principle, once he has been identified as a *ranguma* techniques of persuasion or retaliation can be used. On the other hand, even if by some chance an ordinary man can strike first, he is always on the defensive against a *ranguma*. A *ranguma* is considered to have the initiative, no one knows when or how he will strike. Thus identification, some means of knowing what kind of man he is likely to be, is of the first importance.

Habitually thought of as a tall, bony man with red-rimmed eyes and the splay hand and long fingers of a strangler, a *ranguma* is unsociable, surly, a man who walks by himself. Not all men with red-rimmed eyes are *ranguova*, but one only has oneself to blame in dealing carelessly with such men. A secretive and churlish fellow is not necessarily a *ranguma* simply because he is secretive and churlish—'But,' Tangu remark, 'why

---

[1] *Infra*, pp. 152–3.
[2] The 'nastiness' and '*ranguma*' define each other. So that someone who is obviously bent on some nastiness is clearly a *ranguma*.

does he not gossip and pass the time of day as other men do, if he is not about some *ranguma*-like activity?' The solitary and lonely man who is nursing a grudge tends to brood over his fire, smoking, and his eyes become bloodshot. Such men are dangerous. As a long-legged man probably runs swiftly, so a man with large hands and fingers is the better able to strangle than a man with small hands and fingers. And stranglers do not leap forward openly in front of a man. They creep up from behind, or they wait until the victim is sleeping. A man who seizes the opportunity to take an axe carelessly left lying is simply a thief. But if a man deliberately plans a theft, and is prepared to break open and enter a hut while the owners are away, then he is a *ranguma* or like a *ranguma*. A *ranguma* is a purposive and ruthless adulterer who sets out to steal another man's wife. Only a *ranguma* could, or would, intentionally cause sickness or kill outside an open situation of warfare or feud. A *ranguma* has that within him which normal men have not: both the desire and the ability to thieve, trespass, commit adultery, cause sickness, and kill, either for his own ends or on behalf of those who share his desires but not his ability. And the means a *ranguma* uses, Tangu consider, may be potent charms or spells, gestures, poisons, strangulation, the spear, or a club. If to a European the translation of *ranguma* must depend on the circumstances of his alleged activities, to Tangu, who allow for different kinds of *ranguma*, it is what *ranguova* have in common that justifies the single category, that distinguishes them from other men. A *ranguma* is he who deliberately places himself outside the system of reciprocities which characterizes the moral order: a singular man, any man who behaves thus singularly.

A shameless one, thought to blacken his face when he goes about his business, a *ranguma* is associated with the night and is especially feared after sunset, when counteraction is difficult. Women and children, who cannot themselves retaliate, or who are thought not to be able to, are considered particularly vulnerable to *ranguova*. Children are regularly brought to heel by being told—seriously and anxiously—that a *ranguma* may strike if they do not do as they are told. By day a *ranguma* may hide near the gardens or stalk the forest on the look-out for unaccompanied women and children. At night he is expected to creep round the forested fringes of a settlement seeking his opportunity. Because he may crawl under the floorboards of a house to entice the womenfolk out, a careful husband whose wife and daughters are not sleeping well, or who hears a rustle from below, will thrust his spear down through gaps in the flooring in order to frighten off, or wound, or kill the suspected marauder. No man walks abroad after nightfall, not even to answer a call of nature, without a light and a weapon. To be without a light after dusk is suggestive of something peculiar afoot, and therefore to lay oneself open to defensive or pre-emptive attack. To have a light not only helps a man to see a *ranguma*, and so retaliate if necessary, but is itself evidence of innocent intentions. Tangu expect trouble from a *ranguma* when they know that a *ranguma* is in the vicinity, and they expect a visitation from a *ranguma* when there is trouble in the settlement. Trouble and the presence of a *ranguma*, or *ranguova*, are closely associated, one tending to imply the other. At night during feasting and dancing exchanges, when *br'ngun'guni* takes place, often the whisper goes round that a *ranguma* is watching. There may be sorties into the bush by small parties armed with spears and, if they find nothing, the dance carries on. But from that moment the atmosphere becomes more restrained than it might have been. Orators in *br'ngun'guni* become more careful, more courteous, less anxious to find fault. Those who eat maintain poker faces and belch appreciatively. Couples who have edged their way into the shadows return to the firelight, sit well within the glare of bamboo torches.

Normally, unless circumstances have led them to believe that it might be 'another kind' of *ranguma*—in which case suspicions of witchcraft are beginning to form in the *mwerkindanger* or mother's brother–sister's son relationships[1]—the members of a settlement prefer to think of a *ranguma* as not being one of themselves. Indeed, since a *ranguma* is *imbatekas*, and *imbatekas* connotes that which does not belong to the normal or preferred order of community relations, a *ranguma* can only be one who, if living in the community, has placed himself outside the system of reciprocities; or one who comes from elsewhere and is, therefore, outside community reciprocities. The most dangerous *ranguova* are thought to live in the areas bordering Tangu, particularly in Tangwattitzir, Andarumitzir, and Diawatitzir-

---

[1] *Infra*, pp. 143–4.

To seaward, it is felt, *ranguova* tend to be less dangerous. And whilst nearly all Tangu have friends or sisters or *mwerkindanger* in the villages towards and on the coast, relatively few can avail themselves of such sanctuaries in the hinterland areas. Within Tangu itself *ranguova* are thought to come from another neighbourhood, another settlement; in particular, residents in the other three neighbourhoods feel that Wanitzir people are more prone than others to become *ranguova*. Then again, in most Tangu settlements there are men who, being the offspring of 'mixed marriages' and having close kin in non-Tangu villages, travel from one settlement to the other, living now in one and then in the other. Trying perhaps to get the best of both worlds, but not making their commitment sufficiently clear, such men, if they are also taciturn or nonconformist in other ways, become the focus of suspicions. Are they or are they not *ranguova*? To Tangu at all events they participate in a *ranguma*-like ambience or atmosphere. And in a sense it is convenient that they should. For such men are known, marked, and easily accessible. They may be collared without undue difficulty or danger, beaten up, forced to confess, made to pay a compensation. To be seen talking to such a one may instil caution in an exchange partner who appears to think he is going 'one up'. On the other hand, because such men appear to participate in that which is *imbatekas*, they may become *ranguma*-killers.

Though a *ranguma*-killer is not necessarily a man of mixed ancestry, he is always considered to participate in the *imbatekas*. He is as like a *ranguma* as it is possible to be without actually being one. An ordinary man is afraid of a *ranguma*, but a *ranguma*-killer is not. He is bolder, more cunning, more patient, more skilled in bushcraft than others. He knows mystical ways of detecting the approach of a *ranguma*, and he has the will and capacity to surprise and kill a *ranguma*. An ordinary man may retaliate against a *ranguma*, but he cannot, as a *ranguma*-killer can, himself take the initiative, seek out and kill a *ranguma*. If some *ranguma*-killers appear simply as men who are bolder, fiercer, and more able than the average, just these extraordinary qualities set them apart from other men and predicate their participation in the *imbatekas*. Other *ranguma*-killers are 'retired' *ranguova*, men who were once considered to be *ranguova* but who, now, put their skills and abilities to work in defence of the moral community instead of against it. More often in the old days, perhaps, but rarely today—though it is alleged still to occur—a *ranguma*-killer was one who had 'eaten *ranguma*', *ranguma brami*,[1] a phrase which refers to a ritual in which several men would foregather, rub eyes and brows with nettles to make them hot, sore, and red, and eat a dead baby,[2] or a live toad, together with a species of chestnut known as *juata-k'mba*.[3] Although, during field-work, there seemed to be some doubt among Tangu whether the rite made a man into a *ranguma*-killer or a *ranguma*, one may see in retrospect that the question would hardly be intelligible if it implied mutually exclusive alternatives. For the purpose of the rite seems to have been to invest a man with the desire, the will, and the ability to kill in cold blood. Any man in passion might wish for the death or sickness of another, and any man may kill if sufficiently provoked. But, Tangu consider, it is no ordinary man who can injure or kill with cool objectivity. A *ranguma* may cause sickness deliberately, without provocation. His is an initiatory act, not necessarily a response to the act of another. He eliminates with professional precision. And a *ranguma*-killer is the same sort of man. He must have the same qualities of cool appraisal, forethought, knowledge and experience, will and capacity. *Ranguma* and *ranguma*-killer are reverse and obverse of the same coin.

On certain occasions Tangu use a *ranguma*-killer as a night guard: when the killer's skin becomes 'hot', or 'creeps', when a *ranguma* is thought to be on the prowl, when there is trouble in the village, when there has been a quarrel, when there is a sense of tension and crisis in the community. Then, without a light, the *ranguma*-killer stands his watch, patrolling the village and its environs. Good men may sleep soundly. Others, indignant and angry men perhaps, with thoughts of surprising an antagonist during the night, also keep to their huts. They know that the *ranguma*-killer, an expert, will pounce on them before they can do what a *ranguma* might do, before they can commit what, in the calm of hindsight, would be an unnecessary or even irreparable injury. Though the presence of a *ranguma* may be

---

[1] The word *brami* means 'to eat', 'partake of', or 'imbibe' (*supra*, p. 84, n. 3).
[2] So it is said.
[3] See *infra*, pp. 295–6.

suspected when, overtly, there seems to be no trouble,[1] it is more often in situations of stress—typically and crucially when it is felt that someone with a grudge does not intend to bring the issue to *br'ngun'guni*—that the idea that a *ranguma* is present becomes immanent. But the task of finding out precisely who the *ranguma* is, while always supposedly urgent, only becomes a matter for active concern if trouble and disquiet continue to the point when somebody is actually hurt. While the *ranguma*'s specific intentions remain vague, plans for counteraction are similarly generalized. Once the intention becomes clear, however, then the responsibility for saying that this or that particular man is a *ranguma* becomes more and more insistent. Sickness, for example, prevents a man from working, damages a manager particularly, and throws uncertainty on the whole complex of reciprocities in which the sick man is involved. When one of their number is sick, especially when that sickness is diagnosed as due to the machinations of a *ranguma*, the members of a community grow anxious and doubtful as current reciprocities become questionable and begin, well-nigh perceptibly, to shift in order to meet the new situation.

Almost any ailment will occasion an examination of conscience, and probably confession afterwards. For no sickness or disability is considered by Tangu to be quite accidental. If it is not due to the caprice of non-mortal beings,[2] a prior transgression probably lies at the root of the matter. Headaches, colds, boils, cuts, or fractures may herald the beginnings of *ranguma* activity, or they may have other causes.[3] When a person vomits, however, and continues to vomit day after day; when boils degenerate into carbuncles; when a man cannot eat or keep his food, has diarrhoea, and begins slowly to waste away; then assuredly a *ranguma* is at work. The sick person should examine his conscience and confess either to a friend or to an old man—formal neutrals who will bruit it abroad that confession has been made.[4] And whether a sickness is considered to flow directly from a wrongdoing—as with most sexual misdemeanours; or from defying the powers of a protective spell—as may happen in

---

[1] For an example see B–1960: 61.
[2] *Infra*, pp. 159–70.   [3] *Infra*, pp. 159–61.
[4] Sometimes Tangu confess to a brother. But his evidence of confession, interested as he is in the sick person's productive potential, cannot but be suspect.

cases of theft or trespass; confession expunges the wrong on one side and also obliges a human initiator of the malady to desist. Ordinary men will feel so obliged, and will act accordingly. But a *ranguma* may not. He is unobliged, without pity. So that if a sickness continues after confession has been made, the notion that a *ranguma* is at work is confirmed. It becomes imperative to identify the *ranguma* as a particular man and make him subject to the community moral by forcing him to stop. Yet who but the sick person, or, conceivably, the *ranguma* or his hirer, can judge whether or not the confession has been complete?

Tangu use three main methods for identifying a *ranguma*: an oracular technique, rarely used today, in which names of suspects are suggested and affirmative or negative answers obtained;[1] eliciting successive confessions which, in giving the names of wronged persons, provide the names of those with a motive; employing dreamer-diviners, specialists who confer closely with the victim and then attempt to dream, intuit, or divine the identity of the *ranguma*. When first a sickness is diagnosed as having been caused by a *ranguma* the victim is likely to threaten revenge, protest his innocence, or—because ultimately a *ranguma* needs no provocation—plead for mercy. First confessions tend to provide the names of wronged persons who live in communities neighbouring Tangu; and through friends and *mwerkindanger* these communities are apprised of the fact of confession. If, then, the sickness continues, it is taken to indicate either that the man causing the sickness is obdurate and wants his last ounce of revenge or self-satisfaction, or that the right name has not yet been obtained. Nothing as yet can be done about the last dread alternative, that the *ranguma*, untouched by the moralities, is going to continue through to the kill. To cover the first assumption members of the victim's community may resort to threats, then to spoliation of the suspects' gardens, incitements to fight, counter-magic, or hiring a man believed to be a *ranguma* to take appropriate action. To cover the doubt regarding names, more confessions and more names are obtained—these last now coming closer to home and including members of the victim's community—and the specialist dreamer-diviners are asked to provide a definitive answer.

[1] *Infra*, p. 178.

In the past, one feels, most such *ranguma* situations would be taken to have been solved in an affray with the outside community: a slain or wounded enemy would afterwards be identified as the *ranguma* responsible. One affray would beget another, and each would temporarily 'resolve' a particular *ranguma* situation. The dreamer-diviners would have played, one may suggest, merely a supporting role. Today, however, as an armed skirmish would certainly come to the ears of the administration and so involve the participants in an uncomfortable official inquiry, such a procedure is unrewarding. Yet since a man has been hurt, made sick, prevented from honouring his reciprocities, and equivalence must be maintained, somebody must be identified as a *ranguma*. One alternative is overtly to drop the matter, leaving the question of identification and revenge or compensation to the victim's kinsfolk—who might employ an assassin or *ranguma*-like person to take action against the suspect or his more immediate family. But if such a course were actively engaged it would re-energize animosities towards the other community and interfere with trading and exchange relations. While an administration enforces the peace, and while influence in the local community depends upon widening interactions and the extension of possible resources, trading relations are preferable to war or feud. Warrior values stand at a discount in relation to productive potential and command over wealth. Consequently, the further alternative of employing dreamer-diviners to select a guilty party from within the community seems to be coming more and more to the fore as a convenient solution. Indigenous detectives, dreamer-diviners reason with the clues provided by the sick man and his circumstances, arriving at an answer which, if largely intuitive, is also contained within the logic of the situation. They pick on the misfit, the partial stranger, the fellow thought to be odd, the man who does not communicate his parts as well as others do. And once so identified the *ranguma* is persuaded or coerced into confessing his guilt and paying compensation to the sick man. When the latter recovers and is able to return to work, he repays the alleged *ranguma* with goods or money equivalent to the compensation—thus leading the *ranguma* further into reciprocal action and leaving him without a pretext for repeating his action later.

When a man begins to suspect that his wife is having adulterous relations with someone unidentified by him, he may express his suspicions by saying that he has dreamed that a *ranguma* has designs on his wife. Or, to put it another way, when a man dreams that a *ranguma* is threatening members of his household, particularly his wife, it is more than likely that behind the announcement that he has dreamed of *ranguova* lies the suspicion of adultery. And by making it explicit that he thinks *ranguova* are about he minimizes the opportunities for adulterous relations, makes it difficult for adventurers or *ranguova* to interfere with his wife or daughters. The community assumes a state of preparedness, the *ranguma*-killer keeps his watch. Either the lover—if there is one—will have to come out into the open and bear his responsibilities, or he will desist, or he must accept the considerable risks which attend his continuing the affair.

A wife is the fulcrum of the husband's relations with mother's brothers on the one hand, and *mwerkindanger* or wife's brothers on the other. And with both of these categories, it will be remembered, the husband is in a quarrelling relationship—not only through the exchanges in which he must participate through his wife, but also because wife's father and wife's brothers have residual claims on the wife and should protect her. Mother's brothers (or wife's fathers) are always ambiguously placed in relation to sister's sons; and *mwerkindanger*, whose own exchange interests lie in their sister, like to be sure that her husband is working to full capacity. So that a man who is an unsatisfactory husband, and either feels it or is made to feel it through regular *br'ngun'guni* or outside it, cannot but regard *mwerkindanger* and mother's brothers with suspicion if ill luck befalls him. Though it is typically a witchcraft situation, Tangu do not explicitly recognize it as one radically different from any other situation involving a *ranguma*. They simply point out, *sotto voce*, that when categories of close or putatively close kin are involved, 'another kind' of *ranguma* is at work.

If *mwerkindanger*, or mother's brothers and sister's sons, were regularly to accuse each other of being *ranguova*, no amount of verbalizing about 'different sorts' of *ranguova* could qualify the ultimate implications of the accusations. Little in the way of a community would remain. And, one suspects, just this possibly happened during the period of the epidemic sickness when,

with an alarming increase in the number of deaths, the opportunities for identifying slain or wounded outsiders as *ranguova* began to be outstripped by the numbers of deaths to be
accounted for. Today, a husband tends to throw out hints that
mother's brothers and *mwerkindanger* are worrying him, and
talks loudly about the presence of unidentified *ranguova*. In this
way he channels animosities outside the complex of his own
exchange relationships, community and family responsibilities
whilst also implicitly cautioning *mwerkindanger* and mother's
brothers. In addition, he recruits the sympathies of the community in general; he gains time and confidence to gird his
loins and make a better show of it. For their part, if only to
avoid being identified as *ranguova*, both mother's brothers and
mwerkindanger will attempt to deflect suspicions by strenuously
taking the husband's part against the alleged *ranguma* or *ranguova*.
So that by the time the excitement has died down both mother's
brothers and *mwerkindanger* will be behaving towards the husband as though they were in every respect pleased with his
performance.

Representing an amalgam of the classical essentials of both
sorcery and witchcraft, the kinds of relations categorized by the
ranguma complex define equivalent reciprocities by contraposition on the one hand, and serve to enforce the same reciprocities on the other. While, for Tangu, the worst kind of *ranguma*
is a man innately without shame, unobliged, one who is quite
capable of striking an innocent—and children are considered
his most vulnerable target—it is also the case that Tangu find
it hard to believe that an adult can be without stain and wholly
undeserving of a *ranguma*'s attentions. Though, therefore, it is
thought that a *ranguma*, being self-willed, may kill without
provocation, in fact for the most part the activities of suspected
ranguova relate directly to the state of current reciprocities.
Everyone protects property and claims by means of charms and
spells, and within the reciprocities typical of a Tangu community anyone may be a wrongdoer, even unwittingly. Hence,
upon being hurt, it is first necessary to look back over the past
and examine one's conscience, and then confess. So soon as
wrongdoing and guilt are thereby admitted the automatic

consequences of a wrongdoing are nullified: ordinary men are under obligation to neutralize the power of spells or charms which they may have initiated. Normally they do so or are taken to have done so, the victim's recovery being taken as evidence that they have. But if the victim does not recover reasonably quickly it is taken to mean either that a full confession has not been made, or that there exists someone who considers himself unobliged. So the label '*ranguma*' goes looking for a particular man, and the victim returns to searching his conscience in order to make a fuller confession. Again, recovery evidences a full confession as well as the fact that a *ranguma*-like fellow has undone his spell or charm.

Yet a risk has been taken. And if there is a fair consensus regarding the identity of the *ranguma*-like fellow, he becomes a marked man. He is watched. Should the affair reach the stage at which a *ranguma* or his hirer is positively identified, then confession by either or both erases their guilt in the matter. For through confession they acknowledge explicitly that as men they are subject to the community moral. And the compensation exchange which follows on the confessional exchange maintains and re-expresses public equivalences, reiterates the triumph of morality. Self-willedness is overcome, reciprocities and self-restraint are honoured in the deed.

In the majority of cases the recovery of a victim makes it unnecessary actually to identify who the *ranguma* or *ranguma*-like fellow is, and in some cases recovery follows upon identification and the confessional exchange.[1] But when the victim does not recover, and dies, then it is taken as certain that the *ranguma* is an outsider. In the past an expedition to exact vengeance would have been mounted. Today, the brothers of the womb might continue investigating in order to extract either a compensation which, though not formally repayable, should be repaid at least in part if further action by the alleged *ranguma* is not to be taken; or they might execute a revenge killing, directly or by employing a *ranguma* or *ranguma*-like person. More often, however, since the brothers may not be agreed on

---

[1] One case observed in the field took some seven months to play itself out. The victim, formerly an extremely robust young man, was unable to hold his food, and was eventually reduced to a scarcely breathing skeleton. At last the alleged *ranguma*, identified and coerced by dreamer-diviners, confessed. Within a week the victim was on his feet and out and about.

the matter, and because there are trading and exchange relations to consider, the affair simmers on uneasily, possible deaths
on either hand being laid at the doors of the parties involved,
mutual suspicions alternately gathering to the point of explo-
sion and lying dormant as more immediate concerns engage
attention.[1]

Children in Tangu play a game they call 'Ranguma'. Players
gather on the dancing-space and start the game by dashing
about in a mêlée of weaving and jinking bodies. No player may
touch another. Gradually, however, they bunch closer and
closer. What seems like a consensus begins to germinate. In a
trice the mob of scurrying children melts into an ordered circle,
one poor lad being left in the middle. He is 'it', Ranguma. He
smiles weakly, embarrassed, whilst those in the circle hurl abuse,
leap forward to touch, poke, or strike, retiring to the safety of
the circle before the victim can riposte. 'Ranguma! Ranguma!'
they scream, pointing derisively.

The victim defends himself as best he can. But he cannot
escape until the circled children have tired of the game.[2]

It was noticeable in the field-work situation that the same few
boys repeatedly found themselves alone in the centre of the
circle. They were as though *imbatekas*.[3] They knew the rules of
the game and what would occur, but were unable to keep
abreast of the developing consensus. Unlike the majority of
their companions—who seized the moment precisely—the isolates who found themselves dubbed 'Ranguma' were some
seconds too slow. Perhaps such boys try to make self-conscious

[1] During the Japanese occupation, when there was no adequate administrative
supervision, and when trade and communications were at a low ebb, this kind of
situation seems to have developed into an armed affray (*supra*, p. 26).

[2] It is of interest to compare this game with the Tangu cargo activities described
in B–1960: 1–3. In the game an individual who is different is being selected. And
this difference, while it connotes a somewhat greater potential, is at the same time
one that is rejected. In the cargo rites, by contrast, very much the same technique
was used to select a new man, a different kind of individual whose potential was
represented as being most desirable. Common to both procedures is the selection of
self-willedness. (See *infra*, pp. 370–2.)

[3] Since children are not responsibly involved in reciprocities, and *imbatekas* only
has meaning in relation to the normative moralities, particularly mutually enforceable reciprocities, the boy in the middle can only represent a 'pretence at being',
or 'almost' or 'as though' *imbatekas*.

judgements—for during the initial mêlée they try to edge outwards. To no purpose. In the end they are caught in the middle,
alone. Do these boys think and feel in the same ways as their
companions, have they the same mutual appreciations? If they
were 'on the same wavelength' as the others, surely they would
have been able to participate in the forming consensus? In
relation to their age-mates boys such as these are indeed 'odd'
or 'different' or 'peculiar'—qualities which can only appear as
inherent or innate. Literally 'singular' boys without friends,
abrupt in manner, prickly, they tend to play private games by
themselves, and seem to prefer their own company or that of
the intimate household to playing with other boys. Perhaps
their mothers were cruel or careless, perhaps they are genetic
mutants. . . . At any rate, almost as soon as they can run little
boys join in the game, and he who is different, who cannot
engage in the forming rapport or consensus as quickly as the
others, is left in the middle of the circle. In relation to his
fellows he is an odd one. And when such a boy, once having
been selected as different, does essay a game with the others, he
tends to be picked on, teased, and forced further into himself
and away from the focuses of mutual interaction. Some children
may work their way out of this position and become much the
same as their playfellows, able to project their parts and sense
or receive those of others. But a few do not or cannot. And if by
the time they reach puberty they are still unable or unwilling to
communicate their parts like others, it seems probable that they
become the adults who are identified as *ranguova* or *ranguma*-like
fellows.[1]

To a European the *ranguma* might appear in most contexts as
a useful fiction created *post hoc* to explain or account for certain
situations: an imaginative projection which, personifying the
unobliged and non-reciprocal, still prevents ordinary men from
overtly behaving as though they themselves were *ranguova*. But
for Christians and pagans alike in Tangu he is always a man of
flesh and blood, a part of total reality, an odd one. There can

---

[1] While it would be impossible to 'prove' the suggestion either way without
close observation of Tangu over the period of a generation, Tangu themselves
incline to regard the suggestion as being generally true. Yet, because so much stems
from being odd or self-willed, Tangu would not be Tangu if they did not seize on
any and every indication of the abnormal and tuck it away in memory for future
reference.

be little doubt that as a result of mission and administrative influence the incidence of deaths by violence in revenge for *ranguma* killings has decreased. Yet since suspicions of *ranguma* activity are so intimately related to the maintenance of reciprocities it is debatable whether the numbers of *ranguma* cases have been materially affected.[1] Christians in Tangu do not always take the kinds of active counter measures that their pagan brothers would like them to take. Still, they are as involved in reciprocities, confession, and the modes of identification as pagans are. Christians are members of the local community as well as of one that is world-wide, and Christians also fall sick and die. Whether Christian or pagan, in any community there are those who are, at the least, criminally minded, or who are odd or different in some way from the majority of their fellows. And in any relatively closed community, whose members have to jog along together, there will be mutual animosities and harsh feelings whose expressions must be conventionally controlled if the community is not to disrupt altogether. Among Tangu, the announcement that a *ranguma* has committed a theft, has trespassed, is trying to get at the womenfolk, or is determined to induce sickness or death, recruits the support of the community at large. A man who feels insufficiently secure, unwilling or unable to venture into *br'ngun'guni* can always turn a personal problem into one of community interest by remarking on the presence of *ranguova*. Indeed, in a small community particular and personal problems inevitably tend to become community problems. So soon as the idea that *ranguova* are present is made explicit, men and women going about their daily tasks keep a sharper look-out, take care, behave with restraint. *Ranguma*-killers stand their guard at night, a situation of nervous tension and preparedness is brought into being. No ordinary thief, trespasser, or adulterer would risk himself. The odds would be against him, and the penalty might be a spear in his side. Often the tension is such that if there is a wrongdoer in the community he will confess and make restitution. Otherwise, anxiety and suspicions gradually relax until it becomes clear that a particular *ranguma* is either quiescent or has decided to go elsewhere.

[1] See *supra*, p. 26. So soon as the conditions making for restraint were removed, killings restarted.

If Tangu are asked not 'Why are there *ranguova?*'—for this is tantamount to asking why they themselves exist—but 'When are *ranguova* most active?', they reply at once, 'When there is trouble over garden produce, when there is trouble over a division of meat—especially a pig—and when there is trouble over women.' That is, one is returned immediately to the heart of the complex of reciprocities: to food and its distribution and equivalent repayment; to women who, as between groups of allied men or, in terms of the model, as between lines of male filiation, are exchanged in marriage; to women through whom men come into exchange relationships and express their rivalry, opposition, amity, co-operative ability, restraint, and self-willedness. Defining current allocations of power, the *ranguma* sharpens the quality and content of both personal relationships and social categories. Conversely, the quality and content of community relations define the *ranguma*. For if the *ranguma* is always a man, and many kinds of man, he is also a potential moral being who is at the same time discovered to be different from other moral beings. And his difference resides in the fact that more than being simply a thief, a trespasser, an adulterer, a criminal, a singular or maladjusted fellow, or even a witch, he is inordinately self-willed, arrogant, and unobliged. Exemplifying *hubris*, ultimately he is taken to consider himself either a superior sort of man, or something more than ordinary men.

A man who acts covertly rather than openly through *br'ngun-'guni*, or whose spells appear as only too potent, has taken the first steps towards being something other than an ordinary man. He is becoming like a *ranguma*, an extra-ordinary man. And the adjectives and phrases by which he may be described in English are but particular projections and translations of the single word *imbatekas*: the odd, self-willed, and unobliged. Hence it is that a man who is *imbatekas* causes trouble and a trouble-maker is *imbatekas*—one who considers himself unobliged by the reciprocities which the members of community acknowledge. And since the notion of trouble is itself defined by the breach of reciprocities, Tangu are justified in bracketing together the many other kinds of man a *ranguma* might be. Some men readily confess to being *ranguova*: it makes them feared, may be profitable. And given that a man who realizes that he is going to be forced to confess might just as well do so before he is beaten,

Tangu argue that only a *ranguma*, or a man like a *ranguma*, would actually make such a confession, and thereby separate himself from his fellows whilst at the same time overtly rejoining them. Most men, Tangu say, are ordinary men, good conformists who reckon themselves under obligation. But some are different. These either choose to be different or wicked or self-willed, or in spite of themselves cannot control the evil or oddness or singularity that is in them. They are *imbatekas*. They cause trouble, and the trouble they cause derives from what they are. Tangu allow that any man—but especially a manager—might become a *ranguma*, or like a *ranguma*, and that all men are prone to arrogance, or greed, or selfishness, or lust. But whereas most men will attempt to curb actual expressions of such vices, a *ranguma* not only has the ability to develop, exploit, and manipulate the wickedness in himself and others, but does so. Identifying a man as a *ranguma* pulls him back into the moral order. His confession acknowledges guilt and wrongdoing, and the compensation exchange that follows demonstrates an overt willingness to become obliged and beholden to others. Yet what a man has done once he might do again. Suspicions remain dormant, becoming explicit and overt again when troubles start. So that while any man may be like a *ranguma*, one who might have been a *ranguma* tends to become a *ranguma*, and outright condemnation is reserved for the stranger who kills and who may never be identified.

In general, Europeans do not engage in reciprocal relations with Tangu. And, selecting the quality of unobligedness or self-willedness as definitive in the context, Tangu tend to classify Europeans as *ranguova*, as human beings who manifest the *imbatekas*.[1] On another projection Tangu admit that *ranguova* may not exist in the world of white men, and that white men themselves are not only invulnerable to *ranguova* but may, by their presence, provide sanctuary from the designs of a *ranguma*. The presence of a European, that is, evokes the open society as distinct from the relatively closed community of Tangu. Yet when a European begins to speak the Tangu language and

---

[1] Though a man who feels shame whitens his face, and a *ranguma* is thought to blacken his face, white men are still classified as *ranguova*.

becomes accepted into the Tangu community, then he becomes as vulnerable to *ranguova* as Tangu themselves.[1] 'If', Tangu say, 'we were like white men, then things would be different and we would not suffer from *ranguova*. Perhaps we would suffer from *gems* (germs) instead . . .' As most Europeans are members of another moral order, however, what Tangu are saying is that if they possessed a different kind of moral order, then they would be living in the terms of a different moral order. Without the *ranguma* there would be either no moral order or a quite different moral order: he defines by antithesis.

In spite of the fact that Europeans are generally thought to inhibit a *ranguma*, there are still many who, once a sickness has been diagnosed as having been caused by a *ranguma*, will refuse treatment at the hands of Europeans and will object to taking a sick kinsman to see a European doctor. Apart from the fact that the sick man would always be under an obligation to those who carried him down to the coast, and thus himself permanently discountenanced, Tangu say that such action might annoy the *ranguma* or his hirer and so encourage either to have done without delay. Irrespective of the attitude that asks how many patients come out of a hospital alive and well, the apparent contradiction is resolved when it is realized that so soon as the label '*ranguma*' begins to grow flesh it becomes possible to draw a particular man into the moral order and persuade him to undo his work. The axiom is not that a man is ill because some germ or virus has entered his bloodstream, but that a *ranguma* is causing the sickness. Recognizing some kinds of sickness as being physiological or fortuitous, Tangu treat them with medicines. But the kinds of sickness diagnosed as caused by a *ranguma* express, and derive from, moral rather than physiological lesion: they indicate maladies in the distribution of power, maladies in the body politic. The explanation of certain kinds of sickness, that is, is moral or psychological rather than medical, and is treated accordingly. So that though a European prevents a *ranguma* from acting because his presence evokes the open society and vitiates the reciprocities within which a *ranguma* is significant, once a *ranguma* has started his work, the help of a European—who is unobliged in terms of Tangu reciprocities—cannot but force the *ranguma* to appear unobliged also. Or, the

[1] See B–1960: 70.

intervention of a European into a process that has already started under one set of rules does not suffice to change the rules in mid-course.

The existence in Tangu of different sets of rules indicating quite different assumptions about the nature of things calls for working compromises—or cargo movements. Both Christians and pagans use holy water, prayers, and the Sign of the Cross as magical counters against *ranguova*. And for both Christians and pagans a *ranguma* is *imbatekas*, unobliged and self-willed. But whereas Christians have become involved in a system of dogmatics that invites them to engage in particular kinds of relations with beings or powers or representations conveniently described in these pages as divine, but which are not necessarily *imbatekas*, pagans are beginning to forget the kinds of relations they traditionally had with beings and representations which, also conveniently referred to in this book as divine, were nearly always described by Tangu themselves as *imbatekas*. And though the two terms *imbatekas* and divine have overlapping fields of relevance, the difference between them is in a sense the one difference that matters. By the same token convergences of meaning are equally important. So it is as well to be explicit. The use of *imbatekas*, then, is and was generally—but not always —contingent, *ad hoc*, in particular circumstances. It refers to a quality or attribute which things or humans or other kinds of beings might exhibit at some times though not necessarily at all times. The word divine, on the other hand, whilst covering the meanings of *imbatekas*, has a wider field of reference which does not in any way necessarily connote the good.[1] Like *imbatekas*, divine refers in general to the non-reciprocal, to the self-willed or unobliged: it describes that which, in the circumstances, is odd or in contrast with the normative moralities, particularly mutually enforceable reciprocities. Unlike *imbatekas*, divine is a more general and inclusive term which, in taking account of Christian representations, enables one to appreciate convergences and correspondences as well as differences.

---

[1] Many Europeans, Christians or otherwise, incline to regard the word divine as connoting the good or beneficent or ineffable and omnipotent. They tend to forget that the devil is or was also divine.

Although a *ranguma* is *imbatekas*, divine or touched with the divine, and participates in the divine or *imbatekas*, he is but human. Yet many Christians among Tangu tend to see in the *ranguma* a manifestation of the devil, or Satan, without properly distinguishing between a *ranguma* who is always a man, and the devil who was never a man. More sophisticated Christians remember that Christ was a man, separate the terms 'devil' and '*ranguma*', and see the devil as in, or as possessing, the *ranguma*, where the majority regard devil and *ranguma* as virtually synonymous. Further, building on the distinctions between 'different kinds' of *ranguova*, some Christians have begun to differentiate kinds of *ranguova* on a scale which at one end identifies the *ranguma* with the devil, bad absolutely, and at the other end describes him as merely humanly erring. That is, whilst traditionally the *ranguma* was judged in relation to his supposed activities on a scale between the reciprocal and non-reciprocal, now some Tangu are beginning to separate act and actor and judge the *ranguma* on a scale between good and bad—where 'good' and 'bad' tend to carry the values of the greater Christian community.

The description '*imbatekas*' may seem to a European an undifferentiated mingling of what he (the European) might distinguish as 'ineffable' or 'good' or 'bad' or 'worthy' or 'wicked'. But for Tangu *imbatekas* simply defines by antithesis the normative moralities of community life, and only merits epithets such as 'good' or 'bad' in relation to the viewpoints of particular individuals at particular times. In Tangu, Christian teaching—which presses the distinctions, differentiations, and relations between the divine and the moral, and good and evil —is ever pitted against a traditional conceptual system which on the one hand describes the moral order by reference to normative relations, and on the other describes the divine and defines the moral by reference to the *imbatekas*.

Tangu Christians have cheerfully adapted themselves to the Christian form of confession which, involving an awareness or knowledge of the self, sin, and the divine, expresses a relation between an individual and the divine through an intermediary who may insist upon certain penitentiary and restitutory measures, but who may not divulge what has been confessed. And with this the traditional confession to a friend after some sexual misdemeanour is, up to a point, in a fairly close correspondence. For the boils or sickness which may follow from the act itself are taken to derive ultimately from the divine—which is not under obligation to cure or restore to health. While the covert dissemination of the fact and content of the confession covertly re-engages the wrongdoers in a moral rapport with the remainder of the community, nothing can undo the act itself. It is an expression of unobligedness, it is in itself *imbatekas* and the consequences may be uncontrollable: boils may continue despite the confession. On the other hand, the moralities have been satisfied, and in Tangu—as elsewhere—a man can do little more.

When a man confesses a breach of equivalence that would have occasioned shame had it been discovered and made public, he may be trying to avert the possibility of sickness which a *ranguma* might be waiting to induce, he may feel a sense of guilt in relation to his fellows, or he might—after a generation of Christian influence—feel a sense of sin. Yet, whatever his state of mind, what he is accomplishing by his confession is a restoration of mutual reciprocities. He is acting in terms of the moral, he is making the covert overt, he is communicating his parts to those with whom he is engaged in community relations. When a man's sickness is diagnosed as having been caused by a *ranguma*, the confessional procedures that follow are almost entirely related to the reciprocities involved. If an examination of past activities must lead into an awareness of the self, of wrongdoing, of retribution stemming from or through the divine—a *ranguma* is *imbatekas*, his spell or charm is a manipulation of divine elements[1]—what is being sought is an end to the sickness by restoring reciprocities. And if this can be achieved without a full and complete confession or communication of the parts, so much the better. Each man likes to hold something in reserve.

A *ranguma* is considered not to recognize confession to a Christian priest. Not simply a blanket reaction on the part of traditionalists against the new or Christian or European, confession to a priest by-passes the essential reciprocities involved, and the *ranguma* has no means of knowing what has been con-

[1] *Infra*, pp. 182–90.

fessed. Christian confession introduces both secrecy and one who—even if he were a native-born Tangu—must stand outside the Tangu moral order as it is because he may not co-operate in the procedures necessary to clear up the affair. Moreover, Christian confession invokes as significant that part of the divine which Tangu as a whole do not yet fully comprehend, and which, even if they did comprehend it, is not—and possibly cannot be—articulated to the qualities of Tangu reciprocities. If the devil may be thought to be in a *ranguma*, the latter, unlike the devil, is a man who may be forced into reciprocal relationship the while he assumes unobligedness. As we shall see presently, though the word *imbatekas* gathers meaning when focused on the non-human and therefore quite unobliged, because a *ranguma* arrogates to himself, or participates in, the same kind of unobligedness, he is *imbatekas*. But since he is a man, who ought to be involved in reciprocities, while he remains unobliged he is touched with the divine and usurps the divine. Where Christian confession emphasizes an awareness of the self and the divine, and a relation between the self and the divine— at the expense, some might say, of the relations between the self and community—the traditional modes of confession in Tangu stress relations between the self and others. So, while the dilemma for Christians is how to excise the connotations of *imbatekas* from those of the (Christian) divine, in Tangu they bow to necessity and solve the problems posed by the *ranguma* by using both the Christian and the traditional modes of confession.

Some of the narratives (N. 14–N. 21) round off Tangu attitudes towards the *ranguma* as a man. But it is to the remaining narratives that we have to look if we are to appreciate the *ranguma* as a representation or inclusive category of being.

The Divine and the Imbatekas: *Preliminary*

By becoming *mngwotngwotiki* through due process in *br'ngun'guni* men and women realize the basic structural pattern of the community, attain a redemption. By bringing the overt breach of reciprocities before the public, *br'ngun'guni* openly maintains and regulates the equivalences necessary to becoming *mngwotngwotiki*. In one sense a *ranguma* vitiates all this. But when objectively viewed the *ranguma* becomes an integral part of the pattern. Selecting a man to be a *ranguma* externalizes the covert breach of equivalence. The *ranguma* has a punitive and corrective role, enforcing equivalences from outside. He prevents most men from being like *ranguova*; his activities, actual or alleged, bring the ethic to the forefront of men's minds; he precipitates moral conflicts; he provides others with the opportunity to develop their own moral strengths; he makes men aware of themselves both as individuals and as parts of the community. In himself, however, the *ranguma* is, and personifies, the unmoral or non-moral and even amoral. When he kills he is considered to do so not because custom obliges him, but because he is different, because it is in him to kill wilfully and unconstrainedly. And since it is possible that he may never be identified, he may escape the moral net in which others are caught. So far as Tangu can know a *ranguma* in his actions he is culpable. Confession—the admission of fault, the rejection of *hubris*, the reacceptance of open and equivalent reciprocities—draws him back into the moral order, overtly makes him a part of it again. Nevertheless, through his self-willedness and singularity a *ranguma* usurps the divine. He participates in, and manifests, what is *imbatekas*.

Storms, floods, thunder, lightning, and earthquakes, not being men, or personalized, or subject to equivalent reciprocities, are non-moral, distinct from the moral order, outside, beyond or above morality. But Tangu invest these natural phenomena with a punitive, corrective role. Always on the fringes of the meaning of *imbatekas*, severe manifestations are certainly *imbatekas*. While rain, 'ordinary rain', is a partial exception—for a few men, themselves participating in the *imbatekas*, are believed to possess spells which enable them to 'call on' the rain or prevent it from falling[1]—all these natural events, particularly when close at hand or violent, conjure presentiments of evil and tribulation and, being beyond the control of man, are considered to 'act' entirely self-willedly and unobligedly.

When a thunderstorm occurs guilty consciences are pricked: not so far as to elicit a confession perhaps, but certainly into noting a past misdemeanour. *The* earthquake, Tangu assert,

[1] See *infra*, pp. 187-9.

harking to their narratives, will happen only once more. Then, with accompanying thunder, lightning, rain, and flood the world will turn over itself. With each storm that breaks over Tangu a normally dormant awareness is briefly fanned: this might be the last. In severe storms Tangu sit quietly, heads bowed, talking desultorily. Some will squat in the porches of their huts, banging a handdrum and singing. Just such storms end many a narrative, and in narratives just such storms herald radical changes—the act or omission which starts mythical beings on the road to becoming men, creation itself, or the end of man as Tangu know him. Both in life and in narratives thunderstorms and earthquakes are associated with the presence, and particularly the killing, of large snakes or snake-like beings. Large snakes are associated with those patches of forest or bush that are considered to be *imbatekas*;[1] and to enter such a portion of forest or bush is almost sure to bring on a thunderstorm, a flood, or an earthquake. After an earthquake, even a minor tremor, investigations are set on foot to discover who has killed a large snake, or who has entered a portion of forest known to be *imbatekas*, or who may have been to an unfrequented place, which, though not thought of as *imbatekas* hitherto, will in future participate in the *imbatekas*. Stories about men and women becoming involved with *ranguova* usually include an otherwise unnecessary storm or rain shower to introduce the situation in which a *ranguma* sets about his work.[2] Large snakes are said to inhabit marshy and eerie portions of bush or forest; the *juata-k'mba* chestnuts, associated with *ranguova*, only grow in such marshy and eerie places; such marshy and eerie places are usually regarded as *imbatekas*. And just as the *ranguma* is on one level harmful and culpable, but on another level serves the community by enforcing the ethic, so in some narratives the snake is also ambivalent: like the storm, destructive, initiating troubles; also like the storm, pregnant with the possibilities of a new moral order.

While *imbatekas* connotes the anomalous, the unconstrainable and unobliged, it also evokes the generative and originating impulse. Still, Tangu do not venture into places that are known to be *imbatekas* because, as they say, they might not be able to

---

[1] But see *infra*, pp. 167–70, in relation to the Founder.
[2] *Infra*, pp. 281–4.

deal with the consequences. The same hazard attaches to the exchange which is not equivalent: expectations become uncertain, someone is arrogating to himself the attribute of being unobliged, anxieties find a focus in suspicions of sorcery, a *ranguma* is thought to be about his business, community energies are mobilized to restore the *status quo*. The man or woman[1] who provides too large a feast is *imbatekas* because, by providing too much for the others to repay within the limits of the resources at their disposal, they are putting themselves outside the complex of equivalent reciprocities which bind men and women together into a moral community. Like *ranguova*, they are arrogating to themselves that which does not properly belong to them as moral beings. They are behaving self-willedly, as though unobliged. Boils and sicknesses and injuries may be described as *imbatekas*: they prevent a man from maintaining equivalence. If a *ranguma* is thought to be responsible for a sickness, then not only is the latter in itself *imbatekas*, but it is so also because it derives from one who is himself *imbatekas*. Conversely, a *ranguma* is *imbatekas* because he acts in ways that are *imbatekas*. If a non-human agency is thought to be responsible for a hurt, this agency is contingently described as *imbatekas*: it has done something which is in itself *imbatekas*, and there is no way of retaliating. Sex relations within the brother–sister relationship, or coition within the sweetheart relationship, are *imbatekas*, and so are the actors: the consequences of the acts may be uncontrollable, nothing can undo the acts themselves, nothing can restore the previous relationships. For though confession restores the controllable moralities, that which is *imbatekas* is ultimately quite unobliged, and boils and sickness may continue their course in spite of the confession. When a sickness is thought to derive from a wrongdoing which has energized the latent powers of a protective spell, wrongdoing, sickness, overpowerful spell, and the caster of the spell are initially described as *imbatekas*—Who knows beforehand whether the whole was not the work of a *ranguma*? Ordinary men, who may involuntarily cast overpowerful spells, usually nullify the effects of their spells—but supposing they did not, or could not?

Contraposed to the normally functioning reciprocities of the moral order, *imbatekas* connotes a non-reciprocal intrusion

[1] *Infra*, p. 325.

predicating trouble and change. Critical, qualitative, and with degrees of intensity—so indicating degrees of controllability—*imbatekas* may refer to anything that happens to interfere with the smooth operation of current obligations, and it always refers to that with which reciprocal relations are impossible or relatively uncontrollable or unpredictable. So it is that Europeans may be described initially as *imbatekas*, and fit into the category '*ranguma*'.

Divine Beings

The Tangu word *puok* (pl. *puoker*) generally refers to beings which, having certain parallelisms with man, may be said to inhabit the divine order of being. A *puok* is self-willed, unobliged, non-reciprocal. In a more specific reference the word *puok* is used of, and describes, those whose adventures are recorded in narratives. But the most revealing reference, perhaps, is to the fire-fly which, itself normally invisible, still makes its presence evident at night in flashes of luminosity. When a *puok* so impinges on the life of man as to cause some loss or hurt or interference with current reciprocities, then it is described as *imbatekas*. A *puok* cannot be constrained or held under obligation:[1] it can scarcely impinge on the life of man without causing an interference in current reciprocities; it is a divine being, *imbatekas*.

A *pap'ta*, a water being, is loosely thought of as a *puok*, though it is almost always actually referred to simply as a *pap'ta*. Generally accorded a punitive role, when a *pap'ta* acts it is described as *imbatekas*. A *pap'ta* has no personal name. Men have no control over its activities, cannot successfully plead with one, placate it, or enforce its service—though some may try. Normally thought of as striking at trespassers, a *pap'ta* may, however, strike at anyone. Solitary and rather large boils on the inside of the thigh have a fair incidence in Tangu: and if a man walks in a stream, or fishes in it, and afterwards develops such a boil, the *pap'ta* residing in the stream is considered to have caused it. The boil is lanced when ripe by a specialist in such matters and, when he recovers, the victim avoids that part of the stream where it is judged that the *pap'ta* struck him. The *pap'ta* clearly disapproved—Why? To answer the question a man

[1] For a partial exception see *infra*, pp. 177-9.

might quickly examine his conscience. But it is also possible that the *pap'ta* may have attacked the man at that particular time and place out of caprice or whimsy or self-will—for no reason that the victim can project from his own personal circumstances. Should the victim at a later date enter the same part of the stream with no ill effects, the conclusion is that the *pap'ta* now has no objections. And because it is as capricious as that a *pap'ta* may have an oracular as well as a punitive role. Thus, should a man be attempting to exercise claims to fish in a particular stream, a point in his favour is that since he has not suffered from boils after walking in the water the *pap'ta* does not object to him. On the other hand, a *pap'ta* is not precluded from attacking a man who has fished in a stream for as long as he can remember. Though it is considered that a *pap'ta* generally strikes trespassers, it may strike one who has always fished there, and no man will continue attempting to exercise claims in waters where he suffers repeated attacks from the *pap'ta*. Ultimately, therefore, a whimsical *pap'ta*, unobliged by men's moralities, can decide who is a trespasser and who is not.

Tangu consider it possible that all the particulars in their physical environment, though not, generally, those which have been moulded or constrained by the hand of man, may be possessed of, or inhabited by, inner identities or guardian beings described as *puoker*. But it is only when the *puok* in a rock, say, becomes active that it is recognized as a *puok*. Whether it is one *puok* inhabiting all things, many *puoker* inhabiting a quantity of particulars, or millions of *puoker* each individually inhabiting single things, are irrelevant questions. For though men and women may stub their toes on roots and rocks it is also the case that a *puok* may 'enter into' the root or rock and strike the toe as it passes. And this the *puok* does perhaps to give men a start, a jolt, a goading, but essentially because a *puok* is self-willed. If the man is hurt, the *puok* which hurt him is *imbatekas*. A youth may fall from a tree and injure himself. But it might also be that a *puok* in the tree caused the fall and so the injury. And if the injured person cannot, because of the injury, maintain his equivalences, then the *puok* is described as *imbatekas*. The head of an axe or hammer may fly off its haft: if someone is hurt, then a *puok* in the tool is to blame, and is *imbatekas*. If no one is hurt, no problem arises, no explanation is necessary. So that although the notion of *puoker* inhabiting things is *a priori*, the notion becomes explicit only in particular instances, *post hoc*, when someone is hurt. And then the *puok* is *imbatekas*. In the case of things made by man an obvious fault in the manufacture is merely an obvious fault in the manufacture. But when the artifact does not behave as it should, and there is no obvious fault in its construction or use, then a *puok* is considered to have entered the implement and behaved in a way that is *imbatekas*. Finally, though *puoker* are thought, hopefully, to act against thieves or trespassers rather than against those with acknowledged claims, it is conceded that they may act whimsically or capriciously, oblivious of the moralities.

Narratives, Dreams, and Ghosts

While narratives as such are not described as *imbatekas*, they may be taken to belong with the divine. Narratives are about *puoker* and, not considered to have been made up by men, are taken to have originated from *puoker*, or at least from some source not a part of the moral order. Nor are narratives in principle constrainable. Considered to have an ideal form and content, whether they came into being in the beginning, having been handed down by the ancestors, or more recently, narratives are still thought to contain truth or truths which are neither the conscious creations of man himself nor subject to reciprocal obligation. By criticizing a delivery, by reminding the story-teller of omissions or additions, Tangu attempt to maintain the form and content of a narrative, and so the truths contained in it, even though they may not wholly comprehend those truths. But if one man says this is a truth, and another denies it, who is to judge? Both the narrative and the *puoker* within it remain unobliged. Narratives are thought to exist in the way that they do, irrespective of what this man or that might prefer them to be like. They are essentially oblivious, oracular: it is up to men and women to extract such truths as are contained in them and to accept the consequences of doing so. And if a narrative so impinges on the awareness of a listener as to predicate a quality of being different from that which characterizes his own moral order, then he is likely to ejaculate '*Imbatekas-ake!*'[1]

[1] The suffix *-ake!* is a fortifier or emphasizer.

To relate a narrative is to talk about *puoker—puok'ptiek*. And though telling a story about ordinary human beings is also normally *puok'ptiek*, today a circumlocutory distinction is often made: 'This story', some say, 'is not about *puoker*. It is a *sitori nating*.'[1] However, there is no consensus regarding what is a story, *sitori nating*, and what is a story, *puok'ptiek*, though most are agreed on what is *tok tasol*, just talk, gossip, and anecdote. As we shall see, though the distinction between one kind of tale and another tends to turn on its form, and whether the characters involved show themselves subject to obligation,[2] in general the *puoker* of narratives, though they cannot but be anthropomorphic in certain particulars, being named or categorized, are neither men nor women, are neither involved in reciprocal relations nor bound by morality. They do not suffer from *ranguova*,[3] and if certain activities could be construed as theft, trespass, or adultery, it is not evident that the *puoker* concerned regard them in that light or react to them as humans might. *Puoker* are not bound by amity and equivalence, and, with a single but notable exception, they do not take part in *br'ngun-'guni*.[4] Yet anthropomorphic they are. For as they appear in narratives *puoker* are sexed, and may be babies, youths, maidens, adults, or aged. They have kinsfolk, they hunt, gather, garden, work, dress, and live very much as single individuals in Tangu do today. But *puoker* are not organized into communities. Settlement, village, and community appear as abstractions, back-cloths to the activities of singular *puoker*. Like human beings, *puoker* in narratives have their troubles and their tiffs. Unlike Tangu themselves, *puoker* are 'selves' freed from the burdens of community and morality. They marry their sisters, kill their wives, eat stones, feast without working, grow up in a trice, travel great distances, do not have to participate in *br'ngun'guni*. . . . And while it is true that men may impute particular reasons for the activities of *puoker*, or glean a meaning from the variety of acts and their contexts, or perceive a reflection of their own inner feelings, on the face of it what a *puok* does it does for no reason, whimsically, impulsively, self-willedly. Only those

[1] A pidgin phrase meaning 'only a story'. The point is further discussed *infra*, pp. 197–8.
[2] *Infra*, pp. 281–90.
[3] Tales about *ranguova* (*infra*, pp. 281–97) are explicitly about men and women.
[4] See *infra*, p. 325.

who live in a moral order need to have reasons for acting, and need to impute a reason or meanings in the activities of *puoker*. Why should a *puok* have a reason for doing anything? If Tangu are asked why so-and-so did such-and-such, they simply shrug their shoulders and answer, '*Puok-ake!*'[1] At the same time the *puoker* of narratives do not normally pop out of one narrative and into another. They have an ordered mode of being within the form and content of the narratives in which they appear. And they seem to maintain this mode of existence, as well as their own internal interrelationships, down the generations.

Even if it were not axiomatic that narratives contain truth, or truths, it would not be unreasonable for Tangu to infer that their narratives should or might contain truth, or truths. It seems as necessary to appreciate that the *puoker* of narratives are anthropomorphic, are like men and women, are as though men and women, as it is to preserve the distinction. The environment and activities of *puoker* are sufficiently like the Tangu environment and Tangu themselves to draw attention and capture interest. So far as what is apparently strange and distinctive is penetrated by the familiar, so far are chords of awareness touched. When the apparently strange appears simply as strange, then, one may assume, awareness ceases and the ejaculation '*Imbatekas-ake!*' is likely. But until this point is reached— and it is worth noting that different individuals become aware of the strange at differing levels of penetration—Tangu are extracting truths from their narratives. If some take their narratives at face value and dismiss them with a scornful '*sitori nating!*', or, after a short pause, with an '*imbatekas-ake!*', others ponder rather longer, attempt to explain what meaning might be intended, and then, when the impasse is reached, when awareness is exhausted, the explication is finished with an '*Imbatekas-ake!*' Independent of the degree of penetration, that is, narratives are always oracular, enigmatic, unobliged to men in community. On the other hand, it is also true that in the course of regarding their narratives in relation to their own particular circumstances and awarenesses, individuals among Tangu may either confirm, or perceive alternatives to, current beliefs and activities. And, in causing such a flux—albeit momentary—or questioning in relation to current moralities, narratives bear

[1] It [He/She] is [existing] (emphatic) [a] *puok*!

the same kind of relation to Tangu themselves as does the *ranguma*, a violent storm, or an earthquake.

As narratives contain truth, or truths, so, Tangu consider, do dreams. And it is for men to try and understand what these truths are. But whereas narratives have an objective existence, and have the same overt form and content, irrespective of the different kinds of awareness particular individuals may cull from them, dreams are always intensely personal experiences, particular dreams are thought to come to particular men, particular men are visited with particular dreams. Yet like narratives, dreams predicate the potential of flux in current relationships. If, having had a dream, a man interprets it in a certain way, and despite the apparent warnings or instructions in the dream misfortunes follow fast, then in disgust the dreamer will say that his dream was *imbatekas*. Within the relationship dreamer–dream the dream has caused the dreamer to suffer, and has impaired his ability to honour his obligations. If, on the other hand, all had gone well, then the dream would have been described as '*schwari*, good, sweet, or beautiful'. A dream is as though self-willed, unobliged by the moralities of community life. And though it may be given to some to dream more effectively than others—as, for example, in the case of dreamer-diviners—no man can dream what he may think he wants to dream, and he is unable to say precisely what he will dream—if he could, why dream it? Considered not to flow from the will and purpose of man, both dreams and narratives exist, occur, or are experienced irrespective of particular intentions and conscious motives. But while narratives-as-wholes have certain parallelisms with dreams-as-wholes, the *puoker* of narratives—different from the *pap'ta* or *puoker* thought to be in rocks, plants, trees, or artifacts, but still *puoker*—are regarded as distinct from the characters which appear in dreams. These are dream-images or visitants or 'ghosts'. Not *puoker*, still they are like *puoker*: self-willed and unobliged.

Those who most often and significantly reveal themselves in dreams are the ghosts or images of dead kinsmen, usually the father or an elder brother.[1] Normally referred to in the kin idiom simply—'I saw my father last night', it being common

---

[1] It will be remembered (*supra*, p. 113) that elder brother, *ambwerk*, may take the father's place.

knowledge that the father is dead—such a ghost might be identified as an ancestor, *nduor*,[1] but is not thought of as a *puok*, even though it behaves very much like a *puok* and may, eventually, become assimilated to the world of *puoker*. Ghosts are considered to have some sympathy with the problems of living in community—they have, after all, experienced the problems at first hand. But since they are no longer among the living, cannot 'die' again, and are not bound by either space or time, they are not expected to behave as though subject to the same rules and reciprocities as order the lives of those who still live. Not *puoker*, ghosts still have very much the same kind of being as *puoker* possess. Generally appearing in dreams to advise, remonstrate, or admonish, ghosts cannot be said to appear as aggressive.[2] Yet no dreamer can know precisely from what point of view the advice or admonition is being given, or whether his own interpretation of the dream is a correct one. Thus if a man, as the result of an experience with a ghost, determines to give a feast, and it turns out disastrously, he may in a first irritated flush—though he knows it is fruitless to do so—blame the ghost for wrong advice and think of it as *imbatekas*. It has harmed him and there is no way of getting even with it. But when the dreamer calms down and reflects on the matter, he knows he cannot blame anybody but himself. After all, he need not have taken the advice. It is given already, and accepted, that the dream may be a trick or deception,[3] or that he may have interpreted the advice mistakenly, or that there may be some other consideration for which the disaster is an unpleasant but necessary preliminary. If a ghost comes to see his live descendant it is not for the former to explain himself—in what terms might a living man understand a dead man's reasons if he had any?—but for the dreamer, who needs reasons, to work his way to an answer in relation to his own experience and motives, to wrestle with his conscience. A dreamer may invite a ghost to

---

[1] *Nduor* is properly 'an ancestor' or 'ancestors', and not, usually, a particular and named person known to have existed. Though the word *nduor* may be used of a known and named ancestor, the term has a community rather than individual reference. Thus while a ghost is relevant only to the particular man whom it visits, an ancestor is relevant to all in the community. He must be linked to most if not all.

[2] Cf. R. F. Fortune 1935 *Manus Religion*, Memoir of the American Philosophical Society, No. 3, Philadelphia.

[3] '*Bengemamamake!*—It was a deception, it was deceiving (me)!'

reveal itself: but a ghost cannot be put under compulsion and only reveals itself at its own behest. Though a man might seek advice from a ghost, the latter is under no obligation to give clear or good advice, or even the advice the dreamer might think he wants. Intractable, self-willed, a ghost pleases itself, forces a man to come to terms with himself. And should a man attempt to re-create with a ghost the relationship he enjoyed when the ghost was a man, then he has only himself to blame if the ghost does not comply. A ghost is unobliged, it is up to the living man to fuse his divine and moral experience to his best advantage. And on the whole, this is just what capable men do, or are taken to have done.

Not all dreams feature a ghost. There are times when men dream of pigs, or a feast, or yams, or copulation, or wake with a cry, sweating and trembling, having dreamed of a *ranguma*. Yet, whatever the dream may be, Tangu consider that a man cannot lie down and dream what he might like to dream. Dreams 'come' or are 'sent'. So that when a man does have a dream it is up to him to take notice. He must act. A dream carries an imperative, even if that imperative is oracular or ambiguous. Never experienced for nothing, for no reason, a dream also tends to realize or foretell a future. Should a man dream of a pig he may build a trap in the sure expectation of taking a pig; if he has already built a trap he will visit it, expecting a pig to have been caught; or he will confidently await the pig he has been expecting in an exchange. If a man dreams of *ranguova* he takes the necessary precautions. He would be considered a fool if he did not—Why else should a *ranguma* appear in a dream? In relation to the dream as such, as well as in relation to its content, relevance emerges from the interrelations of dream, dreamer's circumstances, and the general moralities. Subsequent action decisions, which are political decisions, or decisions having political implications, are reached by resolving the situation the dreamer perceives between his dream and his own expectations, experience, motives, and ambitions in relation to the moralities obtaining.

In a general kind of way *puoker*, whether as *pap'ta* or in things, bear upon women as much as men. But because women are primarily child-bearers and workers, and not sources of overt decision, their relationship to narratives, dreams, and dream-images is only of limited significance. Women may scrutinize narratives with consummate skill and insight, yet, being but women, they can rarely make their awareness overtly relevant. That anyone should take a woman's dream seriously is regarded by Tangu men as laughable—though covertly, of course, it may be another matter. Women in Tangu may reveal their ideas to their husbands and goad them into action. But in the context of community affairs they are not held to be wholly responsible. Dreams, dreaming, and dream-images or ghosts go together with the social responsibility that adheres to men. Men, one might say, need the support of dreams and ghosts if they are to search into themselves and their circumstances the better and more responsibly to project and communicate their parts. Women may be themselves.

Founders and Patrons

The founding ancestor of an ancient settlement site, who has no context in known time, is known as an *angai'ek*, an uncivil word which we may translate as 'Founder'. To be distinguished from the founders of recently settled sites, who, even where their names have been forgotten, have context in known historical time, a Founder, loosely classified as a *puok*, and presumptively the first ancestor, *nduor*, is strictly neither man nor *puok* nor *nduor*. He or she or it belongs to a locality. Unlike an ancestor, *nduor*, who while loosely thought of as a *puok* seems to have been perpetually on passage from the world of men to that of *puoker*, a Founder, contrariwise, marks the transition from the world of *puoker*, or *puoker*-like beings, to the world of men. A Patron, identified by a specific personal name, is loosely thought of as a *puok*, is sometimes thought of as *tzienga*—a word which may refer to an emergence hole in the earth,[1] a hole in an old tin can, an eye-socket, the eye itself, or any bodily orifice—and may be identified as, or at least closely associated with, a Founder. But while a Founder had territorial relevances, a Patron seems to have been associated with a group of persons. Whether this group was the *gagai*, the *GAGAI*, those who were 'one womb', a line of male filiation, or one or other

---

[1] This kind of hole refers to the narratives (*infra*, N. 25, pp. 320–5) in which it is related that men and women emerged on to the earth from a hole therein. This may be associated with men and women being born from the womb.

combination of these categories in different parts of Tangu remains uncertain. The close association with a Founder indicates the *gagai* or *GAGAI*; the meanings of *tzienga* indicate *mwerz ungunwan* or one womb; and the close connection between a Patron and the pig of the circumcision (which father had to provide for his son, and in which the image of father seems to have been contained),[1] indicates a line of male filiation. When in the past a man shouted 'Garamun!' or 'Twankovan!'—names of Patrons —as he thrust his spear into a pig, he was calling on the Patron in whose honour, and on whose behalf, the pig was being killed: which is indicative of a prestatory group.[2]

While it is possible that Patron and Founder were expected to guide or help or protect the social or socio-territorial groups with which they were associated, there is no evidence that they were under any obligation to do so. Today, pleas for help or protection are reserved, by both pagans and Christians, for ghosts or dream-images, God, the Holy Ghost, Jesus, the Virgin Mary, and some saints. And these, as seems probably to have been the case with both Patron and Founder, are not considered by Tangu to be under any obligation to respond, though they may do so at their own behest. Founders are today mostly forgotten, and for those who claim to know something about Patrons their role has become honorary merely, the names of a few being associated with some surviving dance masks which are infrequently worn.

In the past a Founder seems to have been thought to reside in, or to be more immanent or concentrated in, those tracts of forest or bush which were considered to be *imbatekas*. When hunting on home lands, calling on the Patron seems also to have bidden the Founder to witness, and, since in such a case Founder and Patron would have been closely associated, rather less danger seems to have attached to entering a portion of forest described as *imbatekas*. When trespassing, however, calling on the Patron would seem to have implied some kind of protection from the Founder over whose associated lands the hunter was trespassing. Yet in either case one who entered a tract of

---

[1] *Infra*, pp. 397–9.

[2] As we shall see (*infra*, pp. 397–9), the relevances of pig are such that it is probable that the Patron was in some way imaged or contained in the pig, particularly the pig of the circumcision.

imbatekas bush was in grave danger of being attacked by a large snake into which the Founder had entered—an act typical of *puoker*, especially as they occur in narratives—or of being caught in a violent storm and drowned in the subsequent flood, or of being driven crazy or deaf, or of becoming prone to hearing disturbing noises when other men hear nothing. . . . But then, as we have seen, trespassing has become quite common, people move relatively freely from settlement to settlement over other men's lands. Moreover, since there do not appear to be many large snakes in the forest nowadays, and no one can remember anybody actually being killed by a large snake, it has become evident to Tangu on a pragmatic basis that a Founder is at present more or less satisfied with having founded an ancient settlement site. Particular portions of bush remain *imbatekas*, and new portions of bush are becoming *imbatekas* in terms of the associations with flood, marsh, chestnuts, and *ranguova*. The former close association of Founder and *imbatekas* tracts is today neglected by the elderly and mature, and is virtually unknown to the younger generation. As a distinctive representation, that is, the Founder has been merging into the associative complex of large snakes, storm, flood, chestnuts, and *ranguova*. Further, while one may assume that such beneficence as may have been thought to attach to a Founder has been absorbed in Christian representations—the only other beneficent representations in Tangu today—it is reasonable to suggest that its punitive and spiteful associations have been transferred to the *ranguma* or devil.

A Founder provides the only example of a *puok* who participates in *br'ngun'guni*.[1] And though only one narrative about a Founder has survived in coherent form, while it is still told so he or it moves from being as a *puok* to being as a man and first ancestor, without at any time coinciding precisely with any one of these categories. As a *puok* a Founder could enter into a large snake and, unobliged, kill those who passed too near. As far as a Founder was considered to act in defence of territory, so far was it acting like a man; as far as a Founder founded an ancient settlement site, so far was he an ancestor. Though clearly a part of the divine, and associated with the local community, large snakes, and *imbatekas* bush, a Founder, like a *ranguma*, yet tends to bridge the distinction between the moral and

[1] *Infra*, p. 325.

the divine. So that the suggestion that a Founder's punitive associations have become absorbed in the *ranguma* is not wholly implausible.

What may be said of a Patron? Did it provide protection against one or other kind of *ranguma*, and if so, whom did it protect? Perhaps there was once a more explicit connection between a Patron and 'eating *ranguma*',[1] perhaps the self-willedness associated with 'eating *ranguma*' referred to the self-willedness of a Patron as well as a *ranguma*. . . . We can but hazard the suggestion that, given the connection with the pig of the circumcision, a Patron was probably most closely associated with the line of male filiation.

That the evidence relating to Founders and Patrons should be so unsatisfactory is hardly surprising. Their contexts of relevance lay in stable associations with territory, in the filiatory values definitively expressed, in the relations between *GAGAWA* and *gagawa*, and, since circumcision had some connection with a Patron, in club-house life. Yet, as we have seen, precisely these features were most affected by Tangu history. With the movements that followed both the introduction of artificial dogs' teeth and the epidemic sickness, with the breakdown of *GAGAWA* and *gagawa* combined with the diminishing importance of the filiatory values, with the disappearance of the club-houses, and, finally, with the inability of Patrons and Founders to manifest themselves in significant ways, it is to be expected that their relevances would be oblivescent. Yet even from what little we know of them we can appreciate that, like other representations of the divine, Founders and Patrons made men aware both of themselves and of the rules which make them a community.

The Club-houses

Tangu club-houses, together with Founders and Patrons and other categories which connote particular groupings of persons within the community, belong to a traditional and relatively integrated social order and community life in which responsibility could be shifted on to the group. But, as we have seen, over the last three generations householders have been becoming

[1] *Supra*, p. 139.

PLATE IV

a. Preparing the harvest exchange

b. Dancing round the yams of a harvest exchange

the best judges of their own interests, and have been taking more
and more responsibility into their own hands. Neither Patron
nor *mwerz ungunwan* can any longer certainly recruit the group.
Private oracular techniques such as dreaming have been
becoming more rather than less significant.[1] If the punitive relevances of the Founder have indeed become merged in the *ranguma*, it is no accident: for where a Founder related to a group
within the community, the *ranguma* relates on one level to the
individual and his household, and on another to the community
as a whole. As we have seen, current alliances or combinations
of households within the community are merely temporary.
And the disappearance of Tangu club-houses is entirely consistent with this decreasing importance given to the 'middle
categories' or constituent groupings within the community in
favour of an emphasis on the individual and his household on
the one hand, and the community as a whole on the other. In
the past, as we shall see more pertinently, the club-houses
provided just that ambience in which mature and responsible
members of the constituent but rivalrous groups within the
community could meet in fellowship and mutual dependence.
'Cross-cutting' institutions which transcended sectional rivalries, club-houses and the life associated with them must have
eased considerably the strains of personal decision and responsibility. Today, with no club-house to resort to, a householder
must assume his responsibilities within a context of general
rivalry. When a man retires alone to his hunting-lodge he is
only temporarily releasing himself from household cares: going
away on contract labour is his only provided and explicit
opportunity for enjoying the company of his fellows outside his
role as a householder and within a grouped association. And
yet, as the narratives will show, unlike Founders and Patrons,
the club-houses were essential to the making of traditional man.
The question that Tangu ask now is, what kind of organization
or association of men will make the new man?

The more mature among Tangu say that there used to be two
kinds of club-house in Tangu, the *garamb* and the *ginangin*. In
both of these the householder might relax, gossip, and pursue

[1] It may be noted in parentheses here that Tangu cargo activities, which engaged
the attentions of the community as a whole, or of communities as wholes, were
triggered off by the dreams of individuals (B–1960: 1–2).

ends which revealed him as a man among men rather than as a domestic comptroller; both offered him a context of release from the obligations inhering in the kin categories combined with a more general fellowship. The *garamb* was a men's club-house where pre-nubile girls might spend the time of day when appropriate, and in which boys, at about puberty, had to spend a probationary period culminating in circumcision before they could attain full membership as men. A largish building raised on stilts, with end-walls panelled with bark paintings representative of the *gagawa* which had combined to build it, the *garamb* was generally associated with a *gagai*, a *mwenk*, or group of proximate *mwenker* and *gagawa*. With the exception of Ungiar and old Andemarup, which are said to have had a *ginangin* only, the *garamb* seems to have been common to all Tangu, and Tangumar is reputed to have had both a *garamb* and a *ginangin*. Located openly in the *mwenk*, the *garamb* was associated with community life. But the *ginangin*, either a low shelter in the deep bush where it was attended by men only, or a building in the forest environs of a *mwenk* for the use of adult women only, is today generally associated with secret rites and dark mysteries.

Entering the *garamb* towards puberty, when beginning to resent their fathers, boys came under the supervision of mother's brothers. Partially secluded in the *garamb* for varying periods, at circumcision—which rite seems to have been conditional on father taking a large pig in his *juaka* trap[1]—the boy 'came down' from the *garamb* and was admitted to the community of men. During the probationary period boys were allowed to see and talk to the girls who had access to the club-house, but otherwise they were supposed to stay in the *garamb* building, answering calls of nature from a platform at the rear end abutting on the forest. When hungry they signalled mothers and sisters by whistling, or by sounding a trump or single-stringed zither or toy slit-gong of bamboo.[2] They were not permitted contact with mothers and nubile sisters. For most of this period in the *garamb* the boys were harshly treated, exercised in

[1] A large dead-fall trap for a pig (see *infra*, N. 29, pp. 385, 388–9).

[2] 'Trump', I think, is better than 'Jew's harp'—which is awkward and inelegant. A zither was made from a piece of hardwood palm, a thread of which was held in tension by a small chock. All these instruments (trump, zither, toy slit-gong) are associated with immaturity, boyishness.

self-control,[1] and taught traditional lore. For specific purposes the boys were escorted from the *garamb*: for instruction in manly skills, in fighting tactics, stalking, hunting, and trapping; so that they could be ambushed by parties of adults who thrashed them with thorns and nettles; to be taught how to make a *mar*, a breechclout of barkcloth;[2] to gather cane for weaving into anklets, armbands, wristlets, and waistbands.

The rite of circumcision, Tangu say, 'made a boy into a man'. When father had killed an appropriately sized pig in his *juaka* trap, and before the operation itself, the boy drank a potion of *awunga* leaves, nettles. He was then beaten on groin and buttocks with thorns and nettles. Thus prepared, the boy was held by father and circumcised by a mother's brother. The foreskin was pulled forward over the penis, cut off with a bamboo razor, and thrown into a cluster of wild bananas. Recovering from his ordeal in the *garamb*, in the course of a few days the boy donned his breechclout for the first time, put on his cane decorations, clotted his hair with clay and red ochre, and greased his skin with pig fat reddened with ochre or red pandanus juice. Then, to the blasts of conch shells and the acclamations of his brothers, the youth emerged from the *garamb* in his finery. No longer a boy, he was a newly made man, ready to marry and play his part in community affairs. The pig of the circumcision, provided by father, seems to have expressed not only the solidarity of the line of male filiation but also, it seems, to have brought a youth into relationship with his Patron. Whether the Patron was incarnate or manifest in the pig is not at all clear, but more certainly, as we shall see,[3] it was through this pig that father transmitted to son sense of obligation and social responsibility.

Girls received no ceremonial treatment at puberty—though at first menstruation they were incised in the small of the back and on the shoulders as a sign of their marriageable state. Paraphrasing the Tangu idiom, 'Boys have to be made into men; girls grow naturally into women.'

---

[1] It is said, for example, that the boys had to sit still for hours at a time, being beaten by their mother's brothers if they moved.

[2] A breechclout was made by stripping off the inner bark of a *deamar* tree (unidentified), and alternately soaking the pulp in a stream, beating it with a wooden hammer or mallet on a stone anvil, and drying it in the sun.

[3] Evidence as to the significance of the Patron must remain hazy. But the meaning of this pig comes out well in N. 29 *infra*, pp. 385, 388-9.

Unlike the *garamb*, the *ginangin* was for adults only, either for men only or for women only. The women's *ginangin* was a more or less permanent structure, but the men's was built in the forest when needed. In both cases the club-house was used for feasting on a large pig outside the complex of community reciprocities. The women's pig was carved and apportioned by the father or full brother of the woman in whose name the pig was being provided. But before they started their feast the women armed themselves with spears, lifted their skirts to show their genitals,[1] and chased the men from the vicinity. 'They did this', Tangu explain, 'so that they could eat the pig by themselves.'[2] For the men, meeting secretly, the pig-feast was accompanied by fluting which, exclusive to adult males, seems to have invoked a divinity or power that became manifest or incarnate in the pig. Some informants refer explicitly to the Patron in this connection, others to *ranguma brami*, eating *ranguma*. In both cases the feasts were of sectional interest only, assertions of maleness against femaleness and vice versa. But if men did indeed 'eat *ranguma*' then it looks as though they were trying to obtain a particular kind of self-willedness.[3]

Those informants living in settlements once most closely associated with the *ginangin* treat the derogatory imputations of others with some contempt, saying that the *ginangin* was simply a place where men, or women, could get together and feast on a pig outside the complex of community reciprocities and its attendant *br'ngun'guni*.[4] On the other hand, since the *ginangin* is associated with Wanitzir, and members of the other three neighbourhoods feel there are more *ranguova* in Wanitzir than elsewhere in Tangu, they link the *ginangin* with *ranguova* and 'eating *ranguma*'. Further, everywhere in Tangu today fluting

---

[1] English is reasonably well endowed with words for male and female genitalia, and although they are warmer and more appropriate to the context than the more usual Latin words, I have, perforce, used only a few of them. Where they fit the context better, the Latin words are used. The words that Tangu usually use, three, are translatable as 'penis', 'testicles', 'vulva'.

[2] As the narratives will show, women coming into association with 'pig' and 'spear' is most unusual. But, as we shall see, the narratives concentrate on the theme of the *garamb* and do not mention the *ginangin*.

[3] The *ginangin*, be it noted, excludes the community values of self-restraint and relationship with others through women.

[4] Again note that community values, the enforcement of reciprocities through *br'ngun'guni*, are excluded.

has become associated either with *ranguova* or with secretive rites which can bode no good. Yet it may be that this last is but a recent development. For since, as Tangu see it, all club-houses have been stigmatized by both mission and administration as '*samting nogut*, a nasty business', and both European organizations regard fluting as indicative of secretive, and therefore nefarious, rites, it is quite possible that Tangu have taken over and conformed to the European attitude. Certainly, no one in Tangu today openly blows a flute or admits to possessing one. And those who want to be secretive about something talk darkly about going into the forest to *windim mambu*, blow flutes.[1]

Though the narratives will fill out the meaning of the *garamb*, direct evidence concerning both kinds of club-house must, perforce, remain slight. While elderly folk sometimes say they regret the passing of the club-houses, they add that perhaps it was all for the best. Men tended to gossip and laze in the *garamb*, they say, leaving the burden of garden work to their wives. And for their part most women agree that if the club-houses were of some use to the men, they themselves had little share in the benefits, and that on the whole life is easier and simpler without them. 'Now we have the mission', they remark. As to the *ginangin* in particular, only those who have reputations for being like *ranguova* openly state their regrets. For most in Tangu the *ginangin* has become too closely associated with clandestine activities to be missed with any nostalgia.

The Mind, Thinking, and Speech

Founders, Patrons, *GAGAWA*, and *gagawa* belong to a vanished past of which only memories remain: their relevances have faded with the groups and activities with which they were associated. But, as we shall see, the meaning of the *garamb* is still relevant— what kind of 'new *garamb*' will make the new man?—and those beings or representations or categories which relate either to individuals in themselves or to the community as a whole still play a significant part in Tangu life. Narratives, the *puoker* in narratives, *puoker* which contingently inhabit or 'enter into' a variety of things, *pap'ta*, dreams, ghosts—all relate to the

---

[1] As in other parts of New Guinea and in the neighbouring areas, flutes were played in pairs, flautists standing chest to chest, one foot advanced, the flute parallel with the left shoulder, the music contrapuntal.

community at large, or to single individuals, but not to particularized groups within the community. To this list we may add
the *gnek*, a word which may be translated as 'soul', 'mind', '*nous*',
'psyche', or even 'conscience', but which is probably best
thought of simply as *gnek*; the *niemur*, which has elsewhere been
translated as 'sprite',[1] but is here kept as *niemur*; and *nduor*,
'ancestor'. The *gnek* is definitely not a *puok*, though *gnek* and *puok*
have much in common; and whilst *niemur* and *nduor* are not
puoker, they behave much as *puoker* do and are often assimilated
or loosely classified with them.

Each human being today is deemed whilst alive to have a
gnek. But it is probable that in the past only an adult man was
thought to have a *gnek*. For the *gnek* is, or appears as, the
immediate source of responsible behaviour. The active verbal
form, *gnek'gneki*, means 'to think, ponder, cogitate, rack one's
brains'. And though Tangu have no word which of itself may be
translated as 'confession', when a man sets to examining his
conscience, when he searches in memory to see whom he may
have wronged, or where he may have transgressed, he is said
to be *gnek'gneki*, thinking on what he has done. In revealing,
afterwards, what he has been thinking about, he is surely confessing. Among pagans today it is supposed that after death a
gnek becomes a *niemur*, then a ghost, then an ancestor, *nduor*. But
in the past it is probable that only a woman became a *niemur*,
and that a man went straight through to becoming a ghost.
Though, in present thought, a *niemur* is nearer to the living than
a ghost, and may appear in a dream as a ghost does, it is much
more like a *puok* than a ghost. For whereas a ghost is always the
ghost of someone, a *niemur* often tends to be regarded as a quite
separate entity, having a being of its own and unrelated to the
human it once was. *Gnek* and *niemur* and ghost, in short, appear
to enjoy much the same kinds of being, but at different stages
of maturity. Through a Founder, *puoker*, which were never
human, generate humans with *gneker*.[2] At death the *gnek*
becomes a *niemur* and then a ghost. Yet though by becoming
nduor an ancestor is virtually reassimilated to the kind of world
which *puoker* inhabit, whereas *puoker* are generally punitive or
spiteful, ancestors are rarely so. Having reference to the community as whole, rather than to an individual within it, an

---

[1] B–1965: 243.   [2] Singular *gnek*, plural *gneker*.

ancestor or the ancestors are invested with an as yet unrealized benevolence. Rather vaguely, they look after the living, or have their interests at heart, though no demands are made upon them explicitly. One day, some Tangu opine, the ancestors will return to the land of the living. And their return will predicate a new order of being. There will be no obligedness, no tension between self-will and self-restraint, no thinking on past wrongdoings, no wondering which of two will have the edge on the other. All the parts of creation, in short, will be in a state of *mngwotngwotiki* with each other.

Once upon a time, so the story goes, wife died . . .

Upon the death of his wife, husband went into the garden, as was the custom, to destroy her foodstuffs.[1] But on returning to his house who should be waiting for him, sitting in the porch, but the *niemur* of wife.

'What are you doing here?' husband demanded. 'I buried you under the porch, piling the earth on top, and yet here you are again —I thought I had done with you!'

'I am not dead,' wife replied. 'I came up from the grave, following the kingpost of the house.'

Now husband, having destroyed all her yams and taros, was very angry. So he took the half of a coconut, the half without holes, and gave it to his wife. 'Here, pull this over your head,' he said, 'and let it come down over your eyes.'

Wife did as she was asked and slid down the kingpost back into her grave.

'And that is why', Tangu say, 'we cannot see the dead. Now if that man had given his wife the other half of the coconut, the half with holes in it, we would be able to see each other. Most of the time we are blinded by that half coconut. Sometimes, though, we put on the other half. Then we can see each other— as in dreams.' Clearly, when a person dies he or she is separated from the reciprocities that interlink the living. For without food it is not possible to participate in the reciprocities characteristic of the moral order. On the other hand, equally clearly, people who die are not completely dead: they enjoy another kind of being not characterized by the reciprocities of the moral order.

Though a *niemur* cannot itself be seen, except perhaps in a dream, Tangu concur in saying that it may see the living and may manifest itself to the living as a rat, a noise, or a whitish

[1] Formerly apparently general, this usage is not in vogue today.

luminous glow which moves over the tops of the trees in the valleys. A *niemur* croons softly, like a melancholy dove; it crackles and sighs in the bush, slithers loose pebbles down a hillside, mutters in the eaves of a hut, and pokes its way into a woman's vulva, tickling it. Though mischievous, a *niemur* is neither harmful nor directly punitive. Yet it may, on occasion, be described as *imbatekas*. A *niemur* is apt to pinch the legs of the living, startling and irritating them. When a man lays down his axe to have a smoke, and then cannot put his hand on the axe when he resumes, a *niemur* or a *puok* is considered to have moved it or taken it away. If one is sitting on a log on a hillside, or on a stool, and the log slides or the stool topples, then a *niemur* is surely up to its tricks. Upon a death the hut of the deceased is vacated for a few nights and food is left in the half shell of a coconut just inside the porch.[1] The *niemur*, usually in the form of a rat which, it is supposed, climbs up the kingpost of the hut, eats the food. When a person dies or is killed, close kinsfolk watch at the graveside to see whether the *niemur* will appear to tell them something about the death. If it is thought that the dead person, man or woman,[2] has been slain by a *ranguma*, then kinsfolk (usually of the womb) may proceed to an oracular rite. Pebbles or knucklebones and scraps of beard or the nail parings of the dead person are placed in a bamboo barrel to which are lashed two crossed staves. Squatting opposite each other, gripping the staves with outstretched arms, two men attempt to steady the barrel about a foot from the ground. Others then recite the names of possible guilty men, and the *niemur* of the deceased is conjured, or invited, into the barrel by means of a spell. As the barrel is delicately balanced and held in extreme muscular tension, any positive reactions on the parts of the holders of the barrel are likely to rattle the stones or knucklebones inside the barrel. In this way affirmative or negative answers to particular names may be obtained. But for Tangu it is the *niemur* inside the barrel which causes different kinds of rattle; and it is the *niemur* which may even sound the guilty person's slit-gong call-sign.[3]

---

[1] Compare the story above, p. 177.

[2] This seems to contradict the suggestion that only women became *niemur*. But it may be that in the past a man's ghost did what a woman's *niemur* did.

[3] For slit-gongs and call-signs see *infra*, pp. 275–8.

A spell, as we shall see in more detail below, constrains. And in the rite above the general expectation is that a *niemur* will come and give answers. Having only recently been a part of the moral order, the *niemur* is considered to have an interest in identifying the guilty man. On the other hand, Tangu admit that the *niemur* need not come, need not give answers. It is unobliged.

Through his *gnek*, which survives death to pass out of the moral order to become in turn *niemur*, ghost, *nduor*, and so almost wholly a part of the divine, man participates in, without necessarily usurping, the divine. By virtue of his *gnek* man is aware of the divine, apprehends something of the conflict in himself and his relationships with others which gives him access to the divine. In possessing a *gnek* man is unique, a moral being aware of himself and the ties of community. Centred on a clearing in the forest, his culture is an island of obligedness and morality. Yet between the divine on the one hand, and the wild forest and its denizens on the other, man still participates in both forms of being. And though, because of their common contraposition to culture and the moral, divine and wild frequently merge or overlap, they are not identical. Pigs and other animals, insects, minerals, and flora of the wild all have their parts to play in narratives. But they are not *puoker*, though *puoker* may enter into them. Man exerts his powers on the material stuffs of the wild to create and maintain his culture: *puoker* and other representations of the divine exert their pressures on man so as to maintain the moral community. On both hands one may perceive the images of conscience and impulse as well as the imprint of man's will, thought, and creative energies.

In the past the only mammals in Tangu were man, his dog, a rat, (the *niemur* rat?), and the pig which, next to man in the scale of animal life, was wild and fecund but domesticable. Men, Tangu say, were originally made from the flesh of a pig: and women were fashioned from the stomach and entrails. Credited with a certain understanding, domestic pigs may be suckled at the breast,[1] are named, talked to, allocated slit-gong call-signs, mourned when killed for a feast. But, since domestic sows mate and farrow in the bush, all pigs originate in the wild, and a pig

---

[1] But women often put piglets, as well as pups, to the breast simply to relieve themselves when, for instance, a new-born child has died.

does not have a *gnek*. It is killed and absorbed into the tissue of animal man, making him strong. If man did not have a *gnek* he would be very much like a pig: meat. Corpses are referred to as pigs: the *gnek* has been loosed from its animal prison and has become a *niemur* or ghost. Some in Tangu, who once were cannibals, expatiate on the delicacy of human flesh. But there is no hint that they hoped to absorb anything of the dead man's personality. On the contrary, without a *gnek* and lacking the connotations and evocations of 'pig', human flesh seems to have been 'victory meat' at most. A wild boar is described as *imbatekas*: like a *puok* it is wilful and unobliged. But unlike a *puok* it may be pinned with a spear. A Patron, if not manifest or incarnate in a pig, was at least closely associated with 'pig'—and probably a wild one.[1] Father had to provide a wild pig caught in his *juaka* trap to celebrate the circumcision and budding manhood of his son.[2] In narrative, father, or some part of the meaning or essence of father or fatherhood, enters into a pig so that son may slay it.[3] A wild pig seems to have been appropriate to a feast specifically having to do with men's affairs: it evoked male qualities, the unobligedness of a wild pig being associated with those elements of self-willedness peculiar to a male;[4] it also goes with the non-reciprocity of the father-son relationship. A domestic pig, on the other hand, was more appropriate to community affairs, affairs involving women as much as men. All important feasts centre round the distribution of pork and, conversely, while no feast has primary importance without pork, it is insulting to give what ought to be an important feast without providing pork. If pork is not scrupulously apportioned at a feast *ranguova* are thought to become more active, and when a man does not divide his pig fairly at a feast he receives scant sympathy should a *ranguma* begin to operate against him. Pigs so enable man to define and realize his moral condition that, like *puoker*, they are vehicles of an inheritance of self-understanding. Unlike *puoker*, pigs are controllable and food for the animal parts as well as the *gnek*.

When, in relation to Europeans, Tangu say they were like pigs,[5] they are using metaphor to indicate relative capacities. For speech, the ability to articulate thought and communicate

---

[1] *Supra*, p. 168. [2] *Supra*, p. 170.
[3] *Infra*, N. 29, pp. 384–5. [4] *Infra*, p. 398. [5] *Supra*, p. 24.

in words, and *a fortiori* to talk well, as in *br'ngun'guni*, is for Tangu a manifestation of man's power over himself and his environment. Thought, the activities of the *gnek*,[1] enables man to venture into the wild, bring its products into the fields of culture and morality. By means of thought and speech man creates those rules to which he subjects himself; speech makes the moral order significant, articulates the moral sense, and makes awareness explicit. Words, proceeding as they do from the *gnek*, are thought of as powers in themselves. If the consequences of saying something may be mitigated, words themselves cannot be unsaid and, coming to rest in men's minds, may precipitate trouble or change. The oath or insult to which there is no reply is described as *imbatekas*: hence the desideratum that those who speak in *br'ngun'guni* should be responsible men, aware. Before doing anything, Tangu say, it is first necessary to think (*gnek'-gneki*) things out. If Tangu are asked how they came to learn a traditional technique, they answer that in the dim long ago *puoker* showed the ancestors, and that each generation has handed down this knowledge to the generation following. But they may also say, as some *puoker* in narratives do, that they have thought the matter out for themselves. Between these two poles Tangu rely on their narratives. For contained in them are a large variety of subsistence and manufacturing techniques. And while on the one hand, through narratives, *puoker* are still telling men how to go about their work, on the other hand men have to articulate narratives to understand what *puoker* are saying. So that, given the possibility of origination, which itself derives from the *gnek*, part of the divine, within a wide field of making and doing Tangu are imitating or learning from *puoker*. Through his *gnek* man looks about him, envisages, appreciates, and realizes.

The values of both speech and technological ability are interassociated in the slit-gong, an instrument which Tangu use to communicate with each other over considerable distances. Originally, Tangu say, the slit-gong could speak for itself: it was as though possessed of a *gnek*. But because of what happened in those far-away days man now has to labour to make a slit-gong and he has to cause it to speak for him.[2] He has, moreover, to

[1] *gnek'gneki* = 'think, ponder, cogitate'.
[2] *Infra*, N. 12, p. 272.

bring it in from the wild and make it as though a member of the moral community. In the past a slit-gong was made in the forest from the centre section of a wild tree and, with accompanying rituals, was finally brought into the village. A feast and the killing of a large pig were required to 'initiate' the instrument and make it into a slit-gong which would 'speak for' a man. If the memories of older folk are to be trusted, a part of the initiatory ritual consisted of a man's inserting his penis into the slit of the gong and ejaculating into the body of the instrument.[1] There was also a significant substitution: before being set up in the village, it is said, the gong was brought into association with a human, usually a child, who was buried under the slit-gong.[2] Further, as in the case of the pig of the circumcision, the pig of the slit-gong had to be caught in a *juaka* trap. So that, whether the gong was brought into association with the female and siblingship, with father and fatherhood,[3] or whether the rite was an analogue of circumcision, such fragmentary evidence as remains still points to a process whereby the instrument was brought in from the wild and, having been made a part of the cultural ambience, was inducted into the moral order as a slit-gong.

Today both men and women, though in the past possibly not women, mourn for dead kinsfolk on their slit-gongs, the slow rhythms echoing through the valleys. By means of a slit-gong feasts, dances, complaints, claims, anger, threats, confession, warnings, the birth of a child, betrothals, marriage, the killing of a pig or cassowary, divisions of meat, anniversaries—any known social situation may be announced. And whether a slit-gong signal advertises an event or intention, or is an invitation, request, plea, or simply the expression of a mood or disposition, it is always a publication, a definitive and public statement from which a man retreats at his peril. Through his slit-gong a man expresses and re-expresses his membership of the social order, his moral nature, his involvement in reciprocal obligation. In using his slit-gong a man is saying something which all can hear. He is being as open as he would be in *br'ngun'guni*, he is eschewing secrecy and the private nursing of grudges, he is publicly communicating his parts. In narratives, as we shall see,[4] slit-

---

[1] Compare the ritual for the making of a new garden site, *supra*, p. 75.
[2] *Sic*. But compare the narrative N. 4, *infra*, p. 221.
[3] *Infra*, pp. 272-4.   [4] *Infra*, pp. 275-81.

gongs are associated with a generative or initiatory process: and this is precisely their role in community. A man who announces on his slit-gong that he is going to give a feast is committed to making the necessary arrangements and providing the feast. He is also precipitating a situation which, if familiar in general form, may also be unique in its particulars. From it may emerge shifts in alliance, new personal relationships.

In the past men, though perhaps not women, were closely associated with their own slit-gongs. The use of a particular instrument was limited to its owner, and only in emergencies was this use extended to a member of the immediate family. Upon the owner's death a slit-gong was destroyed. In a sense identified with its owner, as well as representative of him, a slit-gong speaks for a man as, if not more powerfully than, his voice. It makes decisions overt, public, and definite. As a man who participates in *br'ngun'guni* should be responsible, aware, so he who would use a slit-gong should also be aware and responsible. A slit-gong should speak as a man, responsibly.

Man lives in his village, cultivates gardens, hunts in the forest, makes artifacts, is moral. Through his *gnek* he participates in the divine. Like a *puok* or other manifestations of the divine, he may become self-willed; like a pig he may run wild. Unlike a pig, but as figured in the slit-gong, a man has a *gnek*, can think and talk, and must be presumed to be aware. Beings and things of the divine and wild are not aware. And when they reveal themselves thus they are *imbatekas*. A *ranguma*, both a man and *imbatekas*, is culpable because, presumed aware, he does not seem to care.

The Divine, Charms, and Europeans

In Tangu today men and women are much more concerned with day-to-day tasks, with exchanges, feasts, maintaining equivalences, and their fears of *ranguova* than they are with those elements of the divine which, non-reciprocal, have no rewards to offer, do not smile, will not bargain or exchange, cannot be manipulated. At best oracular, reformulating the problems which man ultimately has to resolve for himself, the divine brings retribution and punishment, or provides a decision which,

oblivious of what may seem to have been the balance of moralities between the particular persons involved, in rearranging
numbers of personal relations continues to enforce expressions
of the self-same moral principles. Death releases man from the
rewards, punishments, prestations, prescriptions, restrictions,
and preferences characteristic of the moral order. Virtue in this
life is its own reward, the more so if others appreciate it. If a
ranguma escapes detection no hell awaits him. Nor is there a
paradise reserved for good managers. Whatever may have been
done in life the *gnek* becomes a *niemur* or a ghost, and eventually
a *puok* or something like a *puok*. Then, indeed, brother may
marry sister. Otherwise, to be remembered by descendants
either by name for a short while, or in general and anony-
mously as *nduor*, ancestor, may seem a good hope. Yet when there
is some conflict of mind, or when narratives are told, dreams
dreamed, and thunderstorms and earthquakes occur; when
large snakes are encountered, or when a man pauses before a
boar at bay, hears a noise in the stillness, sees a glow on the hillside, or a rat, Tangu become aware of an order of being distinct
from their own, become aware of themselves.

Traditionally, one may suppose, the dynamic of social relations as between living persons and their categories could be
seen and understood in terms of the interactions between moral
and divine or wild. Changing particulars within a relationship
could be explained as the interplay of unchanging general
principles. When *br'ngun'guni* failed to maintain reciprocities, a
variety of particulars described as *imbatekas* might be invoked:
a ghost might deceive, a dream could be misinterpreted, a
narrative misunderstood; a storm might destroy, a *puok* injure;
much of the wit and cunning of a manager might be set at
nought by a whimsical *pap'ta*. But Europeans have brought
with them an ambience in which relationships are existential,
uncertain, and not always predictable. And, apart from the
narratives about Duongangwongar and Mambu,[1] there is as
yet no coherent and generally acceptable mode of explanation
for this field of European experience. Traditionalists attempt to
pull the features of the new environment into conformity with
traditional conceptions and, indeed, to a large extent succeed
in doing so—but only at the price of warping it. Though some

[1] *Supra*, pp. 30–4, and *infra*, N. 30 and N. 31, pp. 400–4, respectively.

moderns treat with contempt the notion that it was a *puok*
which caused a man to fall from a tree, saying that he merely
fell, there remains the muttered question as to why an agile
climber should fall. Whether or not the characters in some
narratives are *puoker* may be matter for argument. Still, the
same characters do much the same things as they did in the past
and they provoke the same questions. An economy in which all
members of the community must participate in the same set of
subsistence activities if they are to gain respect and influence,
exerts its own pressures. Life in community demands reciprocal
exchanges of foodstuffs worked out through *br'ngun'guni* and
becoming *mngwotngwotiki*. Confession is necessary, *ranguova* are
still active, men become angry with one another, feel shame, try to
enlarge their claims and personalities. A few years after he has returned from a spell of contract labour, as his experience of the open
society grows dim, the once superior and sophisticated pagan
tends to readopt traditional attitudes and explanatory categories.

At least part of the missionary purpose in Tangu is to attempt
to prevent such reversions, to maintain, foster, and guide newly
awakened awarenesses. Unlike their pagan brothers, Christians
in Tangu are being taught an alternative schema. For them
there are heaven and hell; and there are divinities who, if
unconstrainable, are not necessarily punitive in their interventions and may even consent to help mankind. If most Europeans
are generally regarded as a species of *ranguma*, men who remain
unobliged by Tangu reciprocities, it is mainly through Christian
teaching that more and more Tangu are coming to see them as
ordinary human beings whose capacities and command over
wealth they might one day equal. The hierarchy 'European,
Tangu, Pig' is no longer seen as fixed and permanent. On the
other hand, Christians are as involved in community reciprocities as pagans and, even if explanatory categories do not
necessarily derive from the empirical experience, the habitual
insistence on reciprocal relations in daily life must tend to become the standard by which other kinds of relations are
measured. So *puoker* begin to reassert themselves, ghosts appear
in dreams, and a man who gets a boil on the inside of his thigh
cannot but think of a *pap'ta*: they are there, extant representations. Though Christians may strive to escape from the traditional symbolic system, the latter is still a part of them and

they have to participate in it when interacting with pagans. Since experiences in the open society of trade stores, offices, plantations, hierarchy, commerce, and specialization tend to remain unrelated to rationalizations having a general consensus, they are inevitably reduced to traditional terms. Christian divinities are as self-willed and unobliged as *puoker* or thunderstorms; prayer may strive after and beseech, but does not command; there are plenty of rich Europeans who never say a prayer. Causation and efficacy in the European world must either remain highly mysterious, or they may be explained in traditional ways.

Traditionally, among Tangu, command, the power to move or undo, resides in the divine. By using that in himself which participates in the divine, the *gnek*, man has some access to such power and command. In this all pagans and most Christians explicitly or tacitly acquiesce. For Tangu there is power in the word itself, in the sounds that proceed from the *gnek*, whether they are intelligible as language or not. Indeed, the strange or uncommon word may, potentially, have more power than words in normal use. There is power, too, perhaps by analogy with the storm and rain, in blowing and spitting. If a child hears a man swearing he ought to stop his ears, spit, blow, and run away. To swear at a trap when, say, the trip mechanism seems recalcitrant, may render the trap ineffective. To swear at or on a new garden site may make the soil infertile. But words specifically arranged into a formula, a spell (*kam imbatekas*),[1] usually conjoined with a loose rite or medicine-making, in all a charm, has more positive powers.

The test of the power and efficacy of charms is severely pragmatic. Whether revealed in dreams, or bought from other New Guinea peoples, or taken from European procedures and phrases which seem to Tangu to be, or to be like, charms, new charms are continuously replacing those which all Tangu have in common, or which men have inherited from fathers or mother's brothers, or which women have inherited from mothers.[2] Yet no

---

[1] *kam imbatekas* (*kam* = 'word, talk, language'). Both 'swear' and 'spell' are referred to as *kam imbatekas*: both are essentially non-reciprocal uses of language, and while the first is irresponsible both carry the potential of demanding that others conform to the powers released.

[2] Women's spells are supposed to act only in circumstances having specifically to do with women's affairs—e.g. in childbirth, menstruation, etc.

charm is sacrosanct: it is abandoned if and when it seems to have become ineffective. Blowing, spitting, blowing spittle in a fine cloud of spray, and certain procedures of medicine-making are common to most charms. European habits and phrases, thought of by some as charms, have a more limited distribution. But it is the spell, the formula of words, which is regarded as the powerful and causative element. And a spell, thought of as inherently *imbatekas*, acts or moves at the behest of the initiator.

Everyone has charms, everyone has spells. When a man builds a series of traps in the forest he cordons the area with saplings lashed to tree trunks, blows his spittle on the barrier, and utters a favourite spell: trespassers into the area are expected to sicken. When the trespasser confesses a second charm will nullify the effects of the first. Only a more powerful charm, such as a *ranguma* might use, will enable a trespasser to pass unscathed; and only a *ranguma* will not at once nullify the effects of a charm when a trespasser has confessed. On the other hand, should a known trespasser who is not thought to be a *ranguma* remain unharmed, then it is time to find a new spell. To blow spittle in a fine cloud of spray is a first line of protection against inimical intentions; to blow urine is better; to spit on an axe or spear may make it more effective. But a spell both protects and, as it were, retaliates. In the past, if a man wanted to marry a certain woman, and there was some impediment, he took some tobacco[1] or an areca-nut with the cup or 'eye' removed,[2] and either impregnated the tobacco with sweat from face, armpits, and crutch, or inserted the salivations of an aphis-like insect together with his body sweat into the areca-nut. Then, calling on the name of the woman he wanted, he gave the tobacco or areca-nut to a child to give to the woman. If the woman ate the areca-nut, or smoked the tobacco, she was expected to go crazy. She broke cooking-pots and food bowls, would not cook or work in the gardens. . . . In the end, it was thought, she would leave her home and go to the house of the man who had worked the charm. He then restored her to normality by blowing in her ears. Afterwards they would marry. A charm known to all and derived from a narrative,[3] Tangu say that it could only be used

---

[1] Which first grew from the vulva. In the past tobacco was smoked by rolling the leaf into a thick cigar.

[2] See N. 8, *infra*, pp. 243–5.   [3] Ibid.

where marriage, not mere sexual adventure, was the end in view. If the man used the charm merely to satisfy sexual appetite, then the spell, which gave the charm particularity and efficacy, would rebound to the user's detriment.

To make rain a coconut was filled with water, blown over, spelled on, and hurled into a stream with a great splash. And anyone could follow this procedure. But only a man with a particularly powerful spell could actually constrain the rain to fall. Unlike the woman in the love charm example, where the power of the spell was held in a matrix of moral requirements, rain is not amenable to moral persuasion, but it is, as we shall see, closely associated with semen; and while males, in virtue of having semen, may try to constrain the rain with a spell, Tangu feel that only those men with plenty of powerful semen could actually have the sort of spell that would cause the rain to fall. So that although a spell is generally considered to be efficacious of itself, its power and effects may be limited by the procedural matrix or intentions or personality of the initiator. An ineffective man will have ineffective charms, just as a *ranguma* will have bad and powerful ones. Otherwise, how could a man become a *ranguma*?

Formerly a valuable inheritance, charms today may be bought and sold quite cheaply; subtleties of usage have decayed, and confidence in the spell as distinct from its matrix appears to be losing ground. Whether in relation to aphrodisiacs, conception, contraception; or to make a trap effective, a spear fly true, to counter *ranguova*, to protect house or hunting-lodge or garden shelter, to prevent trespass or theft; the turnover is substantial as Tangu experiment with the Sign of the Cross, holy water stolen from a mission chapel, garbled English phrases, mysterious signs pencilled on scraps of paper, European notes and chits, stolen cheque forms, rubber stamps, and a host of other expedients which seem to Tangu to have effectiveness for Europeans. The powers that Europeans deploy are evidently so much more potent than those available to Tangu that, clearly, if they are to compete with Europeans then they must make a start with European techniques. The principle of the causative nature of a charm, particularly the formula of words embedded in it, the spell, is not so much in doubt. The question for Tangu is, 'Have we got the right words, the right medicines, the right procedures?' In what, many Tangu ask, lies the efficacy of European techniques? Do they have a closely guarded secret which they refuse to divulge to others? Why is it that a piece of coloured paper written on or signed by a European will persuade a banker or storekeeper to supply money or goods, whilst another piece of paper signed by a man from Tangu is quite useless?

Appreciating European techniques and procedures on a level of apprehension merely, Tangu do not yet comprehend them. For Tangu, man has such powers as he possesses as a moral being in virtue of his *gnek*, in virtue of his participation in the divine through his *gnek*. And the operations of the traditional *gnek* are closely bounded by the terms of the traditional moral order which, in turn, is related to the ways in which Tangu conceive the operations of the divine. If when contemplating the powers of Europeans many Tangu are forced into asking themselves whether, if Europeans are but human, they themselves are not more closely related to the wild things of the forest, in their own lives and within their own environment they preserve a common-sense balance. While, for example, ageing managers search for charms and spells to compensate their ebbing physical strength and mental robustness, younger men point to spindling shanks, grey hairs, and hanging skin. Though no one expects to remain young and strong for ever, few would not attempt to stave off decay by attempting a freer access to that which never decays. Until Tangu come round to accepting new categories of thought and causation, the charm, particularly the spell, remains the only accepted mode of constraining the powers that reside in the divine.

For Christians in Tangu the categories of intellection have been widened, the *gnek* has a broader operational field and is correspondingly more capable of grasping other theories of causation. Yet for Christians as well as for the more sophisticated pagans, the habits of daily life, the continuous re-engagement of reciprocities, tend to close the door on those avenues which the *gnek* might more fruitfully explore. Moreover, the stimulus of the more gifted and capable is generally lacking. The schoolboy who is above average goes away to Alexishafen for further training, the more capable find they can exercise their abilities more profitably outside Tangu. Additionally, though each individual in Tangu covets that privileged access to the divine which will enable him to deal more easily or efficiently with his fellows or his own problems, no one in Tangu will brook open evidence of such access in others. Only a *ranguma*, or *ranguma-*like fellow, is admitted to have that kind of access. On the other hand, when such an ability or afflatus receives expression in a stranger, as in the case of Europeans, for example, or Mambu, then it is accorded respect and even obedience. It is not a capacity which has been gained at the expense of other Tangu, nor is it one which, in the winning, has necessarily contravened the requirements of the Tangu moral order.

Tangu sometimes hazard the existence of two beings whom, they admit, they know very little about. The first, Mngungerp, a name related to the word for earthquake, *gungepake*, is supposed to cause storms and earthquakes, and is regarded as located 'on high' as well as 'below'. Sometimes likened to the 'King of England' who, it is supposed by a few, causes earthquakes by shifting on his throne, Mngungerp tends most often to be identified with the Christian God—'like God', Tangu say. The second being, Yameung, mother, may at one time have been Mngungerp's consort, but is today more closely associated with, and even assimilated to, Christian teaching on the Virgin Mary. An example, again, of oblivescence on the one hand and cognoscence on the other.

Nevertheless, though Christian teaching and the European experience are beginning to bridge the divide, Tangu life is still dominated by the two contraposed categories of power represented in the terms 'moral' and 'divine'. Self-willed and creative if also apparently destructive and punitive, the divine *is* before men were, and will not be obliged. For most in Tangu today the acts and omissions of men and women in community earn their deserts, or the consequences are dealt with, in terms of the moral order or not at all. While many Tangu Christians might demur, pointing out that man does not escape consequences by dying, for most purposes in Tangu the struggle between self-will and morality is ended at death. The *gnek* is released from the flesh and the constraints of morality, and becomes a part of the divine where morality as such is irrele-

vant. Among Tangu death is very matter of fact. Within an
hour or so pagans are under the sod, and if a Christian may have
had the benefit of a prayer by a catechist it is not long before
people are about their workaday tasks, gardening and hunting
as usual. When the heart aches for one who was loved and is
lost, then Tangu mourn on their slit-gongs. Ghosts and *niemur*
cause troubles rather than joy, the benevolence of ancestors may
be realized at death or in an inscrutable future. Growing
numbers of pagans as well as Christians go to mass on Sundays
and holy days, and mission sermons and schooling provide
the impetus towards a new kind of life. But Tangu still take
departure from the common engagement in subsistence
activities, and are most deeply touched by those expressions in
the living which lie within or outside the requirements of
equivalence. Becoming *mngwotngwotiki* is still the most practical
and intelligible means of redemption.

For most Tangu the basis of awareness lies in the *gnek*, or in a
soul that is very much like a *gnek*. By listening to narratives and
reflecting on his dreams and his encounters with ghosts, man,
through his *gnek*, is given the opportunity to perceive and resolve moral problems for himself. The activities of the *gnek* imply
conscience. Yet the moralities themselves remain fixed. Inviting
fresh resolutions of new particulars within the same normative
terms, interventions of the divine impose a rearrangement of
persons in relation to one another, provide a new departure
for expressing the self-same moralities. Realigned, individuals
interact within the same normative rules, reattempt the same
redemption from different bases. But an appropriate redemption depends on awareness, on a full understanding and acknowledgement of the relations between the moral and the divine.
Not to demonstrate awareness—which must be done in *br'ngun-
'guni*—is a denial of the distinctive nature of being human, is an
attempt to resolve the problem between morality and self-
willedness by becoming as though divine, wholly self-willed and
oblivious, whilst still within the moral order. Though most of
the colour, muscularity, and verve—even the illusions—of
traditional life have wasted away, Tangu remain on their guard
against the contempt of moral being, insist on redemption
through becoming *mngwotngwotiki*.

PART TWO

MYTHOLOGY

4

THE NARRATIVES (I)

WE turn now to consider Tangu formal statements about themselves and their experience—their myths, folk-tales, stories, and legends, summed up as 'narratives'. Accepting that the purpose of narratives is to provide a logical model capable of overcoming inconsistencies,[1] we shall see something of the way in which Tangu narratives do this job. Nevertheless while this 'purpose' is entailed in, or emerges from, the analyses that follow, our specific interest is in the experiential content of the narratives. Given that to a large extent narratives are, and must be, 'reflections' of social life, what is of greater concern here is the way in which Tangu use their narratives in their conduct of social relations, and change their narratives in the light of a wider positive experience. Finally, through a conversation between the narratives and other aspects of Tangu culture,[2] we hope to sketch the content of the developing cultural experience in which Tangu are involved.

The general structure of the narratives cannot but be governed by the logic of Tangu social relations. The terms reciprocal and non-reciprocal, culture and the wild or natural, moral and divine, provide the widest referents, and we have seen something of their behavioural content. Men are held to be responsible; women are workers and child-bearers; males are opposed to females. The basic design of the community consists of mutually opposed lines of filiation wherein paired lines of males and females are related as brother and sister on the one hand, and as husband and wife on the other. The incest taboo entails differentiation, a communication of parts between brother-and-sister and husband-and-wife until each is implied

---

[1] See Claude Lévi-Strauss 1968: 229 (*Structural Anthropology*, Basic Books, London), where he says that 'the purpose of myth is to provide a logical model capable of overcoming a (real) contradiction'.

[2] *Supra*, p. xiv.

in the other. The normative but non-reciprocal values in filiation call for resolutions between self-willedness and self-restraint; values in filiation are contraposed to the reciprocal values of siblingship; the resultant tensions are resolved in becoming *mngwotngwotiki*, unobliged and in stasis. With each generation the moral order and the material wealth of the community are recreated: those who contribute the most foodstuffs, and who efficiently communicate their parts within the terms of equivalence, gain prestige and extend their influence. The redemptive process is summed up in becoming *mngwotngwotiki*, equivalent and unobliged within the terms of morality. The advent of Europeans and cash notwithstanding, subsistence activities and not money measure and define the man, provide the redemptive medium. These features give the narratives their context.[1] But we shall find *br'ngun'guni* mentioned only once;[2] and confession, the *gnek*, and becoming *mngwotngwotiki* not at all—though 'thinking' is mentioned, and is of course directly implied in knowing, recounting, and listening to a narrative.

The Narrative Idiom

Traditionally, narratives belong with the divine rather than the moral: they are concerned with the activities of *puoker*, endure, may impinge on the moral order so as to initiate changes, are considered by Tangu to contain truth or truths. But because the *puoker* of narratives are anthropomorphic it becomes possible to appreciate the 'play within a play', to contemplate successive developments of the primary oppositions of Tangu culture, to penetrate the strange by means of the familiar, to realize deeper levels of being—or at least gain the illusion of doing so. Moreover, at the moment when *puoker* begin overtly to be non-anthropomorphic, when they begin to appear strange, so that we, or Tangu, might say '*Imbatekas-ake!*'—then one is in touch with what *imbatekas* connotes: the occasions and refractions of self-willedness or unobligedness, impulse, and assertions of the self outside the bounds of morality.

---

[1] The narratives presented in this and the two chapters which follow do not represent the whole *corpus* of Tangu narratives. They are those which are remembered reasonably well, which have a minimum coherence. Those which are not remembered, or which are not remembered very well, are hardly relevant to our purpose.

[2] *Infra*, p. 325.

Though traditionally it would seem to have been otherwise, Tangu today distinguish between two kinds of narrative: the *sitori*,[1] or story, which is taken to be about men and women merely, and those other narratives which are about *puoker*. However, the distinction cannot be expressed in the Tangu language, and the verb *puok'ptiek*, to talk about *puoker*, is used of both kinds of narrative. That Tangu can only distinguish between the two sorts of narrative in pidgin carries its own obvious significance. Further, when deciding whether a particular narrative is about *puoker* or about men and women, or when discussing what differences such a distinction might entail, a consensus is lacking. Christians as well as pagan progressives are inclined to regard the vast bulk of traditional narratives in each case as '*sitori nating*, just a story', but they continue to tell them and admit that they contain kinds of truth. At the other extreme, pagan conservatives tend to recognize all traditional narratives as true or as containing truths. And if some regard the traditional narratives as slightly less true than the Bible and moral stories they have learned from missionaries and other Europeans, what is in question is not whether narratives contain truths, but what these truths are and how they may be recognized as such. For it remains that a possible *sitori* is apt to include *puoker*; that, like other narratives, the *sitori* and its characters tends to persist through the generations; that no narrative or *sitori* is dismissed as not containing truth or truths; that if the *puoker* of narratives are often like men and women, the men and women of a *sitori* are as often very like *puoker*. Finally, in their attitude towards narratives that are quite clearly new,[2] the great majority of Tangu are agreed: they are true or contain truths.

It seems reasonable, therefore, especially in relation to the developmental experience, to regard all those narratives which Tangu can relate and remember as evidences of the same rather than different kind. The traditional attitude towards narratives holds good even though there may be disagreements as to which particular narratives, or parts of narratives, actually illustrate the principle. The use of the inclusive term 'narrative' seems justified, and though the reader might select from the narratives

---

[1] Pidgin 'story'.
[2] The 'Duongangwongar' and 'Mambu' narratives, N. 30 and N. 31, *infra*, pp. 400–4.

presented here and label them 'legend' or 'fairy story' or 'just-so story' or 'folk-tale' or 'myth', such categories, derived from the European experience and perhaps of use in the European context, are not only not relevant to Tangu but tend to obscure rather than clarify the Tangu situation. Just as the reciprocities of the moral community are ordered and made known within the terms of friendship and the kinship idiom, so the narratives articulate other kinds of awareness within the terms of a particular idiom. All Tangu narratives have in common the fact that they are social or cultural facts which, being collective representations, are also modes of cognition. Listening to a narrative, or telling a narrative, involves a communication of knowledge, of awareness.

For Tangu, only a few of whom are literate,[1] a narrative exists in perceptible form only through articulation in speech. Not a part of private gossip, the tales are told in public. Their form and content are public knowledge, seized of the community at large, however particular renderings or criticisms may vary, and despite the different ranges of remembrance encountered among Tangu today. At each telling a narrative is criticized and welded into a community asset with community support by promptings from the audience, reminders and arguments as to the correct ordering of events and their content. That there is a discoverable relationship between narrative, story-teller, and audience is hardly to be doubted; that this relationship pertains to cognition is a reasonable inference. Story-tellers may innovate, whether by way of embellishment or by the introduction of popular anecdote: but such innovations are subject to the lively criticism and consent of the audience. On both hands the mental faculties are engaged. Thought, recollection, choice of words, articulation in speech, approval, and criticism all involve the *gnek*, direct the *gnek* towards a particular kind of awareness. Experiential in themselves as well as expressive of experience, the words of a narrative are not simply spoken and listened to: there is both appraisal of, and identification with, what is being said. The images evoked may be seen 'objectively', at a distance, as well as internally felt or appreciated in varying degrees. Yet if a narrative is generally apprehended it is not

---

[1] Literacy among adults, of low standard, is about 3 per cent. Among children, only a few of whom do not go to the mission school, it may reach 35 or 40 per cent.

always comprehended. To ask Tangu what a tale is about may elicit a longish précis, a repetition of the last few sentences, or even a synopsis of the events of the tale. This is to apprehend or grasp the story. Comprehension goes much further. It requires the perception of an inner meaning, an interpretation, a correlation of the circumstances set forth in the narrative with other kinds of experience outside the context of the narrative itself. And in achieving such a comprehension each of the different and correlated kinds of experience serves to illumine and inform the others: comprehension and awareness result from entering a conversation between the narratives and other aspects of culture.

Some among Tangu who are aware of what life was like in the old days are able to relate the circumstances of those days to what is told in narratives. They comprehend something of what it is that the narrative is, or might be, communicating. For others, however, these particular kinds of comprehension are not always possible: the circumstances which might have thrown light on the tale, or which the narrative itself might have been able to inform, no longer exist as parts of their total and active awareness. Hopeful and partially explanatory promptings, it is true, sometimes awaken dormant memories. But while comprehensions must vary with particular individuals, one may generally assume that the traditional narratives are experienced for the most part on a level of apprehension merely. On the other hand, when it comes to the Duongangwongar and Mambu stories Tangu are quite able to make their own interpretations for themselves. And, where Tangu are at a loss, there seems to be no reason why a European, with the advantages of literacy, time for reflection, and a wider experience, should not suggest those kinds of correlation which yield a comprehension. Yet a *caveat* is necessary: narratives are apt to be as complex, profound, and varied as the intelligence and experience which is contemplating them; the wider experience of a European might uncover layer after layer of meaning. Some limits must therefore be drawn. And here, on the whole, imagination is held in check by what we know of Tangu social relations and the features of the narrative idiom.

Among Tangu sense of time, whether cyclical (in the sense of horticultural and life cycles) or linear (in the sense that these cycles have repeated themselves through unnumbered years from the days of the Founders), is taken from flux or change in the relations of physical and social space. An event in the past is said to have occurred when a boy was as high as father's hip joint, or when a man was gardening a particular ridge, or when grandfather was in the *garamb*, at the time of the first taros in the new hunting lodge, when the Pleiades in the heavens were thus, when the missionary first came to Wanitzir. . . . Without such spatial co-ordinates Tangu would simply 'be'. The senses are occupied with spatial relations, with relative sizes, the position in the skies of heavenly bodies, the location of places, people, and things relative to one another, relative positions in terms of the idioms of kinship and friendship. By noting change or flux or movement in these relations Tangu are able to construct intervals which may be interpreted as 'time'. Yet it is precisely these spatial categories and relations which Tangu narratives tend to ignore, negate, or ask a listener to abandon. The *puoker* of narratives or men and women of stories tend to be oblivious of both time and space however conceived: to them neither space nor time seem to exist, they 'are'. The narratives in which they have their being persist through the generations, and they themselves exist outside of Tangu spatial relations, and therefore outside of Tangu time.[1] But living Tangu have being both in space and in time. And it is difficult to conceive how ordinary living beings could comprehend events that had no context in either space or time. Yet a narrative is for mortals, not *puoker*, to tell and listen to, and mortals must have some potential for apprehending and then comprehending the tale. In Tangu, one finds, though most of the action might be happening anywhere in New Guinea, in addition to the introductory '*arin*, long ago', specific and emphatic spatial correlates are mentioned: 'by such-and-such a stream . . .' or 'on such-and-such a ridge . . .' or 'at dawn . . .' or 'at dusk . . .'. So *puoker* are brought into the world of men and women and made anthropomorphic. On the other hand the different events in a narrative occur, as they must, in succession, one after the other, without reference to those spatial co-ordinates which would yield inter-

---

[1] It is possible in some contexts to impute to men and women of stories an awareness of space, and so of time. Perhaps this is why they are men and women, and not *puoker*, and why a narrative may be regarded as a *sitori* and so distinguished from other narratives. . . . But there are too many inconsistencies to formulate a general principle—though it would be nice if one could.

vals of 'time': a feature which represents an insistence on time as flux merely, and not, as it is among living Tangu, as inferred from relations in space. In this perhaps limited sense the technique of narration itself provides 'pure' time or timelessness, or that which seems eternal. On the one hand the activities of *puoker* are brought within the range of human comprehension, on the other that which is to be comprehended is as though timeless or eternal.

The recurring feature of 'origin' in Tangu narratives goes overtly to event rather than to first cause or principle. In comprehending the narrative, on the other hand, as some Tangu can, it is possible to appreciate that the tale is communicating that which is not necessarily bound either by time or by space. It is communicating not particular events but axioms or principles which indicate being, and so, potentially, awareness of being. Since a narrative is concerned with *puoker* or beings like *puoker*, and *puoker* themselves are represented as existing irrespective of time or space, the apparent events in which *puoker* or beings like *puoker* take part, or in which they become involved, are not really events at all—for events take place within particular spatial relations from which location and a value in relative chronology may be inferred—but those primary truths that, determining the nature of being, have a persistent validity so long as the culture of which they form a part continues to exist. And the activities of *puoker*, whether in the guise of animals or persons or categories, invite awareness of the interplay of principles of being and their refractions. Still, in providing dramatic effect by relating the events of a narrative to known topographical features or the parts of the horticultural cycle, Tangu succeed in imprisoning the contents of a narrative in known spatial relations, and so into relative chronologies: principles or axioms tend to be reconverted into events and persons. The movement from apprehension to comprehension requires, therefore, a penetration of those obstacles which themselves bring the interior truths within the range of comprehension. Moreover, since history is decisively trapped in spatial relations which may be converted into relative chronologies, Tangu are enabled to insist on the historicity of many of their narratives: a typical euhemerism.[1] On the other hand, though history may

---

[1] In principle, that is. Some narratives which were once regarded as having historical validity are now not regarded as history.

enter into a narrative as history, and the narrative may be regarded as history, when history enters a narrative it takes on the qualities of narrative: if events and persons remain significant in themselves they also become susceptible to comprehension in terms of eternal or timeless principle.

The Tangu narrative uses words which are normally directly apprehended. Yet some of these words may be signs, pointers, or symbols which, when apprehended, require some process of thought, inspection, reflection, and wit to arrive at a comprehension. Always having meaning in terms of the culture of which it is a part, a word may still assume a central position within a constellation of rather different meanings. It may have connotations, carry overtones and implications, be a substitute or perhaps a euphemism. It may correspond in meaning with another word, or it may be ambiguous or ambivalent, and thus mediate between words which refer distinctly and severally to some of the meanings contained in the mediator. But to decide definitively that a particular word is itself or any one of the features mentioned surely negates the essential quality of a narrative. Words and sentences must be assumed to be not haphazard collections but meaningful choices and arrangements; and though among Tangu the possibility of genuine mistakes is fairly wide, the interchange of referents inhering in a word is the very stuff of the narrative idiom. While a first hearing may start the mind towards a particular comprehension, different nuances of tone on subsequent occasions may predicate subtly variant apprehensions which, in turn, open the way to other kinds of comprehension. That is why a narrative is a narrative, persists through time, and remains seminal. Keywords or phrases or events are capable of speeding the mind through the whole gamut of the culture. But for practical purposes some points of closure there must be. And again, in the chapters that follow, the narrative idiom, suggestions and cross-references in other narratives, and what we know of other aspects of Tangu culture, plot these points.

In discussing the relations between Tangu and their narratives we are, clearly, re-entering the dialectic between the reciprocal and the non-reciprocal. But at a quite different level. While the narratives show forth the same sets of oppositions that we have already encountered, we, like Tangu, may also experience something more: that awareness which is derived from the synthesis of differently based universes of knowledge. We begin to realize that the contrapositions, never static, always imply movements to synthesis. As the narratives take us, or Tangu, from the more familiar to the less familiar, and so to the strange, they communicate an awareness of the creative ecstasy. In picking our way through the intricate shifts of the father–son relationship, for example, we begin to appreciate that if one kind of creation lies in begetting a son, further heights are conquered by providing son with a conscience through an appropriate begetting in marriage, and by training him to be responsible, aware of conscience. On this, we learn, the moral order and culture depend. Brother-and-sister unions imply an undifferentiated state: but they also evoke the incest taboo, appropriate marriage between husband and wife, and so that differentiation and communication of parts which enables the culture to thrive. While semen and milk are figured as nourishing stuffs, other kinds of nourishment are brought to mind only to return to their anchorage in semen and milk: mind and narrative come back to their starting-points. But in the meantime there has been an exploratory journey, a journey which reveals the contours of experience and awareness.

The traditional Tangu narratives generally adopt a dialogue form. Here and there we find actors referred to in terms of more generalized categories such as old man, manager, youth, maiden, or baby; and in the more anecdotal narratives[1] we find actors assuming the personal names of living Tangu. But for the most part we shall find a series of dialogues between actors designated in the terms of the categories of kinship and friend-ship; and these dialogues are mediated either by things or situations, or by a few named characters who are certainly not men and women. Because they are few, these named characters carry heavy burdens of meaning which seem almost inexhaust-ible. Mediating between successive pairs of categories and so loading the categories with relevance, these named characters— bundles of multi-faceted principle—are thereby invested with added significance. As we gather together the series of dialogues between father and son, adults and children, men and women, husband and wife, brother and sister, elder sibling and younger

[1] N. 14., N. 15, N. 16, N. 17, N. 18, N. 20, N. 31, for example.

sibling, mother's brother and sister's son, members of community, and the *ranguma*—to mention but a few—we begin to see that if, in Tangu thought, the peak of creative essence is in the end beyond the reach of man, he still has sufficient *nous* to explore his condition and manage his own affairs. But the latter he can only do well if he knows something about the former. Parts or refractions of the creative essence continually intervene in human affairs, and man has to learn to recognize them for what they are, gird his loins, and use his initiative.

These and other themes are worked out through a variety of categories, characters, signs, and pointers in the narratives that follow. One should first of all 'think in pictures', sketch on the canvas of awareness the events and patterns of social life, paint in the colours derived from the narratives, harmonize colour with pattern. Then one should bear in mind that though the narratives, and the events within them, cannot but be presented in succession, each is more accurately imagined as lying on the circumference of a circle pointing to a centre of being. Awareness blooms only in an intimate knowledge of the narratives: when they can be appreciated as wholes as well as in their parts; when, as with a child listening to a story he has been told over and over, each event is appraised within a context of what has gone before and what is to follow; when the events of one narrative are illumined by events in another; when the narratives are framed in the texture of a positive experience of social life. To the perceptive and orderly mind, prepared to do these things, the logic and structure of the narratives emerge by themselves. As the reader plunges into the discussion he will find himself being asked to take the relevances of some signals for granted, he will find himself referred to another narrative. Let him not despair. As he becomes accustomed to the idiom, narratives and signals will unfold themselves.[1]

Adults and Children

Framed within a primary dialogue between adults and children, the three narratives below also have in common a concern with rocks and stones.

---

[1] A summary of primary signals and their indications is provided in Appendix I. This may be used as a guide while reading the narratives.

N. 1: *Orphans in the Rain*

Once upon a time a leading man[1] of Wasamb was fishing by the light of his bamboo torch in Cipenderp stream when it came on to rain. He and all the other good[2] men and women of the village took shelter under the lee of a large rock. The last to come were a boy and his sister, orphans, who were unwashed, dirty, and smelly.[3]

'Hey! You two can't come in here!' exclaimed the leading man. 'You smell too much!'

The storm increased, the rain poured down, the two orphans went off and found shelter in a hollow tree.

Now seeing what had happened out there, and sympathizing with the orphans, the Great One[4] decided to deal with the villagers. He caused the rock to envelop them.

The orphans returned to their *mwenk*, mourning their fellow villagers. Later, they came back to the large stone and tried to crack it open. But it was no use. The stone was immovable. Then, with the help of some neighbours, they killed all the pigs in the village, collected heaps of yams and taros and some cockerels—all the foodstuffs they could lay their hands on—and placed them beside the rock. To no purpose. All those imprisoned in the stone died of hunger inside.

N. 2: *The Fairy-woman*

Once upon a time the men of Baikunai killed all the pigs in the village and divided the flesh between the grown-ups. The children had none. Even when the children cried out in protest the parents would not be persuaded. They wanted all the meat for themselves.

Thinking on the matter for a while, at last the children took up their fishing spears and bows and arrows and went down into the valley to the stream. Then, wending their way up-stream, they had barely reached Rangwatz, where the big stone lies today, when it came on to rain and storm.

[1] *Wunika ruma*, big man or manager.
[2] The word used is *aran*. When not used as a kin term (sister's son) *aran* means 'good' or 'wholesome' or 'complying with reciprocal obligation'. *Aran* connotes the opposite of *imbatekas*.
[3] Here summed up as *imbatekas*. Tangu comment on the orphans, odd, set apart, and different, was simply '*Imbatekas-ake!*'
[4] Igoe'ika. This being, of whom Tangu could say little, other than refer one to the narrative itself, was thought to correspond with God—in the pidgin, *bigpela antap*, 'Great One on high'—and was also identified as Mngungerp the earthmover (*supra*, p. 190). That Igoe'ika is associated with rain and storm, and that *wigoea*, as strange-sounding on Tangu lips as Igoe'ika, but very like, means semen, suggests a correspondence between semen and 'germ of being', and rain and vegetation.

The children went under the large stone to shelter from the rain, not knowing that the stone was the house of a fairy-woman.[1] She heard them chattering as they sheltered from the storm and, going out to see what the noise was about, she saw the children and invited them into her home.

The children were delighted. They gave the fairy-woman the fish they had caught, and she prepared a sumptuous meal of yams. They feasted together, and afterwards, their bellies full, those children lolled drowsily where they sat until sleep overcame them. And because they were too sleepy to get up and go, the fairy herself went out, shutting the door behind her and making her way to another stone in another part of the stream.

During the night one of the smallest of the children woke up. He wanted to stool. He tried to wake up his brother, but he was too sleepy. And when he went to the door of the house he found it locked. So he squatted in a corner and delivered himself on to a piece of firewood. Later on, another boy did the same.

Now the parents in the village got anxious. They waited and waited, but no children came home. So, deciding to look for them, the parents tracked the children to the stream, and followed the trail up-stream until they eventually came to the large rock. They saw their children's fishing spears and bows and arrows stacked outside the rock. And they could hear their children crying out to them from inside the stone, begging to be let out.

There was little the parents could do. They quarrelled among themselves, blaming each other for not giving any meat to the children. They collected all the foodstuffs they had and laid them beside the stone. But it was no use. Weeping, they returned to the village, leaving their children in the stone.

But the fairy had not forgotten the children. She took pity on them. She struck the stone at the top with a wand and opened a doorway. Two lads stumbled out, the sun beating on their eyelids, waking them, as they made their way slowly back to the village.

When the parents saw these two lads they welcomed them joyously, asking what had happened to the others. But the two lads were too hungry to speak. So the parents prepared hot soup and yams, and massaged the lips and stomachs of the two boys until they could swallow. Then, as their lips began hesitantly to move, as their stomachs filled with food, the boys told their tale. . . .

Too late. When the parents returned to the stone the door was shut. All the other children starved in the stone.

---

[1] *Puokamainya*—literally, '*puok*-woman'.

N. 3: *The Yam-man*

Once upon a time while he was out hunting a man happened to notice the vine of a wild yam, a *warika* yam, growing by the side of the forest path.

The vine was only about four feet or so long, and the tuber, the man decided, must still be quite small. So, binding the vine with creeper and strands of grass to show that he had reserved the yam for himself, the fellow went on his way. 'Later on, when it has grown big, I'll come back and dig it up', he thought to himself.

Came the time for making new gardens; for cutting the underbrush, clearing, lopping, drying, burning, raking, and planting; for the children to make tops and spin them into coconut spines stuck in the ground;[1] for the man to take a look at the *warika* he had marked for his own.

The *warika* had grown. It had grown as huge as a rock. Carefully, the man dug out the yam and strapped it to a pole as though it was a pig. Four men, each of them with a shoulder under the pole, were needed to carry the *warika*, so large a wild yam was it. And when they got back to the village they placed the *warika* in the porch of the man's house, slinging the pole from two forked supports, for all the world as though that yam had been a pig.

Considering the matter, husband thought he would keep the *warika* until the season of dearth, when cultivated yams would be scarce and the new taros not ripe enough for the eating.

One day the slit-gongs sounded for Juangam.[2] All the children of the village decorated themselves, boys painting themselves on the forehead and across the nose and over the eyes, whilst the girls limed their cheeks. But those children did not dress themselves properly. Their parents, busy with their own decorations and paraphernalia, could not be bothered to see to their children.

Now it happened that mother passed close to the *warika*. She noticed that it had turned into a man, well and properly decorated but still trussed to the pole like a pig. . . .

Mother complimented the *warika*-man and went on her way.

That night, even though the children were improperly dressed

---

[1] For an account of this game see B-1957(*b*): The game is played by spinning tops, made from the halves of dried fruit rinds pierced by wooden spindles, into an array of coconut spines stuck vertically into the ground. The object of the game is to reach equivalence, as between two teams, in terms of the spines hit or missed. It compares, in an opposite sense, with the game '*Ranguma*', described *supra*, p. 146–7.

[2] Juangam, the harvest dance, danced by men, women, and children together.

and painted, the villagers feasted and danced. And as the dawn broke the *warika*-man sounded a slit-gong, announcing Manjaip.[1]

Husband and wife consulted together. They decided it was time to eat the wild yam.

Now as soon as the *warika*-man learned of this he told the children of the village that on the morrow they must make their excuses and leave the village. For the parents were going to eat him, and the children should on no account do so.

The next day, after husband had split the *warika* with his bamboo razor,[2] cut the yam into pieces, and offered a piece to all in the village, the children excused themselves. 'We will go down to the stream to fish', they said.

The parents were only too pleased—they would have all the more for themselves. Yet when they tried to cook that *warika* yam, boiling and boiling it again, they found that it remained as hard as a rock, quite indigestible. They had to be content with meat only.

The parents slept heavily that night. But the children, who remembered what the *warika*-man had said, slept outside the village.

And well it was that they did so! For during the night a large rock grew out of the ground, first encircling then growing over the *mwenk* until the settlement was wholly enclosed. . . .

One man, taken short in his sleep and rising to piddle, hit his head on the underside of the rock as he stretched himself. Reeling dizzily, he shouted that he was going crazy, that something very peculiar indeed was happening. . . . The rock bore down and crushed him.

Next morning when the children returned to the village there was only the rock to be seen. They called to their parents inside the hard stone and heard them answering. But they could do nothing.

'You see what has happened?' the children shouted. 'You would not decorate us properly for the dance—and now what a business!'

That was the end of the village. All the parents died in the stone, and the children had to build a new village for themselves.

Each of the three narratives above is concerned with large stones or rocks which are associated with *puoker*, which grow or move, which are in a sense punitive, and which imprison people inside them. The question whether the tales 'reflect' the association of large stones with *puoker*, or whether the association of stones with *puoker* is derived from the narratives, is answered definitively by Tangu: 'Because the story says so, It is in the

---

[1] Manjaip, danced in late harvest time, or even early dearth.
[2] *zaka*, a razor made from a split-bamboo sliver; circumcision knife.

story, That is the story and that is how it is.' Empirically, *puoker* and stones are associated. And so far as Tangu are concerned, the association derives from the evidence provided by the narrative. Not only is it a matter of dogma or axiom that narratives contain truths, but since *puoker* are in fact associated with large stones it is empirically verifiable that narratives contain truths.

The Tangu word for 'orphans' is *mnduner*, a plural form without a singular. As such, orphans occur only in narratives, in pairs, brother and sister. In life the ordering of kin relationships makes it virtually impossible for a child to be without some kind of parental guardianship.[1] And here in N. 1 the orphans are not only set apart from the community by virtue of being orphans, oddities, but they are further described as smelly and dirty: features which Tangu summed up as *imbatekas*.[2] Emphasizing the non-reciprocal nature of orphans, the impossibility of engaging in reciprocities with them, those in community are described as *aran*—good people, people who engage in reciprocities. Those in community are allowed into the shelter, the orphans are not: they are dirty. As will be appreciated more fully later, being dirty and smelly prevents boys from entering the *garamb* clubhouse.[3] And the idea of 'shelter' when otherwise unqualified evokes the *garamb*.[4] Whilst those in community are associated with shelter and *garamb*, that is, the orphans cannot enter the *garamb* or be a part of the community.

The spokesman for the community is a leading man, a manager, one who has experienced *garamb* life, one who is mature and responsible. And his discovery fishing by the light of a bamboo torch strengthens the evocations of responsibility in community contraposed to the divine and non-reciprocal. For, apart from the contraries 'light' (responsibility in community) and 'darkness' (wild and/or divine),[5] as we shall see reiterated again and again, since circumcision took place in the *garamb*, and the circumcision knife was a bamboo sliver, the mention of 'bamboo' in a narrative takes the mind to circumcision, the

---

[1] *Supra*, pp. 93–4.
[2] Tangu might have said that the orphans were '*buokotiki*, bad, no good', but they didn't.
[3] *Infra*, p. 324.   [4] *Infra*, p. 366.
[5] On the associations between 'light', 'seeing', and 'responsibility' see *infra*, pp. 212–3. But note here that 'white' (light) ≡ 'shame, awareness'; and that 'black' (darkness) ≡ *ranguma* (*supra*, pp. 130, 136).

garamb, and the process of becoming a responsible man.[1] The dialogue between adults and children is also a contraposition between the responsible and the not yet responsible. Here the children are odd ones, orphans, dirty and smelly, unable to enter the *garamb*. They belong with the wild or divine because they do not properly belong with the moral; without kin who could enforce mutual reciprocities, selfwilledness is written into them.

The orphans take shelter from the rain—itself non-reciprocal —in a hollow tree, a home or refuge not for men and women in community but for wild and non-reciprocal things.[2] The rain increases to a storm, and the Great One, the earth-mover, takes pity[3] on the orphans: so that the orphans become associated with the power in the divine rather than the wild. And from the standpoint of those in community the divine intervenes punitively: *aran* people are buried under the stone; one may presume an earthquake.[4] Yet the divine remains unobliged. The orphans are not restored to amicable relations with the community—as might happen in an Andersenian folk-tale. They have been decisively cut off from the moral, brought into association with the divine. Even when the orphans, anthropomorphic, are as it were shown to have a moral sense by their placing food against the stone—perhaps a reference to the now obsolete custom of destroying the foodstuffs of the dead—the divine is not to be persuaded. Nor is death sudden. Those inside the stone fade away, starve, make the passage into death.

Stone is not only the most durable material in Tangu, evoking perhaps the permanence and inevitability of death. In association with community, stone also reminds one of the tools without which Tangu would hardly have been able to clear a site for cultivation, without which traditional culture could not have survived. And if the story communicates the information that culture is dependent on the permanence of tools, it also conveys an awareness that culture continues despite, or because of, the inevitability of human deaths.[5] Still, in placing foodstuffs, pigs,

---

[1] Bamboo has, of course, many other uses. But circumcision is the most dramatic and pertinent use.

[2] Compare the hollow tree in N. 4, *infra*, p. 221, and in N. 11, *infra*, p. 259.

[3] '*Mandyungangarai*, to be sorry for, to sympathize with' (*supra*, p. 129).

[4] The 'Great One' is the earth-mover, Igoe'ika or Mngungerp (*supra*, p. 190).

[5] All the way through, of course, one may add the words 'the story communicates or conveys . . .'.

and cockerels by the stone the orphans are exhibiting sense of obligation. And, one feels, they are thus brought back into an association with the moral for a purpose. Cockerels herald the dawn,[1] the coming of sunlight and daylight—evocations of awareness and the moral order. Fire-flies, it will be remembered,[2] are like *puoker* in that, whilst themselves invisible in the dark, they are evident as light and make men aware of *puoker*, and so of themselves and their condition. The orphans are helped by neighbours, neighbourly. And since the community from which the orphans have been separated fades away inside the stone, it may be presumed that community life starts again from brother and sister, orphans, a pair without known antecedents, whose survival is due to their association with the divine and wild. Certainly nature and/or the divine fructifies; and whilst the permanent relevance of brother-and-sister mating or intimacy is a divine one, belonging to self-willedness and impulse, this in itself begets its antithesis, the moral imperative of the incest taboo.

There are two decisive acts in the story: the leading and responsible man excluding the orphans; and the Great One who, thought of as male and associated with earthquake, storm, and rain—which latter seems often associated with semen[2]—sympathizes with the orphans. Bringing the two acts together, it seems clear, that so long as the moralities endure, men or that which pertains to maleness—the predicative and generative—may act so as to alter the relationships which express the moralities. And because men can act thus self-willedly and according to impulse, they should be aware of the distinction between that which pertains to the wild or divine, and that which pertains to the moral. They are responsible.

In N. 2 children, who cannot be fully and actively engaged in reciprocities, are separated from their parents, who can be and are involved in reciprocities through a division of meat. The children, wayward and not yet responsible, are associated with the divine or wild, and cannot use their *gneker* appropriately: their thinking leads them into danger, a situation defined

---

[1] Compare the cockerels in N. 11, *infra*, p. 260; N. 25, *infra*, p. 324; N. 29, *infra*, p. 385. Compare also the sun and daylight in N. 2, *supra*, p. 206, and N. 29, *infra*, p. 385.

[2] *Supra*, p. 159.   [3] *Supra*, p. 205, n. 4, and many instances below.

by stream, storm, stone, and fairy. Storm, as we have seen, predicates the intervention of the divine. Streams harbour *pap'ta*, but stream itself is not simply wild, non-moral, deriving from rain and storm. When brought into relation with the moral it is creative and continuing, indicative of growth and maturation—particularly when youths or children walk upstream.[1] In N. 1 'stone' or 'rock' was associated with community, particularly as 'shelter' which evoked the *garamb*. Here in N. 2 the stone is the home of a fairy and the children enter into it: they are separated from the world of community and reciprocities. They eat heavily and go to sleep: the divine is unobliged, leaves them. The parents track their children to the stone and find their fishing-spears which, traditionally, were made from bamboo, and their bows and arrows, also traditionally made from bamboo.[2] If the stone itself does not evoke the *garamb*, the bamboo implements do. And since it may be assumed that the implements have been left outside the stone for a purpose, the point seems to be that the children have not been circumcised, have not been in the *garamb*, and are therefore liable to be 'taken' by the divine. Certainly the theme is one which repeats itself throughout the narratives. Bows and arrows are particularly associated with boys who are becoming sexually mature, with youths whose thoughts are beginning to turn towards girls and enjoyment. It is a dangerous period, they may be taken. And, as we know, in this instance only two young lads come through their ordeal into the light.

Having imprisoned the children the fairy, unobliged but associated with the children through her sympathy for them, opens a door in the stone without, however, taking any steps to see that the children are made aware of the fact. That is for them to discover for themselves. It happens that two lads seize their chance, totter out, and return to community. Coming from darkness, they are wakened to light, community, and responsibility by the sun beating on their eyelids. In time they can see. The same process is connoted in being circumcised and making the passage of the *garamb*. As fire-flies may remind us, 'seeing'

---

[1] See *supra*, pp. 75–6, regarding *ringertiam* and *ringertingertiki*, and many instances below.

[2] Men's fishing spears may also be made of bamboo today, but they are more usually made from a species of hardwood.

and 'light' evoke awareness and responsibility. The lads are revived by being given cooked—that is community-treated—food, and are encouraged to speech by lip massage.[1] Though the narrative does not tell us the kind of wood from which the fairy's wand was made, it would be a good guess that it was either of bamboo—indicating the entry into community of those boys who had been wakened to maturity and responsibility—or of the hardwood from which spears are made: spears being used by, and so signalling, the responsible man.

In N. 3 a man finds a wild yam, thinks about it, reserves it for himself by an ordinary and common means: a charm. Man, wild, yam, *gnek*, and charm are brought together. In time the wild yam grows to huge proportions—so large that it passes from the class 'yam' to the class 'pig'. Carried back to the village, not in a string bag as is usual with ordinary yams, but by men as though it were a pig, as 'pig'—from whose flesh men were made—it turns into a man. Mother compliments the yam-pig-man on his decorations as she passes by—Why? We are not told what decorations the yam-pig-man was wearing, but since he is later cut with a bamboo razor, and he has already been associated with pig, it is not going much beyond the evidence to suggest that mother was complimenting a young man who has been, or is about to be, circumcised; who has qualified to receive his pig of the circumcision; who is formally ready to play his part in the adult community. If so, then the implication surely is that the pig of the circumcision is not simply representative of father,[2] but of son as well, and therefore of the link between father and son: male filiation.

Though the children have already been separated from that part of the community which is fully engaged in reciprocities, when the parents do not supervise the children's preparations for the Juangam dance, a further and more explicit separation of children from parents takes place. Juangam is a harvest dance usually followed, towards the beginning of the dearth, by dance Manjaip; children normally participate in Juangam. Though in life parents normally take great care to see that their children

---

[1] Compare the description of Tangu cargo activities in B-1960: 1–2, where those 'possessed' or 'taken' by the divine were brought into the 'new community', or were brought back into the light as new men, by massaging the lips. On the significance of speech see *supra*, pp. 175–83.

[2] *Supra*, p. 170, and *infra*, pp. 397–8.

are properly dressed for Juangam, if a parent should take such supervision a little casually the child will remind him or her of this particular story. On a level of apprehension the gist or moral of the tale is clear. However, following their separation from the reciprocal the children are brought into association with the only other orders of being available: the divine and/or wild as represented in the yam-man. He takes their part. That which divides children from adults—association with the divine or non-reciprocal—and that which makes children into adults—the *garamb*, circumcision, and the pig of the circumcision (which includes male filiation)—are contained in the one refracted element: wild yam-pig-man.

Husband and wife consult together and decide to feast on the *warika*. And this, it would seem, is tantamount to eating one's own progeny. The *warika* has been associated with the children, and through the representation of circumcision surely contains the potential of the next generation. On a converging projection, no matter how long the parents cook the *warika*, it remains, as in life, hard, like a stone, indigestible and obdurate. Children are similarly wild and obdurate in relation to the quality of the moral community: they are not responsible, and can only be drawn into being responsible as stone is made into tools, and yams are cultivated in the garden. Following upon their attempt to eat the *warika* the parents are enclosed in a rock: they die, they have not nurtured their children as they should, their community dies. As in N. 1, however, the children are returned to the moral order of being. They scold their parents inside the rock and, presumably, restart community life elsewhere. If in N.2 the children in the rock are crying to be born, only two reach responsible being; and if the parents here are bewailing their careless self-concern, they are too old and too late. Culture belongs to those who, aware of the divine, can realize the meaning of circumcision and the *garamb*.

There is nothing untoward in (N. 2) a child getting up during the night to stool on a piece of firewood in the house, or in a man breaking sleep (N. 3) to urinate. But if the former indicates childishness, the latter entails a discovery. When a child is taken short at night he or she will either waken an elder sibling or parent to see him safely outside, or defecate quietly inside the house on a piece of firewood. To go outside the hut at night is to invite the attentions of a *ranguma*, so that a responsible guard is required. Stooling on a piece of firewood wakens nobody, and in the morning the dried stool may be thrown into the forest. Men, on the other hand, urinate outside the house. And when they do so they may see something strange or have a thought. In life a nocturnal urination always makes a good talking point: the strange or mysterious or odd is evoked from the start, it is the kind of occasion when a man is likely to think he has seen a *ranguma*. Then again, urination and defecation are wild or animal acts which, if they can be socialized, cannot always be put under control. Inevitably, therefore, when these acts are not under normal control they are associated with the non-moral aspect of being. At the same time, since urination and defecation are acts which have to be performed by moral beings, when they are not under control moral and divine are brought into significant relationship, and the strange or odd or troublesome or generative is predicated.

There is no happy ending to these narratives, nor is what humans may take to be virtue rewarded. Events occur. In whatever way one would prefer to regard the *puoker*, animals, and things of narrative, the narrative itself cannot but stand both inside and outside narrator or listener, inviting him to reflect on his own nature, his relations with others, and his and their places in the cosmos. Far from connoting static or absolute values, the contrapositions are relational: if all humans are moral in relation to the divine or wild, where adults—fully involved in reciprocities—are moral, in relation to them children—not involved in reciprocities—are divine or wild. Any Tangu situation, whether in life or in narrative, can evoke the relatively non-reciprocal in relation to the relatively reciprocal: this is the distinctive element in Tangu culture.

Thus far, let us say, the narratives have informed us that children are in danger of being taken by the divine, are likely to be lost to the moral community. But through the signals evoking circumcision and the *garamb* the narratives communicate something of the process by which children may be removed from their initial association with the divine and brought into a fuller association with the moral, the ambience of community reciprocities. And the same theme of drawing elements out of, or from, the divine or wild and bringing them into the moral is reiterated in other contexts. Stone may become 'cave' or 'shelter' or '*garamb*' or 'tool'. And because stone is the most durable material within the Tangu environment we are surely being told of the persistent and eternal: the significances of '*garamb*' and 'tool' to culture and community life: the relevances of orphans and kin relationships, of brother-and-sister mating and incest. We are also, if only implicitly, being told something about the convergence of moral and divine: as *puoker* brother and sister may mate; as humans they may not. But in becoming *mngwotngwotiki*, being as *puok* and being as human merge and form one. The wild yam becomes as pig, a wild animal which Tangu bring into the cultural community to express their reciprocities in relation to the non-reciprocal.[1] As pig the *warika* becomes man, and man was made from the flesh of a pig. As man the *warika* is circumcised, brought fully into the field of reciprocal action and made into a potentially responsible man. So that in itself the *warika* evokes the wild contraposed to culture, gardens, and cultivated yams; animal contraposed to man; the child or youth who is not yet responsible contraposed to the responsible man; the progress or movement from one condition to the other. Further, behaviour over the *warika* reveals a theme common to all three narratives: the difficulties attendant on the non-reciprocal relations between parents and children, and some of the occasions and qualities of the opposition between self-willedness and self-restraint characteristic of relationships of filiation.

How may wild stuffs be brought into the field of culture and be made into cultural stuffs? How may children develop and mature into responsible beings capable of maintaining culture? How may they be made aware of the reciprocities that order community life? How nurture the young into an awareness of their condition as moral beings? The conversation yields a variety of suggestions. In particular, it points to a generating initiative adhering to males; to the incest taboo between brother and sister; to circumcision and admission to the *garamb*; to the capacity for distinguishing between duty and impulse, moral

---

[1] Note (*supra*, p. 46) that all pigs originate in the wild.

and divine; to the necessity for establishing particular and appropriate relations between moral and divine. Seized of an awareness of these features, a thing like an animal may become man.

Elder and Younger Brother

Overtly concerned with the dialogue between Ambwerk and Tuman, elder brother and younger brother, the three narratives which follow add to our knowledge of the *garamb* and further illustrate the process of drawing the moral out of the divine.

N. 4: *Nuakai and the Sago Palm*

One day long ago as old grandmother Nuakai was sweeping the space under the floorboards of the house, grandson, who was playing close by, called to her: 'Oh grandmother, I'm hungry!' he cried. 'May I have some sago whey?'

Nuakai took a pinch of sago flour from her store, mixed it with water, and gave it to grandson.

Grandson swallowed the mite and returned to his play. But very soon he was back with an 'Oh grandmother, grandmother! I'm so hungry now—may I have something to eat?'

Nuakai gave him a little lump of dry sago. Then, with her sweeping completed, she went down to the stream with a load of empty barrels to draw water. On her return she fetched some firewood, made up a fire, and set a pot of water to boil. She waited until the pot was bubbling merrily. Then, putting the tiniest piece of sago flour into an eating bowl, she poured all the hot water on top.[1] Which done, she armed herself with a barkcloth mallet and seated herself on the platform under the porch of her house. 'Hey, there, grandson!' she shouted. 'Your whey is ready now—come and get it!'

Famished, grandson came running. But Nuakai was fooling him. As soon as the lad was close enough she jumped to her feet, cracked him across the eyes with her mallet, and, taking him into her ropy-strong arms, hurled him into an *awupa* thorn tree. There he stuck.

Now it happened that in a little while Ambwerk, grandson's elder brother, who had been out hunting, returned to the village with a pig, a wallaby, some bush-rats, and a bandicoot which he had taken. 'Where is Tuman?' he asked.

---

[1] Sago whey is made by adding hot or boiling water in small quantities to the dried sago flour and stirring hard.

'Here I am!' shouted Tuman. 'Here I am—in this *awupa* thorn where Nuakai threw me after hitting me with a barkcloth mallet!'

At once Ambwerk went off to rescue his brother. He eased Tuman out of the thorns, brought him to the ground, helped him on to the *pekas*. Together they cut the meat into strips, stuffed it into bamboo barrels,[1] cooked it, and ate well. 'Tomorrow', said Ambwerk, 'you and I will go down to the swamp to leach sago.'

Next morning, as the pair made ready, elder brother turned to Nuakai. 'You go to the garden, old grandmother', he told her. 'You go and dig out some yams while we two go and wash sago.'

When they arrived at the swamp the two brothers cut down a ripe palm. They split the bark from the trunk, and while Tuman pounded out the pith Ambwerk stood over the bath, washing the flour from the fibres and straining the dissolved flour into a basin.

Nuakai, meanwhile, had gone to the garden, dug out some yams, and returned to the village. She helped herself to some of the meat which had been left over from the night before, and put the yams in the embers to bake. Then, when the yams were nice and soft, she ate all the good ones herself, keeping only rotten ones for the brothers—even so, she split open those rotten yams with a bamboo razor, blew her nose, put the snottle into the yams, and closed them again. . . .

She called to the brothers, inviting them to come for a meal.

So the brothers returned to the village, took the yams which Nuakai gave them, and broke them open—'What's this?' they exclaimed as they examined the mucus inside. 'Ugh!'

Disgusted, the brothers threw away their yams and returned to the swamp to leach some more sago. But Tuman was fretful—'I'm hungry, I'm hungry!' he wailed.

Ambwerk suggested to Tuman that he should climb a *kura* tree near by, strip off the seed twigs, and eat the seeds.

Tuman climbed the *kura* tree, crawled out along a branch, collecting seeds as he went, and then—'A cuscus!' he cried excitedly, shaking the branch and throwing the animal to the ground.[2]

Nuakai bounded into the clearing. 'The head and the liver for me!' she cried.

'Certainly not!' Tuman retorted. 'You hit me yesterday—I'll deal with this myself!'

Tuman ate the *kura* seeds he had gathered, carved the cuscus, stuffed the meat into a bamboo barrel, and cooked it. He gave the

---

[1] Stuffing meat and/or tubers into a green bamboo barrel, stoppering the ends, and then steam-pressure-cooking the food by laying the barrel on an open fire, is a popular and traditional way of preparing food.

[2] The cuscus is a nocturnal marsupial which may be found dozing in a *kura* tree by day.

stomach and intestines to Nuakai. 'Here, grandmother!' he shouted. 'You can have these. Take them away and wash them in the river—don't wash them here!'

So soon as Nuakai had gone off to the river with the stomach and intestines, the two brothers packed their sago flour into palm-frond packets, filled their string bags with packets of sago and barrels of meat, and broke up the used sago trunk. Then, choosing a tall sago palm, they climbed into the bushy fronds at the top with all their supplies. They built themselves a shelter up there, making themselves comfortable.

Now after Nuakai had washed the stomach and intestines, she opened her mouth, swallowed them whole, and returned to the sago swamp to look for the brothers. She could find them nowhere. It started to rain.

Nuakai was furious. She stamped up and down the spoiled palm and ate up the fibres. Then, streaming wet, she took shelter under a palm, pressing herself close to the trunk, hugging it with her arms. But the rain came through, dripping on to her shoulders. So she went to another palm—the very one in which the brothers had built their shelter—and she found it nice and dry at the foot. The shelter above kept off the rain.

Ambwerk and Tuman split a barrel of meat and started to eat. Some drops of hot water spilled from the barrel and trickled on to Nuakai below. 'Oooh!' she cried, startled.

She tasted the liquid that had spilled on her, and, finding it was only water, decided she had been stung by an ant. Then more hot water splashed on her. And this time, looking up into the fronds of the palm, she saw the shelter the brothers had built. 'Oho!' she cried in threatening delight. 'So there you are!'

Nuakai decided to cut down the palm. First she tried with her little finger, then with the fourth finger, after that with the middle, the index, and lastly with her thumb.[1] No use. So she pressed herself close to the trunk and put her quim to the palm. No use. Hastening back to the village, then, Nuakai found an old axe and returned to the clearing, determined to cut down the palm. But as she laid to with the axe the brothers quietly moved out of their shelter and into another palm.

So it was that when at last the palm fell with a crash, search through the fronds as she might the old woman could not find the two brothers. Raging, she stamped on the tree in temper, rending it in pieces, then eating it—just like that, without first leaching out the flour!

[1] Compare N. 29, *infra*, p. 375.

When Nuakai had done with the palm she searched for the brothers again. And finding them, she started to hew at their refuge. She had almost cut her way through, and the palm was about to fall, when the brothers jumped into a *nuonga* tree!

This time Nuakai was so angry at not finding the brothers in the fronds that, before setting to work on the *nuonga*, she swallowed it whole—fronds, bark—everything.

But by now the brothers were desperate. There wasn't another tree close enough for them to jump into—only a tall *vinga* tree, far away over towards Barit. Still, they called out to that *vinga*—and lo! The *vinga* bent down over the forest towards them. 'Hold tight to me, now', the *vinga* cautioned the brothers. 'When the *nuonga* falls I will spring back like a bow.'

Nuakai's axe cut through the *nuonga*. And as it crashed to the ground the brothers hurtled over the forest towards Barit, clinging tightly to the boughs of the *vinga*. . . .

Nuakai searched through the litter of broken branches, stamped the *nuonga* to pieces in her rage, ate it, and returned to the village.

High up in the branches of the *vinga* the brothers ate sago, content.

After the brothers had been in the *vinga* five days, Ambwerk thought to return to the village to see how the land lay. 'You stay here,' he said to Tuman, 'and I'll signal you if all is right. Don't move until you hear me signal.'

With that, Ambwerk threw his basket to the ground, slid down the trunk, and set off for the village. Arrived, nothing seemed untoward. So at first light next day he signalled his brother on his slit-gong.

Hearing the signal, Tuman decided to return to the village on the morrow. He slept. At dawn he put his basket under his arm and started to climb down the *vinga*.

About half-way down, Tuman threw his basket to the ground and jumped—landing all of a heap on his buttocks, arms and legs flying. He was hurt—and worse! For when he tried to get up and walk, it was so painful that he had to crawl on all fours. Still, taking his basket with him, Tuman dragged himself through the forest until, weary and exhausted, he found himself close to Nuakai's garden. Then, unable to go any further, he took some bananas to eat and hid himself in a hollow *manyapa* tree.

Away out in the forest then a wasp was stinging Nuakai on the arm. She swatted it and ate it. 'Tomorrow', she said to herself, 'I'll go to my garden for some banana fronds. If I rub them on this sting they will soothe it.'

At dawn, then, Nuakai set out for her garden. She noticed that some of her bananas were missing. So, thinking it might have been a cuscus, she returned to the village for her dogs, Monbang, Cienengar, and Kwanraiap. Then, with her string bag over her shoulder and adze in hand, Nuakai set her dogs on the scent.

They made straight for the *manyapa* tree, barking and scuffling around the trunk.

First Nuakai sent in Monbang. Tuman, who was waiting, pierced him through the nose with the sharpened thigh bone of a wallaby. Monbang fell dead. Nuakai grasped his paws, pulled him clear, and sent in Cienengar. Tuman served him as he had Monbang. And when Nuakai had hauled Cienengar clear and sent in Kwanraiap, Tuman killed Kwanraiap too.

So it was that Nuakai, seeing her three dogs dead on the ground, decided to cut down the tree with her adze. Chipping and chopping she worked her way slowly to Tuman—until he could stand it no longer: 'It's only me up here!' he shouted to Nuakai. 'Don't chop any more—it's only me, I tell you!'

'Kill my dogs, would you?' shrilled Nuakai, laying to with vigour renewed. 'You just wait, my lad!'

Nuakai hewed and hewed until she split the *manyapa* tree from one end to the other. She hauled Tuman out of the wreckage by the scruff of his neck and, holding him underfoot, she filled her string bag with thorns, nettles, bees, ants, and wasps. 'Oh my poor little laddie!' she crooned. 'Oh my poor little laddie—how tired you must be after all those adventures!'

As she would a baby, Nuakai lifted Tuman by his wrists and his ankles, put him in her string bag, and, slinging him over her shoulders, set off for home.

'Oh! Oh! Oh!' Tuman wailed. 'I'm being stung and bitten and prickled all over!'

'There, there, little laddie!' Nuakai said soothingly. 'It's only my bony old hip bones my dear. . . .'

'Oh! Oh! Oh!' Tuman screamed.

'Hush there, my dearie!' Nuakai crooned as she walked. 'It's only your granny's old hip bones!'

When she got back to the village Nuakai dug a deep hole. She thrust Tuman into it, piled the earth on top, and dragged a large slit-gong over all. Then, spent with her efforts, she slept. Next day she went off to her garden.

But Ambwerk was worried. Tuman ought to have arrived by this time. He decided to signal again on the slit-gong. He pounded his call-sign. Then, in the silence which followed, he heard cries and scratchings and shufflings from under the gong. So, pulling the instrument aside, Ambwerk dug out the earth beneath.

Tuman came out.

Now Nuakai's husband and brothers had gone into the forest to clear a new garden site. So that when the old woman came back to the village after visiting her garden she was alone. Tuman surprised her. He smashed her across the chest with the dead Cienengar and killed her. Then he cut her into little pieces. He put a pot of water to boil, and he threw in some yams which Nuakai had already cleaned and made ready. He cut out Nuakai's old cunt, set it aside for her husband, and hung her intestines on a smelly *gemban* tree by the village latrine. 'Presently', Tuman said grimly, addressing the intestines, 'your husband will come home. He will come here to blow his stinking wind and empty his bowels. He will sniff your stench and he will shout that your old belly stinks!'

In a little while, then, husband and his brothers returned from the forest. 'Where is the wife?' he asked.

'She has gone to make turds', Tuman answered him, sharing out the meat and giving Nuakai's cunt and skirt to her husband.

Husband looked at the thing, very dubious, thinking how peculiar it was. He wondered if the brothers had killed his wife.

'Oh! Oh, my belly! Oh my belly is aching!' wailed Nuakai's intestines.

'Never mind that now!' husband replied. 'Come here and have something to eat!' Then he noticed the intestines hanging from the *gemban* tree. His mien became serious, brows drawn in thought. . . .

When husband had finished his meal, he and his brothers consulted together. They would have to deal with Ambwerk and Tuman. They sharpened their spears.

But Ambwerk and Tuman were too quick for them. First hiding themselves in the *garamb*, of a sudden the brothers burst out in wrath, laying about them furiously. Ambwerk killed only a few, choosing those whom he thought to be bad. But Tuman killed anyone he could lay hands on.

After the slaughter was over, the two brothers fetched out two bamboo barrels and went down to the stream to draw water so as to wash the corpses of those they had killed. Tuman, who had killed many, finished his barrel. But Ambwerk, who had killed but a few, had plenty left over. 'Look at this now', remarked Ambwerk. 'You have used up all your water, my brother. You must have killed lots. But I still have plenty of water left me. Why such a killing?'

'I was hit with a mallet across the eyes', Tuman replied. 'I was flung into a thorn tree. I fell from the *vinga* and hurt myself. I had to crawl through the forest. I was attacked by each of three dogs. I was forced from my refuge and stuffed into a string bag filled with ants, wasps, bees, nettles, and thorns. I was stung and I was pricked. A deep hole was dug and I was put into it. I was buried deep in the earth as though dead . . .'

N. 5: *Faeces and the Wild Yam*

Once upon a time two brothers were in the forest. Tuman noticed a little dark lump in the undergrowth. He thought it might be a turd. So he called to Ambwerk to come and examine it.

Elder brother, who had just stripped down some inner bark for making a breechclout, came over to have a close look. He picked up the little black lump, scraped it. 'Aha!' he exclaimed. 'This is not a turd—it is a wild yam, a *bu*!'

Ambwerk returned the *bu* to his brother. Tuman put it in his string bag. The two brothers set off through the forest for home.

Arrived back at the village, Ambwerk asked Tuman to hammer out the bark for his breechclout while he himself cooked the wild yam. Tuman agreed, gave the *bu* to Ambwerk, and started to pound away at the bark which his elder brother had brought home.

After a while Tuman felt hungry. 'Hey! Is that yam cooked yet?' he hailed.

'Not yet!' Ambwerk returned.

But he was lying. Not only had he already cooked the wild yam, but he had eaten the greater part, leaving only a tiny piece for his brother. And this little piece he wedged between the rafters and roof thatch of their house.

By and by Ambwerk called to Tuman to eat his share of the *bu*. Tuman fetched it down from the rafters, waxing indignant. 'This is too small!' he compained. 'You must get me a larger piece!'

Ambwerk fetched Tuman a small lizard. Tuman refused it. Next morning Ambwerk shot a bird and offered it to Tuman. Tuman refused it. Ambwerk shot more birds—large ones. Tuman refused them all. . . . Night fell and the brothers slept.

Next morning the brothers went hunting for pig, using a fire-surround. Tuman took the firebrand, running round in a wide circle, firing the *kunai* grass, while Ambwerk stood ready with a spear. The flames roared. . . .

In a few minutes a small pig came squealing through the gap in the ring of fire where Ambwerk was waiting. 'Will this satisfy you? Shall I spear it?'

'No!' Tuman returned. 'That pig is too small.'

Another pig came rushing through the gap. 'How about this one?' shouted Ambwerk.

'Not big enough!'

Ambwerk waited. Sure enough, in a little while a really large pig came snorting and grunting, making ready to charge. Ambwerk lunged, and his aim was true. Tuman was satisfied.

Strapping the pig to a large pole to carry it home, the two brothers set off through the forest, gathering edible leaves to eat with the pork. Then, deciding to return to the scene of the hunt, where they could eat their meat by themselves, they went back on their tracks. But the fire had gone out, and so had their slow-match.

'Look here', suggested Ambwerk. 'You guard the pig and I will go to the village and get a firebrand from Nuakai. You wait for me here.'

Tuman agreed.

'What do you want a firebrand for?' Nuakai asked suspiciously when Ambwerk made his request.

Ambwerk was evasive. 'I only want to cook some breadfruit out there in the forest . . .', he replied.

'Why not bring it here?' Nuakai suggested. 'You bring the breadfruit here to the village and we can cook it together.'

But cunning old Nuakai would not be persuaded. So Ambwerk had to tell her the truth. She was overjoyed. She praised the lad, flattering him. 'Oh you strong fellow, you handsome one!' she fawned. 'Here—take some of my fire. Bring me back some succulent meat, meat cut from the inside without any skin or bone to it!'

Ambwerk took the firebrand and made haste through the forest back to Tuman. He told his brother what had chanced with Nuakai, and then, while Tuman saw to the roasting of the pig, he collected a heap of bird droppings, pigs' dung, and men's turds. These, together with some prickly and hairy pig skin, he stuffed into a bamboo barrel.

When they had finished cooking the pig, the brothers feasted themselves, filling their bellies. Then, replete, they took the barrel of foulings to the village, tied it to a high branch, and called to old grandmother Nuakai. 'There you are, old grandmother!' they said. 'We'll leave your share of the meat here. But do not eat it at once. Let it stand for a while. We've got some work to do just now, but when we come back we can eat it together.'

No sooner had the brothers disappeared into the forest, however, than Nuakai had leaped up, snatched at the barrel, and brought it down. Greedily she cracked it open and peeled back the strips of bamboo. The dung fell in a heap to the ground.

Nuakai fetched a bamboo sliver from her hut and started to pick over the turds, looking for a scrap of meat. There was nothing, only foulings.

Nuakai was furious. She armed herself with a stick and sat by her house, waiting for the brothers to return to the village.

Now when the brothers came back they saw that Nuakai was wait-ing for them, and they saw her face, angry and vengeful. They de-cided to hide.

Ambwerk crept into the heap of turds, while Tuman, entering into a land crab, scuttled as fast as he could for a hole.

But Nuakai was too quick for him. She saw him across the *pekas* and bounded to him in a trice, transfixing him with her bamboo sliver before he could reach the hole.

'Let be! Let be!' screamed Tuman in fear. 'Don't kill me! Don't kill me!'

Nuakai would not be persuaded. She sliced the crab into pieces, threw the bits into a pot of boiling water, and went off to her garden to fetch some taros.

Ambwerk, tiring of his hiding-place in the dung heap, came out to see what had happened to Tuman. And, finding him in slices, cooking, he decided to rescue him. First, he collected all the pieces of crab. Then he joined all the pieces together, chewed areca-nut over them, and spat the juice over the pieces and joints. . . .

So was Tuman made whole again.

Ambwerk gave Tuman a spear. While elder brother beat the ground with a bamboo sliver, Tuman raged up and down the dancing-space, waving his spear, yelling he would skewer Nuakai when she came back from the gardens.

They waited in the *garamb*.

When Nuakai returned to the village she went straight to her cooking pot to see how her meat was doing. 'Oh my meat!' she wailed when she saw that her pieces of crab had gone. 'What has happened to my meat?'

Hearing her keening in this way, the brothers rushed from the *garamb* and thrust their spears into the old woman, killing her.

They buried Nuakai, and then they chased the old hag's daughter. She escaped by turning herself into a rat and running down the kingpost of her house into the earth. . . .

That is the end.

N. 6: *Nimbamung*

Once upon a time there was a blind man called Nimbamung who lived alone with his dog. One evening, as he was thinking of collect-ing some tree grubs on the morrow, he hafted a stone axe-blade, not taking to his pallet until he was satisfied with the balance.

Next morning, taking bow and arrows and the newly hafted axe, he set off into the forest to look for tree grubs, his dog showing him the way. They found a right good tree where tree grubs should be and, ripping away the bark with his axe, Nimbamung started to flick the grubs into the bamboo barrel he had brought with him.

Now Ambwerk happened to be close by at the time. He heard the old fellow at his work and he thought he would see what was happening. So, creeping through the undergrowth, he hid himself at the edge of the clearing. Who was this man? he wondered. Why was he behaving so strangely?

Ambwerk waited for a while, watching closely. Suddenly he understood. The fellow must be blind!

Stepping carefully so as not to make a noise, Ambwerk eased his way through the clearing and started to scuffle Nimbamung's grubs into a barrel of his own. . . .

'Out of my way! Leave my grubs alone!' Nimbamung scolded, thinking his dog was stealing the grubs.

Ambwerk stayed with Nimbamung the whole day long, filling his barrels with the grubs which Nimbamung and his dog had found. Afterwards, he followed Nimbamung to his home.

The fellow took a strange trail, eventually stopping in front of a *wamunga* shrub. Creeping close, Ambwerk waited to see what would happen.

Nimbamung blew his spittle over the bush and uttered a spell: the leaves of the *wamunga* shrub parted to reveal an open door leading into a hole in the ground.

Ambwerk memorized the spell. Then, as the dog led the way down, Ambwerk followed close behind, leaving Nimbamung to bring up the rear and shut the shrubbery door.

Down inside the hole, Ambwerk saw they had come on a beautiful *mwenk*. Coconuts a-plenty grew around the perimeter, arecanuts hung in thick clusters, the bananas were bending with fruit. Ambwerk started to help himself. And Nimbamung, hearing the sounds of eating and thinking again that it was his dog, scolded the animal, shouting to it to stop.

Inside Nimbamung's house quantities of meat hung from the rafters, and a large heap of yams was piled on the floorboards. Ambwerk set to on the meat.

Nimbamung took a small yam, scraped it clean, cut it into small pieces and put them into his stew-pot. Ambwerk followed suit—with a large yam, a hunk of wallaby meat, and some saltwood. He took a coconut, scraped out the meat and mixed the latter with coconut milk. Ambwerk did himself proud, eating hugely, very quickly, while Nimbamung, eating slowly, cursed the dog which he thought was eating all his food.

They slept.

Next morning, Nimbamung rose early to go hunting. Ambwerk slept on. When he awoke he gorged himself on all the good food that was there, collected as much as he could carry and, remembering the spell, opened the shrubbery door and set off for home.

Arrived back at his village, Ambwerk showed his younger brother all the food he had stolen, hanging his spoils from the rafters.

'Where did you get all that food?' asked Tuman.

Ambwerk told Tuman all about Nimbamung, that he was blind, what a lot of food he had, and how easy it was to rob him. Tuman was excited. 'I'll go along tomorrow!' he exclaimed. 'I'll go and collect as much as I can and bring it back here!'

But Ambwerk had not finished. 'Mind now', he cautioned. 'When the old fellow opens the door you must get in after the dog and before he does—he shuts the door behind him. When you get into his *mwenk*, eat as much as you like—but leave his dog alone. Let the dog eat as much as it wants.'

Next morning, Tuman went off into the forest to look for Nimbamung. He found him where Ambwerk had said he would be, and he did as Ambwerk had told him to do. He filled his own barrels with grubs while Nimbamung, cursing his dog, shovelled pith and rotting bark into his own. He followed the old man to the *wamunga* shrub, crept close as the fellow blew his spittle over the shrub and uttered the spell, then darted in ahead of him, following the dog down into the *mwenk*.

There it was, just as Ambwerk had told him. He picked some bananas.

'Stop eating my food!' Nimbamung shouted crossly. 'Get out of it, there!' Still he thought it was his dog. Grumbling and scolding, he put a pot on the fire, sliced a small yam, and threw the pieces into the pot.

Tuman followed suit with a large yam, some saltwood, and grubs. The water bubbled merrily, the food was cooked, and Tuman ate fast and furiously while Nimbamung, groping blindly, eating little, muttered and swore at his dog.

Then, as often may happen, Nimbamung's dog nosed its way into Tuman's food. He hit it on the snout. The dog yelped.

'What's that?' Nimbamung roared. 'Who hit my dog?' he raged, rising to his feet and taking down his adze. 'Who is in here eating my food?'

Tuman fled to the back of the hut and hid himself behind a pile of water barrels. And Nimbamung, stumbling blindly, thrusting and swinging his adze, crashed against the pile of barrels as he brought the weapon down in a wild overhand stroke. . . .

Tuman could do nothing. The blade struck him between the eyes and he fell lifeless to the floor.

Nimbamung carved the corpse, cooked the flesh, and ate it. Head and bones he hung under the porch of his house.

After five days of waiting, Ambwerk knew that something had gone awry with his brother. So, taking his bow and arrows, he went to the *wamunga* shrub, blew his spittle over it, and uttered the spell. The door opened and he went down into Nimbamung's *mwenk*. He saw the bones hanging in the porch, he recognized the head.

Ambwerk returned to his village at once. He selected a large pig and placed it on the *pekas* in front of his house. Then he fetched bunches of areca-nuts and placed them beside the pig. All the men of the village gathered round to hear what was afoot.

Ambwerk told them about Nimbamung and what had happened to Tuman. Something would have to be done.

Next day, then, the villagers shouldered their spears and set off for Nimbamung's home. Ambwerk uttered the spell and blew his spittle over the *wamunga* shrub. The door opened and the party trooped down to the *mwenk*.

Ambwerk was first with his spear, thrusting it deep into Nimbamung's side. Then each of the others followed Ambwerk's example, turn by turn, until all had had a share in the killing. They killed Nimbamung's dog too, packed all the meat and foodstuffs they could carry into string bags, and then piled faggots around the outside of Nimbamung's house.

When the pyre was ready, they placed Nimbamung and his dog on the top and set it alight. They waited there until house, man, and dog had been entirely consumed, burnt in the flames. Then they returned to their village.

Structured within the terms of a dialogue between Ambwerk and Tuman, mediated either by Nuakai or Nimbamung, each of the narratives above could be said to be concerned with either or both of two purposes: (i) providing a logical model capable of overcoming the inconsistencies between the moral and divine, reciprocity and non-reciprocity, siblingship and filiation, and self-restraint and self-willedness; (ii) demonstrating the vicissitudes attendant on establishing proper but progressive and developing relations between the predicates of the same sets of terms. The two tasks converge, but are not quite the same. Still, as we shall see, in doing the one the other is also accomplished.

Ambwerk appears as the reasonable, competent, and responsible man. Not by any means perfect, he is still the 'man in community', foil to Tuman who is only becoming a man, who may be childish, silly, demanding, or wilful. Both Nuakai and Nimbamung are old. If they carry the affirmations of their sexes, they are essentially sexually neutral. The one is past childbearing; the other is not, and is in any case past being, a husband in any sexual sense. In life, old grandmothers may scold, be greedy or cunning. But, generally helpful and of value to a household, they do not normally behave in the ways depicted in the narratives above. A blind man in Tangu might be able to survive in a context of family: but alone—albeit with a dog—in the midst of plenty is fantasy. So that, though all the characters in narratives are *puoker*, it may be taken that Nuakai and Nimbamung represent particularly relevant hinges of meaning. They and what they represent cannot but inform social life. Like storm, stream, thought, the Great One, and the yam-pig-rock-man, Nuakai and Nimbamung represent and reveal kinds of awareness. They provide the paired contrapositions with context and content.

With N. 4 and N. 5 the *garamb* is encountered directly. Never far away in a traditional Tangu narrative, the *garamb* and its associated activities and ideas also informs N. 6. Indeed, if we knew more about the *garamb* from direct observation, and if we knew more accurately how in fact it was regarded before it disappeared, we should be in a better position to comprehend the narratives. Still, we do know something about the *garamb*, and the narratives themselves will tell us much more. We know that a boy went into the *garamb* to become a man; that he was separated from nubile women; that he was beaten with nettles, prickles, and thorns; that he was circumcised by a mother's brother using a bamboo razor; that the severed foreskin was thrown into a clump of bananas; that after circumcision or while he was in the *garamb* a boy made and donned his first breechclout. If the key to the understanding of N. 4 and N. 5 lies in their endings, in Ambwerk and Tuman bursting from the *garamb*, the themes of theft and blindness in N. 6 set the context for the youth who cannot learn discretion, who fails to make the passage through the *garamb*, who cannot learn to distinguish his parts.

The opening scene of N. 4 discovers grandson, Tuman, as a baby; and as a baby he whines for food. In life grandmother would certainly accede to his demands. But she is not a real grandmother, she is a *puok*. She tricks the boy rather nastily, hits him over the eyes with a mallet, and throws him into a thorn tree. We have already come across a reference to eyes, to 'eyes being opened to community':[1] and Tuman in N. 6 was killed by being struck between the eyes with an adze. There will be many more instances, and each seems to be a refraction of the first. Here in N. 4 barkcloth mallet and thorn tree evoke the *garamb*: a boy made his first breechclout in the *garamb*, there he was beaten with thorns. Tuman is ready for, or about to go into, the *garamb*. Beating the boy over the eyes with the mallet surely suggests that a growing child should cease seeing life with the eyes of a child, and should on the contrary begin to see life through the eyes of an adult—demonstrate sense of shame, restraint, responsibility. And throwing him into the thorn tree evokes that which will make the boy into a man: circumcision.[2] Nuakai makes herself unpleasant again with another contemptuous reference to childishness: the mucus in the yams reminds one of the runny noses of Tangu children.

Nuakai's behaviour also carries the suggestion of disdain for males as a class. The fouled yams are given to Ambwerk as well as Tuman, and the former is, or is as, a responsible man. He has been out hunting and returned with meat;[3] he has rescued Tuman from the thorn tree; he teaches Tuman how to leach sago. He is Tuman's tutor and guardian. Together Ambwerk and Tuman connote a line of male filiation, in opposition to Nuakai the female. Through the idea of the female—divine or wild in relation to a male, who is moral—the dialogue between the responsible man and the unrestrained child who is not yet subject to reciprocities, and who is, therefore, more closely associated with the divine or wild, femaleness, becomes the more intelligible. For if he is to become responsible Tuman must rid himself of the female in himself. Protagonist and antagonist are really male and female, or male and hypostatic female—which latter is figured in Nuakai.

---

[1] *Supra*, p. 206.

[2] Both before and after circumcision boys were beaten with thorns (*supra*, p. 173).

[3] Hunting is a male occupation, and successful hunting—getting meat—qualifies a man for sexual intercourse and being husband (*infra*, pp. 260, 263).

PLATE V

a. Placing joists for the floor of a new house

b. Putting on roof thatch: the man in the foreground with strips of cane

In the vernacular the separate processes of leaching sago are itemized: the cutting of the palm, the pounding of the pith, washing the fibres, straining out the dissolved flour, evaporating the solution. And together with the lesson on how to leach sago is a wrinkle on the cuscus. For this animal eats *kura* seeds and may often be found dozing in the branches of a *kura* tree, from whence it may be dislodged and dispatched. With the killing of the cuscus, demonstrating the successful hunter,[1] Tuman seems to be growing up. He makes up his own mind on the division of meat. No longer the whining and puling infant, he asserts himself, rejects belly and intestines and gives them to Nuakai. Towards the end of the narrative, belly, intestines, and Nuakai are again brought together; the same word, *mwerz*, is used for stomach, belly, and womb; intestines are often associated with the afterbirth. Since stomach and intestines signal the female,[2] the indication here surely is that Tuman is not only giving Nuakai that which pertains to her, but he is rejecting childishness, dependence on women, his own close association with women. Further, as becomes more evident later in the narrative, in freeing himself from association with women Tuman is also engaged in overcoming the hypostatic female, the femaleness in himself. When the brothers build a shelter in the fronds of the sago palm, a proper manhood is envisaged. Tuman is gathering semen, must fling clear of womanliness, mature, make the passage of the *garamb*, and become a man. For shelter evokes the *garamb*, and so the meaning of the *garamb*, protection from the storm, the divine and unobliged; sago fronds are used as roof thatch, and roof thatch evokes the *garamb* and shelter;[3] the woods of the *vinga* and *nuonga* trees were used in the construction of the main frame of the *garamb*;[4] trees and trunks of trees are usually associated with competent maleness.[5] The barkcloth mallet, wielded by Nuakai, is a male tool used for making a breechclout, the male garment worn after circumcision.

[1] See p. 230, n. 3, above.
[2] Women were made from the stomach and intestines of a pig (*supra*, p. 179, and *infra*, p. 385).
[3] For the associations of roof thatch see *infra*, pp. 366–7.
[4] And now used in the construction of ordinary dwelling-houses. In the past, it will be remembered (*supra*, p. 4), most dwelling-houses were built down to the earth on hardened ground, whilst the *garamb* was larger and built on stilts.
[5] *Infra*, p. 283.

Then—again the allusion to gathering semen—it starts to rain. Nuakai seeks shelter. . . . When the brothers spill hot water on her she thinks she has been bitten by an ant. Later on in the story she is stung by a wasp, and Tuman is put into a string bag together with stinging animals and plants: again, surely, circumcision, the *garamb*, and the meaning of the *garamb*. Yet because of their apparent carelessness Nuakai discovers the whereabouts of the brothers. She tries to cut down the palm, and so have at them, first with fingers and thumb, then with her vulva. Children suck their thumbs, using them as teats or dummies; a woman will often insert a finger into a child's mouth to comfort him when giving him the breast is inopportune. The evocation is with breast nipples and so with the milk which nourishes a child, causes it to grow. Further, as we shall see,[1] finger (thumb), nipple, and penis are also interassociated. Add to this semen-as-rain, and we become aware not only of growth, but of the correspondence between different kinds of growth at different stages in the life cycle. If much might be extrapolated from Nuakai's action with her vulva, it indicates an end point in the maturation process, sexual intercourse—tree and vulva—whilst also evoking a general notion of circumcision, *vagina dentata*, combined with the escape from womanliness and overcoming the hypostatic female through the *garamb*. For succour is at hand: maleness in the shape of a *vinga* tree, itself evoking the *garamb*, erects and extends itself to carry both brothers to safety—but only after they have stayed awhile in the *nuonga*, a thorn tree, and only after the *vinga* has associated itself with bow and arrow, an indicator, as we shall see more abundantly,[2] of the male coming to sexual maturity, of the boy learning to be a man.

Ambwerk has no difficulty in leaving the *vinga*, the *garamb*, after a period of five days—perhaps five days was the interval between circumcision and an effective healing of the wound. . . . And, arrived at the village, Ambwerk signals Tuman that it is safe to come out. But Tuman is not quite ready. He is still not quite a man. The careless ass jumps down after his basket and hurts himself. But it is his loin-parts which are damaged, and he crawls through the forest as he might have done had he just been circumcised. He comes at length to Nuakai's bananas.

---

[1] *Infra*, p. 389.   [2] *Infra*, p. 324.

Now Nuakai's bananas are not only where Tuman's severed foreskin might be,[1] but banana fibres are used to make a woman's underskirt. Poor Tuman, weary and exhausted, might well wish that he did not have to become a man, that he might be a child again, safe with his mother, with women! And his wish or feelings or impulses are realized. For bananas, the juice from whose fronds is used as a salve for bee or wasp stings, lead straight back to Nuakai, the devouring female who has, it will be remembered, eaten sago palms and *nuonga* tree trunk, pith, branches, and all. Though Tuman, from his refuge in the *manyapa* tree,[2] manages to kill Nuakai's three dogs—if it exhibits a certain manly skill, in the past a wallaby bone was a child's weapon, adults using a heavier implement of cassowary bone— Nuakai inevitably gets him in the end. But to chop down the tree she uses an adze, the tool or weapon associated with the mother's brother, the customary circumcisor, the male on the mother's side, the female-man-or-father. All of which seems appropriate, because Nuakai herself, a woman past childbearing, a mannish female, represents in this context very much the same elements as a mother's brother does. When Nuakai takes hold of the lad she treats him both as a woman would a baby, and as a mother's brother would a sister's son in the *garamb*. She picks him up as babes are picked up, by the wrists and ankles; she puts him into a string bag as babes are put into string-bag cradles; as a baby she carries him home to the village. She is as mother. But in the string bag, instead of a soft pad of leaves and barkcloth, there are nettles, thorns, wasps, ants. . . . She gives Tuman the same sort of treatment as a mother's brother metes out to a sister's son in the *garamb*.

Back at the village childhood is finally put away, buried under a slit-gong.[3] If association with a slit-gong indicates responsible manhood,[4] when Tuman is rescued by Ambwerk, his childhood dead, he is a man ready to deal with the female or females with

---

[1] *Supra*, p. 173.

[2] There seem to be no explicit associations with the *manyapa* tree except that the first two syllables are *manya-* or *mainya-*, 'woman'.

[3] Compare the burial of the 'child Tuman' under a slit-gong with the fragmentary reference (*supra*, p. 182) that in order to initiate a slit-gong into the moral order a child might have to die or be killed.

[4] See *supra*, pp. 182–3, regarding the way a slit-gong 'speaks' responsibly for a man, and *infra*, pp. 280–1.

decision. He kills Nuakai by smashing her across the chest with a dog: dogs are hunting animals, associated with men, and Tuman has finished with breasts. He carves Nuakai, giving vulva and skirt to the husband—who is only now introduced, and to whom alone both rightfully belong. Only a husband has an acknowledged access to the vulva; and the giving of the skirt surely emphasizes that only as a husband does a man have sexual claims over a woman. But if Tuman is as a man he is not yet a husband. The lad then places Nuakai's stomach and intestines—representing the female—on a *gemban* tree, a tree which exudes a pungent odour and which is also associated both with a woman in her period and with a latrine or place of defecation: hence the gusty reference to the husband easing himself. Stomach and intestines speak to husband, complaining. Now whether hunger, pain, or desire are implied, husband's reaction takes the mind to the closely associated notions that a husband has the task not only of supplying his wife with meat and tubers, but of feeding through his penis the babe which lies in the womb:[1] an obligation to the wife that goes together with the claims to sexual rights over her and the assuagement of sexual appetites in her. Upon seeing skirt and vulva, and so realizing what has happened to wife, husband consults with his brothers on the action to be taken. They sharpen their spears. Yet if husband has responsibilities and reciprocities to nurture, so now has Tuman. He is becoming a man. Forestalling the husband and his brothers, but together with his own elder brother, he bursts from the *garamb* to make up for every injury done to him. It is the *garamb* which has made him a man, the *garamb* which is the source of his manhood. In contrast to Ambwerk, however, he clearly goes too far. He has something of the *ranguma* in him, he is still divine in relation to Ambwerk who is moral, more responsible.

N. 5 provides a slighter and more oblique comment on the passage from childhood to manhood, on the ambience of aware-ness in which, in Tangu, it was possible to participate. Like many a child, Tuman is interested in turds: and from time to time during the course of the narrative the mention of faeces brings the listener back to this point of departure. As in N. 4, divine to Ambwerk's moral, Tuman appears over-demanding.

[1] See *infra*, pp. 375, 389, and *supra*, p. 84.

The wild yam known as *bu* is the size of a plum. On the other hand, placing the *bu* in the rafters evokes the *garamb*,[1] the references to bamboo slivers—one of which is used to slice Tuman—evoke circumcision, and at the end of the narrative Tuman rushes out of the *garamb*. The *bu* is a wild thing, unconstrained. Like Tuman, it is or should be brought into community and socialized, brought from the wild into the moral, cooked. Placing the *bu* in the rafters evokes the *garamb*, where Tuman ought to go. Tuman it is who actually works on the breechclout. And it seems likely that the large pig which Tuman insists that Ambwerk should kill for him is the pig of the circumcision, the pig that is his due after having been circumcised in the *garamb*. In life small lizards and birds are food for small children: clearly Tuman reckons he has finished with that. He is maturing and wants his pig. And in the description of his obtaining it the listener is told of the fire-surround technique for hunting pig in grassland, and implicitly warned about keeping a firestick or slow-match alight. Nuakai is rejected from the start. Until she chases Tuman-as-crab and succeeds in cutting him with a bamboo razor, so playing the part of the mother's brother in the *garamb*, she is the hypostatic female. She is associated with childhood, with faeces;[2] in life it is mother, grandmother, or sister who cleans up a child's foulings, never a man. That Nuakai gets faeces, not pork—which is for men—emphasizes her rejection both by men and by boys who are becoming men. For although it is through Nuakai and the loan of her firebrand that Ambwerk and Tuman are enabled to cook their pig and have their pig, as the female she is cunning and unobliged, wilful. She must be outwitted, neutralized, or eliminated: the qualities she represents should not form a part of the being of the responsible man, even though, in other contexts, other refractions of her nature are essential to the making of a mature and responsible man.[3]

The association of Ambwerk with faeces is perhaps more ambiguous than it need be. He is not, as a child might be, directly interested or fascinated by faeces: he simply makes use of them to hide from Nuakai. He also, quite deliberately,

---

[1] See *infra*, pp. 366–7.
[2] Compare *supra*, p. 86, on a father's fears of being fouled by his child.
[3] See, for example, *infra*, pp. 245, 251–2.

collected them together. On the whole the suggestion seems to be that as a responsible man Ambwerk may not only deal with faeces purposively without coming to any harm, but also that he may use them to gain a point. For, as is made clear in N. 6, a mature and responsible man may undertake in safety those tasks and activities which are dangerous for a boy or un-circumcised youth. When Tuman-as-crab is caught by Nuakai —in this instance again acting as or representing mother's brother—he pleads for mercy. But he is cut, circumcised, all the same. As soon as Nuakai as mother's brother, and Nuakai as herself, are out of the way, Ambwerk rescues Tuman, cures and makes him whole again with areca-nut juice. Areca-nut juice is thought to have curative and creative properties.[1] It is frequent-ly used in the treatment of cuts and abrasions today; it was probably used on circumcision wounds in the past. While Tangu would say, first, that areca-nut juice was curative and creative because the narrative implies that it is, they might add that since areca-nut juice is efficacious the narrative is true or contains truth.

Nuakai is finally disposed of by the brothers who, coming out of the *garamb*, spear her. Boys and growing youths have bows and arrows; spears are the weapons of responsible men. Tuman has grown into a man. And this he has done by eliminating from himself those aspects of the female which would prevent him becoming a man. His experience of the *garamb* has made him into a proper man. While the mention of Nuakai's daughter turning into a rat and running down the kingpost of a house into the earth is a reference to *niemur*, in the field situation the incident seemed to have been added as an afterthought. The suggestion is that only women or females became *niemur*: a final re-emphasis of the difference between the nature of being ap-propriate to a man, and the nature or mode of being associated with women.[2]

N. 6 reveals other aspects of the process of becoming a man. Tuman does not stay the full course. And the themes of the context in which he meets his death are, overtly, blindness and theft. Nimbamung is blind, his home is underground, he kills

[1] See also *infra*, pp. 247–8.
[2] While the question must remain open (*supra*, p. 178), the same suggestion occurs in other narratives.

Tuman with an adze. And in Nimbamung's home there is plenty of food to be had without working for it. If, as seems probable, the correct association here is that of incubation and safety in the womb,[1] then the association of Nimbamung with mother's brother—in virtue of his adze[2]—tells us something about the nature of the *garamb*: it represented a 'male womb' in which boys matured and from which they were reborn as men.[3] Given this, the burden of the narrative becomes clearer: to become a man a boy must make the passage of the *garamb*, he must not succumb to Nimbamung. And whatever principle of being Nimbamung may represent, though blind—and so possessed of insight?—he does not make exceptions for ignorance or carelessness. His nature, the ways in which he operates, should be known—features which Ambwerk takes care to emphasize. Tuman cannot escape Nimbamung by continuing in childishness and irresponsibility.

Nimbamung gathers tree grubs—generally thought by Tangu to be blind, without eyes;[4] and Tuman is killed by a blow between the eyes. Irony, yes. But also a reference to Tuman's obtuseness, to his inability to see and appreciate with the eyes of an adult,[5] to his stupid lack of restraint in relation to the dog after he had been warned not to strike it. Nor is it any accident, surely, that before he is killed Tuman tries to take refuge behind a stack of water barrels—which are made from bamboo. Yet if Tuman fails to make the passage into manhood because of his unawareness of Nimbamung, Ambwerk, a responsible man, is also a sober and successful thief who is careful, takes pains, and has regard for the habits and nature of Nimbamung and his dog. When Ambwerk steals, he steals from 'under a man's eyes';[6] and he who is stolen from is blind, or as though blind. But even a blind man cannot ignore a carelessness when it is brought to his notice, more especially when that carelessness is also an injury to himself. Tuman has been told quite specifically by Ambwerk what to do and what not to do. A dog pertains

---

[1] Men and women first emerged on the earth through a hole from underground (*supra*, p. 133, and also *infra*, pp. 325, 355).

[2] *Supra*, p. 89, n. 1.

[3] If the association seems tenuous in this particular context, further acquaintance with the narratives (*infra*, pp. 329–31) will confirm that this is a proper judgement.

[4] No eyes are visible.   [5] *Supra*, p. 212.

[6] *Supra*, p. 129.

to a man, to the responsible hunter who knows how to care for and treat his dog. Tuman does not know how to treat a dog, he is not responsible, he is not aware of himself in relation to Nimbamung. Nor can he avoid his fate by simply ignoring instructions, by attempting to take refuge in continuing childishness. He should grow up, become aware.

When Tuman does not return to the village, Ambwerk, responsible for him, sets off in search. But, be it noted, he has waited five days, a period which, it has been suggested, possibly represents the time it took for the circumcision wound to heal.[1] Moreover, cutting back, it will be remembered that when Ambwerk returned to the village with his spoils he hung them from the rafters of his house: the *garamb* evoked. Ambwerk goes to the *wamunga* bush (upon whose leaves, in life, tree grubs are served), utters the spell (which is efficacious of itself, whoever uses it), and goes down into Nimbamung's *mwenk*. There he recognizes the skull or head of his brother.[2] The *wamunga* bush is, however, a 'door'; and a 'door', as in N. 2 when the two lads came out of the stone into daylight, divides one kind of being from another. When Ambwerk sets off to look for Tuman he arms himself with bow and arrows. He is, as it were, backtracking, re-entering his childhood, which was the womb of his manhood. Ambwerk seems to be searching into the wild or impulsive or instinctual. Yet for a man who has already made the passage of the *garamb*, and who has become responsible, the dangers of so doing may be overcome. Ambwerk knows the way back. He can re-enter his childhood or youth, his wild or impulsive being, because he knows what his childhood was about. And he proves his awareness of others in community by not undertaking his vengeance alone. He comes back to the village, places a pig and a bunch of areca-nuts on the *pekas*, and not until after he has consulted with the others and gained their sanction and approval does he mount his expedition. The company take spears, pertaining to men and responsibility, and Nimbamung is killed not by Ambwerk alone but by all in turn.[3]

---

[1] *Supra*, p. 232. By 'heal', of course, one means that the blood has clotted and that the wound is no longer as excruciatingly uncomfortable as it was.

[2] So far as it can be ascertained, the hanging of skull and bones in the porch of a hut was never a Tangu usage. But it is a practice in other parts of New Guinea (see N. 30, *infra*, p. 400).

[3] See also N. 28, *infra*, p. 357.

Then Nimbamung and all that belongs to him is burned. Fire is used for cooking, for socializing food; and fire it is which, burning the wild litter off a garden site, readies the plots for planting and cultivation. Whatever the meaning of Nimbamung, it is underground and covert or impulsive with a fruitful relevance when socialized and brought into awareness. By implication, successful passage of the *garamb* brings the meaning of Nimbamung into an appropriate field of awareness.

Nuakai figures the hypostatic female, the bitch:[1] she is also the mannish woman in whom the female man, the man on the female side, the mother's brother, is figured. Nimbamung is blind, the opposite of being aware and able to see and appreciate with the eyes of a responsible man. As a *ranguma* is wilful, may kill, and may have more insight than others, so Nimbamung is unrestrained, the killer of Tuman and, perhaps, representative of insight. When Tangu confess to an old man they confess to one who is removed from the focal interplay of reciprocities, who is as though blind, for whom reciprocities are no longer related to ambition, desire, material interests.[2] As life in community must be regulated, ruled by defined expectations —and the placement of pig and areca-nuts on the *pekas* as well as the consultation and teamwork in the killing are good examples of such—so, it would seem, the responsible members of community should kill or exclude the blind, the unforeseeable, the irresponsible. They should be aware—of the moralities on the one hand, and of particular interests on the other.

If we cast back to the beginning of the narrative we might have guessed that, by taking up bow and arrows, Nimbamung was going to behave in a unrestrained way. Apart from the oddity of being blind, Nimbamung is, from the start, signalled as wilful as an uncircumcised boy. He does not have the eyes of a responsible man: which makes him like a *ranguma*. Conversely, an uncircumcised youth might be as *ranguma*-like, odd, blind, and unrestrained as Nimbamung. A *ranguma* is a man, most of the a-social aspects of man converge in the *ranguma*; so that one who is more a-social than another is like a

---

[1] Those who have observed, or who know much about, the mating habits of dogs and bitches will know what Englishmen mean by 'bitch' and, therefore, something of the content of meaning in hypostatic female.

[2] *Supra*, p. 140.

ranguma in relation to that other. Not only was Tuman killed because he was careless in his encounter with Nimbamung, and because he ignored the rules which Ambwerk was trying to teach him, but because Tuman, in the nature of his being as it is revealed in the narrative, belongs in the same category with Nimbamung in relation to the responsible or more responsible. Both die, both are killed. The one by the divine, or wild, which is self-willed, blind, unable to see with the eyes of morality; the other by members of community who could see and who are responsible for maintaining the moralities. Finally, Ambwerk, who was a responsible man, could, with care, engage the divine or wild and increase his awareness of the whole. Tuman, not yet responsible and not yet aware, could not.

Let us epitomize Nimbamung as that which becomes perceptiveness in one who is aware, and rashness in one who is not.

In each of the narratives considered, as indeed in those that follow, events follow fast on each other, indicate flux or change. Flux or change in what? Primarily, one would answer, in the condition of man as he grows in awareness. Further, once it is appreciated that the events of narrative indicate principles of being, it becomes evident that the tales are communicating an awareness of those eternal or abiding principles which govern the growth and development of man. Endings inhere in beginnings. If all the events of a narrative could be communicated in the same instant of time, as perhaps in a picture, then the tale might be more efficient than it is. Hence the value of knowing a narrative, of telling it over and over again.

Men and Women

Since children cannot be as involved in reciprocities as adults, it follows that they will be more closely associated with the divine or wild than with the moral. Babies are bundles of instinct and impulse, children are fickle and subject to impulse: the divine is apt to intervene on their behalf, they are in an intimate association with the divine. If children are to become adult members of community, impulse and instinct must be brought under control: they must be removed from the divine and brought into the ambience of the moral. Either a growing boy makes the passage through circumcision and the *garamb* and, reborn as an adult, is firmly set on the path to responsible manhood, or he fails, is lost to community and taken by the divine. Learning to see through the eyes of an adult, the growing boy should become aware of himself and others, should recognize the distinction between moral and divine, should temper self-will with restraint, should loose himself from his childish association with women, should overcome Nuakai. And Nuakai is wanton, the wantonness typical of the female: this wantonness, both in himself and in others, a youth must learn to master. Whether children are divine because of their necessary association with women, or vice versa, is a false problem: their intimate interaction with each other, and the quality of caprice they have in common, classes them together in relation to the responsible man, husband or father. Parents are to children as men to women, man to youth or boy, Ambwerk to Tuman.

Again and again the narratives take up the theme of how boys may be made into responsible men, moral beings in the fullest sense. Represented as the culture bearers, men maintain the moral community as against the inroads of the divine, the wild, and the wanton. Men should overcome impulse and accommodate themselves to the needs of culture and community life. But girls are considered to grow into women quite naturally. Not held responsible, regarded as inherently subject to impulse—and so wild or divine in relation to men—women have to be constrained by men who are stamped with responsibility and awareness. If there were no such awareness there would be no incest taboo, promiscuity would be general, there would be no culture or community to maintain.

In the narratives that follow immediately we turn to dialogues which are explicitly between men and women. As might be expected, Nuakai intervenes. But while her interventions in the situation boy-becoming-man have one series of connotations, constituting a challenge to growing manhood, where this manhood is proven and the context is male–female or husband–wife or youth–maiden we encounter quite another series of connotations or refractions of meaning.

N. 7: *Lime and Ashes*

Once upon a time long ago, the women of the village went down to the stream to fish. The men stayed at home, chewing areca-nut with ash. Yet the mixture of areca-nut and ash was not very appetizing. And when the women returned to the village and started to chew areca-nut with ash from their cooking fires, their faces wrinkled in distaste.

Next day, the men went out hunting, and the women remained behind in the village, chewing areca-nut. But they did not use ash. They chewed their nuts with lime which they took from a large globular gourd. They found the mixture exciting, tasty, and juicy.

When they had finished their chewing they hid the gourd in a clump of bananas.

Returning from their hunting, the men noticed that the *pekas* was speckled with bright red splashes of spittle. 'Aha!' they exclaimed. 'The women have had a fine chewing today indeed!'

They sat down at once to chew areca-nut, using the ash from their fires. Alas! They found little joy in it.

Puzzled and disappointed, the men fell to thinking on the matter and discussing what they should do. So it was that next day, after the women had gone to fish, they selected a small boy, put him in a string-bag cradle, and told him to watch closely on the morrow—to find out what it was that enabled the women to have such a fine chewing of areca-nut.

On the following day, therefore, while the men were out hunting, the boy kept a watch on the women from his hiding-place in the string bag. He saw them fetch the gourd from its hiding-place in the clump of bananas, and he saw them go down to the stream to make lime. . . .

That evening, after the men had come home to a *pekas* freshly marked with red spittle, the boy told them what he had seen.

They slept.

Next morning, after the women had gone down to the stream to fish, the men fetched the gourd from its hiding place and they chewed their areca-nut with lime. They covered the *pekas* with red spittle. And afterwards, when they had finished, they refilled the gourd with ash, sprinkled a little of the remaining lime on top, and replaced the gourd in the bananas.

Next day, after the men had gone hunting, the women fetched the gourd and started to chew areca-nut. It was horrible. There was no lime in the gourd, only ash. They were furious.

While all the women chattered and bickered, wondering what they should do, old Nuakai began to palm some string on her thigh. She worked hard, without stopping, until the string she was making seemed to her to be long enough. Then, throwing one end of the line high into the air, she told the women to climb upwards. . . .

Now by the time the men had come back from their hunting, most of the women had already gone up into the sky. Only Nuakai, two maidens, and a little girl remained on the *pekas*. And the men, seeing what was happening, rushed forward to catch the two maidens.

But the maidens were nimble. They jumped at the string, caught hold, and climbed swiftly upwards—gathering the string behind them as they went. The little girl was left behind.

Nuakai entered into a bird—you can hear her today in the dawning, complaining as all old women do. The little girl grew up to bear children—yet she was only one woman among many men. That is why, today, there are never enough women for the men of a village. They all went up into the sky on that day long ago.

N. 8: *Friends*[1]

Once upon a time there were two villages. In the first of these all the women had perished, leaving men and boys only, and in the second there were no men or boys, only women and girls.

One day, dance Juangam was signalled in the women's village. And as the sun went down the women decorated themselves and started the dance.

The deep booming of their handdrums carried through the still night air over hill and valley to the far-away village of the men. 'If only it were noon', a young lad mused as he wakened and listened to the rhythm of the drums, 'I would go along and join them. But it is night, too dark and too late . . . I'd better sleep. Some other time, perhaps, I'll listen out for the signal. . . . I'll make sure to hear it in good time—then I will go and visit them . . .'

The women danced through the night until dawn. Then they betook themselves to the tops of their areca-nut palms to sleep. Only old grandmother Nuakai remained below on the ground.

The following morning the women again signalled Juangam on their slit-gongs and prepared for the dance. Far away in his village the lad, Kwav,[2] heard the signal and decided to go to the dance. He cut himself a piece of inner bark from a *deamar*, hammered it out by the stream, and hung it in the sun to dry. After drying it, he suppled and shaped his new red-brown breechclout, girding it about his loins so that the apron in front came down to his ankles. He made up a slow-match, furbished his handdrum, tightening the head and sticking on buttons of resin. Then, with decorations and bird of paradise plumes in a basket under his arm, he set off through the

---

[1] This narrative was presented in shortened form, in a slightly different context, in B–1957(*a*): 182.

[2] Kwav and Wvert (*infra*, same narrative) are alternative words for 'friend'. They have been used here as proper names to prevent confusion.

forest to the village of women. He travelled all night, not arriving until dawn was breaking. And there on a *pekas* strewn with shreds of croton and palm he saw Nuakai sitting by herself, making a string bag. He was too late. The dance was over.

Kwav strode on to the *pekas*. 'Where has everyone gone?' he asked the old woman.

'They've all gone to their beds long since', Nuakai informed him.

As the lad stood there wondering what he should do next, Nuakai set aside her string bag, put a pot on the fire, and invited the visitor to share a meal. Gratefully, Kwav accepted.

After they had eaten, Nuakai turned to the lad and, 'Climb one of those areca palms', she suggested. 'Pick two small nuts. Don't pick the large ones—only two small ones. And be careful how you pick them. Take them eyes and all!'

Kwav grasped a palm in his hands, gripped with his knees, and soon climbed to the top. He picked his first nut—with the eye. But with the second he was careless. Tugging rather too sharply, he parted the nut from its cup. . . . Still, putting the nuts in his basket he slid down the trunk and set off for home.

As Kwav walked on his way through the forest he came to a stream, the water clear and cool. 'I'll have a swim', he thought. 'I'll wash off the sweat and dust.'

He threw his basket on the foreshore, stripped off his breechclout —folding it and putting it on the top of his basket—and splashed into the shallows, wandering slowly up-stream.[1]

Suddenly the glade rang with gay laughter—'He! He! He!'

'Who can that be?' the lad wondered, amazed. Then, thinking it might be someone after his areca-nuts, he hurried down-stream to where he had left his belongings.

Two maidens were sitting on his breechclout.

'Hey there!' Kwav shouted, crouching behind a bush. 'That is my breechclout you're sitting on—go away! I want to put on my breechclout!'

The maidens giggled. 'Well, come out and get it!' they returned.

There was nothing else for it. Kwav had to come out of the stream to put on his breechclout. Then he saw that his areca-nuts had gone —and he rounded on the maidens, accusing them of taking his nuts.

'No, no, no!' they protested. 'We haven't taken your nuts—we *are* the areca-nuts you picked! You've been carrying us in your basket all day!'

Kwav noticed that one of the maidens had only one eye. 'When

---

[1] At once one ought to think of maturation, creativity (compare N. 2 and *infra*, pp. 352, 383).

you picked me,' she explained, 'you left my eye behind. But you
picked the other nut eye and all—and she is unblemished.'

Kwav took the two maidens home with him and showed them to
his friend, Wvert.

'You have one for a wife,' suggested Wvert, 'and let me have the
other. You take the pretty one, and I'll take the one-eyed.'

'No!' Kwav countered. 'I want the pair of them. But look—they'll
probably signal a dance for tomorrow. Why not go over yourself and
get two wives of your own?'

Next morning the booming of the slit-gongs from the women's
village signalled a dance. So Wvert cut himself a strip of inner bark,
hammered out a new breechclout, dried it, suppled it, and wound
it on to his loins. He fetched down his bird of paradise plumes, his
decorations, his handdrum. Then, making up a slow-match, he set
off for the women's village.

Wvert walked very fast all night. Yet even so he did not arrive till
the dawning. The dance was over, the *pekas* strewn with croton and
palm leaves. Only Nuakai was there.

'Where has everybody gone?' asked Wvert.

'They have all gone to sleep', came the reply.

Then, as had happened with Kwav, Nuakai asked Wvert to share
some food.

After they had eaten, and were sitting contented, Nuakai suggested to Wvert that he should pick two areca-nuts together with
their eyes.

Wvert did so. And as he made his way homewards through the
forest he stopped by a stream to bathe and refresh himself. He was
splashing about and enjoying himself when he heard sounds of gay
laughter. Two maidens were sitting by his breechclout, and they
challenged him to come out of the stream and fetch his breechclout
for himself. Like his friend, Wvert did so, and took the two maidens
home to his village.

Kwav greeted him when he arrived. 'So you have got your two
wives!' he exclaimed. 'And each of them has two eyes!'

'Yes indeed!' replied Wvert. 'When you picked your nuts you left
the eye of one of them behind. That is why one of your wives has only
one eye. I picked my nuts carefully—eyes and all.'

The wives bore children to their husbands, and their children
married and remarried, the son of one friend marrying the daughter
of the other. They all lived together in the village, and it prospered.
So that though that village had been small, without any women, now
it became large, with men and women living together.

N. 9: *Sisters and the Snake-brothers*

One day two sisters went fishing. They had spent all day by the stream when, having caught only one fish between them, they decided to give it up and return to the village.

It started to rain.

As the two sisters hurried home through the forest they noticed the leaves of a clump of sugar-cane—good sugar-cane, not the wild sort —tossing in the breeze. They stopped, wondering how such cane should come to be in that part of the forest. Thinking to take some of the cane, Ambwerk searched the forest on one side, and Tuman looked round the other. No, there seemed to be no one about. . . . They cut a few shoots and stowed them in their string bags.

But someone had seen them. Kuokavalik,[1] whose cane it was, and who had been hiding near by, saw everything they did. And as the sisters continued on their way to their village he followed them— shouting the halloo that men use when they have killed a cassowary.

The sisters thought it might be their father, or perhaps their brothers, returning to the village with their kill. So they sat down by the side of the path to wait. Kuokavalik said nothing. Puzzled that no hunting party should some into view down the path, the sisters shouldered their bags and went on their way. At once Kuokavalik roared the successful cassowary hunter's halloo—'Meaghoo! . . . Meaghoo! Kundu meaghoo! Re! Re! Re!'

'Aha!' Ambwerk exclaimed in relief. 'Here they are at last!'

The two sisters sat down by the path, took some sugar-cane from their string bags, peeled it, and started to eat. Kuokavalik said nothing. All was silent.

More perplexed than ever, at last the sisters got up and walked home. Kuokavalik followed them to the boundaries of the village, marked which house they entered, and turned back through the forest to his home.

'Two sisters took some of our sugar-cane today', Kuokavalik remarked to his younger brother, Cipnangk'der.[2] 'And they ate some of it. I followed them back to their village, and I made sure where they live.'

Agreeing that something ought to be done, the two brothers waited in their home until nightfall.

That night, after the two sisters had retired, loosed off their skirts

[1] Kuokavalik (*kuok* = 'snake') is a general term for small snakes (which tend to be found in clumps of sugar-cane), and has the added connotation of 'snake-man'. Kuokavalik is NOT the name of a species of snake.

[2] A *cipnangk'der* is a particular species of small snake. Along with other kinds of small snake it may be found in clumps of sugar-cane.

and lain down to sleep, the two brothers crept up to their house in the darkness and crawled in under the wall. They saw the two sisters lying there, quite naked. Without more ado they slipped between their legs into their quims: Kuokavalik, Ambwerk, into elder sister, and Cipnangk'der, Tuman, into younger sister. Through to their wombs they went, growing huge, into their stomachs and so at last out of their mouths. . . .

Next morning, father noticed that though it was long past dawn his daughters had not left their hut. He told mother to see what had happened.

Mother peeped through a hole in the wall. She trembled. For there were her daughters lying quite still on the floor, huge snakes coming from their mouths, lolling coiled on their torsos. 'Snakes!' she screamed. 'Snakes! Snakes!'

While the villagers gathered round the sisters' house, their own brothers collected heaps of firewood and piled it around the walls. Then, when all had been made ready, and having armed themselves with bamboo razors, the brothers rushed into the house and sliced the snakes into little pieces. . . .

They carried out the bodies of their sisters for burial. Then they set a torch to the piles of faggots, watching as the flames consumed the house and the remains of the two snakes.

That is the end of the story. Sugar-cane makes your stomach swell up, and young people should not eat too much of it.

Male and female are opposed, enjoy different but complementary kinds of being. Yet on either hand fulfilment in community is through ordered sexual relations centred in marriage. Still, how did it all start—with a brother and sister who had to commit incest if a community was to exist, or with men who were friends using their initiative to find a village of women? In N. 7 Nuakai deprives the men of their women, but fails to prevent them getting a small girl. In N. 8 she negotiates the marriage. N. 9 comments on sexual relations outside the marriage bond, particularly when impulse is not under control, when undertaken prior to circumcision. Taken together the three narratives pose the question of the relations between men and women, particularly the problem of appropriate sexual access.

In N. 7 men go hunting on alternate days, women fish every other day, men and women take it in turns to rest in the village: a routine which should be seen against a basic sexual division of labour in which husband and wife form a complete working unit. But their chewing areca-nut takes awareness to deeper levels of significance. When Tangu have no lime to chew with their areca-nut they use ash as a substitute. The taste is woolly, spittle colourless. When areca-nut is taken with lime, however, the mixture is sharp and stimulating, saliva is freely secreted, spittle is bright red. As we have seen, spittle is associated with charms, perhaps with rain, with causation, and with curing or making whole again. Spitting chewed areca-nut juice on the severed parts of Tuman-as-crab made him whole again.[1] Redness is associated with the menstrual flow, with the evidence of the procreative capacity as well as with blood and life. In the past circumcised youths who were ready to come down from the *garamb* as marriageable men dressed their hair with clay and red pigment. Adult males periodically dressed their hair with clay and red pigment. Today sexually mature youths and men mix oil or pig fat with red pigment or pandanus juice to rub on their bodies when decorating themselves for a dance. But children may not do so. 'Redness' indicates life, creative maturity; and reddened hair or head imply a creative *gnek*.[2] But a man who demonstrates shame whitens his face, and, as the narrative informs us, it is white lime that makes for redness in spittle, lime which is in the exclusive possession of women, lime which is made next to that which evokes the line of male filiation: a stream.[3] Appropriate redness (creativity) grows from whiteness (morality).

In the days before screw-top tobacco tins found their way into Tangu, men used long sausage-shaped gourds as lime containers, and women used coconuts or spherical gourds: the sexual associations are clear. In the narrative, lime, white as milk, is in a globular gourd hidden in a clump of bananas—themselves, as we have seen, associated with women, from which women make their underskirts, into which the childishness of men, the foreskin, is thrown. The men gain access to the lime

---

[1] *Supra*, p. 247–8. Note that ash is also fertile and effective—wood ash fertilizes a garden plot—but it is not red.

[2] Even where 'redness' represents the blood of a pig, it still refers to sexual maturity, the capacity to generate or procreate, as well as to life-stuff or blood. Further, since sexual maturity is associated with adulthood, redness also comes to stand for moral maturity and awareness.

[3] See *supra*, p. 75, on the evocations of *ringertingertiki*. We shall see the specific association between stream and male filiation building up as we go along.

through a small boy, a male associated with women. And in doing so they gain access to a property or capacity hitherto exclusive to women: the ability to give birth. As has been remarked, and as we shall see more pertinently,[1] through the *garamb* and the rite of circumcision in or near the *garamb*, men as a collectivity united in the *garamb* were enabled to give birth to men. For though women bear the children which men nourish or generate in the womb,[2] to make a man a period of probation in the *garamb* and circumcision were necessary. The mother's brother, a male on the female side, was the circumcisor; and the same relevance of female-in-male is represented in the boy who, associated with women, gives men access to the lime. Men give birth to men, that is, in terms of the junction of the male and female in them, through the *garamb* in which the male and female parts of men conjoin. Men are responsible, decide, initiate: the germ of responsible being is in men, men nourish and generate responsible being. And this they do through their embodiment in the *garamb* of conjoined lines of male and female filiation.

Nuakai and the small boy are mediators who complement each other in the primary dialogue between male and female. The small boy, male but associated with women, is hidden in a string bag, in which babies are normally carried; women make string bags. Nuakai, female but no longer having the distinctive quality of women, the ability to bear children, is discovered making string. Making string is women's work, perhaps more closely associated with grandmothers, for whom it is one of a small variety of jobs, than with mothers, for whom it is one of a much larger variety of tasks. Though string is and was used for crocheting bags, pouches, and plaques, in the old days it was particularly associated with making new gardens, with that process of growth and maturation in the cultural field which starts with planting seed. Lengths of string were used to mark out the several plots in a site, and the shapes and sizes of the plots were determined by reeling the string on a spindle, holding the free end of string, and throwing the spindle across the site: the unreeled string marked the borders of the plot, the landing points of the spindle the corners. Here, by means of her string, Nuakai puts the distinctive quality of women out of the reach

[1] *Infra*, p. 342.   [2] *Supra*, p. 84.

of men: men cannot bear children. Yet she also marks out that part of the whole female to which men do have access, which cannot escape, and which is necessary to community life: wife. Nuakai herself, hypostatic female, goes into a bird, for ever outside the moral community but not outside the range of awareness and experience. The men are left with a little girl whom they have to educate into being a wife.

We know that little girls—just such a girl as was left behind when the maidens went up into the sky and drew the string up behind them—were allowed into the *garamb*. What happened to them while they were there? What did the men say or do to them? We do not know. Yet it is possible that a man's view of what a good wife should be was impressed on them. Men are the culture bearers, responsible. They take the initiative, make decisions, play the man. Women do not initiate unless through their husbands; their work is routine. The discussion the women have when they discover that their lime has been stolen is pointedly irrelevant. Nuakai intervenes. And the women, following their natures and being themselves, climb into the sky. Men, on the other hand, may not follow their natures. They have to hold their parts on a rein, managing community affairs. The female is divine, as a wild thing, until she is made relevant to the community as wife. In this sense, until they are circumcised, boys are wild things, like women, like *ranguova*. To them restraint is a stranger. The period of probation in the *garamb*, culminating in circumcision, represents being born into awareness and responsibility. It is, as will more surely be borne in on us, a rebirth as men of men, the moral bearing and begetting the moral.

It cannot be too often emphasized that within the narrative idiom neither men nor women nor children are indivisible entities, persons. Nor are they necessarily categories in a direct and formal sense. They are *puoker*, beings revealing elements or aspects or axioms or refractions of meaning. The reader or listener is informed on particular parts in relationship, on the relations between particular principles of being. He is not necessarily being informed on the relations between types or categories of persons as they occur in the moral order. Thus N. 8 reiterates the notion that the 'female' or 'femaleness' is of relevance within the community as 'wife', but is otherwise either outside it, as though non-social or non-cultural, or at any rate a danger to managing a moral order. In a context placing males and females an unknown distance apart, contraposed to each other, a female who is not yet a wife, but who is becoming a social being and who is already a part of cultural life, is as though an areca-nut, a nurtured product, until brought into close proximity with a breechclout. And this contains or is associated with penis and testicles. On the one hand, the raw material for a breechclout is taken from a wild forest tree, hammered out by a stream in the forest, exposed to the sun and daylight to dry, and is eventually worn only by sexually mature males; on the other hand, areca-nut represents the curative and generative, areca-nuts resemble testicles, testicles and areca-nuts are generative, and areca-nuts are also maidens ready to bear children. Through the breechclout which signals the circumcised male, the areca-nuts, conjoining male and female maturities, become maidens who become wives.[1]

Though Nuakai is discovered on the *pekas* making a string bag (whereas in N. 7 she was simply making string), and the other women of the village are above, towards the sky, in the areca-nut palms (whereas in N. 7 they went into the above for ever), here in N. 8, instead of overtly separating male from female, Nuakai negotiates the encounter between youth about to become husband and maidens about to become wives. Yet she did just this in N. 7 when, if she separated male from female, she was unable to separate husband from wife, and could not prevent men as husbands educating the little girl to be wife. Often adamantine where boys are becoming men, and representative of an experience or awareness which boys have to overcome or accommodate if they are to become men, Nuakai is more than soft when male and female are to become husband and wife. For 'wife' is the relevant aspect of the female in community. Only through 'wife' may a responsible man fully and appropriately come into relation with the female. But to become

[1] It will be remembered (*supra*, p. 187) that when a man wants to marry a woman who is in some way distanced from him, he may compound a love potion whose main ingredients are an areca-nut together with its cup or 'eye' and sweat from the inner leg—where the breechclout rubs. Bearing in mind the associative complex of areca-nuts together with redness from chewing areca-nuts, we are not surprised to be told towards the end of the story that the marriages were fruitful and that the village prospered.

'husband' a boy must slough off his earlier close associations with women and the female: the foreskin in the banana clump surely represents the unrestrainedness or wildness of youth or childhood being cut off, excluded, and returned to its association with women. If as 'wife', under the domination of husband, a female is effectively under control, she is still apt to be wild, herself, a refraction of the hypostatic female, following her nature and instinct or whim. With this mode of being, the suggestion goes, responsible men should have nothing to do.

In N.8 it is Juangam, the harvest dance in which men, women, and children participate together, which provides the opportunity for boy to meet girl—as indeed it does for young lovers in life today. The youths take with them their bird of paradise plumes: and birds of paradise and their plumes are, as we shall see more fully,[1] indicative of maidens about to become wives, or youths about to become husbands. The more significant themes of friendship are adumbrated. If Kwav had given Wvert a wife there would have been created between them an obligation not proper to friendship. Instead, as a true friend, Kwav puts Wvert in the way of obtaining two wives for himself. While friend has helped friend, no specie has changed hands, no working service has been done by the one on behalf of the other, neither is obliged to the other. Then, and this is another rider to N. 7, we are told of a mode of marriage which is fertile, which links those between whom there was no prior kinship, which creates moral relationship between members of communities separate and distant from one another.

In N. 9 there are echoes from the Nimbamung story. The primary dialogue is worked out between Ambwerk and Tuman on both sides, and while the female pair are undifferentiated in role, the males play varied parts. In life a surfeit of sugar-cane swells the stomach, and a swollen stomach may be indicative of pregnancy. Small snakes[2] may be found in clusters of sugar-cane. In the narrative the brothers are figured as two small snakes— youths whose maleness might be expected to extend to more ample proportions when in close proximity to sleeping and naked maidens. But, as the action of the sisters' brothers later

---

[1] *Infra*, p. 371.

[2] Tangu indicated that these small snakes were about the size of a little finger (about 2 inches long).

seems to indicate, Ambwerk and Tuman have not yet been circumcised. They are wild males, youths who have not learned restraint. And, since crawling under the walls of a house at night is the kind of thing a *ranguma* might do, through the common quality of unrestrainedness *ranguova* and uncircumcised youths are likened to each other, particularly in relation to their sexual proclivities and impulses.

The sisters have been fishing: a circumstance which generally indicates the generative or fecund, the advent of sexual maturity.[1] When the women made the lime which gave the areca-nut juice its redness, they went to the stream to do so. But between them the sisters catch only one fish: not wholly competent, they do not yet rate as 'wives'. Then it rains. Semen is being secreted, the events of the tale are precipitated. Not only is sexual activity being anticipated, but the events of the tale are set in train by, and made to hinge on, a capacity and power peculiar to the male. In stealing cultivated sugar-cane the sisters know they are offending because they are careful to guard against being seen —an oblique on the requirement that the moralities must be overt, should be seen to be observed. But, like Tuman in N. 6, the sisters are stupid, not competent, unaware. They are seen and pursued. Elder brother plays the successful cassowary hunter, roaring what is, in life, the signal for a cassowary kill. And it is a cassowary, perhaps, because while killing a cassowary is an act associated with responsible men—and the sisters are eager to re-enter the safety of community relations—the killing of a pig would throw the mind towards a responsible and appropriate male filiation.[2] And this last is the precise opposite of what is being evoked. Ambwerk has not killed a cassowary. He is simply pretending to be a responsible man, he is deceiving the maidens, he is going to assault one of them. Hearing the halloo, however, the sisters stop, wait, think, and consider. Nothing comes of it. They are but girls, unaware and being deceived as young maidens frequently are. Yet in stealing the sugar-cane— which makes the stomach swell up as in pregnancy—the maids have committed themselves. They have aroused the two

[1] See in particular N. 25, *infra*, p. 321; N. 27, *infra*, p. 350; and N. 28, *infra*, p. 358.
[2] See in particular N. 29, *infra*, p. 377. But we could, from this narrative, make a first approximation as to the evocations of 'cassowary', and say that it signalled a sexual assault. Unfortunately, supporting evidence is lacking. On the whole, a cassowary in itself is female rather than male.

brothers, invited copulation. So, after Ambwerk has ascertained where they live, into the sisters' house the two brothers go. Penetrating the sisters, the small snakes become large ones.

In the morning father, a responsible man, wonders what has happened and sends his wife to find out. She, a wife and a mother and so persuaded of the virtues of restraint, is horrified at the consequences of unrestrainedness and irresponsibility. Still, removed by their brothers, the sisters are acknowledged as members of community by burial. They have stolen, their mistake was in being seen, they were deceived: faults to which all mortals are prone. But the snake-brothers came from the wild, what they did was wild, and vengeance belongs to the brothers who slice the snakes with a bamboo razor.

Why circumcise after the event? Perhaps this is an oblique on the representation of two lines of male filiation intermarrying with two lines of female filiation, carrying the rider that the males concerned should, properly, be circumcised. An alternative answer lies in the conjunction of two notions: first, that circumcision constitutes admission into the moral community; second, that *ranguova* may be readmitted to the moral community through confession. Because, it might be said, *ranguova* and uncircumcised youths have a quality in common, on this projection circumcision and confession have much the same relevance: admission into the moral community. Moreover, the burning of Nimbamung (N. 6) and the burning of the snake-brothers seem to meet the same idea: the principles or modes of being which they represent—blindness to the moralities on the one hand, unrestrainedness and the pursuit of mere sexual satisfaction on the other—should be wholly excluded from the mode of being proper to the moral community. For if life in community depends on creative perceptiveness, it also insists upon restraint and awareness of self and others; it cannot brook the unrestrained and blind or unaware.

Sex and Marriage

Within the primary dialogues thus far encountered the most persistent theme has been the development of the distinctive human quality, moral being. Through such features as storm, rain, pig, Nuakai, Nimbamung, areca-nut, lime, *garamb*, stream, and snake in relation to the contrapositions males/females, husband/wife, parents/children, Ambwerk/Tuman, friend/ friend, father/daughter, mother/daughter, brother-and-sister-union/marriage-in-community, *ranguma*/community, and mother's brother/sister's-son we have begun to see the interior relevances of reciprocity/non-reciprocity, moral/divine or wild, siblingship/filiation, self-restraint/self-willedness. And all these relations cohere in metamorphosis, developmental process rather than static oppositions. The signals pack the narratives.

For Tangu the passage from conception to birth takes place unseen in the womb. Upon death the body rots. If Tangu notions of what happens before birth itself, and after death, can only be theories—founded perhaps on observation of plant and animal life—which have hardened into articles of faith, the passage from childhood into adulthood may be experienced, remembered, observed, and described. Paps become globes, menstruation occurs, maidenheads are surrendered; a beard grows, testicles drop, features and muscles coarsen and harden, a penis begins to ejaculate more than urine. With these biological changes come changes in moral obligation. Because now a girl can bear a child it becomes appropriate that she should do so in an ordered and approved way. Because now a youth can beget a child it becomes appropriate that he should learn how to do so responsibly. Bundles of instincts have to be nurtured into moral awareness. Puberty is the most dangerous period: impulses are strong and supported by ability, restraint barely learned. Still, the passage from divine into moral must be made, and a successful passage connotes a movement from the divine or wild to the moral. The process of birth corresponds to this movement, the one kind of movement is a model for the other. An unsuccessful passage into adulthood represents a movement in the opposite direction, from the moral or potentially moral to the divine: social death. And a movement from moral to divine is what occurs at physical death.

In all the narratives presented here the viewpoint is essentially that of a mature and responsible man. If women may have secret narratives of their own, because they are secret they cannot be relevant to the community at large, they can make little difference to the ordering of community relations.[1] It is the responsibility and privilege of men to maintain and order

---

[1] But see *supra*, p. xiv.

community life. So long as women remain effectively under the control of men, girls may blossom into maidens and become wives; as wives women become indispensable. As females simply, on the other hand, they are represented as highly dangerous, wild and wanton. Yet the men who must do the controlling are boys before they are men, and boys are represented as being unable naturally to grow into men. In Tangu tradition restraint and moral sense are not represented as a development coming naturally with puberty: they had to be taught and implanted so that the youths of today could become the protectors and guardians of the moral tomorrow. The dangers that traditionally confronted Tangu culture from within were that a man might become unrestrained, go wild, become a *ranguma* or like a *ranguma*; that boys and youths might act upon impulse, wildly, just so much too often; that women might merge into their prototype, the hypostatic female, and become wholly wanton and unmanageable. And *ranguova*, women, children, and young boys are associated with the divine or wild in relation to responsible men. Given that community life should continue, that the youths of the present will have to become the responsible men of the future, it is to the institutional means of making men, circumcision and the passage of the *garamb*, that the narratives repeatedly return.

N. 10: *The Brothers who Misbehaved*

One day long ago two brothers misbehaved themselves behind the *garamb*. Father saw them. 'Get out of the village, you pair of knaves!' he shouted in anger. 'Go away! Unprincipled jugglers[1] like you have no place in the village! Off into the forest with you! Only decent and proper[2] folk can stay in a village!'

The two brothers ran off through the forest to their gardens where they thought they would spend the night. As they prepared their pallets in the garden shelter, two birds of paradise came to roost in a wild banana near by. When night fell the brothers slept. So did the birds.

With the dawning, as is their wont, the two birds of paradise voiced

---

[1] 'Unprincipled': in the vernacular *imbatekas*. 'Jugglers': it seemed clear in the field situation either that the brothers were urinating in a very unusual way (the boys' latrine was behind the *garamb*) or that they were engaging in some form of self-abuse.

[2] 'Decent and proper': in the vernacular *'aran*, good, moral'.

their harsh clamour. The brothers awoke. Quickly taking their bows
and arrows they slipped out of the shelter and, bent double, weaving
swiftly through the garden, they came to the wild bananas. Arrows
to bowstrings, the brothers took aim.

'Don't shoot! Don't shoot!' one of the birds called out as it saw
them. 'We're not really birds—we're maidens!'

The brothers lowered their bows. Ambwerk took one of the birds
and Tuman took the other. They returned to the garden shelter, and
there brothers and maidens[1] pleasured each other until sleep closed
their eyes.

Next day, whilst the maids hid themselves in the forest, the
brothers went hunting. They took some small game, cleaned it,
carved the meat and brought it back to the shelter for the maidens
to cook. After they had eaten they had their pleasure of each other,
then slept. So it went, night after day. . . .

The day came, however, when father and mother, coming to the
garden to dig out some yams, sat down by the shelter to smoke. They
noticed two skirts lying on the ground. 'What are those skirts doing
here?' father asked of his sons. 'Are you trysting in secret? Have you
got a couple of girl-friends hidden somewhere about?'

'Oh no!' the brothers protested. 'We are not hiding anybody!
You can see for yourself there are no maidens about. We've been
in the shelter here all the time, sleeping alone. How could there be
any maidens out here?'

Father and mother set to work. They dug up the yams and taros
they wanted, packed them into string bags, and returned to the
village.

When their parents had gone the two brothers hastened down to
the garden border where their wives[2] lay hidden. Together they
returned to the shelter, set out some food, cooked it, ate, and retired
to their pallets. Ambwerk had enjoyment of his wife, Tuman of his.

Next morning, as usual, the maidens went into hiding in the clump
of bananas at the bottom of the garden whilst the two brothers went
hunting. And away in the village father also went hunting. Mother
and sister[3] came to the garden to do some weeding.

Now, as she was working in the garden, sister felt the need to pass
water. She scrambled over the fence at the bottom of the garden and
crouched by a bush a few paces outside the fence. She thought she
could see something in the underbrush. She craned forward, peering
closely—Yes!

---

[1] 'maidens' it is, but 'sisters' could easily be evoked or understood.

[2] *Sic.*

[3] Daughter of 'mother' and 'father', sister to the two brothers.

S

'Oh! Oh! Oh!' shrilled sister, jumping to her feet and hurrying back over the fence. 'Mother! Mother! There are two girls hidden down here and they're making skirts for themselves! Mother! Mother! My brothers' wives are down here and I've found them!'

Mother trotted down to see for herself. 'Hey you!' she called to the two maidens when she espied them. 'Don't move! Just stay where you are and don't go away!'

Mother and daughter repaired to the shelter, packed some yams into their string bags, and returned to the village.

When the brothers got back from their hunting that evening they went straight to the shelter to clean their meat, carve it, and put it into the pot to cook. Then they went down to the bottom of the garden and fetched their wives.

'Your mother and sister saw us this morning', the girls told them. 'Your sister came here to ease herself and saw us making skirts. She told your mother you were hiding us. Then both of them came down here and your mother told us to stay where we were and not to move.'

The brothers were embarrassed. 'We're not hiding you!' they protested. But of course they were lying. . . .

The brothers and their wives ate together, then slept.

Next morning father came to the garden. 'Oho, my daughters-in-law!' he shouted. 'Oho, my sons' wives!'

The following day the villagers started to make preparations for weddings that were to take place in the village. They went into the forest to cut cane for making armbands, waistbelts, and anklets. And having cut the cane in convenient lengths, they coiled it and returned to the village to sleep. Next day they put the cane out in the sun to dry, and afterwards they scraped and suppled it.

Out in the forest the two brothers were doing just the same. They wove waistbelts of cane for their wives, made anklets, bracelets, and armbands for them. . . .

When all was ready the brothers in the forest and the villagers in the village sounded their slit-gongs.

Father went to the garden on the following day to dig up some taros. He looked over the plot with some pride, noting how many tubers he had, pleased that he had more than enough. 'They've good and large piles of foodstuffs back in the village', he thought to himself. 'But I, I also have more than enough!'

That night the villagers feasted and danced. In the forest the two brothers did the same.

Next day at dawn each of the husbands in the village decorated his bride with chaplets of dogs' teeth, pigs' tusks, and long cassowary nose bones. They dressed their brides in their waistbelts, helped them on with their bracelets, anklets, and armbands. Then they went to sit in the *garamb*.

In the forest the two brothers did likewise.

Father then rose to his feet. 'Hey, you two out there!' he called to his sons in the forest. 'Hey there! Your mother's brothers await you!'

But the villagers took up their spears, indignantly crying in protest.

'My sons! My sons!' father cried in alarm. 'Stay where you are! The villagers here have taken up their spears against you—stay where you are in the forest!'

Then father turned on the assembled villagers and raised his adze in defiance. 'You stubborn, obdurate bunch!' he exclaimed. 'All right! If you won't allow my sons to come into the village—I at least can go out and see them!'

So father went out of the village and wended his way through the forest. He saw Ambwerk with his wife, and he saw Tuman with his. . . .

Then he returned to the village.

N. 11: *Ruongaptiamkan*

Once upon a time there was a man whose name was Ruongaptiamkan. He was walking through the forest on a fine day when he thought he would take some of the fruit of a wild breadfruit tree. He laid to with his axe.

'What do you think you're doing?'

A woman had put her head out of a hole in the tree. 'This is not your breadfruit tree!' the woman scolded. 'This is my home!'

Ruongaptiamkan stepped back in alarm and surprise.

But the woman was friendly. 'Why not come in for a while?' she invited.

Ruongaptiamkan stepped into the tree. Inside, the woman lay on her back, legs spread, enticing. They embraced in their pleasure.

By and by the woman bore a son. . . .

One day Ruongaptiamkan decorated the boy with chaplets of dogs' teeth. They did not become him. Then, seeing that the boy had sores on his anus,[1] Ruongaptiamkan pinched him, making him scream with pain.

'What is the matter?' asked mother.

'The lad is hungry', Ruongaptiamkan replied. 'Take him away and give him some food!'

'But the child is your son—you ought to feed him!'[2] mother riposted.

---

[1] See *supra*, p. 205, and *infra*, p. 324.   [2] See *infra*, p. 384.

'Not so!' Ruongaptiamkan replied. 'He belongs only to you!'

With that, Ruongaptiamkan started to lop the branches of the breadfruit tree. And afterwards, when the woman had cooked him his evening meal, he only pretended to eat, stuffing his food into a hole at the bottom of the tree when the woman was not looking. . . . Then, the meal over, he cut down the tree altogether.

That night, in bright moonlight, Ruongaptiamkan went hunting.

At home, the woman dreamed that Ruongaptiamkan had charmed a cock's feather and put it into her quim.

Ruongaptiamkan hunted well that night, filling his string bag with meat. But he did not return to the woman in the breadfruit tree. He went back to his wife in the village.

When in the dawning the woman awoke, she wondered where Ruongaptiamkan had gone. She waited and waited until, suddenly, realization came. 'Oh!' she exclaimed in a rage. 'He has gone away and left me with his son!'

Remembering the dream she had had in the night, however, the woman charmed a cock's feather and put it into her quim. Then she set out after her lover. Whenever she came to a fork in the trail she would try first one way then the other. If she took the wrong turning the cock's feather would droop. But if the path was the right one then the feather would stiffen, erect. . . . So it was that she was able to find out where Ruongaptiamkan had gone.

Arrived at the village, the woman found Ruongaptiamkan seated with his wife. 'What are you doing with all that meat?' she raged at the wife. 'That meat belongs to me! He is my man—not yours!'

Wife said nothing. She grasped her heavy digging-stick tightly in both hands—lunging and striking with all her strength.

Woman and boy fell dead at her feet.

Each of the two narratives set down above is probably corrupt. In the course of the narration, bystanders commented that they were not quite right—adding that, though some might tell the stories one way, others might tell them rather differently. Even so, though some links or signals would seem to have been omitted, those who volunteered corrections lost themselves in quite different narratives and had to give up. Still, they are not so corrupt as to be without meaning.

The back of the *garamb* (N. 10) was the normal and proper place for boys to urinate whilst in the *garamb*: yet father expelled them. What were they doing? The normal posture for urinating in Tangu is resting on the haunches; and the term used here is a combination of 'stand' and 'urinate'. Tangu refused to comment any further, saying they would be ashamed to put actual words to the deed, that in any case such a thing would never occur today. Evidently, what occurred behind the *garamb* was something rather more heinous than a question of stance: it would be inappropriate to expel them from community for that. For, whatever it was that they did behind the *garamb*, the theme of their lack of restraint is continued: they encounter wild maidens in the forest, they marry them without benefit of community, they remain in the forest cut off from village and community, the latter will have nothing to do with them. They are sexually mature males who grossly misbehaved themselves in the club-house lavatory. Their behaviour is contraposed to that expected of good and decent village folk, *aran* people, and they are sent out of community into the forest.

The birds of paradise are discovered in association with the wild banana, in which, later, they make their skirts. Whether as birds of paradise, maids, or wives, the couple belong with the divine, the wild: and to this order also the two brothers belong when they are expelled from community. In life, only the sexually mature are allowed to wear bird of paradise plumes in their hair. If one asks Tangu to explain the usage they point out that in this narrative the birds of paradise are maidens; that the harsh cry of the bird of paradise puts them in mind of a nagging wife; that birds of paradise are as maidens or women.[1] The plumes worn as decorations evoke the birds and represent the desire and capacity to have what the birds represent: sexual intercourse. Also, of course, courtship, marriage, and family are evoked.[2] Roused by the raucous cries of the two birds, then, the brothers stalk them with bows and arrows which, if threatening, are signals indicating the sexually maturing but not yet responsible male who is about to marry or engage in sexual relations. And as soon as the brothers are informed that the birds are themselves maidens they take them to the garden shelter and bed them. Further, once the sexual relationship has been established, the linguistic shift into 'wife' occurs, and the brothers go hunting to obtain meat for their wives to cook—a feature reiterated in N. 11: a man hunts and obtains meat for the woman

[1] *Supra*, p. 105.   [2] See especially N. 28, *infra*, pp. 358–9.

with whom he is having regular sexual relations, ideally and properly the wife. Meat is good for both kinds of milk.

Though it is father, the responsible man, who first notices the skirts of the brothers' wives, it is sister urinating—thus returning the listener to the opening scene—who actually discovers the wives themselves. And she has to go outside the garden fence, into the wild, to perform an essentially animal act, to do so.[1] The immediate family is reconciled. Father, indeed, seems happy. His announcement is one of pride and assertion. But the brothers have denied that they have wives, and they also lie to their wives, telling them they have not been hiding them. Why? It is here perhaps that the signals are missing. For though from one point of view a kind of awareness is indicated, it is not clear whether this awareness hinges on circumcision, the nature of the wives as wild ones, or the association of the wives with sister. From another point of view, since the brothers have been described as *imbatekas*, it may be that what is being indicated is unobligedness, a complete unawareness of the demands of morality. What is clear, when the preparations for the weddings are detailed, is the presentation of parallel antitheses which cannot be reconciled with each other. The brothers and their wives (sisters?) belong with the divine, the wild; and the members of community, proper and decent folk, take up their spears —the sign of responsible men—against them. Though father attempts to mediate between the two antitheses, his endeavours are vain. The brothers have gone too far. Though their mother's brothers await them—presumably to make proper men of them—the community is obdurate, will not take them back. By taking wild wives and becoming wild husbands the brothers have committed themselves to the wild or divine. If the brothers had renounced their wild wives, one might suppose, they might have been able to return to community—as Ruongaptiamkan does in N. 11. The procedures of engagement, betrothal, and marriage, however, make it clear that the brothers are as committed to their wild wives as the village lads to their wives in community.

N. 11 carries the same theme of the wild contraposed to the controlled, only here protagonist is a whole man who knows the limits. He stands in contrast to the young brothers of N. 10

[1] Compare the man in N. 3, *supra*, p. 208.

who did not. In life, breadfruit-picking parties are associated with flirtations and, by extension, with a certain amount of sexual licence. But, being permissive occasions, the consequences which might flow from an amorous encounter are not handled as though they flowed from an adultery. Thus here, in N. 11, in association with a wild breadfruit, Ruongaptiamkan meets —as though in a flash of libidinous fantasy born of the flirtatious situation—a woman of the wild who, following her nature, unrestrainedly invites him into her hollow tree of a home for pleasure. The result is a son. Decorating the boy with dogs' teeth as though he was about to enter or come down from the *garamb*, Ruongaptiamkan rejects him. He has sores on his anus; such sores debar him from the *garamb*. Born in, or in association with, a hollow tree, the boy is offspring of the wild, does not belong to community. Without a mother's brother, he cannot have that placement in filiation which circumcision and the pig of the circumcision would give him. By pointedly not eating the food which the woman cooks for him, Ruongaptiamkan not only avoids binding himself to her but shows some maturity and forethought. His association with an axe reveals him as more or less responsible. And though the woman clearly desires a more permanent arrangement, wants to become wife, from Ruongaptiamkan's point of view the whole episode is to be thought of as temporary merely. He is not an adulterer in the full sense, for the woman is wild and not another man's wife. He is injuring the claims of no one in community. In the village he already has a wife. Belonging to the community himself, Ruongaptiamkan has no obligations to a child who is wild, who cannot enter the *garamb*.

During the night, therefore, Ruongaptiamkan leaves the wild woman, goes hunting, and takes his game back to the village: thus signalling the relationship between husband and wife. He provides game for her, she will cook for him. This act is Ruongaptiamkan's ticket back to community. Unlike the brothers in N. 10 who committed themselves to the wild and their wild wives, Ruongaptiamkan renounces his association with the wild and returns to his wife. In cutting down the breadfruit tree with his axe he severs the fleeting and wild or impulsive sexual link between himself and the wild woman. The flirtation is over, the fantasy done. Then, emphasizing the theme of lust or impulsive sexual relations, and also illustrating how in life a dream may be put to use, the wild woman finds her way to the village by a technique that does not have its analogue in Tangu today. 'It was her way', Tangu remark, 'not our way.' And if 'cock' may have obvious sexual overtones, cocks or cockerels also herald the dawn, emergent reciprocities. While the wild woman wants an appropriate marital relationship with her lover, Ruongaptiamkan himself is about to re-engage community reciprocities by going back to his wife. Further, as in life, the consequences of acting on a dream are not always foreseeable: a dream may deceive, interpretation may be misguided. Still, a deception is no bar to the inexorable flow of events. Hence the lessons of being aware and not being deceived which the narratives repeatedly offer. Like Tuman in N. 6, or the two sisters in N. 9, the wild woman has no awareness. She is wild, she is deceived.

In N. 10 husbands and wives in the wild were contraposed to husbands and wives in community. Here the wild woman—representing the sexual wantonness of a female who cannot become wife, who cannot be as wife unless a man hunts for her, provides for her, and also goes wild—is contraposed to the wife in community, to the female under control. Brought face to face, there can be no mediation: mutually opposed valuations confront each other. While metamorphosis and change, or maturation and the developmental process, movement from the wild or divine to the moral, appropriately relate moral and divine, decisive movement in the opposite direction means death—removal from the moral community. The *gnek* becomes a *niemur* or ghost; a living man becomes a *ranguma* or like a *ranguma*; an uncircumcised boy strays, may become like a *ranguma*, dies at the hands of a Nimbamung; a woman merges into her prototype, the hypostatic female. If it is possible to rescue one who has begun to move away from the moral, the committal on either hand points sharply to the mutual exclusiveness of the two orders of being. In N. 10 father attempted to mediate—in vain. Ruongaptiamkan does nothing, there is little he can or should do. Adding to our appreciation of the meaning of husband bringing back game for his wife, the wild woman stakes her claim. But it will not do. As the villagers took up their spears against the brothers, so wife takes a digging-stick and deals with the wild woman and her child. But where men were reluctant to kill, responsibly controlling their impulses, the female follows her nature and realizes her impulse. She kills.

Both men and women use digging-sticks in garden work, to plant seed crops or dig out ripened tubers: men and women came out of a hole in the earth,[1] the hole was made with a digging-stick.[2] As a man feeds the 'germ of being' in a woman so that it may become a boy or girl, in the same way he plants a tuber in the womb of earth to grow and develop on the semen of rain. Thus, while a digging-stick in itself is an image of maleness, begetting and planting emerge as corresponding processes.[3] The womanly weapon, in narratives at least, is most often a digging-stick.[4] And the association with gardens, womanly, together with its maleness, invest the digging-stick with an ambience proper to culture: a combination of the male and female. Since the most responsible kind of woman is the female as wife, when she takes the initiative and kills she is a female right enough, but she is exercising an attribute of the male: her action is touched with maleness and responsibility, what she does is in defence of the community. A digging-stick is appropriately wielded by wife, the moral female; and it is fitting that she should confront the wild woman. The implications of being one rather than the other are in stark contrast. Denied the *garamb*, the wild son has a begetter but no appropriate filiation. Denied circumcision by a mother's brother, he is simply the issue of a breadfruit party which has gone further than it might have done: the fantasy is followed to the conclusion it would have reached had it been realized. More than a priding cock's feather, 'husband' and 'father' are moral categories, more properly filled and informed with self-restraint and responsibility. On the other side, death is the fate of the issue of an impulse vented irresponsibly, outside the bounds of morality: not necessarily physical death, but certainly a social or

---

[1] *Supra*, p. 133.

[2] *Infra*, pp. 325, 355.

[3] The garden is associated with women rather than with men (*supra*, p. 55), and with wife (woman under control) rather than with female.

[4] In life too, for the most part. In private combat women use digging-sticks. In the past, in situations of armed conflict with outsiders, women were ammunition carriers. They filled their string bags with suitably sized pebbles, which their men-folk used either in slings or simply to throw.

community death. That it is not the fault of the child that he should be born of such a union is both beside the point and apposite. He is a *puok*, an impulse proceeding from the impulsive—itself and its consequences begotten of the nature of things as they are.

Narratives are told mainly in the gardens, particularly when new sites are being cleared and planted. Childen quickly appreciate that growing crops, like *puoker* and things of the wild, are not subject to moral laws—though they enable man to express his own distinctive condition and become aware of its limitations. And though Tangu ideas on natural and moral development must tend to interpenetrate each other, moral rules are imposed upon nature and can only hold firm in an awareness of things as they are. But wild and divine are not to be confused. They meet in that which is *imbatekas*, and they seperate when new thoughts and initiatives gain consent to a new morality.

5

THE NARRATIVES (II)

ADULT men who have made the passage of the *garamb*, and who are married, are represented as forming the heart and core of the moral community. They are the most fully involved in reciprocities, they carry responsibility, they manage community affairs, only they can speak fully and effectively in *br'ngun'guni*, on them lies the onus of dealing with the consequences of what might be said. They are, the narratives suggest, the guardians of community life. Children on the other hand are least involved in reciprocities. Initially quite unaware, children grow into awareness. The divine is etched with the qualities of 'child', 'child' stands in antithesis to 'adult'. In the first flush of their new strengths youths who have not been circumcised may become non-reciprocal persons, should be steered through the *garamb* and circumcision into responsibility. Their involvements with 'woman', in the shapes of mother, grandmother, and sister, should be so transmuted that they are ready to enter into a relationship with 'wife'. Circumcision inducts a youth into the moral community, takes a boy from his mother's skirts, removes from him that which pertains to women, the foreskin, and returns the foreskin to the bananas from which women's underskirts are made. In relation to men who are moral, women are wild or divine, wanton or self-willed. Beyond their necessary association with children the being of women appears as rooted in their sexuality, essentially unrestrained, a refraction of Nuakai, the hypostatic female. Women are the sisters eating sugarcane, an invitation to the sexual act whatever their thoughts or motives may be; they are the two areca-nuts which, brought into association with a breechclout, predicate a youth coming out of the stream to take them as wives; they are represented in the wild woman who, having invited Ruongaptiamkan into her home for enjoyment, cannot make her femaleness morally significant as woman unless she can persuade a man to accept her as wife. Only as wife does the female fully belong to the moral community.

As morally unaware, divine and wild belong together and are contraposed to the moral community and culture. *Puoker* are divine, abound in the wild. As 'roof' and 'shelter' are wild stuffs moulded by culture and constrained by man to protect him from the storm, so the *garamb* protects men from the divine and rescues youths for culture and the moral. As 'child' becomes 'growing boy' and eventually 'responsible man', so forest and bush may become gardens, wild trees may become slit-gongs, handdrums, food bowls, and other artifacts. But where Tangu themselves may venture into, and constrain, the wild, they have to bow before the divine as they bow before the storm, seeking shelter in the *garamb* and the maintenance of reciprocities. Yet while the wild as forest and bush is on the whole neutral, the divine is not: it is predicative, and may appear as vindictive or punitive. Neither divine nor wild are 'bad', for though 'bad' is often a convenient translation of *imbatekas*, like the 'good' the 'bad' is defined by the capacity to be reciprocal. But as far as interventions of the divine are departures for rearranging moral relationships in favour of some at the expense of others, so far do the interventions seem 'good' or 'bad' to particular individuals. Moreover, since culture and the moral community depend upon adherence to rules and regularities of expectation, rearrangements are fraught with danger, and humans who attempt to promote changes cannot but be initially associated with the divine or wild.

Interaction between divine or wild and the cultural or moral is appropriate when an attribute of the divine or wild is transformed into a moral quality. The human life cycle is represented as a progress from the divine or wild to the moral, until, in becoming *mngwotngwotiki*, divine and moral converge in the equipoise of stasis. Movement in the opposite direction, from moral to divine or wild, means death, both physical and social. When the divine or wild is manifested in men, members of community may—because they can—attempt to restrain. Those in community view the *ranguma* as 'bad': he should know how to restrain himself. On the other hand, from that exterior point of view which can appreciate not just the moral but the moral in relation to the divine, a *ranguma* strengthens the moralities, operates to the 'good', has much the same effect on human affairs as a *puok* or storm.[1] Moreover, as we shall see later,[2] the *ranguma* is figured as instinct with that initiative and sexual and generative power which, when appropriately used, is essential to the maintenance of community life. As a boy is made into a responsible man, and a girl is led into becoming a wife, so Tangu attempt to bring the *ranguma* into the moral community. Appropriately directed, his qualities are valuable. But for the unmitigated *ranguma* who has committed himself to a movement from the moral to the wild or divine only death or exclusion are appropriate.

If today an ancestor were to listen to the narratives related by a descendant, he would no doubt be indignant over what he would regard as inaccuracies, or at the way in which technological instructions were hurried through or omitted altogether. But as he looked about him he would see that there was no need for instructions on how to make a stone adze, a wooden bowl, a shield, or a painting on the *garamb* walls. For since these things are no longer made, and there is no apparent need to make them, they are truths which are no longer relevant. With the instructions regarding the production of a variety of foodstuffs, on the other hand, he would be quite familiar. For the most part they would be as in his day. Neither *GAGAWA* nor *gagawa* would be evident, however, and he would notice the absence of a club-house, the decay in ritual practices, the lack of any sustained and systematic knowledge about the divine. There would be no youths swaggering about the club-house in long breechclouts, no layabouts to be compared with the industrious, no old men in honourable retirement. Something of an egalitarian himself, perhaps, he might be startled at the way in which the notion of equivalence had developed. Yet he would know that in narratives much of his own tradition lived on in the present generation, even though they were not able to comprehend it as well as he himself could. On the other hand, he might well wonder, as he began to understand the present social organization, whether he had really come back to the people he had left.

Tradition seems contained not so much in organization as in a complex of related ideas. *Puoker* are not organized, with one

<hr />

[1] *Supra*, pp. 158–60.   [2] *Infra*, p. 372.

exception do not *br'ngun'guni*.[1] If the *puoker* of narratives were seen to be organized as though they were members of community, thus instructing men and women how they should organize themselves, they could scarcely be considered as belonging to the divine. *Puoker* detail the processes of production, reveal the nature and propensities of men and women and children, tell humans how to make artifacts, inform them as to how the divine may help them to maintain themselves. But it is for men, the culture bearers, to determine how they should organize themselves within the principles of being revealed by *puoker*. Men are possessed of *gneker*, they dream, they have access to the charms and truths revealed in dreams and narratives. Their problem, as moral beings, is to discover those organizational forms which contain their awareness: an appropriate movement from the divine to the moral. And just such a movement—the realization in organizational form of awareness in and through narratives —was what Tangu were attempting when they engaged in cargo activities.[2] Further, despite the disappearance of the *garamb* and its procedures, the essential relevances of the *garamb*[3] are still being conveyed and articulated in narratives—a feature whose importance we shall appreciate later.[4]

If one asks Tangu whether, in N. 1, the leading man of Wasamb was 'right' or 'wrong' to exclude the orphans, they shrug their shoulders and say that that is what he did. 'Right' and 'wrong' are moral issues for men in community to decide. For *puoker* the terms are irrelevant. If a man is asked whether, in a similar situation, he would or would not exclude the orphans, his answer is that he might or he might not. If he allowed them in there would probably be trouble: the orphans were smelly, someone would drop a remark, he as a responsible man would be obliged to make a reply and there might be a quarrel. If he did not invite them in there might be an earthquake which would bury them. . . . On the whole, Tangu agree, it is best to avoid being found in such a situation—it is a bad business, *imbatekas*. Yet if a man is asked why he leaches sago in the way it is leached in a narrative, his answer is because that is the way sago is leached, that is the way the *puoker* taught the

---

[1] The Founder, *supra*, p. 169, and *infra*, p. 325.   [2] B-1960: 217–28.
[3] The procedures, of course, would have guided and assisted comprehension of the narratives.   [4] *Infra*, pp. 454–7.

PLATE VI

a. Preparing the feast

b. Pounding the pith preparatory to leaching sago

ancestors to leach sago, and that is the way *puoker* are teaching the living to leach sago. So that where, as in the last case, the encounter between Tangu and their narratives bears upon activities that do not necessarily presuppose moral or organizational relations between members of community, then the truth is direct and comprehension follows fast on the initial apprehension. But where, as in the first instance, the encounter bears upon moral and organizational relations, then the narrative is both prophetic and oracular.

As with the technological process, so in most instances with the charm.[1] For though the latter is considered to have powers of causation, it does not necessarily predicate the kinds of organizational or moral relations between the members of the community in which its power will be effective. If a man deliberately chooses to do to another man what one *puok* does to another, regarding the *puok* directly as exemplar, he does so at his peril. He is engaged in reciprocities, and *puoker* are not. Should he go deeper than a mere apprehension, arriving at a comprehension, still the narrative remains both prophetic and oracular. For while a narrative may reveal certain principles of being, this is all it can do. Decision one way or another is a moral act which cannot be made by a *puok*, which can only be made by one who has moral being, who is aware. And the deeper the comprehension and awareness the more complex the issues become, the harder it is to make a decision. Yet assuming that behind the scrutiny of a narrative there lie well-defined motives and interests, the tale may be more helpful than tossing a coin. If in life a father were to find his sons misbehaving behind the *garamb*—Should he expel them from the village? If he did so— Would the sons be permanently lost to the village? Does the story mean that a father ought to keep an eye on the back of the *garamb*, looking out for possible acts of a heinous kind so as to guard against them? Or does the tale carry an opposite gist, that it is silly for a father to watch the back of the *garamb*?

Such questions are predicated by the oracular nature of a narrative. They raise moral issues which the divine cannot answer directly, which the living have to answer for themselves. In fact, even at the level of apprehension, a father with reciprocities to nurture would have taken the point that discretion is

[1] But see *supra*, pp. 187–9.

often the better part of virtue. And should a foolish father have decided to act like the father in the narrative, then the narrative would have been prophetic. For, given the moralities, the sons would have been so shamed at the discovery of their mis-behaviour, and their subsequent expulsion from the village, that they would never have returned, had they, indeed, been able or allowed to do so. They would have been lost to the community in very truth.

Should a father, then, turn a blind eye to what might be going on behind the *garamb*?

A father is a responsible man. To one who is perceptive a narrative may yield knowledge, perhaps a deeper and wider understanding of predicament and dilemma in the human con-dition. Though the divine may be distanced or bridled with ritual, it remains unobliged, intervenes at its own behest. And it does so to put the moralities in issue. In seeking the aid of a narrative in coming to a particular decision, therefore, a man should reflect and look into himself, be aware that truth is compounded of irony.

The Slit-gong

Tangu have two narratives about the origin of the slit-gong,[1] the one figuring father and son, the other husband and wife. Both dialogues reach towards, and comment upon, particular kinds of responsibility.

N. 12: *The Slit-gong and a Foolish Father*

Once upon a time father and son were sitting quietly by their house in the village.

Thinking, on an impulse, that he would like a coconut, son fetched out a length of old barkcloth, knotted the ends together, put his feet into the circlet and clambered nimbly up a nearby palm. Arrived in the fronds, as he was twisting a nut from its stem, he thought he heard a noise in the forest. . . . Was it a pig?

Son paused, looking closely through the undergrowth—Surely that was a scuffle, something moving in the shrubbery?

Son slithered down the palm to the ground. 'Father! Father!' he hissed. 'I think there is a pig in the forest just there!'

---

[1] Both these narratives have been published before in B-1959(*d*). And see *supra*, pp. 181–3.

Father jumped to his feet, took down his spear, and made off to where son was excitedly pointing. Slipping silently through the bushes, he saw a shadow in the underbrush. . . . Father halted abruptly, gathered himself, hurled his spear straight and true to the shadow.

Squeal of pain there was none. No snort of rage told of a wound. . . .

Cautiously, for a wounded pig is cunning and dangerous, father crept foward to see what had happened.

There was no pig in the underbrush. His spear was embedded in a slit-gong.

That night there was a terrible storm.

Father, who was sleeping in the forest, built himself a temporary shelter. But the earth shook, the rain poured down, the flood waters rose. Father's shelter collapsed and was washed away. The slit-gong was swept to the bottom of the valley and cast up on the rocks of a stream.

The following night, as father slept, the slit-gong spoke to him. 'I am not a pig—so why spear me? Nor am I a man—so why did you try to kill me with your spear? If I wanted to I could break up your house and the houses of all of you in the village. . . . Now get up and go into the forest and hunt for some game! Go to your garden also and dig up heaps and heaps of yams and taros. Bring all your foodstuffs to this place, and then tell all the villagers that you are going to give a feast.'

Father girded his loins. He took some game in the forest, brought it back to the village, laid it out in his hut. Then he went to his garden to fetch yams and taros. He loaded the tubers into a string bag, returned to the village, packed his meat on top of the tubers, and took all his foodstuffs to the stream.

Father walked along the banks of the stream, showing his food-stuffs to the waters. And by the time he came to the slit-gong poised on its rocks in the stream the waters were mollified, no longer angry with him.

All the villagers were invited to come down to the stream, to see the slit-gong, to feast on the food that father had collected together.

The villagers ate and ate, and still they had room for more. But father's string bag was empty. He had not collected enough.

The waters were angered, thunder roared, lightning flashed, rain poured down, the winds blew, the flood rose. . . . The villagers were afraid, and went back to the village. The slit-gong stayed where it was, in the stream.

So it was that men have to make their slit-gongs for themselves. They have to cut down the tree which makes the barrel, they have to hollow it out, and they have to carve it all by themselves. The slit-gongs that men make today do not understand what is happening to them. But the first slit-gong, the slit-gong in the stream, that slit-gong understands. It was this first slit-gong which gave to all the other slit-gongs that have come after the power of making themselves understood.

N. 13: *The Slit-gong and a Clever Husband*

Once upon a time long ago there were no slit-gongs. Men had trumps of bamboo.

On one fine day, when wife had gone into the forest to forage for edible leaves, husband, who had stayed behind in his hut to rest, played on his trump.

Wife heard the notes of the trump and returned to the village at once to see what was happening. Husband, seeing her coming, hid the trump.

'What was that noise just now?' wife asked. 'What were you doing?'

'Noise? What noise?' husband protested. 'I was doing nothing!'

Next morning in the garden, wife asked her children if they had seen where father had hidden his something.

'You ask him yourself', the children replied. 'We did not see him do anything.'

The following day, as soon as husband had gone off into the forest to hunt, wife started a search of the house. High and low she searched diligently and carefully into every part of the hut—until at last she had the trump in her hands.

Wife put the trump to her lips and started to play. But she was clumsy and unused to the thing. She broke the vibrant—Poinnng!

Away in the forest husband heard it. 'Oh!' he exclaimed in vexation as he started back to the village. 'My slit-gong [*sic*] is broken! My slit-gong is no good any more!'

Husband brought no game back with him to the village. 'Why did you break my slit-gong?' he demanded, going straight to his wife. 'It was my slit-gong. Now what can I play on?'

They slept.

Early next morning husband took his axe and adze and went into the forest to cut himself a slit-gong. He came to the right place, chose the right tree. He decided to cut down the tree and make himself a slit-gong. Then he slept.

Next morning husband cut down the tree. He stripped off the branches, chopped out the centre section of trunk, and chipped it with his adze into the shape of a slit-gong. He incised the outside, gouging and carving a handsome design. He carved out the lug, made a slit along the top of the body, and hollowed out the inside. And when all had been done he cut himself a hardwood wand and struck the slit-gong with the butt.

In the village wife heard the deep booms carrying over the forest. 'What is that?' she wondered. 'Can it be a slit-gong?'

When husband returned to the village he told his wife what he had done. 'I have made a slit-gong for myself', he told her. 'It is mine, I made it. I cut down a *mngwota* tree,[1] carved it, and hollowed it—I did it all by myself! Call your brothers—they can haul my slit-gong through the forest and bring it here to the village. We will feast them. You go to the garden and dig out as many yams and taros as you can. I will go hunting and find meat for them.'

So the feast was prepared. On the appointed day wife's brothers were called to go into the forest to haul the slit-gong back to the village. They feasted at the place where the slit-gong had been made, eating well. Then, after each of the brothers had taken his turn at striking the slit-gong, they tied strong vines to the lug of the instrument and hauled it over the ground back to the village.

When they arrived at the borders of the village, they halted. Wife gave them more food, the brothers eating their fill until nothing was left. Then they brought the slit-gong into the village.

Husband waited until four moons had waxed and waned, and then, when all the nights had been counted, he chewed areca-nut over the slit-gong and threw the broken trump into its belly. He took up his hardwood wand and struck the gong with the butt, showing it how it should speak, what it should say, and the directions in which its voice should go.

The *garamb* no longer exists, the associated procedures are no longer practised. But the relevances of the *garamb*, which would have been more accessible through the procedures, are still potentially communicable through narratives. Slit-gongs, on the other hand, still exist, are still used. And though the rituals and feastings which accompanied the manufacture and positioning of slit-gongs have been abandoned, the narratives remain, and as between narratives and slit-gong fields of awareness are generated and communicated.

A gong rather than a drum, for there are no membranes,[2] a

---

[1] In Tangu slit-gongs are made from the *mngwota* tree. I am unable to give the botanical name.

[2] But if gong and drum are defined by the mode of sound production then a slit-gong is a drum. For the sound does not appear to proceed from the qualities of resonance in the wood so much as from the reverberations in the sound box.

slit-gong is cut from the straight, middle portion of the *mngwota* tree, hollowed, and carved on the outside faces. Echoing the process of construction set down in N. 13, the tools are the axe and adze. Either a man will make his own slit-gong, or he will persuade others to make one for him, feasting them as they work in the forest. In both cases, though, a party of men, usually wife's brothers, are required to haul the instrument from the forest where it is made to the village or hunting-lodge where it will be used. Hauliers are usually feasted, both in the forest preparatory to transport, and then afterwards on arrival at the settlement. Once there, the gong is normally set clear of the ground, in the horizontal plane, on wooden or stone wedges. By striking the gong on its upper face near the central slit with the butt end of a hardwood stave, but never with the flat, a booming note is obtained which may carry some three or four miles, depending on position, wind, and general weather conditions. A slit-gong belongs to the husband of a household, and only he may use it as against the world. Wife, children of the household,[1] co-operating brothers, and members of the latters' households may use it in an emergency, or as a particular convenience. Others are not normally allowed to use the instrument unless specifically permitted to do so.

Slit-gong signals are usually rhythmical phrases taken from songs, linguistic rhythms, or jingles: sometimes a man may invent a rhythm for his own personal use. Each person of mature age in Tangu has a call-sign, or several call-signs. Just as everyone in Tangu has a personal name by which most people know them, and several other different names by which they are known to particular people, so he or she has a general call-sign and a series of particular call-signs. Personal signals and knowledge of call-signs go with close and affective relationships. Humans apart, domestic pigs—but not hunting dogs—are allocated, and respond to, call-signs. Particular phrases identify named topographical features and localities as well as common and well-known social situations. Each dance is known by a different phrase, and feasts, number of days in the future, discoveries of theft or trespass, the death of a person or domestic pig or hunting-dog, mourning, success in the chase,

---

[1] Though today children do from time to time use a slit-gong—particularly the school slit-gong—they are still not formally allowed to do so.

suspicions of sorcery, a confession made, the approach of an administrative officer, anger, ill will, pleas for help, warnings to keep clear, the birth of children, betrothal, accident, general recall to the village, or the call to school or mission service—all have their own phrases and rhythms. Having little to do with morse and other codes dependent on a written language, the system of signalling is not as complex as might at first be thought. It depends upon situation and a general knowledge of current affairs.[1] Thus though a signal might contain the call-signs of addressees, the phrase for the situation—say a pig slain in a *juaka* trap—followed by the identification of the locality, the call-sign of those required to help the hunter carry his kill back to the village, and finally the call-sign or signature of the originator, it can be considerably shortened by presuming a knowledge of situation and affairs. For those who hear and do not understand, the signal has neither meaning nor concern nor relevance: it is not a broadcast to the world, but a message to particular people within terms which those in community have in common. Because co-operators will know that one of their number has gone to look at his *juaka*, where the latter is, and that they—and only they—may be required to help with the carrying, all that the successful trapper need do is signal 'pig killed'. Those in exchange relationships will not have been backward in informing themselves of the hunter's intentions: ears will be cocked, listening for the signal. Later, when the pig has been brought back to the village, they will listen to hear if their own call-signs are among those signalled to come for a share of the meat.

Tangu children learn the meanings of slit-gong signals as they learn their language and the names of people and places. Indeed, through their knowledge of slit-gong signals, children come to have an explicit and objective awareness of social situations, and the ways in which they may develop, long before they actually experience them. From apprehending the signals— which constitute a formal taxonomy in rhythmical terms of most of the situations likely to be encountered in social life—a six year old moves towards comprehension and a deeper knowledge of what a situation may entail in terms of satisfied or disappointed expectations. Having an intensely personal value,

[1] See B-1959(*d*): 138–43.

slit-gong signals are also publications.[1] A slit-gong signal is news, news which affects everyone in a small community. It starts a train of events which are going to affect the mutual interrelationships of all in the community to a greater or lesser extent. Moreover, the signals a man makes on his slit-gong reveal his hunting prowess, his capacity to provide feasts, the dances he knows, his favourite dances ('There goes old Mangai again!'), his judgement, whether he has so offended as to bring *ranguova* into action against him, for whom he gives feasts, to whom he distributes the fruits of his hunting and gardening activities, how often he is involved in cases of theft or trespass, his proneness to accident. . . . And for those who are familiar with a man's mode of signalling it is also possible to interpret his mood and temper. A man's behaviour in relation to his slit-gong accurately defines his being as a social personality, is as suggestive of himself as personal acquaintance.

The two narratives about the slit-gong provide different but complementary approaches to the kinds of awareness which the slit-gong represents to Tangu. N. 13 concentrates on the slit-gong as an instrument, on the way in which it is made by a man who uses his *gnek*, who can think of a technological process, who uses the right wood, who can make arrangements for having the instrument set up in a place where it can be effective. Husband is competent, resourceful, and responsible. Led into making a slit-gong by analogizing from the trump or Jew's harp, he still has to chew areca-nut over the instrument to make it effective as a slit-gong. Not only is the slit-gong brought into an association with the divine, with being, by figuring as a major theme in a narrative, but in the play within a play this feature is further emphasized. Being consists in an awareness of both moral and divine as well as in an awareness of the relations between moral and divine. The ingenuity of the cultural and technological animal is explained in relation to the divine and not in terms of itself. N. 12 contains no technological advice, but still it relates the moral and the divine. Like storm and flood, the slit-gong is represented as having the potential to 'break up your house and the houses of all of you in the village'. The central theme con-

[1] *Supra*, pp. 181–3. And see also B-1959(*d*): 142.

cerns communication, understanding. If a slit-gong is ordinarily a vehicle of communication, in the narrative it becomes a vehicle of awareness—the communication of that which belongs to comprehension rather than apprehension.[1] And, as in N. 6, the tale of Nimbamung, it draws attention to a failure in awareness, to the failure to distinguish the moral from the divine, to the failure to realize the relations between the moral and divine.

The opening scene of N. 12 has father and son quietly minding their own business. Son is divine in relation to father, and son it is who climbs the coconut, hears what he thinks is a pig, and mediates between—or relates—his father and the divine. Through son father is pushed into flux, development, and change. Successively the slit-gong is associated with pig, storm, flood, man, talking, dream, stream, and stones. Further, father receives advice from the gong in a dream—something which he would normally get from the ghost of his dead father or elder brother. At one time, perhaps, a slit-gong may have been represented as the shrine or dwelling-place of a ghost. Indeed, if this were so, it would explain more pertinently why father and son in particular are involved in the opening episode, and why the slit-gong was first thought to be a pig. Before being circumcised, it will be remembered, Tuman was buried under a slit-gong;[2] the pig of the circumcision was supplied by the father, and both the pig of the circumcision and the pig of the slit-gong should be caught in a *juaka* trap;[3] father is elsewhere represented as virtually incarnate in a pig;[4] and father will be dream-image or ghost to son. . . . Father builds a shelter—evoking *garamb*, circumcision, protection from the storm, divine—but it is swept away. Taking up the associations of slit-gong with pig and the pig of the circumcision, father feasts the gong. But he cannot provide enough. The waters are angry—as others would be if father did not provide a large enough feast on the occasion of a son's emergence from the *garamb*—storm and flood follow, and the slit-gong which can speak for itself, and which has been cast on to stones in the stream as in life it is laid on stone or wooden wedges, remains in the stream. Man has to make a slit-gong for himself.

Not simply evoking male filiation, the father–son, circumcision,

---

[1] These particular facets of relevance find more appropriate scope for analysis in narratives that follow.
[2] *Supra*, p. 221.   [3] *Supra*, p. 168.   [4] *Infra*, pp. 397–9.

the *garamb*, and father's duty of making son into a responsible member of community, these themes seem to be attached to the gong itself. Made in the forest from a wild tree, the slit-gong has a responsible role to perform in community. Itself may not have a *gnek*, but it has to amplify the overt activities of *gneker*. Moreover, since the amplifications are also publications, a slit-gong should speak as though responsibly. It is going to precipitate events in community, it is going to make decisions overt and explicit. As a boy is gradually inducted into the moral community, his impulses excised, so a slit-gong is pulled out of the wild and into community. And, since it speaks for a responsible man, it is itself made as though responsible.

In the second of the two narratives, N. 13, the gong-as-trump starts in the moral order, is broken, comes into association with *gnek* or thought, is found in the wild or divine, brought back into the village, and finally culturally reassociated with the divine through chewing areca-nut—a feature which also implies a generative quality in the slit-gong. Husband is juxtaposed with wife and children, and it is wife, divine in relation to himself, who breaks the trump and sets husband on the way to using his *gnek*. As soon as he knows that his trump has been broken, husband brings back no game: he has no husbandly favours for the wife who has been wilful, who has become—albeit temporarily—more woman than wife. No longer in use today, in the past trumps were used for serenading, or for amusing oneself when passing the time. Their associations are with young men about to be married, with the newly married, with men who have not yet been fully aroused to the extent and meaning of their responsibilities. A male toy, a trump which is broken by a wife seems to be a signal wakening a husband to a larger sense of awareness. Here it results in the husband using his *gnek*: he goes into the forest to make a slit-gong. Proud of his achievement, he has a new air of authority about him as he instructs his wife on how to proceed for the feast. And she is meekly obedient. Fully engaged in feasting reciprocities, husband now has a slit-gong, is a fully responsible man—features which are re-emphasized towards the end of the narrative when husband throws his broken trump into the belly of the slit-gong. He has finished with trumperies. He is now ready, with and through his slit-gong, to assume his larger responsibilities.

Though the behaviour of the children is here different from that of the children in the other 'trump situations' which we shall presently encounter,[1] their presence serves to emphasize that when a man has married a wife and begotten children he should give up the trump—and what a trump represents—and take to a slit-gong—and what it is that a slit-gong represents: responsible use of the *gnek*; technological skills; responsible initiatives; effective articulation and communication of thought; management of affairs; obligations to son and the *garamb* through which boys may be made into men; a control over wife; the provision of feasts; acknowledgement of reciprocities, particularly with wife's brothers; the use of dreams and charms; maintaining the moral order; recognition of appropriate relations with the divine; the creation of culture from wild and divine. Such capacities spell out awareness.

Tales of Sorcerers

Sorcerers or *ranguova* are men. So that narratives about *ranguova* are about men and women, not about *puoker*. Yet as *puoker* are anthropomorphic, so the characters in narratives about *ranguova* tend to be like *puoker*. Still, framed within two kinds of dialogue, *ranguma*/community and *ranguma*/individual, the stories that follow convey a more obvious awareness than stories about *puoker*: the message is simple and direct.

N. 14: *The Men in the Pig-trap*

One night a band of *ranguova* from a village in the vicinity of Moresapa came prowling into the bushlands of Tangu. . . .

Clouds gathered, a storm broke, it started to rain.

Now it chanced that as the rain sheeted down the *ranguova* were passing close to a *juaka* pig-trap. And as the owner of the trap had placed some coconut fronds over the bundle of logs, the wretched fellows thought it would make a fine shelter for them. So in they went, seating themselves in two rows inside the *juaka*. One of them,

---

[1] *Infra*, pp. 302–3, 382–3. Here, unlike other 'trump situations', the children do not betray their father. Yet would it have made any difference to the gist of this particular story had they done so? I think not. Their presence here simply seems to indicate the state of maturity of the husband when related to trump, and invites the expectation of maturation which is realized when husband makes his gong. As we shall see, where there is a betrayal of father the act is followed up and adumbrated. Here there is no need to do so.

a *girili*, a man whose skin was dry and flaked and peeling from ringworm, sat in the middle.

The night was dark, made darker by the storm.

The *ranguova* had not been sitting in the *juaka* for long when one of them, by accident, sprang the trap.

Down on top of them came the pile of logs.

All the *ranguova* were killed—except for one, the *girili*. He lay under the logs, imprisoned but alive.

Next morning the owner of the trap, coming to examine his *juaka*, heard the *bunjera* bird chuckling over the trap. And knowing by this that he had caught something, he broke into a run and hurried to his *juaka*.

The logs had fallen—that was all right. But what was that moving inside?

'What kind of pig have I caught?' wondered that man as he thrust his spear into the scaly flesh. 'What kind of a pig has skin like that?'

The man returned to his hunting-lodge, sounded his slit-gong, and went back again to the trap. He cleared away the logs, laid out the bodies, counted them.

When his brothers, having heard the slit-gong, arrived to help him with his kill, the man told them what had happened. They trussed the bodies of the *ranguova* on to poles as though they were pigs and set off for the village. Arrived, the man sounded his slit-gong, asking the neighbouring villagers to come and identify and collect their dead.

First came men from Amuk. They looked at the bodies, shook their heads. 'These are not men from Amuk', they said.

When those from Amuk had gone, some from Andemarup came. But they too shook their heads and departed. For the *ranguova* were not from Andemarup. After them came men from all the other villages around, from Jumpitzir and beyond. They did not know the *ranguova*.

Then, last of all, the man signalled for the men of Moresapa to come. Not a single one came.

'Aha!' the villagers exclaimed. 'So! These *ranguova* are Moresapa fellows!'

The villagers cut the dead *ranguova* into strips, stuffed the meat into bamboo barrels, cooked it, and ate it. They gave some of the meat to folk in neighbouring villages, and those who did not like fat on their meat ate the *girili*.

N. 15: *The Woman in the Woodpile*

It happened one day that a husband had occasion to beat his wife. And she, being sorely vexed and sorry for herself, went off alone to spend the night in her garden shelter.

Arrived in the garden, she grew anxious and afraid. So, thinking to protect herself, she gathered together a large pile of firewood, heaped it in the middle of the floor in the shelter, and made herself a comfortable nest. When night came she repaired to the shelter, lay in her nest, and, pulling some of the sticks over her body so as to hide herself, lay down to sleep.

Clouds gathered in the night, the storm broke, rain poured down.

Now it happened that a band of *ranguova* from Wanitzir were prowling in the vicinity. They saw that woman's garden shelter in the darkness, and they decided to take cover. So, entering into the shelter, they sat down in two lines along the walls. But one of them did not. He sat in the middle by the pile of firewood.

The *ranguova* had not been in the shelter very long when one of them remarked on the cold. 'How about making a fire?' he suggested.

The band was agreed. The man by the woodpile began to pick out some pieces. Fumbling in the darkness as he looked for suitable bits, suddenly his fingers curled round a nipple! Cautiously, feeling further into the woodpile, he knew a breast was cupped in his palm.

'Ssh!' whispered the woman, holding his wrist.

'Who are you?' breathed the *ranguma*.

'Never mind who I am! Don't talk—wait!'

So, saying nothing of what he had found in the woodpile, the *ranguma* continued to hand out pieces of firewood to the others.

The rain streamed down, drumming on the roof. The fire was warm, the atmosphere in the hut grew drowsy. Very soon all the *ranguova*—except for that one—had fallen asleep, snoring contentedly.

'Now', demanded the *ranguma*, 'tell me—'

'Sssh!' the woman cut in. 'Don't waken the others—you and I can have pleasure!'

Straightway the *ranguma* loosened his breechclout, freed his tool, and gave it to the woman.

She cradled it in her hands, stroking and chafing until that maleness stood as long and straight and stiff as a tree. Then, freeing one arm, she eased her cane armband down over her forearm and hand so that it encircled that tool. She brought it into her quim. . . .

All ready now, gripping him tightly in her quim, the woman twisted that armband, tightening and pulling and tugging with all the strength that she had.

The *ranguma* bellowed with pain—shriek upon shriek, arms and legs flailing. The others, wakened by the clamour, struggled and fought in the darkness as they tried to gain the door of the shelter.

In a few moments it was over. As the *ranguova* scattered into the forest, the woman jumped from her nest in the woodpile and ran to the village as fast as her legs could take her.

She arrived screaming, waking the whole village with her wailing and screeching. And when the villagers asked her what the matter was, she could make no reply. She could only scream and laugh and weep by turns, running up and down the *pekas* as though crazy.

The *ranguma*, meanwhile, had gone down to the stream to bathe his sore tool. As it softened and drooped in the cool waters, he was able to remove the cane armband. Then, after resting, he went to look for his companions.

By and by, when all the band had found each other in the darkness, they talked of what had happened. They resolved that the woman should die. So, whetting their spears, they returned to the shelter.

But, as we know, the woman had gone. No one was there.

N. 16: *A Sorcerer Worsted*

One night a *ranguma* decided to strike[1] one of the boys in the *garamb*. He stole silently up to the *garamb*, unlatched the cross-bolts over the door, crept in. . . .

It happened, however, that one of the boys in the *garamb* had been unable to sleep that night. He heard the *ranguma* fumbling with the bolts on the door. And knowing that such stealth could bode no good, he slipped from his pallet, hid behind the kingpost, and waited. . . .

The door opened, the *ranguma* came in.

The boy leapt at the man. Before that *ranguma* could know what was happening the boy had grasped him by his matted hair and thrown him to the floor!

The noise wakened all the boys in the *garamb*. They set upon the *ranguma*, pummelling and beating him till he was dead. Then they took the body out of the *garamb* and on to the *pekas*, laid it out, and called to their fathers—'Wake up! Wake up! Come on the *pekas*! Come and see the pig we have caught!'

So all the men of the village awoke and came on to the *pekas* to see the dead fellow. They examined the body, then threw it away in the forest.

N. 17: *Mariap Alert*

One day a man, whose name was Mariap, decided to catch a pig in a pit-fall. So he went into the forest, chose a suitable place, dug a

---

[1] A *ranguma* is said to 'strike'. The same verbal root is used for 'striking' a slit-gong, 'striking' (spearing) a pig, or where one man strikes or cuffs another.

deep hole and, fixing some sharpened stakes at the bottom, covered the top with a framework of sticks and leaves. Then he returned to his hunting-lodge.

Now there were some *ranguova* who had determined to deal with Mariap. So during the night they went to the pit-fall to prepare an ambush. One of their number, they decided, should lie on the ground close to the pit-fall covered over with leaves. Then, when Mariap came to examine his trap in the morning, the fellow under the leaves would trip Mariap by the ankles, whilst the others, hiding near by, would rush him.

Next morning Mariap came to look at his trap. He noticed a slight bump in the ground alongside his pit-fall. . . . He stopped to consider. 'That bump wasn't there yesterday', he mused. 'It might be a snake under there, or again it might be a —?'

Mariap stood quite still, looking carefully around and listening. 'A *ranguma*!' he decided. 'Much more likely than a snake . . .'

Mariap shifted his breechclout, peed into cupped hands. Then he drank. He held the last mouthful in his cheeks, blew it out in a fine spray over his spear and into the air around. Thus fortified, he rushed forward and plunged his spear into the mound of leaves.

Because of what he had done Mariap was quite safe. Those other *ranguova*, hiding in the forest and waiting to pounce on him, were helpless. Unable to move, as though rooted in the ground, they could only watch as Mariap went about his business.

Mariap swept the leaves aside and called to his father to come and look at the pig he had caught. And father, waiting in the hunting-lodge, came running. Together they laid out the body and carved it in pieces.

When they had done, father and son returned to the village, leaving the pieces of meat in the forest.

As soon as Mariap and his father were safely away, the *ranguova* were freed and able to move. They came out of their hiding-places, collected the fragments of their dead comrade, and buried them.

They were all Moresapa men. They wanted to kill Mariap because of some trouble they had had with his father's brother over a pig.

N. 18: *Nuok Resigned*

One day Nuok and his brother set traps in the forest, in Savangi bush, to catch bush-rats and possums. Then they returned to their hunting-lodge.

Now some *ranguova* had decided to deal with poor Nuok, and during the night they laid an ambush close to the traps.

Next day, when Nuok came to look at his traps, the *ranguova* surprised him as he bent down to examine a trap. They hit him across the back of the neck with a heavy stick.

Nuok fell senseless. The *ranguova* worked their medicines on him and set a day for his death.

When Nuok regained consciousness he returned to the village much troubled. Some of the villagers told him that a gang of *ranguova*, their faces blackened, had been seen skulking in the forest. Nuok knew then that his days were numbered.

Next day Nuok took his nephew[1] with him to examine the traps. They found a small possum, stuffed it into a string bag, and reset the trap.

As they did so there was a rumbling and snorting in the bush close by.

'What can that be?' the boy asked, much alarmed.

'Only a pig . . .', Nuok replied, not wanting to frighten the child.

But Nuok knew that the noise had been made by *ranguova* hiding in the bush. He accompanied his nephew back to the village, the possum slung from his shoulder.

A few days later, whilst in his hunting-lodge, Nuok fell ill. His brothers made a stretcher for him and carried him back to the village, where he would be safer. But it wasn't much use. In a couple of days Nuok was dead.

Who did it?

No one knows. Nuok's brothers are still looking for the culprits.

N. 19: *A Sorcerer Born*

One day, a woman who was pregnant with a son went to her garden to dig out some yams and taros. She was alone that day.

As she worked in the garden a *ranguma* struck her and worked on her.

The villagers found the woman a little while later, lying unconscious. Her brothers rallied to help her, forcing ginger and pepper down her throat, uttering many good spells to counter those of the *ranguma*.

By and by the woman returned to her senses, wholly recovering.

But the babe in her womb had heard all the spells. They were in him, so that he would always remember them. He had absorbed the power of the pepper and ginger, he was at one with the *ranguma* who had struck at his mother.

The woman bore her son in due course.

When this boy was about two years old mother took him with

---

[1] Sister's son.

her to the garden one day. She killed a small lizard for the child to play with, to keep him quiet while she worked.

The boy played with the dead lizard for a while, and then, taking a yam thorn and piercing the lizard's head, front paws, hind paws, and flanks, he uttered a spell.

At once the lizard revived.

The boy screamed with delight, holding the wriggling lizard by the tail, calling to his mother and telling her he had brought the animal back to life.

'Don't talk nonsense, my child!' mother scolded, thinking that son was trying to trick her with another, live, lizard which he had caught.

Son allowed the lizard to run off through the underbrush, and he and his mother returned to the village.

When the boy had grown somewhat, and was about nine years old, he asked father if he could go with him when he went to examine his traps.

Father was delighted. Together they set off into the forest.

In the first pit-fall they found a dead wallaby. It had drowned in the water at the bottom of the pit-fall. Father hoisted the animal out and asked son to watch it while he went to look at some other traps he had set.

Son plucked a thorn from a nearby vine, pierced the head, limbs, and flanks of the drowned wallaby, and uttered a spell.

The wallaby revived.

Holding the struggling wallaby by the tail, son yelled to his father to come and see what was happening.

Father came running—but he was not quick enough. As he entered the clearing the wallaby broke loose and bounded away into the forest.

Son explained to his father that the wallaby had only been pretending to be dead, that it had started to try and break free as soon as father had gone off to look at his other traps.

But father was puzzled. It didn't seem right. Surely that wallaby was dead when he had taken it from the pit-fall? And later, when that evening he recounted the adventures of the day to his wife, she listened very quietly. She remembered the time she had given son a dead lizard and he had claimed to have brought it back to life. She thought too of that day when, with son in her womb, the *ranguma* had struck her while she was in the garden alone. . . . But she held her peace.

One day father and son again went out together to examine their traps. In one of the large pit-falls father had dug they found a sizeable pig. It had been drowned in the water at the bottom.

Father hauled the pig from the hole, laid it down by the side of the pit-fall, and told his son to watch over it while he went to examine the other traps. But, remembering what had happened in the case of the wallaby, no sooner had he passed from view into the forest than he doubled back to see what his son would do. He hid himself in the bushes and waited.[1]

Son searched for a vine, plucked a thorn, pierced the pig in head, forelegs, hindlegs, and flanks, and uttered his spell.

At once the pig revived.

Son yelled to his father for help. But father knew what he would have to do. He balanced his spear in his palm, steadied, hurled the weapon with all his strength at his son.

The boy fell, transfixed.

Father threw the body of his son into the same pit-fall from which the pig had been taken, and he shovelled all the earth on top. Then he returned to the village.

'Where is our son?' mother asked.

Father told his story, missing no detail. 'So I killed him', he finished at last. 'I ran him through with my spear and buried him in the pit-fall out in the forest there.'

Wife was silent. Then, 'My brothers will have no quarrel with you', she said. 'Long ago, you remember, a *ranguma* struck me when I was in the garden alone. It was with a thorn that he struck me. . . . No! My brothers can have no quarrel with you for killing our son.'

But son was not really dead. He cured his wounds with the spells he had in his head, with the spells which had been born in him. He scrambled through the loose earth piled on top of him, and he returned to the village.

When son had reached puberty, thoughts of revenge took shape in his mind. 'Now!' he thought. 'Now I will pay him back!'

So it was that one day when father had gone out into the forest to examine his traps and dig a pit-fall, son waited in ambush. He waited until father had almost finished digging his pit-fall, then he struck him from behind, pushing him into the hole.

Son considered the matter for some minutes. . . . Then he dragged father out of the pit-fall, laid him by the side of the hole, and pierced head, arms, legs, and flanks with a bone from the wing of a flying-fox.

Father shook his head and revived.

'The time was', son said, 'when you tried to kill and bury me. Now I am paying you back. You will go back to the village and eat the

---

[1] Going into the forest and doubling back is, as we shall see, a father's favourite stratagem.

meal which mother is preparing for you. Then, after you have eaten, you will drop dead.'

And so it was. Father returned to the village and went to his hut, where his wife had just finished cooking a meal. He ate well. He was just rolling himself a cigar after his supper when he keeled over, dead.

'Some while ago,' son said to his mother, 'father speared me and buried me. Now I have paid him back. I marked him and I struck him. He is dead.'

Son dug a deep hole, threw the body of father to the bottom, and piled the earth on top.

N. 20: *Warrior Unmanned*

One day a man from Riekitzir was walking through the forest when, chancing to trespass into lands belonging to Andarumitzir, he fell into a pit-fall which had been dug for a pig.

The Andarum fellow, who had made the pit-fall, and who had been waiting close by, put his shield over the mouth of the hole and mocked the Rieken inside.

'Ha! Ha! You yam-eater—you!' laughed the fellow. 'Haven't you got enough yams in your garden that you want to come trespassing down here? Did you want some of our sago, then? Yah-ha! What a fine pig I have in my pit-fall!'

The Rieken was desperate. But on looking up at his enemy he noticed that he had not fastened his breechclout properly, that his balls were hanging outside. . . .

Quick as thought that Rieken leapt from the hole. Grasping those ballocks, he wrenched hard, tearing them off!

The man from Andarum fainted, lying prone as though dead.

The Rieken scrambled from the pit-fall, smashed the fellow's head with his shield,[1] and made off through the forest back to his village. Arrived, he told everyone what he had done, boasting to his wife of his strength.

After all, if he had not killed that man from Andarum he himself would have been killed and then eaten.

N. 21: *Chestnuts*

Once upon a time an old woman went with her brother's young son to pick *juatak'mba*[2] chestnuts.

---

[1] In parenthesis one may note here that Tangu say that in the past it was general practice to go hunting accoutred with shields.

[2] Botanical name not certainly identified. Strictly speaking the suffix *-mba* is an isolate. Thus when the word occurs in a sentence 'chestnuts' are *juatak* merely. But when one says 'chestnuts' in isolation, then the suffix *-mba* is added.

Arrived at the marsh where the chestnut trees grew, the woman marked off one of the trees, started to fence it about, and breathed a spell over the fence as she worked.

'Hey! What d'you think you're doing?' demanded the youth. 'Stop that at once or I'll hit you with my adze!'

So saying, he pushed the old woman aside and breathed his own spell over the fence.

'That's my tree!' screamed the old woman, rushing to the trunk and starting to climb into the branches. 'You can't put your spell on it!'

'I can and I will!' shouted the youth in a rage.

His auntie[1] began to pelt him with chestnuts.

Furious, the youth climbed into the branches where the old woman was still screaming at him, and he knocked her to the ground, where she lay senseless.

Then the youth chopped her into little pieces with his adze, stuffing flesh and chestnuts alternately into his bamboo barrels. He put the barrels in a stagnant pool in the marsh to ferment.

But the old woman had turned into a sting-fly, and she stung the lad on the inside of his thigh.

'Oah! What's biting me?' shouted the lad. 'I see what it is—it's a sting-fly!'

The youth caught the sting-fly between finger and thumb and squashed it.

Days passed, the youth returned to the pool to fetch his fermented chestnuts and meat. He took the barrels from the water, slung them over his shoulder and made his way back to the village. Then, meaning to eat the contents on the morrow, he stowed the barrels in his hut.

But the old woman had gone into a rat. She gobbled up the chestnuts as they lay in their barrels in the hut.

Next morning the young man went hunting. He took his barrels of chestnuts with him, but noticed that they seemed lighter than they should be. So he stopped on the path, removed the stoppers, and looked inside.

They were empty. All the food had been eaten.

The narratives about *ranguova*, above, have a different atmosphere from that of the other narratives thus far presented. If they are about men and women who are like *puoker* in certain respects, they are also about men and women who are not *puoker*. *Puoker* act, and the listener or reader follows panting behind,

---

[1] Father's sister.

knowing there will be no reason for what a *puok* may do next. Always signalling related awarenesses, their surface activities cannot be predicted. Always relating the moral to the divine, they invite the listener to reflect on the meaning of things. In these *ranguma* stories, however, the main themes concern reciprocal interaction. Characters act and forcibly react within the same terms. Time is spatially framed, actors are bone and flesh rather than bundles of principle. The dialogue is between those who are obliged and those who think of themselves as exempt, between those in community and those who might be in community but who have opted out of conformity and who are as though divine.

In N. 14 and N. 15 the advent of *ranguova* is heralded by a storm: and 'storm' epitomizes the wild, the unconstrained. In both narratives the *ranguova* take up positions seated in two lines, with one of them, the odd man out and chief antagonist, in the middle. Perhaps these seating arrangements refer to a *ginangin* club-house usage, or to what might have been included in *ranguma brami*. They also suggest that since a typical Tangu community is divided into two exchanging halves, *ranguova*, similarly divided between themselves, are properly to be classified together with those in community, though they usurp the divine and place themselves temporarily outside community. Further, there is the hint that even in a sub-community such as a band of *ranguova* represent there will be the odd one, the man who does not wholly belong. Both narratives were told in Riekitzir, and in each of them the *ranguova* are strangers from other villages who go about their nefarious activities after nightfall.

In N. 14 the strangers, *ranguova*, are eaten. They have been brought into association with 'pig'; they were found in a *juaka* pig-trap; they were trussed to poles like pigs; the members of the community to which they formally belonged, Moresapa, did not collect them for burial. They are as pigs, their *gneker* are elsewhere, they are acknowledged by no community, nobody claims them, only the flesh which is as pig meat remains. Or, since 'pig' is 'man without *gnek*', is as man without man's moral sense, a *ranguma* is like a pig because, though he has a *gnek*, he acts as though he had no *gnek*, no moral sense. Moreover, these *ranguova* are as meat, perhaps, because they have been caught in a *juaka* pig-trap. In N. 16, when a *ranguma* invades the *garamb*, the very shrine of the community, though he is referred to as a pig after he has been killed, he is thrown into the forest, returned to the wild from whence he came. Unlike the *ranguova* in N. 14 and N. 15, who were organized into a band, the one who attacked the *garamb* was a singular fellow, an odd and arrogant one indeed. Burial is for men in community. In N. 17 the *ranguma* is killed and referred to as a pig: but it is for his comrades, his fellow *ranguova*, to bury him. In three cases, that is, *ranguova* are recognized as human by being given burial. The fourth case evokes the unmitigated *ranguma*: the man who, in assaulting the *garamb*, aggressively opposes and attacks the association of men responsible for maintaining the moral order.

In N. 15 a wife has been beaten by her husband and she goes into the garden to sleep alone. Rain, flowing semen, brings the *ranguova* to her hut. They seat themselves in two lines with one in the middle. The encounter which follows brings out the sexual aspect of the *ranguma* complex and reveals that quality of unrestrainedness which *ranguova* and women are represented as having in common. Wanton women are likely to commit adultery, a *ranguma* is an adulterer. Husbands who believe their wives are having adulterous relations tend to dream of *ranguova*. And if the mind has moved to the snake-brothers who assaulted the sisters,[1] here male sexuality is explicitly associated with 'tree' rather than with 'snake'. As we shall see,[2] while a tree, wild, evokes the male sexual impulse only, snake has other connotations also. In this case, N. 15—because she has been beaten by her husband, perhaps, and is, therefore, under some kind of control or constraint—the woman who is also a wife worsts the *ranguma*. Echoing Nuakai as she appears in N. 4,[3] the vulva has an active potency. Even a *ranguma* may be a biter bit. Though the woman might have given in to the *ranguma* (Why not? She was heavily outnumbered, she might have been killed), her association with firewood enjoins us to believe that at heart she is a good woman: a good wife always sees to it that there is sufficient firewood in home and garden shelter. So, hurting the *ranguma* in his pride as only a woman could, she hastens back to the village. Yet her re-entry into community cannot be easy. She has been too intimately associated with *ranguova*, dark

---

[1] *Supra*, p. 247.   [2] *Infra*, pp. 433–4.   [3] *Supra*, p. 219.

impulse, and wanton sexuality. She is as though crazy, runs up and down the *pekas* screaming and shouting. Only time, perhaps, only a prolonged probationary period of reassociation with the reciprocities of the moral order will give her back her sanity. She is as though wild, and one may presume that she was not beaten by her husband for nothing.

In N. 14 *ranguova* are thwarted in association with a *juaka* trap: and the *juaka* evokes the notion of filiation as well as circumcision.[1] In N. 15 *ranguova* are thwarted by a woman who is also essentially 'wife': 'wife' is the most responsible kind of woman. In N. 16 the *ranguma* attempts to enter the *garamb*, the home of responsible men and those learning how to become responsible men: the *ranguma* is worsted. In N. 17 Mariap escapes because he is on his toes, alert, with an expert knowledge of charms, responsible, aware. It is not every man who, in a dangerous situation, even if he may urinate involuntarily, can remain cool enough to drink. By contrast, in N. 18 Nuok takes no precautions and falls victim. Nuok is clearly a kindly man. But where Mariap is competent, collected, thoughtful, and determined to be master of his own fate, Nuok submits meekly to what he thinks is inevitable. Yet, since we are told that Mariap had had trouble over a pig, he could be expected to be wary of *ranguova*. Nuok, on the other hand, seems to have done nothing in particular that was offensive to anyone. *Ranguova* had simply decided to remove him. And precisely this quality in a man characterizes the worst kind of *ranguma*. Defeated by the competent and prepared, by the responsible and by wife, by an adherence to male filiation, the *ranguma* may still find his victim. While in N. 19 father had to kill son, in the end son it was who killed father.

The technique, in N. 18, of dealing with a man in mystical ways after he has been knocked unconscious, and then naming a date for his death, is reiterated in N. 19. Alleged to be one of the ways in which *ranguova* go about their business, it is encountered less commonly in Tangu than on the coast. For there the sorcerer (in pidgin *sangguma* or *tangguma*)[2] is generally thought

---

[1] *Infra*, p. 385.
[2] It is sometimes said by Tangu and others that the pidgin term for 'sorcerer', *sangguma* or *tangguma*, is derived from the place-name Tangumar or Sangumar. Though the idea tallies with the fact that Wanitzir people have or had the reputation of being expert sorcerers, and that the *ginangin* had some renown in the surrounding country, the connection—though plausible—seems tenuous.

to render his victim unconscious, pierce him with thorns or bones—as the boy does in N. 19—and then set a time for the victim's death. The victim, so it is said, recovers consciousness after the initial attack, usually starts to behave oddly or crazily, and then dies at the time set. Still, though the method is not common in Tangu, Nuok himself lived in Tangu, and Nuok's brothers 'are still looking for the culprits'.

In N. 19 the characters are in a sense more like *puoker* than in the other *ranguma* stories—despite the accent on 'paying back'. The essential attributes of a *ranguma* are attached to the child while he is still in the womb. He knows techniques, spells, and charms which are not accessible to ordinary men, and which are 'in' him, inborn—in the head, the seat of the *gnek*: that is why, when he is 'killed' and buried, he can bring himself back to life and get out of his grave. And it is this access to divine powers which, presumably, enables him to bridge the gulf between 'life' and 'death' in relation to animals as well as to his father. So that though the game 'Ranguma' may be a means of making *ranguova*, it is also a means of finding out who might have been born a *ranguma*.

If ordinary men are involved in reciprocities, in 'paying back', they do not find themselves in situations where it seems an overt and necessary obligation to 'pay back' father. Father and son are not in a position to make exchanges and become *mngwot-ngwotiki*: the relations between them are of quite another kind. If a father had inadvertently injured a son of tender years it would be considered an inevitable part of growing up. The effects might emerge in particular kinds of attitudes and awareness in relation to father, but they would not emerge as generalized factors to be acknowledged in the maintenance of community life. No ordinary son would feel that he should realize the impulse to exact vengeance on his father. Not only does a son owe his very being to his father,[1] but, if a father should wrong a son it is for the mother's brothers, not the son, to exact amends. And here we are told explicitly that father was within his rights in attempting to kill the boy after he had exhibited such dangerous powers: the mother's brothers would have no quarrel with him. Son is an odd one and born so. At puberty boys begin to resent their fathers: this one kills his father. All boys as they

[1] *Infra*, p. 386.

come towards puberty are thought to be unrestrained, self-willed, associated with the divine: this one is so much more so that he usurps the prerogatives of the divine. Where most sons 'kill' their fathers in approved societal or cultural terms by becoming independent of them, this one, even though he is 'as if' in community, acts within terms of himself, much as a woman is thought to act. Instead of playing the man, in him moral and divine are undifferentiated, covert and overt are not distinguished: irrespective of their appropriateness or inappropriateness to community life, his impulses are self-willedly realized. Further, since there is no evidence that the son has been circumcised—and the context, particularly his age, directly implies that he was not—like Ruongaptiamkan's son,[1] this one has no appropriate male filiation. That is, boys without an appropriate male filiation are likely to be, or become, *ranguova*—self-willed.

N. 20 bears the same anecdotal marks as N. 17 and N. 19, the stories of Mariap and Nuok. It demonstrates the *ranguma* as a stranger or foreigner, though it is a member of the in-group, a man from Riekitzir, who first puts himself in the wrong by trespassing. Yet there is a balance. For the trespasser, who is an outsider in relation to the Andarum folk, is in their eyes a wrongdoer, as a pig, flesh to be eaten. It is made explicit that the Andarum man would have eaten the Rieken had he been able to do so. The Rieken, however, has a *gnek*, and he uses it. He seizes his chance—and in doing so evokes the sexual qualities and dangers inherent in all *ranguova*—kills his captor, and returns to the village to boast of his prowess to the very person to whom, in his eyes, the stranger-*ranguma* might have been a menace: his wife.

Though the word '*ranguma*' is not mentioned either in N. 20 or in N. 21, both tales were narrated in response to specific requests for stories about *ranguova*. If the notion of 'stranger-*ranguma*' makes it clear why N. 20 is thought by Tangu to be about *ranguova*, in the case of N. 21 the associations are not so straightforward. The activity of gathering *juatak'mba* chestnuts is itself associated with *ranguova*. The nuts grow in dank and dripping marshy places—*imbatekas* places; a sudden storm is liable to cause rapid flooding of the areas in which the chestnuts grow; large snakes, which feed on marsh frogs, are more common where chestnuts grow than in other places; leeches, gnats,

[1] *Supra*, pp. 259–60.

mosquitoes, and stinging insects abound. Marsh odours are never pleasant, but when, after fermentation, the nuts are unpacked from their parcel of leaves for stuffing into bamboo barrels, the stench is execrable.[1] The whole atmosphere round chestnut groves is eerie, made more so by the fact that when villagers go there they speak only in whispers or in hushed tones. Given, then, that the places where the chestnuts grow are *imbatekas* places, that *ranguova* are *imbatekas*, the chestnuts are likely to be associated with *ranguova*. Despite the unpleasant spatial associations, however, the nuts themselves are considered a great delicacy. Chestnut trees are few in number, they only grow in these rather nasty places, the nuts are in demand, he who has access to a tract of marsh with chestnut trees must guard them jealously if he is to reap a harvest and advantage from them.[2] Powerful spells are required to protect the nuts from trespassers, and the main danger is from stranger-trespassers, *ranguova*, those who have access to extra-powerful spells, who will use them unrestrainedly to steal, to whom the dangerous associations of the chestnut-growing areas mean relatively less.

When the old lady enters into a sting-fly, and then stings the youth in just the place where a boil caused by a *pap'ta* might emerge, she is behaving like a *puok*. Later she goes into a rat, becomes as though a *niemur*, and eats all the fermented chestnuts. In stuffing the pieces of his auntie into the barrels the youth cannot be said to be regarding her as a member of community: she appears as much more like Nuakai—a feature which may derive from the strongly textured elements of the *imbatekas* found in chestnut groves. Yet the action turns on reciprocities, on a quarrel over the ownership of the chestnut trees and who is entitled to put a spell on them. Further, the youth, at a stage of maturity strongly associated with the divine, self-willedness at the expense of self-restraint, is tangling with a father's sister whose household might be in a competitive and exchange relationship with his own. Then, to kill his aunt the youth uses an adze, normally the sign of the mother's brother,

---

[1] Tangu also find the stench repellent at this stage.

[2] Chestnuts are exchangeable, but not necessarily against each other. Other things being equal, those who have access to chestnuts always have an edge on those who do not.

but here presumably evoking what the adze also connotes: the 'cross-relationship' between the two generations. On the whole, therefore, it would seem that we are being told of conflicts of interest in the 'cross-relationships', and, giving the context of heavily concentrated divine elements their full value, it is possible that we are also being told that, just as man is ultimately helpless before manifestations of the divine, so there are certain kinds of conflict which he cannot avoid. He should be aware that they are inevitable. So that if gathering a valuable resource from the wild for use in exchanges in the moral community is clearly instinct with dangers, these latter seem to focus on the *ranguma* and the adze. The quality of the *ranguma* in this case, that is, is that quality which adheres to the phrase 'another kind of *ranguma*': the *ranguma* as witch.[1]

It will not have gone unnoticed that *ranguova* tend to be encountered by women when alone in the garden, by uncircumcised boys, and by men when they are out hunting in the forest by themselves. On those occasions, that is, when self-willedness is opposed only by self-restraint. But when self-restraint is supported by moral awareness or those social relations in which the moralities are secreted and made manifest, then the *ranguma* is worsted. The antithesis of those possessed by a responsible man, inborn in some, appearing in the stranger or outsider, in the father–son and in affinal relationships, the qualities of a *ranguma* are primarily self-assertion and sexual potency—qualities most dangerous to husband and wife, marriage, and appropriate male filiation. Potent in penis and testicles, there also is a *ranguma* vulnerable. An inappropriate male filiation and *ranguma* qualities go together, but a right-thinking wife and a husband who exerts his authority responsibly will probably defeat him: he and his qualities are totally excluded from, and defeated by, the association of responsible men in the *garamb*. Yet though a *ranguma* and a responsible man are related as night is to day, black to white, and arrogance to shame, the important point is that living men often tend to veer between these poles.

The Path to Manhood

Though moral and divine stand in antithesis, each field of experience thus investing the other with meaning, the

[1] *Supra*, pp. 137, 143–4.

reverberations of a particular experience ripple and re-echo within a totality that includes both moral and divine. Life in community requires an awareness of this whole, an awareness of the relations and distinctions between the opposed fields of experience. And just such an awareness, the narratives imply, is proper to responsible men. Yet all men in Tangu are wont to experience in youth, as well as in later life, that arrogance and self-willedness characteristic of the *ranguma* and the divine: each man covets that reserve of power which will enable him to be more equal than others. Nevertheless, a self-willed youth has to be taught the proper distinctions between the moral and divine, so that, being aware, he may become a responsible man. Should he then express *ranguma*-like qualities, he is culpable.

N. 22: *A Youth and his Handdrum*

One morning long ago a youth came down from the *garamb* and went into the forest to make himself a new breechclout of barkcloth. Coming to a glade by a stream, where a *deamar*[1] grew, he ripped off a length of bark, soaked it in the stream, and took up his mallet to pound the pulp.

Thump! Thump! Thump!

He had scarcely started when two little birds settled in the branches of the *deamar*, chirruping and twittering to the beat of the mallet.

Put out, losing rhythm, the youth laid aside his mallet and took up his bow. One by one he shot his arrows at the birds.

All missed. As the arrows hummed by, the birds caught them in their beaks and flew off with them into the forest.

Angry now, the lad threw a lump of clay at the birds—then his mallet, followed by the stone on which he had been hammering his breechclout. It was no use. The birds caught clay, mallet, and stone and carried them off into the forest.

Thinking, then, simply to ignore those birds, the lad started to play on his handdrum. But the birds in the *deamar* followed his rhythms, trilling and chirruping to the beat of his handdrum.

Furious at their impertinence, the youth hurled his drum at the birds. They caught the drum as it sailed through the air, and they flew away with it into the forest.

That night, as he listened to the throbbing of handdrums as the other villagers sang, made merry, and danced, the youth grieved

---

[1] The *deamar* tree: the tree from whose inner bark Tangu make barkcloth for breechclouts. The Tangu word for breechclout is *mar*.

over his loss, tossing and turning on his pallet, trying to sleep—How
he wished he too could join in the dance!

Sleep came at last. And in his sleep he dreamed. He dreamed that
he was in the forest and that he saw his handdrum coming towards
him.

At first light, therefore, the youth rose from his bed and went out
into the forest to look for his handdrum. He searched far and wide
through the underbrush until, exhausted and in tears, he rested
against a small areca palm.

'Pssst!'

The lad looked up, surprised. It was the areca palm.

'What is the matter? Why are you weeping so?'

'I've lost my handdrum', the lad explained. 'I threw it at two
cheeky little birds who were pestering me with their twittering—and
they took it away with them into the forest.'

'Come now, don't grieve so!' comforted the areca. 'Look now—
you go off hunting! Get some meat for me, bring it here at sundown.
You'll see! Everything will turn out all right—you'll see!'

Much cheered, the youth went off into the forest to set some traps.
He took some bush-rats, and in the evening he brought them to the
areca palm.

The areca was satisfied.

'Now then, take off your breechclout, wrap it around your ankles,
then climb me', the areca instructed.

As the areca had told him, so the youth did. The palm had seemed
to be a small one, but, as he climbed upwards, gripping the trunk
with his breechclout and steadying himself with his hands, it grew
longer and larger, taller and taller until, the lad reaching the top, it
bent over the highest trees in the forest and down into a clearing
where there was a settlement.

Two maidens lived there—the same two maidens who had been
in those birds! And as the areca lowered the youth into the clearing
they came out of their house to greet him.

'I am looking for my handdrum which I lost earlier today', the
lad said at once. 'I think you have it here.'

Now it is true that the maidens had taken his handdrum. They
had wrapped it in their skirts and hidden it under the bed in their
house. But they denied it, telling the lad that he had come to the
wrong place.

The youth was adamant. He insisted they had it, he would not
go away. And at last the maidens admitted they had it. They invited
the lad into their house.

'You cannot take your handdrum away', they warned him. 'If

you were to do so our father would kill us. So why not stay the night here with us? We can tie the areca with vines, and then in the morning you can go back to your village. . . .'

The youth agreed. Together they tied down the palm with stout vines. Then they went into the maidens' home. They talked and joked with each other, the lad stroking the breasts of those maidens, sucking their nipples, and feeling the down in their thighs, while the maidens giggled and gurgled in delight. They made such a noise, in fact, that father, next door, awoke. 'What's going on in there?' he roared. 'Go to sleep you two girls! Don't chatter so—I want some sleep!'

At this they quieted, and the youth lay down between the two sisters, pleasuring now one, then the other, all the night through—It had to be thus, because until he had begotten children he would not be able to get back his handdrum.

Next morning at dawn the youth crept out of the house and returned to his mother by the areca-palm road. She scolded him for having been out all night—Where had he been? Why did he swagger so proudly?

The lad was evasive. He made lots of excuses. He promised he would spend the day hunting.

Mother was mollified.

Towards evening, the lad returned from the forest, his string bag full of good meat which he gave to his mother to cook. They supped together, then slept.

The following night the youth went back along the areca-palm road to the two maidens. He pleasured them in their house as he had before, first one then the other all the night through. And so it went on for many a night.

At last the day came when father, noticing that the bellies of his daughters were large and swollen, sat down to consider the matter. . . .

'Has a man been visiting you?' he asked his daughters after he had thought for some time.

Hotly, they denied it.

But father was not convinced. And he determined to find out the truth.

Next day, then, only pretending to go to the gardens, father doubled back through the forest and hid himself in the bushes on the borders of the settlement. There he waited.

As dusk was falling, father saw the areca palm hover over the village and then stoop down towards it. He saw the youth jump to the ground, lash the palm tight, and go into his daughters' house.

Father sharpened his adze. He tested it on a creeper to make sure that the edge was keen. Then he went to examine the palm, looking closely at the way it was secured—So!

Father raised his adze, brought it down as hard as he could—Gdeung!

The adze cut right through that vine, and the areca sprang back, whirling over the forest to the young man's village.

Inside the maidens' house the youth heard the sound and started up, lower lip trembling in fright. 'Your father has cut the vine!' he exclaimed. 'Now he will kill me!'

'You must hide, you must hide!' fluttered Ambwerk.

'Get into the yam bin!' Tuman urged.

In a trice the young man was there, pulling the lid over the top.

Next morning, before they went to the gardens, the two maidens made doubly sure that the door of their house was shut and securely lashed. But father had been watching them. As soon as they had gone he forced open the door of the house and began searching around inside. He came to the yam bin at last, removed the lid, and gazed for a moment at the youth inside. 'Aha!' he exclaimed. 'So there you are—My son-in-law!'

Satisfied, father shut the yam bin again, went out of the hut—carefully shutting and fastening the door behind him—and awaited the return of his daughters.

Towards evening the two maidens returned to the village. They boiled some tubers in a pot, ate, and took to their pallets. Husband[1] remained in the yam bin.

The following morning, father called to his dog and went hunting. He killed five pigs. All the villagers helped him carry his pigs back to the village, carve them, and stuff the meat into bamboo barrels.

They slept.

At daybreak the sisters' brothers came to help with the preparations for the wedding. They cut posts on which to hang all the food-stuffs for the feast, and at father's suggestion they built a long platform in front of the house so that all the visitors might have somewhere to sit. They spent the whole day on these tasks.

Next day wife[2] went into the gardens to fetch tubers. She drew many barrels of water from the stream, collected large heaps of firewood for the cooking of the feast.

They slept well that night.

Next morning, while the villagers started to cook all the food, preparing the feast, the youth in the yam bin made himself a new breechclout, wove cane anklets, armbands, wristlets, and

---

[1] *Sic.*
[2] The wife, that is, of 'father'.

knee-straps. He washed himself clean, wound himself into his new breechclout, dressed his hair with clay and red pigment.

When all was ready, father sounded his slit-gong. The guests assembled.

The bridegroom came out of the yam bin.

'See!' the villagers cried. 'There is the youth who has been hiding in the yam bin!'

'Behold my son-in-law!' father announced.

'Behold our brother-in-law!' shouted the sisters' brothers. 'See what a strong and handsome man he is!'

All who were present saw and admired the young man.

By and by the sisters bore children, Ambwerk a son, Tuman a daughter. And because it was the season for making new gardens, husband suggested to father-in-law that they should clear a new site and make a new garden for themselves. For now there were children to feed.

They chose the new site together. Father-in-law worked in one part, husband in another. With the help of the sisters' many brothers all the clearing away was soon done. Next day they burnt off the litter, and on the following day they planted the taros. Afterwards they put in the yams.

The days passed. The new taros ripened, they dug them out and ate them. The sisters found themselves busy with weeding, keeping the yam vines clear and free. . . .

Now it happened one day, while his wives were out in the garden weeding, that husband stayed at home, whittling a piece of bamboo. Cutting and scraping and filing, he made a trump for himself. Then he played it, strumming the rhythm 'many visitors have arrived'.

The wives in their garden heard the signal quite clearly. 'Listen!' each urged on the other. 'Lots of visitors have come—we had better collect as much food as we can and go back to the village at once!'

Making haste, the wives filled their string bags with tubers and returned to the village. Only husband was there, sitting in the porch of his hut.

'What's happening? Who called us?' demanded the wives.

'Nothing is happening', husband answered. 'I did not call you. Perhaps it was someone from another village—?'

'We were sure you were calling us', the wives insisted.

But husband denied it.

That night the elder of the two wives, Ambwerk, took her son to one side and told him to hide in the yam bin the next day. 'Keep a good watch on your father', she told him. 'Take care. But see everything he does.'

The following day, then, after wives and daughter had gone to the garden to weed, husband fetched his trump from its hiding-place in the roof thatch and started to strum. He recalled his wives from the garden.

'Listen!' exclaimed the wives when they heard the signal. 'Our husband wants us. Lots of visitors have arrived and we shall have to entertain them.'

They filled their string bags with tubers and returned to the village.

'Who called you back?' husband demanded when he saw them. 'Go back to the garden and get on with your weeding.'

He, their husband, had recalled them, the wives protested. But he denied it. So back to the garden they had to go.

Next day husband went hunting whilst wives and children stayed in the village. Son, who had watched all that his father had done on the preceding day, told his tale to mother. 'Father has made himself a trump. He plays it while you're in the garden, then he hides it in the roof thatch.'

Mother looked in the roof. She found the trump, started to strum —Poinng!

She broke the tongue!

Away in the forest husband heard the sound of his trump breaking, and guessed what had happened. He returned to the village with lots of game,[1] gave it all to his wives to cook, and sat down to think about his broken trump. . . .

He supped, then slept.

Next morning, after wives and children had left for the garden, husband fetched his trump from the roof, confirmed it had been broken. . . . He had been considering the matter all night, and he had been thinking, too, of his handdrum, that though he now had two wives and two children, he had not got it back. . . .

Something would have to be done.

Husband unwrapped his handdrum from the skirts of his two wives. He put a string bag over his shoulder, took up his spear and, with his handdrum under his arm, set off through the forest back to his village. There he signalled on his slit-gong.

In the garden the two sisters were laughing and chuckling together. 'Ha! Ha!' they giggled. 'We shall do a good day's weeding today—husband cannot disturb us with his trump!'

Then they heard the booming of husband's slit-gong.

They frowned, puzzled. They recognized the signal, they knew it was meant for them. Yet it had not come from their own village, but from another—husband's village!

[1] Compare N. 13, *supra*, p. 274.

As the truth of the matter dawned on them, the two women started
to scold—'It was your idea to make son spy on our husband', Tuman
accused. 'You broke his trump. He's found out, he's gone off and
left us!'

Sadly, Ambwerk put her son on her shoulders and led the way
home, Tuman following with daughter. Yes, they had guessed
aright. Husband had gone. The two women fell to weeping, griev-
ing for their husband, unable to sleep for thinking on what had
occurred.

Slowly the night passed. As dawn broke they heard their husband
signal dance Juangam from his village.

Ambwerk went to the garden, sad and despondent. She dug out
some taros and returned to the village to eat. She thought and she
pondered, turning the matter over in her mind, wondering what
she should do, until, towards evening, her mind was decided.

She would go to see husband.

Ambwerk summoned all her courage, put son on her shoulder, and
set off through the forest to the dance. Arrived at husband's village,
she stood in the shadows at the edge of the *pekas*, watching the
dancers, not daring to come any closer.

Son recognized his father in the lines of dancers. He saw how well
decorated he was, how brave he looked in his finery, and he pressed
forward to greet him.

But mother held him back. 'Hush now, my son!' she enjoined.
'Don't let your father see you—he is very angry with us!'

Yet son would not be gainsaid. As the festivities continued he
pushed his way forward into the weaving lines of dancers and touched
his father on the shoulder.

Father straightened, turned, gazed at his wife and son.

'Why have you left us?' wife asked from the shadows. 'We did not
sleep last night after hearing your signal on the slit-gong. Then,
when we heard you announce Juangam this morning, I thought and
thought until, at last, I decided to come here with your son. . . .'

'The food you gave me was bad', husband replied. 'And you did
not give me sufficient.'

'From now on', wife replied humbly, 'we will give you lots and
lots of good food—the best!'

'Then you did well to come here and see me. . . . Come now! Let
us dance together!'

So husband and wife danced the night through. Now that at long
last husband had got back his handdrum, he was no longer shamed
by having to go to dances with a bamboo barrel instead of a proper
handdrum.

Dealing with the passage from youth to responsible manhood within terms of a dialogue between husband and wife, some of the themes in N. 22 will have become familiar. With the first sentence—'coming down'[1] from the *garamb*—we may presume circumcision and sexual maturity. A lad goes to a stream to make his breechclout, he encounters two maidens as birds, he tries to shoot them with bow and arrows, he misses: a sexually mature young man who is thinking of sexual relations or marriage, he is not quite ready.[2] Yet the maidens have invited his advances, keep the arrows, entreat desire. The bark-cloth-mallet and stone, male tools associated with the breech-clout and so with sexual maturity or its onset, are also accepted. The clod of earth or clay[3] surely evokes the cooking-pot in which a husband and wife cook their food, or the garden they might, and in the event do, make together. Aroused by the twittering of the maidens-as-birds, the youth hurls his handdrum at them. As is explained twice in the narrative, possession of a handdrum signals maturity of manhood: it enables a man to take his proper part in dances—in which feasting, connoting reciprocities, necessarily takes place; the lad cannot get it back until he has begotten children in whose name he may give feasts. While the youth matures, his handdrum is kept wrapped in the maidens' (wives') skirts; he only regains it when he has begotten children on his wives, when he begins to assert himself as master of his household. Then, forgoing his trump, he goes to a slit-gong to announce a feast and dance. So demonstrating himself as the responsible head of a household, he brings his wives to order, instructs them to supply him with plenty of foodstuffs. He must give feasts, honour exchanges. Only by acting thus may he progress into full maturity, responsibility, and awareness.

To return to the opening scene. Deeply distressed at the loss of his handdrum, at being unable to participate in dances as he might or should have done, the youth dreams. Through and because of the dream he meets the areca palm. We know

---

[1] Since the *garamb* was raised on stilts, and in the past other houses were not, and it is said that whilst in the *garamb* a boy was not supposed to touch ground, the phrase 'coming down' from the *garamb* is apposite when implying the termination of a boy's stay in the *garamb*. He 'comes down' when he has been circumcised.

[2] See *infra*, p. 324, where an accurate 'hit' implies readiness.

[3] The narrative is not clear whether earth or clay was intended or both.

something about areca-nut juice; we have seen areca-nuts both as maidens and, when covered by a breechclout, as evoking the relevance of testicles as makers of wives or mothers. Here, breechclout and areca palm are brought together. Remembering the *ranguma* and the woman in the woodpile, the palm's growth and extension to the maidens' village after receiving meat evoke the youth's reaction to the coquettish taking of the handdrum: fulfilment for priding phallus. But before he can respond to the maidens' appeal and nature's gift to his age, the disconsolate youth, sentimental and weepy, has to prove his competence as a hunter. When he has done so the areca gives him access to the maids. He makes love to them, they enjoy each other. But every alternate morning the youth goes back along the areca-palm road to his mother in his natal village. Sexually and economically competent, his awareness is not yet that of a man. He is bound to his mother, as if uncircumcised, as if the umbilical cord remained uncut. His is as yet an adolescent lust.

The father of the two maidens, standing to the youth as wife's father or mother's brother, solves the problem with his adze. In the past, as we have seen, it was customary for the mother's brother to greet a sister's son with a threatening flourish of his adze.[1] And the adze, besides being in particular the sign and symbol of the mother's brother, necessarily also signals the 'cross-relationship' between the generations. The circumcisor of the sister's son, mother's brother, in weaning son from mother through the act of circumcision, in the same act signalled the lad's rebirth into the community of men—not as a mature and responsible man, but as a 'baby-man'. For maturity is not attained simply by a rite. It has to be earned through children, feasts, wife management, initiative, and thought and awareness. Here, in cutting the vine not with an axe or a knife but with an adze, the maidens' father—or youth's mother's brother—cuts the bond between mother and son, evokes the whole process of boy growing into manhood, and commits the youth to his marriage. As the areca goes back to mother over the forest, one may say, so is the foreskin returned to the banana clump.[2] When a boy finishes with his mother's skirts, his manhood

---

[1] *Supra*, p. 89, n. 1.

[2] One might like to add 'as the afterbirth and umbilical cord are laid in a banana clump'. But I regret that I have no evidence that this was indeed the practice.

is to be found in the skirts of his wives. He must take it from there.

With the cutting of the vine the youth is on his own; his lower lip trembles with nervousness: the mother's brother may kill him. As in life indeed he does. For in order to make the boy into a man, the child in him, the dependence on women, has to be 'killed' or eliminated. Elder sister fusses, and it is left to Tuman to give practical advice: the youth hides in a yam bin. Certainly the latter has its economic significance: a household working-team is forming, one may remember the lump of clay or earth flung at the birds. At a deeper level lies the association of preg-nancy and fecundity with the fertility and multiplication of crops.[1] When a crafty father discovers the youth in the yam bin he is not angry. He looks in, stares, and again solves the problem at a stroke. 'My son-in-law!' he exclaims.[2] And from now on the youth is referred to by the term for 'husband'. Yet the associa-tion of mother's brother, youth, and yam bin, coupled with what happens later—the youth-husband in the yam bin making a new breechclout, anklets, armbands, and wristlets, pigment-ing his hair as if in the *garamb* and about to claim his pig of the circumcision—suggests a further phase of maturation. For as the *garamb* was the place where, initially, boys were turned into young men, sexually and economically competent, ready to take their places in community life, so the yam bin seems to represent a parallel process between betrothal and the consum-mation of the marriage. From childhood to the *garamb*, culmin-ating in circumcision; from circumcision through a period of experiment[3] and disengagement from mother to the decisive encounter with maidens; from betrothal to marriage. Nor is this the whole story. If upon the discovery in the yam bin the narrative proceeds to involvements with feasting, ceremonial, guests to be looked after, wife's brothers to be satisfied, and preparatory tasks, it is not until after he has married, had children, and accepted the loss of his trump that the young husband shows his final growth into manhood by signalling on a slit-gong.

As soon as children are born to the young husband and his

[1] *Supra*, p. 99, and also *infra*, pp. 378–90.
[2] Compare father in N. 10 (*supra*, p. 258) when he discovers sons' wives.
[3] Perhaps with *gangariner* (*supra*, pp. 96–7)?

wives, they turn to making a separate garden: involvements
with wives' kin are reiterated. Then husband makes himself a
trump. Evidently he can think and is technically competent.[1]
Still, like Tuman who wished he did not have to be circumcised,
and who might have wished he could remain a little boy,[2] the
young husband is, as it were, wishing himself a carefree young
man again. His wives, busy with their children and garden
tasks, are, as we understand more clearly later in the narrative,
neglecting him. Petulantly, the young husband uses the trump
to call them back. They come at his signal, thinking there are
visitors, that their husband has become well known and sought
after. But there is no one there. Husband has nothing in his
mind that he can say he wants them to do, he even denies that
he has called them back. He is acting irresponsibly, and the
suggestion is that he has yet to learn how to take responsibility,
how to act responsibly. He is no longer the romantic and unrestrained young lover. He has children and gardens. The sisters
cannot give him the attention they gave him in the past: they
must bring up their children and attend to their weeding. And
it is wife who precipitates his further education by telling son to
spy on him from the yam bin. Boy, trump (youth and young
husband), yam bin (*garamb*, entering upon manhood), father,
husband, mother, wife, and children are all brought together
to sum up the gist of the narrative: distinct processes of maturation which yet refer to the prime model of all maturation, the
garamb, movement from the divine or wild to the moral.

Son, ambivalent, is the link between father and mother,
husband and wife. In the trump incident son, associated with
women but male, acts so as to disrupt the relationship between
father and mother. At Juangam, the harvest dance in which
men, women, and children participate together, son repairs the
relationship. We have already seen how son must break from
mother through mother's brother or wife's father if he is to
become husband, and we have seen how in becoming husband
a man comes into relationship with wife's brothers. Now we see
son moving from a position of close association with mother,
and obedience to her wishes as against father's, to the point
where, acting contrary to mother's expressed injunction, in
joining father he also joins mother to father. That is, within the

---

[1] Compare N. 13, *supra*, p. 274.   [2] *Supra*, p. 221.

context of male maturation we are made aware of the see-saw process between filiation and siblingship which maturation entails.

Despite the breaking of his trump husband brought back meat for his wives. It may be that this is a slip.[1] Perhaps he brought back meat because he was not sure that the trump had in fact been broken. Or perhaps the incident is meant to indicate that the young husband, by acting in terms of routine merely and not taking cognizance of a changed situation, has not yet learned to think and act for himself as he should. At any rate, it is not until he confirms that the trump has been broken that he brings his mind to bear on the matter. Then he unwraps his handdrum—which he had seen in his dream coming towards him from the forest, the wild or divine—from the skirts of his wives: he is no longer in thrall to them. Finished with bow and arrows, he takes up his spear: the sign of the responsible man. On his own initiative and by his own decision he returns to his natal village. Next morning he announces Juangam, his first harvest dance, on a slit-gong. He is responsible, has come to full manhood. Ambwerk, who broke the trump, and who was scolded by Tuman for doing so, comes to him to apologize.

Is the wife's thinking and pondering of any account? Is she not doing what she would have done anyway? Is she not here being as much herself, a woman, following her nature, as when she twittered in the *deamar*, invited the missiles, enjoined the youth to stay for the night? But if, on balance, the suggestion that a woman is perhaps wasting her time by attempting to think seems confirmed by the ending, it should be remembered that the woman is a wife, the most responsible kind of female. She apologizes, thereby admitting the authority of her husband. As a *ranguma*-like man is readmitted to the community by the act of confession, so is a wife who acknowledges her husband and his status acting responsibly. If she had not apologized, if she had not promised lots of good food in the future—who would have protected her and her children, who would have brought meat for the family? And, like a responsible man, husband accepts the apology. He needs a wife. Without a wife

---

[1] Compare N. 13 (*supra*, p. 274), where husband does not bring back meat when he guesses that his trump has been broken.

he would not be able to give feasts, would not be able to demonstrate and communicate his parts.[1]

The maidens hid the handdrum in their skirts, father hid in the bush, the youth hid in a yam bin, the young husband hid his trump in the roof thatch. . . . In many of the narratives presented people or things hide or are hidden, and, on the whole, the hiding-places are appropriate. For a hiding-place and what is hidden together evoke a process of becoming, a present mode of being in relation to an emergent or future mode of being.[2] A handdrum represents young manhood, and a handdrum is appropriately hidden in the skirts of maidens who become wives: through courtship and marriage a youth attains a more responsible manhood. Father hides in the forest, and it is from the wild that he brings the pig of the circumcision, the meat and vigour necessary for feeding wives and children. The youth hides in a yam bin, and a yam bin evokes the husband who is to take charge of the gardening activities upon which the welfare of his family depends. A trump, which evokes the not fully responsible man, is hidden in roof thatch; roof thatch evokes the *garamb*; the *garamb* evokes circumcision; the *garamb* is where responsible men are forgathered. As we know from N. 13, upon attaining his slit-gong a man throws his trump into its belly. Wife and small son hide in the darkness at the edge of the *pekas*, husband and father brings them into the light of community.

It becomes evident now that the gist of the narrative was predicated in the first paragraph. A youth makes his first breechclout whilst in the *garamb*. He goes into the forest, strips some inner bark from a wild tree, soaks it in a stream.[3] Moulding the wild stuff and bringing it into the cultural ambience, he dries the beaten pulp in the sun.[4] Then he wraps the finished breechclout about those parts which are apt to become self-willed. . . . Whether one views a narrative as sequential, or, in the European idiom, as a series of flashbacks, the *garamb*

[1] See *supra*, p. 104, n. 2.

[2] One may compare particularly, for example, the lime gourd in the banana clump (N. 7); the friends in the bushes (N. 8); the wife in the woodpile (N. 15); the variety of hiding-places in N. 23 and N. 24, below; the descendants underground in N. 25 and N. 27, below. There are many other instances.

[3] Creativity, the lines of filiation.

[4] Light and responsibility.

emerges as the primary model for a series of metamorphoses. Cutting the umbilical cord separates the child from its mother, circumcision separates childhood from manhood. But until a man takes up his spear and has a slit-gong of his own, vestiges of childhood remain. Successful courtship is intimately related to cutting the motherly ties. Whilst any mature male might be able to engage in sexual activity, marriage and becoming a father entail further processes of maturation, a growth into full masculinity.

Awareness Achieved

Dealing mainly with metamorphoses, the contexts in which impulse and self-willedness may overcome qualities of restraint and morality, the narratives so far presented have communicated an awareness of the self in relation to a variety of categories and representations, and have drawn attention to the importance of being aware of the distinctions and relations between different orders of being. The fundamental error for Tangu, let us say, is to confuse the orders of being; to realize an impulse which should be suppressed or realized in some more appropriate way; to be unaware of the unconstrainable and inevitable. A failure to distinguish between exemplar and the oracular is likely during metamorphoses. Instead of a movement into a wider moral awareness, one in the opposite direction might take place. What may be appropriate to one condition of being is not appropriate in another, and in moving from the one to the other confusions are probable. And while appropriate qualities of being and behaviour may be defined in the first instance by the categories of relationship involved, these are themselves dependent on the interplay between moral and divine evoked by the particular situation.

These themes are further adumbrated in the narratives which follow. But the comment is exterior rather than interior. Where more basic assumptions have been largely implicit, the narratives now communicate an awareness of the nature of the assumptions themselves. The *garamb* is given a broader and deeper framework of relevance. The incest taboo, hitherto taken almost for granted, is brought to the forefront of awareness. The implications of filiation, siblingship, and marriage are now bedded in the attempt to discuss why filiation, siblingship, and marriage should exist at all. Separable pieces of experience grope for the generalization dogma and, in turn, rough maxims are refined in specific experience. Manipulations of a few multifaceted symbols within an accessible total awareness, narratives remain unobliged, oracular, ambiguous exemplars. While those who live by equivalent reciprocities may always assert the moral against the divine or wild, proper men should respond with a fully purposive awareness, not simply react.

N. 23: *Wvawvasikai*

It happened one day long ago, as she was enjoying the sight of green taro leaves and spreading yam vines, looking to see if any of the plots needed weeding, that wife's eyes came to rest on a cluster of pit-pit canes, heads ripe and hanging heavy with seed. Two little birds, she noticed, were hovering over the canes, darting in and out to peck at the bolls.

'Aha!' wife thought to herself. 'Husband is in the village just now, making a bow and some arrows. I'll go and fetch him. He can shoot those two birds!'

Wife hurried to the village and told her husband about the two birds. He welcomed the news, took up his newly made bow and arrows, called to his dog, and set off for the garden.

As he entered the garden, husband marked the two birds over the cane brake. Pausing for a moment to don his shell breast ornament, he crept cautiously through the garden until, coming right up to the canes, he lifted his bow and took aim. . . .

Wvawvasikai leapt at him out of the pit-pit.[1]

Husband loosed his arrow at once. It was useless. Wvawvasikai opened his terrible jaws and swallowed man and dog together in a single gulp. Then he smashed his way through the garden fence, slithered down the hillside to the stream at the bottom of the gully, and dived deep into the waters. There he slept, snoring.

When the villagers discovered what had happened, one of them cut himself a bamboo razor and went off to the garden to see what he could do. He came to the clump of pit-pit canes, followed the trail through the breach in the garden fence and down the hillside to the stream. He dived into the stream, going deep, and came at last upon Wvawvasikai asleep in the depths.

Quickly and without hesitation the man thrust his razor into Wvawvasikai's anus. Thrusting on higher into the colon and so into the stomach, he ripped it wide open.

[1] Wvawvasikai is described as 'like a snake', a 'snake-man'.

Husband and dog hurried out. Rescuer and rescued hastened back to the village. They called the villagers together to discuss the affair.

Now, knowing how fierce the wrath of Wvawvasikai could be, the villagers decided to flee, to take their fire with them and abandon the village. But so sudden and precipitate was their flight as they ran away into the forest, they forgot about the children and old grandmother Nuakai.

When Wvawvasikai awoke, his rage knew no bounds! He set off at once through the forest in a fury, until, arriving at the outskirts of the settlement, he hid himself in a clump of bamboos. Then, tying a shell to his tail, he stretched it out on to the *pekas*, shaking and rattling the shell.

The children were amused. They crowded round the shell, pointing and laughing, curious to see what would happen.

Wvawvasikai slowly withdrew his tail from the *pekas* into the forest. . . . And the children followed the shell, followed it right up to the clump of bamboos. . . .

Wvawvasikai gobbled them up.

Nuakai, who had seen all this, trembled in fear, wondering where she could hide. And as Wvawvasikai emerged from the bamboo and started on to the *pekas*, she jumped into a slit-gong.

Wvawvasikai made straight for the slit-gong where Nuakai was hiding. He sat on that slit-gong, chewing areca-nut with lime and pepper and spitting the good red juice all around him and into the slit-gong. He never noticed Nuakai inside, terrified and expecting the worst. . . .

It happened that there was a small lizard in this slit-gong. And as time passed and her appetite grew keener and keener, Nuakai ate the lizard, swallowing it through her quim.

Her belly swelled in her pregnancy. First she bore Ambwerk, a son, and then Tuman, a younger brother.

The two brothers grew, waxing strong. Nuakai told them about Wvawvasikai, how he had swallowed husband and dog, how the villagers had fled after the rescue, how he had swallowed all the children, that they should beware of him and keep out of his way.

But the brothers showed no fear. Instead, they planned vengeance. They made hardwood shields for themselves, incising them and decorating them. They made sharp-pointed spears of hardwood. They made bows and many-barbed arrows. And having armed themselves thus they set off in search of Wvawvasikai.

Searching high and low, they found Wvawvasikai on the ridge of Iwop in Sasa'nyipitek.[1]

---

[1] The name of the forest locality around the area of Murinap (see Map 2).

Wvawvasikai rose: 'Where do you think you're going?' he demanded as the brothers approached. 'Why have you come to my place? Advance a pace further and I will strike you—I will swallow you up!'

The brothers trembled in fear. They turned in their tracks and ran as fast as they could back to the village. Nuakai prepared a meal for them; they supped. Afterwards they slept.

Next morning the brothers decided they would truly give battle. Ambwerk fixed a golden bird of paradise plume in his hair, Tuman donned one of rich ruddy brown. Bravely they took up their arms and set off for Iwop.

Wvawvasikai was waiting for them. He was armed and magnificently decorated.

Now, seeing Wvawvasikai thus fresh and ready for the fray, and because he himself was tired from the walk, Tuman walked a little way into the forest to rest. . . .

So it was that Ambwerk, alone, advanced to meet his adversary. 'Now!' he announced boldly. 'Now I will kill you!'

Wvawvasikai laughed.

Yet Ambwerk was determined. He charged, came right up to Wvawvasikai, and thrust his spear deep.

Wvawvasikai reeled back—'Oh! Oh!' he gasped between chokings. 'By this act of yours, by what you have done today, you two brothers will die!'

With that Wvawvasikai fell. Ambwerk roused Tuman from his sleep. Together they disembowelled the great Wvawvasikai, afterwards carrying him back to the village.

Nuakai, meanwhile, had started to prepare a meal for the brothers. And while the food was cooking she took her digging-stick and set to work, making a large hole in the middle of the *pekas*.

When the brothers got back to the village, carrying Wvawvasikai between them, they asked Nuakai to make the hole much larger and to boil lots and lots of hot water. Then, stripping Wvawvasikai of his decorations, and remembering especially to remove the shell on his tail, they threw him into that hole in the *pekas*. Nuakai dragged the pot of boiling water to the hole, poured it out over the corpse, and pierced Wvawvasikai through with her digging-stick.

Ambwerk was satisfied. Taking up a hardwood wand, he addressed himself to his slit-gong. Pounding his gong, Ambwerk signalled the victory, the death of Wvawvasikai. He called the villagers back to the village.

Out in the forest, where they had taken refuge, the villagers heard the booming notes of the slit-gong. Still, they were wary, and one of them, mother's brother, decided to go ahead and spy out the position in case it might be a trick.

Creeping carefully through the forest until he could see on to the *pekas*, mother's brother hid himself in a clump of bananas.

Now it chanced that Nuakai, collecting the scraps left over from a meal, and coming to the edge of the *pekas* to throw the remains into the forest, saw the man. 'Why—my brother!' she exclaimed.

Ambwerk sprang to his feet. 'Come out of hiding and show yourself!' he shouted.

Mother's brother trembled with fright, his urine streaming out from between his legs and over the ground.

Tuman joined his brother Ambwerk, angrily calling to mother's brother to come out of hiding. And he, creeping bent and shamefaced from the clump of bananas, came forward on to the *pekas*, excusing himself. 'I did not see you at first. . . . I did not think there was anybody here. . . .'

Ambwerk cut him short, taking him by the arm and making him sit down. 'Now, listen!' he commanded. 'We have been living here for some time. And we have killed Wvawvasikai! We have put his body into that hole you see in the *pekas* there. We have poured streams of boiling water on top of him. You have done nothing! You helped us not a whit! What we did we did alone, without help! We are big men, truly big men! Go out into the forest and find all the other villagers! Find them and tell them to come back to the village! Tell them that Wvawvasikai is dead! Tell them who killed him! While you are in the forest collecting the others, we shall carve the great Wvawvasikai, we shall carve him into lots of little pieces! Then we shall feast! We have killed him and will feast on him! In this village will we feast on him! From this time forward this village is the first, the finest of villages!'

So the brothers carved the body of Wvawvasikai, giving a portion to each of the villagers. The brothers themselves took the head—that is here in Mangigum. Others were given the stomach—that is over there across the valley. And the people of Andarum—they have the tail. . . .

To this day the blood of Wvawvasikai—which, as you must know, was spattered round and about—can be seen on the green leaves of the bushes of Rumeyep.[1]

---

[1] Rumeyep is towards Sasa'nyipitek near Iwop. There is a species of shrub here with red splashes on the green leaves. Rumeyep ridge also leads into the hinterland to Andarum country, where *ranguova* are thought to be plentiful and dangerous.

N. 24: *Zawapai*

One morning long ago, after two brothers had finished pointing and feathering their arrows for shooting at lizards, Ambwerk decided to test the flights.

The first arrow he loosed fell into a clump of thorns and nettles. The second lodged in the prickly branches of a wild breadfruit tree. And the third went into a spiny pandanus.

'Fetch those arrows for me, will you?' asked Ambwerk, turning to Tuman. 'When I marry, you may lie with my wife in the garden and take your pleasure.'

Tuman went to fetch the arrows. He went into the thorns and nettles, and he climbed the wild breadfruit and the pandanus. The nettles stung him, the thorns pierced his flesh, the blood coursed down his body.

'When I marry', Tuman said to Ambwerk as he gave the arrows back to his brother, 'I will lie with my own wife in the garden, and there we shall pleasure each other. But until that time comes you have promised me your wife. . . .'

On a day when Ambwerk had gone hunting, therefore, Tuman went to his elder brother's garden, where he knew his brother's wife would be weeding. He entered in, sat down, and wept.

'What ails you then—are you hungry?' asked elder brother's wife.

'No', replied Tuman between sobs, 'I am not hungry.'

'What then? Do you want to stroke and fondle and suck my breasts?'

'No', Tuman replied, 'I do not want your breasts.'

'Well. . . . Is it my quim that you want?'

'Yes!' Tuman replied, drying his tears. 'My brother promised you to me on the day that I fetched his arrows for him.'

'Why did you not say so at first?' she chided him. 'See! Here it is—take it!'

They embraced in the garden in pleasure.

When they had done, Tuman wiped his hands and his man with the fronds of a tangked palm,[1] dropping the shredded leaf at the foot of a yam pole. Then he accompanied his elder brother's wife back to the village.

Next morning Ambwerk and his wife repaired to their garden. On viewing his yam plot, Ambwerk noticed a cloud of flies buzzing around a certain pole. . . . Puzzled, drawing closer, he saw the crumpled pieces of tangked.

'Hey! What is the meaning of this?'

---

[1] *Taetsia fruticosa*—planted on the grave of a dead man.

Wife told him. 'Yesterday, while you were out hunting, your brother and I took our pleasure just here', she explained. 'He used that tangked to wipe his hands and man.'

No more was said. Husband and wife dug out some yams and taros and, packing the food into their string bags, they returned to the village to cook a meal. They supped, and afterwards they retired to their hut.

But husband did not sleep. While wife lay on her pallet husband was not there beside her. He was sharpening his spear.

At dawn the following day the couple set off through the forest, wife with a cooking-pot and bananas in her string bag, husband leading the way through the trees with his spear.

They walked on until, coming to a place where a wildfowl had nested, husband paused as though thinking. Then, turning in his tracks, he raised his spear and lunged.

Wife fell, transfixed.

Husband eased his spear from the body, cut down a wild banana, and wrapped the corpse in the fronds. Then he stuffed the package into the wildfowl's nest and covered it with bird droppings and loose earth which the bird had scratched up around the nest.

'Hullo!' Tuman greeted when Ambwerk got back to the village. 'All alone? Where's the wife?'

Ambwerk shrugged. 'She's gone to visit her brother', he replied.

Three days passed. The brothers went hunting together, Ambwerk leading the way along the same trail he had taken with his wife. As he drew abreast of the wildfowl's nest he slowed, then stopped.

'Aha!' Tuman exclaimed, excited. 'There is something very peculiar in here—look!'

Ambwerk stood quietly on the path, leaning on his spear while Tuman, squatting on his haunches, peered into the nest and began to remove the banana fronds. First one leaf, then the next, and the one following. . . . Suddenly he knew what it was—turned in alarm!

Ambwerk stood over him, spear at the ready. 'Eat her!' he ordered. 'Eat her—in such a way did you enjoy her! Eat her I say—or I'll run you through with my spear!'

Tuman ate until his stomach swelled and distended over his legs, almost bursting. Ambwerk was satisfied. First he called on the rain. Then, leaving Tuman by the path, he returned to the village.

The storm broke, rain poured down.

Tuman crawled through the forest, his swollen belly weighing him down, crawled on his hands and knees into the shelter of the large board roots of a ficus tree. There he sat, shivering with cold.

Now, though Tuman did not know it at the time, high above him

in the branches of that ficus sat Kuokavalik, the snake-man.[1] He had
seen Tuman taking shelter in the roots of the ficus.

Kuokavalik dropped a firebrand from on high. It fell at Tuman's
feet.

'Why—what is that?' Tuman faltered, looking up. He saw
Kuokavalik. 'I see you up there!' he cried.

'What brings you here?' Kuokavalik demanded.

'I took my pleasure with elder brother's wife', Tuman explained.
'He killed her when he found out, and then he forced me to eat her.
Afterwards he called on the rain and left me. I couldn't walk. I
crawled into these roots to take shelter.'

Kuokavalik slipped down from the high branches of the ficus and
joined Tuman in the roots. He blew up the firebrand, built a fire,
and threw a few chunks of saltwood on the flames. Waiting until
the saltwood had burned to ash, he allowed it to cool and mixed it
with ginger and pepper. Then he gave the medicine to Tuman. 'Eat
this!' he said.

Tuman ate, then vomited. His stomach contracted. He felt better.

Then Kuokavalik took a cooking-pot—that same one which wife
had brought with her and which Ambwerk had placed in the wildfowl's nest along with the body—and stewed a handful of *galip* nuts.[2]

Kuokavalik gave some of the nuts to Tuman, and he ate the others
himself. They slept.

Next morning Kuokavalik greeted Tuman. 'Last night when we
met,' he said, 'I was a snake. Now, as you see, I am a man. Have no
fear—all will be well yet!'

The following day Tuman awoke feeling very hungry. 'Father!'
he cried. 'Father! I am hungry—what shall I eat?' And Tuman
called to his sisters to fetch him some food.

Kuokavalik vomited huge piles of yams, taros, bananas—all sorts
of foodstuffs—and gave them to the sisters. 'Here are foodstuffs for
you', he said. 'You take charge of them—I have my own business to
see to!'

They cooked the food, ate, and slept.

Tuman fell to thinking. 'I ought to prepare a garden site', he said
to himself. 'I ought to clear away a site and plant all these foodstuffs
that father has given me. . . .'

That night Kuokavalik—whose real name was Zawapai—cleared
away the underbrush on the site which Tuman had selected.

So it was that when son awoke in the morning and repaired to his
site he found that Zawapai had already cleared it for him. Accordingly, he set to lopping the trees. He laboured all day. And at dusk as

---

[1] Kuokavalik (see *supra*, p. 246), 'snake-man'.   [2] South Seas Almond.

he made his way home he called to his father—'Father! All the underbrush has been cleared and I have spent the whole day lopping the trees.'

That night, while son slept, Zawapai finished off the lopping.

Next day Zawapai said to son: 'You see, son, during the night I finished the lopping. You must wait, now, for the rubbish and litter to dry in the sun. Then you can fire it.'

Son waited three days, and then—'The litter is dry now', he said to Zawapai. 'Tomorrow, as soon as the sun has dried off the dew, I will go to the site and burn it off.'

It was a long day. The rubbish burned very slowly, and son had to come home in the evening with the burning only half done.

During the night Zawapai finished the job.

On the following morning, then, when son went out to the garden, he saw that the site was ready for planting. 'We are ready to start planting', son said to father. 'We must fetch taro suckers, lay them on the ground well spaced apart, then plant them.'

So it was that son prepared his taros for planting, returned home in the evening, and slept.

During the night Zawapai planted the taros.

And it was the same with the different kinds of yams, the bananas, sugar-cane, pit-pit, squashes, and all the other crops to be found in a garden. Zawapai planted them all, each in its proper turn and season.

One day a dance was signalled—from Pariakenam it was. But they postponed it, and son, who had meant to go to the dance, slept all day instead.

Next day he decided to make a breechclout.

'Strip the bark from a *deamar* tree and then soak it', said Zawapai. 'After soaking it well, hammer it and beat it on a suitable stone with a mallet all morning until the sun is at its highest and starts to fall to the west. Then hang up your breechclout to dry.'

Son did as father told him.

Next day the slit-gongs of Pariakenam boomed their announcement of the dance.

'Go to the dance in your new breechclout', father advised. 'And afterwards, when you get back to your village, you must signal a dance in return.'

Son danced the night through at Pariakenam. He met a maiden there who would make him a good wife, and he brought her back to the village with him. He went to his slit-gong to announce a return dance, and he signalled a feast to celebrate his wedding.

Hearing son signal these feasts, and listening to him banging his handdrum, so cocky and arrogant, father ran away into the bush to hide. He trembled for the food that would be needed for two feasts at once. He shivered and was fearful at the coming of a wife. . . .

By and by wife's mother came to visit the newly-wed husband and wife, and she went to see what their garden was like. There were no wild bananas, she noticed, and no pandanus. And because these were necessary for her daughter to make herself under- and over-skirts, she went into the forest a little way to look for some cuttings.

There in the forest she saw Zawapai in hiding.

'Oh! Oh! Oh! My son-in-law!' she screamed as she turned and ran all the way back to the village. 'Oh my son-in-law! There is a great snake lying in the forest close to your garden—go and get rid of it at once!'

Son-in-law went into the forest, killed a small snake, and brought it back to his mother-in-law.

'Oh no!' she exclaimed when she saw the small snake. 'Not that tiny little thing! The snake that I saw was a huge one—that is the one you must kill!'

So son went off into the forest again, looking for father.

Son found Zawapai behind a bush. He lifted his spear and drove it well home.

Zawapai fell. 'Take out my stomach and colon while they are still warm', he gasped in his death throes. 'Stuff them into bamboo barrels, cook them, and eat them. From now on you will have to make your garden by yourself. You and your wife will have to do the clearing, the lopping, the burning of the litter, the cleaning and the planting. . . . You will have to do everything, everything for yourselves.'

Son returned to his *mwenk*.

While it was still daylight mother and daughter dug out some tubers from the garden, packed them into string bags, and returned to the village.

They cooked the tubers, ate, then slept.

That night the earth shook, heaving itself over and over. The whole village was turned upside down.

N. 25: *Maribun*

This is the story of Maribun, killer of men, who is like Satan, who is in the bush all around us, in storm and in flood, in thunder and lightning. . . .

One day long ago husband and wife went down to the stream with their son and daughter to fish. They fished all morning till noon.

Then husband, who wanted to make some repairs to his house, and wife, who wanted to get on with the cooking, returned to the village. They left son and daughter playing by the stream.

Brother and sister played by that stream all afternoon until, seeing how late it was, sister suggested they should return to the village.

Now it happened that sister was sitting by the stream on a large flat stone, a reddish stone that gleamed in the rays of the westering sun. And as she made to rise to her feet to go home, she found she could not get up. She was stuck fast to the stone.

Brother gave her a hand, trying hard to pull her off. It was no use, the stone held her tight.

Hurrying back to the village to fetch help, son told mother and father what had happened. Father left his repairs at once, coming down to the stream to see what could be done. Yet, try as he might, pushing and pulling with all his strength, he could not dislodge the maid from that stone. At last he turned to his son. 'Look', he said. 'You'll have to stay here by the stream and watch your sister. See what happens. I must get back to the village.'

Son made himself comfortable on the bank of the stream and settled to his vigil.

A little after dusk, as son watched, the stream waters parted. . . .

Maribun emerged from the deep.

His skin shining russet, strong and handsome of aspect, Maribun stood in the waters. His breechclout hung low, broad and clean and reaching to his ankles; scarlet-threaded cane-work covered his shins and swelled over his calves, encircled his wrists and forearms. Streamers from knees and elbows fluttered in the breeze. Through his nose septum there was a long cassowary bone, a pair of boar's tusks hung from his neck between the nipples of his chest. And to crown all, behind and on top of his head a halo of golden bird of paradise plumes glowed in the afterlight. . . .

The maiden was numb on the stone.

Maribun spoke: 'The villagers hereabout are an unprincipled lot!'[1] he declared. 'But you', he continued, turning to the maid, 'you will be mine! I will take you to my dwelling and you will live with me there!'

Maribun stooped. Lifting the girl from the stone, he bore her away.

As soon as he had recovered from his astonishment, son took to his heels and ran back to the village to tell of what he had seen.

They did nothing.

Wife bore Maribun a son, and the boy grew, strong and supple of limb.

[1] *Imbatekas.*

One day, as the lad was walking through the forest, a snake reared from the undergrowth and made as though to strike at the boy's newly dropped testicles. . . .

Son stepped nimbly aside, killed the snake with a stick. It was only a very small snake.

Now, though some say that son himself took the little snake back to the village, others have it that son left it there in the forest and that a passer-by picked it up and took it home with him. But, however this may be, someone it was who took that snake back to the village and threw it into one of the huts. And during the night, while all the villagers slept, the little snake grew and grew, swelled and extended itself so that it filled the hut, coiling around and around itself.

Next day, seeing such a monstrous snake, the villagers were very frightened. They banded together, and they speared the snake, chopping it into small pieces and distributing portions to all in the village—except two young orphans, a brother and a sister. These two were given only a scale and a fragment of fat to share between them.

When wife came to Maribun with her portion of snake, and told him of what had passed in the village, his anger was terrible to see!

He struck son over the eyes with a bundle of coconut spines. Then he sought out the two orphans. And learning that they had not eaten the portions of snake which had been given them, he told them to go into the topmost fronds of a high coconut. 'Take with you all that you need', he instructed them. 'Take fire and food, adze and spear, household stuff, your dog, and other animals. Stay there at the top of the coconut and do not come down.'

The orphans got their belongings together and started taking them to the top of the highest coconut in the village. The others crowded around them, mocking and laughing—'For shame!' they cried. 'Brother and sister together in a coconut!'

As soon as the orphans were safely settled, all their gear with them, Maribun summoned the billowing black clouds, thunder, lightning, and rain. The storm gathered, the sky darkened. Lightning flashed, thunder roared, rain streamed down in torrents. Higher and higher the flood waters rose, filling the valleys, topping the ridges, crumbling the village into ruins, and rising over it and drowning all who lived there.

Only the two orphans remained, safe in the high coconut.

By and by the rain stopped, the flood waters receded, and brother threw down a coconut from their place in the palm. He heard it splash in the waters below and he knew it was not safe to go down.

Day by day he tested the depth of the flood in this way until, one morning, he heard the coconut thud on dry ground. 'Aha!' he remarked to his sister. 'Now we may go down.'

What a sight met their eyes! All that had lived was dead! Men and women who had been drowned in their coupling lay there together, cocks in quims, all dead.

Brother and sister gazed long at the desolate scene. And as brother was wondering what he should do, all the animals they had had with them in the coconut scampered off into the forest. Brother and sister were alone.

Brother decided they must have somewhere to live. So he brought down all the supplies and equipment they had saved from the flood, cleared a space, and built a house. Then he strung his bow and set off into the forest to look for some game.

Whilst brother was away hunting, a pigeon lighted on a branch close to where sister was sitting in front of the house. The pigeon cooed softly.

Sister looked up. 'What is it?' she asked.

'Sit with your legs apart and your skirt lifted', the pigeon said gently.

Sister was puzzled, clumsy and awkward.

'Oh—sit thus in front of your house!' the pigeon rapped crossly, showing her how.

All this was necessary, for she and her brother must couple, man into woman.

Brother returned from his hunting without any meat. 'What's the matter with you?' he asked, scratching his head, in perplexed at the way sister was sitting. 'Why are you sitting like that?'

'A pigeon told me to do so', sister explained.

Brother shrugged his shoulders. He didn't understand.

Next day, after brother had gone hunting again, the pigeon came back to the house. It was very cross and it scolded the girl. 'Today', the pigeon added severely, 'you must wait for your brother lying on your back, legs wide apart, and your skirt lifted up. Perhaps then he will understand what he must do.'

Brother returned empty-handed again. There was no game in his bag. He glanced at his sister lying on her back and frowned. He could not think what it all meant.

Next morning, after brother had gone hunting, the pigeon came to the house yet again. Angrily now, it upbraided the sister. And sister, only wanting to please, waited for brother, lying on her back, legs wide apart, skirt lifted clear.

This time brother returned from his hunting with game in his bag, with meat sliced up and ready to cook. And he saw sister lying on her back. . . .

Some say that brother understood at once what to do. But others have it that he did not quite understand yet. They say that the pigeon had stayed in the tree, that when brother saw it he shot it with an arrow from his bow, and that only when he saw his arrow entering the quim of the pigeon did he understand what it was he himself had to do. . . .

Whichever was the way of it, brother understood. He went to his sister and pleasured her, man in woman.

This was a sin,[1] as we know. But in that time, so long ago, they did it.

Sister bore a son and a daughter. Son and daughter lay with each other, and she bore more sons and daughters. These sons and daughters married each other and had more sons and daughters, who married each other and begot yet more sons and daughters. . . . They hid themselves under the earth in the forest. There they multiplied, only brother and sister remaining above ground, on top of the earth, with a son and a daughter.

Now brother, whose name was Daroomi, had a friend called Niangarai, who lived in a village some distance away. And the two friends decided to build a *garamb*, arranging to do the work in turns.

When Niangarai was away hunting, Daroomi would call on his many descendants hidden under the earth; and they would come out through a hole and help him with his work. Then, before Niangarai came back from hunting, they would all go back into hiding again under the earth. . . . Niangarai was amazed at the way his friend Daroomi seemed to get on with his share of the work.

'Who is helping you with your work, my friend?' Niangarai asked Daroomi one day.

'No one is helping me', Daroomi replied, 'I and I alone am doing my part of the work.'

So it went on, day after day, until the *garamb* was finished.

Now it happened that some of the boys and girls who went up into the *garamb* at that time had sores on their bottoms—though some say that it was only the daughter of Daroomi who had such sores. . . Yet, however it be, those who were clean threw out those who were dirty. For only those whose skins are clean and without boils or sores may sit in the *garamb*.

One day, while he was out hunting, Daroomi espied a cockerel which belonged to Niangarai. He shot it with bow and arrow.

'Why did you shoot my cockerel?' Niangarai asked afterwards, grieved at his loss.

---

[1] Pidgin—*pekato*.

'I did not mean to shoot your cockerel', Daroomi explained. 'I did not know it was your cockerel. I thought it was a wild guinea-fowl.'

Niangarai said nothing.

A few days later Daroomi gave a feast. His wife brought huge piles of foodstuffs for the guests—unprincipled[1] woman that she was!

Now some say that Daroomi boasted overmuch in *br'ngun'guni*; and others have it that Niangarai, moved at the sight of so much food, remarked that wife was *imbatekas*. Then again, while some say that Daroomi himself, vexed at what Niangarai had said, took a digging-stick and opened a hole in the earth for his descendants to come out, others say that it was wife who took the digging-stick, who rammed that digging-stick into the earth and so opened a way for the descendants to come out.

But, whether it was Daroomi or his wife who made this hole, who used the digging-stick, one of them did it, a hole was made, and out of it came all those descendants, men and women, who were to people the earth. The first of them—who was waiting just under the earth—was struck on the head by the digging-stick. He is the ancestor of all bald-headed folk, of *gagai* Mnamnier. . . .

The last fellow to come out of the hole was a *ranguma*. He brought poison with him, sickness and death. He was arrogant and proud, and as he emerged through the hole he cried out that all things were his.

The hole was at Andarum, where so many *ranguova* live.

As for Niangarai—he was so afraid at the sight of so many descendants coming out of the hole that he took to his heels and ran as fast as he could. He ran all the way to Biampitzir, where he stayed and founded the *mwenker* that lie on and around the hill.

Communicating an awareness of husband, father, manager, and *garamb*, the images contained in Maribun, Zawapai, and Wvawvasikai also invite a listener to reflect on the grounds of culture and the means whereby an animal crossed the threshold to become man. Each of the principal representations is figured as male; Wvawvasikai and Zawapai are explicitly 'snake' or 'as snake' or 'snake-man'. Though Maribun is only circumstantially associated with 'snake', subsequent conversations with Tangu revealed the association to be more explicit: 'like a snake'. Zawapai is associated with fire, salt, ginger, pepper, *galip*-nuts, and making gardens, as well as with the ficus in whose twining and sinuous branches he is discovered. Wvawvasikai is associated with pit-pit, stream, bamboo, shell,

---

[1] *Imbatekas.*

areca-nut, and the twisting ridges of the countryside. Maribun comes from the stream which jinks between the ridges; he is associated with storm, rain, thunder, lightning, and flood. While the Wvawvasikai narrative considers the relevances to culture of the assumptions underlying the *garamb*, the Zawapai tale takes up the theme of male filiation, and the Maribun story deals with siblingship, with husband-and-wife and brother-and-sister, with the basis of community life itself. Wvawvasikai relates the *garamb* to Nuakai, mother's brother, slit-gong, Ambwerk and Tuman, is concerned with the movement from impulse to thought, from childishness to manliness. Zawapai refracts the father–son into gardening, marriage, Ambwerk and Tuman. Maribun finds male filiation at the heart of the *garamb*; deals with friendship, the incest taboo, and the correspondence between husband-and-wife and brother-and-sister. Snake, stream, and storm[1] are the elemental symbols whose facets of meaning inform Tangu culture as a whole.

In the opening scene of N. 23 wife surveys her garden, she precipitates the action. Husband is figured as pre-cultural, without awareness, as not yet a husband-as-though-in-community. While he has a dog, an animal which normally pertains to the responsible man, since Nuakai may also have dogs the signal cannot be taken as conclusive. Much more telling are the facts that pit-pit is a delicacy appreciated more by the young than by the mature, and that a supposed 'husband' goes to shoot two birds with a bow and arrows. He is youthful, childish or womanish, impulsive. This is a husband to whom the requirements of appropriate being as a husband have not yet been revealed.

Wvawvasikai springs from the clump of pit-pit, he swallows both husband and dog, smashes his way through the garden fence—the boundary between culture or the cultivated and the wild or divine—and goes into the depths of a stream to sleep. Then husband is rescued. He is taken out of the stomach of the snake by a member of community, a villager, who uses a bamboo razor, the circumcision instrument, and he comes into a renewed form of being from the stream. If for the moment we may read 'coming from the stream' as signalling that effective-

---

[1] When not otherwise refracted, the category 'storm' may be taken to include thunder, lightning, rain, flood, and earthquake.

ness which, residing in maleness, is properly constrained in an appropriate male filiation,[1] then circumcision, the signal continues, rescues a male from the divine and unconstrained—here figured in Wvawvasikai, male and unconstrained—and admits him into the moral community. But, since circumcision actually took place in or by the *garamb*, and the rescue here is from the stomach or womb of a snake, figured as male, it becomes more evident that the *garamb* is represented in Wvawvasikai. At the end of the story Wvawvasikai is 'killed' or 'tamed', brought into community and made subject to responsible men: the *garamb* was an association of responsible men with, now we see more clearly, the female quality of being able to bear, or give birth to, men. Hence the appropriateness of the circumcisor being a man on the female side, a mother's brother. And though it is not explicit here that the rescuer was in fact a mother's brother, Tangu quickly identify him with the mother's brother who makes an appearance towards the end of the narrative.

Whether one prefers to regard the narrative as back-tracking through time, or as attempting to provide a logical antecedent, since, as we have seen, circumcision and the *garamb* model the maturation processes, on either view we can say, not simply that husband is maturing, but that the category 'husband' is developing. As if in answer to the question, 'How may a male be made into a responsible husband?' the narrative replies, 'He comes from the stream; there should be a *garamb*, an association of responsible men; he should be circumcised, reborn as a man from the *garamb*; he should have an appropriate male filiation.' Then the narrative proceeds to show what might happen if these recommendations are ignored. For now Wvawvasikai, still maleness unconstrained—for he has not yet been tamed and brought into community—confronts the community directly. Community life breaks down, the villagers disperse into the forest to live like animals. Only Nuakai and the forgotten children remain in the village. But Wvawvasikai does not come roaring in. He hides in a clump of bamboo, from which the circumcision knife is made. Then, taking advantage of the wayward curiosity of children, he entices them close and swallows them. And this, as we know, is a danger to which children are

---

[1] We already know something about the imagery of *ringertingertiki*, and the fuller relevances of 'coming from the stream' will become clearer in due course.

represented as being particularly vulnerable: they may not survive to become full members of community, they are associated
with the wild or divine, they may be struck by *ranguova* who, like
Wvawvasikai, may lurk in the forest environs of a settlement.[1]
On the other hand, given that Wvawvasikai represents the
garamb, then children are indeed lost or swallowed in the *garamb*.
For though women are the childbearers, it is in and through
the *garamb* that the child or childhood is lost so that boys
may be reborn as men in masculinity. As Nuakai is herself,
revealing the nature of the female, so Wvawvasikai—like other
male representations—shows forth the parts into which men
may enter.

The shell breast ornament which the husband put on when
he was about to shoot the two birds may have been a 'gold lip'
oyster shell. But in any case only mature men may wear shell
breast ornaments. And a man who wears such an emblem, and
who yet goes chasing after maidens (the two birds, and the bow
and arrow) in an immature way, surely deserves to be gobbled
up. If the shell that Wvawvasikai tied to his tail was a similar
kind of shell, then, so it would seem, the premature desire to
wear the emblem may lead into Wvawvasikai's maw. On the
other hand, if children are to aspire to wear this emblem of
maturity, become mature, then the proper route is through
circumcision—Wvawvasikai hiding in the bamboo—and association with and in the *garamb*. It may be, though, that what
Wvawvasikai tied to his tail was a conch shell, a shell used as a
trumpet in *garamb* ceremonial. And a conch shell—a shell with
clear female connotations, but blown by a man—is precisely
what one would like to specify that this shell was if one were
re-creating rather than reporting the narrative. But the fact is
that we do not know that it was a conch. Nevertheless, we are
told at the end of the story that the shell is preserved as an item
of value, and it is brought into association with feasting, the
activity of responsible men. Whether conch, 'gold lip', or other
kind of shell, the process being evoked is that of maturation, and
the model for maturation is contained in the *garamb*.

With the swallowing of the children, Nuakai hides in a slit-
gong, itself the sign or attribute of the responsible man.

[1] Note too, casting forward, that mother's brother, also caught lurking in the
forest environs of a settlement, may be a 'kind of' *ranguna* (*supra*, p. 137).

Wvawvasikai sits on the slit-gong, chews areca-nut over it,[1] spits red spittle all around. Lime and pepper are there too. These features, crowding Nuakai with the fertile and effective, together with the act of eating the lizard through her vulva, bespeak or explain the births of Ambwerk and Tuman. Small lizards such as may be found in a slit-gong in life are food for children, and, as we have seen, Tangu have it that children are born after they have been fed and nurtured in the womb by the husband's semen or 'milk'. If Wvawvasikai has quickened Nuakai with germs of being, these last still need sustenance if they are to develop into babes and be born. The lizard, food for children, and penis-like perhaps, provides this sustenance.

Though, initially, the brothers must be born of woman, it is Wvawvasikai who causes their births. They are begotten by maleness and the *garamb*—male with female qualities—of a mannish female in a slit-gong: they are born as though men, with, it may be assumed, an approprite male filiation. Indeed, it is as responsible men that the brothers, through Nuakai, destroy that which is dangerous to community: Wvawvasikai, the unconstrained in the male. Then, bringing Wvawvasikai into the village, the brothers proceed to give the corpse cultural treatment: thus taming maleness, or killing unconstrained maleness, and providing male filiation with its quality of appropriateness. But before they do so Ambwerk and Tuman make arms for themselves, so asserting themselves and the community not only against the unconstrained male—in effect the *ranguma*, or the qualities which are taken to adhere to the *ranguma*—but against wild animals and other communities as well. Arms are only appropriately used against *ranguova*, wild animals, and outsiders. In the event, however, the brothers do not accoutre themselves properly, they have to retreat from their first encounter with Wvawvasikai. Only after they have put on appropriate war dress, only after they have recognized that they have a partnership with women—for they must wear bird of paradise plumes, and for men these plumes represent the desire for maidens as spouses[2]—can they give battle successfully.

---

[1] *Supra*, p. 225.
[2] See especially *infra*, p. 359. But note that Tuman, usually less responsible than Ambwerk, has a darker feather than Ambwerk, and is thus midway between Ambwerk (sunny, golden, light) and a *ranguma* (who paints his face black).

Tuman tires, sleeps in the forest: in relation to Ambwerk he is associated with the divine, the wild. Ambwerk, responsible, deals with Wvawvasikai by himself. But the price of establishing the *garamb*—bringing Wvawvasikai into community, giving him cultural treatment, expunging unconstrainedness from the maleness represented in Wvawvasikai—and of vindicating or distinguishing the moral order as against, or in relation to, the divine, is death. It is characteristic of men and women in the moral community that they die, and of elements of the divine that they do not. And perhaps, just as human beings continue in life by that intervention of, and association with, the divine which results in their being able to reproduce themselves, so the *garamb*, proceeding from the divine, keeps the moral order in existence.

Though Tuman did not take part in the actual killing—which indicates, again, Tuman's lack of moral awareness in relation to Ambwerk—Wvawvasikai expressly associates Tuman with Ambwerk. Never as fully responsible as Ambwerk, always more divine and self-willed in relation to Ambwerk, Tuman is still human and subject to the same death. Though the capacity for wholly and properly distinguishing between moral and divine, and so acting, belongs to the responsible man, Ambwerk, to Tuman—defined by Ambwerk—is given a peculiar ability to become associated with the divine. To put it another way, though Ambwerk is always responsible for Tuman, Tuman can never be responsible for Ambwerk.

As the narrative draws to a close, mother's brother is (re)-introduced. Nominally the guardian of Nuakai and her children, he has not done his job properly. Associated with the female, he hides in a clump of bananas; associated with the handling of children, he urinates involuntarily. Nuakai, femaleness, brings him on stage. Indeed, the significance of the mother's brother in relation to the *garamb* is his association with women and children. He is *mother*'s brother, *wife*'s father; he deflowers a bride. He is the circumcisor who removes from a boy that which pertains to women or womanliness, and who returns it to that which pertains to womanliness, the banana clump.[1] He shows

---

[1] Whether the foreskin was associated with the lips of the vulva, or with the umbilical cord—which might have been secreted in a banana clump—or with the puckered end-piece of the wild banana or plantain, is impossible to say.

forth the female aspect of the *garamb*. By contrast, Ambwerk and Tuman are by definition joined in a common male filiation. Proceeding from the self-same lizard out of Nuakai, they were born in responsibility, in a slit-gong. Though Wvawvasikai, as yet unconstrained, made it all possible, having dragged mother's brother on to the *pekas* Ambwerk launches into a paean of self-praise which reflects unfavourably on mother's brother. Within the contraposition siblingship/filiation, that is, we are surely being told that while the mother's brother is necessary in relation to the *garamb*, and may, by circumcision, put a lad on the path to manhood, responsibility and initiative of themselves derive essentially from the fact of filiation. Ambwerk was able to think, use his *gnek*, and initiate without benefit of a mother's brother's ministrations. So that while the appropriate route to conformist manhood is by way of the *garamb*, mother's brother, and circumcision, responsible initiatives are ultimately rooted in filiation. Yet the distinction between responsible and irresponsible initiatives is a delicate one. On the one hand appropriate initiatives are rooted in divine and/or moral consent, in appropriate filiation, in their derivation from the stream, in their issuance from a slit-gong. On the other hand, while a *ranguma* was never necessarily an uncircumcised man, a man whose father is unknown, whose male filiation is insecure or doubtful, is quite likely to be thought an odd one, a *ranguma*.[1] Tuman donned a dark bird of paradise plume.

In his refraction as father, Wvawvasikai is killed, and Ambwerk and Tuman become independent of him, no longer under his control. The corpse is put into a hole in the *pekas*, Nuakai pierces it through with a digging-stick. And it is Nuakai who, elsewhere negotiating marriages[1] and here remaining always in the village and associated with mother's brother, evokes the socialization processes connoted by the values of siblingship by pouring boiling water, water given cultural treatment, over Wvawvasikai's corpse—which was earlier on associated with stream, wild water. Having thus been brought into the cultural ambience, tamed, Wvawvasikai's body provides that most human of organized community activities, a feast. The digging-stick evokes the partnership of men and women in the nurturing of crops, and the latter—if digging-stick itself has not—takes

---

[1] *Supra*, p. 138.   [2] N. 8, *supra*, pp. 244–5.

the mind to the nurturing of children. Life in community, cultural life, commences. But the price of culture is the transformation of maleness unconstrained, and the bases or sources of culture emerge from the gathered relevances of Ambwerk and Wvawvasikai: a resolute but controlled exercise of the will to engage and overcome the adversary; an appropriate male filiation which enables the self to restrain the self; channeling the potent effectiveness in maleness by the procedures inhering in the *garamb*—filiation ordered by siblingship; and the fructification of Nuakai, femaleness, by Wvawvasikai, maleness—filiation working on siblingship.

Where the Wvawvasikai tale draws attention to the ultimate value of restraint of the self by the self, but lays stress on the *garamb* and socialization of male powers, the Zawapai story takes male powers and male filiation as its main theme. As was the case in the Wvawvasikai tale, the first scenes deal with a state that is logically prior to culture. Ambwerk, presented as sexually mature, with a wife, has the male power of calling on the rain, semen. He puts Tuman through the trials of the *garamb* by making him suffer from thorns and nettles, he offers access to a wife as reward. Yet, like the husband in N. 23, Ambwerk's association with bow and arrows, and the promise of access to his own wife, reveal both himself and Tuman as but in progress towards a state of cultural awareness. And though Tuman is, as usual, presented as less aware and responsible than Ambwerk, it is Tuman who, stripped of the brotherly relationship and becoming himself, son, under the care of father, Zawapai, is going to make the values of male filiation explicit.

Like the *ranguma*-boy in N. 19, Tuman, as yet unconstrained, is determined to hold Ambwerk to his promise. And though the general context is one of unrestrainedness, the idea of emerging restrainedness cannot but be there. The thorns and nettles evoke the *garamb*, and the fact that Tuman bleeds copiously in a context that includes the *garamb* carries the mind to circumcision and its meaning. Yet unrestrainedness is the dominant note, and Tuman indulges the impulses of a sexual appetite. The fact that he goes into the branches of a breadfruit tree—which, as we know from the tale of Ruongaptiamkan,[1] is

---

[1] *Supra*, p. 259.

a signal for unrestrained sexual relations—might have given warning of what is to follow. In three sentences Tuman's encounter with elder brother's wife summarizes the male life cycle: a child cries when it is hungry, a youth fondles the breasts of his sweetheart, a quim is for a man. Tuman leaves Ambwerk a clue, wife confesses, tangked palms are planted on graves: Tuman has predicated at least one kind of death. Ambwerk sharpens his spear.

A danger to community, particularly in relation to the unconstrained male, wife is brought into association with cooking-pot and bananas, female images. Ambwerk dispatches her with his spear. Gradually that which is prior progresses to cultural being. For though wife has shown no moral awareness of the relevance of her act, she is immediately brought forward into direct association with culture through the cooking-pot and bananas. And it is in this situation that Ambwerk acts with the symbol of responsible manhood, the spear. Now we know that what she did was wrong, now we know that in such a situation the responsible man may be ruthless.[1] Yet Tuman runs true to form. The nest of the wildfowl is a messy affair of leaves, grass, nodules of earth, and droppings; this litter, particularly perhaps the droppings,[2] attracts Tuman's attention. Poor fellow! Ambwerk forces him to eat the body; the distinction between satisfying a sexual appetite, and ordered and controlled sexual relations, is made explicit. Ambwerk calls on the rain, semen, and it pours. Within a context provided by phases of the life cycle, the *garamb*, circumcision, sexual intercourse, responsibility, and rain or semen, Tuman is to become son and enter into that process which starts with being fed in the womb with father's semen, proceeds to birth, childhood, and the passage of the *garamb*, through to marriage, and then comes round again to conception, feeding, and male filiation.

With Ambwerk off-stage, Tuman is simply himself, becoming, a germ of being which is to develop into son, experience the father–son until, finally, the implications of father–son (male filiation) are contraposed to those of husband–wife (siblingship) as he himself prepares for fatherhood. Evoking pregnancy and the foetus, rain or semen sends him with swollen belly, crawling

---

[1] Brothers, it will be remembered, may decline responsibility for a sister who is a marital bad risk (*supra*, p. 107).   [2] Compare Tuman in N. 5, *supra*, p. 223.

like a child to the ficus in which Kuokavalik (the snake-man who is to reveal himself as Zawapai, father-provider) is hidden. In the Wvawvasikai tale, it will be remembered, though physical beginnings are referred to the lizard and the potency of the snake-man, cultural beginnings are referred to the taming or constraint of maleness. The emphasis is on the cultural or moral content in changes of being. Here, Kuokavalik—snake-man, maleness, associated with rain—is as begetter or genitor. He also gives son fire, salt, ginger, and pepper,[1] makes him vomit (makes that which was in the belly come out, the *garamb* evoked, birth evoked), and then gives him cooked, culturally treated, *galip*-nuts. And it is these last which—reddish, associated with goodness and fertility,[2] and found wild—seem to emphasize the junction of natural and cultural elements required to beget a son who will have cultural being. For it is after this that Kuokavalik, snake-man, becomes Zawapai, the father-provider in whom are imaged the values of male filiation, culture-creator, and culture-bearer and guardian.

Zawapai vomits forth foodstuffs, sisters are called on to cook for brother, father-provider has more important things to do: he provides but does not cook. Still, filiation is being contraposed to siblingship. Father provides, does the work: all that son has to do is to make a start, learn the techniques. Yet it is son, not Zawapai, who thinks he may need a garden for himself, who by his own volition makes the transition from being divinely supported to supporting himself. Then, after the lesson on how to make a new garden, the stage is reached when son is told how to make a new breechclout. He is growing up fast. He attends a dance, gets himself a wife, undertakes feasting responsibilities, signals on a slit-gong. He is as though responsible, has become independent of father, must do things for himself, may no longer rely upon father. Father foresees his own exclusion: the event is made to hinge on the amount of food to be provided for the wedding feast and return dance. And the wife's mother, as though Nuakai, makes sure of it. Until now the garden has been a male affair, something between father and son, and there has been no specific provision for female needs, for the pandanus

---

[1] Salt is often used as an emetic. Ginger and pepper are the ingredients of many medicines. Like areca-nut, they are thought to have efficacy. They make a patient sweat, a reaction which Tangu regard as therapeutic.　　[2] *Infra*, p. 392.

and bananas which are required for making string bags and women's skirts. Mother-in-law alters all that, insists that her son-in-law, reluctant at first, kills the large snake. For if son-husband is himself to become a father and a responsible guardian of community in his generation, father or reliance-on-father must be eliminated.

Son kills father Zawapai with a spear—the sign of the responsible man. If the implications of Zawapai's instructions regarding his colon are not entirely clear, the association of stomach and intestines with femaleness,[1] the man and his dog being rescued from Wvawvasikai's stomach, and Wvawvasikai as *garamb*, suggest what Zawapai goes on to make explicit: from that moment man and woman, as husband and wife, will have to work in partnership by and for themselves. Then the earth overturns.

If we assume that this overturning or reversal connotes some sort of ending, then we may take it that until the end of time the process of sons dealing with their fathers and taking their places will be repeated. Yet the Tangu word for 'overturn'—*pupu'riem'riembaki*—not only contains the root of the words for 'die' or 'death' (*ariem'*, *ariemi*) but also has the meaning of 'back to front' and 'reversed' or 'upside down', as well as connoting the motion of rolling over and over. So that, remembering the tale of the *niemur* and the coconut,[2] and bearing in mind that after death the *gnek* passes over into the divine and becomes a ghost, it is possible that what is being indicated here is not only the existence of the two orders, moral and divine, but also the corresponding orders of the overt and covert: social or cultural being, as contrasted with wild or divine or instinctual being. With one primal earthquake *puoker* become moral beings joined in community; with the next primal earthquake men and women will become *puoker* again; the world as it is will have come to an end.[3] Meanwhile, father's ghost, conscience, reminds a man of the grounds of his morality.

Maribun is introduced as killer of men, in the forest and bush, in the storm, flood, thunder, and lightning. He is maleness

---

[1] *Supra*, pp. 219–22.

[2] *Supra*, p. 177. Compare also *supra*, p. 133, and *infra*, p. 355, where *puoker* emerge from under the earth to become men and women and *ranguova*.

[3] Compare *supra*, p. 157.

unconstrained by community ties. The association with *ranguma* is made explicit at the end of the narrative; both terms meet in the narrator's opinion that Maribun is 'like Satan'. If Christian influences are clearly present, the associations are none the less appropriate. The devil is thought by some to be in the *ranguma*, a *ranguma* is male and unrestrained, Maribun is maleness unrestrained.

A family goes to the stream to fish. Because mother has some cooking to get on with, and because father wants to make some repairs to his house—probably, as Tangu comment, to his roof thatch[1]—brother and sister are isolated, a feature which recurs several times in the course of the narrative. With this first isolation sister is held to a red stone in the ruddy glow of the setting sun. Something good and fertile is starting, and something is coming to an end. Knowing, however, that she is going to be taken to wife, we may take it that the girl is finishing with childhood on the one hand, and becoming sexually mature—perhaps in her first menstrual period[2]—and ready for marriage on the other. Brother is the guardian of sister, and he takes up his watching role.

Watching for what? As an activity in itself, 'watching' seems to evoke the emergence, or maintenance, of reciprocities, the moral community. As we know, if Tangu are to maintain reciprocities they have to watch each other closely.[3] At the same time, no amount of 'watching' can prevent the interventions of the divine, the development of certain kinds of inevitability. Here, neither son nor father can do anything to alter the course of events. While boys have to be treated with great care if they are to grow into responsible men, culture bearers, it is in the nature of girls inevitably to grow into women. That is their way. The girl is probably menstruating, or at any rate ready for marriage. If she is to become relevant, she must become wife: Maribun will come. Culture is the reverse of the natural: it is an imposition upon natural or wild or impulsive being, it is the product of self-conscious constraint, awareness, watchfulness. Yet there are some situations into which the natural or wild or

[1] Thus bringing to mind the notion of *garamb* (*supra*, p. 209, and *infra*, p. 366).
[2] Compare *infra*, p. 350.
[3] 'Watching' has to be done with 'eyes open'. Eyes come in pairs (*infra*, p. 344 ff).

impulsive intervene inexorably. And women, intimately associated with these features, tend to bring on the action.

Maribun emerges from the stream, evoking the essence of
maleness. He is the epitome of what a man should be. Handsome
and well muscled, in full regalia, with his head haloed in bird
of paradise plumes, he is aware. He cuts through the gist of the
story as though he had foreknowledge of the eating of the snake,
as though he knew how the villagers would be discovered after
the flood. 'The villagers hereabout are an unprincipled lot!' he
exclaims. Then he takes the girl and she bears him a son. In the
context a better word than 'unprincipled' might be 'promiscuous'. Both words are adequate translations of *imbatekas*, and
'promiscuity'—a mode of being that eschews the rules which,
by regulating marriage, make community possible—is surely
what is indicated by the address of the villagers to each other
after the flood. Moreover, later in the narrative brother-and-
sister marriages occur. Marriage and its regulation, siblingship,
are at the heart of the matter, and male filiation and the survival
of culture and community cannot but be closely related.

Very briefly the narrative refers to the difficulties of the
growing boy. He is startled by a small snake—which makes for
his testicles—and he kills it. The idea of castration may come to
mind, but it is scarcely borne out by the evidence of the narrative. The connection is rather that when a small snake—in
association with a small boy—is taken into the village, into
community, it is capable of growing to huge proportions. One
may recall the snake-brothers and the sisters who ate the
sugar-cane;[1] one may probe more fruitfully into the meaning
or relevance of snake, maleness, and responsible manhood; one
may take up the themes of Nuakai, Zawapai, and Wvawvasikai
and their association with male filiation, the *garamb*, and femaleness. The issue is not the excision of male potency, but the
control of that power.

The villagers, an unprincipled lot, kill the snake and eat it.
Maribun is furious. Clearly they have killed that which pertains
to himself, Maribun, figured as husband, aware. They have
also killed that which, in community, is capable of growth and
development. The villagers have evidently broken a rule vital
to the survival of culture and community: because of their act

[1] *Supra*, p. 247.

they are destroyed, in effect destroy themselves. They have, in a sense, been eating themselves, eating that which is vital to themselves and community life: the relevance of snake.[1]

When wife brings husband the news of the eating of the snake, it is her last line. She has mediated between Maribun and the villagers,[2] it is time for Maribun to address himself to the villagers directly. Wife fades from the scene, son is cruelly punished (perhaps he has seen what he ought not to have seen, perhaps he has been irresponsible simply, perhaps he has become aware of his own maleness too soon, and in doing so has been stupid enough to kill its effectiveness[3]), and Maribun confronts the two orphans, brother and sister. These two have been selected to survive the flood. Both as orphans and by virtue of not having eaten the snake they are different, or separated, from those who are as though in community. As in N. 1, the survival of the orphans is connected with their exclusion from community, and with their association with divine male power.

When the villagers see brother and sister going into a coconut they jeer and cry 'Shame!' Since coconuts are associated with marriage,[4] the villagers, as though in community, are now making it explicit that intimacy of this kind between brother and sister is not appropriate to community relationships. The narrator himself, influenced by Christian teaching, says later on, in an aside, that the mating of brother and sister is a sin (*pekato*), but that in those far-away days it was done. He might perhaps have added that as *puoker* in narratives brother and sister still mate or 'marry'; that with each alternate generation a line of male filiation intermarries with a sisterly line of female filiation; that a union between brother and sister on one plane of awareness corresponds with a marriage between husband and wife on another; that by observing the incest taboo, and then entering upon a series of exchanges until becoming *mngwotngwotiki*, brother and sister might be able to realize an awareness in which the implications of the divine and moral are met, become one, in stasis.

Why does brother have to test the flood? Why cannot he

[1] An earthquake, it will be remembered, occasions a search for one who has killed a large snake. Further, since 'snake' and *ranguma* are connected, it may be that there is here an oblique reference to *ranguma brami*.
[2] What every wife does through the exchange relationships she initiates on becoming a wife.　　[3] But see *infra*, p. 364.　　[4] See *supra*, p. 99, and *infra*, p. 395.

simply look down to see if it has receded? The answer seems to lie in the implications of the tale of the *niemur* and the coconut,[1] in the lads rubbing their eyes as they come out of their rock-prison into the daylight,[2] in the refractions of meaning attaching to Nimbamung's blindness,[3] in the earth turning over or reversing itself as in the Zawapai story,[4] in Maribun hitting his son over the eyes, in brother and sister being separated from descendants who live underground hidden from sight, until they emerge into the light and become men and women. Brother and sister cannot see with the eyes of moral beings, their union belongs to the reverse or underside or covert side of being—which should not receive overt community expression. For them the incestuous union, for moral beings the incest taboo.

Brother knows how to make a house, string a bow, and go hunting. But he does not know what to do with his sister-wife until he has brought back meat for her. Even so, as some say, it requires the further use of his bow and arrow before he can begin to be aware of his maleness. The pigeon, a bird which secretes a milky fluid in its crop to feed its fledglings, a wild thing generally associated with women or the female, reveals the sister's nature to herself. And brother, a successful hunter with bow and arrow—but not, be it noted, with a spear—follows his arrow. Man into woman means children.

The primary theme thus far has been the incest taboo and its relation to the power in maleness, a part of siblingship/filiation. Now the narrative shifts into the dialogue between friends mediated by the building of a *garamb*. If it was not brother and sister who gave rise to community, perhaps it was two friends?[5] The brother becomes Daroomi, friend of Niangarai.[6] A cockerel—which heralds the dawn, and so the emerging moral community, reciprocal obligation—is killed by Daroomi. And Daroomi, associated with Andarumitzir, and therefore with the *ranguova* considered by Tangu to be plentiful there, goes on to re-emphasize what a singular man he is, how unobliged by the requirements of friendship he is. While the building of the *garamb* evokes the creation of the core of community life, the

---

[1] *Supra*, p. 177.   [2] *Supra*, p. 206.   [3] *Supra*, p. 239.
[4] *Supra*, p. 320.   [5] Compare N. 8, *supra*, p. 243–5.
[6] Note that here the friends are named, whereas in N. 8 they are referred to as 'friends'.

behaviour of the two friends comments on the relations between Tangu and Andarumitzir, Daroomi prefigures the presence of *ranguova* in community life. The moral community is beginning to emerge from the activities of *puoker*.

Why are those with sores on their buttocks or anus not allowed to enter the *garamb*? Among Tangu a clear skin is taken as a general indication of a clear conscience, and those with skin sores or boils tend to be regarded with some suspicion. Not that those with skin troubles are regarded as necessarily bad or like *ranguova*: rather is it that those who do not know their own minds, and who, therefore, in all sincerity may find good reasons for not meeting their obligations, are thought by Tangu to show their uncertain state of mind by having skin troubles. Echoing the attitude to men with red-rimmed eyes who are surly,[1] Tangu feel that a man has only himself to blame if he expects the same kind of integrity from one with skin sores as he might from one with a clear and shining skin. Maribun has a shining skin. Since those with sores on their buttocks may not enter the *garamb*, the *garamb*—and aspirations to Maribun—is not for those whose integrity is thus overtly in doubt. Conversely, the *garamb* is for those of integrity, for those whose self-willedness is tempered by qualities of self-restraint, for those who are aware. Further, as we may gather from the tale of Ruongaptiamkan,[2] the lack of integrity associated with skin troubles is also associated with an inappropriate male filiation.

Whether it was Daroomi or his sister-wife who wielded the digging-stick which released the descendants hiding under the earth, the wife it is who is described as *imbatekas*. . . . She it is who releases humans, including *ranguova*. Still, Daroomi also has something to do with it. If women give birth, Maribun and Daroomi are male, men and women are jointly responsible for humans.[3] While *ranguova* and the qualities they image emerge as inevitable parts of life in community, they particularly belong with male filiation on the one hand, and the tension between brother-and-sister and husband-and-wife on the other. Or, *ranguma* qualities are associated with inappropriate male filiation

---

[1] *Supra*, p. 135. And compare the *girili* (N. 14), the *ranguma* caught in a pig-trap.
[2] *Supra*, p. 259.
[3] Would it not have been more appropriate for Daroomi to use the digging-stick here? Maybe Tangu were misremembering the narrative. . . . But then Daroomi is a *ranguma*-like being!

PLATE VII

a. Boy among yam vines

b. Pig awaiting its moment

c. Maidens going down to the stream to draw water in bamboo barrels

and a failure to resolve the marital-sibling relationship. Finally, in the last few words, through Daroomi and his sister-wife and their relations with Niàngarai, we encounter, first, a Founder, and then the qualities of the *imbatekas* contraposed to involvement in *br'ngun'guni*. Culture and the moral community have come into being.

In a very real sense life in Tangu seems traditionally to have been, and to a great extent still is, concerned with resolving the tensions between opposed orders or qualities of being: controlled and responsible behaviour as against the impulsive or wild, maintaining reciprocities as against contriving a dominance, the imperative to conformity in others as against a more generous allowance for the self; the overt and above-ground as against the covert and underground; light and seeing in contrast to darkness and blindness, awareness as opposed to the unaware; male qualities as against female, adults as against children, Ambwerk as against Tuman. . . . But these and other contrapositions are not simply word lists. Through the narratives, modes of cognition, they communicate the possibilities of the cultural awareness. When *gnek* and narrative are brought into relationship, fields of awareness are generated. On one plane of awareness a man may come into union with his sister, kill his father, or deceive a friend. On another plane he knows he may not marry his sister; should become independent of, but not kill, his father; is being silly, if human, in deceiving a friend. Though a narrative might be regarded with detachment, even scorn, in lending an ear an individual cannot but come into relationship with it. Like most Tangu today in relation to their traditional narratives, he might not be able to realize the full awareness which his culture, by means of its narratives, allows and attempts to communicate to him. Still, whatever his attitude, and sluggish of wit though he may be, if he knows something about himself and his place in community he must, surely, by simply listening to a narrative gain an awareness of being which differs from the predicates of the moral order in itself. Conforming to the dictates of morality is but a part of realizable being. Narratives allow an actor to distinguish between himself and his parts.

The source of culture and the moral community, we learn,

and the responsibility for maintaining them, are rooted in maleness, and particularly in male filiation. These features, working
on the female and wild stuffs, realize their potential through the
garamb in terms of siblingship. Maribun is a representation of
total awareness. Though he is in the storm, he has power to
command it. He knows what ought to be done, and why. Yet he
himself is unobliged. In one sense beyond the reach of man,
through the narrative Maribun is brought within the range of
comprehension. Before a man may aspire to Maribun, one may
say, he should become husband. But to do so he must deal with
Zawapai, the father who teaches him a variety of techniques,
who gives him his crops, who helps him make a garden. And
before he can deal with Zawapai and so become seized of the
possibilities of social being, he must face up to Wvawvasikai. He
must be 'swallowed' by the *garamb*, circumcised, and be reborn
as a man by and out of maleness or men. Freeing himself from
mother, by overcoming Nuakai he may engage her help in
finding a wife. Not until he has mastered tendencies to succumb
to femaleness, not until he is aware of the implications of the
power of his maleness, is he fit to become husband. Since the
female is represented as wanton, the onus is on the male to
restrain himself and not behave as do the snake-brothers in N. 9
or as Tuman in N. 24. He should engage the divine with eyes
open, aware, distinguishing between the moral or appropriate,
and the impulsive or wild. Then, by marrying a wife who is not
his sister; by winning his handdrum from the skirts of wives;
by passing through the phases represented in yam bin, trump,
and slit-gong; by being obliged and communicating his parts
across the brother-and-sister link—by doing these things he
may yet achieve that stasis or state of unobligedness represented
in becoming *mngwotngwotiki*. And at this point, having run the
gamut of obligedness through participation in *br'ngun'guni* and
become unobliged, he realizes a state of being which corresponds
with a brother-and-sister marriage. Like Maribun, he has become wholly aware of the implications of the incest taboo. But if
he chooses to rest there, self-satisfied, he becomes, again like
Maribun, very like a *ranguma*.

6

THE NARRATIVES (III)

So far as traditional Tangu notions of being are accessible to an outside observer, creation and experience appear as successively divisible into contraposed qualities which are conveniently summed up as moral and divine or wild. Moral qualities are capable of generating an equal and opposite reaction, are subject to reciprocal obligation, under control or controllable; divine or wild qualities are self-willed, not apparently subject to reciprocities, and in a relative sense not controllable. Men and women in community are manageable, and so moral, in relation to thunder and lightning or *puoker* which, not being controllable, are divine. Within the community men are considered more able to control themselves and exert self-restraint than women are: hence men stand to women as moral to wild or divine. And the same relation holds between ordinary men and *ranguova*, adults and children, Ambwerk and Tuman, brother and sister, husband and wife, father and son, mother and daughter. . . .

In a non-literate culture such as Tangu was, and virtually still is, the majority of adults could be presumed to have had much the same moral experience. Deriving from the mutual interactions of community life, the moral experience predicates that basic consensus regarding normative behaviour without which life in community would not be possible. Experience of the divine, on the other hand, is subject to variation. Awarenesses differ, experience of the divine or impulsive or non-moral quickens awareness. Through his *gnek* man is both moral and divine, experiences, and is in differing degrees aware of, the relevances of the divine and the moral. And the corpus of narratives seems to contain or indicate that basic cultural experience within which the awarenesses of particular individuals may move, develop, and so differ from one another. If there are limits to the kinds of experience which a non-literate culture can offer its members, its narratives probably define them. While, therefore, a whole and entire comprehension of all Tangu narratives would be tantamount to exhausting the possibilities of awareness contained in the culture, it is quite safe to say that no one in Tangu has actually realized them. Apart from the fact that the traditional narratives are oblivescent, that Tangu either cannot or will not—as we have done—enter a sustained conversation between their narratives and their daily experience,[1] there remains the point that, once we have become aware of the significance of the contrapositions, an appreciation of the singular is also required.

The conversation between the narratives and other aspects of Tangu culture has shown the principle of bifurcation—of contraposition or pairings—to be general. None the less, though the cosmos itself is divided into moral and divine, and though all moral elements bifurcate into pairs, so far as the moral does not penetrate the divine, thus far is the divine represented as singular. Within the categories of the moral community bifurcation is typical. Equivalent reciprocities demand bifurcation and pairings. Without them equivalence would be simply unworkable. Not only is an individual both *gnek* and tissue, with the *gnek* itself participating in both moral and divine, but it is difficult to see how, traditionally, a person could be visualized outside a further pairing, as being anything other than a part of brother-and-sister, Ambwerk-and-Tuman, husband-and-wife, siblings-in-law, father-and-son, mother-and-daughter. . . . The categories of the idioms of kinship and friendship describe the range of moral relationships, and each category cannot but connote a pairing. As a collectivity men are not simply males: so far as they, and only they, through their association in the *garamb*, may give birth to the most responsible beings, men, so far do they reveal a female aspect. The Tangu language possesses a dual form, and numeration—reflecting the appropriate units of community life—is mainly in couples. But while complementary wholeness within the moral order appears as represented by a pair related as moral to divine, when like is paired with like the whole is formed of oppositional halves. Thus though man-and-woman, husband-and-wife, brother-and-sister, Amb-

---

[1] N. 30 and N. 31 are exceptions. These are new narratives and Tangu attack them with zest.

werk-and-Tuman, father-and-son, mother-and-daughter are complementary wholes, two husbands-and-wives form the oppositional halves of a larger whole; two siblings of the same sex, not explicitly designated Ambwerk and Tuman, are in opposition; so also are two friends and two *mwerkindanger*. We have seen that local communities used to be divided into two halves, *GAGAWA*, and that communities still bifurcate into oppositional halves, though they do so in rather different terms.

The bifurcations of the moral order,[1] which go together with the insistence on equivalent reciprocities, are, however, always subject to the interventions of divine elements. And these, always relatively singular and self-willed, are informed by the absolutely singular and self-willed. *Puoker* in general, *ranguova*, dream-image or ghost, *niemur*, *pap'ta*, Founder, Patron, narratives, dreams, denizens of the wild, and certain natural or meteorological phenomena are all, relative to the moral order, singular, self-willed, and unobliged. Still, from the point of view of certain individuals they may act co-operatively or reciprocally. And so far as they do so, even if only momentarily, so far do they express bifurcated qualities, so far are they penetrated by the moral. A *puok* may strike an enemy, a *ranguma* may confess, a ghost may give excellent advice, a *niemur* may be persuaded into a bamboo barrel to give pertinent signals, a *pap'ta* may attack a trespasser, Founder and Patron may help, narratives and dreams may yield understanding and insights, denizens of the wild may fall into a trap or not attack, rain may come when it is needed. The *puoker* of narratives, anthropomorphic and for the most part categorized in the terms of friendship and kinship, are paired or connote pairings. Even those *puoker* which appear as singular show contraposed qualities. But the storm—earthquake, thunder and lightning—is indisputably itself, unbifurcated and without opposite, wholly singular and uninhibitedly self-willed.

This singular power and quality of the storm informs all elements of the divine or wild. Random in femaleness, women, and children, in maleness and men it may emerge as a creative initiative. Mngungerp and Igoe'ika are figured as male;[2] in

---

[1] It will be appreciated that the paragraph above does not represent a complete summary of the bifurcations of the moral order. It merely serves to remind.

[2] *Supra*, pp. 190 and 84, n. 5.

narratives storms are caused by male *puoker*; in life storm and the anger of men are closely associated. Rain, which derives from the storm and is an image of semen, may be controlled by rain-makers or rain-checkers who are men. The *ranguma*, associated with storm and rain, is male, singleton and odd. And though the *ranguma* is contraposed to those in community—he is human and potentially moral—the variety of qualities he subsumes figure the 'one and the many' rather than a pairing. As we shall see further, the singular power and quality of storm is in fact penetrated by the moral in terms of male filiation and the *ranguma*. Still, whereas men only *appear* to exhibit complete self-willedness, the storm remains itself, divine, utterly self-willed and uncontrollable, wholly singular and unobliged.

Traditionally, the moral seems to have penetrated the divine to the point where, arrived at the storm, the bifurcations of the moral order disappear and the singular becomes apparent. With the advent of Europeans, however, particularly the mission, an opposite process may be discerned. The singular has begun to penetrate the moral. Europeans, classed with *ranguova*, singular elements, have become a part of daily experience. Whereas in the past a household could not have been conceptualized outside a pairing, today a household tends to be regarded as one of many like units which may shift alignments and relationships as opportunities occur. Rather than being thought of as the half of a pair, the individual is beginning to emerge as a personality in himself: a singular being. If in the past a woman was represented as not having a *gnek*, now she is definitely thought to have either a *gnek* or a soul. The process of individuation has started, and Christian teaching is clearly largely responsible.[1] On the other hand, money—a system of numerical and factorial relations going together with the notion of the 'one and the many', the handling of which is an exercise in individuation and differentiation—still simply purchases. It measures European goods, measures itself in terms of itself, has little relevance in Tangu to the differentiation and measurement of moral virtues, skills, and kinds of prestige.

[1] Briefly, and in parenthesis, Christian teaching emphasizes the unities, whether at the level of community, the family, or the individual; holds women to have the same kind of soul as men; emphasizes union with, rather than separation from, the divine; concerns itself with the problem of the 'one and the many'.

As, gradually, Tangu abandon the attempt to understand Europeans and their ways in their own traditional terms, and begin taking over the categories in which Europeans understand themselves, so will they become less and less traditional Tangu and more and more the new man. The mounting range of European goods which come within the horizons of apprehension cannot be fitted into the traditional scheme of bifurcations. As Tangu find themselves making continual exceptions to the traditional categories, slowly these very exceptions will become the rule rather than the exception. And as the traditional categories become less precise, as the situations which gave them clarity become forgotten, so Tangu will lose the ability to understand the tradition from which they have sprung. Cargo activities seem particularly to indicate that phase in the process of individuation when, with tradition inevitably slipping away, the singularities of money and the open community are not quite within grasp. On the one hand the reciprocities of community life in Tangu insist upon pairings, on the other hand the *ranguma*, the Christian, the European, money, and life on the coast do not. Whilst Tangu measure themselves by character, industry, and skill coupled to reciprocal obligation and performance in subsistence activities, on the coast money and singular qualities are the basic measures of man.

The narratives that follow add to our appreciation of the singular. Like the other narratives, they are historical documents which yield not events but relations. They widen and deepen our knowledge of Tangu tradition, they also show the singular qualities of the new man taking shape.

The Powers of Men

In these three narratives familiar themes are reworked. In addition, we are given a more rounded account of the predicative powers which are seen as attaching to men. For if men are to maintain the community they must initiate appropriately.

N. 26: *Paki*

Once upon a time, long ago, men and women ate the bark of trees, seeds, and roots. They knew nothing about gardening and cultivating crops. Paki showed us how to do it. Paki made the different tubers, Paki brought them to us, Paki showed us how they should be cultivated.

In those days, then, Paki had a garden in which he cultivated crops in much the same way as we do today. He was the only one with a garden. No one else had a garden. Men and women wandered about the forest.

One day it happened that a man picked up a rotten banana that Paki had thrown away. And the man planted the banana. But of course nothing came of it. He did not know that to grow a banana you must plant out the shoot.

Now, seeing the ignorance of the fellow, Paki decided he would show men how to cultivate. So when he harvested his crops he hung them on a huge feasting pole that reached into the sky. The poles we use today, of course, are but trees which we have cut down and lopped clean. Paki's poles were enormous, not trees at all—though like them—and they towered high, high into the sky!

Paki told men and women that they could have all the crops that hung from the pole if they could cut it down. So the people of that time took up their stone axes and set to work. They hewed and hewed at the pole all the day through. But in the evening when they returned to their village to rest and sleep the pole was still standing.

Early next morning the villagers returned to their work. They laboured all day until, at dusk, they tired and returned to the village to sleep. But that pole still stood where it was.

Now it happened that as they had worked that day a chip from the pole had struck one of the men, leaving a splinter in his leg. He nursed his wound when he got home that evening, drew out the splinter, and threw it into the fire.

Next morning, when the villagers repaired again to Paki's pole, they discovered that all the chips they had hacked out on the previous day had returned into the body of the pole—but one little gap remained. And the man remembered that he had thrown just such a sized splinter into the fire!

Thinking about it, the villagers decided to burn all the chips as they cut their way through the pole. So, working hard, burning the chips, at last the pole was in two.

But it still remained upright.

Wondering why the pole would not fall, the villagers noticed that it was being held in position at the top by a stout piece of cane—as may often happen today when we are clearing a patch of thick forest. They called a small boy, sent him up the pole with a knife to cut that cane.

Paki, however, went into the cane. And although the boy slashed and sawed the cane with his knife he could not sever it.

'Hey there!' called Paki-in-the-cane. 'It is I, Paki, not just an ordinary piece of cane you are trying to cut. You cannot cut me! But you tell all those men and women down there to pleasure each other—and then you'll see!'

Now the lad was only young. And he was ashamed to tell all those grown men and women to do such a thing. So he slid down the pole, saying that he could not cut the cane because a bee was worrying him.

The villagers sent up a slightly older boy. But he, too, was ashamed to repeat what Paki told him. And, making some excuse, he also came down without cutting the cane.

The third lad to climb the pole was a braggart, one of those fellows who is for ever boasting of his loves and affairs. And when he heard what Paki had to say he shouted to the villagers below, telling them to fall to and pleasure each other, so that the pole might fall.

They did so, man into woman. And the pole crashed to the earth, scattering foodstuffs all over the place, distributing to each of the villages the special kinds of yams and foodstuffs they grow today.

Except for two orphans, brother and sister, all the men and women took their foodstuffs and ate them. Knowing nothing about cultivation, they did not understand about keeping seed crops, planting them, tending them, weeding. But the orphans kept their share carefully, watching the others fill their bellies with foodstuffs until they had eaten all they had. . . .

One night, Paki came to the orphans in a dream. And in that dream he told them how they should choose a site for a garden, looking to the mulch of dead leaves, noting what kinds of plants already grew there. He showed them how to take the soil in their hands and crumble it to make sure it was light and airy; how they should cut down some of the trees on the new site, but leave others for shade and for holding the soil; how they should lop the trees before cutting them down, save the straight limbs, strip them clean, and stack them by to make yam poles and parts of the garden fence; how they should burn the chips in the cut of a tree so as to fell it more quickly; how they should wait for the sun to dry all the litter of the clearing, burn it off in a day, and then rake the ashes over the site; how man and woman, husband and wife, should work together in the garden, one doing this job, the other that, dividing the work between them. . . . And Paki told them that if they would have good and plentiful crops from their garden they should pleasure each other there, mixing the milks of their pleasure with coconut milk, bark shavings, and blood from the trencher, and afterwards burying it all in the soil of their garden. . . .

That is our way—the way which Paki marked out for us.

The orphans did what Paki told them to do. They became man and wife, prospered, and had many descendants.

The others? They died.

N. 27: *Dumban* (*i*)

Long ago, one day, father and mother decided to leave daughter at home while they went out to the garden to work. She was young, in the throes of the curse for the first time. 'Stay indoors and rest today', her father said. 'Your mother and I will do what work has to be done.'

Mother and father collected their gear and went on their way.

Now Dumban—who had been hiding in the scrub at the edge of the village clearing, watching and waiting for his opportunity—crept into the maiden's hut. He gave her a wristlet of cane he had woven. And she slipped it on, well pleased. 'I live near that large stone in the stream where the village folk go fishing', Dumban told her. 'If you want to see me again, sit on that stone when next you go fishing. I will come to you and show you my home.'

Next morning, going with the other women of the village to the stream, the maiden made for the stone which Dumban had mentioned, sat on it, and made herself comfortable.

All morning the women fished. And though no one else could catch any fish the maiden herself had caught quite a number[1] when, of a sudden, a storm gathered. The wind came in stiff gusts, lightning flashed, thunder boomed, and the rain came roaring through the forest under a darkening sky.

Mother and father packed up their belongings, shouting to daughter to hurry and come home with them. But she could not move from the stone. Dumban had bound her. Try as they would, pushing and pulling with all their might, they could not drag her from the stone. Dumban held her fast.

'It's no use—we can't move her!' father exclaimed. 'We'll have to go home without her. Here, son! You stay by her, keep watch, see what happens. We'd better be off.'

So, whilst mother and father returned to the village, the lad nestled in the shelter of a small shrub, watching his sister.

Dumban emerged. He rose from the stream, the waters parting on either side of him. He was lithe and straight limbed with a skin that glistened over smooth moving muscles, well shaped and strong. Red pigment covered his eyes, the broad band of white lime on his forehead spread down over his nose and cheeks to cover his full mouth and chin. Golden plumes of the bird of paradise circled his head.

---

[1] Compare the two sisters in N. 9, *supra*, p. 246.

Dumban stood silent, gazing at the maid on the stone. 'Come with me to my house', he invited at last.

The maid trembled, fearing to plunge into the depths.

But Dumban noticed her trembling, and sank back into the waters—to reappear in a few moments with a cooking-pot in one hand and a piece of roof thatch in the other. 'You see?' he said encouragingly. 'My house is down there at the bottom of the stream. Don't be afraid—with me you'll be quite safe!'

Still trembling, but reassured by Dumban's demeanour, the maid rose to her feet and dived to the deeps. The waters closed over her.

Young brother, amazed, and staring entranced at the ripples flowing outwards from the stone, waited only a few moments while he gathered his wits. Then he raced back to the village to tell his parents what had happened.

Meanwhile, in Dumban's house in the stream, all the mother's brothers, snakes, crowded about the new wife, calling to her and greeting her as the wife of their sister's son. She was terrified, thinking the snakes were about to kill her.

Dumban tried to comfort her. 'Don't be afraid—these snakes are but my *awuker*![1] They will do you no harm. . . . Besides', he added, 'after nightfall I myself am a snake.'

At this the maiden was more frightened than ever. But again Dumban reassured her. 'A snake at night I may be', he said. 'But during the day I am a man.'

So the maid became wife. And that night Kuokavalik, a small snake, the youngest of the mother's brothers, lay with her.

She bore a son, then a daughter.

One day these two children, brother and sister, went down to the stream to play. And whilst playing it came on to rain. . . . Thunder boomed, lightning flashed, the flood waters rose.

Sister hurried home at once. But brother decided to stay by the stream. He plucked a *boan*, an orange-coloured fruit as large as his fist, and he hurled it on the flood to use as a target for his arrows.

Taking his bow, he loosed all his arrows at the *boan*. But with not one did he hit.

The lad sat down on the bank, crying and weeping. Then he jumped to his feet, smashed his bow into pieces, cut and gashed himself with the slivers. . . . And thus, with blood streaming from his wounds, he made his way home through the forest.

Father and mother were distressed and worried. 'How did it happen?' they asked.

[1] Mother's brothers.

'A stranger ambushed me in the forest', son told them. 'He threw me to the ground, then slashed me with his spear.'

Next morning, after son had made a new bow and arrows and had gone again to the stream to play, father and mother took daughter aside. 'Go now, follow your brother!' they instructed. 'Hide yourself well, don't let him see you—but see what he does!'

So sister followed brother to the stream. She saw him pick a *boan*, throw it on the swollen waters of the stream, shoot at it, and loose all his arrows without once hitting the fruit. And, as she watched, brother broke his bow into pieces and cut himself with the slivers. 'So that is what he does!' sister exclaimed as she slipped from her hiding-place and made for home.

'No stranger attacked my brother', she told her mother and father. 'He did it himself.'

Dumban said not a thing. He climbed a coconut palm, cut down some nuts and fronds. Then he stripped the fronds, putting the stiff and sinewy spines in the bottom of an eating bowl. Finishing, he poured coconut milk over the spines and mixed in some slices of soft white coconut meat.

When son returned home Dumban gave him the dish to share with his sister. Both ate with appetite, soon finishing the milk and coconut meat. Then, 'Hey—what's this?' they cried, seeing the spines.

With slow deliberation, Dumban took the spines from the bowl. He bundled them closely, grasping them firmly in his hand. Then he beat them, first son, then daughter.

'Go away—the pair of you!' mother shouted. 'You, daughter, go seek the mother![1] And you, son, find your mother's brother! But take care! Whatever you do, do not enter into a snake!'

Brother and sister set off through the forest, brother following a stream down its course, winding along the valley bottoms, whilst sister went directly over the hills. So it was that sister arrived first. She sat down and waited for brother.

After a while, tired of waiting, sister walked up the stream.

'What happened?' she asked when at last she met her brother coming down-stream. 'Why have you taken so long?'

'Oh—I'm so tired!' brother sighed. 'It's been such a long way!'

Sister sympathized, and then—'I know what to do!' she exclaimed. 'You go into a snake, and I'll go into a frog—that way we can both swim down-stream instead of walking!'

So brother, forgetting what mother had said, entered into a

[1] '*Amai*, mother.' In the context it might mean 'my mother'—i.e. grandmother or Nuakai; or, more simply, 'motherhood'.

cipnangk'der, a tiny snake, and wriggled off down the current; and sister went into a frog and followed him.

They swam on until sister, tiring—she wasn't used to swimming like a frog—stopped to rest in the roots of a banana palm. Brother went on for a while, then rested by a sago palm.

Now it happened that mother's father[1] was just there, stitching sago fronds for roof thatch. He saw the *cipnangk'der*, struck it without thinking, and put the little snake into his string bag together with some edible leaves. He went home, caching the *cipnangk'der* 'twixt rafter and thatch where it would be safe from the dog.

Soon after this, grandmother Nuakai finished sweeping under the house, and put a pot of water on the fire to boil. She asked daughter to bring her the snake so that she could cook it.

But that little *cipnangk'der* had swelled, and daughter could not dislodge it from the rafters. So grandmother asked elder daughter to fetch it. The *cipnangk'der*, growing bigger and bigger, was too much even for her. Finally, grandmother herself went into the hut. She wrenched the *cipnangk'der* from the rafters, flung it outside, slit it up the belly, and cut it up into little pieces. These she apportioned to all in the village.

Sister saw all that had happened. 'Oh my poor brother!' she sobbed as she ran home to mother to tell her. 'They've killed my brother!'

Mother listened grimly to daughter's account. Then, arming herself with a heavy digging-stick, she set off for the village.

Arrived at the village, mother discovered that only the head and tail of the snake remained, and that these had been given to a small boy and his sister. So, begging the parts from the young couple, mother put them into her string bag. Then she warned the children to collect all their belongings and take them with them into a high coconut. . . .

Dumban, meanwhile, was collecting the waters of the world, summoning the thunder, the lightning, and the rain. He gathered them into a huge storm and sent them, thundering and lightening and roaring to the village where the people, sated after their feast on the snake, were sleeping as though dead.

That brother and sister, however, despite the angry jeers of their fellow villagers, had done as mother had advised them. They had taken themselves and their equipment into a high coconut. They were safe up there, safe from the waters which Dumban sent swirling into the village. Far below them fires fizzed out one after the other, houses collapsed, only the *garamb* remained as the flood waters rose.

---

[1] *Sic*: but perhaps mother's brother was meant.

Inside the *garamb* the boys were feeling cold. So they sent the youngest lad to fetch some fire from outside. He stepped out on to the porch, slipped, screamed once, and was swallowed in the flood.

Then the boys sent a bigger and older boy. It was no good. He too slipped and was swept away.

Finally a grown man went to the door—alas! The flood, rising higher and higher, roared down upon him, covering the *garamb*, drowning all living things, until it lapped at the feet of brother and sister in the coconut. There it stopped, rising no more.

By and by, high up in the coconut, brother picked a green nut and flung it to the ground. He listened, heard a splash, knew that the waters still covered the earth.

Brother waited. Then, throwing a ripe coconut down, he heard a soft thud as it landed on dry ground. He knew it was safe to come down.

The village was in ruins. Men and women lay rotting where they had been drowned in their sleep. Pigs, dogs, birds, lizards—everything was dead. And yet, as brother and sister picked their way through the wreckage, brother found a little piece of pork which was still good to eat. He put it in his string bag, called to his sister to follow, and set off through the forest.

After a while, growing weary, brother suggested they should rest, make a fire, and cook the pork. 'I'll go to the top of that hill yonder', he added, 'and take a look round, while you get the fire started.'

Sister collected some tinder, got a spark, and blew on the embers.

From the hilltop brother saw the smoke from the fire curling into the sky. He trembled and grew afraid, hurrying back to his sister to make her douse the fire. They shouldered their bags and continued their journey.

Some time later, almost exhausted, brother thought they might try again to cook their little piece of pork. So, while sister made up the fire, he climbed a nearby hill to see how it smoked.

He saw nothing. 'We'll stay here', he said to his sister. 'Blow hard on the fire and let's have a blaze!'

Brother and sister sat down by their fire, took the piece of pork from the string bag and—

'Who are you? What are you doing here?' hissed a soft voice.

Brother and sister were terrified. 'It's only us . . .' they faltered.

A possum came out from behind a bush. 'Well now—you'd better come into my burrow!' it said. 'You'll sleep better in there.'

Brother and sister followed the possum into his hole.

Next day the possum had a chat with the couple. 'You', he said to brother, 'are husband. And you'—turning to sister—'are wife.

You, husband, must give your baby-maker to your wife. And you, wife, must give your quim to your husband. You must come together and pleasure each other.'

It was in this way, then, that brother and sister became husband and wife, enjoying each other. She bore children who married each other and had more children until all the descendants living in that burrow underground could be numbered in scores.

One day the possum told brother, Daroomi, that he ought to build a *garamb* for all the men and young folk to use.

So it was that Daroomi built a *garamb*—it was in the region around Andarum. He sent all his descendants down into the burrow and sounded his slit-gong, inviting his friend Niangarai, who lived in Biampitzir, to come and see him.

Niangarai came, bringing a party of men with him. He looked around him, puzzled. 'Is there no one to sit in the fine *garamb* you have made?' he asked Daroomi.

'Alas! I have no men to sit there!'

At that wife snatched a digging-stick. She struck it into the ground, opening up a hole—so that all the descendants, men and women, came swarming out.

At the sight of so many descendants Niangarai grew afraid. And though Daroomi entreated him to stay, trying to calm him and allay his fears, Niangarai broke loose and ran away back to his own place in Biampitzir.

That is how it all happened. From that time on men inhabited the earth. They—and all the other *gagawa*—came out of the hole.

N. 28: *Dumban (ii)*

Dumban was in the stream, rippling the surface. . . .

One day, wife went down to the stream to wash and to catch some fish. Hours later she returned to the village, cooked the fish she had caught, ate it with husband, and retired to sleep.

Next morning, husband went hunting. He took some game, returned to the village, and gave it to wife to cook. They ate together, then slept.

The following morning wife went fishing. Afterwards she went to the garden to help husband dig out some tubers. In the evening husband and wife returned to the village, cooked some tubers and fish, supped, then retired to their pallets.

Next day, at dawn, wife went down to the stream with all the other women of the village. They cast their nets, started to fish.

Dumban emerged. . . .

Dumban came all-shining out of the stream towards them. Wife and all those other women who were with her loosed their skirts and lay down in two lines as Dumban took his pleasure with them, satisfying each in her turn, first one line then the other, until the last was content. Then Dumban returned to his home in the stream, and the women returned to their village.

Next morning all the wives stayed in the village while their husbands went hunting, taking their dogs. On their return they gave their wives the game they had taken. And for their part the women went down to the stream to fish. They cast their nets—and there! Dumban emerged. . . .

As before, so now. The women took off their skirts, lay down in two lines, and awaited their pleasure with Dumban, first one line then the other, until each had been favoured.

Now, having spent their time thus, when the women returned to the village they had no fish to bring with them.

'No fish? Why haven't you caught any fish?' the husbands demanded.

'There were no fish in the stream today', the wives replied.

Next day the husbands went hunting. They took pig, cassowary, bush-rats, possums, and wallabies—and all this meat they gave to their wives to cook. They supped very well that night, each eating his fill. And afterwards, husbands with wives, they retired to their huts to sleep.

At dawn on the following day, as the women prepared to go down to the stream to fish, father took his son Borkei[1] by the shoulder. 'Yesterday there were no fish in the stream', he started. 'Yet there have always been fish there before. . . . You go with your mother today, hide in her string bag, keep a sharp look-out—see what's going on down there!'

So it was that when mother and the other women went down to the stream that day, Borkei was in her string bag, pretending to sleep.

Arrived at the stream, mother cut a sapling, pointed one end, thrust the stake firmly into the ground, and slung Borkei in his cradle from a notch she had made for the purpose. Borkei could see all that went on.

Dumban emerged. . . .

He came from the stream, muscles rippling under the glistening skin, face painted red and white, streamers fluttering from arms and knees, woven cane-work vivid and bright. . . .

'I am Dumban, Dumban who comes to you out of the stream!'

---

[1] This name was interjected by the narrator, indicating a living boy who corresponded with 'son'.

Immediately all the women took off their skirts and lay down in two lines. And he enjoyed each one in her turn, first one line then the other.

Later that evening, after the women had returned to the village, cooked for their husbands, and eaten, Borkei went to the *garamb*, where he knew his father awaited him.

'Well? What happened? What did your mother do?'

'I lay in my string-bag cradle pretending to sleep, but keeping a watch', son replied. 'A large and handsome man, strong and powerfully built—with superb decorations—came out of the stream. "I am Dumban!" he said. "I am Dumban who comes to you out of the stream!" Then mother and all the other women took off their skirts, lay down in two lines, and waited while Dumban pleasured them in turn, first one line, then the other, each one.'

Father's mien was grim. Taking a bunch of areca-nuts, he distributed them to each in the *garamb*. Something would have to be done.

Next morning, therefore, as the women filed down to the stream, the husbands took up their spears—slipping like shadows through the forest as they followed their wives to the stream. Hiding in the undergrowth, they surrounded the fishing place and waited to see what would happen.

And as they watched they saw the women loosen their girdles, throw off their skirts, and start singing for Dumban to come to them.

He came. He came from the stream, skin shining and sparkling, the water cascading down his shoulders. The women lay down in two lines to enjoy him.

From their hiding-places in the forest the men watched Dumban in his pleasure, watched him until he had done, until he had satisfied each of the women lying there on the foreshore. Then they came storming from the bushes—each thrusting his spear into Dumban as the women stood naked on the beach, trembling, full of fear at the sight of Dumban lying on the sand, bleeding from so many spear thrusts.

Even so the men were scarcely content. Not until they had chopped Dumban into scores of little pieces did they feel satisfied that their work was done. Then they shouldered their spears and returned to the village.

Not so the women. They waited in numb silence until the last man had gone. Then they seized Dumban's huge fellow—slicing it small, each taking a portion and putting it into her quim.

When the women got back to the village, they sat down, inert and silent. 'Why are you not cooking our suppers?' the husbands demanded angrily. 'What is the matter with you?'

The women said nothing.

The husbands leapt to their feet, enraged. Each one took hold of his wife, jerked her to her feet and thumped her hard on the buttocks.

The pieces of Dumban's big fellow fell from their quims.

Now all those little pieces came together in the village, joined, and flew off to Ariangon, coming to rest at a place where women draw water from the stream. There the huge fellow, mended and whole, mewed and cried like a baby.

It happened that two maids of Ariangon, friends, heard the babyish cries as they drew water from the stream. So, searching in the shrubbery to find out the cause, they found Dumban's huge fellow. They put it into a string bag and took it home with them, hiding it in the yam bin.

That night, after the maidens had finished their cooking, supped, rested, and laid themselves down on their pallets to sleep, Dumban's huge fellow came out of the yam bin and rejoiced them in turn, first one then the other, until dawn.

Next morning the two maidens took the huge fellow outside the hut and flung it away towards Dimuk. It fell at a place where women come to draw water, and there, behind a bush, it whimpered and grizzled like a baby.

Two maidens, who had come to the stream to fish, heard the cries and went to investigate. 'Aha!' they exclaimed when they saw Dumban's huge fellow. 'Here is a little son for us! Here is a little son who will work for us in our gardens!'

The two maidens took the fellow home with them, hid it in the yam bin, cooked food, ate, and retired to their pallets. During the night Dumban pleasured each of them in turn, first one then the other, all the night through.

In the morning the two maidens took the fellow outside and threw it over towards Wasamb. It landed at a place where women come to draw water, and there it began to snivel and chuckle like a baby.

Two maidens who had come down to the stream found the fellow. They took it home with them and hid it in the yam bin. And when the two maidens lay down to sleep Dumban pleasured them both, each in her turn, all the night through.

From Wasamb, Dumban's big fellow came to Mariap; and from Mariap it was thrown over to Pariakenam. And from Pariakenam it came at last to a pool in the neighbourhood. There Dumban started to sing—

> I am Dumban
> Dumban who comes from the stream!
> Dumban the handsome,
> The great one, the strong one!
> Li-la-o! Maria-la! Li-la-o!

A small boy heard Dumban singing in the pool, and he and other little boys—who were wont to use the pool as a bathing-place—came to listen and to learn the song.

When Dumban had finished, the boys returned to their village and practised the song Dumban had taught them. Day after day he taught them his songs and his dances—Juangam, Maridar, Rak'mba, Birituk—and many others which the boys kept to themselves, learning them and practising them secretly.

One day the boys came into the village to sing. Their parents were astounded. 'Where did you learn all those songs?' they demanded. 'Who taught you those dances? Who showed you how to decorate yourselves so?'

'No one taught us', a little boy piped. 'We thought of them on our own, then we taught ourselves.'

The parents cried out in alarm and disbelief. They stopped the dancing immediately. They chased the boys out of the village and into the forest where, cornered, the boys admitted that it was Dumban who had taught them all that they knew.

So, that was the way of it. Through their children who got them from Dumban, men and women came to know the songs and dances of our people. And though Dumban had said that his home was in the pool, the day came—during dance Rak'mba, which is danced in the sunlight—when he strode from the pool, handsome, powerful, resplendent, to feast in the village.

All that day Dumban danced with the villagers. And it chanced that as he was dancing two plumes from his bird of paradise headdress fell to the ground, and two maidens picked them from the dust. They were comely, and Dumban smiled on them as they returned his feathers to him.

So it came about that Dumban decided to stay in the village, taking the two maidens as wives.

Although narrator and bystanders claimed the Paki story as complete, because its themes are important it is possible that in the past they received longer and more leisurely treatment. The cutting of the cane and pole, the bee sting, and a bloodied trencher evoke circumcision. A brother-and-sister union merges into a marriage between husband and wife; human fecundity and increase are shown to correspond with the planting, cultivation, and fructification of crops. Paki, male and singular as well as creative and generative, is directly contraposed to, and so defines, community. Paki, the cane, the feasting-pole, the foodstuffs, and the maturation of the male (represented in the three lads who climb the pole) together evoke male filiation which, in turn, is contraposed to brother and sister, siblingship.

In order to teach men and women the techniques of cultivation, and so make them human, Paki conjoins earth and sky, moral and divine, with a magical feasting-pole (itself as tree, trencher, or the power of penis) which is hung with cultivated crops. This link between the two orders of being men and women have to sever (circumcise, distinguish) if they are to cross the threshold of the wild, become human and, instead of eating seeds and bark, live in community by the fruits of their labour and intelligence. But the transition from one order of being to the other is made conditional on felling the pole: and this, as the braggart makes clear, depends on an awareness of the nature of sexual intercourse, on an awareness of the rules which regulate it. The villagers who fell to and pleasured each other (promiscuously) also ate up their foodstuffs and perished as a result. But brother and sister who waited and who had foresight, who gained an appropriate access to the divine through a dream—is Paki here not equivalent to a dream-image or ghost? —and thus learned how to cultivate properly, become husband and wife. They survive and have many descendants. As with other orphaned brothers and sisters, survival is associated with the exercise of a divine and singular power figured as male, proceeding particularly from father (Paki as ghost or dream-image) or through male filiation.

The incident of the chips is a comment on the traditional technique for felling large trees with stone axes—chips used to be placed in the cut, fired, and allowed to smoulder through what remained of the trunk[1]—and also refers to the current practice of making small bonfires of chippings, whose ashes are afterwards raked over and into the topsoil as fertilizer. The mind goes to the making of new gardens. . . . Paki, however, has gone into a stout cane, and this prevents the pole from falling. It often happens in the clearing of a new garden site that a tree whose trunk has been cut through will not fall, because its branches are interlaced with, and bound by canes and vines to, other trees. Normally, to prevent such a situation arising, trees are lopped before felling, and lopping and cutting

---

[1] This technique is still used.

away the tangle of canes and vines are tasks generally undertaken by youths. Since the job is not without its dangers, and
smaller boys may fall, and are not, in any case, strong enough
to do the work effectively, the appropriate person is a strong and
nimble youth in the first flush of young manhood. And such
youths, sexually mature and eager to demonstrate their prowess
and daring, are also those who like to talk of their love affairs
and conquests. Hence it is apposite that just such a youth should
be sent up the pole to cut the vine and pass on Paki's instructions. The bee sting reminds us of Nuakai, Tuman, and the
advent of circumcision; and the second lad is still not quite
old enough to appreciate the sense of Paki's message. But the
third is sexually aware, technologically proficient, ready to communicate his parts. Only then can the cane—which is Paki,
male and creative as well as singular—be cut or circumcised,
made morally relevant, be so placed as to receive and pass on
an appropriate male filiation.

Now that the singular power residing in the divine has been
appropriately brought into the moral by or through male
filiation, male filiation has to come into relation with siblingship. For their more important feasts Tangu erect poles on
which they hang a variety of cultivated and nurtured foodstuffs: Paki's pole and Tangu feasting-poles correspond with
each other. Within this context, which holds the promise of
moral activity, brother and sister become husband and wife.
Or, since narratives deal so often with the reverse or covert
side of experience, it might be more accurate to say that husband and wife become as though brother and sister. At any
rate, it is as husband and wife that they engage in sexual intercourse in their new garden,[1] and it is as husband and wife that
they hand on their seed crops and knowledge of cultivation to
their descendants. Community life and culture, that is, proceed
from male power. Men quicken the 'germ of being' in a woman;
men make boys into men through the *garamb*; men decide and
are responsible; men are the culture bearers.

The first of the Dumban narratives, N. 27, has clear simil-
arities with the Maribun tale. Maribun, Paki, and Dumban (i),

[1] *Supra*, p. 99.

indeed, belong together. Maleness, singular and potent, has to become relevant in moral terms as husband and father; has to be related to wife through marriage; must be shown as ordered by the *garamb* and circumcision. First, though, the meaning of the red stone in the Maribun tale is here made more explicit: the maiden is in her first menstrual period, mature, and marriageable. And she receives what is in fact a typical token of affection and earnest of marriage—only those about to marry make cane waistbelts or wristlets for each other—from Dumban. But he waits until the parents have gone before he makes his intentions clear, and his lurking in the bushes at the verges of the village clearing carries a flavour of the *ranguma*, of the unbridled and sexually potent. Then, as in the Maribun tale, the girl cannot be loosed from the stone which Dumban has told her to sit on. Comes the storm which moves, creates, precipitates the flow of events; and the parents return to the village. Brother watches over sister. Dumban comes.... Handsome and strong, with shining skin and well decorated, it is not until he produces a piece of roof thatch and a cooking-pot that he can overcome the maiden's fears and hesitations and persuade her to accompany him to his home in the stream.

Cooking-pot and roof thatch are evidence of a properly equipped house somewhere under the water. While both evoke marriage and the household, 'roof thatch' carries us to the *garamb*.[1] Though a bride's brothers usually provide her with household equipment, here, it would seem, Dumban is telling the maiden that there is no need to worry over such matters. He is equipped. Like a *ranguma*, he is taking his woman without regard to the conventions. Nevertheless, despite these pertinent asides, the main theme—following on the gift of the wristlet—is that the girl should be given the confidence to follow Dumban to his house in the stream. Dumban, she discovers, is a snakeman, a man in the daytime, a snake at night: the mind turns to Zawapai's introduction to Tuman, to the snake-brothers and the two sisters who ate their sugar-cane.[2] The girl is scared. She has never before encountered the generative power and force in maleness. Yet it is a small snake, Kuokavalik, a mother's brother, who deflowers her.[3]

---

[1] *Supra*, p. 209, and more especially *infra*, pp. 366-7.
[2] *Supra*, pp. 247 and 318.
[3] *Supra*, p. 246.

The process of creation proceeds. And with the birth of children the narrative takes up a fresh brother-and-sister situation. But a reversal occurs: sister now watches brother. The stream floods, brother puts bow and arrows to use. Tangu say that the *boan* fruit may 'stand for' a pig, that the presentation of a *boan* is a declaration of intention to provide a pig. The bow and arrows signal the onset of sexual maturity and desire; the boy wants to shoot that which stands for a pig—though he fails to do so; he slashes himself with the slivers of a bow which, when used by small boys, is usually made of bamboo. . . . Is not son trying to make himself a man, trying to circumcise himself, trying to kill his own pig of the circumcision? Later on, arising from the self-mutilation, mother tells son to go to his mother's brothers, circumcisors and sponsors of incipient manhood. Dumban, skulking in the bushes, and a snake at night, has already evoked the *ranguma* and his self-willedness and disregard of others. Here, surely, the self-regard of youth, *ranguma*-like, is being contraposed to interaction and relationship with others.

Before brother and sister are brought into relationship with those whose influence is necessary for their maturation and growth into community, both are cruelly beaten by father. Both eat from the same bowl, both are beaten with coconut-frond spines after eating coconut meat mixed with coconut milk. And later brother and sister take refuge from the flood in a high coconut—at which the villagers jeer. The play is upon coconut and the associations of coconut with marriage; upon brother and sister in a context of intimacy predicating marriage. If the general situation permits one to say 'punished by father', the pretext is on the surface vague and unprecise. Because brother slashed himself, told lies? Because sister spied upon brother? Or because brother and sister were too intimately related to each other by eating coconut milk and meat from the one dish? Tangu say simply that he, Dumban, beat them. And it is this dead-pan comment which, since the whole narrative is concerned with 'brother and sister', suggests that the beating is not so much linked to one particular episode as to the general gist of the narrative: male filiation and the incest taboo (siblingship).

Though brother-and-sister marriage is prohibited to those in community, the significance of a brother-and-sister union, stasis, is realizable through becoming *mngwotngwotiki*, through a process of substitution and exchange. Further, a brother-and-sister union is realizable in terms of the self's interior experience. Men, if not women, are figured as having both male and female qualities; and a union of these qualities would, it seems, produce the same kind of stasis as is indicated by a brother-and-sister union. This brings us to the coconut—a fruit which reproduces itself from within itself—and refers back to the self-regarding boy who seems to have wanted to circumcise himself. In another narrative father beats brother and sister over the eyes with coconut spines after they have eaten from a common bowl;[1] and it is possible that, in the days when narratives were remembered more accurately, Dumban also struck the couple over the eyes. If so, then the indication is that the relationship between brother and sister being demonstrated is not one that is appropriate to overt community life. Brother-and-sister union —especially if they were twins as well as orphans—solves the problem of the historical or temporal priorities as between filiation and siblingship; and it also solves the problem of the logical priorities between filiation and siblingship. If in life brothers were to marry their sisters, the tension between filiation and siblingship would be resolved. But there would no longer be a community. If in life human beings were so narcissistic as to desire only a union of the qualities within themselves, again the community would cease to exist. Community life demands the communication of parts between one and others, demands ordered interactions. Brother and sister should look outwards, aware of others and community, not inwards to each other or into themselves. Circumcision in the *garamb*—an appropriate balance between the mother's brother who circumcises and the father who provides the pig of the circumcision—leads a youth into awareness of community and the demands of responsibility. As we know from N. 10, self-enjoyment leads into the wild.

The next brother-and-sister situation sees them journeying to mother's brother and grandmother: it is the solution to the problem posed by the preceding situation. For the mother's brother is the circumcisor who brings a growing boy into the association of men in the *garamb*, who leads a boy into that responsible maleness which father initiates and completes with

[1] *Infra*, p. 383.

the pig of the circumcision; and grandmother Nuakai is the appropriate person to bring a girl into a fuller association with that which is essentially female. The girl goes by a direct route, the boy takes the meandering course of the stream. And Tangu say the episode shows that girls grow into women quickly and directly, whilst boys have a longer and more tiresome route to manhood. Elsewhere, as we shall see,[1] brother goes over the hills and finds the going difficult, sister follows the stream and gets there first. Yet despite the reversal of illustrative representation the same point is made: boys take longer.[2] On the whole, however, the stream route is perhaps the more appropriate for boys. Maribun and both Dumbans come from the stream; a stream twists and turns; snakes, associated with stream, also twist and turn; Maribun and Dumban (i) are associated with snake; Maribun and both Dumbans are indicative of the power in maleness; women go to streams to fish, to have pleasure with Dumban (ii), to find husbands and babies.

Inevitably, a tired brother does exactly what mother had warned him not to do: on sister's suggestion he goes into a snake. A male, now he enters into his maleness. Though snakes eat frogs, there is no hint here that brother might eat sister. The *cipnangk'der* is a small snake—small boy—quite unable to cope with the large and fatty frogs of Tangu streams. But 'snake' combined with the way in which a frog swims, and its plenitude of spawn,[3] evokes the onset of two sexual maturities; and the mind leaps forward to the mating of brother and sister. But brother runs into trouble. He is struck by mother's father,[4] who is making roof thatch, he is put into a string bag with gathered foods, he is finally lodged between rafters and thatch. Then, where younger women fail, it is old grandmother, sinewy Nuakai, who dislodges the swollen snake from the rafters, who disembowels it, who carves and distributes the portions, who precipitates the final brother-and-sister situation which results in *puoker* becoming men and women. Because they have not

---

[1] *Infra*, p. 383.

[2] Differences in route, but not in substantive meaning, may relate to patrilineal and matrilineal biases.

[3] Tangu regard frog spawn as a delicacy with aphrodisiac properties.

[4] *Amaikawai*, the father of mother. Maybe a mistake or slip, maybe not. But since mother's brother and mother's father are in the same line of male filiation, the 'circumcising line' seems to be indicated.

eaten their portion of the snake, brother and sister are selected for survival: their significance survives, survival depends on their significance.

The relevances of roof thatch may now be brought together. Roof thatch is shelter from the storm, brother and sister escape from the effects of the storm by sheltering in a coconut from whose fronds roof thatch is sometimes made. The wild yam *bu* was placed between rafters and roof thatch;[1] trumps are hidden in roof thatch;[2] Ambwerk and Tuman make a shelter in a sago palm, from whose fronds roof thatch is more commonly made;[3] in the Maribun tale father is thought to have left son and daughter by the stream in order to make repairs to his roof thatch.[4] Dumban (i) shows his future wife a piece of roof thatch when persuading her to come with him into the stream.[5] Sister, as a frog, hides in a banana clump, and women make their underskirts from banana fibres; brother, as a snake, rests in the roots of a sago palm, from whose fronds roof thatch is generally made. Before he went into a snake the young boy—who has tried to circumcise himself—was told by mother to find his mother's brother: he meets the mother's father, who is making roof thatch. When the small snake, brother, is struck, it is put into a string bag, as a baby is,[6] together with gathered foods, which have womanly, not male associations; the man who uses the string bag is a male on the female side.

When the small snake is placed between rafters and roof thatch it grows and grows. . . . Here and in other narratives where roof thatch is especially mentioned the context is one of growth and maturation, a process to which circumcision is central. Here specifically, when the narrative here deals with the end of one order of being and the beginning of another, the *garamb* is introduced; and when proceeding to a point much closer to the human condition the theme of the *garamb* becomes even more insistent. In sheltering men and women from the storm, roof thatch divides the moral from the divine, protects moral beings from the power in the divine. But, since Tangu build roofed shelters over the graves of the newly dead, the notions of protection, distinction, and maturation evoked

---

[1] *Supra*, p. 223.   [2] *Supra*, p. 303.   [3] *Supra*, p. 219.
[4] *Supra*, p. 336.   [5] *Supra*, p. 351.
[6] One remembers Nuakai and Tuman *supra*, p. 221.

by the relations beteen roof thatch and *garamb* would seem to be contained in the more general notion of transition from one order of being to another. Still, where youths are concerned, roof thatch seems to indicate the distinction between moral and divine, awareness of the relations between the two orders, a transition from the random and instinctual to a progressively fuller containment in the ordered and moral.

Dumban, meanwhile, gathers the waters of the world, and the storm breaks. Fires fizz out in the rain, culture dies: the snake has been inappropriately treated. Nor is the *garamb* any protection when the challenge is thus explicit. Without its relevance the *garamb* is merely a building. A small boy, an elder boy, and a grown man—signalling a male life-cycle in the *garamb*—try to save their fire, their culture. That is their responsibility. But the flood sweeps them away, the village is submerged. Only brother and sister in the coconut escape: they have co-operated with the divine, have not defied it, have not eaten the snake. And, as in the Maribun tale, brother does not look down to see whether the flood has subsided: he tests the situation with coconuts. The green and unripe fruit—the connection is simple—falls into water, but the ripened fruit, as it does in life if left to ripen on the palm, falls with a thud on the dry ground below. Brother knows that it is safe to descend; his connection with the previous order of being is the piece of pork which he finds in the ruins of the old village, and which is to sustain him and his sister as they set off through the forest.

Why should brother be afraid of smoke from the cooking fire? Are there enemies about who might thus find them? Is this an anticipation of the quarrel between Daroomi and Niangarai, of the enmity between the peoples of Tangu and Andarum? Or does brother not want it to be known that his sister is going to cook for him as a wife does for her husband? The interior associations are obscure. Yet it might be that smoke rising skywards has here the same kinds of association as Paki's poles reaching from earth to heaven, or that length of string which Nuakai made, and which enabled the women to climb to the sky until men in community stopped them. If so, brother might well be anxious. For the new order he is about to start crucially depends on the separation of the divine or wild from the moral. The smoke might join them again—there has just been an almighty flood due to an inability to distinguish the moral from the divine. But all is well. Whatever the basis of brother's fears regarding the smoke, a possum finds them, invites them underground, persuades them into sexual congress and marriage—underground, not where community is normally to be found. Again the suggestion is that brother-and-sister marriage is to be thought of as an interior experience, or a categorical union, not as an actual union between real persons living in community.

From this point the narrative briefly recites the Daroomi–Niangarai episode. The opposition between the two friends is considerably toned down as compared with the Maribun tale, but otherwise there is little to add. Wife makes the hole, *gagawa* come out. Niangarai flees in alarm from the *garamb* in Andarum to his own place in Biampitzir.

The second of the Dumban tales, N. 28, has clear and strong associations with the dance known as Rak'mba in which— as originally danced—Christians have been forbidden by the mission to take part. Rak'mba, one of the very few dances in Tangu which take place during daylight hours, used to be—as older Tangu report it—an essentially satirical saturnalia in which participants, masked and excessively decorated, acted out in dance and mime the known, reported, or suspected sexual misdemeanours or perversions of members of the community. Specifically an occasion when several local communities congregated together, no names seem to have been mentioned explicitly, and much of the attraction of the dance seems to have lain in guessing whom the mimings were meant to represent on the one hand, and in the covert invitations actually to engage in particular kinds of eroticism at some later date on the other. Misinterpretations of meaning might add to the zest. Then again, though in many Tangu dances both men and women participate together, they do so as separate collectivities, playing the complementary roles familiar in most folk dances. In Rak'mba, however, this does not seem to have been the case. Men and women mingled, made erotic advances, and together acted out either their suspicions of what others had done, or what they themselves would like to do, or both. Given the missionary role, it is hardly surprising that action was taken against continuing Rak'mba in its original form. Even today, much modified though it is, many might blush or find themselves roused. Yet it should not be thought that mission objections referred solely to the eroticisms of the dance. No dance is without erotic undertones. The more substantial basis for opposition was the fact that the actual or alleged sexual activities of particular individuals were being brought to the notice of the community in general. And this feature, bearing as vitally as it does on the Christian view of the domains of the public and private, community affairs and the individual conscience, on the difference between the Christian and traditional forms of confession—and so, in the end, on the differences between the Christian and traditional conceptions of the relations between the moral and divine—could not be allowed to continue.

Rak'mba, in particular, then, sets the context of sexual licence in which the Dumban of N. 28, Dumban (ii), gathers meaning. And the covert invitation to sexual engagement inherent in all dances, for Dumban taught men and women many dances, provides the more general atmosphere.

The narrative begins with the men and women of the village in opposed but complementary roles: the men go hunting, and the women fish, on alternate days: matter of routine. But Dumban interrupts this workaday programme. At sight of him rising from the stream,[1] the women throw off their skirts and lie down in two lines. He pleasures them—both lines of female filiation. And if Dumban concerns everyone, not just one of the two halves into which a community is divided, the situation itself evokes the *ranguova* going into the *juaka*,[2] taking cover in the garden shelter, and encountering a wife hidden in the woodpile.[3] Yet not until ordinary routine is interrupted by the failure of the women to take fish are the men's suspicions aroused. Then, they are clear, something odd is occurring. So a small boy, male but in association with women, acts the spy by pretending to sleep in his string-bag cradle. He watches, evoking emergent reciprocities, and he reports back to his father, not privately

---

[1] With Dumban, as with others, though it is no doubt the water which causes skin to glisten, the point is that a shining skin evokes integrity and awareness, the reverse or opposite of what is evoked by skin sores or buttock sores.

[2] *Supra*, p. 281.   [3] *Supra*, p. 283.

but in the *garamb*: maleness in the wild and maleness in community are contraposed to each other. Areca-nut is eaten by all in the *garamb*, and, as was the case with Nimbamung,[1] a co-operative expedition is set on foot. Dumban is treated as an enemy, as a *ranguma*. All the responsible men sanction, and share in, the subsequent killing. Dumban has been pleasuring other men's wives, engaging his sexual capacities outside the marriage bond. He is maleness in the wild, maleness unconstrained, an adulterer, singular, as though a *ranguma*.

The indignant husbands may succeed in killing and then dismembering Dumban, but they cannot eradicate his meaning. This survives, is a part of all men. Though the wives want to keep Dumban or his meaning or possibilities with and inside them, the husbands will not tolerate it. They externalize Dumban, making the hidden interior experience or pieces of experience into a recognizable and exterior whole. At this point, one might say, the inherent wantonness of Tangu women becomes controllable and manageable by being externalized and contained in the *ranguma* complex. When an unconstrained male is believed to be around, a *ranguma*-killer keeps watch.

Dumban's phallus is surely in essence his singular self. When it moves through the peripheries of Tangu, touching at Wasamb within Tangu, it travels through those areas where, commonly, *ranguova* are thought to exist more prevalently. The narrator was from Riekitzir, and Wasamb as well as Amuk are thought by Riekitzir people to be the likeliest places in Tangu where *ranguova* might be.[2] But Dumban is not simply a *ranguma*. *Ranguova* are men and Dumban is a *puok*. Dumban is, and in a consequential sense means, babies also. It is as 'baby' that the pairs of maidens recognize him; friendship is specifically evoked. Though in the past Riekitzir people regarded Amuk and Wasamb with some hostility, they still sought friends there and concluded intermarriages. While Tangu generally regard Ariangon, Dimuk, Mariap, and Pariakenam as places where *ranguova* were, and are, likely to be encountered, both in the past and currently they have sought to maintain friendships as well as kin relationships in these places. For where there are

---

[1] *Supra*, p. 228.
[2] *Supra*, pp. 137–8.

ranguova there must be friends, brothers, and sisters who will serve as sanctuaries, and where there are in-laws and trading partners there are likely to be varieties of *ranguova*.[1] Further, in the matrilineally-biased parts of Tangu, while women would tend to stay in the *mwenk* of birth, men would marry out, thus producing a travelling line of male filiation.[2] So, though Dumban as unconstrained maleness from the outside or wild evokes the *ranguma*, as a power under control he evokes babies, the result of intermarriages with members of other communities.

Both aspects of Dumban are in line with other indications in the narrative. At the start Dumban is outside community. At the end he comes to a community dance—danced in the day-time, in sunlight—and, upon two maidens picking up his bird of paradise plumes, he is brought into community through marriage.[3] He becomes maleness under control, maleness contained within the normative moralities. Dumban is associated with dances in general, with Rak'mba in particular: and Rak'mba is an intercommunity dance which, in effect, both controlled and invited extra-marital sexual activities. Dances provide occasions for members of different communities to meet and arrange marriages—which Dumban illustrates—and during dances the feeling that *ranguova* may be lurking close by often becomes acute.[4] Dumban teaches dances to boys, boys used to be taught dances in the *garamb*, a boy brings Dumban to the notice of the husbands, Dumban's phallus is sliced by women, Dumban means babies. . . . Is not Dumban being circumcised by the female side, being brought under control? When the slices of Dumban's phallus are lodged in the genitals of the wives and knocked out by the husbands—are not foreskin and banana clump evoked? Does not a man have to control his wife as well as himself? With Dumban's maleness and singular vigour made potentially moral, the pieces of phallus immediately come together into a singular whole again, and then gad about the country as a *ranguma* or recently circumcised boy might do. The phallus is as baby; it generates desire for

---

[1] Note that while Daroomi and Niangarai are friends, their villages are traditional enemies, and each expects to find *ranguova* in the other. Indeed, in the Maribun story Daroomi is more *ranguma*-like than friendly.

[2] See B-1956(*b*): 427.

[3] Now the meaning of bird of paradise plumes is made explicit.

[4] *Supra*, p. 137.

babies; presumably it begets babies; it is hidden in yam bins. And yam bins, as we have seen, evoke the *garamb* or a parallel process of maturation, and also associate gardening competence and fertility of crops with sexual maturity, human fecundity, and marriage.

Nearer to humans than Maribun, Dumban, too, suggests the singular power in maleness and men. On the one hand the qualities he figures belong to the *ranguma*, to the self-willed man who, sexually potent and outside community, may be persuaded to conform to the moral and enter community; on the other hand, while the same qualities go with an appropriate male filiation, without self-restraint they may run wild and turn a man into a *ranguma*. The balance is precarious and, as we know, while Tangu insist that others should conform, each man covets a reserve of self-willedness.

Father and Son, Husband and Wife, Brother and Sister

It will have become apparent that in Tangu tradition women, though imbued with the qualities of Nuakai, tend simply to *be*.... In themselves rather like *puoker*, they are represented as bundles of impulse. But unlike *puoker*, women are subject to the constraints of men who, having positive being, should communicate their parts with thought and decision. As a garden yields its fruits when it is cultivated and controlled, but may otherwise run riot with weeds, so women, associated with gardens, are represented as workers and childbearers upon whose latent fecundity men may exercise their creative parts. Similarly as between male filiation and siblingship. Where the former is positive and creative, the latter is the receptive medium through which positive creativity becomes morally relevant. Yet men could not properly fulfil their roles as culture bearers and guardians of community in terms of an awareness which simply coincided with the implications of those pairings which order the moral community. This would be following in the wake of community, puppetry. As Maribun and Dumban (i) exemplify, men should command community, possess or aspire to that larger awareness which, encompassing community arrangements, is also capable of appreciating the singular and perceiving itself as aware. For only by oneself being as though singular may the community be perceived and comprehended. Only by comprehending the community as a whole may the singular become aware of itself.

Though the storm is contraposed to community, it has no opposite. Mngungerp and Igoe'ika command the storm—but we know only very little about them. On the other hand, Maribun and Dumban (i) also command the storm. And they, aware and possessing just that commanding awareness of which we speak, are figured as fathers and husbands. Being both inside the community and able to appreciate it from the outside, they create or initiate the incest taboo. Through them the *garamb* and the moral community come into existence, male filiation is given its potency and brought into relation with siblingship. Paki shows us how sexual awareness, circumcision, and male filiation go together; how these features become morally relevant through the garden, marriage, and siblingship. And Dumban (ii) shows us how the singular power and awareness attaching to the male may shift between a position of command within the community and in conformity with the normative moralities, and a position outside the community whence a man may attempt to command as a *ranguma*: an appropriate as against an inappropriate male filiation. Wild before he was tamed by a responsible man, Wvawvasikai figures the *garamb*— an institutional resolution, as we shall see more clearly,[1] of the tensions between filiation and siblingship. Ambwerk may call on the rain, showering uncontrolled semen. But it is not until Zawapai, father-provider, meets and is aware of son that he can come from the storm with fire and a variety of cultural techniques and appurtenances. Even so, in emphasizing what it is that son owes to father, Zawapai sharpens the tension between filiation and siblingship.

With the narrative that follows, the meanings of fatherhood and the singular power attaching to the male and male filiation are given further precision. And the role of the *garamb*, which appropriately contains this power for the service of culture and community life, is respun. Still, if it is to contemplate others as well as itself and aspire to commanding awareness, the singular power of males and male filiation can only become morally relevant in relation to siblingship. Son has a sister, but must find a wife if he is to become father himself.

[1] *Infra*, pp. 452–5.

N. 29: *Mazienengai*[1]

One day, long ago, husband and wife with baby in a string-bag cradle went to a hillside to burn off the dried litter of their new garden. They chose a shady place under a tree at the edge of the clearing, slung son from a low branch, and sat down to smoke before starting their work. Then, while husband went hunting in the forest, wife collected the dried scrub into piles, fired them, and began raking over the burning embers and ashes. Smoke billowed over the new site, clouding the sun.

Wife did not see the hawk wheeling above her. Her mind on her work, she did not see the great bird dive down through the smoke, hook its talons into the cradle, and soar up and away down the valley of the Iwarum. It was only when she went to see whether her son had awakened that mother discovered her loss.

Sobbing, peering distractedly through the smoke, at last mother spotted the hawk sailing into the distance, son in his cradle hanging from the talons.

She gave chase at once. Running along the hillside, keeping the great bird in sight as it flew across to Igom, up along the ridge to Mangigum, and so over Tangu towards Mariap, mother marked the hawk as it alighted in the branches of a *galip*, a wild almond tree.

When mother came at length to the foot of this *galip* she saw that her baby, Mazienengai, was dangling from a bough near the top. So she started to climb to the rescue.

She could not find a sure hold. Again and again as she attacked that thick trunk she slipped and slithered to the ground. She clawed the bark with her nails, she wailed, she screamed until, exhausted and overcome with grief, she sat down at the foot of the *galip* and wept.

By and by mother recovered herself. She collected her things and made off to her village. There she met husband, just back from hunting, and she told him what had happened. Together they hastened back to the *galip*.

By the time they arrived, however, it seemed to mother that the tree was much higher than it had been. And father, looking up at Mazienengai so far away at the top of the tree, stopped to consider what best might be done. 'This', he said, 'is something for mother's brother to deal with.'

So husband and wife returned to the village, found mother's brother, and told him their problem. 'You leave it to me!' he said with assurance. 'I'll get him down!'

[1] Previously published, in a slightly different translation, as 'The Story of Mazienengai', B-1959(*b*).

When the trio got back to the *galip*, however, they found that it had grown even higher. And mother's brother, pretending he could not see Mazienengai hanging there, walked round and round the trunk of that *galip*, gazing up into the high branches and muttering over and over—'Hah! I cannot see my sister's son, I do not think he is there at all—I cannot see my sister's son!'

So it is with mother's brothers today. When they meet their sister's sons they pretend not to see them.

But in the end mother's brother admitted he could see Mazienengai hanging there. And he tried to climb up the trunk. But as it was with mother, so with him. He could find no hold. With each attempt he slithered back to the ground.

Mother's brother considered the matter. And, having thought, he cut a length of bamboo—meaning to hook the cradle off the bough and lower it down. It was too short. So, cutting another piece of bamboo and joining the two lengths together, he tried again. Still too short. Mother's brother cut a third length of bamboo and lashed it to the other two. . . .

It was no use, he could not reach Mazienengai.

Again mother's brother pondered the matter. 'If I got a piece of barkcloth from my garden, tied the ends, and put my feet in the circle,' he thought, 'I might be able to get a better grip on the trunk. . . .'

But even after going to his garden, fetching some barkcloth, making a circlet, and then trying to climb the tree, he still could not do it. Each time it seemed he had a grip, he slithered back to the ground. So, giving it up, the three of them returned to the village.

Mazienengai, meanwhile, was wakened by hunger. He started to cry. He put his little finger in his mouth, sucked, felt comforted, dozed.

But not for long. In a few moments he woke again, crying even more desperately, and sucking his third finger, then the middle finger, then the index. . . . No use.

But when he put his thumb in his mouth and sucked it, he was consoled and slept.

After a while, though, hunger moved Mazienengai again. And he woke, howling to be fed.

Namai the hawk heard him. Seeing the babe so hungry he flew down to the cradle and put his man into Mazienengai's mouth. Mazienengai sucked, content. Father [*sic*] urged his milk [*sic*] forth.[1]

So it was that father fed the baby Mazienengai. The little chap

[1] Semen is referred to as '*geumb*, milk' for the child 'to eat, *brami*'—see *supra*, p. 84.

ate, slept peacefully, and began to grow big. Came the time as the lad grew stronger and larger that father Namai brought him meat to eat, made him a bow and arrows, taught him how to shoot lizards in the dawning, gut them, and hang them in the sun to dry. Then, when the growing Mazienengai had learnt that meat gave him strength, father Namai taught him how to shoot birds, how to make fire, how yams and taros should be cooked. . . .

Father taught son how to do everything.

When all the teaching was done and it seemed as though son had no more to learn, Mazienengai gathered his bow and arrows, his firestick, his yams and his taros, and he climbed down the wild almond tree. 'I must go', he said to Namai. 'You must needs go on eating berries and such, but I—I have yams and taros to eat.'

Father, no longer needed, soared into the sky and away.

Mazienengai walked by himself through the forest until—there was father in front of him!

Father was terrified. He set arrow to bowstring, bent his good bow, and came to the aim.

'Don't shoot!' Mazienengai shouted. 'Do you not recognize me? I am Mazienengai, Mazienengai your son!'

Father lowered his bow, wary and ready as Mazienengai came forward to greet him. Yet all was well, and they sat down together.

Mazienengai took some yams from his bag, blew up his firestick, made a fire, and started to cook. . . .

Father was astounded—he had never seen cooking before and was accustomed only to eating stones.

When the yams had been cooked, Mazienengai gave some to father to eat. Very gingerly, father tasted the yam, chewing very carefully and thinking about it. Then he took another bite, and another and another—big mouthfuls, each bolted down one after the other. He vomited. 'I don't think I like eating your kind of food,' father complained, 'I would rather go on eating what I am used to.'

'As you like', Mazienengai replied. 'It is for you to choose. You can go on eating stones by yourself, whilst I, Mazienengai, will eat yams and taros.'

They parted, father going his way, son his.

Now it happened that as Mazienengai walked through the forest his mother's brothers—the hornbill, the crested pigeon, and all the other birds of the air—came to him, telling him to clear a site and build himself a home, instructing him as to how he should build his house. They flew away when they had finished their counsel.

So Mazienengai went hunting next morning. He came across a pig, killed it with a stone and, dragging the beast through the forest

until he came to a suitable place, suddenly made up his mind—
'Here is the place!' he decided. 'I will build my house here!'

Father had also gone hunting, killing a pig as Mazienengai had
done, and sounding his slit-gong to tell everyone what he had
done.

The following morning, after measuring the ground carefully,
Mazienengai cleared the site he had chosen. He cut some stout poles,
lopping them to size and bedding them in holes he had dug on the
site. Setting the main verticals straight, he bound on the horizontals,
framed the gables and the walls, and put the roof-beams and the
lintels in their places. Then, tying the joists to the base, he placed
poles and split arecapalm trunks across them as the floorboards of
his house. Thus, the framework completed, he set off into the forest,
where he stalked and killed a cassowary.[1]

Next day Mazienengai gathered a heap of sago fronds and stitched
them together round staves as roof thatching. And when he had
finished he went hunting, killing a pig. This time he sounded his
slit-gong to tell everyone what he had done.

The following day Mazienengai set the thatching to the roof,
binding each length of stitched thatch to the beams and rafters under-
neath. Afterwards he went hunting, killing a cassowary, which he
brought back to his house.

That night Mazienengai slept well.

Next morning the hornbill came to help Mazienengai paint the
sheets of bark which were to form the walls of his house, stitch the
panels together, and place them in position. They shared a meal of
yams and taros when they had finished, and the hornbill, mother's
brother, returned to his home.

Father, meanwhile, had been hunting. He killed a pig, took it
home to the village, and, announcing a feast and a dance on his slit-
gong, started to make his preparations. The hornbill, the crested
pigeon, the bird of paradise—all the mother's brothers—saw to the
lizard-skin heads of their handdrums, fixed fresh buttons of resin to
the newly-taut membranes, and decorated themselves for the feast.

Each sang as was his wont, dancing the while, and returning to
his home when all the festivities were done.

Next morning Mazienengai went hunting. He killed a cassowary,[2]
brought it home with him, and signalled a dance on his slit-gong.

---

[1] On the evidence of N. 9 (*supra*, p. 253, n. 3) we could say that the cassowary
here introduces the idea of sexual assault, or at least the idea of burgeoning
sexuality.

[2] Unlike the snake-brothers of N. 9, who did not go into the *garamb*, Mazienengai
is going to deal with his sexual desire in an appropriate way: he is going into the
garamb.

Then, blowing a blast on his conch, he went into his home—the first *garamb*.

Three months Mazienengai stayed there, plaiting cane into wristlets, armbands, and anklets. He made a waistband of woven cane for himself, threading it with a pattern of red-dyed strips. He hammered out a long strip of barkcloth as a breechclout for wrapping around his loins and his privates.

Then the proper day came. He went down to the stream in the early morning to wash himself, returning afterwards to the *garamb* to array himself in armlets, wristlets, anklets, and waistband. He twirled himself into his breechclout, tying the abdomen tight, knotting the back firmly and allowing the apron in front to skirt the ground by his ankles. Then, with chaplets of dogs' teeth on his brow and about his neck, with boars' tusks and pearly shell on his breast, he repaired to his slit-gong, calling his friends, his mother's brothers, and his sisters to see him.

So Mazienengai entered into manhood, and the *garamb* was finished. The mothers' brothers returned to their homes. And though father stayed on for a while, he too went off on his business at last. Mazienengai slept.

With the dawning, next day, Mazienengai roused himself and went down to the banks of the Iwarum. There he climbed into the branches of a high *galip*, and sat comfortably combing his hair.

By and by two maidens, sisters who had been helping mother and father clear a new garden site close at hand, came down to the stream to draw water. They bent down over the pool to fill their barrels—and there, mirrored in the still water, they saw Mazienengai, comely and strong, combing his hair.

Elder sister leaned closer, stretching out her hand to the image in the stream—Mazienengai vanished in the ripples!

'Stupid girl—now see what you've done!' scolded Tuman. 'You've spoilt it!'

Then they heard father shouting from the garden, 'Hey there! Hurry along with the water, you two!'

'Oh do come along, then!' Tuman fretted impatiently. 'Father will be so angry with us if we don't go at once!'

'Go? Why go?'

The sisters turned their faces up to Mazienengai in the branches of the *galip*. 'Because our father is calling us', Ambwerk started to explain. 'He will be angry with us if we don't take him his water.'

Yet neither of the maidens could move. Entranced, as though rooted, they gazed at Mazienengai.

Now father, working on the new site with his wife and young son, was becoming hot and sweaty, riled and impatient. 'Go and see what's keeping your sisters!' he snapped to his son.

The boy slipped through the forest to the stream, gently parting the bushes as he came to the bank. He saw his sisters gazing up at Mazienengai, and he watched them, held there, deaf to the angry shouts of his father.

Father lost patience. He made for the stream in a fury, determined to see for himself what was happening. Yet when he got there he had to stop short in surprise, all anger gone. For there was elder daughter clasping the trunk of the *galip* at about shoulder height, whilst younger daughter was hugging it a little lower down. . . .

'What can you be doing?' father demanded. 'Why have you not brought me my water? Why are you hugging that *galip*?'

So the two girls explained that Mazienengai, a strong and handsome young man, was in the topmost branches of the *galip*—'And we want him for our husband!' they finished.

'What? You talk to me thus?' Angrily, father took the two girls firmly by the arms and dragged them back to the village.

Now the following day, having decided to cut down that tree, all the villagers repaired to the *galip*. Ginunk people started to chop at the bottom, Mnduopa people a little higher up, and Mnduor people a little higher still.[1] There was no trace of Mazienengai.

All day those villagers hewed with their axes of stone, but they could not bring the tree down. Some say that a thick vine at the top of the tree, roping it to others around it, prevented it from falling, and that not until the vine was cut would it fall. Others have it that when the people rested from their labours that night the chips they had cut from the trunk flew into it again; but that one little chip struck a boy on the shin, cutting him; and he, hurt and annoyed, threw the chip into the fire—so that next morning when they came back to the tree to cut it down, noticing that the burned chip had not re-entered the tree, they decided to make a large fire and burn all the chips as they cut them out. Now, whichever is the truth of it —for even today, as you know, trees may be held up by vines and canes, and we have fires to burn the chips as we cut them out when we clear land for a new garden—this much is certain: Not until Ginunk and Mnduor and Mnduopa people had enjoyed each other was it possible for the tree to fall down. Then, when it did fall—after all the pleasuring—it scattered the different kinds of yams to the various villages on the ridges hereabouts. . . .

But still no one could see Mazienengai.

[1] In some versions the positions of Ginunk and Mnduor are reversed, in others Mnduopa does not appear at all.

Father and daughters searched high and low in the litter of crushed and broken branches of the *galip*, walking up and down, looking carefully through the wreckage, trying to find Mazienengai.

Father it was who at last saw Mazienengai—huddled in a yam vine. But he said nothing. He walked up and down as though he were still searching, humming a song, the song of Mazienengai—

Oh Mazienengai! Oh Mazienengai!
What a dance you have led us,
What a dance you have given us!

At last father told his daughters where Mazienengai was. They pounced on him, each taking an arm. 'He is mine!' cried Ambwerk. 'I am the elder!'

But Tuman only held on the more tightly, surrendering nothing. For his part, father left them, going on his way.

Deciding in the end to share him, the two sisters took Mazienengai back to their house in the village and hid him in their yam bin. And later that night, as they set out their pallets for sleep, they opened the yam bin and asked Mazienengai to join them.

Mazienengai did so. He lay between the two maidens, pleasuring each in turn, now one, then the other, all the night through. For ten nights in succession Mazienengai pleasured the sisters, first one, then the other, through each of all of those ten nights.

By and by the bellies of the sisters swelled out. And father, seeing them thus, was puzzled. How had it happened? He decided to find out for himself. He would go to the garden as usual on the following day, but, as soon as the daughters had gone out to work, he would double back through the forest and search through their hut.

Next morning, then, taking his adze and spear as usual, father started off along the path to the garden—doubling back to the village when he was sure his daughters had left. He unlatched the door to his daughters' house, quietly went inside. There was no one, it seemed. So, humming to himself as though he had come into the house for no reason, he searched through the hut until, coming to the yam bin, he lifted the lid and looked down inside—'Aha!' he exclaimed, seeing Mazienengai there. 'So it is you—now just you stay where you are!'

Father replaced the lid on the yam bin, crept softly outside, re-latched the door securely behind him. And that night, lying with his wife, he told her what he had done. 'We have a son-in-law now!' he said. 'We have a son-in-law in our daughters' house!'

Next morning, very early, before the others were awake, father went over to his daughters' house, opened the door and looked inside. 'Ah!' father observed, seeing Mazienengai lying between his two daughters, pleasuring them in turn. 'I can see you are busy—doing what you should do.'

He shut the door gently behind him and went off to his garden.

So it was that Mazienengai got two wives for himself. While they went out to the gardens to plant yams and weed the plots, he would think about dancing and singing songs, practising the steps and repeating the melodies.

One day, all their near kinsfolk having died, the sisters became orphans. 'What is to become of us now?' they wailed. 'Where shall we go? We have used up all our foodstuffs in feasting and dancing and now we have nothing!'—For you must know that though their gardens were large, and they had sown much, they had little to eat at the time, and now there was no one to help them. Also, Mazienengai was tiring. He was still pleasuring his wives the whole night through, feeding the babes within them.

Mazienengai thought of a plan. He made a small hole in the roof over his sleeping mat and, during the night, after pleasuring one of his wives, he would complain that the rain was coming in through the hole. Then he would go outside and pretend to repair the roof. Once outside, however, he would take his trump from its hiding-place near the hole he had made, go out into the bush a little way and make music. Afterwards, he would come back into the hut, lie down with the other wife and feed her babe with his milk.

The sisters, meanwhile, grew larger and larger, the one with a son, the other with a daughter. During the day Mazienengai would go hunting, filling his wives' string bags with the game he took—pig, cassowary, bush-rat, and wallaby—returning home in the late afternoon to cook the meat and eat. Then, after the meal, while his wives slept, Mazienengai would leave the house, fetch his trump from its hiding-place in the roof, and go into the forest a little way to play a tune.

One day, when his wives were in the forest gathering relishes, Mazienengai, who had stayed behind in the village, thought he would play his trump. Through the trees went the music, through the trees to his wives.

'Whatever can it be?' they wondered, immediately slinging their bags and making haste to return to the village.

Mazienengai saw them coming down the path, quickly hid his trump in the roof thatch.

'What was that we heard just now?' the wives demanded. 'We were in the forest gathering relishes when we heard music like the *jangaliwawa* of a trump.'

'Oh? Perhaps what you heard were noises in the forest—forest noises?'

'No such thing!' the wives contradicted. 'We heard music, music coming from the village here. We heard a trump! Instead of hunting and getting meat for us, and instead of feeding the babes in our wombs, you laze in the village all day playing on a trump!'

'A trump? I played no trump!' Mazienengai denied. 'What you heard was probably just the babes stirring in your wombs. . . .'

Next day Mazienengai went hunting. He caught a small pig, a small wallaby, a small bush-rat, a small lizard, and a small possum. He put the meat into two small string bags, one for each of his wives. They stuffed the meat into bamboo barrels, cooked it, supped, and retired to bed.

The following morning, after finishing what remained of the meat, the two wives went fishing. Each caught a *wiambaran* fish. Then, floating through the forest, they heard the twangly-jangle of a trump. And at once, running all the way, they returned to the village. 'Well? Was it you making that music?' they asked their husband Mazienengai.

'Music? What music? I wasn't playing a trump and I've seen no one else around here. It must be your children stirring inside you!'

There was no meat that day. So they cooked yams and taros, ate, and slept.

The day came when Ambwerk bore a son, Tuman a daughter. Father continued his daily round of hunting, taking game, stuffing the meat into bamboo barrels, and returning to the village to cook, eat, and sleep. One morning, however, instead of going hunting, Mazienengai went only a short way into the forest, sat down in a comfortable place, and played his trump.

When he got home his wives were there to meet him. 'Who was playing that trump just now?' they asked Mazienengai.

'I don't know', he replied. 'It must have been something playing itself.'

They cooked tubers, ate their meal, and retired to their pallets. But the wives had determined to settle the matter of the trump. They told son and daughter to keep awake that night, pretend they were sleeping, and watch what father did.

When, therefore, later that night, Mazienengai, having slept with one wife, started to complain of the rain coming in through the roof, saying he would go out and make some repairs,[1] son and daughter quietly followed him outside. They saw him take his trump from its

---

[1] Tangu men are not really obsessed with repairing their roofs. But they are, or were, concerned with maintaining the community.

hiding-place in the roof thatch and, following him a little way into the forest, they saw him sit down and play some tunes.

On his getting back to the house, one of the wives asked Mazien-engai what it was she had heard in the night—for she was sure she had heard music in the forest.

'Oh no!' Mazienengai told her. 'It was something playing by itself.'

Next morning they had yams to break their fast. And while husband went hunting, mothers and children stayed in the village. 'Well?' the women asked, so soon as Mazienengai had gone, 'what did you see last night?'

'He played a trump!' son and daughter replied together. 'He hides it in the roof thatch there!'

Mother went round to the back of the hut, rummaged in the thatch and, finding the trump hidden there, examined it closely, turning it over and over in her hands, clumsily pulling the tongue. . . .

POINNNG! She had broken the tongue.

Away out in the forest husband heard the noise and guessed what had happened. He speared a small pig, put it in his string bag, returned to the village. Glancing at the thatch as he came to his home, Mazienengai saw it had been disturbed. Angry now, still he said nothing. He gave the meat to his wives, and they cooked it.

Mazienengai supped with his family, then slept.

Next day, while the wives went down to the stream with their fishing-nets, husband stayed at home in the village. He picked a coconut, split it, and poured the milk into a bowl. Then he scraped the meat from the nut, mixed the meat with the milk. Lastly, taking some coconut fronds, he stripped the leaf from the spines and, binding the spines into a tight bundle, he hid the bundle. 'Oh, son! Oh, daughter!' he called. 'Come and see what a lovely dish of coconut meat and milk I've made for you!'

Son and daughter came running, and fell to the dish with a will.

Father waited until his children had almost finished. Then he fetched out his bundle of sinewy spines, and he thrashed his son and daughter over the eyes.

Screaming, the children ran off into the forest to their mothers. Sister made straight for the stream and followed it down between the banks until she came to her mother. But brother picked his way through the forest over the hills and down the valleys. Long after sister had found her mother, brother found his.

'What is the matter? Why are you crying?' the mothers asked.

'Father found out that we spied on him. He knows that you broke his trump, and he beat us over the eyes with coconut spines.'

Mother rounded on son. 'Why did you take so long to get here?'
she demanded. 'Your sister here—she grew up on her mother's milk
and she got here almost at once. But you—you took a long time! Go
away! Be off with you! Go and drink your father's milk—that'll
make you strong!'

So son went into the *garamb*.

When mothers and children had returned to the village, the
wives scolded Mazienengai for what he had done. 'You grew up on
your father's milk', they shrilled. 'We grew up on our mother's milk!
And now you have beaten our children! Go away from here—go
back to your father!'

Saying nothing, Mazienengai rose to his feet. He fetched his spear,
girded his areca-nut bag, slung a larger string bag over his shoulders.
Then he walked off down the path from the village, children and
wives—still scolding—following closely behind. He walked on until,
arriving at the edge of the forest and suddenly turning in his tracks,
he lunged four times with his spear. Wives, son, and daughter fell
dead, turning to stone.

You may see the four stones on the top of Bolivol hill today.

Mazienengai walked by himself through the forest, looking for
father, calling to his mother's brothers, the birds of the air: 'Have
you seen my father, O my mother's brothers? Where is my father,
do you know? I am here in the forest, my mother's brothers, looking
for my father!'

The mother's brothers came down from the tree tops to Mazienengai, guiding him as he circled the ridges of Tangu, went down
through Mangigum, and came at length to Igom. Father awaited
him.

'What is the news? What have you been doing? Why have you
left your home and come here to me?' father asked son.

'I married two wives and they bore me a son and a daughter',
Mazienengai explained. 'They nagged me when I played my trump.
They tricked me, found out where I had hidden my trump, and then
they broke it. I beat son and daughter over the eyes with coconut
spines for spying on me and betraying my secret. Then my wives
nagged me again, scolding me and telling me to be off and go and
look for you. I speared them, each one. Now I have come to you. I
am tired, hungry, and weak—but I have found you at last!'

When Mazienengai had rested and regained his strength, father
told him how he might make a *juaka* pig-trap. So, being keen to try
for himself, Mazienengai went off into the forest to make one. He
cut down a wild sago palm and bound it with vines as though it was
a pig.

Father shook his head sadly. 'No, no!' he said. 'That isn't the way!'

Father showed Mazienengai how a *juaka* should be made. To-gether they cut down some boughs, cleaned them, sized them, and bedded them firmly into the ground, describing three sides of a rectangle. Then, leaving one of the narrow ends open, with enough space inside for a man to lie comfortably, they bound the posts upright and tightly to each other with vines. Next, having cut and gathered some heavy logs, they bound them into a hollow and semi-circular bundle, placing them on top and between the longer parallel lines of the fence. Lastly, father showed Mazienengai how to make the trigger and the slip, how to bait the trap with sago seeds and flour. 'Now,' he said, stepping back to look at the trap, well pleased with what they had done, 'now you will see!'

Next morning father entered a pig. He walked right into the trap which he and Mazienengai had made, and he deliberately stepped on the trigger.

Down came the bundle of logs.

Having proved the trap in this way, father returned to the village. 'Why don't you go and have a look at your *juaka*?' father suggested to Mazienengai. 'Perhaps you have caught a pig!'

Mazienengai strode off through the forest, saw the pig pinned under the logs. He speared it.

Father taught Mazienengai how he should lift the bundle of logs with a lever, drag the pig out, and bind it to a stout pole with vines, so that it could be carried on the shoulders of two men. He taught Mazienengai how the meat should be carved, how the cuts should be stuffed into bamboo barrels for cooking. 'Now then,' father said when they had finished, 'take these barrels of meat and place them on the ridges in the vicinity here. Tomorrow you will see what you will see. Sleep well until dawn. Wake up at cock-crow, when you hear the birds starting to sing in the trees.'

Mazienengai did as he was told. He placed the barrels of meat on the ridges, and then he retired to sleep.

That night there was a tremendous storm. Rain poured in torrents, lightning flashed, thunder boomed, the earth shook—some say that it turned right over. And in the morning, then as now, Mazienengai woke to the chorus of birds in the dawning. He found the world as it is today. The barrels of pig meat had turned into villages with men and women, the small barrels into small villages, the larger barrels into larger villages. The stomach and entrails of the pig—which had not been stuffed into barrels—had turned into wives for Mazienengai. There were kinsfolk, men and women had come into the world.

Now as Mazienengai sat there on a log, thinking, his sister came and sat down beside him. 'It was my father,' Mazienengai said to himself as he pondered what had happened, 'it was my father who made the land as it is, who made men, who gave them a language so that they could speak, who taught them to understand one another, who brought men and women together in villages—'

Mazienengai glanced at his wives. 'But I, I sit with my sister', he finished.

So Mazienengai sat by the fire with his sister, eating with her, and talking to her.

That is how it is.

The central theme of the Mazienengai narrative is the cycle of fatherhood from the begetting through birth, growth, and maturation to generation again. It deals with the singular power and awareness pertaining to men, and its containment in male filiation and the *garamb*. And it also deals, as it must, with the incest taboo and marriage. Occurring as they do in the stories of Wvawvasikai, Zawapai, Paki, Maribun, Dumban (i), and Dumban (ii), the themes are already familiar. Now they are woven together. More penetrating than the Zawapai narrative, perhaps, the Mazienengai story repeatedly presents us with the father–son in opposition to the husband–wife. Not until the end are the father–son and the husband–wife brought into relation with brother–sister. Then the comment is pertinent.

The opening episode is the making of a new garden. The mind turns to Paki, to the incest taboo, to the association between fertility of crops and the pleasure of husband and wife in a new garden, to the twin notions of germination and generation. Later in the narrative, when Mazienengai meets the two sisters whom he is to marry, make pregnant, and have children by, a family at work on a new garden site again forms the general situational referent. The *galip* tree, the nuts of which we have already met in association with Zawapai, father-provider, is central to both situations. Like Paki's feasting-pole hung with the fruits of cultivation and reaching skywards, when the tall *galip* is felled it distributes yams to all the villages in and around Tangu. As a tree the *galip* participates in the general nature of trees, maleness, and its nut is red, creative. In addition to the generative power in maleness, what is abstracted from 'maleness' is the quality of 'father'. For if the two sisters hugging the *galip* remind one of Nuakai and the sago palm,[1] or the woman in the woodpile,[2] the hawk, the father of the two sisters, and Mazienengai himself shift attention to the relevance of 'father'. Zawapai brought fire and medicines, made gardens, and provided for son. Yet if the emphasis here is upon the generative and physically creative qualities of father, father it is who also initiates the cultural community. 'Father taught son how to do everything.' It was 'father who made the land as it is, who made men, who gave them a language so that they could speak, who taught them to understand one another, who brought men and women together in villages'.

When the hawk steals the babe it traces in its flight the borders of the area occupied by Tangu-speaking peoples. And in doing so it suggests, perhaps, the priority of fatherhood, of filiation as against siblingship. But if a priority is intended it cannot last very long. Siblingship is there almost at once. Mother's reaction to the hawk is motherly and womanly, following her nature. She chases the hawk and, without a thought, flings herself at the *galip*. She is quite ineffective. Apprised of the situation, father thinks, considers the matter, is judicious: mother's brother is the authority, the guardian of the child. It is for mother's brother, the circumcisor, the man chiefly responsible for initiating a boy into that process which will lead him into becoming a responsible member of community, to bring the boy back into the community from which he has been abducted. And, as we know, mother's brother connotes the interactions of siblingship, the interactions of community life. Father begets and teaches his son, mother's brother introduces him to the responsibilities of community life.

After first identifying himself as a typical mother's brother by pretending not to see his sister's son, mother's brother tries to rescue the babe for community with the aid of lengths of bamboo: circumcision with a bamboo razor is surely evoked. But he fails. He fails, too, with barkcloth—from which breechclouts and only breechclouts are made.[3] A *galip* cannot be climbed as though it were an areca or coconut palm, no bamboo pole could have fetched a baby down through the interlaced branches

[1] *Supra*, p. 219.　　　　　　　　　　　　　　　　　[2] *Supra*, p. 283.
[3] Whatever uses pieces of barkcloth might have in Tangu—pads, pillows, bandannas, wraps or wrapping, climbing aid—every little piece was originally part of a breechclout.

of a *galip*: neither of the methods selected by mother's brother are practical propositions in the circumstances. But since bamboo signals circumcision, and a breechclout signals sexual maturity after the passage of the *garamb*, their place in the narrative is, surely, to show that father's solution to the problem of a young son's being taken by the divine or going wild is to put him in the *garamb* under the supervision of a mother's brother. Yet mother's brother fails. Mazienengai seems to possess a quality with which the *garamb* alone cannot deal. For though mother's brother, the *garamb*, and circumcision are the instruments of socialization, introducing the growing youth to the complexities of siblingship, that singular awareness which is exterior to community whilst participating in it, which perceives the singular and suffers and commands the pairs, adheres to filiation. As we learned from the Wvawvasikai story, when Ambwerk hauled a urinating mother's brother from a clump of bananas,[1] a proper man commands the community he lives in. Mother's brother is simply an appropriate instrument for—quite literally—dealing with the singular by cutting it.

We have seen childhood. Puberty and the *garamb* have been evoked. Now with the notion of *garamb* alive in his mind, the listener is taken by the narrative to the process of conception. Physical and social birth are represented as analogous or parallel processes. The *garamb* is represented as the womb in which, by and through men, boys are reborn as, or are made into, men with the potential of acting responsibly. Tangu say, as we have seen, that the 'germ of being' is contained in the womb of the mother, and that if it is to develop and be born into the world as a human child it must eat, or be fed by, the father's milk or semen. When the hawk feeds Mazienengai through his penis there is a linguistic shift from Namai ('*namai* = hawk') to 'father, *abwvai* or *avai*': the hawk is procreator, doing for Mazienengai what the latter does for his own babes in the wombs of his wives. Yet the hawk is not simply male. A hawk is a bird, birds are figured mainly as female, the mother's brothers are figured as birds. The hawk is male-in-relation-to-female, appropriate fatherhood, and it is also as *garamb*, male and female parts in the male.

Before being fed on father's semen or milk Mazienengai sucks

[1] *Supra*, p. 315.

each of his fingers in turn, eventually being comforted by sucking his thumb: usual enough, for children generally comfort
themselves by sucking their thumbs. But there are more
nuances of meaning than this. For the thumb is a singular digit
opposed to two pairs of fingers: the singular opposed to the
pairs, the singular and non-reciprocal opposed to the four lines
of filiation which, in terms of the model,[1] connote the community. In N. 4 Nuakai tried, but failed, to cut the sago palm—
phallus—with her thumb; and her vulva, a pair of lips, was
also ineffective.[2] The exercise of the singular pertains to the
male. An old woman beyond the menopause, but a female all the
same, Nuakai has to use an axe, a tool with male or ambivalent
associations.[3] In the present context, however, the thumb is
also, surely, a substitute for teat or breast nipple. And Mazienengai does not find the substitute satisfactory: he wakes and
cries again, he cannot appropriately nourish himself on his own
singular being. Yet as soon as the hawk feeds Mazienengai with
the milk of his penis, the babe is satisfied—just as he would be
in life if put to the breast. Breast nipple and penis, then, are
associated: each, female and male, similarly shaped with
erectile properties, produces a nutritive and milky fluid.[4] Later
on, when mother scolds son for taking so long to get to her,
saying that he grew up on his father's milk, the comment and
implied riposte are immediate: he enters the *garamb*. Again, the
hawk is both as father and as *garamb*; birth and the passage of
the *garamb* are analogous. While appropriate fatherhood is contained in the engagement of male and female parts, and while
a father is both 'father' and 'mother' to his son, in that he begets,
cares for, and teaches him, the *garamb*, figured as possessing both
male and female parts, is as father and mother to the man if not
to the child. Mother's brother, figured as bird, a male on the
female side, circumcises a boy. By contrast, an inappropriate
'fatherhood' is exampled in the *ranguma*, or in the tale of
Ruongaptiamkan.

Though, in terms of the surface events, the feeding of Mazienengai might seem to be a reversal of the 'natural' order of
events, the associative logic of the narrative provides a deeper
sense of what is involved, or represented as involved, in physical

[1] *Supra*, pp. 69–71.   [2] *Supra*, p. 219.   [3] *Infra*, p. 466.
[4] One might, of course, add 'seminal' to 'nutritive'.

and social metamorphoses. For through it the hinterland of meaning contained within the Tangu theory of conception becomes clearer, the complexities of the relevances of the *garamb* emerge, and each both illumines and is illuminated by the meaning of father and fatherhood. Further, within the associative complex of milk-breast-nipple-penis-semen-milk, one may appreciate the significance of the coconut in marriage, particularly where a brother and sister are concerned. A coconut, like brother-and-sister in narrative and husband-and-wife in life, is a reproducing unit, reproduces itself from itself, from the meat and milk inside it. Coconuts are as testicles as well as breasts: all have within them a milky fluid which, already associated with human fecundity, is also associated with the fertility of crops. Milk is powerful stuff. On the other hand, though the central theme in procreation and metamorphosis is the junction of male and female elements, the essential quality of synthesis seems to adhere to the peculiar and generative singularity of maleness and men. Not all coconuts germinate and mature. Some rot, others wilt and die. In Tangu men, and only men, are charged with the nurture, care, and planting of germinating nuts. Only males are positively dealt with in the *garamb*, and one job of the *garamb* is the socialization of male powers. If a woman's two breasts are to swell with milk, she must first receive the milk of maleness from that singular part which stands out from between a pair of areca-nuts.

As the episode of feeding Mazienengai comes to an end, father is presented in his role as tutor to son: a role which is re-emphasized immediately and explicitly, as well as at the end of the narrative. And in both contexts, though the fields of meaning do not quite coincide, once the teaching is done son is separated from father. In this instance, competent and equipped with certain essentials of culture, knowing that meat gives him strength—the necessary strength to qualify as husband—son takes his leave of Namai. Almost at once, however, Mazienengai encounters father again. But of course it is a different father, father in another aspect. The father–son relationship is changing. In descending from the *galip* and becoming independent of father on one level, son is ready to go into the *garamb* and re-engage with father on another level. For father Namai, a hawk, wild stuffs will serve. So, confident and cocky, with fire and yams and taros and the ability to cook, Mazienengai strides away through the forest. He is becoming human, a cultural being.

When Mazienengai meets father, the latter brings his bow to the ready. This acute oppositional relationship, which we have noted as occurring in life when son comes to puberty and should go into the *garamb*, is smoothed over. But it is soon apparent that if son now thinks he can teach father a thing or two, it is not for father to learn from son. Father vomits and goes on his way, independent. Yet father has not behaved quite as a responsible father should. His use of a bow and arrow suggests that in openly revealing an opposition to son he is behaving like a stripling and not like a responsible man, and in doing so he also exhibits that which is prior to culture and cultural awareness. He eats stones—wild and untreated material. But stones are not only permanent and durable, they contain the possibility of tools. And in vomiting cultural stuffs father is surely revealing himself as a source of culture. Vomiting seems indicative of a new beginning, a cleansing out of the old and uncomfortable or indigestible, a renewal. When Tangu feel over-seedy, lethargic, and glum, an emetic is considered a useful medicine. Tuman, becoming son, is freed from the consequences of his prior being by the ministrations of Zawapai: he vomits. So here, vomiting sets the scene for a new beginning. Mazienengai enters community, becomes more human, prepares to go into the *garamb* and free himself from the personal domination of father. Father, figured as inhabiting a different order of being, begins to dissolve into the wider notion of fatherhood, into broadening fields of relevance: partly into an association with hawk, the wild or divine and instinctual begetter; partly to that aspect of father which is pertinent to the *garamb*; partly to the point where the appropriate transmission of singularity, initiative, and cultural tradition now passes to the younger generation; partly to the phase when, as ghost or dream-image, father becomes a divine confidant who may play tricks or be misunderstood.

Distanced from father, under the supervision of mother's brothers, Mazienengai builds the first *garamb*. And, since the mother's brothers are birds, usually figured in narratives as female, we are brought back to the meaning of the *garamb*: males on the mother's side training boys to be men; males in community generating men from their female aspect. While the *garamb* is building father does not neglect his duties in providing feasts for the mother's brothers—who are in charge of the growing boy, and who are to himself as wife's brothers. And Mazienengai, who has hitherto only shot at birds and lizards with a bow and arrows, a boy's pastime, now begins to hunt the kind of game that men hunt: wallaby, cassowary—a boy become sexually virile[1]—and pig. Moreover, no sooner has he got his sago roof thatch stitched together than he uses a slit-gong to tell everyone that he has killed a pig. Yet father himself has already killed a pig and used a slit-gong to tell everyone. And if the one pig which Mazienengai has killed brings 'slit-gong' and 'roof thatch' into association, revealing on the one hand the imitation of father and on the other the budding of manhood and responsibility, the first pig, the one Mazienengai killed with a stone, is as significant. Not yet a man, Mazienengai could not have used a spear, nor is it fitting in the context that a bow and arrow should account for a pig. But father ate stones, and stone tools are, perhaps, father's gift to community; a pig is evidently needed to build the *garamb*; towards the end of the narrative father enters a pig so that Mazienengai may trap it; pig-meat becomes men and women; in life it is father who provides the pig of the circumcision. Thus fatherhood is again included in the notion of the *garamb*. Moreover, we are also told how a *garamb* house is built: idea and meaning, mental creations and activities, are brought into relation with beams, spars, flooring, walls, and roof, so that on the one hand 'notion' is given its necessary anchorage in space, on the other a trigger or series of triggers is provided for evoking the notion or notions.

Mazienengai prepares himself for 'coming down' from the *garamb*. He washes, dons the canework decorations he has made, winds on his breechclout, arrays himself in shell ornaments and dogs' teeth. Blowing on the conch shell perhaps represents an acknowledgement of the pig of the circumcision, and Mazienengai's replacement in the *galip*, in an ambience of redness, seems equivalent to oiling the skin with pig fat and red pigment, and daubing the hair with clay and red ochre. Father, as usual, goes off on his business. Mazienengai is as a man, sexually mature, ready to generate, handsome, strong, meticulous in his

---

[1] Note the evocation of 'cassowary', *supra*, p. 253, n. 2.

appearance. He is seated in what is to be the source of all yams, the *galip*, which has already been associated with the hawk as generative fatherhood. And then, like Maribun, Dumban (i), and Dumban (ii), each of whom was of aspect magnificent, Mazienengai comes to the cognizance of the two sisters in a stream. In her eagerness elder sister destroys the image in the pool. But this only serves to bring the two girls into more vital contact with Mazienengai himself. A new garden is in the making, sexual intercourse and marriage and children are predicated. When little brother is sent to see what the sisters are doing we feel we already know he will look on helplessly while the sisters, unable to move, will remain entranced with Mazienengai. The encounter itself is decisive.

The sisters hug the *galip*, revealing it as essentially male. Their action evokes the theme of a trencher and a couple of areca-nuts,[1] a tree and two pairs of breasts turn the mind to thumb and four fingers. And their relative positions bespeak the two main *GAGAWA*, Mnduor and Ginunk. Does this suggest that *GAGAWA* had a matrilineal bias? Is the intrusion of Mnduopa people a mistake, a later addition, or has it a more substantive significance? No definite answers arise from the evidence. Though, as has been pointed out,[2] *GAGAWA* were primarily territorial divisions, it is true that the general tendency would have been for any local group outside Wanitzir to have had a matrilineal bias. On the second point more conservative Tangu roundly assert that Mnduopa people are wrongly included, that Mnduopa was always a 'small' *gagai*, that there were only two *GAGAWA*, Mnduor and Ginunk. Yet, whether or not these answers are acceptable, it seems clear that both points refer to those kinds of almost incidental organizational forms which do not significantly pertain to the being and awareness of Tangu. What does pertain to the nature of being and awareness in the mention of *GAGAWA* has already been encountered in the Paki narrative. Before the tree can fall the chips have to be burned, the vine has to be cut. Before the fruits of cultivation can be made available, man and woman or wife from different *GAGAWA* must pleasure each other. New garden, fertility of crops, pleasure, and the importance of being a circumcised penis are all inter-associated in survival and

[1] *Supra*, p. 244.   [2] *Supra*, pp. 8–23.

fecundity. Yet when the *galip* actually falls and distributes the yams, Mazienengai himself cannot be found. A fresh episode, a new facet of meaning, is being introduced.

The theme returns explicitly to father. Father it is who finds Mazienengai in the yam vine, who is inspired to sing the song known as 'Mazienengai', who brings Mazienengai to the notice of his daughters. Then he goes on his way. As yams are vital to men in community, so man is as vital to cultivated yams. Mazienengai and yams belong together. And if it is father who discovers and is responsible for this association, he also brings boy and girl together. On both hands germination and generation are rooted in fatherhood. The daughters, each of whom would like to have Mazienengai to herself, compromise, decide to share, hide him in their yam bin in their house. And 'yam bin', as we have seen, evokes the *garamb*, the fertility of crops, the begetting of babies, and a further phase of maturation. Dumban's great phallus goes into a yam bin before it can father babies; the youth who lost his handdrum was sexually competent and a good hunter, but he went into a yam bin when marriage and children were in view. Mazienengai is associated with the source of all yams, but he has to be placed in a yam bin before he can be considered as married, before he can generate children as a father.[1] Mazienengai's creative powers are being socialized, made manageable; the good gardener is being signalled.

It will have been noted that at no point in the narrative is father excluded from the context. He may come, he may go about his affairs, but he is always there in his different aspects. We have seen him as procreator of babies and crops; we have seen him in the context of family; he has appeared in relation to wife's brothers (children's mother's brothers), the *garamb*, son, and daughters. Now, having left Mazienengai with his daughters —so that Mazienengai can himself become a father—father, like the father in N. 22,[2] uses a stratagem to find out whether and how his daughters are pregnant. He finds Mazienengai in the yam bin; he satisfies himself that what ought to be happening is actually taking place. Then, having completed the play of a father with daughters, father dies, the children become

---

[1] Few yam bins remain in Tangu today. Instead, harvested yams are stored on the floor of a living-hut or garden shelter, carefully piled in a conical heap.

[2] *Supra*, p. 300.

wives—and orphans—and Mazienengai becomes the father of a son and daughter (brother and sister) as well as husband. The problem of wife's brothers (children's mother's brothers) has already been considered. By representing the wives as orphans all exterior problems of interrelationships are excluded. The narrative concentrates on father as husband, and the theme is worked out through two signals, trump and roof thatch. As we know, these belong together—the first is found in the second— and signal the young husband who has yet to grow into his full maturity, become father and responsible.[1] The jangle of a trump may be a forest noise, or it might be music generating itself. Suggestive of father generating son who is to become a father himself, trump music may also be indicative of a babe stirring in the womb. Mazienengai is maturing, becoming father: a process corresponding with being formed in the womb and with the passage through the *garamb*—where boys used trumps to summon their mothers and sisters.[2]

Nevertheless, the episode as a whole takes maturity and the process of maturation on to another plane of awareness: children, feasting, slit-gong, and participation in *br'ngun'guni* certainly— but the conclusion of the narrative, the contraposition of husband-and-wife and brother-and-sister, is also being anticipated. Brother and sister are beaten over the eyes for betraying father to mother, or wives, in a context in which each has been eating coconut meat and milk from the same dish. The coconut and its meat and milk evoke the idea of marriage, and a responsible man, a father, should surely see to it that brother and sister do not marry. A responsible man is a guardian of community, the survival of community depends upon maintaining the incest taboo, looking outwards and communicating the parts. Brother and sister are behaving through their eyes in a way they should not. In the intimacy of a coconut and a forthcoming union—a union which in community terms is appropriately realized by becoming *mngwotngwotiki*—brother cannot see that the flood has retreated: he is not aware, he is actually going to pleasure his sister.[3] Eyes come in pairs. When a mother's brother pretends not to see a sister's son, he is surely temporarily rejecting a community awareness in favour of a singular act. He has to

[1] *Supra*, N. 13, pp. 274–5; and N. 22, pp. 302–3.   [2] *Supra*, p. 172.
[3] *Supra*, N. 25, p. 323; N. 27, p. 354.

thrash and circumcise the boy in order to lead him into self-restraint and responsibility. As a father generates physical being by using his singular part, his penis, so the mother's brother is singular in initiating social being. As filiation is related to siblingship, so is the singular related to the pairs. Their mutual engagement—as when *puoker* or *ranguova* are active—maintains the community. The singular act of enforcing the incest taboo, separating brother from sister, entails that communication of parts followed by stasis or union which is implied by the design of community life.

After the incident of the coconut spines, evoking the price of community, boy and girl go to their mothers. And though the routes they take are interchanged when compared with those in the Dumban tale,[1] the gist is identical in both narratives: the boy takes longer. A girl simply begins to menstruate, her breasts swell, she becomes available as a weeder, wife, and childbearer. In order to become a husband and father, a boy has to go into the *garamb*, be circumcised, and through the processes represented by yam bin, trump, and slit-gong, learn an awareness of himself, the community, and his role in community. The allusions to father's and mother's milk[2] refer back to the beginning of the narrative. They indicate the continuities of male filiation, physical procreation, and social and cultural rebirth out of the *garamb* through the male and female parts of maleness on the one hand, and the opposed continuities of female filiation on the other. There follow the bickerings and scoldings which Mazienengai brings to a swift conclusion. He takes up his spear, the sign of the responsible man. He kills wives and children as he walks off into the wild forest. And the evidence that Mazienengai actually did what he is supposed to have done lies in the four rocks which, enduring through time, are to be found on Bolivol hill to this day.

Mazienengai's massacre of his family may suggest numbers of different things.[3] Overtly, Tangu themselves are unable to offer any clues. It was, after all, the act of a *puok*. Yet the children's

---

[1] *Supra*, p. 352.

[2] The different 'milks', a variety of minor leads and the matter of *gnek* (*supra*, p. 177) could indicate that women were once thought to bear girls parthenogenetically, while the births of boys needed fathers. But conclusive evidence is lacking.

[3] See, for example, B-1959(*b*): 193.

behaviour has been irritating and disloyal; and the wives have been nagging. Might not a young husband wish them dead or out of the way? Through *puoker* a narrative identifies kinds of impulse, shows forth their consequences and, through the engagement with listener or narrator, communicates an awareness of the relationship between *puoker* and the requirements of community life. That wives and children become stones suggests the eternal or durable: wives and children are the stuff of community, while community exists wives and children will be there. In relation to husband and father, wives and children are a responsibility, often intractable, often a nuisance. But, since Mazienengai is on his way back to father, once again the values represented as inherent in maleness and male filiation are being contrasted with those of siblingship and community life. Moreover, if the episode—an impulsive gesture rather than a moral undertaking—is an object lesson to wives and children, in the act of killing them Mazienengai isolates himself and brings the notion of death to the foreground.

Isolation from the community is a kind of death. A man unto himself interacts with himself, is incestuous, is as though dead; filiation without siblingship is death to the community; death removes the *gnek* from participation in the moral community. No sooner does Mazienengai isolate himself than he calls on the mother's brothers to help him find father and so re-establish the community engagement in terms of male filiation. The crisis is over. Mother's brothers evoke the *garamb*, the fellowship and company of men in the *garamb*, community values. Chaos is turned, order restored, Mazienengai is going to win through, all will be well. With the help of his mother's brothers Mazienengai finds father, the meaning of father: for the mother's brothers guide Mazienengai to father-as-bird, his community relevance. At once the father–son projects into teacher–pupil, and father listens while son tells him his troubles: the category 'father' is now as dream-visitant or ghost. Father gives advice, shows Mazienengai how to make a *juaka* and trap a pig. If teaching is shown to be as much matter of example and demonstration as of exhortation, in life it is precisely when a *juaka* has been built that a man's expectations of being visited by the ghost of his father are considered to be the most lively.[1]

[1] *Supra*, p. 165.

And, as may often happen in life, Mazienengai misinterprets the advice of his father-ghost. Still, in binding a sago trunk with vines Mazienengai evokes Paki, roof thatch, *garamb*, and so the ways in which mother's brothers interact with father to guide a man into that appropriate maturation which will enable him to interpret a ghost's advice to his own and the community's advantage.

As a husband a man is the central concern of his wives. But when he becomes father the wives turn their attentions to gardens and children, and, as in N. 22, husband is neglected, nagged, and scolded. As a father a man is alone, 'eating stones': it is the price of independence, of being able to decide and initiate for himself, of possessing a singular awareness. Dependants, on the other hand, bear one another's burdens, do not initiate, assume a collective responsibility. Yet no man-in-community can live quite alone, and as a dependant he is hardly a man. Between these extremes, in Tangu, a man with initiative has recourse to dreams, obtains advice from father-as-ghost, and in the past could rely on that aspect of fatherhood which was contained within the meaning of the *garamb*. In the *garamb* he found companionship, opportunities to communicate and exercise his parts within a fellowship of responsible men. Represented as both womb and quickener of social being, the *garamb*, through mother's brothers, offered an appropriate re-engagement with father, the source of culture and own being.

Mazienengai traps a pig in his *juaka*. It was father who took the pig into the trap by entering into it, fatherhood enables the pig to be caught, and, after the storm, the flesh of the pig in bamboo barrels becomes men while the stomach and intestines become women: procreation both physical and cultural. Now though it is but a calculated guess that the circumcision pig had to be caught in a *juaka*, and had some connection with the Patron,[1] it is evident from the narrative that male filiation was represented by a pig caught in a *juaka*, and it is a fair inference that fatherhood or male filiation was incarnate in, or represented in, the pig of the circumcision. Appropriate male being, that is, is transmitted from father to son through a wild pig trapped in a *juaka*.[2] Yet this being has to be realized through

[1] *Supra*, pp. 168.
[2] If it be asked why, in particular, a *juaka* trap, the answer seems to lie in the

siblingship: which leads back to the central importance of pork in feasting exchanges, as well as to the rider that he who abuses his male filiation by unfairly dividing his pork deserves the attentions of a *ranguma* whose male filiation is inappropriate.

As the narrative draws to a close with a brief recapitulation of the meaning of fatherhood and male filiation, Mazienengai is made the fulcrum of brother-and-sister on the one hand, and husband-and-wife on the other. He awakes at cock-crow, at the dawning when sun and light herald awareness. Birds—maidens and mother's brothers and the meaning of hawk—sing merrily in the trees, maleness. Has the world overturned or reversed itself? Some say that it did, but there remains a doubt: the meanings of tradition, we know, are presently in question. Nevertheless, that final episode—as so often in narratives— summarizes the narrative. How may a man reconcile impulse and self-willedness with the claims of culture and community? How may son seize from father responsibility for culture and the management of community affairs without impugning the notion of fatherhood upon which the cultural heritage depends? How may a man enter on the complexities of marriage and fatherhood and also attain that stasis connoted by a brother-and-sister union? How may the authoritative initiative and awareness pertaining to men be made subject to, involved in, and responsible for, the ordering of community life?

To these questions, not of much relevance to women who may be themselves, and who are under the control of men, men, who have to learn to communicate their parts and play the man, give answer in terms of those institutions which they are represented as having initiated, and for whose maintenance they are represented as being responsible.

A New Awareness

The two narratives which follow have been discussed elsewhere, in the context of Tangu cargo-cult activities.[1] Now,

facts that a *juaka* is constructed after the manner of a house, and the deadfall is roofed over with sago thatch. So the *juaka* evokes both houses—marriage—and the *garamb*—community life. On the other side, illustrating an inappropriate male filiation, it will be remembered that *ranguova*, described as pigs, were caught in a *juaka* (*supra*, p. 282).

[1] B-1960: 155–76; 177–96; and *passim*. Both narratives have been retranslated, but there is no difference in meaning. Perhaps they now read more smoothly.

whilst summarizing their relevance to the cargo situation, the context is broadened into an attempt to gain a deeper understanding of them, and the new kinds of awareness they convey, by relating them to the main body of Tangu narratives.

N. 30: *Duongangwongar*[1]

One day long ago the men of the village decided to hunt for pig by burning off a tract of ginger plants. Duongangwongar, an odd sort of fellow,[2] who had a mother, Gundakar by name, but who had no father or mother's brothers, went with them.

When, in due course, the hunting party came to the ginger plants, no one wanted to have anything to do with Duongangwongar. He was told to go away.

So Duongangwongar wandered off on his own.

Presently, though, seeing a pig-run leading into a patch of *kunai* grass, Duongangwongar followed it. Almost immediately he saw a pig right there in front of him.

Quickly taking an arrow, Duongangwongar set it to bowstring, took aim, and loosed off. He wounded the pig, and started shouting for the others to come and help him.

Hearing the commotion, the other men rushed from the ginger into the *kunai*, surrounded the pig, and speared it. Then, as each man drew his spear from the pig, he plunged it into Duongangwongar.

Duongangwongar fell dead.

The villagers placed Duongangwongar's body on a small platform in the exposed roots of a tree, and returned to the village. There Gundakar, seeing that her son was not with the others, asked where he was. They said they did not know.

That night Gundakar had a dream, and in the dream her son Duongangwongar appeared before her and told her he was dead, hidden in the roots of a tree in the forest. So, next morning, as soon as it was light, Gundakar set out to look for the body of her son.

As she walked, a little bird, into which Duongangwongar had entered, settled on her shoulders and showed her the way. She found the body, took it from the roots, put it into her string bag, and returned to the village. Then, collecting some yams, taros, bananas, and sweet potatoes, she put them into her string bag with the body of Duongangwongar and left the village.

The first village she came to was W'tsiapet in Riekitzir. She asked if the villagers would allow her to bury her son there. They refused.

---

[1] Elsewhere called the Primal Myth (B-1960: 154; and *supra*, pp. 30–6).
[2] *Imbatekas*.

So she went on to Amuk in Wanitzir, whence she was sent on to Mariap. From Mariap she was told to go on to Kangwan, and from there she had to go on to Lilau. She rested by the sea at Lilau, and afterwards came to Dogoi, where a man lay with her, agreeing to become her husband and helpmeet.

Gundakar dug a hole near Dogoi, and in it she buried Duongang-wongar, covering the corpse with coconut fronds. There the body lay, rotting and becoming putrid in the grave.

Gundakar bore sons to her husband.

One day it happened that, being alone in the village and in need of some water, Gundakar went to the grave of Duongangwongar, drew aside the coconut fronds and, finding salt water and fish in his nostrils, filled her pot. Later, she cooked the fish and salt water for the evening meal. Some say that husband and son vomited when they ate the fish and salt water, others that they found the meal good. But, however it was, during the night son grew and matured.

Next day, when husband's younger brother, Tuman, came to visit them and saw how his nephew had grown, he was amazed. 'How your son has grown!' he exclaimed. 'My own sons are still small—what has been going on here?'

They gave him no answer.

The following day, collecting the skins of her yams, taros, and *mami*, Gundakar threw them on to the garden plot, which husband had just cleared and burnt off. They took root, reached down into soil, and became tubers. Then Gundakar returned to the grave of Duongangwongar, took some water and one small fish from his nostrils, cooked them for husband and son.

That night son grew into a man.

Next day, coming to visit, Tuman was so surprised at what had happened that he insisted on knowing how it was done. So Gundakar turned to his wife and told her what to do. 'Go to the grave of my son Duongangwongar', she said. 'Draw aside the coconut fronds, take water from his nostrils and one small fish. You will see there other, larger fish. Do not take them. Take only one small fish.'

Tuman's wife went to the grave, removed the coconut fronds, and drew some water. Then, looking into the putrefying nostrils, she saw a large *ramatzka*, a long fish like an eel. She speared it.

At once there was a loud rumbling in the bowels of the earth, as of an earthquake accompanied by thunder. Water gushed out of Duongangwongar's nostrils in a seething torrent of foam and bubbling waves—rising in a flood between Ambwerk and Tuman, forcing them to flee in different directions.

Tuman found safety on a low-lying place. He killed a small bird, cooked it, and threw the bones into the sea. There was a small splash and a soft sssshhh . . . like wavelets over pebbles. Then he killed a crested pigeon, cooked it, threw the bones into the sea. There was a splash and the sea remained calm. He killed a hornbill, treating it as he had the other birds, and the waters rippled. Then at last he killed a cassowary. And on his throwing the bones into the sea the waves rose with a roar and tumbled on the beach.

Tuman was satisfied.

Pondering, then, on the fate of his elder brother, Tuman took a leaf, directed it to Ambwerk, and threw it on the sea.

Ambwerk, who had found refuge on high land, saw the floating leaf and picked it up. 'Oh!' he exclaimed. 'My younger brother is well. He has sent me this leaf to find out how I am. I will return it to him.'

Ambwerk threw the leaf back into the sea.

When Tuman saw the leaf floating back to him he knew that Ambwerk was safe. So he took another leaf, wrote a message on it for Ambwerk, dispatched it, received an answer in return. Then Tuman felled a tree, hollowed it, made a canoe, and went off to visit Ambwerk.

Ambwerk, seeing Tuman coming in the distance, wondered who it could be. And when at last Tuman beached his canoe and showed his brother what he had done, Ambwerk was amazed. 'Who showed you how to make this canoe?' he asked. 'Surely you did not do it by yourself?'

'That I did. I made it myself. I thought of it on my own.'

When Tuman made his farewells and returned home, Ambwerk copied him. He made a canoe for himself and went off to visit Tuman. Afterwards he returned to his village, content.

Tuman started work on a boat. He finished it, had some practice in it, and went off to show it to Ambwerk. Ambwerk was impressed. 'Who showed you how to do it?' he asked. 'Surely somebody showed you how it should be made?'

'I invented it myself. I made it on my own.'

When Tuman had gone, Ambwerk set to work on a boat. He had some practice in it, then set off to Tuman's village to show it to him. Tuman complimented his elder brother on his work. Ambwerk returned to his home, content.

Tuman made a pinnace. He made an engine, fitted it to the craft, had some practice, and went off to show it to Ambwerk. Dumbfounded and impressed, Ambwerk started to make a pinnace for himself, copying Tuman.

Tuman made a motor-car, a motor-bike, and a large ship with tall masts and a siren which went Whoooo! So large a ship was it that it broke elder brother's jetty, and it had to be secured by ropes passed around coconut palms. Tuman made an aeroplane, canned goods, cloth, and all sorts of things. Each time he made something he went to show it to his elder brother. And each time he did so elder brother copied him.

You see, Tuman could use his head. He could understand—like you white folk.

N. 31: *Mambu*[1]

Mambu was a Kanaka from the Bogia region who, after he had finished a spell of contract labour in Rabaul, stowed away on a steamer bound for Australia. But before very long Mambu was discovered and taken before the captain.

The captain was very angry. He was about to have Mambu thrown overboard lest, by going to Australia, he should chance upon the secret of the white man, when his former employer, his 'master', who was on the same ship, intervened and saved him from the captain's wrath.

This master was an Australian and he saw Mambu safely to an Australian port.

Once he had got to Australia, Mambu was clothed and fed. His master showed him the sights, gave him rice, spare clothing, beads, knives, canned goods, razor blades—and heaps of other good things.

All this cargo was packed into cases and sent to the quayside for loading. The master's sister wrote a letter, stuck it into Mambu's hair, and told him to go down to the quay where he would find all his cargo marked with such and such a sign. Mambu was to board a certain ship, together with his cargo, and return to New Guinea. If there was any trouble, or if anyone questioned him, Mambu was to show him the letter.

Mambu boarded his ship. Surviving several attempts by the captain to have him thrown overboard, eventually he got back to Bogia.

If it had not been for that letter he would have been killed.

In Bogia Mambu said he knew the secret of the white men, and that they, being jealous, were preventing Kanakas from obtaining it. Kanakas, said Mambu, should not submit to this. They should be strong and throw the white men out of New Guinea into the sea. But to make themselves strong Kanakas needed money.

So it was that Mambu travelled around the countryside collecting shillings and pennies. But when a missionary reported him to the

[1] Elsewhere called the *Mambu* myth (B-1960: 188; and *supra*, pp. 31–3).

administration for doing so, Mambu was gaoled. He was dangerous to white men and might destroy their overlordship and authority.

When the policemen came to arrest him Mambu said to them: 'You can hit me—never mind! You can maltreat me—never mind! Later, you will understand!'

The policemen were awed, but took him to gaol just the same.

That night, though supposedly behind bars in prison, Mambu was seen chewing areca-nut in a nearby village. He had slipped out of his chains. . . .

The policemen knew about this, but they were too frightened to report it, lest they should be accused of neglecting their duties and punished.

Yet Mambu could not escape altogether, and the administration took him away to Madang in chains.

Before he left he prophesied the War that was to come.

There was another thing which Mambu did. One of the men here went to 'try' him, to see if he was true (genuine). And Mambu drew a banker's 'stick' of money out of thin air for him, and gave the money to the man, who went to a trade store and bought an axe and some beads with it. Mambu said to him: 'You do not understand. You are like a child who has yet to learn much. . . . You do not understand the things that I know. . . .'

Mambu could get more money whenever he wanted to.

In differing degrees, both the Duongangwongar and Mambu narratives stand apart from the main bulk of Tangu narratives. They are not in the same style or genre, they hardly belong. Yet Tangu regard them as in a sense more precious, more meaningful, than their other narratives.

In N. 30 there is mention of certain Tangu communities; Gundakar takes the more frequented Tangu route to the sea, the salt route;[1] and the dialogue between Ambwerk and Tuman has a familiar if not wholly authentic tone. Yet it is apparent that the narrative has its roots elsewhere, among a seafaring or coastwise people, and that it has been adopted by Tangu. Son grows into a man not in relation to the *garamb* but in relation to salt water, fish, and a particular mode of burial. There is nothing in the narrative which evokes the *garamb* directly, nor does the burial of Duongangwongar in the roots of a tree have

[1] See B-1956(*b*): 427.

any relevance to Tangu tradition.[1] That Duongangwongar is odd or different and *imbatekas*; that the men of the village band together to kill him; that he is, like a *ranguma*,[2] particularly touched with the divine; that he is kinless, without father or mother's brother,[3] and so separated from the community—in a general sense all these features might be found in a traditional Tangu narrative. But where in the traditional corpus do we find chief protagonist embodied in the mother–son? Tangu themselves associate Gundakar and her son with those divorced or unsatisfactory women who have to wander from village to village in search of a husband.[4] One may allow the device of a dream—but that son should go into a bird and then become as dream-visitant to mother? While it is possible that such a representation might take shape, there is no evidence in the traditional narratives, or in other aspects of Tangu culture, that it actually does. Where else do we find a wife and mother magically growing tubers in a new garden cleared by husband, mother responsible for the maturation of son, a woman who kills the *ramatzka*-snake and precipitates the creative storm? If the singular fish or phallus in a pair of nostrils is apposite, Tangu women go to the stream to find and take from it that maleness in stream which makes them relevant as wives. They do not spear that maleness; and salting is associated with Zawapai, father-provider, not with women. A Nuakai is capable of ripping open the belly of a 'dead' snake, and a wife in a woodpile may damage a roused *ranguma*: but that a woman or wife should actually kill a snake-like animal, maleness in Tangu thought, goes very much against the grain.

A dialogue between Ambwerk and Tuman might be found almost anywhere in the Melanesian islands. But in Tangu Ambwerk and Tuman go hunting, make bows and arrows, trick Nuakai, evoke the *garamb*. They do not cast the bones of cooked birds on the waters to evoke the sea, they do not make sea voyages. Nor for that matter do they make canoes, pinnaces, ships, and the rest. In all the narratives there have been con-

---

[1] A connection with Tuman in N. 24, the tale of Zawapai (p. 316), may seem plausible but is hardly tenable.

[2] Compare the killing of Dumban (ii), *supra*, p. 357, or Nimbamung, *supra*, p. 228.　　　　　　　　　　　　　　　　[3] See B-1956(*b*): 427.

[4] That Duongangwangar had no mother's brother is, of course, to emphasize his 'unsocial' qualities.

sistent cross references, signals, and indicators whose import becomes clearer as familiarity grows, as different situational contexts are compared. But this is not the case with the Duongangwongar and Mambu narratives. They do not belong to the traditional store of knowledge. They are told only when Tangu are asked to talk about their relations with Europeans, particularly when they are asked to enlarge upon their cargo activities. Though the style of N. 30 is almost traditional, the content is strange, and some of the incidents are recent.[1] And with the Mambu story we are confronted with a narrative wholly sprung from recent historical events and anecdote. Nevertheless, both tales are narratives, modes of cognition within a particular idiom.

Tangu would seem to have become familiar with the Duongangwongar story during the period of their first encounters either with white men themselves, or with other New Guinea peoples who were, or had been, working as labourers for Europeans.[2] On the whole it seems to have been adopted by Tangu from some coastal people. But it is the second half, the dialogue between Ambwerk and Tuman, that Tangu themselves say they find most relevant to their situation. It deals with a common experience, the encounter with Europeans, and it deals with the problem in terms of traditional reciprocities. Versions of the first half differ.[3] And though, as we shall see, the first half has an importance of its own, at the level of a field observation—where the overt is more immediately apparent— this first half appears as but an ill-learned preamble to the dialogue between Ambwerk and Tuman. For the brothers are here representative of black men and white men, and the relations between them pose the possibilities of the relations between black men and white men. Tuman, traditionally non-reciprocal in relation to Ambwerk, represents white men. The problem, as always, is how to bring Tuman into the complex of reciprocities characteristic of community; how to stop Tuman from being lost to the divine and non-reciprocal. And should Tuman be partially lost to the divine, become a *ranguma* or like a *ranguma*, still all is not lost: he may be persuaded to surrender to

[1] The ship breaking the jetty—at Bogia—was an event that actually occurred only a few months before the narrative was recorded.

[2] A calculated guess. Those who tell the story today say that they learned it as children from their parents.

[3] See B-1956(b): 425, and B-1960: 154–65.

the reciprocities of community life through confession. In real life the dilemma is how to persuade white men, *ranguova* or like *ranguova*, into those reciprocal relations which Tangu regard as appropriate to community life, and which, in particular, the Duongangwongar story gives some promise of realizing.[1]

With the Mambu story the theme of coming to terms with Europeans and their modes of thought and behaviour is further developed. Though Mambu himself was a historical person who was known to Tangu, and who was seen by them, the narrative about Mambu is not a piece of historical reporting. The events in which Mambu was concerned have been converted into more durable principle and then retranslated into narrative events. Moreover, the principles that emerge conform not so much to the behaviour of Mambu himself as to the gist of the Duongang-wongar tale. Where the pragmatic experience seemed to confirm the growing belief that Europeans would adamantly persist in a non-reciprocal relationship, the Duongangwongar story gave some promise of realizing a reciprocal relationship. Where the historical and narrative Mambu were at one in saying that, because white men were eschewing the reciprocal relationship, black men should forcibly eject Europeans from New Guinea, the Mambu narrative goes on to develop the themes of the Duon-gangwongar tale in suggesting that certain kinds of European may be persuaded into reciprocal relations, even if others persist in remaining non-reciprocal. Thus, moving from the simple and overall category of 'white men' (figured in Tuman) who, though distinguished among themselves according to task and vocation, and so distinguished by Tangu,[2] have in common the quality of being non-reciprocal persons to Tangu, two internal categories relating to mode of being are brought into cogniz-ance: the captain, and the master or employer and his sister. The captain is inimical and non-reciprocal. He wants to have Mambu thrown overboard lest he should discover the 'secret' of white men—the 'secret' being, essentially, that capacity of access to manufactured goods or cargo which is associated with Europeans. The master and his sister, on the other hand, help

---

[1] As explained in B-1960: 165–76. Though other alternatives are posited, the movement to reciprocal relations was the one most favoured by Tangu on the level of overt and explicit behaviour (*supra*, pp. 30–6).

[2] Such as *kiap*, *kampanimasta*, *misin*, etc. (*supra*, p. 61, n. 3).

Mambu, give him access to cargo. Their behaviour indicates an awareness of the reciprocities of Tangu social life, they represent the 'moral European'—the European who, irrespective of job or status, is imbued with that quality of being which will enable him to engage in reciprocal relations with black men. Moreover, no longer an agitator, a rebel who failed, a gaol-bird, the Mambu of narrative emerges as not only representative of the new man—a black man with European capacities and understanding, a black man competent to deal with the Europeanized environment—but as an individual-in-himself, a singular man.

The bifurcation of the category 'European' is in line with tradition; so is the contraposition 'new man' and 'moral European'. But the representation of Mambu as an individual-in-himself is a development from tradition into a European or Christian mode of thought. The historical Mambu was a stranger to Tangu, an outsider, a *ranguma*-like fellow who yet engaged in reciprocal relations with Tangu. He initiated new rites, he experimented with a new form of baptism, he called himself 'Black King', he attempted to collect taxes—he was a black man, *ranguma*-like, acting the part of a European-missionary-administrator.[1] And his initiative commanded consent. The Mambu of the narrative, Europeanized and significantly touched with the New Testament, more knowledgeable than ordinary black men, but still dependent and not wholly competent, appears as an individual in his own right. In one of their cargo rites[2] Tangu acted out the birth, or the making, of a new man, a new kind of individual. After a communal meal in which the traditional sectionalisms of the community played no part, an individual, a man or a woman, took position in the centre of a circle of chanting villagers, with the intention that he or she should fall into trance, be revived by massaging the mouth, and then utter a message—not in Tangu but in some other language. The themes of a symbolic death and rebirth are clear, so also the links with tradition and the attempt to remodel tradition. As a means of selecting the fellow who is different, singular, and not as reciprocal as he might traditionally be, the rites compare with the game of 'Ranguma'.[3] In order to restore them to the light of community life, the boys who in N. 2

---

[1] B-1960: 254–73.   [2] B-1960: 1–2.   [3] *Supra*, pp. 146–7.

escaped from captivity in the stone had their mouths massaged.[1] Women as well as men are now thought to have *gneker*, or souls, and the rites reveal that the new mode of being to which the entranced was to be awakened pertained to women as well as to men. If we give the Christianity of Mambu full value, we can appreciate the Mambu narrative as being informed by the rough correspondence between Christian teaching on the father-hood of God and the inspiration of the Holy Ghost on the one hand, and the traditional representation that language, culture, and responsibility are, or were, obtained through an appropriate fatherhood or male filiation on the other.

The historical Mambu, the Mambu of narrative, and the cargo rites belong together. From them there emerges the representation of a Christianized *ranguma*-like person, a singular fellow who is to play his part within the moral community: a partial synthesis of the *ranguma* and appropriate male filiation, informed by simplicist Christian understanding. Mambu also belongs with Yali.[2] Like Mambu, Yali was an initiator, a cargo activist who commanded Tangu consent. Unlike Mambu, Yali had a record of achievement in the Europeanized world. He was a black man who became as though a European, a black man who seemed to Tangu as competent as white men, who had come to manhood in European terms. So that while there are some in Tangu today who point to the killing of the *ramatzka* as one of those decisive acts which have resulted in making the present dependence on Europeans inevitable and permanent, the Mambu story reveals a more optimistic groundswell. Through Yali the problem of engaging in reciprocal relations with Europeans was solved in principle. Yali had shown it was possible, in Yali the new man was embodied. Further, in the conjunction of Tuman in the Duongangwongar tale, Mambu, the Mambu of story, the cargo rites, and Yali, the new man emerges with peculiarly significant qualities. Basically reci-procal, he is also a 'black European', an individual-in-himself. But, like a European, and like a *ranguma*, his being seems to be predicated by a wider scope and opportunity for being non-reciprocal within the moral order. To put it another way, the new man will have appropriate being within a moral community which allows him more scope for the exercise of

[1] *Supra*, p. 206.   [2] *Supra*, pp. 31–3.

self-willedness and initiative, more opportunity for the appropriate exercise of that singular and non-reciprocal element in men that current moral imperatives seek to curb and restrain. If and when Tangu use money in the ways it is used by those who mint it, one may say, then the new man will find appropriate conditions in which to exercise his more singular parts.

Tangu narratives run a course in experience, pose problems and suggest solutions. And though both problems and solutions tend to be oracular, forcing men in community to formulate and make the moral decisions for themselves, the process of narration marshals experience, conjures an awareness of what is involved, and so generates further comprehensions. Community is represented as beginning with, and dependent upon, the relations between brother and sister, siblingship and its concomitants. But it is also represented that there is that in the maleness of man which was, and is, prior to siblingship. An attribute of fatherhood, this quality realizes culture through the incest taboo, and is thought of as being passed from generation to generation in the line of male filiation. Originating or manifesting its essence in the storm or storm-mover or earth-mover, figured as emerging from the stream and as bifurcated in the hawk, this quality of maleness is in the end singular, unobliged, and self-willed. Through self-restraint, however, man wrests order and culture from the chaos of self-willedness. With each generation the singular self-willedness of maleness has to be tamed and ordered if community and culture are to survive. Again and again the traditional narratives come round to asking how maleness may be tamed, how boys may become men, how men may become husbands and fathers, how such mature and responsible men may secure the community for the succeeding generation. And repeatedly one is led into the images and procedures evoked by the *garamb*. But there is no longer a *garamb* in Tangu. The responsible man has a wider, more variable, and less stable field in which to exercise his parts. So the newer narratives take up the problem. What is now to be the measure of manhood? What kind of new man will re-create a new order from the present gallimaufry? How will he do it? What kind of filiation will be required?

Over-all, the narratives play an Oedipus tune. The single

most crucial relationship is represented as the father–son, male filiation. Almost any third party, event, or circumstance can be used to vitiate this and so entail the destruction of some part of culture and the moral order. On the other hand, with an appropriate resolution of the father–son, the *ranguma* is worsted, Nuakai is tamed, the moral order is maintained, creativity in culture is assured—even the Ambwerk–Tuman becomes manageable.

The importance to Tangu, on a symbolic level, of Christian teaching on fatherhood can hardly be overrated. Yet though Christianity has provided new solutions to old problems, and some have found a new dignity in becoming Christians, for those who feel they want to be like Europeans the Christian inside them seems almost irrelevant. Engrossed in exchanges of material goods, this is the pragmatist gauge to which Christian dogma and idealism are continually referred. Affluence and what affluence means and portrays are the possible and practical goals. The *ranguma* and what he means as an enemy or rival or sickness or death are the immediate obstacles. The Tangu *gnek* may range more widely than it did, viewing, experimenting, constructing, and then coveting images of what might be. But in order to live Tangu still have to make gardens, cultivate crops, hunt, and gather from the wild. Community life entails marriage, bearing children, engaging in trade, barter, and exchanges of produce. Tangu still have to find their parts and express and communicate them in largely traditional terms. Still attached to that measure of man which concentrates his several parts into the relevances of a single series of activities —the production and exchange of foodstuffs—Tangu exclude the full-time specialist, have not allowed money to differentiate and measure the separated parts. Only a new kind of *gnek*, one might say, a new awareness which is prepared to grasp the nettle, which is prepared to measure the differentiated parts against money, can make the new man. If the historical Mambu was not wholly aware of how this might be achieved, those who comprehend the narrative about him, who seize on the importance of Mambu and money, very soon should be. And despite what this man or that man might contingently say, do, or think, it is evident that Mambu was a new man, that a new *gnek* appropriate to the new man is presently in the making.

PART THREE

NEW CATEGORIES SHAPING

7

DEVELOPING AWARENESS

NARRATIVES have a quality of remaining fecund with meaning: fruitful ambiguities abound. Were we to go into them more deeply many other and further significances might be extracted from the tales presented above. Like an onion, narratives can be shown to have layer upon layer of meanings. The treasures of analytical psychology have not been broached, some links of evidence are missing, there are gaps in the information available. All that has been done is to record the events of daily life in Tangu, talk to Tangu, perceive a pattern in their social relations, record their narratives, and pursue the social contexts of a relatively small part of their total vocabulary. Yet we have seen something of the way in which the spoken narrative is a mode of cognition, communicating the possibilities of awareness. Categories, named characters, things, natural phenomena, animals, and events have revealed themselves as indicative of premises of being. Couched in what is essentially a poetic idiom, certain words in a narrative do not have the references of ordinary language. Exciting the imagination, they evoke images, ideas, awareness of varieties of experience. Not exhausted by the referents of ordinary usage, these words communicate that which ordinary language does not: they evoke the cultural awareness on an objective and collective level, they indicate the possibilities to which an individual in the culture might aspire but not himself be able to realize. The word *gitam*, for example, means 'roof' or 'roof thatch' or 'strips or parts of roof thatch'. And in everyday usage that is all that *gitam* means. But when the word appears in a narrative it invites reflection on the relevance of roof thatch or roof, and—not only on account of a phonetic similarity—it may evoke the *garamb*, and so the experience which the *garamb* and its procedures represent. Moreover, *gitam* has these evocations whether or not particular individuals are aware of the fact that it has them. Growing out of the condensed experience of generations by way of the *gnek*, the spoken words of narratives become symbols and transform the wild and existential world of nature into those purposeful ideas and images and relations which evoke the divine in man.

In thus revealing the meaning of experience the narrative not only differs from ordinary spoken language, it is also unlike a dream. For the latter, though it may be described in words, exists for the dreamer irrespective of words. Yet narrative and dream clearly have much in common. Both are to be appreciated as wholes; each has a locus outside time as normally conceived; events elicit relations and ideas or feelings or attitudes which are not necessarily contained in the way one situation succeeds to another. Whether in dream or in narrative a youth may take up his bow and arrows and shoot a pigeon through the privates. But the reference goes further than simply good shooting. Sometimes in Tangu a man will admit that, in a dream, he has found himself married to, or having sexual relations with, a sister. Such a dream is described as *imbatekas*: it refers to an activity associated with *puoker*, prohibited to men and women in community. Whether the man has been dreaming the part of a narrative, or whether the narrative is articulating the dream of a man at a particular time, or of most men at some time in their lives, is, for our purposes, irrelevant. For though a narrative may provoke a certain kind of dream, and dreams may themselves be sources of narrative, both indicate possibilities in experience and awareness. At the same time, however similar the contents of collections of dreams may turn out to be, a dream is a private experience experienced in private, and a narrative, however exclusive the appreciation of a particular listener, represents an articulate if encoded store of experience and awareness at the level of the collective. Even if a dreamer articulates his dream to himself so that for him it becomes as though a 'private narrative' to which only he happens to be listening, it still remains an articulate dream and does not become a narrative.

A dream which is made public, and which the community accepts, becomes a narrative. For it is then seized of the community in general, expresses a cultural rather than private experience, becomes an explicit collective representation. It

is possible that dreams, and those parts of narratives which find
their sources in dream life, relate to facets of the common human
experience, go beyond the confines of a particular culture. If
so, these aspects are beyond the scope of the present inquiry. Are
Paki's poles or Nuakai's string and Jacob's ladder in any way
corresponding terms? Perhaps. But while the symbolizing that
arises from first awareness may be a universal in human affairs,
the new content that awakened awarenesses feed back into the
symbol is surely product of, and imprisoned in, the cultural
experience. Not an absolute thing-in-itself, a symbol is defined by
its referents, and swings at its anchor in a local an specific
texture of relations.

Among Tangu today the precise form of words in which a
narrative is told is not of particular significance. At some time
in the past, perhaps, the narratives presented here might have
had a more rigid formulation. In a stable and non-literate
society, in which each generation had a similar experience
to the one preceding, not only would narratives not change
appreciably, but one would expect the more positive effort to
prolong a well-founded tradition by an insistence upon a particular form of words. Among Tangu, however, the cultural
experience has been widening and, as yet, there is no form
of systematics capable of comprehending and articulating the
whole of experience. Miming, gesturing, struggling for words,
ready to initiate as well as forgetful, a story-teller may leave out
some passages and incidents, and he may add new ones. Listen-
ers, who know the gist of the tale, who know which characters
and events ought to be awaiting their cues, deride, correct, or
approve both the narrator and each other. Closely approximat-
ing the process of *br'ngun'guni*, each narration runs the gauntlet
of general approval. Traditional incidents become tinged with
overtones of new meaning, a narrative tends to remain charged
with current relevance. Not only do Tangu use their narratives
to think with, and think from, but in their narratives new
thoughts are deposited.

The arguments which ensue when an innovation is made
reveal a three-cornered tussle between conservatives who do
not want to see change, those who acquiesce in the appropriateness or fact of change, and those who wish to promote change.
For the last as well as for the outside observer, narratives will

inevitably tend to appear old-fashioned, behind the times, not really relevant. But a community consists of more than its 'progressive' elements and, in the end, relevance relates to the whole community, not simply to a part of it. Tangu storytellers have their pride. They do not like adding to, or subtracting from, a narrative unless they feel it is going to be acceptable. Interruption and correction in mid-career reflect on the ability of the narrator. And though the process of innovation and correction may be restated as a *rapport* linking storyteller and audience, and relating the genius who knows he can innovate with a public which can appreciate and approve the innovation, the precise factors involved are by no means clear. The first part of N. 30,[1] for example, seems only marginally relevant to Tangu. Yet it is told. Perhaps it is told because it 'belongs' to the second half, whose relevance is undoubted. Since both halves came into Tangu together, perhaps Tangu are giving themselves time to see whether or in what sense the first part is as relevant as the second if they could but perceive it. As has been pointed out,[2] versions of the first part differ. On the other hand, as the odd man out, *ranguma*-like, Duongangwongar himself has a pointed and objective relevance. However the narrative may change in other respects, one feels, so long as the *ranguma* is relevant, so long will Duongangwongar continue to play his part.[3] The incident, towards the end of the story, of the ship breaking the jetty, a recent addition based upon an actual event and scarcely a year old when the story was collected, had already been approved.[4] The Mambu story, which cannot have originated before 1937, and which contains a reference to the War, was in full bloom in the early fifties—how will it run a generation hence?

The life and vitality of a narrative clearly depend upon a give and take between the narrator and his audience. Commit a narrative to writing and the opportunities for change and development are limited. Writing has the effect of concretizing,

---

[1] The tale of Duongangwongar.   [2] *Supra*, pp. 30–1.

[3] One may go further. If the *ranguma* as such were to become irrelevant, but if the problem of the *ranguma* were to remain, intellectualized or rationalized in some other way, would Duongangwongar remain, or would he become someone else with a corresponding relation to the re-rationalized but persisting same problem as Duongangwongar-*ranguma*?

[4] Further discussed below, pp. 421–2.

provides an 'authorized version' which may turn the narrative into an historical document simply. Yet the written form does not necessarily excise the dialectic involved. For where the spoken narrative indicates an active and living dialectic within the terms of a shared if limited symbolic experience and awareness, the written narrative often becomes the focus of an intellectualized awareness and experience. And where the former is characteristically freely associative and self-exploratory, just these features are formally, if not wholly successfully, expunged from the intellectualized awareness.

The stories of Twopingar and how men went to the moon are not presented here. Remembrance of them is so scrappy as to be worthless; presumably the kinds of awareness they evoked did not repay the trouble of remembering. As spoken narratives the tales of Paki, Maribun, Dumban (i), and Mazienengai are beginning to be oblivescent. Hesitances in narration and occasional cries of derision reveal that they belong more to the past than to the present. Concerned as they are with the dialectic between filiation and siblingship in traditional terms, either they must so change as to accommodate current awarenesses, or they must become historical documents. Yet now that they have been written down they may—indeed have—become the focus of an intellectualized awareness. The story of Dumban (ii), on the other hand, is still told with a zest which bears witness to its pertinence in the present. *Ranguova* still threaten, still figure the arrogance of self-concern in a male. The *garamb* building is as obsolete as *GAGAWA* and *gagawa*. But whereas the *garamb* relates to metamorphosis of being, and this must always be relevant, *GAGAWA* and *gagawa* seem only to relate to contingent and expedient organizational forms.

The minor references in the narratives to *GAGAWA* and *gagawa*, compared with the concern for the *garamb*, invite the assumption that remembrance is, if only loosely, connected with awareness of relevance to being. And whereas being would relate to the structure of a society, organization—simply a contingent means of accommodating that structure—would only correspond with the authentic in being so far as it corresponded with the structure. Trumps are no longer used in Tangu, but 'trump' is remembered, and 'trump' refers to changes and maturation in being which are indicative of the structure of Tangu society. Flutes find no mention in narratives —why not? The omission may be simply fortuitous, perhaps they were mentioned in some narrative which has been forgotten, or, since we find no mention of the *ginangin* either, and flutes had some connection with the *ginangin*,[1] perhaps flutes were irrelevant to the structure which contained the *garamb*. Moreover, the *ginangin* was secretive and exclusive, pertaining to a section of the community only. On the other hand, since flutes were made from bamboo—would they have signalled anything different from other bamboo objects? Would mention of them have been superfluous, or does bamboo—in which the pig flesh that became men was stuffed—refer to something more than the meanings attached to circumcision and maturation? Certainly flutes must have had something to do with maleness and the singularity of male powers; bamboo barrels contain water from the stream as well as that which was to become men. Other than its contribution to the purposive matrix of a charm, what significance should we attach to the element of 'blowing' in fluting? The answer eludes us. Still, if we dress 'flute' with the meanings we have gleaned from bamboo, do we not feel we know much more about flutes?

Both the Duongangwongar tale and the Mambu story show how historical events may be sources of narrative. One is entitled to assume that the former would never have gained any currency in Tangu were it not for the fact that it appeared to illumine the relations between black men and white men. While these relations could be known and experienced pragmatically and directly, the significance of the Duongangwongar tale as a narrative surely lies in the way it has selected particular features on either hand to strike at vital differences in being: the reciprocal as against the non-reciprocal; a mode of being determined by pairings as against one habitually touched with the singular; inventiveness, initiative, and intelligence as against a *gnek* of an apparently quite different order. In the space of ten years or so what the historical Mambu actually did had become almost irrelevant. Yet to the extent that Mambu's activities could reveal facets of being relevant to the encounter between blacks and whites, so far does the narrative take cognizance of them and proceed to invention to emphasize

[1] *Supra*, pp. 174-5.

and communicate their meaning. In short, when historical events enter a narrative they are no longer significant as events, but rather as media which illustrate facets or principles of being.

As successive generations of story-tellers, or perhaps the one genius, built and embellished the story of Dumban (i), the idea that roof or roof thatching, *gitam*, should have stood for, or evoked, the *garamb* must have had some basis for acceptance. Roof and thatching provide shelter for men in community, protect them from the storm and rain, divide the ordered from chaos. And this is precisely the relevance of the *garamb*: it connoted the ordered community; it rescued youths from damaging and destructive expressions of the singular powers in maleness, figured in the storm; it contained and ordered this power; it made youths into men capable of becoming the guardians of community. Because *gitam* corresponds with *garamb* in certain respects, the meaning of *garamb* can be projected into *gitam* and vice versa. Again, is that tailpiece about Tuman's ship smashing the jetty a clumsy adornment or a perceptive twist? For Tangu a jetty is a point of departure as well as a point of arrival. When Tangu go away on contract labour they walk down to the coast through a world and environment with which they are familiar, whose values they know. From the jetty at Bogia they take ship for Alexishafen, Madang, or Rabaul. At once they enter into a new world, a world of strangers and Europeans, of manufactured goods and working for cash. Without any kinsfolk around them, bound to the clock, and working regular hours under the orders of a foreman or boss-boy, they enter a mobile and open society where reciprocities as Tangu understand them count for little or nothing. As bamboo evokes birth and becoming as well as circumcision and the passage of the *garamb* into full membership of the moral community, so Tuman's jetty seems to have parallel connotations in relation to the movement from traditional man to new man. Moreover, Tuman represents the European, and the jetty, a European creation, is smashed by Tuman's ship: the initiative in breaking down the barriers that separate the two kinds of being is, surely, in Tuman's hands. Afterwards, Tuman's ship is secured to the black man's world by a familiar environmental feature, a coconut, itself evoking marriage and the productive unit. The two worlds, that is, ought to be married or joined together. So that, far from being an unnecessary ebullience, the incident is significant, relates to the nature of beings in conflict and, indeed, sums up the gist of the tale. Yet we know that the event actually occurred only recently. A ship owned and worked by Europeans rammed the jetty. Someone who had either witnessed or heard about the incident must have perceived how apposite it was. And since the inclusion of the event in the Duongangwongar story has gained approval, others too must have appreciated how appropriate it was.

The point is not that every single word in a narrative relates to being, but that clusters of words, and the situations evoked, point to it. *Br'ngun'guni* is mentioned once, becoming *mngwot-ngwotiki* and confession as such not at all: they are surely organizational devices sustaining the structure. The *gnek* finds no mention, but its activity—*gnek'gneki*, thinking—does, and the *gnek* is surely implied in the existence of a narrative, whatever other name the *gnek* might be known by. The test lies not in asking whether such-and-such actually does or does not relate to being—for that question no one can answer—but in asking whether what is adduced is appropriate and consistent in the circumstances. The objection that such a procedure is merely a 'reading into' the situation is countered by the reply that a particular kind of 'reading into' is what any investigator undertakes to do. Nor is it of much account to say that such a procedure is 'having it both ways': the science of symbols and meanings cannot be other than multidirectional, seeking inter-consistencies and mutually defining relations rather than *ad hoc* political or quasi-political formulations. There are other kinds of tree or palm to which the ship might have been made fast, and to which it might in fact have been made fast. But the story-teller chose 'coconut', and 'coconut' is appropriate and consistent. 'Sago palm' or 'bamboo' or other kinds of tree or palm would have emphasized the passage into manhood, the passage from traditional man to new man. But they would have left out that element of 'marriage', of 'productive unit', so necessary in the context of the relationships between black men and white men. The story of Duongangwongar is, after all, about black men and white men rather than about the new man. As the relationship between white men and black men is resolved, so perhaps 'coconut' will become 'sago' or 'bamboo'. The fact that there are not many trees or palms evocative of particular ideas merely underlines the likelihood of meaningful selection.

The Mambu story tells us something about the meaning of Mambu, little about his historical activities.[1] In the same way the traditional narratives inform us on the meaning of the *garamb* without telling us precisely what went on or was done there. Again, though the cargo rites in which Tangu participated have a close correspondence with the dreams which set them in motion,[2] and are closely related to the significances of N. 30 and N. 31, we have not come across many instances of a direct correspondence between narrative and ritual procedures. Sexual intercourse on the new garden site is indeed an enactment of the Paki story (N. 26). At a further remove the love charm noted on page 187 has a clear contextual relation to the areca-nuts in N. 8. But in what sense is the role of the coconut in the wedding ritual[3] an enactment of, say, the Maribun story? It may be that in the past there was a closer and more direct correspondence between a narrative and ritual activity. We cannot know. On the other hand, again and again we have noted correspondences not so much of 'things' and 'activities' in themselves as of their meanings and significance. Briefly, if A has a significance X, and B also has a significance X, then A and B are equated in relation to X. Or, if a part of A has a significance X, and a part of B has a significance X, then the relevant parts of A and B will be equated. Further, if a part of A has a significance X, then the value of X is likely to be attached to anything resembling A or a part of A. In narrative a coconut is associated with the union of brother and sister; a union between brother and sister implies stasis; a marriage in community implies the progress towards stasis, becoming *mngwot-ngwotiki*. As the common term between the two kinds of union, the coconut mediates between the idea of stasis as contained within a brother-and-sister union and the realization of stasis in community as husband-and-wife.

Tangu are not a ritually minded people. If the authentic is secreted in procedural forms, then Tangu provide only a few pointers to an understanding of their nature of being. Yet that

Tangu are not a ritually minded people is itself revealing. Providing that the arrangements for a marriage result in the formation of a new household in suitable exchange relationships, the ritual procedures of the wedding itself, if any, are left to those most directly concerned. While importance is attached to the reciprocities involved, the particular form of ceremonial has a personal rather than a collective value today. It is not the ceremonial which defines a marriage, but the formation of a household in reciprocal relationships. Again, the principle that charms are effective is not in doubt. What is more important is that a charm should be defined by the effective. Hence, whatever the procedure adopted, that which is effective is a real charm, and a so-called 'charm'—however deeply enmeshed in traditional lore—is discarded as a useless pretence if it does not appear to be effective. *GAGAWA* and *gagawa* were organizational categories which existed in certain conditions of concentration, co-residential association, and active hostility towards outsiders. Today these conditions no longer obtain, and *GAGAWA* and *gagawa* have become obsolete. Yet the division of a community into oppositional halves continues. The radical element involved is clearly the adherence to equivalent reciprocities—for this demands a process of pairings and bifurcations. And it follows that the odd man out, the singular thing, can only be non-reciprocal.

The particular modes by which the characteristic pairings of community are effected and organized appear, then, to be contingencies merely. Whereas being relates directly to equivalent reciprocities and to their opposite, the singular and non-reciprocal, it relates only indirectly to *GAGAWA* and *gagawa*, organizational forms within which and through which, for a time, the authentic was preserved. And not least among the difficulties which beset Tangu today is the lack of appropriate forms within which to contain the authentic. So one is returned to the core of the Tangu dilemma. 'What is to be truly authentic? In what form should the authentic be contained and expressed?' For the moment the exploratory and pragmatic approach suffices. Not until Tangu have gone rather further along the line represented by the movement from apprehension to comprehension, one may opine, will experience and predicative idea cohere in an appropriate form.

The fact that the Tangu language possesses only present and future tenses reinforces the appearance of the Tangu narrative as an ever-present reality, and adds point to the ways in which a narrative may presage the future or appear as exemplar or oracle. The first word in a Tangu narrative is *arin*, long ago, once upon a time.[1] But the action of the narrative is related in the present tense. So that although the word *arin* specifically places the action as having occurred in the past, the use of the present tense cannot but bring the narrative into significant relations with the present: as in the past, so now; as now, so in the past. Yet even if all history is necessarily seen through the lens of the present, Tangu are aware that the past was different from the present. And if not all of the traditional narratives are remembered, some are still told and Tangu are emphatic that narratives are 'true' or contain 'truths'. Assuming, then, that that which is 'true' in a narrative relates to being, or that a particular mode of being recognizes as 'true' whatever in a narrative is appropriate to itself, or that 'truth' in a narrative is an appropriate and efficient articulation of a mode of being which exists, we still have to recognize that though there are common themes through the traditional narratives to the Duongangwongar and Mambu stories, the last two do not connote the same mode of being as the former.

If narratives and the other aspects of culture were related either as identical or opposite twins, the conversation would tend to be dull. Nevertheless, the enagagement would still represent a dialectic as between two kinds of impersonal collective, whose product, synthesis, could still be rephrased as 'the realization of being'. And the process would still represent the living and active dialectic of history. Among Tangu, however, the conversation is dynamic, the dialectic is fraught with potential. When a narrative is told older folk in Tangu tend to reflect on the past, enlarging on the days of their youth. And for those who know there can be no turning back, reflection on the unsatisfactory conditions of the present quickly leads to the construction of images to be realized in the future. Though all narratives begin with *arin*, and are told in the present tense, a crucial difference between the new and the traditional narratives is that while the latter refer to a past in the present, the former refer to a

[1] Translated above in a variety of ways.

future in the present. When Tangu say that the newer tales are 'more true' than the traditional narratives, they seem to intimate that realization of being in the terms of these stories is more possible or relevant or desirable than realization of being in terms of the traditional narratives. Since that which is past is now irrevocably past, the alternative is to fill out the future.

The relationship between the traditional and the newer narratives, and the movement from apprehension to comprehension, represent corresponding processes which meet in the questions, 'What is or may be the measure of man? What parts of traditional being, fusing with what parts of new being, are capable of creating a viable future in the new environment?' Given that the movement from apprehension to comprehension is primarily a matter of mind, a mental activity generally applicable to any phase of developing awareness, it is in itself a process which corresponds with the movement from boy to youth, from youth to encounter with maiden, from yam bin to trump, from trump to slit-gong, from traditional man to new man. The while a scrutiny of the narratives yields up perceptions of the possibilities of awareness, being is realized as the possibilities are fulfilled. But as the possibilities are fulfilled and being is realized, so do the content and range of meanings in narratives become enlarged, so are further possibilities of awareness within an expanding horizon brought into cognizance. The process is a continuing one, an on-going dialectic in which 'synthesis' and 'new man' imply each other.

If one could imagine Tangu as a stable and completely closed society, one could also imagine a point at which the over-all continuing process would stop, at which all experience could be accounted for and explained within the terms of a particular systematic. Nevertheless, with each generation the dialectic would continue within the terms of a regularly reiterated stasis or synthesis. If Tangu represented a stable and settled social order in communication with other social orders, one could still say that there would be a point beyond which only a few individuals would or could develop their awarenesses. And in these few would lie the seeds of a developing awareness capable of becoming more generalized. With each generation the dialectic would be open to slightly differing syntheses. In fact, however, Tangu are involved in a process of drastic change.

They are making the passage from one socio-economic order to another, from one kind of being to another. Still, tradition and pragmatic necessity both brake and steer the course of change as a whole. The dialectic process continues, but the element of synthesis in the larger context is, as it were, 'open-ended', indeterminate, defined only by the meanings connoted by the new man.

The present Tangu social order may be said to be based on a catena of three interdependencies whose values are mutually defining: engagement in certain selected subsistence activities, equivalent reciprocities, and a prestige system which depends on the relation between equivalent reciprocities and the arrangements for engaging in the selected subsistence activities. If individuation on an intellectual level could be realized without a concomitant differentiation in the bases of prestige, it is more certain that given the latter the former would follow more quickly. At present Tangu use money simply as a means of buying those kinds of artifacts and equipment which they would have obtained in the past through part-time specialization. Money does not necessarily yield prestige, nor is it used as a generalized and common medium of exchange. On the whole, money evaluates extras and luxuries, measures itself and not the man. If money were to become in some part the measure of man, then it would help to effect that further differentiation of the parts—as well as that necessary separation of the bases of prestige—which would speed the process of individuation. But a prior requirement is that quality of thought which is capable of perceiving and exercising itself upon the particulars of the new environment. Only when the mind is prepared further to individuate itself is the social order capable of becoming further differentiated.

Traditionally among Tangu no event would so closely represent the undifferentiated state as a marriage between brother and sister. And the first and most elementary process of differentiation that community life demands is made possible by the incest taboo. From this point, primarily in terms of a dialectic between the values of filiation and siblingship, the formalities of the traditional moral order not only ensure a differentiation of the parts but, in becoming *mngwotngwotiki*, also incapsulate a representational return to wholeness or the undifferentiated state: a total coherence within terms of the pairings of the moral order, a coherence only achieved by excluding the singular from moral affairs. Yet it is just this coherence of pairings that has been vanishing as Tangu gradually become absorbed into the greater Europeanized community, which must vanish if the accelerating range of phenomena now apparent to Tangu is to be accommodated, understood, and categorized. The problem for Tangu is how to find a coherence appropriate to the terms of the new environment, how further to separate and differentiate the parts, how to develop their traditional appreciation of the singular, how to include particular kinds of expression of the singular within the moral order. On the political and purposive level any number of alternative methods might be attempted. On the objective level, however, in spite of, or because of, what has happened in history, Tangu narratives reveal that the process of individuation, of accommodating the singular, has already started.

Preliminary and Historical Syntheses

Basing ourselves on the conversation between the narratives and other aspects of Tangu culture, we can say that the progressive communication of parts which results in the realization of being may be summarized, or rephrased, as the synthesis which follows from the interaction between the values of filiation, thesis, and the values of siblingship, antithesis. The cycle of becoming *mngwotngwotiki*, the completion of the passage through obligedness in relation to unobligedness to the point where, within the moral community, unobligedness is in conformity with the terms of morality, represents the synthesis most economically and exhaustively. Marriage, *br'ngun'guni*, the *garamb*, confession, and becoming *mngwotngwotiki* emerge as the primary institutional means whereby the general opposition between the reciprocal and non-reciprocal is engaged, ordered, and co-ordinated; and friendship repeats and reiterates the same dialectic outside the idiom of kinship. Yet the non-reciprocal contains the singular, and the singular is represented as inherent in male filiation and the *ranguma*. So that while, formally, the terms of the moral order are predicated by a system of pairings, the social order as a whole is predicated by the tension or dialectic between the singular and the pairings.

The singular, moreover, is figured as generative and causative; and the movement from apprehension to comprehension within the new Europeanized environment seems closely related to a developing awareness of this singular.

In moral terms the synthesis yielded by the interactions of filiation and siblingship is represented by stasis—the 'sum' or 'balance' of non-reciprocity and reciprocity. Yet because the singular is represented as causative and predicative, and therefore cannot correspond with stasis, the statement that the moral community is characterized by pairings and bifurcations, but that the Tangu social order as a whole connotes an opposition between the singular and the pairings, means that the traditional order contained the possibility of a continuing and developing or historical dialectic. The formal reconciliation of the pairs connotes but a preliminary synthesis, a synthesis in terms of the pairings, bifurcations, and oppositions characteristic of the moral community merely. And since the stasis of *mngwotngwotiki* is only temporary, and in fact breaks down into the pairings which initially composed it, becoming *mngwotngwotiki* represents such a preliminary synthesis. A true or final synthesis, connoting the reconciliation of the singular with the pairs, is never quite within grasp. Nevertheless, the attempt to effect a final synthesis connotes the developmental process or historical dialectic. For though a final synthesis may not be possible, syntheses distinct from the sum or balance of the initial contrapositions may be effected, and these will themselves break down into theses and antitheses which will differ slightly from the oppositions that created the syntheses in the first place.

Given the provisional formulation above, we may now turn to a summary of the implications for Tangu.

Among Tangu filiation is non-reciprocal, traditionally yields continuity of role and the transference of being from generation to generation. A boy grows up on his father's milk, captures his being as a man through the pig caught in a *juaka* trap. Father gives up his being to his son. A girl grows up on her mother's milk, takes over the being of her mother. And of the two the transference of male being is the more dramatic, represented as the more significant. Though father-daughter and mother-son are relationships of filiation, they have only a minor relevance. For whatever the genetic or psychological contents of being that are in fact transferred from the one to the other, daughter cannot succeed to the being of father, and son cannot replace his mother. Filiation provides initial placement, being as a unique personality. But to provide for fatherhood and motherhood there must be husband and wife, marriage, social being: which leads into the implications of siblingship, the reciprocal relations connoted primarily by brother and sister, husband and wife, sweethearts, friends, and *mwerkindanger*. Yet the crucial focus of the engagement between filiation and siblingship lies in the Ambwerk–Tuman and mother's brother–sister's son relationships. For though Ambwerk and Tuman are certainly siblings, their values conflict with one another within a common filiation. And while the mother's brother–sister's son is inherently nonreciprocal, it is the link between the four lines of filiation, is derived from siblingship, and is not a relationship of filiation.

Men, as we have seen, are traditionally the culture bearers. They ensure a continuity of tradition from one generation to the next. Congruent with the fact that with each generation the wealth of the community has to be re-created, it is equally true that with each generation culture has to be regenerated, started anew. And though, as the narratives have revealed, the process of maintaining culture involves Ambwerk and Tuman as well as the more general categories of adults and children, the most crucial phases of transmission are contained in the father-son and in the *garamb*. Father feeds his son with his 'milk', provides the pig of the circumcision, is represented in the *garamb*. From the point where he is but a 'germ of being' in his mother's womb a son has to be so nurtured that, capable of becoming a responsible man and becoming *mngwotngwotiki*, he is himself nurturing his own son. In engendering his son, father, figured as hawk—a bird usually to be seen floating alone between man on the ground and the storm above, singular in essence yet bifurcated into male and female elements—both feeds his son and is as nurse to him. Through filiation son is seized of his being as himself. Next, the tutorial relationship leads into the removal of son from both father and mother so that he may come under the supervision of the mother's brother in the *garamb*. And the *garamb* is revealed as father and mother to the man, the social man, the man who is to become responsible. Through the mother's brother, and upon completion of his probationary period in the *garamb*, son gains social being, is ready to engage in reciprocal relations. Through the *garamb*, being as a unique personality is translated into social and responsible being. Nevertheless, through father, and through hawk, the element of the singular is always there. The pig of the circumcision, which seems to contain the meaning or essence of father, brings father and son together again, re-emphasizes the presence of the singular. Marriage separates father from son, brings son wholly within the field of pairings and reciprocal obligation. When father dies he becomes a ghost or dream-image to his son: the element of the singular re-enters, father and son are rejoined, son becomes significantly involved in a non-reciprocal relationship as well as being maximally engaged in reciprocities. With the birth of a grandson the singular is further emphasized: the middle generation is non-reciprocally engaged with both ghost and son.

The stages of maturation are figured in hawk—begetting, feeding, nursing, teaching the child; Wvawvasikai—the meaning of the progress into and through the *garamb*, circumcision, rebirth as a social being; Zawapai—the father who gives son the appurtenances of culture; the areca palm or *galip* tree—sexual competence, competence in garden and bush or forest, the gathering of seminal potential which leads into marriage; the yam bin—bespeaking children and productive gardens, both to be nurtured into ripeness; the trump—a further maturation leading to mastery over wife or the female; thence through handdrum, spear, and slit-gong to the return to the *garamb*, the companionship of other responsible men, the making of men out of boys before becoming, finally, a dream-image to son. For the kinds of awareness a responsible man should have, if he is to mature further than simply qualifying for slit-gong, we may turn again to Maribun and Mazienengai, Dumban (i) and Dumban (ii).

Son is, however, born out of woman, a particular woman. And this fact remains significant throughout his life. He is 'one womb' with his mother's other sons. Nevertheless, the path to responsibility is figured as lying in successfully encountering features thought of as female—wantonness, unrestrainedness, being oneself, as though wild—as well as in bridling those powers thought of as attaching to maleness. The explicit tutorial relationship with father removes son from the influence of his mother, is a demonstration of the proper exercise of the powers in maleness. A boy's entry into the *garamb* removes him from both mother and father. At the same time, through the mother's brother the meaning of mother, dependence on the female, is transmuted into interdependence, reciprocal obligation. Circumcision and the return of the foreskin to the banana clump emphasize the boy's removal from the female, his budding mastery over the female. Reattached to father as the boy is through the pig of the circumcision, his rebirth as a man from the *garamb* also entails being seized of the essentials of power in maleness: responsibility, awareness, initiative—that ability to overreach the normal or routine and take a first or original step. Before the youth can marry, however, he must kill Zawapai, make an end to his dependence on father, himself become one upon whom others depend. He must overcome Nuakai, wantonness and greed, as well as that which is capable of chopping the snake, smashing the main posts of the *garamb* and eating them, and circumcising with the vulva. His strength proven, clear of Nuakai who will find him a wife if he is bold, the growing youth must represent himself as freed from his mother entirely. For after father gives son his share of the household crops, wife, not mother, must command his attention. Then, having engaged with his wife and so brought himself under the influence of the female again, through trump, handdrum, and slit-gong the maturing man returns to the *garamb*, the association of responsible men. Always seeking to contain his initiating powers, never underestimating Nuakai's resource, if son is to become a responsible father he must distinguish wife from sister, bring the snake under control, and become as, or assimilate the being of, his father through a pig caught in a *juaka*.

There are no apparent difficulties with daughter. She grows up on her mother's milk, father gives feasts in her name so that she may marry and enter into the complications of siblingship. If it is to be presumed that she may become as though Nuakai, she is generally destined to be domesticated by men, become wife, worker, and childbearer, attached to the garden. Wives, it will have been noted, tend to come in pairs. But Nuakai, like husband, is singular. And when she is as Nuakai the female may encounter the snake—which has already been killed by a male

—with aplomb and decision. Her power is not figured as passive, for she can be positively destructive. Rather is it unordered, not wholly aware, incapable of ordering itself. While the power in maleness is imaged as capable of ordering and directing itself, the power of the female is thought of as random or wild. As maiden or wife a female will be destroyed by the live snake—unless a man first brings it under control and orders the power that is represented as residing in it. Nuakai herself is a challenge not so much to maleness as to men whose masculinity is unproven.

The snake is associated with the storm, male; with unrestrainedness in the male, as in the *ranguma*; with brother-and-sister union; with promiscuous sexual relations. The *garamb*, male with female attributes, is figured in snake; snake is as father, by extension a line of male filiation; mother's brother is a snake when deflowering a bride, snake is in husband. A Founder may enter into a snake, and in life killing a snake evokes thoughts of earthquake, perhaps a reversal of the present order of being, a turning-turtle. When in narrative a 'dead' snake is brought into the village it grows huge; killing a snake connotes earthquake and reversal, brings on the storm which sets *puoker* along the road to becoming men and women in community. And restraint and observance of the incest taboo, the reverse of wantonness, unrestrainedness, and brother-and-sister union, also make community possible. Cutting the snake into little pieces may represent that necessary differentiation which makes community life possible: the incest taboo separates brother from sister, four lines of filiation are required to relate brother and sister to husband and wife, the generations are distinguished. Yet, containing both male and female qualities, the snake seems to represent more than the parts of community as such. Itself is singular, all backbone and spine: it also connotes that creative and generative power which, seen as pertaining to the male, is capable of being brought under control and, when under control, makes culture possible and sustains the community. Nuakai butchers the dead snake, threatens unmasculine men. But she does not threaten the qualities of maleness itself: these are figured in the storm.

For the growing youth awareness of snake is awareness of the developing power of maleness in his loins and, implicitly, the ability—which seems to proceed from this awareness—to restrain, control, and order this power. Awareness of snake is the awareness of the nature of community, of the implications of filiation and siblingship, of the meanings and relations between the divine and moral. Given initial being through filiation, a young man communicates his parts in siblingship and, in the course of time, temporarily frees himself from obligation by becoming *mngwotngwotiki*: self and social being are reconciled, the self-willedness of the singular has been as though excised. And even if, because of its temporary nature, *mngwotngwotiki* represents a preliminary synthesis merely, it none the less connotes redemption: self-willedness or impulse or instinctual behaviour and restraint and conformity and awareness merge into one. For a maiden awareness of snake implies an appropriate surrender to the controlled power inhering in the snake: becoming wife. And in becoming wife she may become *mngwotngwotiki*, be redeemed. The alternatives are either her own individual death, as in N. 9, or to become as Nuakai. What she cannot do is kill the snake. Only men can do that. Controlling the power of the snake, men can either kill it or use it responsibly to create and maintain the values of the moral community. But in the *ranguma* the self-willedness of the singular is neither excised nor reconciled with the pairs. In him the snake is rampant and, because rampant or inappropriately controlled, potentially suicidal—both for the *ranguma* and for the community.

The Ambwerk–Tuman relationship is both an extension of the father–son, or, in the case of females, an extension of the mother–daughter, as well as one of siblingship. For males Ambwerk may become, like father, a dream-image or ghost to Tuman. But unlike father, who is never seen attempting to guide son into reciprocal behaviour, Ambwerk attempts just this with Tuman: he becomes as though a mother's brother. Girls grow up naturally and look to men, particularly husbands, to socialize them and bring them into the full ambience of community life as wives. Daughters follow their mothers, are led by husbands into involvements with siblingship and community. If son is to become a responsible man, however, and a father in his turn, he must temporarily sever the line of male filiation, cross over to the mother's brother and find a wife for himself. Only by so doing may he continue the line of male filiation and project himself and the tradition he bears down the generations. Both the Ambwerk–Tuman and the father–son have formally in common the fact that both parties in each pair enjoy the same filiation. But whereas the father–son consists of alternating phases of aggregation and opposition—opposition being a function of association with mother, mother's brother, and wife, siblingship—Ambwerk and Tuman are siblings of the same sex, remain opposed. As boys they compete for the breast, for father's time and attention; as adults they compete in exchange or as co-operators. Within this basic oppositional and competitive relationship Ambwerk has to persuade and guide an obstreperous Tuman into responsibility. And, as we have seen, he may not always succeed. Yet the weight of the evidence suggests that when he does succeed he remains Ambwerk and does not become as father. For, since becoming a ghost is intimately related to the non-reciprocal relationship and alternating phases of acceptance and rejection, if Ambwerk is to become a dream-image to Tuman he ought, it would seem, to realize his relationship to Tuman not by attempting to persuade him into responsibility but by assuming command, being non-reciprocal, and suffering phases of aggregation and rejection in consequence.

Father begets and provides. Son is begotten, succeeds, and inherits. It is a non-reciprocal relationship, in which the one proceeds from the other; consistently the implications of the relationship are adumbrated on the level of the divine, in narrative and ritual. Whether regarded as absolute, a theoretical necessity, or as ideological dogma, continuity between father and son must somehow survive the buffets of opposition and rejection which derive from involvements in marriage and siblingship. Aggregation with father, on the other hand, aligns son with all those representations of power and being—pig, snake, hawk, storm, earthquake, stream—which reveal him as unique, generative, capable of showing initiative. In the father–son the singular is given; it has to be bridled or excised so as to conform with a reconciliation of the pairs; or itself may be reconciled with the pairs when expressed as a self-willed initiative which commands consent. In the Ambwerk–Tuman, however, though reciprocities exist *ab initio*, Ambwerk feels himself responsible for Tuman, may become like father. But Tuman is recalcitrant. The crucial feature in the relationship—which relates directly to the tale of Duongangwongar—is that Ambwerk and Tuman may be as brothers, or as father and son, or as mother's brother and sister's son, yet always remain elder and younger, with elder responsible for younger. A wilful and arbitrary mixing of roles, usually on Tuman's initiative, is not only inappropriate but dangerous—and almost inevitable. Between them Ambwerk and Tuman dart forth sparks.

Siblingship is to filiation as moral to divine. Exercise of the relationship is appropriate and progresses towards the preliminary synthesis of stasis so long as the separable fields of the moral and divine are distinguished and recognized. That further or final synthesis which connotes the progress of the developmental or historical dialectic only starts to be realized when an initiative appropriate to the historical dialectic comes into play, when an initiative commands consent. In fact, however, and as matter of principle, from the point of view of those engaged in community life initiatives which diverge from the norm are most often deemed inappropriate—*ranguma*-like. And whether or not such initiatives are in fact appropriate to the historical dialectic can usually only be determined *post hoc*. If a brother were to pleasure his sister the initiative would clearly be regarded as inappropriate, trouble would result. Such historical dialectic as there was would continue, but so far as the incestuous pair were concerned the preliminary dialectic towards stasis would have been completed by a short-circuit. And if they lived they would be constrained to an appropriate re-engagement of the preliminary dialectic. If all brothers pleasured all their sisters it would put an end to being as human and Tangu, re-introduce being as *puoker*, put an end to the historical dialectic. But, exercising the imagination, it is possible to see that the historical dialectic might recommence in the terms of a more rigorously enforced incest taboo. Particular expressions of fresh initiatives, exercising the power of the singular, invite reassertions of the norm, recommencements of the preliminary dialectic progress to stasis. But were the situation to become generalized, if all men were to start exercising the singular and expressing fresh initiatives, then the world—as Tangu know it—would come to an end, turn-turtle or reverse itself.

Initiatives directed against the self-maintaining reciprocities of the community clearly invite disaster. But, since the singular is represented as attaching to male filiation, within this relationship its exercise might be effective. Thus, were son to attempt to enter reciprocal relations with father, though the initiative would be considered inappropriate, and trouble would ensue, resulting in a recommencement of the preliminary dialectic, a residue pertinent to the historical dialectic might remain, other sons might give a modified consent to the example,[1] a new kind of relationship between father and son might come into being, other relationships would tend to conform to the new father–son, the historical dialectic would be engaged. More crucially—because the relationship contains the values of both filiation and siblingship and is, therefore, inherently hazardous —fresh and troublesome initiatives within the Ambwerk–Tuman are not only more likely, but are apt to be more pertinent to the progress of the historical dialectic. Father-and-son and Ambwerk-and-Tuman are the most persistent themes in narratives. The delicate balance between an appropriate male filiation on the one hand, and an inappropriate male filiation or the *ranguma* on the other, is continually emphasized. In the newer narratives, narratives which made their appearance in the context of a developmental process hinging on the advent of Europeans, the *ranguma*-like fellow (Duongangwongar, Mambu), Ambwerk and Tuman, and male filiation are inter-associated. That is, consistent with the historical dialectic presently being engaged, the role of the singular is being actively explored.

The Syntheses, Roles, and Qualities

Filiation provides continuity and individual being, gives that initial placement from which to engage in siblingship. From the incest taboo are derived those categories within terms of which the community exists and persists as such: mother's brother and sister's son, father's sister's son and mother's brother's daughter,[2] husband and wife, brother and sister, sweethearts, *mwerkindanger*. Friendship relates individuals in different

[1] And precisely this, indeed, seems to have occurred in Tangu history.
[2] The other cross relationships between the generations have only very minor significance.

communities. Of these the most equivocal or ambiguous is the first. For while the others may be worked out and realized in concrete expressions, in the passage and counter of specie and services, mother's brother and sister's son cannot maintain reciprocities, and are not in a filiatory relationship equivalent to father and son. On the other hand, as we have noted, it contains something of both filiation and siblingship. For the sister's son a mother's brother is the explicit disciplinary authority, a *ranguma*-like person, the circumcisor, the man who beats him with thorns and nettles, who has a *ius prima nocte* over his bride, whose clumsiness may cost him his maleness, who may piddle in a clump of bamboo when decision and deftness are most required. For the mother's brother a sister's son may seem a desirable ally. But he is ultimately a tiresome and unrewarding responsibility who may involve him in inopportune clashes with the *mwerkindang*, who attempts to maintain claims on him as against his own sons, to whom he ought to give, from whom —whatever his expectations—he usually gets recriminations and recalcitrance. When in the past a mother's brother thrashed a sister's son with thorns and nettles, he might just as well have done so with gusto and enjoyment. For the other part, a sister's son will get little from a mother's brother unless he exploits to the full the ambiguities in the quadrilateral formed by himself, father, mother, and mother's brother. Yet a mother's brother 'makes a man' of the sister's son and initiates him into responsible manhood. Through the *garamb*, values in filiation and siblingship, which appear as conflicts and ambivalences in the mother's brother–sister's son, emerge as complementary. Precisely at those times—towards puberty, at circumcision, when asserting independence, at marriage, when attempting to succeed to claims—when the oppositional relationship between father and son might so develop as to injure the filiatory values irreparably, the animosities of the succeeding generation are formally deflected from the father to the mother's brother. Conversely, at those times when father is obdurate the mother's brother is conciliatory, and there to receive the brunt of the youth's frustrations.

    Male filiation, mother's brother–sister's son, and the *garamb* are clearly interdependent values, finely tuned to a sensitive mutual adjustment. And each of the terms is intimately related to the *ranguma*. So that, given vagaries in one of the terms, the supports contained in the others are also likely to alter or vary. In fact, as we have noted, in Tangu history *ranguova* suddenly appeared to become more active; the mother's brother–sister's son has changed; the *garamb* has disappeared; values in filiation depreciated significantly. Whether or not a man is 'one womb' with another is wholly a matter of the pragmatic experience, of simply observing the physical facts of birth. But paternity cannot be certain, can only be taken for granted. The narratives contain no explicit reference to the significance of being 'one womb': they stress the kind of being derived from, or involved in, male filiation. Though the narratives do not ignore the terms of being involved in siblingship, these may be directly realized in life through the communication of parts, in exchange, barter, trade, and participation in *br'ngun'guni*. Mutually enforceable reciprocities exert their own controls. Values in male filiation, on the other hand, non-reciprocal and subject to alternating phases of opposition and aggregation, are controlled dogmatically rather than pragmatically. The appropriate modes of realizing the father–son are contained in narratives, and only minds which are capable of appreciating and accepting the kinds of awareness that a narrative reveals can come to know the appropriate modes and realize them. The father–son is not a mutually and pragmatically enforceable relationship. Son may oppose, defy, or neglect his father; father may not provide for his son, the dream-image may deceive. Lacking a mutual consent as to what is appropriate to the relationship, and lacking a common awareness as to why the appropriate should be appropriate, neither father nor son can hold the other to what he himself thinks fitting. In short, largely contained as they are in narratives, in the divine, values in male filiation are mainly matters of dogma, of ideology, of the metaphysic of being. Moreover, a reversal of the terms seems also to hold: the metaphysic of being appears as attached to male filiation.

Knowing that values in male filiation in Tangu have been depreciating over the past half-century or so; knowing that Tangu today lack any sustained metaphysic which might explain or help to explain their present condition; and accepting provisionally that Tangu cargo activities represent an attempt to grasp just such a coherence—is a connection between depreciating values in male filiation and growing anomy so very tenuous? The converse suggests that it is not. For though the mission may have been hastening the obsequies of traditional life, in doing so it has brought Tangu the promise of a new life. Largely through the efforts of the mission Tangu have themselves started to try to strengthen the filiatory values. Christianity lays stress on filiation, male filiation in particular. Europeans are generally more prone to refer significantly to the father–son than to the father–daughter or mother–son. If the Mambu narrative is touched with the New Testament, is Mambu not also inevitably touched with Father and Son? It may seem to be going too far to suggest that the new man is dependent on a re-ordering of the father–son, or, to put it in another way, to suggest that when Tangu have given the father–son a coherence appropriate to present conditions they will have made their new man. Yet, as we shall see presently, the suggestions are more firmly based than they seem. Provisionally, at least, one may point to the father–son as crucial to the stable ordering of other relationships. Where the Ambwerk–Tuman and mother's brother–sister's son are inherently troublesome, the anchor of ordered relations as well as of a coherent metaphysic seems to have lain partly in the *garamb* but particularly in consent to an appropriate father–son. Further, let it be remembered that the *ranguma* and male filiation are reverse and obverse of the same singular, a feature which may be related back to *ranguma brami*, possibly an esoteric exercise of the singular outside the complex of community reciprocities.

In the narratives marriage takes place between man and woman who become husband and wife, between the son and daughter of two friends, and, if the point is permitted, between brother and sister. There is no reference to marriage between father's sister's son and mother's brother's daughter. Yet in the moral community this last is the most common and preferred form of marriage. Thus, though these terms must correspond with 'husband' and 'wife' in narrative, either they are confined to the moral experience—the common component 'husband-and-wife' having a divine or metaphysical as well as a moral significance—or they correspond with, or relate to, the union of brother and sister. Assuming the developmental experience to be substantially the same whatever the previous categories of husband and wife, the awareness of husband has to pass through the meanings and evocations of, chiefly, snake, *garamb*, bow and arrow, Nuakai, areca palm, yam bin, trump, handdrum, spear, slit-gong, and eliminating Zawapai. . . . The female develops naturally, does not have to make the same kinds of distinction between the self and social being, is of animal or wild rather than cultural stuff until she becomes wife, bears children, and comes into a more meaningful association with garden. Seized of these awarenesses most of the metaphysic of marriage is grasped. But no narrative treats of a developmental experience between husband and wife who are figured as brother and sister; no on-going process is envisaged; brother-and-sister union is wholly within the divine, a part of the metaphysic of marriage. Indeed, there can be no developmental process between a brother and sister who are as though spouses: the situation represents stasis, a short-circuit of the preliminary dialectic. This, in life, is only achieved through a series of exchanges and the communication of parts until, in becoming *mngwotngwotiki*, the constellations of pairings which characterize the Tangu moral order are reconciled or in balance. Then a marital relationship actually realizes just that stasis connoted by a brother-and-sister union.

Effecting the preliminary dialectic is, however, not wholly matter of routine. From the narratives there emerges that representation of the singular and male from which a creative imbalance proceeds. We have seen how divine elements intervene so as to upset a given set of maintained reciprocities; and we have seen how this results in renewed efforts to reassert an equilibrium. This, broadly, is the cycle of the preliminary dialectic in action. The normative and persistent relations which connote the moral community are preserved in terms of the changing relationships between particular people. On the other hand, while expressions of the divine and singular promote changes which result in a re-engagement of the preliminary dialectic, they also carry that potential of change and development which is pertinent to the historical dialectic. Mngungerp, Igoe'ika, Zawapai, Wvawvasikai, Paki, Maribun, Dumban (i), and Dumban (ii) are representations which figure in a variety of aspects the singular and creative power in maleness which can never be tamed by the requirements of reciprocities and siblingship. The storm—earthquake, thunder, lightning, flood—is singular, unbifurcated, uncontrollable, wholly self-willed, and unobliged. But rain, which derives from the storm, is as semen; and both rain and the flow of semen may be controlled by men. Stream, which derives from storm and rain, and which in most instances represents a line of male filiation, is also that from which the qualities of husband, father, initiative and responsibility emerge. Coming closer to men themselves, snake and hawk are bifurcated into male and female aspects. Storm, rain, stream, hawk, and snake are figured as generative and as male or as pertaining to the male; the kinds of power implied appear as appropriately transmitted down the generations from father to son in the line of male filiation. But though men in community are bifurcated, the power of the singular still inheres in them.

Whilst a man exercises his powers to maintain reciprocities, he also, as we have noted, likes to hold in reserve those powers which will enable him to act non-reciprocally, as a singular being. Appropriately exercised, male powers may be seen as bent in the first instance to the maintenance of reciprocities, to the stasis of the preliminary dialectic. And in the second instance these same powers may express those fresh initiatives which, commanding consent, engage the historical dialectic: they promote change not only in interpersonal relationships but in the normative relations as well. But the *ranguma*, as figured in Dumban (ii), also comes from the stream. A singular man with potent sexual parts, in whom the power of snake is rampant, a *ranguma* is a man often alleged to be of dubious parentage or filiation. He is the sort of person any man is on the verge of becoming, he acts so as to upset a given stasis; he forces members of community to reassert the stasis, re-engage the preliminary dialectic. Because he is but a man he may be appropriately bifurcated by being forced to the exercise of self-restraint through confession. Yet, as the circumstances of Tangu history imply, the activities of *ranguova* may also promote the engagement of the historical dialectic. Though the *ranguma* does not command consent, he is singular, enforces change, may be the vehicle of the historical dialectic. So that, while the singular power of maleness finds its most common and moderate expression in an appropriate male filiation that results in a responsible communication of parts, maintains reciprocities, and engages the preliminary dialectic proceeding to stasis, it may also find expression in the *ranguma* on the one hand, and in the fresh initiative which commands consent on the other: engagement of the historical dialectic.

Women emerge from the narratives as the housemaids of a culture ordered and managed by men, in which—since domesticated male animals are emasculated—the only generative males are men.[1] Figured as basically of wild or animal stuff, women have to be socialized by men if they are to become relevant as wives, workers, and childbearers. Largely confined to settlement and gardens, the environs of culture, women forage and gather whilst on their way to and from the gardens, or whilst accompanying men on their journeys. But even so, forest and bush are not for them. For a woman to go out into the forest alone is to court the attentions of a *ranguma*. Represented as given to wantonness, as instinctual rather than given to intellection, a woman in the forest by herself may become like her surroundings, may revert to her wild and animal nature. Should she do so she is a threat to ordered relations. Consequently, women are appropriately confined to the cultural environment. Women may be themselves, are not thought of as wholly able to control themselves. Where maleness is considered as generally subject to the control of males or men, the quality of the female is represented as requiring or even seeking control by maleness and men if it is not to become random. Men go into the wild to hunt because, possessed of *gneker* and able to think and initiate, they can do so. Through their *gneker* men participate in the generative divine. Like Maribun, they are aware. In and through them the powers in the divine are made to support the moral community.

Though the survival of community depends on the incest taboo, and upon observing the rules of siblingship, these very rules appear to depend on what is meant by 'control of the

---

[1] With the significant exception of cockerels which herald the dawn, and whose feathers are used by men for decorative purposes.

snake': self-restraint, an appropriate restraint of the self by the self. And this is precisely what a *ranguma* does not do. He does not control himself, in him the snake is not under control. Since, ultimately, no one can prevent a man from becoming a *ranguma* or like a *ranguma*, so, by the same token, engagement of the rules of community ultimately depends on a voluntary submission to them. Just this is implied in the traditional modes of confession, and no less is implied in Tangu expressions of shame. Bearing in mind the imagery contained in the meaning of *ringertingertiki*, we can, perhaps, appreciate more readily that the reciprocities contained within siblingship are, as it were, the banks between which the streams of that power, figured as male and represented as peculiarly attached to male filiation, may restrain itself. When men become *ranguova* they deny their fathers, deny the tradition handed down to them by their fathers, break the banks and become like the flood—destructive, but at the same time creative. And women who are not restrained by their menfolk may become as Nuakai—wilful and random.

Self-restraint and self-willedness appear as essential components of both the preliminary and the historical dialectics. And they interact with each other so as to progress towards, and then realize, awareness. In women and children the element of self-willedness—more accurately wantonness and wilfulness—is represented as inherent, as instinctual and animal-like. But, acted upon by responsible men who know restraint, it is channelled into awareness—into that preliminary synthesis in which the rules are acknowledged and obeyed because the reasons for them are known and appreciated. Expressions of self-willedness in adult men, however, are regarded as matters of volition. They reveal either a lack of awareness, which is inappropriate to an adult man, or arrogance. One who knows and appreciates, or who ought to know and appreciate, the meaning of restraint, has it in him to restrain self-willedness. So that if he does not restrain himself he is allowing self-willedness its expression, or, more positively, he is giving vent to self-willedness.

When the community of responsible men reacts to expressions of self-willedness, it attempts first to foster, and then to enforce, an overt and voluntary restraint. Tangu are critical of each other, watch each other closely. While *br'ngun'guni* orders and maintains reciprocities, enforces restraint, in the traditional confessional procedures and in expressions of shame we can see the self exerting a restraint on itself. The *ranguma* is not simply restrained or restricted: he is made to confess, become aware, and articulate this awareness to himself and to others. Total awareness connotes the synthesis pertinent to the historical dialectic—that fresh initiative which, accurately perceiving and appreciating the current social order, can yet thrust forward and command consent to another. To this kind of awareness Mambu and Yali aspired. They wanted to re-order community life, they articulated fresh initiatives, they commanded consent. But they were only human. It is for Maribun, Dumban (i), and Dumban (ii) to reveal the likeness of total awareness; for the *ranguma* to point to its likeness. Maribun evokes the *ranguma*, so do Dumban (i) and Dumban (ii); Europeans are thought of as like *ranguova*; had Mambu and Yali not commanded consent, they would have been considered as, or like, *ranguova*. When a *ranguma* acts, new syntheses ensue.

Puoker, not responsible men, engage in brother-and-sister unions. And *puoker* are wholly self-willed. Dreams in which brother and sister engage in sexual relations are described as *imbatekas*: they are involuntary experiences, proceed from impulse. Such dreams are not appropriate to moral behaviour. But, by exercising restraint and engaging in reciprocal relations until becoming *mngwotngwotiki*, impulse and moral behaviour converge. The oppositions within the father–son relationship may well give rise to an impulse on son's part to eliminate or even kill father. For not until father is dead does son become wholly seized of his being as a man. Awareness consists in appreciating that the impulse relates to budding independence, to the passage of creative responsibility from one generation to the next. If son is to become a man like father, he must assert himself against one who has fed, taught, and dominated him. Only then may he feed, teach, and dominate in his turn. The appropriate and social awareness which proceeds from the interaction of self-will and self-restraint results in son's killing not father but Zawapai, the provider in father. In this way filiation is maintained and son may become a responsible man, engage in reciprocities. The *ranguma*-son[1] demonstrates the

[1] *Supra*, N. 19, pp. 286–9.

converse. Being born a *ranguma,* he is self-willed, does not or cannot distinguish between the impulse to be rid of father as a whole and the social requirement to differentiate the parts, to rid himself of certain parts of father's influence. The most direct way of becoming quite independent of father is to kill him; and the most direct way of becoming unobliged is for brother to marry sister. But, if community is to exist, the requirements of community must intervene. Brother may not marry his sister. Instead there is a process of differentiating and communicating the parts until brother and sister become unobliged to each other, *mngwotngwotiki.* Son may not kill father. Son distinguishes the parts, succeeds to the responsibilities of father, himself becomes father. Community life continues.

In killing wives and children Mazienengai took the most direct way of ridding himself of responsibility and the obligations of marriage and siblingship. Self-willed, the act led to the reaggregation of father and son, filiation simply, dominance/dependence, a non-reciprocal relationship. But, in opposition to those impulses either to dominance or to dependence, the requirements of community intervene. Mazienengai called to his mother's brothers to lead him to father-as-hawk, father in whom the male and female are conjoined. As we know from the Zawapai story, if son is to marry and become father he cannot continue to be dependent on father; and in relying on the generosity of Ambwerk, Tuman may overreach himself. In Tangu terms a woman can hardly help herself, that is the way she is. But men are the culture bearers, may be *ranguova.* When a man's bow is bent he should, because he can, take appropriate aim. To mix the metaphor, his spear is burdened with responsibility. Since promiscuous killing and promiscuous sexual relations make an end to community, the impulse towards either must needs be brought under control and ordered if community life is to go on. And on both counts the *ranguma* is taken to regard himself as unobliged, on both counts the *ranguma* not only allows his impulse free rein but positively encourages and develops its potential.

Community life in Tangu may be seen as a kneading of impulse into developing awareness and responsibility. Within terms of the preliminary dialectic individuals develop their awarenesses within a given set of paired relations, progressing to stasis, the reconciliation of the pairs. At the level of the historical dialectic the singular enters effectively, and it is the given relations themselves which develop, mature, and change, or which come to the verge of changing, developing, and maturing. On the one hand a particular tradition is maintained, on the other a particular tradition is changing. But in both cases awareness proceeds from the interactions of self-willedness and self-restraint. While women are allowed a large measure of instinctual life within the terms of the cultural community, their impulses controlled by men and appropriately channelled along cultural paths, men have to control themselves. From the time when he comes under his father's supervision, through to the *garamb*, circumcision, marriage, engagement in *br'ngun'guni*, and becoming *mngwotngwotiki*, the awareness of a Tangu male is developed by exerting restraints upon his self-willedness, by so kneading and constricting his impulses that they bear fruit in the image of a man. And the critical test and exercise lies in confession. For here self-willedness is pitted against the demands of community, here self-restraint is invited to act independently of the pragmatic restraints which might be exerted by members of the moral community. Consequently, the *ranguma* who does not confess is either a man who is simply not aware, and who, therefore, should be forced into awareness or eliminated as a not wholly human—that is, moral—creature; or he is a man who, being aware, is yet capable of asserting himself against the moralities accepted and approved by the community. The *ranguma*, in short, does not demonstrate the kind of awareness which might indicate the normative moral qualities.

So far as every man in Tangu demands reciprocities from others but covets the capacity to refuse or dominate, so far is each man on the brink of becoming a *ranguma* or like a *ranguma*. Assertion of the self against the moral, killing upon impulse, denial of reciprocal relations, and the immediate and promiscuous gratification of mounting desire are, therefore, not so firmly under control that a constant vigilance can be forgone. Egalitarianism demands the constant criticism of others. Because the narratives are well supplied with examples of self-assertion and acting on impulse, it could be said that the stories act as a kind of safety-valve, that they enable Tangu to enjoy in fantasy what they may not realize in fact. Maybe. On the other hand, Tangu represent man as seized of a *gnek*; and because of his *gnek* he can never be an animal, though he may often behave like one. Having a *gnek*, man is enabled to rationalize his activities, knows the tension between self-will and self-restraint, distinguishes between impulse and responsible behaviour, recognizes the appropriate relevances of moral and divine, perceives that the relation between a man and a woman should not correspond with a boar scenting a sow.

That man has a *gnek*, is aware of himself, can think and articulate his thoughts in communicable language, is really the starting-point. Gardening, hunting, and gathering sustain both the flesh and the *gnek*. Activities are ordered, express moral relationships between members of community, comprise the relations which connote the community. So far as sexual desire and other impulses are not immediately and promiscuously gratified, they measure restraint. The moral order proceeds from the *gnek*. On the other hand, though much of that which is regarded as initially unconstrained may yield to thought and so become a part of culture, under control, storm, earthquake, thunder, lightning, and flood are not only unconstrained but unconstrainable. They are manifestations of a supreme power or powers which remain quite unobliged. Against it or them, or against those things or beings which participate in their distinctive qualities, men can only oppose the shelter of the *garamb*, the community of men responsibly communicating their parts. Yet man is unique in creation. Only he has a *gnek*. Only man can show that he is aware of himself and of the community in which he lives. Only man distinguishes between the divine and the moral, only in man does the power of the storm, the epitome of the divine, appear as creative and channelled rather than random or destructive. Rain is a part of storm and is also as semen. As men may control the fall of rain, so also may they control the flow of semen. Traditionally, as we have noted, it is possible that only males were thought to have *gneker*. If so, then it is the *gnek* itself which was properly associated with that power in maleness whose passage from one generation to the next, if it is to be appropriately exercised, is represented as ordered by, and attached to, an appropriate male filiation. That is, an appropriate male filiation was represented as necessary or proper to a quality we cannot name other than conscience.

The Syntheses and History

Traditionally among Tangu, whatever an individual's personal and private experience and awareness might be, he could not but think and act within the ambience of a collective experience and awareness generated on the one hand through marriage, friendship, the *garamb*, confession, *br'ngun'guni*, the *ranguma*, and becoming *mngwotngwotiki*, and on the other hand through the corpus of narratives available. A continuing and developing interactional process between personal being, the narratives, and institutional life, no private awareness could find any lasting expression outside the collective forms. The literary experience did not intervene, the personal experience could not be recorded for future generations. Nevertheless, through incorporation in a narrative, personal reinterpretations of the meaning of experience could become a part of the collective experience and awareness. The narratives do not treat of exchange, neither the *gnek* nor becoming *mngwotngwotiki* is mentioned, confession as such does not occur, *br'ngun'guni* appears but once. Given that equivalent reciprocities should be maintained, the implications of siblingship are, on the whole, self-regulating and self-maintaining. Real difficulties only occur with the entry, then the ordering, of non-reciprocal relations and values. And it is with these that the narratives mainly deal, ordering the non-reciprocal, communicating awareness. Yet it is precisely here that personal interpretations are likely to vary, are likely to include the singular and so predicate change.

Competition and criticism may not be necessarily inherent in equivalent reciprocities. Yet they exist in Tangu. They find expression in Tangu watchfulness, in that reluctance to commit the whole of one's resources and potential whilst maintaining an overt equivalence and insisting that others should be open and frank, give of their all. The impulse to dominate, become singular, contends against the injunction to equivalence. Lacking an established social hierarchy such as a lineage or explicit ranking system might provide, and within terms of which the singular might be more appropriately channelled, Tangu yet seek to contain this impulse within a system of equivalent reciprocities.

Within this primary opposition the father–son, Ambwerk–Tuman, and mother's brother–sister's son emerge as the critical relationships. Exceedingly difficult to order in amity, the three pairs grate on each other. Within the pairs the persons involved tend to be in an ambiguous or dynamic tension; each of the pairs connotes values in general opposition to that hinge of reciprocities and siblingship, marriage or 'husband and wife'. That in the past the four relationships were reconciled, sustained, and ordered through the *garamb* there can be little doubt. Father and son, Ambwerk and Tuman, and husband and wife—particularly in contexts where the first two bear on the last—are the relationships most extensively treated in the narratives. And mother's brother is continually chipping in in one representation or another. Again and again one is returned to the *garamb*. Yet within the dialectic that attempts to reconcile siblingship with filiation, reciprocity with non-reciprocity, there runs the theme that the non-reciprocal is ultimately, like the storm, singular and unbifurcated. If the non-reciprocal is appropriately tamed and brought into relation with the reciprocal, first through the filiatory values and then through the *garamb*, ultimately a singular self-willedness may only engage with the obliged by bifurcating itself through a restraint of the self by the self. And the quality of this last is represented as attached to an appropriate male filiation.

Reaching backwards through time in terms of the dialectic it is possible to appreciate that once the tight interdependence between male filiation, Ambwerk and Tuman, mother's brother and sister's son, marriage, and the *garamb* had been loosened by intermarriages between the several original communities that formerly lived in the Tangu ridges, and then further disrupted by the migrations which followed, the loss in significance in one feature—primarily, one supposes, in male filiation—cannot but have affected all. The migrations removed son from father, sister's son from mother's brother, Tuman from Ambwerk, even husband from wife. The constellation of influences in dynamic tension must have been disrupted. Attention would have been—as, indeed, it seems to have been—focused on existential reciprocities. The disappearance of the *garamb* with little or no active opposition was hardly a historical accident. Nor is the remark that 'the mission has taken the place of the *garamb'* without its own significance. For Christianity lays stress on filiation, male filiation especially.

Though the narratives stress the importance of all expressions of the non-reciprocal, the focus of emphasis is on the father–son on the one hand, and the *ranguma* on the other. If son is to become father and responsible in his turn there must be an appropriate passage of being from father to son: within these terms the singular may be exercised appropriately. But the inappropriate passage of being from father to son, and the inappropriate exercise of the singular, are associated with the *ranguma*—the man who does not exercise restraint, in whom self-willedness is rampant, whose parentage is inappropriate, equivocal, or in doubt. Remembering that the epidemic sickness in Tangu was seen as an increase in *ranguma* activity, and bearing in mind the close association of male filiation and the *ranguma*, it might yet be a more accurate and objective assessment to see this increase in *ranguma* activity as more closely related to weakening values in male filiation than to the sickness.

It is not unreasonable to suppose that in the past the relations between individuals and the categories of siblingship which they occupied were more stable than they are today. Brothers would have been more likely to remain brothers, rather less likely to become *mwerkindanger*. If ambiguity was always a necessary feature in social relationships, enabling each man to find his own most suitable ambience of competitive exchanges, the limits were surely more narrowly drawn. Manipulation of persons and categories doubtless existed in the past. Yet one may assume that it was not as general a feature of social life as it is today. And given these predicates of a more stable society governing and regulating itself without the interference and supervision of administration and mission, values in filiation—if only at the level of succession to prerogatives, inheritance of seed crops, and uniting against suspected *ranguova*—together with the established authority of the mother's brother and the requirements of the *garamb*, would have controlled, or prevented, too many shifts in the nature and content of individuals' obligations to each other. So, as a first approximation, one may speak of the decline in filiatory values, the diminished authority of the mother's brother, and the increase in ambiguity, as inter-dependencies. To check this, recall the current Tangu attitudes to adoption, which reveal a decline in the filiatory values. Though the attitudes towards, as well as the numbers of, adopted persons may also relate to the death-rate of parents, the attitudes themselves belong more properly to that cluster of interdependent relations connoted by increasing ambiguity, the decline in filiation, and the diminished authority of the mother's brother. Death may put an end to a particular relationship, but it does not necessarily change the normative relations.

What started the decline in filiation? The answer must be a number of factors acting in concert which, if they were detailed, would themselves require to be accounted for: an infinite regression. Yet it is possible to point to one feature in which all or most of the factors involved seem to cohere, and whose pro-gressive consequences may be outlined: that intercommunica-tion between the several Tangu communities which enabled individuals to opt out of the requirements of a natal community. We have seen that strangers, those of mixed or dubious parent-age, and those who divide their loyalties between two com-munities, are apt to be thought of as *ranguova*; and it is clear that, since a *ranguma* is a man, and a man's personal or indivi-dual being appears to reside mainly in male filiation or the father–son, dubiety of parentage will also relate to male filiation in particular and filiation generally. In conditions of spatial confinement, when neighbours were enemies and there was no administration to keep the peace, values in filiation—whether of fatherhood or motherhood—and the authority of the mother's brother, combined with association in the *garamb*, would have served to keep the *ranguma* under close control, besides protect-ing the integrity of particular marriages. But once it became possible to move about more freely and intermarry with mem-bers of other communities, the choice of possible mates must have widened, and the opportunities for adultery necessarily increased. Strangers would have been encountered more often, and, owing to the intermarriages, there would have been an increase in the numbers of those whose loyalties would be thought of as split between two communities. With the bases of community life widening in this way, how could one be sure of the parentage of men from other communities who demanded spouses in this? Finally, given a widening choice of spouses and more opportunities for adultery, it follows that both the opportunities for, and the numbers of, divorces would also have increased. Since all these features cohere in the *ranguma*, it is not unreasonable to deduce that suspicions regarding the activities of *ranguova* would have increased—as, indeed, they seem to have done—and that the dangers from his activities would have become more generalized—which, again, actually seems to have occurred.

If there was then a reaction, an attempt to reaffirm values in filiation—and who knows that there was not?—it would seem that the process had already passed beyond the point of no return. That reserve of self-will inhering in every male seems to have broken the bonds of self-restraint which the narratives represent as deriving from male filiation; and exterior restraints were clearly not wholly effective. But, since it is precisely the defeat of self-restraint by self-will which makes a man a *ranguma*, again we are faced with an increase in numbers of *ranguova*. The breaking of betrothal agreements, attempts to exercise claims on both hands, the manipulation of spouses to gain economic advantage—these features demonstrate self-will in action. And with the arrival of artificial dogs' teeth the same catena of relations would have been given an added stimulus. If the epidemic sickness must have brought suspicions of *ranguova* and *ranguma*-like persons to a climax, the increasing numbers of deaths were evidence of increasing numbers of quite unobliged *ranguova*. The ensuing migrations and dispersal over territory in small groups could not have resulted in anything other than a furthering of the process of increasing ambiguity, weakening filiation, growing manipulation of persons and categories, concentration on the *ranguma*. Finally, when cash found its way into the Tangu economy, youths and young men, who had a preferential access to the cash through their labour, and who were as yet without wives, were placed in a position of advantage over fathers and mother's brothers. At the very point when, traditionally, a young man had to exert the utmost in self-control if he was to contain the conflicting loyalties and interests adhering to filiation and siblingship, contract labour and access to cash enabled him to side-step the issues involved. He could exercise self-will with impunity. Father and mother became dependent on son for cash, cash could persuade mother's brother, the self-willed returned labourer could outbid the stay-at-home when looking for wives.

While the traditional values in filiation were disintegrating, however, becoming independent of the self-maintaining reciprocities of siblingship, the mission entered on the scene and started to provide the physical facts of filiation with a new metaphysic, a new ideological content, a new meaning. The *garamb* served to organize and reconcile the opposed values of siblingship and filiation: it had no direct connection with the actual maintenance of reciprocities as such. In this respect *br'ngun'guni*, marriage, exchange relations, becoming *mngwotngwotiki*, and the presence of the *ranguma* were the more pertinent factors involved. So that while the disappearance of the *garamb* would scarcely have affected the maintenance of reciprocities, in the face of growing ambiguities and the decline in the filiatory values combined with the diminishing authority of the mother's brother, the main purpose and justification of the *garamb* were themselves becoming irrelevant. The opposition reciprocity/non-reciprocity held good, but the focus of the dialectic had shifted, or was shifting, from siblingship/filiation to *br'ngun'guni/ranguma*. Thus older conservatives, indoctrinated in childhood with the values in filiation and siblingship, might be expected to deplore the passing of the *garamb*. Conversely, those whose knowledge of traditional filiation/siblingship was hazy or oblivescent, and those who had become Christians, could not be expected to have had forceful views on retaining the *garamb*. And such, indeed, is the import of the fieldwork evidence. Though, therefore, the relevance of the *garamb* in narrative as a maker of responsible men is still a lively issue, as an institution concerned with the reconciliation of values in filiation and siblingship the *garamb* was virtually defunct when mission and administration acted as they did. Had the case been otherwise there would surely have been more energetic opposition to the abolition of the *garamb*. But there is no evidence that there was anything more than murmurings from the old who, again, could be expected to be thus sentimental. Yet on the one hand the relevance of the *garamb* persists in narrative, and on the other hand the mission has 'taken the place of the *garamb*'. It begins to look as though the relevance of making a responsible man is shifting, or has shifted, to the mission.

On one level the making of the new man may be appreciated through the Duongangwongar tale, Mambu himself, the Mambu story, Yali, and Tangu cargo activities.[1] But in the light of the filiatory values we can probe a little deeper. There are some in Tangu who echo the remark made by a Manam islander[2] that Europeans, non-reciprocal persons, might have a quite different origin from black men. And in Tangu thought, since 'different origin' cannot but mean 'different kind of filiation', if the statement were true it would preclude the possibility of moral relations between white men and black men. Yet Christianity quite specifically teaches that all men have a common filiation in the Godhead: and again we are returned to the expression that the mission 'has taken the place of' the *garamb*.

From the standpoint of Tangu tradition two sets of features cohere in the creation of the new kind of filiation which will make the new man. On the one hand there is the inappropriate exercise of the singular which is associated with *ranguova* and Europeans, on the other hand there is the appropriate and responsible containment of the singular in the father–son. Without a *garamb* the variety and elaboration of traditional non-reciprocal elements and their representations have been, and are, declining into oblivescence. Emphases have shifted to the maintenance of reciprocities of themselves. Founder and Patron are almost irrelevant. And whilst the traditional relevances of *gnek*, *niemur*, ghost, and *nduor* are slowly fading, the Christian soul, proceeding from the Godhead and inhering in both men and women, is in cognoscence—as are other varieties of Christian representations. If most Tangu still have some regard for the activities of *puoker* in general, particularly the *pap'ta* and *puoker* of narratives, there are those who definitely do not, and others who are uncertain. The snake, however, still carries meaning; earthquakes and snakes are still associated. The storm, too, still provides a vital line of bearing which carries the meaning and content of the non-reciprocal and singular

[1] The framework of B-1960, *passim.*   [2] B-1960: 244.

through *ranguova* and Europeans to the point where, capable of gathering new meaning, it may reinform the filiatory values. While 'God', figured as male and self-willed, tends now to be regarded as the power behind the storm, unlike traditional representations[1] 'God' is not irrevocably non-reciprocal and may show sympathy for men. Other Christian representations,[2] not so distant and powerful as 'God', are understood to be concerned for mankind and may consent, if asked, to give help. And even if the kind of 'help' that appears to have been given often seems mysterious and inscrutable, it is rarely regarded as simply a mischievous deception. While the principle that *ranguova* are ultimately non-reciprocal remains, in fact most of them may be persuaded into reciprocal behaviour. The singularity of Europeans is now qualified by the moral European who, like Tangu themselves, can by self-restraint and an awareness of why restraint should be exercised, become reciprocal when the situation appears to demand it.

The general impression to be gained from reading the narratives is that of an integrated and intimate community life lived within relatively narrow horizons. Themes are worked out in a series of dialogues within the categories of kinship and friendship, the number of key signals is comparatively few, the narratives themselves are interconsistent. When they are related to the present scene and the remembrances of older folk a coherent picture emerges. Reciprocity/non-reciprocity is translated into siblingship/filiation and self-restraint/self-willedness. The singular power adhering to male filiation is appropriately tamed or contained through the *garamb*, excluded from the community in the *ranguma* when recalcitrant. But while the style of the Duongangwongar tale is familiar—the dialogue form is maintained, actors are paired, reciprocity/non-reciprocity is evident—except in an indirect and substitutive way, through Ambwerk and Tuman, explicit values in male filiation do not appear. As an odd and singular fellow, Duongangwongar evokes the *ranguma*. But the brothers are different, the *garamb* is missing, the passage from boy into man is strange, there is little or no play on filiation/siblingship as traditionally understood. When Tangu adopted the narrative, one might say, the *garamb* had

---

[1] For example, Mngungerp and Igoe'ika, or even Maribun and Dumban (i).
[2] Primarily 'Jesus Christ', the 'Holy Ghost', the 'Virgin Mary', and some saints.

already ceased to serve its traditional purpose, and traditional values in filiation/siblingship were already felt to be obsolescent. But the sexual act is still ordered, the storm is there, and so is a snake-like animal, the *ramatzka*. If the mother–son jars, it may also be thought of as an attempt to try out a new kind of filiation —giving to women that new importance to which their possession of a soul (or *gnek*) now entitles them. The core of the question posed is how to tame or contain and transmit the singular in what new and appropriate kind of filiation.

With the Mambu story we find no sustained and traditional dialogue form. On the contrary, as is characteristic of conditions in the open society, protagonist and antagonist are lone individuals. The *garamb* is missing, but there is that echo of the Christ-like figure which seems to indicate a receptiveness to Christian teaching through the mission: the Christian father–son. And it is this feature in particular which, in conjunction with the community values evoked by brother and sister, perhaps enabled Mambu to gain a qualified access to cargo. Still, the opposition reciprocity/non-reciprocity is maintained, and the captain continues intractable, a *ranguma*-like fellow. If Mambu had had a more certain filiation, one might say, or if he had been as like a *ranguma* as the captain, perhaps he would have got all the cargo he wanted.

The Transference and Development of Categories of Understanding

The major theme running through the narratives is the condition and development of man, 'being and becoming': how culture originated, and how it starts again with each succeeding generation; how culture and the moral community are maintained and continued; how men, the culture bearers, may mature and become so qualified to fulfil their roles that culture and the moral community may be sustained; how metamorphoses in cultural and biological being relate to the origin, growth, and preservation of culture. Reduced to its simplest terms, three primary and interrelated experiences are represented as having to be explained, rendered subject to thought, if culture and the moral order are to continue: the storm; the sexual act and its consequences; and that swift metamorphosis which turns a dependent and skinny little boy into well muscled thought and initiative. Let us ourselves mythologize. . . . Let us say that in the beginning an impulse stirred so that a singular part supported by a pair exerted itself in a burrow framed by a pair. As the storm gathers and a tree sways, thunder cracks, lightning flashes, and rain pours down—so the semen runs, there is a bang in the head, the earth seems to move in quake, and fire-flies wink in the *gnek*. Being commences, life is engendered, the mind becomes aware of itself, culture starts. The creative act must be ordered, the little life nourished and taught how that bang may destroy as well as create. As awareness increases the mind generates and feeds on the objects it contemplates: being becomes gaining a livelihood, utilizing the resources of the immediate and other environments, distributing the fruits of labour, allocating priorities, competing for prestige and power within the terms of agreed moral imperatives, realizing images of thought in experience. The servant of impulse has become master, almost author of himself. The while he identifies and recognizes that to which he is subject, heir, and prone, man bends his mind and newly awakened awareness to the preservation and improvement of the cultural inheritance to which his children belong.

In summarizing their experience and projections of the future in narrative form, Tangu offer each other a chart by means of which they may come to know themselves. But this does not necessarily mean that the chart is used, or that everyone or anyone in Tangu is wholly aware of what is being done. Awarenesses differ, fools are answered according to their folly, wise men keep their own counsel. Still, with the help of Tangu themselves—in the ways they behaved, in what they said—a pattern that was there all the time has been coaxed into view. It is an available pattern, a pattern in which daily life, anecdote, narratives, and thoughtful comment cohere; in which particular awarenesses may move and develop. Its bare outlines may now be reviewed.

In the traditional narratives the general opposition between impulsive or instinctual life, and cultural life, an opposition which connotes both preliminary and historical dialectics, is broken down and illustrated within terms of thirteen primary dialogues: Ambwerk and Tuman, whether as brothers, sisters, or pairs of brothers and sisters; brother and sister; father and daughter; father and son; friends; husband and wife; mother and daughter; mother and son; mother's brother and sister's son; parents or adults and children; community and the *ranguma* or odd man out. Both dialectics continue into the newer narratives, but the opposed values of siblingship and filiation are overlaid by the corresponding opposition between black men and white men. Of the traditional primary dialogues we find in an explicit sense only Ambwerk and Tuman, husband and wife, brother and sister, and community and the *ranguma* or odd man out, in the newer narratives. But we also find in these newer narratives the new man (Mambu) and the captain; the new man (Mambu) and the moral European (Mambu's employer or *masta*); the new man (Mambu) and the traditional man (the man who 'tried' Mambu, who was as a child).

Traditionally the preliminary synthesis was effected by becoming *mngwotngwotiki*, neither obliged nor unobliged, in stasis. And the same sort of stasis seems to be represented in the newer narratives in the relationship between the new man and the moral European: mutual obligedness to the point where each is as though *mngwotngwotiki* with the other. Nevertheless, such stases can only be preliminary stases. The storm, the unobliged *ranguma*, the captain, the fact that *mngwotngwotiki* cannot be preserved for long, and that men covet a reserve of power which will enable them to be self-willed and non-reciprocal—these features illustrate the representation that the singular cannot be fully contained within the terms of a stable community life. Indeed, if this singular and non-reciprocal power could be properly contained within, rather than excluded from, the moral community, then, one may suppose, that perfect synthesis which is incapable of improvement would be achieved and redemption made complete. But it remains that no moral system can abide the uninhibited singular. Such dynamic as exists in community life is due to the fact that a singular and non-reciprocal power cannot be wholly resolved or contained in moral terms. And in spite of efforts to exclude it, the singular enters in. So that, whilst the historical dialectic attempts a progress to that true or final synthesis which always lies one step beyond, the preliminary dialectic provides a temporary alternative synthesis within terms of a stable and unchanging tradition. Traditionally the storm, *puoker*, the *ranguma*, and other representations of the singular and self-willed impinged on community life so as to upset a given equilibrium: in the newer narratives it is the inimical captain who upsets a posited equilibrium between the new man and the moral European. In both cases a progress towards the preliminary dialectic is re-engaged, and an opportunity to engage the historical dialectic is offered. While friendship, which implies an easy partnership between equals, might have been used as a model to illustrate the relations between black men and white men, in fact we find Ambwerk and Tuman: a relationship in which, in Tangu terms, the strains and oppositions are inherently almost impossible to resolve. So that both the Duongangwongar and the Mambu narratives may be said to envisage a continuing historical dialectic.

As we have seen, the use in narratives of familiar and well-known things and categories brings a story within the field of apprehension. Particular signals solicit awareness, comprehensions follow. Of the fifty or so primary signals appearing in the traditional narratives[1] less than a dozen are retained intact in the new narratives[2] which, in turn, invite inspection of some forty Europeanisms.[3] None of the fourteen named characters[4] in the traditional narratives appear in the later ones: instead we are presented with Duongangwongar, Gundakar, and Mambu.[5] In the traditional narratives awareness of the meaning

[1] See Appendix I, 5.

[2] Areca-nut, coconut, fishing, ginger, cooking, storm, vomiting, pig, Ambwerk and Tuman, the *ranguma*-like fellow or odd man out (Duongangwongar, Mambu), the snake-like animal or *ramatzka*.

[3] Administration, aeroplane, Australia, authority, steel axehead, banker, canned goods, captain, cargo, chains, trade cloth, European clothing, contract labour, employer, engine, Europeans, gaol, inventiveness, jetty, kanaka, letter, Mambu's activities and sayings, Master, missionary, money, motor-car, motor-bike, New Guinea, pennies, pinnace, policeman, prison, razor blades, rice, Satan, shillings, ship, sin, writing. . . .

Because of the large numbers of synonyms in English this numeration can only be approximate.

[4] Borkei, Dumban (i), Dumban (ii), (Igoe'ika), Mariap, Maribun, Mazienengai, Nimbamung, (Nuakai), Nuok, Niangarai, Daroomi, Paki, Ruongaptiamkan, Namai, Wvawvasikai, Zawapai.

[5] Though the master, sister, and captain are categories rather than named characters, they may of course be included as named characters if it be thought convenient.

of male filiation is achieved mainly through the following: the storm, figuring uncontrolled power; stream, which represents the line of male filiation itself; rain, which is as semen; Namai the hawk, who nourishes or begets through his penis a germ of being which is already existent in the womb; a variety of refractions in the meaning and relevance of the penis, which, through Maribun, Dumban (i), Dumban (ii), and the snake-brothers reveal the close and interdependent association between male filiation and the *ranguma*; the relevances of a pig (or *ranguova*) caught in a *juaka* trap; Wvawvasikai, Zawapai, Maribun, and Mazienengai, who, in their various ways, relate an appropriate male filiation to siblingship through the *garamb*. Though no signal is unidirectional, the relevances of siblingship spring mainly from fire, which transforms instinct into culture; sunlight and day—awareness; mouth and lips—to form words; the adze, eyes, the snake-brothers, Kuokavalik, Maribun, Paki, Niangarai and Daroomi, Ruongaptiamkan, and orphans. On both hands the categories of the kin idiom and friendship, combined with the behavioural experience within them, provide a context which fills out the meaningful content of the signals. While the relevances of the *ranguma* are re-adumbrated in the *ranguma* stories, Maribun, likened to Satan, has common ground with the *ranguma* as the Devil; and through Dumban (ii) we see the power of the male poised between the *ranguma* and self-concern on the one hand, and an appropriate male filiation engaging with the values of siblingship on the other.

Finger- and thumb-sucking, sores on the buttocks which prohibit any further progress, roof, roof thatch, shelter, *garamb*, bamboo, barkcloth, breechclout, barkcloth mallet, bow and arrows, yam bin, trump, music, handdrum, spear, and slit-gong signal the male life cycle; and hawk, *juaka*, Maribun, Zawapai, Mazienengai Dumban (i), Dumban (ii), Nimbamung, Nuakai, Paki, Wvawvasikai, adze, pig, Ambwerk and Tuman, wife, brother and sister provide the processes of maturation with components in experience and awareness. Modelled as they are on the three primary metamorphoses of birth, death, and the passage of the *garamb*—each of which is an analogue of the others—the stages of maturation are also crises that the growing male may not be able to meet unless he is in some way aware of the problems involved. Stemming from the nature of

Tangu society, these problems each male as he grows into manhood must face and resolve if he is to become responsible, maintain his tradition, and hand on the values of his culture to the
succeeding generation. A *ranguma* does not see these problems
as other men do; for him the established modes of dealing
with them are naïve if not irrelevant. His awareness is singular
and undifferentiated, his appreciation of the collective awareness is critical and finally contemptuous. Because of that
power which is represented as being in him, which he obtains
through his father but which has not been informed with self-
restraint and an awareness of community requirements, the
ranguma, a self-exempted man, is a threat to the community
that an association of responsible men maintains. When they
are appropriately few in numbers such singular men mobilize
the community against themselves, and re-energize community
values by doing so. But when there are too many of them, as
happened in Tangu history, the traditional community begins
to disintegrate.

Not held responsible, freed from the burdens of political
decision, the female has a life cycle represented as relatively
void of crises. Generally subject to the male, female power is
not—as male power is—represented as subject to itself. Women
are the medium through whom men generate and maintain
culture. Without male supervision the female may become as
Nuakai, random and untrammelled. To bring the female to
order, boldness is required of a male. The role of the female
lies not so much in challenging, and so escaping or overcoming
the male, as in making sure that the almost inevitable surrender
is to a capacity worthy of that surrender. And by surrendering
to men, the culture bearers, women become a part of the cultural and moral community. Bird, banana, skirt, quim,
digging-stick, cooking-pot, cooking, and gardening reveal a
progress from the instinctual and wild to that domestication
by man which makes a woman into a good wife, a moral being
with something of the self-restraint which Tangu men have to
nurture and develop in themselves.

A coconut shoots from itself and reproduces progeny from
itself. Men nurture the nut in the open, in the porches of their
huts; and when the young palm sprouts, unfolds its fronds, and
is strong enough, men plant it in earth. The milk of the coconut

evokes both semen and breast milk; the whole nut evokes marriage; husband and wife make a reproducing unit, and so do *puoker* who are brother and sister. While the stem of an areca palm evokes penis, the nuts may be as testicles or maidens. Men have pairs of testicles, women have pairs of breasts. But the importance of testicles resides in their effect on the singular part between them: a husband is singular, wives come in pairs. Unlike a penis, a vulva is not singular. Actively receptive —Nuakai's may bite—it is moulded as a pair of lips: a mouth entered by a penis and fed with its milk, and out of which new lives, as relevant as words, may be brought into light. The colour red evokes the creative, is associated with the menstrual flow on the one hand, and the sexually mature male on the other. The head is the seat of the *gnek*, men and circumcised youths daub their head hair with reddened clay: they are culturally as well as sexually creative. Spittle is thought of as efficacious in itself, lime was taken from women by men. Lime is white. When a man is shamed and is aware of it he whitens his face with lime; white signifies thought and awareness. When areca-nut is chewed with lime, red spittle is secreted—a cycle of efficacies is generated: male thought and awareness combined, or in correspondence, with sexual creativity generate the cultural and moral.

Cane binds trees together, rings a *ranguma*'s pride, and also binds the posts, beams, joists, and rafters of a house or *garamb* building. The *garamb* binds men in responsible association, betrothed couples give each other cane circlets and waistbands, married couples are bound to each other in the household, Paki binds husband and wife to the garden, Paki is in the cane. Paki also binds brother and sister in garden produce, and in exchanging the produce of their gardens brother and sister are bound to each other. Any tree may be as phallus, and cutting trees, making fences, building houses, or carving are men's tasks. The snake is both as capable penis and, when men are bound in association in the *garamb*, as collective or social womb. Snake images the impulses and desires of self-willedness as well as the appropriate control of these desires and impulses. Snakes are found by streams, twist and turn in their movements like streams. A stream is white and creamy and fierce when in spate, effective maleness is found in, and comes from, the stream.

Women go to the stream to fish, to meet Dumban (ii), to find babies. Like fish and Dumban (ii), Maribun, Dumban (i), and Mazienengai come from the stream. Appropriately channelled, a stream is as the music of a trump, the promise of creativity realized. But when in flood a stream lays waste and destroys. A stream derives from the storm, and the storm is itself: a power which creates or destroys as it uninhibitedly exerts itself. Anger in men corresponds with the storm, and self-restraint and self-willedness correspond with the moods of a stream. Yet that part of the power of storm which inheres in men may be controlled, is subject to ordering itself: rain derives from the storm, men may make or check rain, rain fructifies garden crops as well as forest and weeds, rain is an image of semen, and rain is closely associated with *ranguova* who, as uncontrolled in principle as the storm or stream in spate, are thought to be more than normally sexually competent. Rain challenges Nuakai, signals the release of youths from her power, invites Ambwerk and Tuman into the *garamb* where they will learn an appropriate control of their maleness.

Both culture and life itself are represented in the traditional narratives as having been made possible, both in the beginning and with each succeeding generation, by that singular power which pertains to men or the male, and which is seen at its most awesome in the storm. In men this power is such that it can both bind and loose itself. And it is from the former, self-restraint, that culture and the moral community seem principally to spring. The stable pairings of community contained in the meaning of moral start with the incest taboo, the ordering of the sexual act. And change, whether in the sense of the preliminary or historical dialectics, flows from the creative singular. In its procedures analogous to, or representative of, the ordered sexual act and its fruitful consequences, the *garamb* seems to have so controlled male metamorphoses that it gave further relevance to the incest taboo, whilst at the same time gathering and ordering the relevances of storm. While it is possible to see the entire system of Tangu categories and symbols as generated and radiated by the consequences of contemplating the interrelations of meaning contained in the storm, the sexual act, and male metamorphosis, some may prefer to regard these three basic experiences as having been selected by a culture and social order which happened to exist as it did. On either view, however, the *garamb* emerges as playing the dominant institutional role in maintaining the culture and traditional social order.

The relevances of the storm and *garamb* persist today, but the *garamb* itself no longer exists and, in the relatively open society which Tangu now form, an ordering of the sexual act is not the imperative it was. In the Duongangwongar story the *garamb* is missing, and the listener is invited to consider a new or alternative mode of dealing with metamorphosis in the male, a new way of making a new kind of responsible man. The sexual act is ordered in terms of spouses whose natal communities are some distance apart: a comment on the increasingly popular practice of trying to find husbands and wives in more distant rather than in immediately neighbouring communities. The values of the open as opposed to the closed community are emphasized. Gundakar and the mother–son become the more significant when appreciated in the light of Christian teaching generally, but especially in relation to the Virgin Mary. Nor is it to be doubted that while Tangu women are playing a more important part in community affairs than they did, they will play an even more important part in the making of the new man. The children in N. 28, and Ambwerk in N. 23, claimed to have invented things on their own. But in fact they were taught by Dumban (ii) and father respectively. Did the Tuman of the Duongangwongar story really invent so many things on his own? Though some in Tangu feel that it was really 'God' who taught Tuman, and so Europeans, how to make and operate his various contrivances, others are uncertain, and a few—mainly those who feel that black men and white have quite different origins—incline to think that Tuman might really have invented them all by himself. . . . Still, since for most the mission has 'taken the place of the *garamb*', and since the mission also provides tradition with other continuities, the first alternative seems the more securely placed for development.

Of the traditional signals in the Duongangwongar tale, bird and banana are only marginally relevant. But a wife who cooks is relevant, and if bow and arrows and vomit and ginger are connected with storm, flood, stream, *ramatzka*, coconut, and the singular and *ranguma*-like male (Duongangwongar), one may well ask whether, given the general bias of Tangu narratives, in shooting his pig Duongangwongar—who had no father—was trying to capture a new, sure, and appropriate filiation for himself. With the Mambu story community values are represented in the master and his sister. And since these are Europeans they evoke not only a European kind of siblingship and community, but reinforce Mambu's association with a Christian or European kind of filiation. Both the new filiation and the new siblingship are figured as normatively non-reciprocal: subject to self-restraint. That is, while the mutually enforceable reciprocities typical of the subsistence economy and closed community may be seen as abandoned, yielding to reciprocities subject to self-restraint and the legal procedures characteristic of the complex economy and open society, the appropriate exercise of the singular, derived from an appropriate filiation, is given a wider field of relevance. Or, to put it more concretely, the new community will permit the new man an exercise of at least some of those qualities which are presently attached to the *ranguma* and excluded from what is appropriate to the moral community.

Of the traditional signals in the Mambu story, chewing areca-nut and the odd or *ranguma*-like man have their clear significances. There are also 'hiding', and 'axe' associated with money. In the traditional narratives people hide, or things are hidden, in places which evoke emergent kinds of being. And Mambu hides in a ship which is carrying cargo: he figures the emergent new man who will have cargo—European competences. In the narratives axes may be used by almost anybody, but generally by women, children, and youths: an axe does not signal a fully responsible man. Responsible men use spears. In the story an axe was bought with money by a traditional man who did not 'understand the things that Mambu understood', and who was 'like a child'. Mambu himself, on the other hand, claimed to have a proper understanding and awareness. He said that money would make Kanakas strong, he collected money, he articulated the outlines of the new man. As Mambu perhaps perceived, the white man's 'secret' is indeed money, money which differentiates and measures the parts of man.

Conclusion

A missionary familiar with Tangu once remarked over the dinner table that Tangu were 'devil worshippers'. And allowing for peculiarities of idiom he was right. For among Tangu, as indeed elsewhere, while the 'good' may be allowed to take care of itself, the 'bad' or evil hangs broody, moody, and wild. The good man emerges from a proper ordering of social relations, the good is a function or product of that ordering, conformity with the implications of the ordering of the moral community implies the good man, restraint and sense of obligation define what is meant by moral. The problem of the singular, on the other hand, must command constant attention. And since among Tangu expressions of the singular are almost always regarded as 'bad', the attention that they give to the 'bad' often looks very like worship. Lacking those necessary rituals which tend to exclude what is 'bad' in the singular by bringing what is 'good' into cognizance, Tangu cannot but be more concerned with the 'bad' than they are with that 'good' which could transcend a current balance of reciprocal arrangements. It is not only Tangu who jump to the conclusion that an act of self-willedness is probably 'bad' rather than 'good'. Evil is wild and unordered, may make its presence evident anywhere at any time. So that while happy conformists are 'good' because they make no trouble, non-conformists are apt to cause trouble and are therefore 'bad'.

With the coming of the mission Tangu have had their attention drawn to more positive ideas of the good, and Christian charity surely differentiates qualities of badness. That Christianity, peculiarly associated with the one-and-the-many and with redemption in historical terms, should have intruded on Tangu when it did seems apposite and fitting. At a moment when Tangu were being forced by circumstances to accept and then legitimize varying expressions of the singular and self-willed at the expense of their binary categories, Europeans came and gave added impetus to the process. At the same time, if community life was to be preserved Tangu could not but abide the more fiercely by equivalent reciprocities. The qualities of storm and becoming *mngwotngwotiki* became the more acutely opposed, singular and pairs were forced wider and wider apart.

And, since the reconciliation of singular and pairs connotes in our terms the final synthesis, final redemption, this is another way of characterizing what may be meant by anomy. Yet despite the priority given to redemption in terms of becoming *mngwotngwotiki*, the preliminary dialectic, so far as we have knowledge of them Tangu have been acting out the terms of a historical dialectic, the reconciliation of the pairs with the singular. With the passage of time, as Tangu have become more and more familiar with varieties of expression of the singular, encountering quantities of singular things which cannot be fitted into their binary scheme, so the categories of pairings have begun to loosen, singular and pairings have drawn closer together. Tangu cargo activities, which embraced Christian or European ideas and differentiations as well as traditional modes, represent fleeting and temporary climaxes to the onward progress of the historical dialectic.

Since a dialectic implies oppositions and conflicts, the process of imposing an ordered coherence on the varieties of expressions of cultural life can be neither smooth nor short. In rationalizing their activities and experience to themselves through their narratives, Tangu seem to have been particularly aware of variations on the Oedipus theme. Accepting that there must have been several alternative ways of organizing their economic and political life, traditionally they seem to have made such arrangements as were necessary to accommodate what they perceived as prior realities. As between father (husband), mother (wife), son (brother, Ambwerk and Tuman), and daughter (sister), the impulsive vitalities of youth were controlled, and disaster and the untimely destruction of both individuals and culture itself are represented as held at bay, by an appropriate male filiation, the mother's brother, and the institutional life—particularly circumcision and the *garamb*. And that Tangu still tend to make much the same major premise is borne out by the newer narratives. Yet it is clear that the traditional binary discriminations required to control the probabilities of singular action which arise from Tangu oedipal relations will not suffice in the new environment. The open society, money, and the habitual exercise of singular qualities require that the energies released in having children, who have to become adult, be both controlled and utilized in an ambience determined not by kinsfolk, friends, and *ranguova*, but by legislative assembly, law courts, and policemen.

Though Tangu comprehensions of their general condition and prospects still seem a long way behind their apprehensions, they are beginning to distinguish their parts, beginning to differentiate and realize different kinds of 'good' and 'bad', beginning to appreciate that in the open society where cargo is obtainable every man must be prepared not only to exercise his singular qualities, but to recognize and accept their exercise in others. For the moment equivalent reciprocities and the allocation of prestige and influence within the community, as an agglutinated 'package deal', draw the divide. Yet Mambu pointed to the way across. Let money differentiate the parts and measure the man. That this will bring its own problems and difficulties goes without saying. But if Tangu want cargo they will have to put up with them.

APPENDIX I

NARRATIVE SIGNALS

Summary index of the main signals, characters, and elements in the conversation between Tangu narratives and other aspects of culture

1. GENERAL LIST

Administration: Europeanism; authoritative; local village officials confirmed in appointment by (N. 31).

Adze: tool or weapon for cutting, carving, slashing, planing, incising, and butchering; carried by men on shoulders on ceremonial occasions as symbols of responsibility and maturity; raised threateningly by mother's brother when encountering sister's son; evokes the cross-relationships between the generations, mother's brother, siblingship, the appropriate and responsible relation between filiation and siblingship (N. 4, 6, 10, 13, 21, 22, 25, 29).

Aeroplane: Europeanism; capacity to manufacture; Tuman (as European) makes (N. 30).

Ambwerk and Tuman (brothers): primary dialogue; Ambwerk responsible for guiding Tuman into reciprocal behaviour and responsibility; Tuman recalcitrant but with more initiative; Ambwerk as black men, Tuman as white men; siblings with common filiation; imbalance of singular and pairs (N. 4, 5, 6, 9, 10, 23, 24, 30).

Ambwerk and Tuman (brothers and sisters): imbalance of singular and pairs (N. 9).

Ambwerk and Tuman (sisters): may be killed on the one hand, appropriately become co-wives on the other; the pairings of siblingship and community (N. 9, 22, 24, 29).

Anger (and synonyms): analogous to storm; predicative of change; examples the singular (almost all narratives, particularly N. 1, 7, 10, 12, 23, 24, 25, 27, 28, 29, 31).

Anus: clean anus or buttocks qualifies for responsibility; sores on anus or buttocks disqualify for entry into the *garamb* (N. 11, 25).

Areca-nut: stimulant, may cause faint drunkenness; efficacious; makes red spittle when chewed with lime, redness is creative; maidens, testicles; men put areca-nuts on *pekas* when reasserting reciprocities (N. 4, 6, 7, 8, 13, 23, 28, 29, 31).

Areca palm: young but competent penis or phallus (N. 22).

Armband, armlet: of woven *kunai* grass, plain; of woven cane dyed red and black; may throttle penis (N. 15).

Arrows: *see* Bow and.

Ash: substitute for lime; saltwood burnt to; fertilizer for garden; may evoke the predicative or creative or fertile (N. 7, 24, 26, 29).

Australia: Europeanism; where cargo comes from; where Mambu goes (N. 31).

Axe: for cutting trees, making gardens; male or female may use; formerly of stone, now steel bought from stores; man buys axe with money supplied by Mambu; erasing singular, evokes immature responsibility (N. 4, 5, 11, 13, 26, 29, 31).

Baldness: caused by being struck with digging-stick; bald people, *gagai mnamnier*, come out of hole first (N. 25).

Bamboo: used as containers for water, sago flour, fermented chestnuts, feathers, decorations, personal trinkets; used for carrying and steam-cooking meat and tubers; makes razors, torches, trumps; evokes circumcision, maturation, metamorphosis, becoming man, mother's brother, the responsible in man (N. 1, 3, 4, 5, 6, 9, 13, 21, 22, 23, 29).

Banana: fronds used for making women's underskirts; foreskin thrown into clump of; evokes the female and femaleness, the wild, random, or instinctual (N. 4, 6, 7, 10, 23, 24, 26, 27, 30).

Barkcloth: for breechclouts, padding in carrier bags, climbing trees; made by males, by streams; evokes sexually mature males (N. 4, 12, 22, 29). *See* Breechclout.

Barkcloth mallet: for making barkcloth; evokes sexually mature males, or males becoming sexually mature; indicates onset of responsibility (N. 4, 22).

Bird: evokes maidens; as mother's brothers (N. 29); in Duongang-wongar story a dead youth (N. 5, 7, 10, 22, 23, 29, 30).

Bird of Paradise: plumes worn by men as head decorations at dances and ceremonies; golden or red-brown (*paradisea apodea, paradisea rubra*); evokes maidens, competence in males and readiness for wives; mother's brother (N. 8, 10, 23, 25, 27, 28, 29).

Black: *ranguova* alleged to blacken faces; spears blackened for war; night; death; unawareness; Maribun calls on black rain clouds (N. 18, 25).

Blindness: evokes the socially unaware (N. 6). *See* Eyes.

Boan: orange-coloured fruit, stands for pig (N. 27).

Boar's tusks: decorative pendant on chest, sole or paired, bound together in string-work base; worn by men; women may wear (N. 25, 28).

Bow and arrows: for hunting birds and small game; associated with boys or youths; evokes young but sexually mature and desirous male (N. 2, 6, 10, 22, 23, 24, 25, 27, 29, 30).

Bowls: of wood, carved, incised; eating vessels; given by brothers to sisters on marriage; coconut spines put in bottom of (N. 4, 27, 29).

Breadfruit: cultivated or wild tree with edible fruit; evokes sexual intercourse (N. 5, 11, 24).

Breechclout: worn by circumcised males wound round and knotted over cane waistband; evokes sexual competence in males (N. 5, 8, 15, 17, 20, 22, 24, 25, 29).

Br'ngun'guni: moral process; maintains reciprocities (N. 25).

Brother and sister: as humans may not marry, as *puoker* form unions; relationship evokes overcoming of impulse, responsibilities of siblingship, stasis of *mngwotngwotiki*, incest taboo (N. 1, 9, 10, 25, 26, 27, 29, 31). *See* Orphans.

Brothers: helpers, co-operators (N. 4, 13, 18, 19, 22, 24). *See* Ambwerk and Tuman (brothers).

Burn: to destroy; destruction of that wild stuff from which awareness may spring; hence burning of forest litter for garden site, burning of blind, careless, and non-reciprocal (N. 6, 9, 24, 26, 29). *See* Fire.

Cane: for binding house-posts, *garamb* posts; for making waistbands, wristlets, anklets, armlets; evokes marriage, circumcision, men in association in the *garamb* (N. 10, 22, 25, 26, 27, 28, 29).

Canned goods: Europeanism; Tuman makes; evokes cargo (N. 30, 31).

Cannibalism: strangers or *ranguova* or enemies (i.e. non-moral beings) may be eaten; evokes the unrestrained (sexual) appetite (N. 14, 20, 21, 24).

Captain: European, non-reciprocal, singular, shows anger (N. 31).

Cargo: Europeanism; European goods; evokes European competences, abilities, and definitions of manhood (N. 30, 31).

Cassowary: flightless bird; source of meat and feathers; bones used as knives or daggers; evokes premature sexual assault (?), onset of pubes; but responsible men also kill in life; towards the responsible (N. 9, 25, 28, 29, 30).

Charm: effective, efficacious (N. 6, 11, 17, 19, 21).

Cipnangk'der: small snake; evokes small boy or uncircumcised youth coming into sexual maturity (N. 9, 27).

Children: wild or divine or instinctual; not responsible; parents' responsibility (N. 2, 3, 7, 8, 23, 28). *See* Children (small boys), Children (small girls).

Children (small boys): evokes relationship between father and mother (husband and wife) (N. 2, 7, 12, 13, 16, 26, 27, 28).

Children (small girls): evokes relationship between father and mother (husband and wife), portends wife (N. 7, 27).

Cloth: Europeanism; Tuman makes; Mambu is given (N. 30, 31).

Cockerel: heralds the dawn; evokes emergent awareness, reciprocities, community (N. 1, 11, 25, 29).

Coconut: milk and meat eaten, fronds may be used for making roof thatch; evokes marriage; reproductive unit; conjunction of male and female elements; appropriate conjunction of reciprocal and non-reciprocal; containment of singular; appropriate conjunction of values in filiation and values in siblingship; fecundity, fertility, the female treated by the male, emergent community (N. 3, 6, 12, 14, 25, 26, 27, 29, 30).

Colon: *see* Intestines.

Comb: made of bamboo; evokes onset of sexual maturity (N. 29).

Conch: blown at circumcision ceremony; evokes onset of responsible sexual maturity (N. 29).

Contract labour: Europeanism; cash obtained from (N. 31).

Cooking: processing of foodstuffs by responsible persons; in clay pots, bamboo barrels, or direct on fire; evokes community relations; wives cook for husbands, sisters cook for brothers (N. 3, 7, 10, 11, 25, 27, 28, 29, 30).

DAROOMI: a friend; evokes friendship, through *br'ngun'guni* the values of siblingship related to the singular; evokes the group within which reciprocities are observed in opposition to the outsider with whom reciprocities are not normal (except through friendship); *ranguma*-like (N. 25, 27).

Dawn: the start of the day; evokes the start of awareness and community (N. 8, 9, 10, 22, 24, 29).

Day, daylight: day sees the community actively engaging community relationships, aware; evokes awareness (N. 2, 6). *See* Night.

Death: evokes the finish of one mode of being (occurs directly or by implication in all narratives, except in N. 8, 12, 13, 15, 22, 31).

Deception: may occur within any relationship (all narratives, particularly N. 2, 3, 4, 5, 6, 7, 9, 10, 11, 12, 13, 15, 17, 19, 22, 25, 26, 27, 28, 29, 31).

Decoration: pertains to the responsible (N. 2, 3, 8, 10, 11, 22, 23, 25, 27, 28, 29).

Defecation: animal act; evokes non-responsibility, the wild, improper sexual relations (N. 2, 4, 5, 24).

Descendants: come out of hole after being hidden underground (N. 25, 27).

Digging-stick: implement for planting tubers, used by male or female; woman's weapon; evokes wife (the female with male virtues), or the most nearly responsible female, or singular and non-reciprocal female; ambivalent (N. 11, 23, 25, 27).

Dog: hunting companion; pertains to the male; not wholly effective when managed by Nuakai (N. 4, 6, 23, 25, 27).

Dogs' teeth: woven into string-based plaques for wearing on chest or forehead; bridewealth; decoration signifying entry into community responsibilities (N. 10, 11, 29).

Door: fitted to houses and *garamb*; marks division between the responsible on the one hand, and the wild or impulsive or instinctual on the other (N. 2, 6, 16, 22, 29).

Doubling back: father's or responsible man's stratagem (N. 6, 19, 22, 29).

Dream: technique for solving a problem (N. 11, 12, 22, 26, 30).

DUMBAN (i): awareness in a male; the singular in a male (N. 27).

DUMBAN (ii): the two sides of the exercise of the singular by the male; *ranguma* and appropriate male filiation; babies and dances provided by; pleasures women-in-community, wives (N. 28).

DUONGANGWONGAR: odd or singular or *ranguma*-like male from whose rotting body the creative 'snake' or *ramatzka* fish and storm proceed (N. 30).

Earth: wild and cultivated plants grow from; female element; potentially fruitful; responsibility is above ground, the wild or instinctual below ground (N. 4, 5, 6, 19, 22, 25, 27).

Earthquake: result of Mngungerp's activity; results from God's activity; may result from King of England shifting in chair;

powerful and singular act; destructive/creative; reverses or separates divine and moral beings (N. 1, 12, 24, 29, 30).

Employer: *see* Master.

Engine: Europeanism; Tuman fits in pinnace (N. 30).

Eyes: to see with; in pairs; evoke awareness/unawareness (N. 2, 4, 6, 8, 13, 22, 23, 25, 27, 29).

Face: *Ranguova* have blackened faces; shamed man who is thinking whitens his face; Maribun and Dumban have decorated faces (N. 18, 25, 27, 28).

Faeces: *see* Defe   .

Fairywoman: female *puok*; hospitable to children; only allows a few to see the light of day (N. 2).

Father and daughter: dialogue; relationship leads into inevitable marriage of daughter no matter what father does; but may lead into death if not into appropriate marriage (N. 9, 22, 25, 27, 29).

Father and son: dialogue; appropriate passage of singular being; initial placement; made appropriate through *garamb* and circumcision by mother's brother; alternating phases of opposition re-aggregation; normative but non-reciprocal relationship (N. 7, 10, 11, 12, 13, 17, 19, 24, 25, 27, 28, 29).

Fear: expressed in face of non-reciprocal, coming change, or metamorphosis (N. 12, 15, 18, 22, 23, 24, 25, 27, 28, 29, 30).

Feast: expression of reciprocities/singular or non-reciprocal (N. 10, 12, 13, 22, 23, 25, 28).

Fellow: synonym for phallus or penis. *See* Penis.

Ficus: large tree with board roots and twining branches; board roots evoke shelter or *garamb*, twining branches evoke snake; father-provider, Zawapai, comes from ficus as snake (N. 24).

Fingers: evoke breast nipple/penis or phallus; but fingers are in two pairs, and the thumb is singular (N. 4, 21, 29). *See* Thumb.

Fire (firestick, firebrand, firewood): for cooking, forest cleared by fire; evokes cultural and community life, responsibility, excision of wild or impulsive or instinctual life, so that culture and responsibility may obtain (N. 2, 5, 8, 15, 23, 24, 25, 27, 29, 30).

Fish, fishing: women fish with nets, men with hardwood or bamboo spears; evokes the creative, sexual intercourse, marriage, babies, community life (N. 1, 2, 3, 7, 9, 25, 27, 28, 29, 30).

Flood: *see* Storm.

Food, foodstuffs: for eating, exchanging; evokes community, reciprocities (N. 1, 2, 6, 11, 24, 25, 26, 29, 31). *See* Feast.

Forest: the wild and non-cultural; evokes animal or wild or instinctual or impulsive life (N. 5, 6, 8, 9, 10, 11, 12, 13, 14, 15, 16, 17, 18, 19, 20, 21, 22, 23, 24, 25, 27, 29, 30).

Friends: dialogue; evokes reciprocal/non-reciprocal; marriage, children (N. 8, 25, 27, 28).

GAGAI: exogamous category (N. 26, 29).

Gagai: exogamous group (N. 25, 27).

Galip: wild almond tree, reddish nuts; evokes the creative in relation to sex relations, crops, marriage, community; creativity comes from male filiation (N. 24, 29).

Game: *see* Meat.

Games: 'Ranguma' game; spinning tops into coconut spines (N. 3).

Gaol: Europeanism; Mambu is put into (N. 31).

Garamb: men's clubhouse; boys served apprenticeship in; boys circumcised in; shrine of community; reconciled values of siblingship and filiation; evoked by bamboo, shelter, cave, roof, roof thatch, and other signals (N. 4, 5, 10, 16, 22, 25, 27, 28, 29).

Garden: for growing crops in; associated with female; as female; men have to work in or on to make fruitful; evokes values of culture and community (N. 3, 4, 10, 15, 19, 22, 23, 24, 26, 29).

Garden fence: protects garden from wild things; evokes division between culture and wild (N. 10, 25, 26).

Garden shelter: small but stoutly built hut in gardens; used for storing foodstuffs; sometimes lived in for short periods (N. 15).

Gemban: odorous tree; evokes latrine and smells of bodily effusions (N. 4).

Ginger: medicinal herb; evokes revivification (N. 19, 24, 30).

Golden, golden-red-brown: golden plume evokes full awareness; golden-red-brown less mature (N. 23). *See* Bird of Paradise.

Gourd: used as lime containers; men's long, evoking phallus; women's globular, evoking breasts (N. 7).

Grandmother: *see* Nuakai.

Grave: dead put into; evokes change of mode of being (N. 1, 2, 3, 4, 23, 29, 30).

Great one: (Igoe'ika); sends storm (N. 1).

Growing huge: evokes change, phallic potential, growth of community (N. 3, 9, 15, 22, 25, 27, 29, 30).

GUNDAKAR: mother of Duongangwongar; new female effectiveness (N. 30).

Hair: *ranguma* grasped by and thrown; red pigment put on; letter put into Mambu's; *gnek* is under (N. 16, 31).

Handdrum: centrally constricted (hour-glass shaped); open at bottom end; monitor-lizard-skin membrane fitted by means of resinous adhesive; 'buttons' of bread-fruit seed stuck on membrane; played at dances by youths and adult men; evokes budding responsibility (N. 8, 22, 24, 29).

Hawk: *see* NAMAI.

Head: seat of *gnek*; appropriate use of is creative within community (N. 4, 6, 19, 20, 27, 30). *See* Hair.

Hiding-place: Hiding-place and that which is hidden evoke what is to be (e.g. trump in roof thatch); evokes process of metamorphosis (N. 7, 8, 9, 10, 11, 12, 13, 17, 18, 19, 22, 23, 24, 25, 27, 28, 29, 31).

Hole: crucible of emergent being; through which one form of being may view or enter another (N. 4, 5, 6, 11, 19, 23, 25, 27, 30).

Hollow tree: refuge of wild and excluded (N. 1, 4, 11).

Home (house): abode of responsible/non-responsible being (N. 2, 6, 8, 11, 12, 13, 22, 25, 27, 29).

Hornbill: bird; as mother's brother; evokes emergent responsibility and reciprocities (N. 29, 30).

Hunger: evokes dissatisfaction with, or inappropriateness of, a present mode of being (N. 1, 2, 3, 4, 5, 11, 24, 26, 29).

Hunting: male task; successful hunter qualifies for sexual intercourse and wife (N. 3, 4, 5, 6, 7, 10, 11, 12, 13, 21, 22, 24, 25, 28, 29).

Hunting-lodge: men retire to alone for thought and hunting; evokes *ranguova* (N. 14, 17, 18).

Husband and wife: appropriate responsible relationship of male and female in community; many vicissitudes within (N. 3, 4, 7, 8, 10, 11, 12, 13, 15, 19, 20, 22, 23, 24, 25, 26, 27, 28, 29, 30).

Igom: where Namai, Mazienengai go (N. 29). *See* Map 2.

Intestines: women were made from; evokes the female, femaleness (N. 4, 23, 24, 29).

Iwarum: stream beside which Mazienengai sits in *galip* (N. 29). *See* Map 2.

Iwop: ridge which leads from Tangu to Andarum; where Wvawvasikai was found and killed (N. 23).

Jetty (quay): evokes transition from one mode of being to another (N. 30, 31).

Juaka: deadfall pig-trap, built like house; evokes male being, passage of male being (N. 14, 29).

Juangam: harvest dance, in which men, women, and children participate together (N. 3, 8, 22, 28).

KUOKAVALIK: small snake; snake-man; grows large in pleasure (N. 9, 24, 27).

Language: father gives; ability to communicate (N. 29).

Letter: Europeanism; Tuman sends to Ambwerk; in Mambu's hair, keeps him safe (N. 30, 31).

Lightning: *see* Storm.

Lime: white, chewed with areca-nut produces red spittle; evokes creative thought, awareness (N. 7, 23, 27, 28).

Lips: represent awareness (N. 2, 13, 22). *See* Mouth.

Lizard: animal evocative of youthful creativeness; penis (N. 5, 19, 23, 24, 27, 29).

Maidens: as areca-nuts, birds, birds of paradise; meet to become wives, or revert to the wild (N. 7, 8, 10, 22, 24, 28).

Man: *see* Penis.

MAMBU: cargo activist, new man (N. 31).

MARIBUN: total awareness in male (N. 25).

Marriage: forbidden between humans who are brother and sister; *puoker* who are brother and sister may marry or form unions; preferred marriage between father's sister's son and mother's brother's daughter, between offspring of friends; basis of community life; evokes community reciprocities, containment of singular (N. 1, 8, 10, 22, 24, 25, 26, 27, 28, 29).

Master: Europeanism; moral European (N. 31).

MAZIENENGAI: male filiation; passage of male being; reconciliation of filiation and siblingship; brother-and-sister/husband-and-wife (N. 29).

Meat: necessary protein (makes milk in penis and breasts); game, domesticated pigs, slain enemies; makes men strong; evokes the responsible man who gets meat for his family; necessary for feasts (N. 2, 3, 4, 5, 6, 10, 11, 12, 13, 14, 22, 25, 29).

Medicines: for making well, revival; for changing state of being (N. 18, 19, 24).

Milk: powerful stuff; from penis, breast, coconut (N. 26, 29).

Missionary: Europeanism; reports Mambu to administration (N. 31).

Mother: responsible female; contains 'germ of being'; must be worked on by husband (particularly N. 3, 9, 27).

Mother's brother: male on the female side; inducts males into responsibilities of siblingship; figured as bird; link between lines of male and female filiation (N. 10, 23, 27, 29, 30).

Mother and children: may be united against father; children re-unite mother and father (N. 13, 22, 29).

Mother and daughter: act together (N. 10, 29).

Mother and son: mutual attachment; mother raises son initially; necessary parting in favour of father, wife (N. 11, 19, 22, 23, 25, 28, 29, 30).

Motor car: Europeanism; Tuman makes (N. 30).

Mouth: from which words (thoughts) issue through a pair of lips; articulates awareness (N. 2, 13, 22).

Music: made with trump; evokes sexual competence, babies in womb, emergent community responsibilities (N. 22, 29).

NAMAI (hawk): appropriate fatherhood; male and female parts (N. 29).

New Guinea: Europeanism; Mambu returns to (N. 31).

NIANGARAI: friend of Daroomi; flees to Biampitzir (N. 25, 27).

Night: proper time for moral beings to sleep; *ranguma* works at; divine elements work during; sphere of divine (N. 8, 9, 14, 15, 22, 24, 28, 29).

NIMBAMUNG: blind man who lives underground; evokes un-awareness, instinctual, chance (N. 6).

Nipple: from which nourishing milk comes; evokes penis or phallus; creativity and nourishment (N. 15, 22, 24, 29).

Nostrils: salt water and *ramatzka* fish found in; storm comes from (N. 30).

NUAKAI: grandmother; hypostatic female; female with male elements; may join husband and wife (N. 4, 5, 7, 8, 23, 27).

Orphans: unconnected with preceding order by kinship, start new order (N. 1, 25, 26, 29).

Own ('all on my/our . . .'): inventiveness; on part of children, Tuman, Ambwerk (N. 23, 28, 30).

PAKI: in the cane; binds male and female as husband and wife; binds husband and wife to garden and crops; binds men in *garamb*; evokes responsibilities of siblingship for the male (N. 26).

Parents and children: non-reciprocal but normative relationship in which elder must care for younger; parents may learn from children (N. 2, 3, 28).

Pekas: dancing and feasting space in *mwenk* or settlement; evokes reciprocities (N. 7, 8, 15, 16, 22, 23).

Penis (or phallus): male sexual organ from which seminal milk or fluid comes; various synonyms such as man, fellow, tool, etc. (rarely explicitly mentioned, usually in form of 'they copulated'; but explicit in N. 22, 25, 27, 28, 29).

Pennies: Europeanism; Mambu collects (N. 31).

Pepper: effective medicine (N. 19, 23, 24).

Pieces (cut into small): exclusion of wild or divine; transformation of wild or divine or impulsive or instinctive into cultural and responsible (N. 4, 5, 6, 9, 14, 17, 21, 23, 25, 27, 28).

Pigeon: bird; shot through privates with bow and arrow; encourages pleasure; like all birds evokes the responsibilities and irresponsibilities of mating and marriage (N. 25).

Pig: meat; men made from flesh, women from intestines; sacrificial animal; transmission of male being; transformation of instinctual and impulsive into responsible; transformation of singular into reciprocal (N. 1, 2, 3, 4, 5, 6, 7, 10, 12, 14, 17, 18, 19, 20, 22, 25, 27, 28, 29, 30).

Pinnace: Europeanism; Tuman makes (N. 30).

Planting: by divine intervention (N. 24, 26).

Platform: body of Duonganwongar placed on (N. 30).

Pleasure (to have sexual intercourse with): Ambwerk and Tuman, their wives all night through (N. 10); Ruongaptiamkan, the wild woman (N. 11); *ranguma* attempts woman in woodpile (N. 15); youth, two maidens, all night, alternate nights (N. 22); Tuman, Ambwerk's wife in garden; inappropriately an appetite (N. 24); brother and sister (N. 25, 26, 27); mother's brother and sister's son's wife (N. 27); Dumban, women in two lines (N. 28); Fellow, pairs of maidens (N. 28); Mazienengai, all night for ten nights (N. 29). Many other instances.

Poison: *ranguma* brings with him from hole (N. 25).

Policeman: Europeanism; in awe of Mambu (N. 31).

Pots: clay by coil method; made mainly by women; pertains to women as wives; evokes responsibilities of siblingship (N. 4, 5, 6, 8, 23, 24, 27, 30).

Prison: *see* Gaol.

Prophesy: concerning coming war which Mambu makes (N. 31).

Quay: cargo on for Mambu; evokes transition from one kind of being to another (N. 30, 31).

Quim: female sexual organ; snakes, fellows, cock's feather, lizard enter; may circumcise (N. 4, 9, 11, 15, 23, 24, 25, 27, 28).

Rabaul: in New Britain; where Mambu worked (N. 31).

Rafters: *see* Roof.

Rain: derives from storm; under some control of men; may be as semen; generative (N. 1, 2, 4, 9, 12, 14, 15, 24, 25, 27). *See* Storm.

Rak'mba: dance taught by Dumban (ii); daylight dance; satirical; evokes responsibility/non-responsibility (N. 28).

Ramatzka: big snake-like fish killed in Duongangwongar's nostrils (N. 30).

Ranguma: odd or singular person, non-reciprocal (N. 14, 15, 16, 17, 18, 19, 20, 25).

Rat: the abode of the dead female (N. 5, 21).

Razor blades: Europeanism; given to Mambu (N. 31).

Red: men coat head hair with reddened clay, put on skin; from pandanus fruit and red ochreous rock; goodness, effectiveness, fertility, creativity (N. 7, 22, 23, 25, 27, 28, 29).

Red-brown: bird of paradise plume; bravery; between 'golden' (responsible) and 'black' (non-reciprocal) (N. 23).

Revenge: reassertion of reciprocities by responsible men (N. 4, 5, 6, 23, 28); as vindictiveness by non-responsible (N. 15, 19).

Revive: by magical means (N. 18, 19); into community (N. 2).

Rice: Europeanism; given to Mambu (N. 31).

Rock: *see* Stone.

Roof (roof thatch, rafters): of sago or coconut fronds; evokes house or *garamb* (N. 5, 13, 22, 25, 27, 29).

Rumeyep: where bushes with Wvawvasikai's blood are (N. 23).

RUONGAPTIAMKAN: sexual adventurer who knows the limits, awareness (N. 11).

Sago: palm from whose fronds roof thatch is usually made; evokes phallus, *garamb*, responsibilities, awareness (N. 4, 20, 27, 29).

Salt water: in Duongangwongar's nostrils (N. 30).

Saltwood: Ambwerk and Tuman put in Nimbamung's pot; Zawapai burns to ash to make son vomit (N. 6, 24).

Sasa'nyipitek: bush where Wvawvasikai was killed (N. 23).

Satan: compared with Maribun (N. 25).

Sea: Europeanism; Tuman uses, Mambu might have been thrown into (N. 30, 31).

Secret: means of access to Cargo; what Europeans have and Mambu might discover (N. 31).

Sexual intercourse: *see* Pleasure.

Shame: evokes appropriate/inappropriate sexual intercourse (N. 25, 26).

Shelter: evokes *garamb*, reciprocity/non-reciprocity (N. 1, 2, 4, 10, 12, 14, 15, 24, 29).

Shell: conch, formerly used as trumpet in *garamb* ceremonial; gold-lip-oyster and others as breast pendants, or attached to bags and pouches (N. 23).

Shield: of wood, carved from the solid; incised; large rectangular ($4 \times 1\frac{1}{2}$ ft.); offensive/defensive weapon; responsible man uses (N. 20, 23).

Shilling: Europeanism; Mambu produces stick of (N. 31).

Ship: Europeanism; Tuman builds; breaks jetty; Mambu stows away on (N. 30, 31).

Sickness: *ranguma* brings (N. 25).

Sign: Europeanism; Mambu's cargo marked with such and such a sign (N. 31).

Sin: *pekato*; Europeanism; brother and sister in pleasure (N. 25).

Sisters: *see* Ambwerk and Tuman (sisters).

Skirt: made from banana, or pandanus fibres; worn by women; evokes the female; manhood found in (N. 4, 9, 10, 22, 24, 25, 28).

Sky: abode of the divine (N. 7, 25, 26, 29).

Slit-gong: instrument for making publications; evokes responsibility, the responsible man (N. 3, 4, 8, 10, 12, 13, 14, 22, 23, 24, 29).

Sliver (of bamboo): used as razor for shaving and circumcision. *See* Bamboo.

Smoke: brother nervous of smoke from fire; blots out sun (N. 27, 29).

Smelly: evokes the unclean, animal, or wild, not responsible (N. 1, 4).

Snake: representative of community, the *garamb*; conjoins male and female elements; appropriate containment of the singular in the male conjoined with the female; but, principally male, may go wild (N. 9, 17, 23, 24, 25, 27).

Son: *see* Father and, Mother and.

Song: evokes the creative (N. 28, 29).

Sores: generally signifies lack of integrity, awareness (N. 11, 25). *See* Smelly.

Spear: adult man's weapon; sign of responsible man (N. 4, 5, 6, 10, 12, 14, 15, 17, 19, 22, 23, 24, 25, 28, 29, 30).

Spell: *see* Charm.

Spittle: efficacious, especially after chewing areca-nut with lime (N. 6, 7, 17, 23).

Stomach: pertains to the female; incubator of emergent being (N. 2, 4, 9, 13, 22, 23, 24, 27, 29).

Stones: abodes of *puoker* when in the wild; evokes the permanent or lasting, the transition from a wild or instinctual or impulsive life to the cultural and responsible (N. 1, 2, 3, 12, 22, 25, 27, 29).

Storm: includes earthquake, thunder, lightning; uncontrollable, unbifurcated; but rain which is part of, and which derives from storm, is controllable; storm heralds change of being; creative; transition from divine to moral (N. 1, 2, 9, 12, 14, 15, 24, 25, 27, 29, 310).

String, string bags: string made by women; for making carrier bags, pouches, plaques, caps, masks; for use in string-figures illustrating narratives; for marking garden plots; pertains to the female; evokes the female, engagement of male and female in community, community life (N. 4, 5, 6, 7, 8, 10, 12, 18, 22, 24, 25, 27, 28, 29, 30).

Stream: derives from storm, rain; evokes maleness, from which maleness comes, line of male filiation; women go to stream for babies, husbands (N. 1, 2, 3, 4, 7, 8, 12, 15, 22, 23, 25, 27, 28, 29).

Sugar-cane: evokes childishness, the wild, the not responsible, the not responsible pregnancy (N. 9, 24).

Sun: awareness and responsibility, emergent awareness and responsibility; new gardens in the making, breechclouts drying in, male and female about to marry in rays of (N. 2, 8, 24, 25, 26, 29).

Tangked palm: placed on graves; evokes death, passage of being (N. 24).

Testicles: may be as areca-nuts; bifurcated male (N. 20, 25).

Thorns: evoke circumcision; so also nettles, stinging things (N. 24).

Thumb: singular element of hand; where fingers are paired and may represent lines of male and female filiation, and are reasonably effective, the thumb, singular, is the positive element which clinches matters (N. 4, 29).

Thunder: *see* Storm.

Tops: made from a dried rind of jungle fruits, particularly *boan*, pierced with a pointed peg; used for games; B–1957(*b*) (N. 3).

Traps: *see Juaka.*

Trump: or Jew's harp; made from segment of bamboo, pear-shaped; for making music; evokes transition to becoming father and more responsible (N. 13, 22, 29).

Try: man goes to 'try' Mambu, to see if he is genuine (N. 31).

Tuman: *see* Ambwerk and Tuman.

Turds: *see* Defecate.

Underground: descendants are; evokes the divine or covert or wild or impulsive or instinctual 'other side' of life (N. 25, 27).

Urinate: childish or wild or animal act; but has efficacy (N. 3, 10, 17).

Village: abode of culture, community life, morality (all narratives).

Vinga: tree from which house-posts and *garamb* posts are made; in which Ambwerk and Tuman find safety (N. 4).

Vomit: evokes change of being (N. 24, 29, 30).

Vulva (and various synonyms): *see* Quim.

Wamunga: shrub or bush; door to Nimbamung's *mwenk* (N. 6). *See* Door.

War: Mambu prophesies coming of (N. 31).

Warika: wild yam; as man, rock, pig (N. 3).

Watch: evokes maintenance of reciprocities (N. 25, 27, 28, 29).

Water: from stream, for drinking, cleansing, cooking; evokes socialization, socialization of male element (N. 4, 5, 23, 27).

Weep: evokes possibility of loss of complementarity or completion of being (N. 22, 24, 27, 29).

White: lime is; man who feels shame whitens face with lime; thinking, thought; awareness of reciprocities (N. 25, 27, 28).

White men (Europeans): Europeanism; have authority, secret of cargo, ability to use head (N. 30, 31).

Wild almond: *see Galip.*

Wristlets: of woven cane; decorative red and black strips against natural colour; given to each other by lovers, betrothed, sweethearts (N. 27).

Writing: Europeanism (N. 30, 31).

WVAWVASIKAI: snake; maleness and collective male womb; evokes the *garamb* (N. 23).

Yam bin: storage bin for yams; evokes *garamb*, transition to husband, father, and having a family and garden (N. 22, 28, 29).

ZAWAPAI: commences as snake, then is as father-provider (N. 24).

2. PRIMARY DIALOGUES IN TRADITIONAL NARRATIVES

Ambwerk and Tuman (brothers): N. 4, 5, 6, 9, 10, 23, 24.
Ambwerk and Tuman (sisters): N. 9, 10, 22, 29.
Ambwerk and Tuman (brothers and sisters): N. 9.
Brother and sister: N. 1, 9, 10, 25, 26, 27, 29.
Father and daughter: N. 9, 22, 25, 27, 29.
Father and son: N. 7, 10, 11, 12, 13, 17, 19, 24, 25, 27, 28, 29.
Friends: N. 8, 25, 27, 28.
Husband and wife: N. 3, 4, 7, 8, 9, 10, 11, 13, 15, 19, 20, 22, 23, 24, 25, 26, 27, 28, 29.
Mother and daughter: N. 9, 13, 22, 29.
Mother and son: N. 3, 11, 13, 19, 22, 23, 25, 28, 29.
Mother's brother–sister's son: N. 10, 23, 27, 29.
Parents and children: N. 2, 3, 28.
Villagers or community and *ranguma* or odd man out: N. 14, 15, 16, 17, 18, 19, 20, 25, 27, 28.

3. PRIMARY DIALOGUES IN NEW NARRATIVES

Ambwerk and Tuman (brothers): N. 30.
Brother and sister: N. 31.
Husband and wife: N. 30.

Mother and son: N. 30.

New man (Mambu) and captain: N. 31.

New man (Mambu) and master (moral European): N. 31.

New man (Mambu) and traditional man (man to whom Mambu gives money): N. 31.

Villagers or community and *ranguma* or odd man out: N. 30, 31.

4. SOME SERIES OF SIGNALS

Since all signals in the narratives represent interdependent values, any series taken at random will, if followed through, ultimately take one through the whole conversation between the narratives and other aspects of culture.

Some selected series are presented below.

(i) *The singular and the pairs*:

Storm/Hawk; Thumb/Fingers; Penis/Testicles; Penis/Breast nipples; Coconut/Milks; Mouth/lips; Blind/pair of eyes.

(ii) *Pertaining to the male*:

Earthquake—Thunder—Lightning—Hawk; Rain—Stream— Semen; Hawk—Father-son—Father—Pig—Man—Father— Pig—Son; Bow and arrow—Trump—Yam bin—Handdrum— Spear—Slit-gong; Bamboo—Barkcloth—Breechclout—Conch —*Galip*—Comb—Stream; Small snake—Snake growing huge —Snake cut in pieces—Flood—Dumban's penis cut in pieces— *Ranguma*; Stream—Snake—*Garamb*; Dogs' teeth—*Garamb*; Adze—Axe—Decorations—Foodstuffs—Spear—Slit-gong.

(iii) *Pertaining to the female*:

Earth—Intestines—Stomach—Quim; Bird—Quim; Quim— Banana—Skirt—Pot—String bag—Digging-stick—Rat; Breast-milk—Lime—Gourd.

(iv) *Pertaining to male and female*:

Phallus—Semen—Milk—Breast nipples—Coconut; Paradise birds—Breadfruit; Cane—Coconut—Cooking—Foodstuffs— Home—Village—Water—Watch—Stream—Rain—Semen; Stream—Semen—Male—Fish—Fishing nets—Female—Babies; Paradise birds—Skirts—Hunting—Meat—Pleasure; Areca-nuts—Breadfruit—Coconut.

(v) *Pertaining to the divine, wild, and non-reciprocal*:

Forest—Hollow tree—Breadfruit; Defecation—Turds—

Smelly—Sores—Urinate; Anger—*Ranguma*—Sickness
Poison—Tangked palm—Death; Night—Smoke; Sugar cane
—Snake—*Ranguma*.

(vi) *Pertaining to the transition between divine and moral being*:

Eyes—Blind—Seeing; Blackened face—*Ranguma*—Night—
Cockerel—Dawn—Day—White—Whitened face; Raw—
Cooked; Fire—Door—Fence—Hunger—Hole; Underground
Reversal—Earthquake—Above ground—Overt; Hunger—
Weeping.

(vii) *Pertaining to the Europeanized environment*:

Ambwerk—Tuman—Ship—Jetty—European—Moral
European—Cargo; Duongangwongar—Mambu—Captain—
Ranguma—odd man out; Black man—Jetty—Ship—Coconut
—White man; Traditional man—New man—money.

The above are not, and cannot be, exclusive arrangements. Nor,
a fortiori, are they exhaustive. Still, it will be appreciated that,
given the whole list of signals and their meanings, it would be possible to rebuild a completely new set of narratives with the same
burden as those which happen to exist.

5. PRIMARY SIGNALS

Given the named characters and primary dialogues, adumbra-
tions and refractions of the following seem to fill out most of the
meaning adduced most economically.

Adze, areca-nut, ash, axe, bamboo, banana, bird, bow and arrows,
breadfruit, breast nipple, breechclout, cane, cockerel, coconut,
colours (red, black, white), cooking, digging-stick, door, eyes (blindness), fire, fish, forest, garden, handdrum, hollow tree, hiding-place,
hunting, milk, mouth and lips, penis, pig, pleasure, reversal, roof
thatch, salt, skirt, spear, stomach (colon, intestines), stone, storm,
stream, sugar-cane, sun (dawn, day, night), thumb, trump, turd,
vomit, watching.

APPENDIX II

MOVEMENT OVER TERRITORY

The diagram below (Fig. 6), much simplified, exemplifies a situation which could be paralleled for any settlement in Tangu. No one person could have provided the sum of the information given, and what follows results from piecing together the separate accounts of numbers of individuals.

Paras is dead and so are his daughter and all his sons. His grandchildren and great-grandchildren form a not inconsiderable part of the population of Riekitzir. Paras lived in Bwongeram and had three wives, one of whom was a woman from Jumpitzir, whilst the other two, apparently sisters, came from Biampitzir. The sons of Paras grew up in Bwongeram.

Vangai, a man from Jumpitzir who had been gardening in the vicinity of Gadaginamb, married a woman of Biampitzir. But she, reluctant to leave home, insisted that they should settle in Biampitzir. Woperk, son of Paras, married Sanak, the daughter of Vangai, and left Bwongeram for Biampitzir—where he settled with his wife. Ruruwai and Ginambai, other sons of Paras, remained in Bwongeram with their wives.

When the epidemic struck Tangu, Woperk moved from Biampitzir to Wump in Riekitzir. There he and his family were joined by Ruruwai and Ginambai and their families. Later, Woperk moved on to Gadaginamb, where Vangai, having enlarged his hunting-lodge, had now settled after fleeing from Biampitzir. Rumerai and Mariap, two brothers, joined Ruruwai and Ginambai in Wump, and another man, Virai, joined them later. Meanwhile the half-brother Vanai, upon leaving Bwongeram, took his wives and children to found Niapang'tien. The children remained attached to Niapang'tien until Vanai's death comparatively recently. Then they moved to W'tsiapet. Shortly after Ginambai's death his sons and daughter and their families moved to Ukwamb, accompanied by Ruruwai's sons and families. When Virai died the other two brothers remaining in Wump went into the deep bush towards Tangwatt and founded the small settlement of Gunyakarpak'-nuandin. Today the descendants of Ruruwai and Ginambai form the core of the settlement at Ukwamb. Others joined them there, and Rumerai and Mariap, eponymous descendants of the two

brothers who went to Gunyakarpak'nuandin, tend to live in
Ukwamb almost as much as in Gunyakarpak'nuandin.
Vangai and his descendants prospered in Gadaginamb. Ruak'n
took Ringwasar from Biampitzir and some time later married

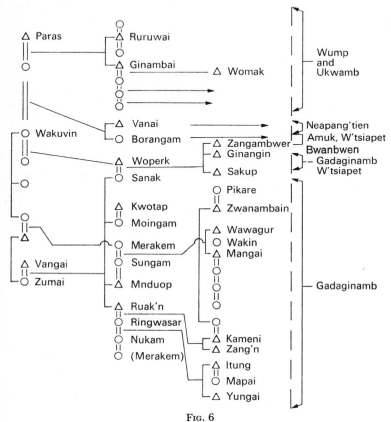

FIG. 6

Nukam from Andemarup. On the death of his brother Mnduop he
took Merakem—who died shortly afterwards—and adopted Mangai. Mnduop's other wife did not long survive him, but she returned
to Biampitzir whence she had come, and her descendants now live
in Riknang'tien. Moingam insisted that Kwotap should come to
live in Biampitzir. And when Vangai went to live in Gadaginamb,
Kwotap and Moingam went with him. Nukam of Andemarup bore
Itung and Yungai. The latter is not married, but Itung quite recently married Mapai of Andemarup. She was a young widow

formerly married to Nukam's sister's son, but after marrying Itung she came to live in Gadaginamb. Zang'n and Kameni, Ruak'n's sons by Ringwasar, are both married, the former to a woman from Biampitzir and the latter to a woman of Jumpitzir. Mangai married Wayamik of Ambungk: she died, and wanting a wife to look after the now motherless children, Mangai took Kwaksai of Biampitzir, who, because she was being beaten by her then husband, left him in favour of Mangai in Gadaginamb. Garuk, Mangai's other wife, was formerly the widow of Mangai's elder brother, who had gone to live with her in Ambungk. When Mangai married her she moved to Gadaginamb. Pikare married Zwanambain of Jumpitzir, who came from his home to be near his sister, concomitants of siblingship which demand interaction with others so as to extend the range of possible claims. Since, too, values in filiation largely depend on a continuing association with the parents in residential propinquity, one may point to the epidemic sickness and the consequent migrations as vital factors in the decline of the filiatory values. On the other hand, the migrations themselves were probably more closely related to the growth of ambiguity and the demands of siblingship, and the readiness to suspect others of sorcery, than to the contingency of the sickness itself.

GENERAL INDEX

Italicized numerals refer to narratives.

K k

PRINTED IN GREAT BRITAIN
AT THE UNIVERSITY PRESS, OXFORD
BY VIVIAN RIDLER
PRINTER TO THE UNIVERSITY